Usborne

Illustrated Dictionary

Edited by Jane Bingham

Designed by Susie McCaffrey

Illustrated by
Sean Wilkinson, Gerald Wood, Nicholas Hewetson,
Ian Jackson, Peter Dennis, Michelle Ross

Definitions by John McIlwain, Sheila Dignen, Jessica Feinstein, Andrew Delahunty

U.S. editors: Scott Ferguson and Carrie Armstrong

YOUR DICTIONARY: A USER'S GUIDE

This dictionary contains over ten thousand entries and over a thousand pictures, many of them surrounded by picture labels. Here is the entry for "satellite" with its labeled picture.

Finding a word

Entries are listed in alphabetical order. Make a guess at the first few letters of your word, for example, for "satellite," find "sat," then try different ways of spelling the next part.

If you can't find a word

- You may have chosen the wrong first letters. Try some alternative spellings and watch for **spelling guides** at the bottom of the page.
- You may be able to find a related word. For example, you would find the word "slothful" under "sloth."
- The word you want may be a **picture label**. Look for it in the **Index of picture labels** at the back of the dictionary.

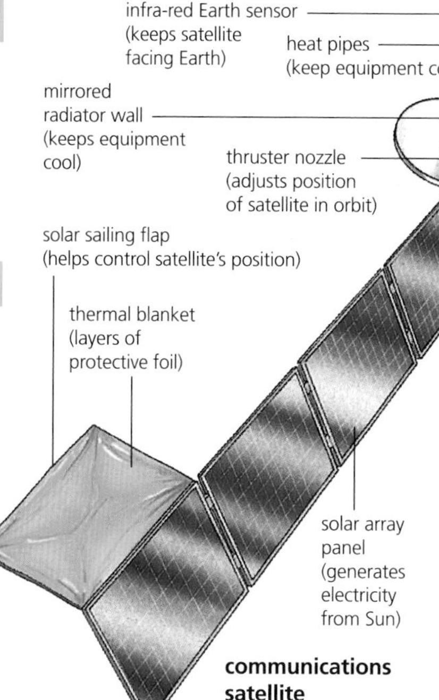

communications satellite

satellite
1 *(n)* a machine that is sent into orbit around the Earth. *The picture shows the main parts of a communications satellite that receives and sends television and telephone signals.*
2 *(n)* a moon or other natural object that moves in orbit around a planet. *See* **Moon**.

Looking at pages

Guide words help you find the right page.

Guide letters help you find the right letter section.

197 Ramadan

a b c d e f g h i j k l m n o p q r s t u v w x y z

2 *(n)* a bone in your lower arm. *See* **skeleton**.
3 *(n)* a circular area around a thing or a place. *Most of my friends live within a radius of a mile from my house.*

raffle *(n)* a way of raising money by selling tickets and then giving prizes to people with winning tickets. **raffle** *(v)*.

raft rafting rafted
1 *(n)* a floating platform often made from logs tied together.
2 *(v)* to travel by raft. **rafting** *(n)*.
3 *(n)* an inflatable rubber craft with a flat bottom. *The picture shows an inflatable raft traveling through fast-moving water.*

inflatable raft

rag
1 *(n)* a piece of old cloth.
2 rags *(plural n)* very old, worn-out clothing.

rage raging raged
1 If you are **in a rage**, you are very angry.
2 *(v)* to be violent or noisy. *The bull raged through the town.*

ragged *(rag-ed)* *(adj)* old, torn, and scruffy. **raggedly** *(adv)*.

raid
1 *(n)* a sudden attack on a place. **raider** *(n)*, **raid** *(v)*.
2 *(n)* a sudden visit by the police to search for criminals, drugs, etc. **raid** *(v)*.

rail
1 *(n)* a fixed bar or metal track.
2 *(n)* the railroad. *Thomas loves traveling by rail.* **rail** *(adj)*.

railing *(n)* a metal bar that is a part of a fence.

railroad *(n)* a path made from metal tracks, which can support cars pulled by locomotives.

rain raining rained
1 *(n)* water that falls from clouds. **rain** *(v)*, **rainy** *(adj)*.
2 *(v)* to fall like rain.

rainbow *(n)* an arc of different colors caused by sunlight shining through raindrops. *See* **spectrum**.

rainfall *(n)* the amount of rain that falls in one place in a certain time.

rain forest *(n)* a thick tropical forest where a lot of rain falls. *The picture below shows the main rain forests of the world, and some examples of rain forest wildlife.* **rain forest** *(adj)*.

rain forests and rain forest wildlife

ruffed lemur (Madagascar), orchid, carpenter bee (Southeast Asia), hyacinth macaw (South America), rain forest, NORTH AMERICA, Central America, Amazonia, SOUTH AMERICA, EUROPE, AFRICA, Congo, ASIA, India, Sumatra, Borneo, Papua New Guinea, AUSTRALIA, Madagascar, palm weevil (Africa), pangolin (Africa), golden cock-of-the-rock (South America), poison dart frog (South America)

raise raising raised
1 *(v)* to lift something up. *Raise your glasses for a toast.*
2 *(v)* If you **raise** money, you collect it for a particular cause or charity.
3 *(v)* to look after children or young animals until they are adults. *Martha has raised five sons.*

raisin *(n)* a dried grape.

rake raking raked
1 *(n)* a garden tool with metal teeth used to level soil or to collect leaves, grass cuttings, etc.
2 *(v)* to use a rake. *Bernard is raking up leaves.*
3 *(v)* *(informal)* If you **rake it in**, you make a lot of money.

rally rallying rallied
1 *(v)* to come together as a group, often to achieve a common goal. *The troops rallied.* **rally** *(n)*.
2 *(n)* An exchange of shots during a racket sport such as tennis.

ram ramming rammed
1 *(n)* a male sheep.
2 *(v)* to crash into something deliberately.
3 *(v)* to push something into a space. *Kitty rammed her clothes into the bag.*

RAM *(n)* the part of a computer's memory that is lost when you switch the computer off. The initials RAM stand for random access memory.

Ramadan *(n)* the ninth month of the Islamic year when Muslims must not eat between sunrise and sunset.

Some words that begin with a "r" sound are spelled "wr."

Spelling guides help you to find tricky words by suggesting other spellings.

Looking at entries

Headwords show how a word is spelled.

Pronunciation guides show how a word is said.

Definitions explain what a word means.

sloth *(rhymes with moth)*
1 *(n)* a very slow-moving South American mammal with a shaggy coat.
2 *(n)* laziness. slothful *(adj)*.
slouch slouches slouching slouched
1 *(v)* to sit, stand, or walk in a lazy way, with your head and shoulders drooping.
2 *(n)* *(slang)* a slow and lazy person. *Dan's no slouch at football.*

Parts of speech identify what a word does in a sentence (see page 3.)

Numbers indicate a separate sense of a word.

Related words introduce words from the same family.

Changing forms show how words change their spelling when they are used in different ways.

Usage guides show that a word is old-fashioned, poetic, informal or slang. Informal words are used in everyday speech, but not in formal or official writing. Slang is usually only spoken.

Example sentences show how a word is used.

Weights, measures, numbers, months, countries, and nationalities are listed on page 284.

PARAMETERS

PARTS OF SPEECH: THE PARTS THAT WORDS PLAY

Each word plays a different part in a sentence, depending on its part of speech. If you know a word's part of speech, you can figure out how to use it. This sentence contains all eight parts of speech.

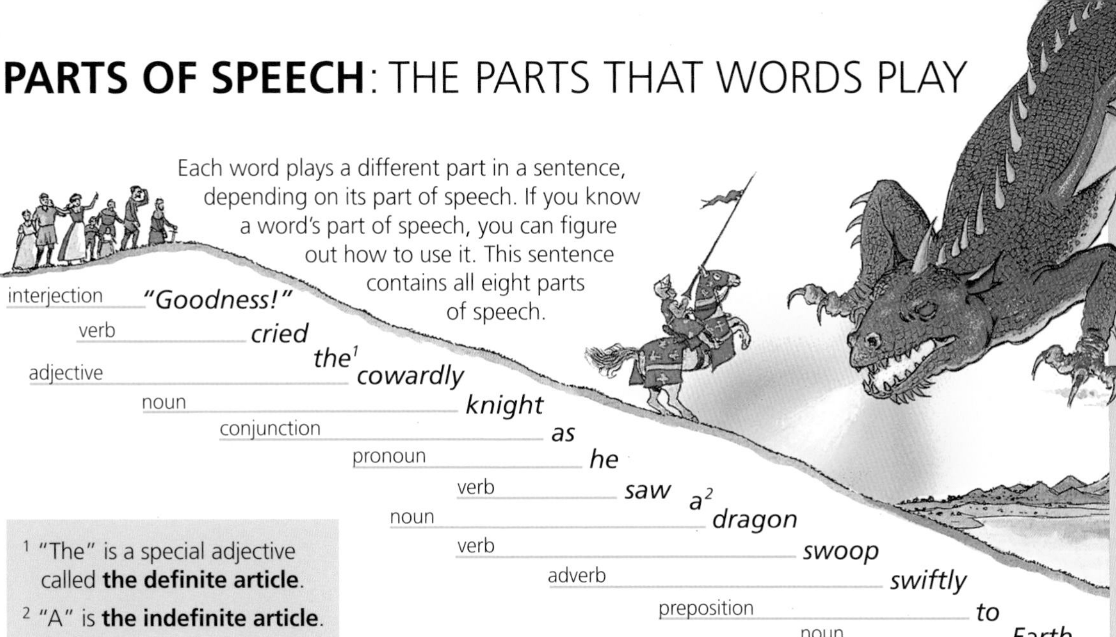

interjection	*"Goodness!"*
verb	*cried*
	the[1]
adjective	*cowardly*
noun	*knight*
conjunction	*as*
pronoun	*he*
verb	*saw*
	a[2]
noun	*dragon*
verb	*swoop*
adverb	*swiftly*
preposition	*to*
noun	*Earth.*

[1] "The" is a special adjective called **the definite article**.

[2] "A" is **the indefinite article**.

noun *(n)* Nouns give the name of a person, animal or thing. They tell you who or what a sentence is about.

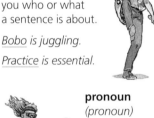

Bobo is juggling.

Practice is essential.

verb *(v)* Verbs are action words. They say what someone or something does, thinks, or feels. All sentences need verbs to tell you what is happening.

Spike loves his dirt bike.

It goes really fast.

preposition *(prep)* Prepositions show where people or things are, or what relation they have to each other.

A Chinese dragon weaves through the streets.

People are dancing under the dragon.

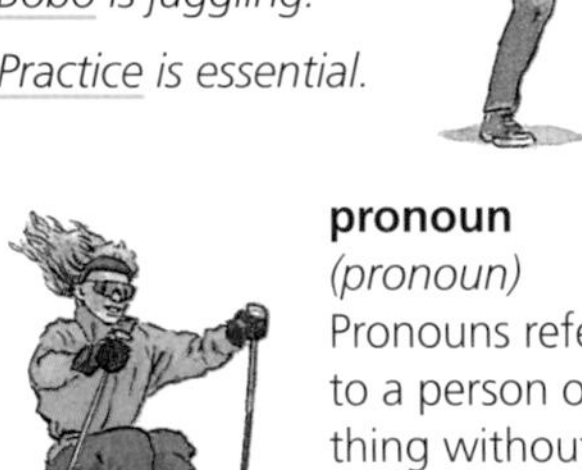

pronoun *(pronoun)* Pronouns refer to a person or thing without naming it. They act like nouns.

(Annie is very good at skiing.)
She is very good at skiing.

(The weather is extremely cold.)
It is extremely cold.

adverb *(adv)* Adverbs tell you how, when, where or why something happens. They are used with verbs.

The horse is bucking wildly.

Its rider may soon fall off.

interjection *(interject)* Interjections are used to show surprise, delight or pain, or to get attention. They are sometimes known as exclamations and often have an exclamation mark.

"Wow!" cried the crowd as the baseball player hit the ball.

"Yippee!" yelled the fielder as he caught it.

adjective *(adj)* Adjectives are descriptive words that tell you more about a person or thing. They are used with nouns and pronouns.

Toucans have enormous beaks.

They are very bright.

conjunction *(conj)* Conjunctions are linking words. They join parts of sentences.

Penguins have wings, but cannot fly.

They breed on land and hunt in water.

Note - Some words in the dictionary are not given a part of speech. This is because they are used with other words or in a phrase.

WRITING ENGLISH: SOME HINTS AND GUIDELINES

These two pages give some help with spelling and punctuation. You should find them useful to refer to when you are writing.

Spelling English

It is sometimes hard to spell English correctly because it is a mixture of so many languages (see pages 6-7). Here are some patterns to follow and spellings to remember, but watch for exceptions and use a dictionary to check your spelling.

dinosaur

Making plurals

Most nouns simply gain an **s** to become plural:

dinosaur - dinosaurs
book - books
garden - gardens
apple - apples
zoo - zoos
day - days
house - houses
bicycle - bicycles

dinosaurs

Some words, however, change differently. Here are some word groups for you to remember:

fox

If a word ends in **ch**, **sh**, **s**, **ss**, **x** or **z**, add **es**:

arch - arches
match - matches
dish - dishes
bus - buses
atlas - atlases
dress - dresses
fox - foxes
waltz - waltzes

foxes

berry

If a word ends in **y** and the letter before the y is not a, e, i, o or u, replace the y with **ies**:

berry - berries
baby - babies
party - parties
pony - ponies
country - countries
city - cities
puppy - puppies
library - libraries

berries

leaf

Many words ending in **f** drop their final f and gain **ves**:

leaf - leaves
half - halves
loaf - loaves
shelf - shelves
wife - wives
thief - thieves
dwarf - dwarves
wolf - wolves

leaves

buffalo

Many words ending in **o** gain **es**:

buffalo - buffaloes
cargo - cargoes
tomato - tomatoes
potato - potatoes
echo - echoes
hero - heroes

buffaloes

Odd plurals

Some words change their spelling dramatically when they become plural. These plurals need to be learned.

woman - women
child - children
man - men
mouse - mice
foot - feet
tooth - teeth

Letter pairs

qu
q is always followed by **u**:

queen *request*
quit *squad*

queen

gh
When **g** and **h** are written together, **g** always comes before **h**:

sleigh
right
ghost
although

sleigh

i and e
It is very easy to get these two letters backward, but this rule should help you:

"i before e, except after c, when the sound is ee."

i before **e**	**e** before **i**
shield	*ceiling*
believe	*receive*
thief	*conceited*
field	*receipt*

Note - there are some exceptions to this rule, such as *seize, weir, weird*.

Doubling up

Watch out for the double letters in these words:

accommodate
accurate
address
beginning
communicate
disappoint
embarrass
necessary
occasion
savanna

One word or two?

Here are some common words and phrases that are often spelled wrongly:

two words	**one word**
thank you	*cannot*
no one	*someone*
high school	*altogether*

Double or single l?

It is sometimes hard to know whether words have a single or a double l. The following words have only one l:

already *careful*
always *until*
awful *welcome*

Remember - when full is added to a word, it drops its final l.

Whenever I see a spider, I am full of fear.

Whenever I see a spider, I am fearful.

Tricky endings

-le or -el
Most words end in **-le**:

battle *bubble*
trouble *table*
able *Bible*

but watch out for:
travel barrel label quarrel

-ic or -ick
Words with two or more sounds (syllables) end in **-ic**. Words with one sound end in **-ick**:

comic *stick*
fantastic *lick*
artistic *trick*

Learning spellings

Follow the four steps below when you are learning to spell a word.

1 LOOK at the word carefully and memorize the order of letters.
2 COVER the word.
3 WRITE it down from memory.
4 CHECK that it is right.

Punctuation

Without punctuation to break them up, your sentences would be impossible to read. These guidelines will help you use some tricky punctuation marks.

Apostrophes

Apostrophes show the owner of something *(The hat that belongs to Ben = Ben's hat)* or mark missing letters *(I am hungry = I'm hungry.)*

Apostrophe s
If the owner is singular, add an **apostrophe s**:
Ben's hat
Charles's hat

If the owner is plural and ends in s, add an **apostrophe only**:
The boys' hats

If the owner is plural, but does not end in s, add an **apostrophe s**:
The children's hats

Never use an apostrophe s to make a plural.

Missing letters
Usually, an apostrophe shows that one letter has been dropped, but sometimes more than one letter is missing:
I'd = I would or *I had*
would've = would have
won't = will not

it's and its

it's is only used to show that a letter has been left out from **it is**:

I'm glad it's a sunny day.

The kangaroo carries its baby in its pouch.

Colons and semi-colons

You can manage without colons and semi-colons in your writing, but they can be very useful. Here are some ways to use them:

Colons can be used to introduce a statement or a list:

At last Harry revealed the secret of his success: three raw carrots every day.

For this trick you need: a pack of cards, a silk scarf and a wand.

Semi-colons are useful for breaking up lists when the items in the list are long and complicated:

We visited the zoo and saw: two giraffes; an elephant with a baby; some performing seals; and a very mischievous monkey.

Quotation marks

You use quotation marks, or speech marks, to show that someone is speaking. Always start someone's spoken words with a capital letter and use a comma to separate speech from the rest of the sentence:

"The view is amazing," said the astronaut.

The astronaut said, "The view is amazing."

"The view," said the astronaut, "is amazing."

THE STORY OF ENGLISH: A HISTORY OF OUR LANGUAGE

People first spoke English fifteen hundred years ago. Since then, our language has changed enormously, both in the way it is spoken and written, and in its range of words. These two pages show how English grew and changed as the British were invaded, visited, and influenced by people from other countries.

Old English: 5th-11th century

Three main groups of people created Old English: the Anglo-Saxon tribes who settled in England, Christian missionaries from Rome, and Viking and Danish invaders and settlers.

Anglo-Saxons

5th-6th century: Tribes of Angles, Saxons and Jutes from mainland Europe and Scandinavia invaded the British Isles and created a new kingdom of England. People in England spoke Anglo-Saxon, the earliest form of English.

Anglo-Saxon helmet

ANGLO-SAXON WORDS		
fire	*day*	*book*
man	*what*	*and*
house	*earth*	*you*

Missionaries from Rome

5th-7th century: Christian missionaries traveled to Britain and founded monasteries. The monks held services in Latin and copied Latin manuscripts.

6th-century monk

LATIN WORDS	
verse	*altar*
angel	*candle*
demon	*school*
pope	*hymn*

Vikings and Danes

8th-11th century: Vikings and Danes from Scandinavia attacked Britain. During the 10th and 11th centuries the Danes ruled over northeast England.

Viking invaders

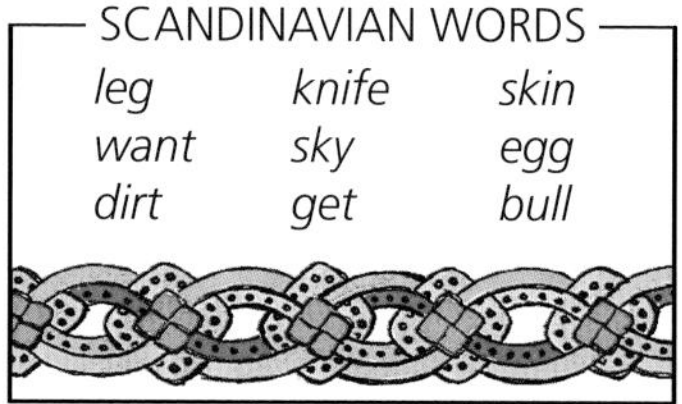

SCANDINAVIAN WORDS		
leg	*knife*	*skin*
want	*sky*	*egg*
dirt	*get*	*bull*

Beowulf - an Old English poem

Written in the 8th century, and over 3,000 lines long, *Beowulf* tells the story of a courageous warrior who fights against monsters to save his people.

"Wiht unhælo, grim ond
The unholy creature, grim and

grædig, gearo sona wæs,
greedy, was soon ready,

reoc ond reþe, ond on
savage and cruel, and from

ræste genam þritig þegna."
their rest seized thirty thanes.

Middle English: Late 11th-15th century

In this period, the Normans added French words to the language, some spellings changed and borrowing from Latin continued.

Normans

1066-1300: In 1066, William of Normandy conquered England. French was spoken by the upper classes and used in parliament and the law courts.

William the Conqueror

FRENCH WORDS		
court	*crime*	*feast*
royal	*fashion*	*music*
attorney	*beauty*	*story*

Spelling changes

12th-15th century: Old English letters were abandoned. French scribes introduced "qu," "gh," "ch," and "ng" spellings.

The Canterbury Tales - a Middle English poem

Geoffrey Chaucer began writing the *Canterbury Tales* around 1387. The poem presents 23 tales, told by pilgrims.

"Thanne longen folk to goon
Then people long to go

on pilgrimages...And specially
on pilgrimages... And specially

from every shires ende of
from the end of every county of

Engelond to Caunterbury
England to Canterbury

they wende."
they travel.

The birth of modern English: Late 15th-18th century

In this period, English gradually became recognizable as the language that we use today.

Caxton and the rise of printing

1476: William Caxton began printing books in English. This led to a great increase in reading and writing.

15th-century printing press

William Shakespeare

1590-1612: William Shakespeare used the English language in new and exciting ways in his plays and poetry.

Shakespeare

PHRASES FROM SHAKESPEARE

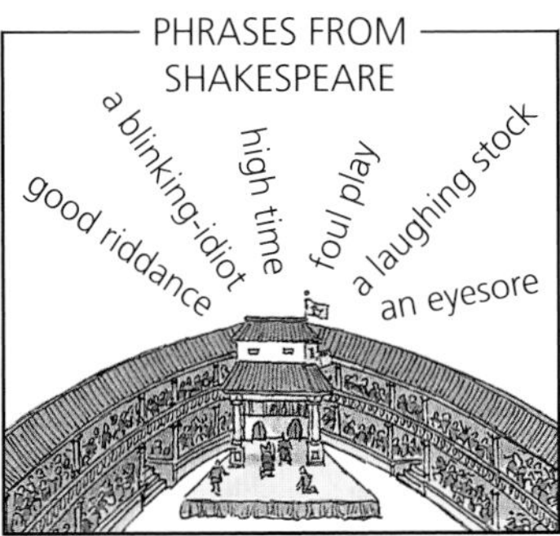

good riddance
a blinking idiot
high time
foul play
a laughing stock
an eyesore

The King James Bible

1611: An English version of the Bible was printed. This version, which was authorized by King James I, was used throughout the country.

PHRASES FROM THE KING JAMES BIBLE

- in the twinkling of an eye
- the skin of my teeth
- a wolf in sheep's clothing
- the salt of the earth
- the apple of my eye
- an eye for an eye

The Renaissance

1475-1650: People became interested in Ancient Greek and Roman writings, and developed new ideas in science and the arts. To express these ideas, they borrowed words from Greek, Latin, French and Italian.

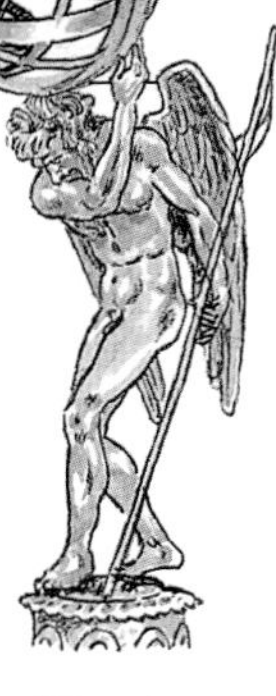

17th-century astronomical sphere

RENAISSANCE WORDS

SCIENTIFIC WORDS
temperature (Latin)
skeleton (Greek)
pneumonia (Greek)
gravity (Latin)
muscle (Latin)
virus (Latin)

MUSICAL WORDS
violin (Italian)
madrigal (Italian)
soprano (Italian)
opera (Italian)
ballet (French)
fugue (French)

ARCHITECTURAL WORDS
cupola (Italian)
balcony (Italian)
grotto (Italian)
dome (French)
portico (Italian)
stucco (Italian)

Dr. Johnson's dictionary

1755: Dr. Samuel Johnson published his *Dictionary of the English Language*. By this time, English spelling was almost standardized.

Dr. Johnson

Traders and explorers

16th-18th century: explorers discovered new countries and merchants traded with them, bringing back new words.

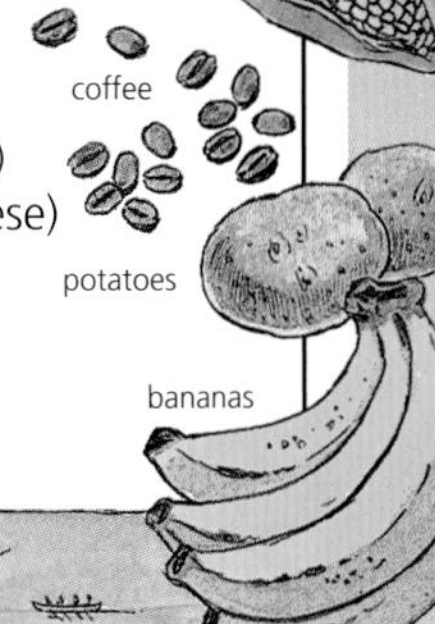

TRADING WORDS

coffee (Turkish)
banana (Spanish)
yam (Portuguese)
apricot (Portuguese)
maize (Spanish)
potato (Spanish)

Gulliver's Travels - an 18th-century novel

Jonathan Swift wrote *Gulliver's Travels* in 1726, using words and spellings that are very close to modern English. In this passage, Gulliver has been captured by tiny Lilliputians.

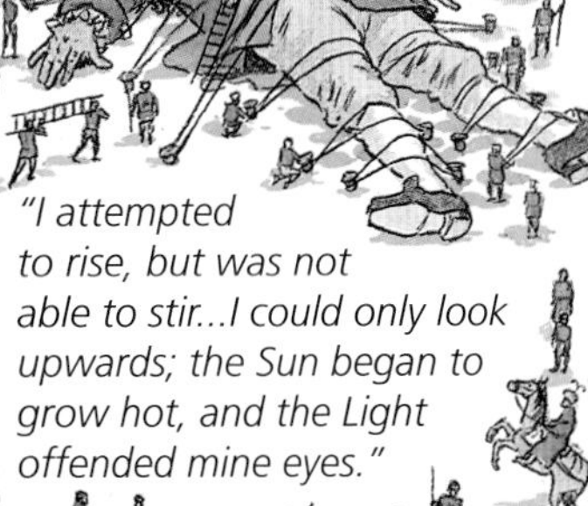

"I attempted to rise, but was not able to stir...I could only look upwards; the Sun began to grow hot, and the Light offended mine eyes."

Modern English: 19th century onward

No major changes took place in the language after 1800, but English spread around the world and gained thousands of new words.

ENGLISH TODAY: ITS RANGE AND VARIETY

English is now a world language, spoken by over 375 million people, with at least 470 million more using it as a second language. Here are some words used by English speakers in different parts of the world.

CANADA

parka - padded jacket
mukluk - eskimo boot
soother - pacifier
reeve - mayor

Niagara Falls

IRELAND

bold - naughty
crack - fun
boreen - lane
bonham - piglet
brack - fruit loaf

Irish harp

WALES

Welsh dragon

cwtch - hug
eisht! - hush!
butty - friend
wass - boy

SCOTLAND

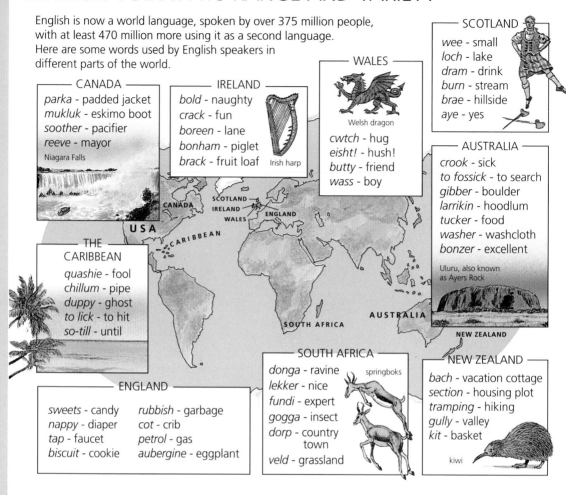

wee - small
loch - lake
dram - drink
burn - stream
brae - hillside
aye - yes

AUSTRALIA

crook - sick
to fossick - to search
gibber - boulder
larrikin - hoodlum
tucker - food
washer - washcloth
bonzer - excellent

Uluru, also known as Ayers Rock

THE CARIBBEAN

quashie - fool
chillum - pipe
duppy - ghost
to lick - to hit
so-till - until

ENGLAND

sweets - candy
nappy - diaper
tap - faucet
biscuit - cookie
rubbish - garbage
cot - crib
petrol - gas
aubergine - eggplant

SOUTH AFRICA

donga - ravine
lekker - nice
fundi - expert
gogga - insect
dorp - country town
veld - grassland

springboks

NEW ZEALAND

bach - vacation cottage
section - housing plot
tramping - hiking
gully - valley
kit - basket

kiwi

New words

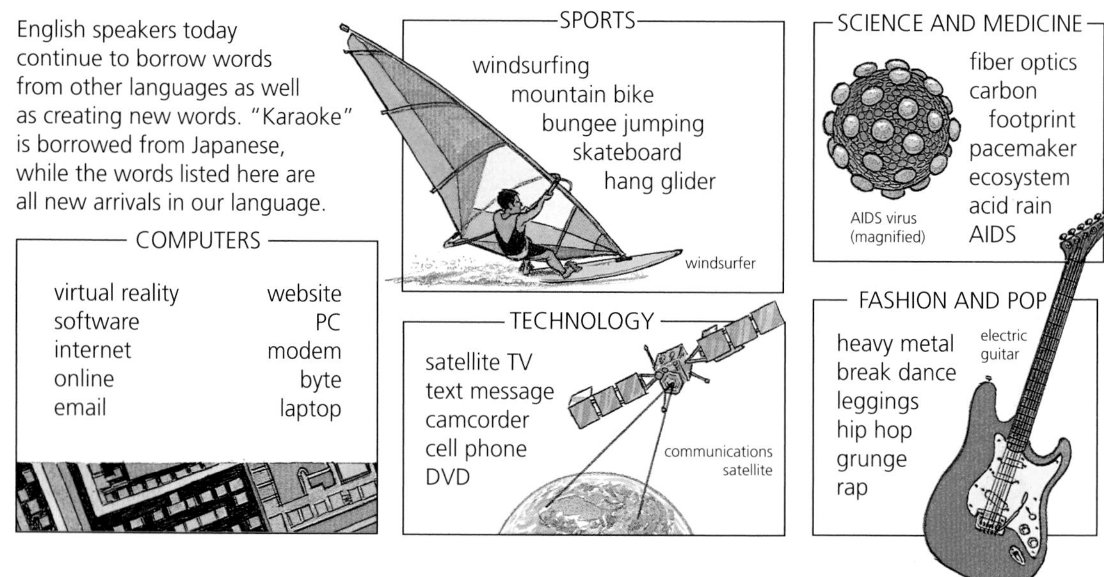

English speakers today continue to borrow words from other languages as well as creating new words. "Karaoke" is borrowed from Japanese, while the words listed here are all new arrivals in our language.

COMPUTERS

virtual reality
software
internet
online
email
website
PC
modem
byte
laptop

SPORTS

windsurfing
mountain bike
bungee jumping
skateboard
hang glider

windsurfer

TECHNOLOGY

satellite TV
text message
camcorder
cell phone
DVD

communications satellite

SCIENCE AND MEDICINE

fiber optics
carbon footprint
pacemaker
ecosystem
acid rain
AIDS

AIDS virus (magnified)

FASHION AND POP

heavy metal
break dance
leggings
hip hop
grunge
rap

electric guitar

Aa

aardvark *(n)*
an African mammal with a long, sticky tongue that it uses to search for insects.

aardvark

abacus abacuses *or* abaci *(n)*
a frame with sliding beads on wires, used for counting.

abandon abandoning abandoned
1 *(v)* to leave forever. *Abandon ship!*
2 *(v)* to give up. *As night fell, we abandoned hope of being rescued.*

abbey *(n)*
a group of buildings where monks or nuns live and work.

abbreviation *(n)*
a short way of writing a word. *CD is an abbreviation for compact disc.* **abbreviated** *(adj).*

abdicate abdicating abdicated *(v)*
to give up being king or queen. **abdication** *(n).*

abdomen
1 *(n)* the part of your body between your chest and hips.
2 *(n)* the back section of an insect's body. *See* **beetle**.

abduct abducting abducted *(v)*
to kidnap someone. **abduction** *(n).*

abhor abhorring abhorred *(v)*
to hate someone or something. **abhorrent** *(adj).*

abide abiding abode *or* abided
1 *(v)* to stay or live somewhere.
2 *(v)* If you **cannot abide** something, you cannot put up with it.

ability abilities *(n)*
1 the power to do something. *I know I have the ability to do better.*
2 *(n)* skill. *Pablo has great ability in art.*

abject *(adj)*
miserable and without dignity. *The refugees lived in abject poverty. Sabrina offered an abject apology.*

ablaze *(adj)* on fire.

able abler ablest
1 *(adj)* If you are **able** to do something, you are capable of doing it.
2 *(adj)* skillful or clever. *Our team has many able players.* **ably** *(adv).*

able-bodied *(adj)*
Someone who is **able-bodied** has no injuries or disabilities.

abnormal *(adj)*
unusual or not normal. **abnormality** *(n).*

aboard *(prep)*
on or into a train, ship, or aircraft. **aboard** *(adv).*

abode *(n) (old-fashioned)*
a home. *Our humble abode.*

abolish
abolishes abolishing abolished *(v)*
to put an end to something officially. *The 13th Amendment to the U.S. Constitution abolished slavery.* **abolition** *(n).*

abominable *(adj)*
horrible or disgusting. *An abominable mess.* **abominably** *(adv).*

Aborigine *(ab-or-**ij**-in-ee) (n)*
one of the native people of Australia who lived there before Europeans arrived. **Aboriginal** *(adj).*

abort aborting aborted *(v)*
to stop something from happening.

abound abounding abounded *(v)*
to be present in large amounts. *The forest abounds with wildlife.*

about
1 *(prep)* on a particular subject. *Tell me about your vacation.*
2 *(adv)* almost, or more or less. *My dad's about 40.*

above
1 *(prep)* higher up, or over. *Above the clouds.*
2 *(prep)* more than. *Above average.*

aboveboard *(adj)* If something that you do is **aboveboard**, it is completely honest and legal.

abrasive
1 *(adj)* rough and grinding, like sandpaper. *An abrasive surface.*
2 *(adj)* rude. *Spike has an abrasive manner.*

abreast *(adv)* side by side. *We walked three abreast.*

abridged *(adj)* shortened. *An abridged novel.* **abridge** *(v).*

abroad *(adv)* in or to another country. *We are going abroad this summer.*

abrupt
1 *(adj)* sudden and unexpected. *The car came to an abrupt halt.* **abruptly** *(adv).*
2 *(adj)* rude and short-tempered. *An abrupt reply.* **abruptly** *(adv).*

abscess *(**ab**-sess)* abscesses *(n)*
a painful swelling, full of a yellow substance called pus.

abscond
absconding absconded *(v)*
to go away suddenly and secretly, usually after doing something wrong.

abseil *(**ab**-sail)*
abseiling abseiled *(v)*
to lower yourself down a steep cliff or mountain face by holding onto a rope. **abseiler** *(n).*

absent *(adj)* not present. **absence** *(n),* **absentee** *(n),* **absenteeism** *(n).*

absentminded *(adj)*
If you are **absentminded**, you are forgetful and do not think about what you are doing. **absentmindedly** *(adv).*

absolute
1 *(adj)* complete or total. *Ben looks like an absolute idiot in that hat.* **absolutely** *(adv).*
2 *(adj)* without any limit. *The dictator had absolute power.*

absolve absolving absolved *(v)*
to pardon someone or free them from blame. **absolution** *(n).*

absorb absorbing absorbed
1 *(v)* to soak up liquid. *The sponge absorbed the juice.* **absorbent** *(adj).*
2 *(v)* to take in information. *The students absorbed all the facts.*
3 *(v)* If something **absorbs** you, it takes up all your attention.

abstain abstaining abstained *(v)*
to stop yourself from doing something. *The prisoners abstained from eating until their demands were met.* **abstention** *(n).*

abstract *(adj)*
based on ideas rather than things. *Abstract artists paint shapes rather than people or objects.*

absurd absurder absurdest *(adj)*
silly or ridiculous. **absurdity** *(n),* **absurdly** *(adv).*

abundant *(adj)*
If there is an **abundant** supply of something, there is plenty of it. **abundance** *(n),* **abundantly** *(adv).*

abuse abusing abused
1 *(ab-**yuce**) (n)* rude or unkind words. **abuse** *(ab-**yooze**) (v),* **abusive** *(adj).*
2 *(ab-**yooze**) (v)* to treat a person or creature cruelly. **abuse** *(ab-**yuce**) (n).*
3 *(ab-**yuce**) (n)* wrong or harmful use of something. *Drug abuse.* **abuse** *(ab-**yooze**) (v).*

abysmal *(uh-biz-mal) (adj)* very bad or terrible. **abysmally** *(adv).*

abyss *(ab-iss)* **abysses** *(n)* a very deep hole that seems to have no bottom.

academic
1 *(adj)* having to do with study and learning. *Anna loves sports, but hates academic work.* **academically** *(adv).*
2 *(n)* someone who teaches in a university or college, or someone who does research.

accelerate
accelerating accelerated *(v)* to get faster and faster. **acceleration** *(n).*

accent
1 *(n)* the way you pronounce words. *Helmut speaks with a German accent.*
2 *(n)* a mark put over a letter in some languages to show how it is pronounced, for example, 'café.'

accentuate accentuating accentuated *(v)* to emphasize or draw attention to something.

accept accepting accepted
1 *(v)* to take something that you are offered. **acceptance** *(n).*
2 *(v)* to agree to something. *Keri won't accept our plan.* **acceptance** *(n),* **acceptable** *(adj).*

access accesses accessing accessed
1 *(n)* an entrance or approach to a place. **accessible** *(adj).*
2 *(n)* the right to see someone. *Lucy lives with her mother, but her father has access on weekends.*
3 *(v)* to open a document, program, or website on a computer.

accessory accessories
1 *(n)* a thing added to make something more useful. *Car accessories.*
2 *(n)* something, like a belt or a scarf, that goes with your clothes.
3 *(n)* An **accessory** to a crime is someone who helps another person to commit a crime.

accident *(n)* something that takes place unexpectedly and that often involves people being hurt. **accidental** *(adj),* **accidentally** *(adv).*

acclimatize
acclimatizing acclimatized *(v)* to get used to a different climate or to new surroundings. **acclimatization** *(n).*

accommodations *(n)* places where people live, especially when traveling. **accommodate** *(v).*

accompany accompanies accompanying accompanied
1 *(v)* to go somewhere with someone.
2 *(v)* to support a musician or singer by playing a musical instrument. **accompaniment** *(n),* **accompanist** *(n).*

accomplice *(uh-kum-pliss) (n)* someone who helps another person to commit a crime.

accomplish accomplishes accomplishing accomplished *(v)* to do something successfully. **accomplishment** *(n).*

accomplished *(adj)* skillful.

accord
1 *(n)* peaceful agreement.
2 If you do something **of your own accord**, you do it without being asked.

according to
1 *(prep)* as someone has said or written. *According to Amy, all boys are stupid!*
2 *(prep)* in a way that is suitable. *You'll be paid according to the amount of work that you do.* **accordingly** *(adv).*

accordion *(n)* a musical instrument that you squeeze to make sound, and play by pressing keys and buttons. *See* **instrument**.

accost accosting accosted *(v)* to approach someone and talk to them, usually in an insulting way.

account accounting accounted
1 *(n)* a description of something that has happened.
2 *(n)* a sum of money in a bank that you can add to or take from, when needed.
3 **accounts** *(plural n)* records of money earned and spent.
4 *(v)* If you **account for** something, you explain it. **accountable** *(adj).*

accountant *(n)* an expert in finance and keeping accounts.

accumulate accumulating accumulated *(v)* to collect things or let them pile up. **accumulation** *(n).*

accurate *(adj)* exactly correct. **accuracy** *(n),* **accurately** *(adv).*

accuse accusing accused *(v)* to say that someone has done something wrong. **accusation** *(n),* **accuser** *(n).*

accustomed
1 *(adj)* usual. *My accustomed seat.*
2 *(adj)* When you are **accustomed to** something, you are used to it.

ace
1 *(n)* a playing card with only one symbol on it.
2 *(n)* a person who excels at something. *A flying ace.*

ache *(rhymes with take) (n)* a dull pain that goes on and on. **ache** *(v).*

achieve *(uh-cheev)* **achieving achieved** *(v)* to do something successfully, especially after a lot of effort. **achievement** *(n).*

acid
1 *(n)* a substance that turns blue litmus paper red. Strong acids can burn your skin. **acidic** *(adj).*
2 *(adj)* sour or bitter.

acid rain *(n)* rain that is polluted by acid in the atmosphere and damages the environment. *The diagram below shows how fumes containing acids from factories, car exhaust, etc. travel until they meet damp air, then fall as acid rain.*

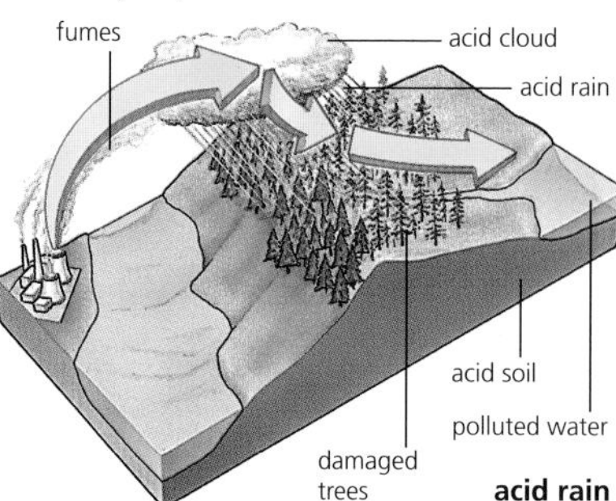

acknowledge
acknowledging acknowledged
1 *(v)* to admit to something. *I acknowledged my mistake.*
2 *(v)* to show that you have seen and recognized someone. *Toby walked past without acknowledging me.*
3 *(v)* to let the sender know that you have received a letter or package. **acknowledgement** *(n).*

acne *(ak-nee) (n)* a lot of red pimples on the skin, especially on the face.

acorn *(n)* the seed of an oak tree.

acoustic *(uh-koo-stik)*
1 *(adj)* to do with sound or hearing.
2 **acoustics** *(plural n)* If a place has good **acoustics**, you can hear sounds and music very clearly there.

acoustic guitar *(n)* a guitar that does not need an amplifier.

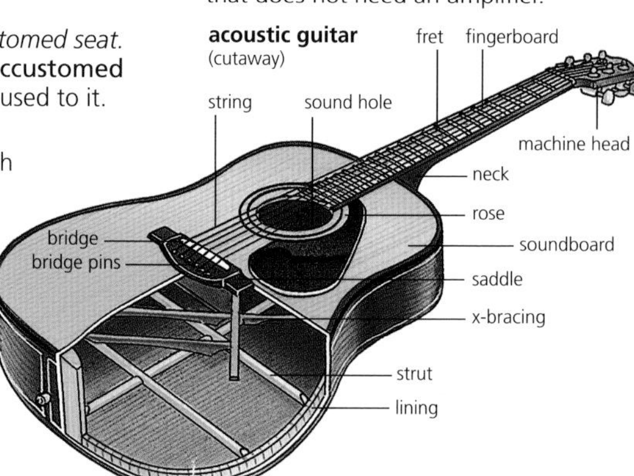

b c d e f g h i j k l m n o p q r s t u v w x y z

acquaintance *(n)* someone you have met, but do not know very well.

acquire acquiring acquired
1 *(v)* to obtain or get something.
2 *(n)* If something is an **acquired taste**, you slowly grow to like it. *Coffee is an acquired taste.*

acquit acquitting acquitted *(v)* to find someone not guilty of a crime. **acquittal** *(n).*

acrobatics *(plural n)* difficult and exciting gymnastic acts, often performed in the air or on a high wire. **acrobat** *(n),* **acrobatic** *(adj).*

acronym *(n)* a word made from the first or first few letters of the words of a phrase. *Radar is an acronym for radio detecting and ranging.*

across
1 *(prep)* from one side to the other. *We ran across the field.*
2 *(prep)* on the other side. *Emma lives across the street from me.*

acrylic *(uh-**krill**-ik) (n)* a chemical substance used to make fibers and paints.

act acting acted
1 *(v)* to do something. *We must act now to save the rain forests.* **act** *(n).*
2 *(v)* to perform in a play, movie, etc.
3 *(v)* to have an effect. *This medicine acts very quickly.*
4 *(n)* a short performance. *A comedy act.*
5 *(n)* one of the parts of a play.
6 *(n)* a law made by Congress.

action
1 *(n)* something that you do to achieve a result. *Nancy's rapid action prevented a serious accident.*
2 When you **take action**, you do something for a purpose.

active
1 *(adj)* energetic and busy.
2 *(adj)* An **active** verb is one where the verb's subject does the action, rather than having something done to it. *In the sentence, "I kicked the ball," the verb is active, but in "The ball was kicked," the verb is passive.*

activity activities
1 *(n)* action or movement. *The playground was full of activity.*
2 *(n)* something that you do for pleasure. *Leisure activities.*

actor *(n)* someone who performs in the theater, movies, television, etc.

actual *(adj)* real or true. **actually** *(adv).*

acupuncture *(**ak**-yoo-punk-cher) (n)* a way of treating illness by pricking parts of the body with small needles.

acute acuter acutest
1 *(adj)* sharp or severe. *Acute pain.*
2 *(adj)* able to detect things easily. *Dogs have an acute sense of smell.* **acuteness** *(n),* **acutely** *(adv).*
3 *(adj)* An **acute** angle is an angle of less than 90 degrees.

A.D. the initials of the Latin phrase *Anno Domini*, which means "In the year of the Lord." A.D. is used to show that a date comes after the birth of Christ. *The American Constitution was written in A.D.1787.*

adapt adapting adapted
1 *(v)* to make something suitable for a different purpose. *We have adapted our garage into a game room.*
2 *(v)* to change because you are in a new situation. *It can be difficult to adapt to life in a foreign country.* **adaptable** *(adj).*

adapter *or* **adaptor** *(n)* a type of electrical plug that you use to connect two or more plugs to one socket.

add adding added
1 *(v)* to put one thing with another. *Add the eggs to the flour.*
2 *(v)* to put numbers together to make a total. **addition** *(n).*

adder
1 *(n)* a small, venomous European snake, sometimes called a viper. *The common adder is found in Britain.*
2 *(n)* a harmless North American snake that hisses and swells its head when threatened.

common adder (male)

addict *(n)* someone who cannot give up doing or using something. *A drug addict.* **addiction** *(n),* **addicted** *(adj).*

addictive *(adj)* If something, such as a drug, is **addictive**, people find it very difficult to give it up. *Cigarettes are addictive.*

additive *(n)* something added to a substance to change it in some way. *Jon tries not to eat food with additives.*

address
addresses addressing addressed
1 *(n)* the details of the place where someone lives. *What's your address?*
2 *(v)* to write an address on a letter, card, or package.
3 *(n)* the series of letters (and sometimes numbers) that you type into a computer to enable a browser to find a particular website or page. *What's the address for that website?*

adenoids *(**ad**-en-oyds) (plural n)* spongy lumps of flesh at the back of your nose.

adequate *(adj)* just enough, or good enough. **adequately** *(adv).*

adhesive *(n)* a substance, such as glue, that makes things stick together. **adhesive** *(adj).*

adjacent *(adj)* close or next to something or someone. *Our families live on adjacent streets.*

adjective *(n)* a word that describes someone or something. *In the phrase, "A tall, handsome stranger," "tall" and "handsome" are adjectives.* **adjectival** *(adj).* *See* page 3.

adjudicate adjudicating adjudicated *(v)* to judge something, such as a competition. **adjudication** *(n),* **adjudicator** *(n).*

adjust adjusting adjusted
1 *(v)* to move or change something slightly. **adjustment** *(n),* **adjustable** *(adj).*
2 *(v)* to get used to something new and different. **adjustment** *(n).*

ad-lib ad-libbing ad-libbed *(v)* to speak in public without preparing first. **ad-lib** *(adv).*

administer
administering administered
1 *(v)* to govern or control something. *Nat administers the team funds.* **administration** *(n).*
2 *(v)* to give something to someone. *The nurse administered the medicine.*

administrate administrating administrated *(v)* to manage and control an organization. **administration** *(n),* **administrator** *(n).*

admiral *(n)* an officer who holds a very high rank in the navy. *The picture shows a statue of Admiral Nelson.*

Admiral Nelson

admire
admiring admired
1 *(v)* to like and respect someone. **admiration** *(n).*
2 *(v)* to look at something and enjoy it.

admit admitting admitted
1 *(v)* to confess to something, or to agree that something is true, often reluctantly. **admission** *(n).*
2 *(v)* to allow someone or something to enter. **admission** *(n),* **admittance** *(n).*

admonish admonishes admonishing admonished *(v)* to tell someone off, or to warn someone. **admonishment** *(n).*

adolescent *(n)* a young person who is more grown-up than a child but is not yet an adult. **adolescence** *(n),* **adolescent** *(adj).*

adopt adopting adopted
1 *(v)* When someone **adopts** a child, they take it into their family and become its legal parents. **adoption** *(n).*
2 *(v)* to accept an idea or a way of doing things. *The government is adopting a tough approach to crime.*

adorable *(adj)* very sweet and lovable. *An adorable kitten.*

adore adoring adored *(v)* to love someone or something very much. **adoration** *(n).*

adorned *(adj)* decorated. **adorn** *(v).*

adrenaline *(n)* a chemical produced by your body when you are excited, frightened, or angry.

adulation *(n)* extreme flattery or praise. **adulate** *(v),* **adulatory** *(adj).*

adult *(n)* a fully grown person or animal. **adulthood** *(n),* **adult** *(adj).*

adulterate adulterating adulterated *(v)* to spoil something by adding something to it.

advance advancing advanced
1 *(v)* to move forward or to make progress. **advancement** *(n).*
2 *(adj)* happening before something else. *Advance warning.*
3 *(v)* to lend money. **advance** *(n).*
4 *(n)* a movement forward by a group of soldiers.

advanced
1 *(adj)* If something has reached an **advanced** stage, it is nearly finished.
2 *(adj)* **Advanced** work is not elementary or easy. *Advanced level science.*

advantage
1 *(n)* something that helps you or is useful to you. **advantageous** *(adj).*
2 *(n)* the first point in a tennis game after the score of deuce.
3 If you **take advantage of** a person or situation, you use them for your own benefit.

advent
1 *(n)* the beginning of something important. *The advent of the computer age.*
2 **Advent** *(n)* the weeks leading up to Christmas in the Christian church.

adventure *(n)* an exciting or dangerous experience. **adventurous** *(adj).*

adverb *(n)* a word usually used to describe a verb. Adverbs tell how, when, where, how often, or how much something happens. *"Slowly," "late,"* and *"soon"* are all adverbs. **adverbial** *(adj).* *See page 3.*

adversary adversaries *(n)* someone who fights or argues against you.

adverse *(adj)* unfavorable or difficult. *Adverse weather conditions.* **adversely** *(adj).*

advertise advertising advertised *(v)* to call attention to something that you want to sell. **advertisement** *(n),* **advertiser** *(n).*

advice *(n)* suggestions about what someone should do. *Sarah gave me good advice on how to fix my bike.*

advisable *(adj)* If something is **advisable**, it is sensible and worth doing. **advisably** *(n).*

advise advising advised *(v)* to give someone information or suggestions so that they can decide what to do. *Tom advised me to stay at home until rush hour was over.* **adviser** *(n),* **advisory** *(adj).*

advocate advocating advocated
1 *(**ad**-voh-kate) (v)* to support an idea or plan. *I would never advocate violence.*
2 *(**ad**-voh-kut) (n)* a person who recommends or supports a policy or cause.

aerial *(**air**-ee-ul) (adj)* happening in the air. *Aerial refueling.*

aerobatics *(plural n)* skillful and sometimes dangerous movements made by aircraft in the sky to entertain people. *The picture shows a plane performing the positive flick roll, an example of aerobatics.* **aerobatic** *(adj).*

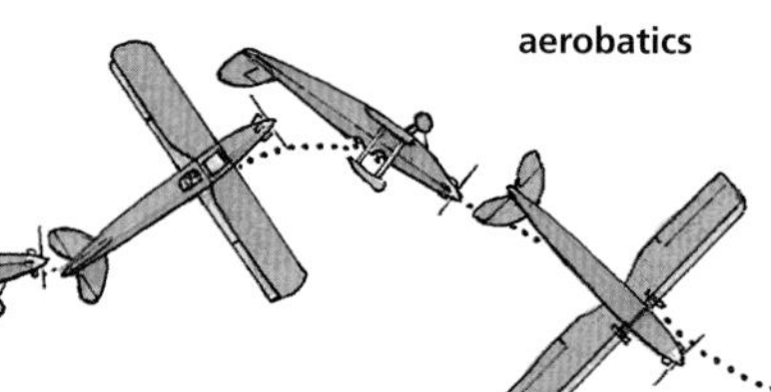
aerobatics

aerodynamic *(adj)* designed to move through the air very easily and quickly. *The streamlined shape of this Suzuki Nuda motorcycle makes it very aerodynamic.*

aerodynamic motorcycle

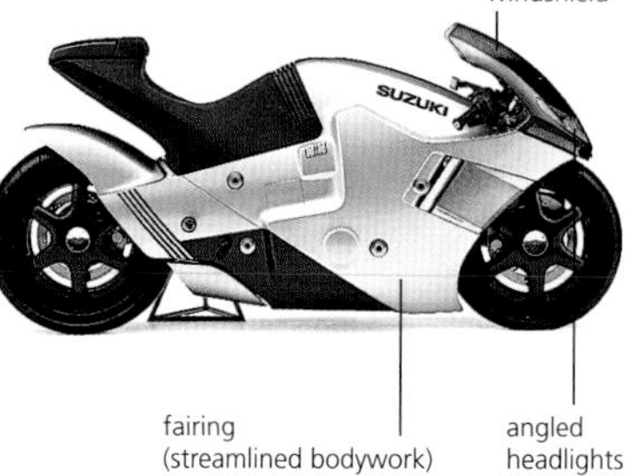

aeronautics *(singular n)* the science and practice of designing and building aircraft. **aeronautical** *(adj).*

aerosol can *(n)* a pressurized can containing liquid that is forced out in a fine spray. When you press the button on an aerosol can, propellant gas pushes liquid up a tube and out through a nozzle. *This picture shows a cross section of an aerosol can.*

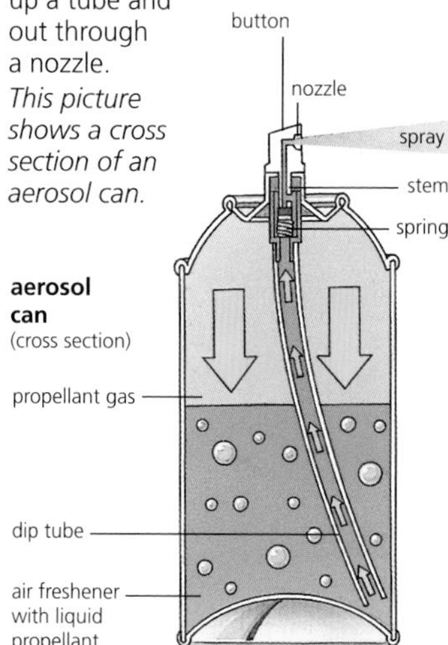

aerosol can (cross section)

affair
1 *(n)* a special event. *The wedding was a grand affair.*
2 **affairs** *(plural n)* business connected with private or public life. *Personal affairs. Business affairs.*

affect affecting affected *(v)* to influence or change someone or something. *Lance's accident affected him badly.*

affected *(adj)* false and unnatural. *Gloria has an affected voice.*

affection *(n)* a fondness or a liking for someone or something.

affectionate *(adj)* loving. **affectionately** *(adv).*

affinity affinities *(n)* If you have an **affinity** for someone or something, you like them and feel close to them.

affliction *(n)* illness or suffering. **afflict** *(v).*

affluent *(adj)* If you are **affluent**, you have plenty of money. **affluence** *(n).*

afford affording afforded
1 *(v)* If you can **afford** something, you have enough money to buy it.
2 *(v)* to have enough time or ability to do something. *I'm so far ahead, that I can afford to relax.*

afloat *(adj)* floating on water.

afraid
1 *(adj)* frightened or worried.
2 *(adj)* sorry. *I'm afraid I can't come to your party.*

afresh *(adv)* When you start **afresh**, you begin something again.

aft *(adv)* toward the back of a ship or an airplane.

after
1 *(prep)* later than. *After lunch.*
2 *(prep)* following. *The puppy ran after her.*
3 *(prep)* trying to catch someone or something. *The police are after him.*

afternoon *(n)* the time of day between noon and about five o'clock in the evening.

afterward *(adv)* later.

again *(adv)* one more time. *Play it again, Sam.*

against
1 *(prep)* next to and touching. *Put your ear against the wall.*
2 *(prep)* competing with. *It's the Chicago Bears against the Miami Dolphins tonight.*
3 *(prep)* opposed to. *I'm against killing whales.*

agate *(n)* a hard, semi-precious stone with bands of color. *The picture shows a piece of agate that has been cut in half and polished.*

agate
(cross section)

age aging aged
1 *(n)* the number of years that someone has lived or that something has existed.
2 *(n)* a period of time in history. *The Stone Age.*
3 *(v)* to become or seem older.

aged
1 *(rhymes with caged) (adj)* being a particular number of years old. *Anyone aged 12 can join our club.*
2 *(ay-jed) (adj)* Someone who is **aged** is very old.

ageism *or* **agism** *(n)* prejudice or discrimination because of age. **ageist** *or* **agist** *(adj).*

agenda *(uh-jen-da) (n)* a list of things that need to be done or discussed.

agent
1 *(n)* someone who arranges things for other people. *Travel agent.* **agency** *(n).*
2 *(n)* a spy. *Secret agent.*

aggravate
aggravating aggravated *(v)* to make a difficult situation even worse.

aggregate *(ag-rig-ut) (n)* a total created by adding together a lot of smaller amounts. *The aggregate of our scores was 25.*

aggression *(n)* fierce or threatening behavior. **aggressive** *(adj),* **aggressively** *(adv).*

aghast *(uh-gast) (adj)* shocked or dismayed.

agile
1 *(adj)* If you are **agile**, you can move fast and easily. **agility** *(n).*
2 *(adj)* Someone with an **agile** mind can think quickly and cleverly. **agility** *(n).*

agism *see* **ageism**.

agitate agitating agitated
1 *(v)* to make someone nervous and worried. **agitation** *(n),* **agitated** *(adj).*
2 *(v)* to stir up a liquid.

agnostic *(n)* someone who believes that you cannot know that God exists. **agnostic** *(adj).*

ago *(adv)* before now or in the past. *Three days ago.*

agony agonies *(n)* great pain or suffering. *David was screaming in agony.* **agonizing** *(adj).*

agree agreeing agreed
1 *(v)* to say yes to something. *I agreed to his plan.* **agreement** *(n).*
2 *(v)* to share the same opinions. *Dan and I always agree on politics.*
3 *(v)* If something **agrees** with you, it suits you, or is good for you.

agreement
1 *(n)* the same way of thinking. *Bill and I are in agreement over that book.*
2 *(n)* an arrangement. *We've made an agreement to share the cost of the party.*

agriculture *(n)* farming. *This picture of agriculture in the Middle Ages shows a group of laborers using scythes to mow a field.* **agricultural** *(adj).* *Also see* **farm**.

medieval agriculture

aground *(adv)* If a boat runs **aground**, it gets stuck on the bottom in shallow water.

ahead
1 *(adv)* in front. *Go on ahead.*
2 *(adv)* in the future. *You must think ahead.*

A.I. *(n) short for* **artificial intelligence**.

aid aiding aided
1 *(v)* to help someone. **aid** *(n).*
2 *(n)* money or equipment for people in need. *Foreign aid.*

AIDS *(n)* an illness in which the body's ability to protect itself against disease is destroyed. AIDS stands for Acquired Immune Deficiency Syndrome.

AIDS virus
(magnified)

aileron *(ay-ler-on) (n)* a hinged piece on an aircraft wing, used to control balance. *See* **aircraft**.

ailment *(n)* an illness, though not usually a serious one.

aim aiming aimed
1 *(v)* to hit, throw, or shoot something in a particular direction. **aim** *(n).*
2 *(v)* to intend to achieve something. *I aim to become a chef.* **aim** *(n).*

air airing aired
1 *(n)* the invisible mixture of gases around you that you need to breathe.
2 *(v)* to let air into a room.
3 *(n)* an appearance or manner. *Wanda has an air of mystery.*

air-conditioning *(n)* a system for keeping the air in a building cool.

aircraft *(n)*
a vehicle that can fly. *The picture shows a Boeing 747-400 aircraft, known as a jumbo jet because of its enormous size. It can carry over 500 passengers and flies at around 570 miles (920km) per hour.*

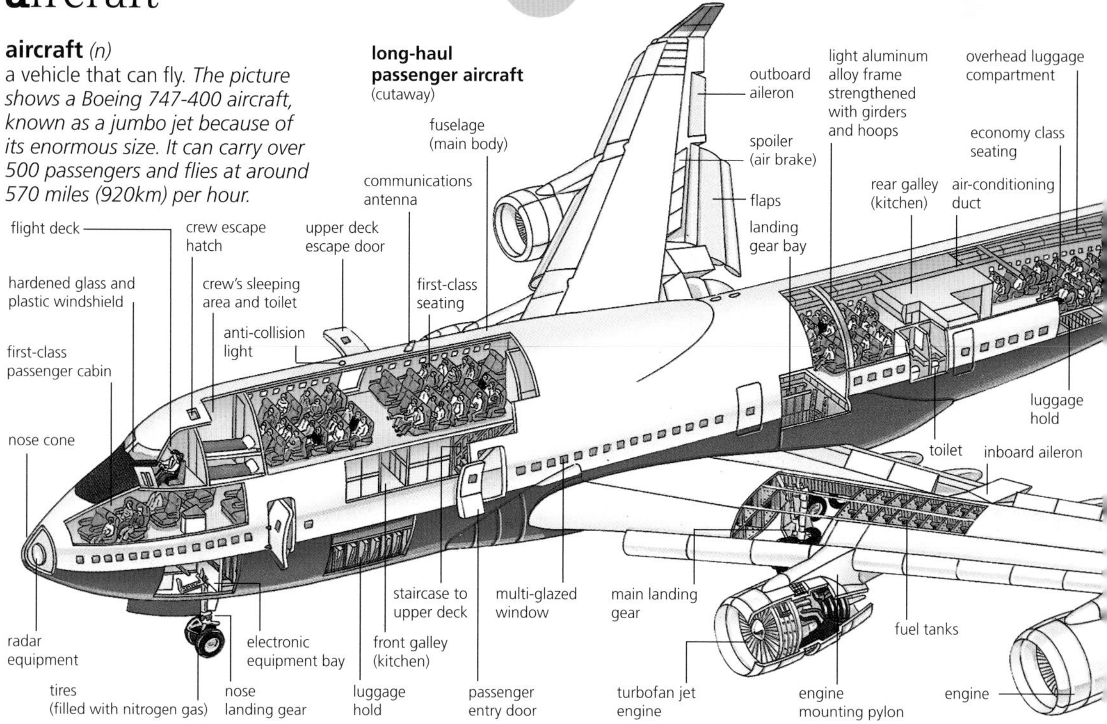

long-haul passenger aircraft (cutaway)

flight deck
crew escape hatch
upper deck escape door
communications antenna
fuselage (main body)
outboard aileron
light aluminum alloy frame strengthened with girders and hoops
overhead luggage compartment
hardened glass and plastic windshield
crew's sleeping area and toilet
anti-collision light
first-class seating
spoiler (air brake)
flaps
landing gear bay
rear galley (kitchen)
economy class seating
air-conditioning duct
first-class passenger cabin
nose cone
luggage hold
toilet
inboard aileron
radar equipment
electronic equipment bay
staircase to upper deck
multi-glazed window
main landing gear
fuel tanks
front galley (kitchen)
tires (filled with nitrogen gas)
nose landing gear
luggage hold
passenger entry door
turbofan jet engine
engine mounting pylon
engine

aircraft carrier *(n)*
a warship with a large, flat deck where aircraft take off and land.

air force *(n)*
part of a country's fighting force that can attack or defend from the air.

airline *(n)* a company that owns and flies aircraft, carrying passengers and goods by air.

airmail *(n)* a postal service by which mail is carried by aircraft.

airplane *(n)* a machine, with wings and an engine, that flies through the air. *See* **aircraft**.

airport *(n)* a place where aircraft take off and land and where people get on and off them.

airship *(n)* a large air balloon with engines and a passenger compartment hanging underneath it.

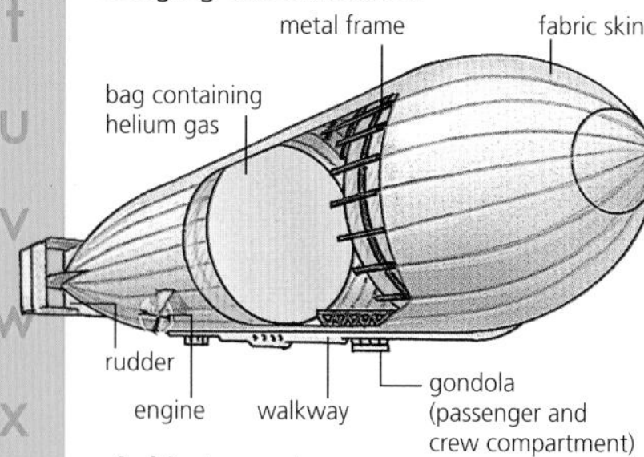

airship (cutaway)

The airship above is a Zeppelin, built in Germany in 1910.

airtight *(adj)*
If a container is **airtight**, it is so well sealed that no air can get in or out.

airy airier airiest
1 *(adj)* An **airy** room is not stuffy.
2 *(adj)* lighthearted or casual. *Camilla gave an airy wave.* **airily** *(adv)*.

aisle *(rhymes with pile) (n)*
the passage that runs between the rows of seats in a church, theater, etc.

ajar *(adj)* If a door is **ajar**, it is partly open. **ajar** *(adv)*.

alarm alarming alarmed
1 *(n)* a device, containing a bell, buzzer, or siren, that wakes someone or warns them of danger.
2 *(n)* a sudden fear that something bad will happen.
3 *(v)* to make someone afraid that something bad might happen. **alarming** *(adj)*, **alarmingly** *(adv)*.

alas *(interject)* unfortunately or sadly. *I'd love to come but, alas, I can't.*

albino *(al-bye-no) (n)* a person or animal born without any natural coloring in their skin, hair, or eyes.

album
1 *(n)* a book in which you keep photographs, stamps, etc.
2 *(n)* a collection of pieces of music recorded on a CD or music player.

alfalfa *(n)* a plant used to feed cattle. Alfalfa sprouts are often eaten as part of a salad or in a sandwich.

alcove *(n)* a part of a room that is set back from the main area.

alert alerting alerted
1 *(adj)* If you are **alert**, you pay attention to what is happening and are ready for action.
2 *(v)* to warn someone that there might be danger. *Alert the police!*
3 *(n)* a warning of danger. *A nuclear alert.*

algae *(al-jee) (plural n)* small plants that grow without roots or stems in water or on damp surfaces.

algebra *(al-jebra) (n)*
a type of mathematics in which signs and letters are used to represent numbers, for example 2x + y = 7.

alias *(ay-lee-us)* **aliases** *(n)*
a false name, especially one used by a criminal.

alibi *(al-i-bye) (n)*
a claim that a person accused of a crime was somewhere else when the crime was committed.

alien *(ay-lee-un)*
1 *(n)* a creature from another planet.
2 *(adj)* different and strange. *Sarah found her new school very alien.*
3 *(n)* a foreigner.

alienate *(ay-lee-un-ate)* **alienating alienated** *(v)* to make other people feel out of place, or to isolate yourself. *Jack alienated his friends by acting strangely.* **alienation** *(n)*.

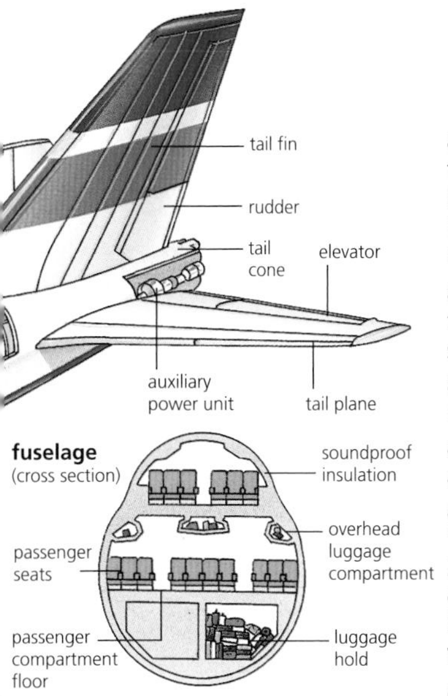

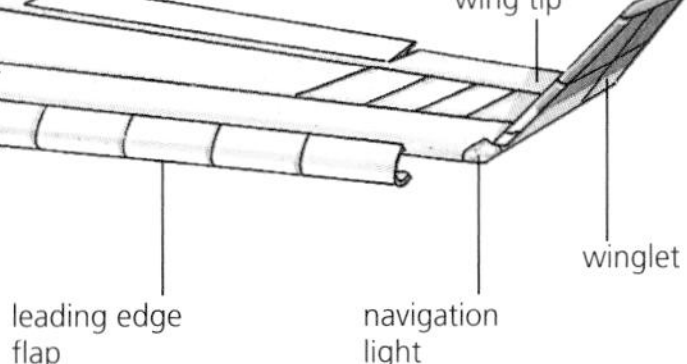

alike
1 *(adj)* looking or acting the same.
2 *(adv)* in a similar way. *All of the children were treated alike.*

alive
1 *(adj)* living.
2 *(adj)* full of life.

alkali *(al-ka-lye) (n)* a substance that turns red litmus paper blue. Strong alkalis can burn your skin. *Toothpaste is an alkali.* **alkaline** *(adj).*

Allah *(n)* the Muslim name for God.

allegiance *(a-lee-jenss) (n)* loyal support for someone or something.

allergic *(adj)* If you are **allergic** to something, it makes you ill. *Joe is allergic to cats.* **allergy** *(n).*

alliance *(n)* a friendly agreement to work together.

alligator *(n)* a large reptile similar to a crocodile, with strong jaws and very sharp teeth. Alligators live in parts of North and South America and China.

alligator

alliteration *(n)* repeated use of the same sound at the beginning of a group of words, for example, "The gruesome ghost gave a ghastly groan." **alliterative** *(adj).*

allocate allocating allocated *(v)* to decide that something should be used for a particular purpose. *We allocated half of the money to charity.* **allocation** *(n).*

allow allowing allowed *(v)* to let someone have or do something. *I won't allow it.*

allowance *(n)* money given to someone regularly.

alloy *(n)* a mixture of two or more metals.

all right
1 *(adj)* good enough or acceptable.
2 *(adj)* not hurt, or not ill. *Helena fell off her horse, but she's all right now.*
3 *(interject)* You say "**all right**" when you agree to do something.

ally *(al-eye)* allies *(n)* a person or a country that gives support to another.

almighty
1 *(adj)* very big. *An almighty crash.*
2 *(adj)* possessing total power.

almost *(adv)* very nearly.

alone *(adj)* by yourself. **alone** *(adv).*

along
1 *(prep)* from one end to the other. *We drove along the street.*
2 **all along** *(adv)* all the time. *I knew all along that Hal was lying.*

aloud *(adv)* in a voice that other people can hear. *Reading aloud.*

alphabet *(n)* all of the letters of a language arranged in order. *The first six letters of the Greek alphabet are shown below.* **alphabetical** *(adj).*

Greek alphabet

α	β	γ	δ	ϵ	ζ
alpha	beta	gamma	delta	epsilon	zeta

already *(adv)* before now. *I've seen that movie already.*

also *(adv)* as well.

altar *(n)* a large table in a church or a temple, used for religious ceremonies.

alter altering altered *(v)* to change something. *We've altered our plans.* **alteration** *(n).*

alternate *(all-ter-nat) (adj)* If something happens on **alternate** days, it happens every other day. **alternate** *(all-ter-nate) (v).*

alternative
1 *(n)* something you can choose to have or do instead of something else. **alternative** *(adj),* **alternatively** *(adv).*
2 *(adj)* different from what is usual. *Alternative medicine.*

although
1 *(conj)* in spite of something. *Although it was wet, we had fun.*
2 *(conj)* but. *Natalie is only nine, although she seems much older.*

altitude *(n)* the height of something above the ground. *This plane can fly at very high altitudes.*

alto
1 *(n)* a singing voice that is quite high for a man and quite low for a woman.
2 *(n)* a singer with an alto voice.

altogether
1 *(adv)* in total. *Barbara has seven hats altogether.*
2 *(adv)* completely or entirely. *What I told you wasn't altogether true.*
3 *(adv)* on the whole. *Altogether, it was a very good party.*

aluminum *(n)* a light, silver-colored metal.

always *(adv)* If something is **always** happening, it happens all of the time or very many times.

Alzheimer's disease *(alts-hi-merz diz-eez) (n)* a disease that affects a person's brain, making it gradually more difficult for them to think clearly or remember things. Alzheimer's disease usually only affects people in old age.

a.m. the initials of the Latin phrase *ante meridiem*, which means "before midday." *I get up at 7 a.m.*

amateur *(n)* someone who takes part in a sport or other activity for pleasure rather than for money.

amaze amazing amazed *(v)* to make someone feel very surprised. **amazement** *(n),* **amazing** *(adj),* **amazingly** *(adv).*

amber
1 *(n)* a yellow-brown color. **amber** *(adj).*
2 *(n)* a yellow-brown substance formed from fossilized tree sap and used for making ornaments and jewelry. *This piece of amber contains an insect that was trapped in the sap before it hardened and fossilized.*

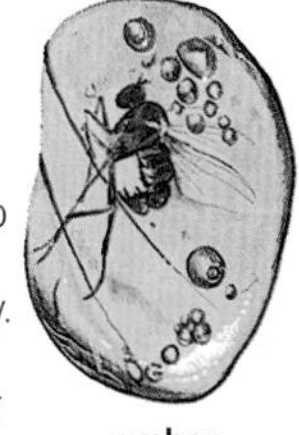
amber

ambidextrous *(adj)* If you are **ambidextrous**, you can use both hands equally well, especially for writing.

ambiguous *(am-big-yoo-us) (adj)* If something is **ambiguous**, it can be understood in more than one way. *Conrad gave an ambiguous answer.* **ambiguity** *(am-big-you-it-ee) (n).*

ambition
1 *(n)* something that you really want to do. *My ambition is to be a movie star.*
2 *(n)* a strong wish to be successful. *Jo is driven by ambition.* **ambitious** *(adj).*

ambivalent *(adj)* If you feel **ambivalent** about something, you are undecided about it. **ambivalence** *(n).*

amble ambling ambled *(v)* to walk slowly because you are not in a hurry.

ambulance *(n)* a vehicle that takes people to the hospital when they are ill.

ambush ambushes ambushing ambushed *(v)* to hide and then attack someone. **ambush** *(n).*

amenity amenities *(n)* something that is available for everyone to use and enjoy, such as a library.

ammonia *(n)* a gas or solution with a strong smell. Some cleaning liquids contain ammonia.

ammunition
1 *(n)* things that can be fired from weapons, such as bullets or arrows.
2 *(n)* information that you can use against someone else.

amnesty amnesties
1 *(n)* an official promise by a government to release prisoners or pardon crimes.
2 *(n)* a chance to hand in something you should not possess, without being punished.

amoeba *(am-ee-bah)* **amoebas** *or* **amoebae** *(n)* a microscopic creature made of only one cell. *The diagram shows the parts of an amoeba.*

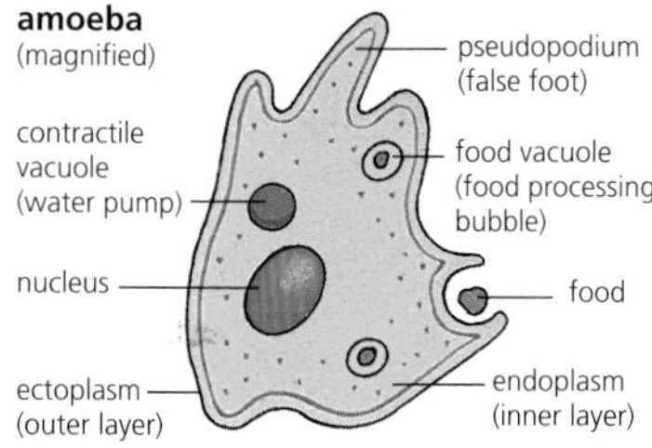

among
1 *(prep)* surrounded by other people or things.
2 *(prep)* If you share something **among** several people, you divide it between them.

amount amounting amounted
1 *(n)* The **amount** of something is how much of it there is.
2 *(v)* If something **amounts to** a total, it adds up to it.

amp *(n)* a unit that measures the strength of an electrical current. Amp is short for ampere.

amphibian
1 *(n)* an animal that lives on land but breeds in water. *Frogs, toads, and newts are amphibians.* **amphibious** *(adj).*
2 *(n)* a vehicle that can travel on land and in water. **amphibious** *(adj).*

amphitheater *(n)* a large, open-air building, built in Roman times, with rows of seats in a high circle around an arena. Amphitheaters were used for public entertainment, such as gladiatorial and animal fights. *The picture shows a famous amphitheater.*

anagram *(n)* a word or phrase made by changing the order of letters in another word or phrase. *"Stop" is an anagram of "post."*

analyze
analyzing analyzed *(v)*
to examine something carefully in order to understand it. *Let's analyze the problem before we do anything.* **analysis** *(n),* **analytical** *(adj).*

anarchy *(n)*
a situation with no order and with no one in control. **anarchist** *(n).*

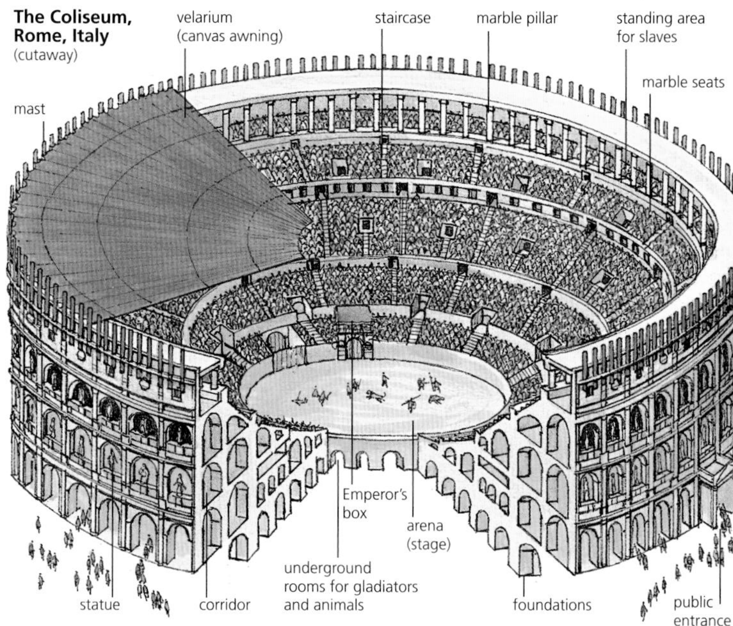

ample
ampler amplest
1 *(adj)* more than enough. *There was ample food for everyone.* **amply** *(adv).*
2 *(adj)* large. *Mara has an ample figure.*

amplifier *(n)*
a piece of equipment that makes sound louder. **amplification** *(n),* **amplify** *(v).*

amputate
amputating amputated *(v)*
to cut off someone's arm or leg because it is damaged or diseased. **amputation** *(n).*

amuse amusing amused
1 *(v)* to make someone laugh or smile. **amusing** *(adj).*
2 *(v)* to keep someone happy and stop them from being bored. *Dad's new camera kept him amused for hours.* **amusement** *(n).*

anatomy
1 *(n)* The **anatomy** of a person or an animal is the structure of their body.
2 *(n)* the study of how the bodies of people and animals fit together. **anatomical** *(adj).*

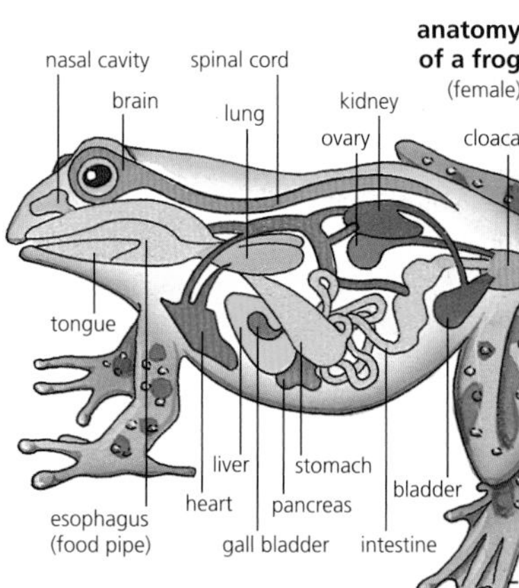

b c d e f g h i j k l m n o p q r s t u v w x y z

ancestor *(n)* Your **ancestors** are members of your family who lived a long time ago. **ancestry** *(n)*, **ancestral** *(adj)*.

anchor *(n)* a heavy metal hook that is lowered from a ship or boat to stop it from drifting. **anchorage** *(n)*, **anchor** *(v)*. *See* **ship**.

ancient *(ayn-chent)*
1 *(adj)* very old.
2 *(adj)* belonging to a time long ago. *Ancient Rome.*

android *(n)* a robot that acts and looks like a human being.

anecdote *(n)* a short, funny story about something that has happened. **anecdotal** *(adj)*.

anemic *(a-nee-mik) (adj)* If you are **anemic**, you become easily tired and weak because your blood does not contain enough iron. **anemia** *(n)*.

anesthetic *(an-es-thet-ik) (n)* a drug or gas given to someone before an operation to prevent them from feeling pain. **anesthetist** *(an-es-thuh-tist) (n)*.

angel
1 *(n)* a messenger of God. **angelic** *(adj)*.
2 *(n)* a very kind, gentle person. **angelic** *(adj)*.

anger *(n)* the feeling of being mad or very annoyed.

angle
1 *(n)* the space between two lines at the point where they touch. *Angles are measured in degrees, for example, 90 degrees.*
2 *(n)* a way of looking at or thinking about something. *Leroy approached the problem from a different angle.*
3 If something is **at an angle**, it is sloping and not straight.

angling *(n)* the sport of fishing with a fishing rod rather than a net. *The picture shows equipment used for freshwater angling.* **angler** *(n)*, **angle** *(v)*.

line
rod ring
carbon fiber rod
float ring
grayling float
split shot
drag nut setting
spool
reel fitting
cork handle
bale arm
reel handle
fixed spool reel
bait on hook

float fishing rod

angora
1 *(n)* a long-haired variety of rabbit, goat, or cat.
2 *(n)* fluffy wool made from the hair of angora rabbits, mixed with sheep's wool.

angora rabbits

angry angrier angriest *(adj)* If you are **angry**, you feel that you want to argue or fight with someone. **angrily** *(adv)*.

anguish *(ang-wish) (n)* a strong feeling of misery or distress. **anguished** *(adj)*.

angular *(adj)* Something that is **angular** has a lot of straight lines and sharp corners. *Carlos had a thin, angular face.*

animal *(n)* any living creature that can breathe and move about.

animated
1 *(adj)* lively. *An animated conversation.* **animation** *(n)*, **animatedly** *(adv)*.
2 *(n)* An **animated movie** is made by showing a series of still images in sequence, very rapidly, to create the illusion of movement. Animated movies can be made using hand drawings, models and computer generated images. **animation** *(n)*, **animate** *(v)*.

animation sequence

animosity animosities *(n)* a strong dislike for someone.

anise *(n)* a strong-smelling seed used in candies and drinks.

ankle *(n)* the joint that connects your foot to your leg.

annex annexes annexing annexed
1 *(v)* When one country **annexes** another, it takes control of it, often by force.
2 *(n)* an extra building joined onto or placed near a main building.

annihilate *(an-eye-ill-ate)* **annihilating annihilated** *(v)* to destroy something completely. **annihilation** *(n)*.

anniversary anniversaries *(n)* a date that people remember because something important happened on that date in the past. *A wedding anniversary.*

annotate **annotating annotated** *(v)* to write notes explaining a piece of writing. **annotation** *(n)*, **annotated** *(adj)*.

announce announcing announced *(v)* to say something officially or publicly. **announcement** *(n)*.

announcer *(n)* someone who introduces programs on television or radio.

annoy annoying annoyed *(v)* to make someone feel angry. *Dudley really annoys me when he talks in that stupid voice.* **annoyance** *(n)*, **annoying** *(adj)*, **annoyingly** *(adv)*.

annual
1 *(adj)* happening once every year or over a period of one year. *The annual writing competition. An annual subscription.* **annually** *(adv)*.
2 *(n)* a book published once per year.
3 *(n)* a plant that lives for only one year. *Sunflowers are annuals.*

anon *(adj)* Anon is short for anonymous.

anonymous *(adj)* written, done, or given by a person whose name is not known. *An anonymous letter.* **anonymity** *(n)*, **anonymously** *(adv)*.

anorak *(n)* a waterproof jacket with a hood.

anorexia *(n)* If someone suffers from **anorexia**, they think that they are too fat and so they eat very little and become dangerously thin. Anorexia is short for anorexia nervosa. **anorexic** *(n)*, **anorexic** *(adj)*.

another
1 *(adj)* one more of the same kind. *Have another cookie.*
2 *(pronoun)* a different one. *I didn't like the red dress, so I chose another.*

answer answering answered
1 *(v)* to say or write something as a reply to a question. **answer** *(n)*.
2 *(n)* the solution to a problem. *Is there an answer to world poverty?*
3 *(v)* something done in response or reaction. *Peggy answered by walking out of the meeting.*
4 If someone has **a lot to answer for**, they have caused a lot of trouble.

answerable *(adj)* responsible. *Each leader is answerable for the safety of her group.*

ant *(n)* a small insect often with no wings that lives in a group called a colony. *See* **desert**, **insect**.

antagonize antagonizing antagonized *(v)* If you **antagonize** someone, you make them feel very angry with you. **antagonism** *(n)*, **antagonist** *(n)*.

Antarctic *(n)* the area around the South Pole. **Antarctic** *(adj)*. *See* **polar**.

anteater *(n)* a South American mammal with a very long tongue that it uses to search for ants and other small insects.

giant anteater

antelope *(n)* a large animal like a deer, which runs very fast. Antelope are from Africa and parts of Asia.

antenna antennas *or* antennae
1 *(n)* a feeler on the head of an insect. *See* **beetle**.
2 *(n)* a piece of wire that receives radio and television signals.

anthem *(n)* a religious or national song.

anthology anthologies *(n)* a collection of poems, stories, music or art by different writers and artists.

anthropology *(singular n)* the study of the beliefs and ways of life of different people around the world. **anthropologist** *(n)*.

antibiotic *(n)* a drug, such as penicillin, that kills bacteria and is used to cure infections.

antibody antibodies *(n)* Your blood makes **antibodies** to fight against infection.

anticipate anticipating anticipated *(v)* to expect something to happen and be prepared for it. *The police anticipate trouble at the rally.* **anticipation** *(n)*.

anticlimax anticlimaxes *(n)* If something is an **anticlimax**, it is not as exciting as you had expected. **anticlimactic** *(adj)*.

anticyclone *(n)* an area of high pressure in the atmosphere that causes settled weather. *In summer, an anticyclone brings clear skies and warm weather.*

antidote *(n)* something that stops a poison from working.

antiperspirant *(n)* a substance that you put on your skin to stop you from sweating too much.

antique *(an-teek)*
1 *(n)* a very old object that is valuable because it is rare or beautiful.
2 *(adj)* very old.

antiseptic *(n)* a substance that kills germs and prevents infection. *An antiseptic wipe.*

antisocial
1 *(adj)* When someone behaves in an **antisocial** way, they do something that upsets or harms other people.
2 *(adj)* If someone is **antisocial**, they do not enjoy being with other people.

antler *(n)* one of the two large, branching, bony structures on a male deer's head. Male deer grow and shed new antlers each year. *The diagram shows a new antler.*

velvet (skin)
antler bone
tine (branch)
pedicel (antler base)
skull bone

male deer's antler (cross section)

anxiety *(ang-zye-it-ee)* anxieties *(n)* a feeling of worry or fear.

anxious *(ank-shuss)*
1 *(adj)* worried. *Mom gets anxious when I'm late.* **anxiously** *(adv)*.
2 *(adj)* wanting to do something. *Sid is anxious to do well on his exams.*

anybody *(pronoun)* any person.

anyhow *(adv)* in any case. *I didn't want to come anyhow.*

anyone *(pronoun)* any person.

anything *(pronoun)* any thing. *I'm not fussy, I'll eat anything.*

anyway *(adv)* in any case. *I never liked him anyway.*

anywhere *(adv)* in or to any place. *I'd follow Jo anywhere.*

apart *(adv)* If two people or things are **apart**, they are separated from each other.

apartheid *(a-par-tide)* *(n)* a political system in which people of different races are kept apart from one another.

apartment *(n)* a set of rooms for living in, usually on one floor of a building.

apathetic *(adj)* If you are **apathetic**, you do not care about anything or want to do anything. **apathy** *(n)*.

ape aping aped
1 *(n)* a large animal like a monkey, but with no tail. Gorillas, gibbons, and chimpanzees are kinds of apes. *The picture shows a type of ape called a chimpanzee, poking a stick into a termite mound to find food.*
2 *(v)* to copy the way another person behaves or speaks.

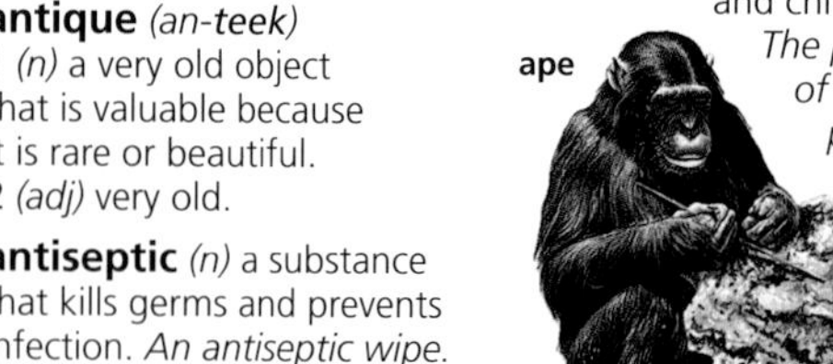
ape

apex apexes *(n)* the highest point of something. *The apex of a triangle.*

apologize apologizing apologized *(v)* to say that you are sorry about something. **apology** *(n)*, **apologetic** *(adj)*.

apostle *(n)* one of the twelve men chosen by Christ to spread his teachings. *This picture of the apostle Matthew is taken from the 7th-century Lindisfarne Gospels.*

apostle

apostrophe *(a-poss-truh-fee)* *(n)* a punctuation mark (') used to show possession, for example, *"Jane's bag,"* or to show that letters have been left out, for example, *"can't."*

app *(n)* *(informal)* a program or game you can download onto your computer or phone.

appalling *(adj)* horrifying and shocking. **appallingly** *(adv)*.

apparatus
1 *(n)* equipment used for performing sports, especially gymnastics.
2 *(n)* equipment or machines used to do a job or laboratory experiment.

laboratory apparatus

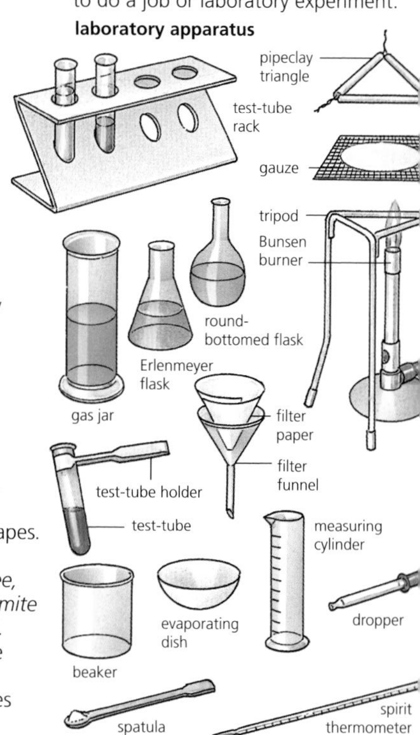

apparent
1 *(adj)* obvious or clear. *Bill's guilt was apparent to us all.*
2 *(adj)* seeming real or true. *Claudia's apparent confidence is really a sham.* **apparently** *(adv).*

appeal appealing appealed
1 *(v)* to ask for something urgently.
2 *(v)* to ask for a decision made by a court to be changed.
3 *(v)* If something **appeals** to you, you like it or find it interesting.

appear appearing appeared
1 *(v)* to come into sight. **appearance** *(n).*
2 *(v)* to seem. *Paul appears to be happy.* **appearance** *(n).*

appendicitis *(n)*
If someone has an **appendicitis**, their appendix is infected and very painful.

appendix
appendixes *or* appendices
1 *(n)* a small, closed tube leading from your bowel. *See* **digestion**.
2 *(n)* extra information at the end of a book.

appetite
1 *(n)* desire for food.
2 *(n)* great enjoyment of something. *Thomas has a real appetite for work.*

appetizing *(adj)*
Food that is **appetizing** looks and smells good to eat.

applaud
applauding applauded *(v)* to show that you like something, usually by clapping your hands. **applause** *(n).*

apple *(n)*
a round, usually crispy, fruit. *See* **fruit**.

appliance *(n)* a machine designed to do a particular job. *Our kitchen is full of modern appliances.*

applicant *(n)*
someone who has written formally, asking for something, such as a job or a place in a class.

application
1 *(n)* a written request for something, like a job. *A job application.*
2 *(n)* a way of using something. *Our computer system has many different applications.*

apply applies applying applied
1 *(v)* to ask for something in writing.
2 *(v)* to be relevant. *These rules don't apply to us.*
3 *(v)* If you **apply yourself** to something, you work hard at it.

appoint appointing appointed
1 *(v)* to choose someone for a job.
2 *(v)* to arrange something officially. *We've already appointed a date for the competition.*

appointment
1 *(n)* an arrangement to meet someone at a certain time.
2 *(n)* a job.

appreciable *(adj)* important enough to be noticed. *The company has lost an appreciable amount of money.*

appreciate
appreciating appreciated
1 *(v)* to enjoy or value someone or something. **appreciation** *(n),* **appreciative** *(adj),* **appreciatively** *(adv).*
2 *(v)* to understand something. *I appreciate your point of view.*
3 *(v)* to increase in value. **appreciation** *(n).*

apprehensive *(adj)*
worried and slightly afraid. *Diana was apprehensive about making her speech.* **apprehension** *(n),* **apprehensively** *(adv).*

apprentice *(n)* someone who learns a trade, craft or profession by working with a professional person. **apprenticeship** *(n).*

approach approaches approaching approached
1 *(v)* to move nearer. **approach** *(n).*
2 *(v)* If you **approach** someone, you go up to them and talk to them.
3 *(v)* When you **approach** a problem, you think of ways to solve it. **approach** *(n).*

approachable *(adj)*
If someone is **approachable**, they are friendly and easy to talk to.

appropriate
appropriating appropriated
1 *(uh-pro-pree-ut) (adj)* suitable or right. **appropriately** *(adv).*
2 *(up-pro-pree-ate) (v)* to take something for a purpose without permission.

approve approving approved
1 *(v)* If you **approve of** someone or something, you think that they are acceptable or good. **approval** *(n).*
2 *(v)* to accept a plan or an idea. **approval** *(n).*

approximate *(adj)*
more or less accurate or correct. *An approximate price.* **approximation** *(n),* **approximately** *(adv).*

apricot *(n)* a small, soft fruit with an orange skin. *See* **fruit**.

apron
1 *(n)* a piece of clothing that you wear to protect your clothes when you are cooking, painting, etc.
2 *(n)* the part of a stage in front of the curtain.

apt
1 *(adj)* very suitable. *An apt reply.*
2 *(adj)* quick to learn things.
3 *(adj)* If you are **apt to** do something, you are likely to do it.

aptitude *(n)*
a natural ability to do something well.

aqualung *(n)* breathing apparatus for diving. An aqualung consists of an air tank with a tube leading to a mouthpiece. *See* **scuba diving**.

aquarium aquariums *or* aquaria *(n)*
a glass tank in which you can keep fish. *The picture shows an aquarium for tropical freshwater fish.*

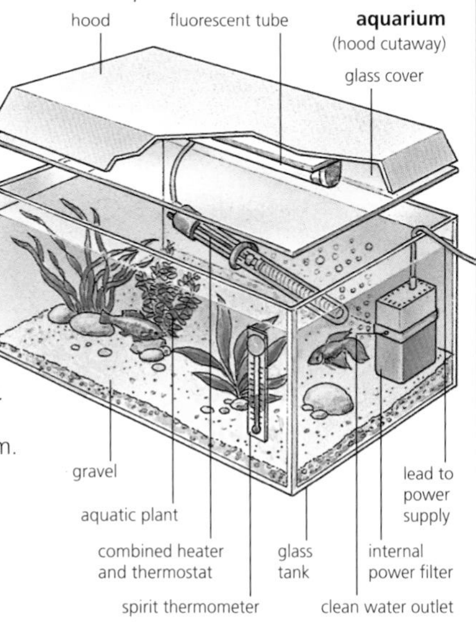

aquatic
1 *(adj)* living or growing in water. *Aquatic plants.*
2 *(adj)* performed in or on water. *Aquatic sports.*

aqueduct *(n)* a large bridge built to carry water across a valley. *The Roman aqueduct shown below was built in France in A.D. 14.*

aqueduct

Arabic
1 *(n)* a language spoken by many people in the Middle East and North Africa.
2 *(n)* **Arabic numerals** are the numbers, such as 1, 2, 3, that we use today. *Arabic numerals are easier to use than Roman numerals.*

a b c d e f g h i j k l m n o p q r s t u v w x y z

arable *(adj)*
Arable land is used for growing crops.

arbitrate
arbitrating arbitrated *(v)*
to help two sides to reach an agreement. **arbitration** *(n)*.

arc
1 *(n)* a curved line.
2 *(n)* An **arc** is part of the circumference of a circle. *See* **circle**.

arcade
1 *(n)* a row of arches in a building.
2 *(n)* a covered area housing a collection of places to visit.
A shopping arcade; a video arcade.

arch
arches arching arched
1 *(n)* a curved structure. Arches often help to support a building or bridge. *The picture below shows four different types of arches.*
2 *(v)* to curve. *The cat arched its back and spat.* **arched** *(adj)*.
3 *(adj)* chief. *Joe is my arch enemy.*

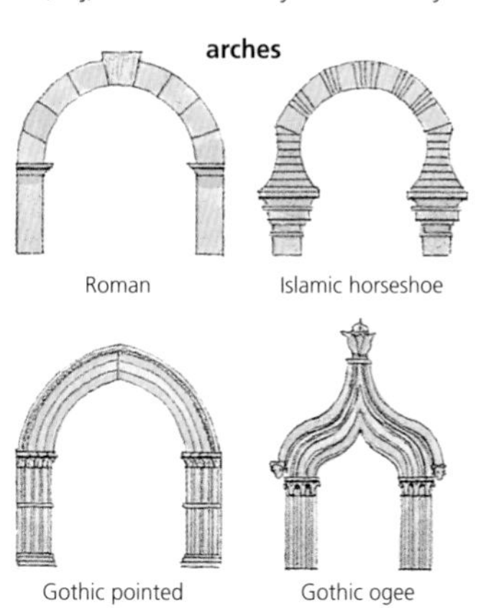

archaeology *or* **archeology**
(ar-kee-ol-ah-jee) (n)
If you study **archaeology**, you learn about the past by digging up old buildings and objects and examining them carefully. **archaeologist** *(n)*, **archaeological** *(adj)*.

archaic *(ar-kay-ik) (adj)* very old-fashioned and not used anymore.

archbishop *(n)*
one of the most important leaders in the Christian church.

archeology *see* **archaeology**.

archery *(n)*
the sport of shooting at targets, using a bow and arrow. **archer** *(n)*.

archipelago *(ar-ki-pel-a-go) (n)*
a group of small islands.

architect *(ar-ki-tekt) (n)*
someone who designs buildings and checks that they are built correctly.

architecture
1 *(n)* the activity of designing buildings.
2 *(n)* the style in which buildings are designed.
This selection of buildings shows how different styles of architecture have been used for places of worship throughout the world and for a range of modern buildings.
architectural *(adj)*.
Also see **building**.

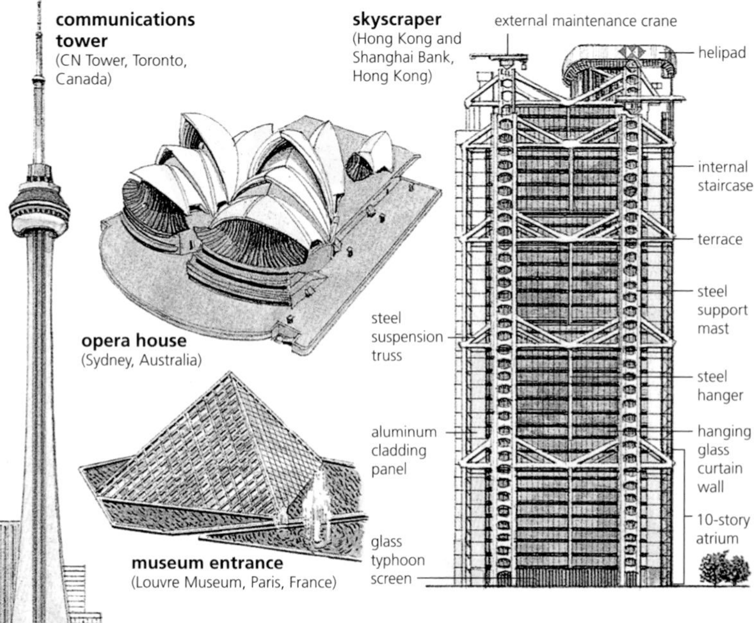

arctic
1 **The Arctic** *(n)* the frozen area around the North Pole. **Arctic** *(adj)*. *See* **polar**.
2 *(adj)* extremely cold and wintry. *Arctic weather conditions.*

ardent *(adj)* If you are **ardent** about something, you feel very strongly about it. **ardently** *(adv)*.

arduous *(ard-yoo-us) (adj)* very difficult and demanding a lot of effort. *An arduous journey.*

area
1 *(n)* the size of a surface. To work out the area of a surface, multiply its length by its width.
2 *(n)* part of a place. *A poor area of the country.*

arena *(n)* a large area, used for sports or entertainment. *See* **amphitheater**, **track and field**.

argue arguing argued
1 *(v)* to disagree with someone angrily. **argument** *(n)*, **argumentative** *(adj)*.
2 *(v)* to give your opinion about something. *Sean argued that hunting was cruel.* **argument** *(n)*.

arid *(adj)*
Land that is **arid** is extremely dry because very little rain has fallen on it.

arise arising arose arisen
1 *(v)* If something, such as a problem, **arises**, it comes into being.
2 *(v) (old-fashioned)* to stand up. *Arise, Sir Francis!*

aristocrat *(n)* a member of the highest social rank, or nobility. **aristocracy** *(n)*, **aristocratic** *(adj)*.

arithmetic *(n)*
calculations with numbers. Addition, subtraction, multiplication, and division are all types of arithmetic.

arm arming armed
1 *(n)* the part of your body between your shoulder and your hand.
2 *(v)* If a country **arms** itself, it gets ready for war.
3 **arms** *(plural n)* weapons.

armadillo *(n)* a mammal covered by hard, bony plates. *The nine-banded armadillo, shown below, is found in North and South America.*

nine-banded armadillo

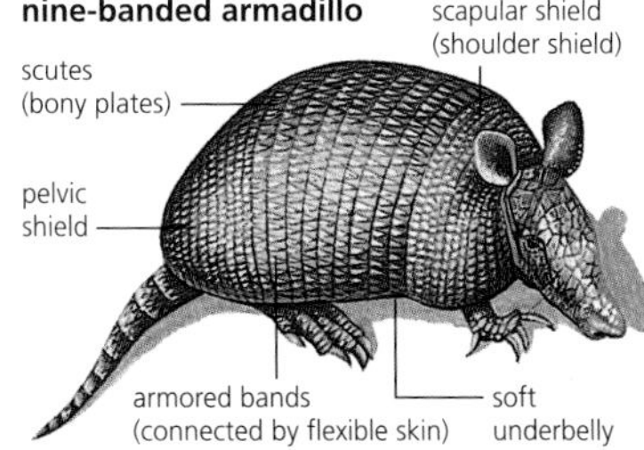

armaments *(plural n)*
weapons and other equipment used for fighting wars.

armchair *(n)* a comfortable chair with supports for your arms.

armistice *(n)*
an agreement to stop fighting a war.

armor
1 *(n)* metal covering worn by soldiers to protect them in battle. *See* **knight**.
2 *(n)* protective scales, spines, or shells that cover some animals, such as armadillos. *See* **armadillo**.

armored vehicle *(n)*
a tank or other military vehicle with a strong metal covering. *This armored vehicle is used for carrying troops.*

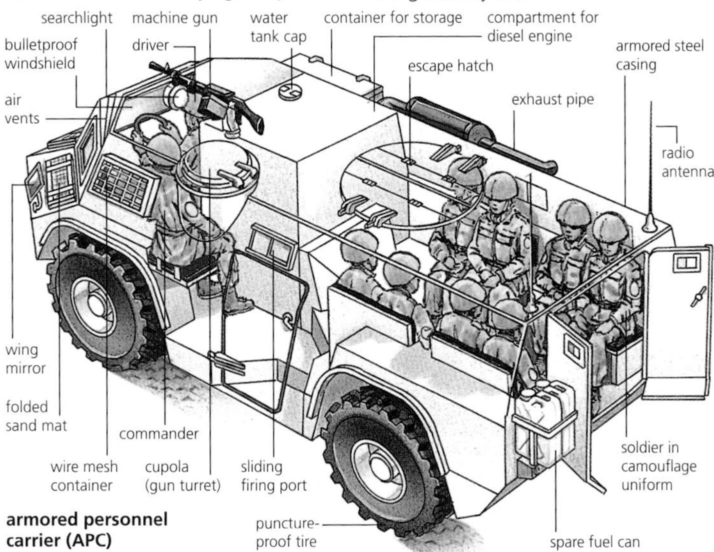

armored personnel carrier (APC)

armpit *(n)* the area under your arm where it joins your shoulder.

army armies *(n)* a large group of people trained to fight on land.

aroma *(n)*
a pleasant smell. **aromatic** *(adj)*.

around
1 *(prep)* surrounding or in a circle. *He tied a rope around the tree.*
2 *(adv)* in many different parts of a place. *We traveled around Spain.*
3 *(adv)* more or less. *There were around 30 of us.*

arouse arousing aroused
1 *(v)* to wake someone.
2 *(v)* to stir up a feeling. *Joe's strange behavior aroused my curiosity.* **arousal** *(n)*.

arrange arranging arranged
1 *(v)* to make plans for something to happen. **arrangement** *(n)*.
2 *(v)* to place things so that they look attractive. **arrangement** *(n)*.
3 *(v)* to change a piece of music slightly, so that it can be played on different instruments. **arrangement** *(n)*.
4 *(n)* If someone has an **arranged marriage**, their parents have chosen a husband or wife for them.

arrest arresting arrested
1 *(v)* to take someone prisoner. **arrest** *(n)*.
2 *(v)* to stop something from developing or happening anymore.

arrive arriving arrived
1 *(v)* to reach a place. *We arrived home early.* **arrival** *(n)*.
2 *(v)* to come. *At last, the great day arrived.*

arrogant *(adj)* conceited and proud. **arrogance** *(n)*, **arrogantly** *(adv)*.

arrow
1 *(n)* a pointed stick shot from a bow.
2 *(n)* a sign showing a direction.

arson *(n)* If someone commits **arson**, they deliberately and wrongly set fire to something.

art
1 *(n)* the skill of creating something by drawing, painting, or making things.
2 *(n)* something that requires a lot of skill. *The art of Chinese cooking.*
3 **the arts** *(plural n)*
forms of entertainment, such as music, theater, and film.

artery arteries *(n)* one of the tubes that carry blood from your heart to all of the other parts of your body. **arterial** *(adj)*. *See* **circulation**.

arthritis *(n)* a disease that makes people's joints swollen and painful.

article
1 *(n)* an object or a thing.
2 *(n)* a piece of writing published in a newspaper, magazine or online.
3 *(n)* a word such as "a," "the," or "some," that goes before a noun.

articulate *(adj)* If you are **articulate**, you can express yourself clearly and well in words. **articulately** *(adv).*

articulated truck *(n)*
a truck with a cab and a trailer linked by a flexible joint so that the truck can turn round corners easily. *See* **truck**.

artificial *(adj)*
false, not real, or not natural. *Artificial flowers.* **artificially** *(adv).*

artificial intelligence *(n)*
the use of computers to do things that previously needed human intelligence, such as understanding language.

artillery
1 *(n)* large, powerful guns.
2 *(n)* the part of an army that uses large guns.

artist *(n)* someone very skilled at painting, drawing, or making things. *This picture shows a range of tools and materials used by artists.* **artistic** *(adj),* **artistically** *(adv).*

aside
1 *(adv)* to one side, or out of the way. *Sarah pushed her brothers aside.*
2 *(n)* a remark made quietly so that not everyone can hear it.

ask asking asked
1 *(v)* to make a request of or put a question to someone.
2 *(v)* to invite someone to do something. *I've asked Tim to lunch.*

askew *(uh-skyoo) (adj)* crooked.

asleep *(adj)* sleeping. *The baby soon fell asleep.*

aspect *(n)* one feature or characteristic of something. *Robbie enjoys most aspects of school life.*

asphyxiate *(a-sfix-ee-ate)* **asphyxiating asphyxiated** *(v)* to suffocate. **asphyxiation** *(n).*

aspiration *(n)*
a strong desire to do something great or important. **aspire** *(v).*

aspirin *(n)* a drug that relieves pain and reduces fever.

assassinate assassinating **assassinated** *(v)* to murder an important person, such as a president. **assassin** *(n),* **assassination** *(n).*

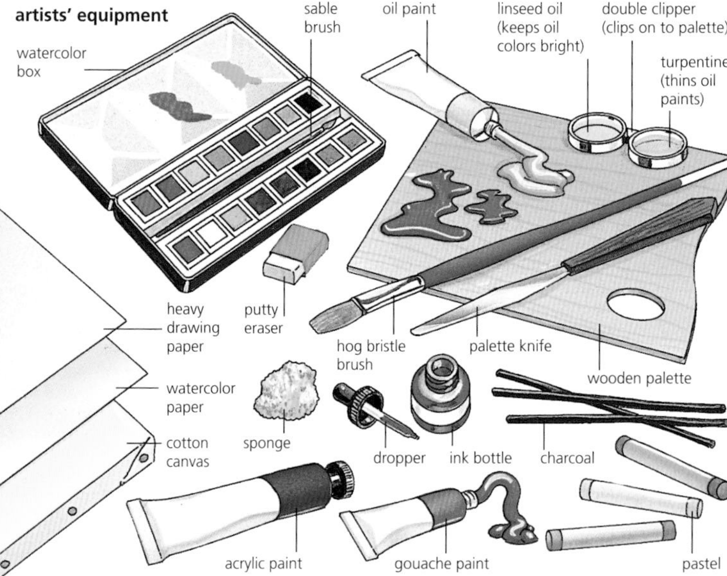

ascend *(a-send)*
ascending ascended *(v)*
to move upward. **ascent** *(n).*

ash ashes
1 *(n)* the powder that remains after something has been burned.
2 *(n)* a tree with long, thin leaves.

ashamed *(adj)* If you are **ashamed**, you feel embarrassed and guilty.

assault assaulting assaulted *(v)* to attack someone or something violently. **assault** *(n).*

assemble assembling assembled
1 *(v)* to gather together in one place. *Everyone from the school assembled in the hall.*
2 *(v)* to put all the parts of something together. *Follow the instructions to assemble this model.*

assembly
1 *(n)* a meeting of a lot of people.
2 **assembly line** *(n)* a series of machines and workers in a factory that each do a particular job.

assent assenting assented *(v)* to agree to something. **assent** *(n).*

assert asserting asserted *(v)*
If you **assert yourself**, you behave in a strong, confident way so that people take notice of you.

assertive *(adj)*
able to stand up for yourself and tell other people what you think or want. **assertiveness** *(n),* **assertively** *(adv).*

assess
assesses assessing assessed *(v)*
to judge how good or bad something is. **assessment** *(n),* **assessor** *(n).*

asset *(n)*
something or someone who is helpful or useful. *Kate is an asset to our team.*

assignment *(n)* a special job that is given to someone. **assign** *(v).*

assistance *(n)*
If someone gives you **assistance**, they do something to help you or to make things easier for you. **assist** *(v).*

assistant *(n)* a person who helps someone else to do a task or job.

association
1 *(n)* an organization, club, or society.
2 *(n)* a connection that you make in your mind between different things. *Our vacation home has many happy associations for me.* **associate** *(v).*

assonance *(n)*
repeated use of the same vowel sound in words that are close together, for example, "How now brown cow?".

assortment *(n)* a mixture of different things. **assorted** *(adj).*

assume assuming assumed
1 *(v)* to suppose that something is true, without checking it. *I assume that you're right.* **assumption** *(n).*
2 *(v)* If you **assume** responsibility for something, you agree to take care of it.
3 An **assumed name** is a false name.

assurance
1 *(n)* a firm promise.
2 *(n)* confidence in yourself and in what you can do. *Self-assurance.*

assure assuring assured
1 *(v)* to promise something or say something positively. *Annie assured me of her support.*
2 *(v)* If you **assure yourself** about something, you make certain about it.

asterisk *(n)* a mark (*) used in printing and writing.

b
c
d
e
f
g
h
i
j
k
l
m
n
o
w
x
y
z

asteroid *(n)* an object in space that is smaller than a planet and orbits around a star.

asthma *(az-ma) (n)* a condition of the lungs. If you have **asthma**, you sometimes wheeze and find it hard to breathe. **asthmatic** *(n)*, **asthmatic** *(adj)*.

astonish astonishes astonishing astonished *(v)* to make someone feel very surprised. **astonishment** *(n)*, **astonishing** *(adj)*, **astonishingly** *(adv)*.

astray
1 *(adv)* If something has gone **astray**, it has been lost.
2 If someone **leads you astray**, they encourage you to do something wrong.

astride *(prep)*
If you sit **astride** something, such as a horse or a bicycle, you sit with a leg on either side of it.

astrology *(n)*
the study of stars and planets and the ways in which they might affect people's lives. **astrologer** *(n)*, **astrological** *(adj)*.

astronaut *(n)*
someone who travels in space. *The picture shows an astronaut operating a manned maneuvering unit (MMU), which is used for moving around outside the spaceship.*

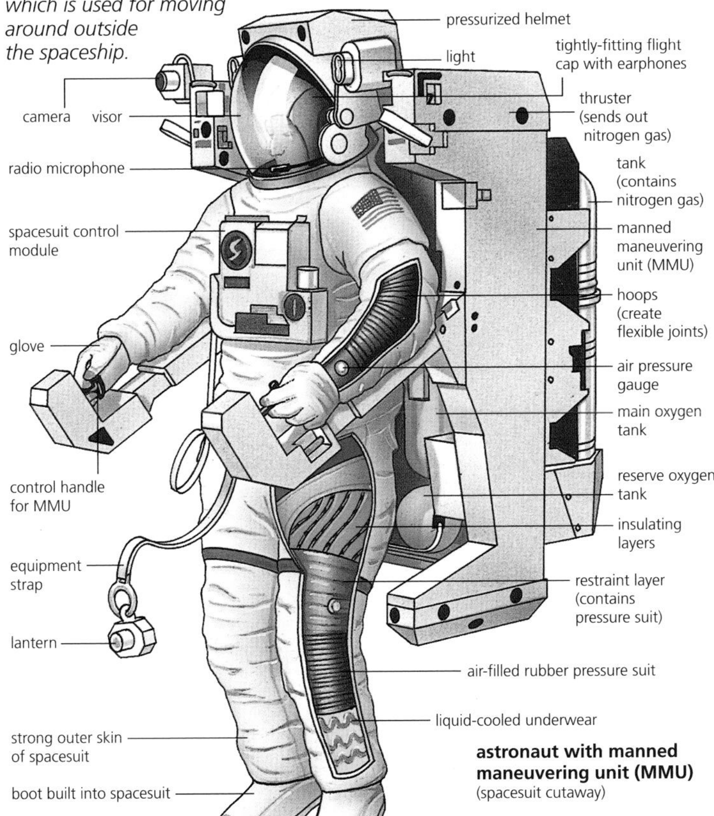

astronaut with manned maneuvering unit (MMU)
(spacesuit cutaway)

astronomical sphere

astronomical
1 *(adj)* related to astronomy. *The astronomical instrument shown here dates from the 16th century and was used to work out the positions of the stars.*
2 *(adj)* very large. *An astronomical amount of money.* **astronomically** *(adv)*.

astronomy *(n)* the study of stars, planets, and space. **astronomer** *(n)*.

astute *(uh-stoot) (adj)*
If someone is **astute**, they understand situations and people clearly and quickly.

asunder *(adv) (old-fashioned)* in or into pieces. *The veil was torn asunder.*

asylum *(uh-sigh-lum)*
1 *(n)* protection given by a country to someone escaping from danger in their own country.
2 *(n) (old-fashioned)* a hospital for people who are mentally ill.

asymmetrical *(adj)*
A shape that is **asymmetrical** cannot be divided into two equal halves.

atheist *(ay-thee-ist) (n)*
someone who does not believe that there is a God. **atheism** *(n)*.

athlete *(n)* someone who is trained in or is very good at sports or games that require strength, speed and skill.

athletics *(n)* competitive sports that involve running, jumping, or throwing. **athletic** *(adj)*. *See* **track and field**.

atlas *(n)* a book of maps.

atmosphere *(at-muss-fear)*
1 *(n)* the mixture of gases that surround a planet. *The layers of the Earth's atmosphere are shown in this diagram.*
2 *(n)* the air in a particular place. *The atmosphere in some of our cities is very polluted.* **atmospheric** *(adj)*.
3 *(n)* a mood or feeling created by a place or a work of art. *I didn't like the atmosphere in Uncle Max's house.* **atmospheric** *(adj)*.

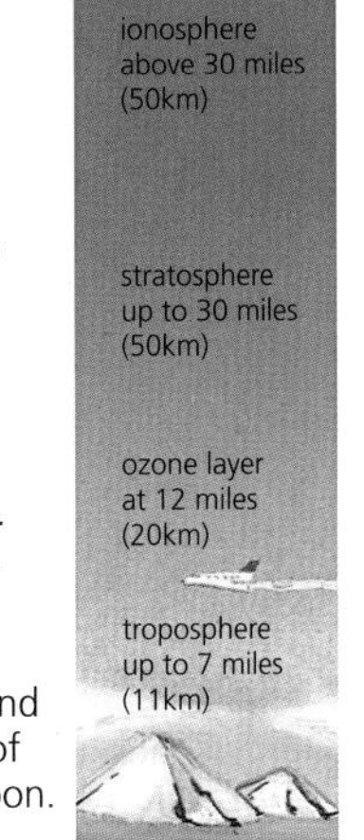

layers of the atmosphere

atoll *(n)*
a coral reef that grows in a circle, and surrounds a body of water called a lagoon.

atom *(n)*
the smallest part of an element. Everything is made up of atoms. *The diagram below shows the main parts of an atom.*

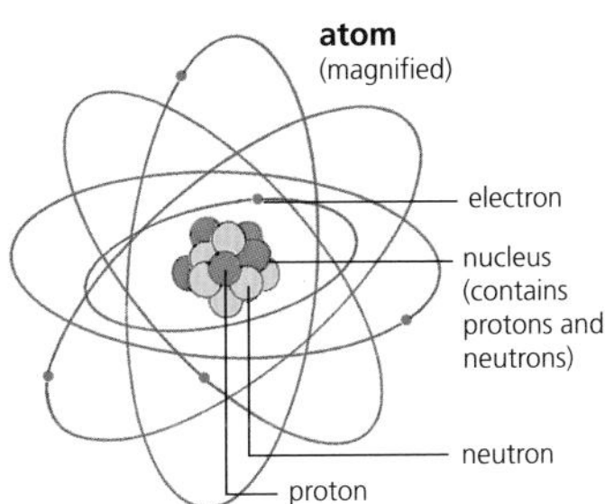

atomic
1 *(adj)* having to do with atoms. *Atomic structure.*
2 *(adj)* using the power created when atoms are split. *Atomic energy.*

atone atoning atoned *(v)*
If you **atone** for something, you make up for it. *Carrie atoned for her lateness by working extra hard.*

atrocious *(uh-tro-shuss) (adj)*
disgusting or terrible.

atrocity atrocities *(n)* a very wicked or cruel act, often involving killing.

attach attaches attaching attached
1 *(v)* to join or fix one thing to another. **attachment** *(n).*
2 If you are **attached to** someone, you are very fond of them. **attachment** *(n).*

attack attacking attacked
1 *(v)* to try to hurt someone or something. **attack** *(n),* **attacker** *(n).*
2 *(v)* to criticize someone strongly. **attack** *(n).*
3 *(v)* to try to defeat an enemy or capture a place where the enemy is. *Troops attacked the castle.* **attack** *(n).*
4 *(n)* a sudden period of illness. *A bad attack of flu.*

attainment *(n)* an achievement. **attain** *(v),* **attainable** *(adj).*

attempt attempting attempted *(v)* to try to do something. **attempt** *(n).*

attend attending attended
1 *(v)* to be present in a place or at an event. *Thousands of people attended the concert.* **attendance** *(n).*
2 *(v)* If you **attend to** something, you deal with it.

attendant *(n)* someone who looks after a person or place. *A museum attendant.*

attention
1 *(n)* concentration and careful thought. *Attention to detail.*
2 If you **pay attention**, you concentrate on something.
3 When soldiers **stand at attention**, they stand up straight, with their feet together and their arms by their sides.

attic *(n)*
a room under the roof of a building.

attitude
1 *(n)* your opinions and feelings about someone or something. *Aidan has a positive attitude toward his work.*
2 *(n)* the position in which you are standing or sitting.

attorney *(uh-ter-ney) (n)* a lawyer.

attract attracting attracted
1 *(v)* If something **attracts** you, you are interested in it. **attraction** *(n).*
2 *(v)* If a person **attracts** you, you like the person. **attraction** *(n).*
3 *(v)* If something **attracts** objects or people to itself, it pulls them toward itself. *Magnets attract iron and steel.* **attraction** *(n).*

attractive
1 *(adj)* pleasant or pretty to look at. **attractiveness** *(n),* **attractively** *(adv).*
2 *(adj)* interesting or exciting. *An attractive plan.* **attractiveness** *(n).*

auburn *(ah-burn) (n)*
a red-brown color. **auburn** *(adj).*

auction *(n)* a sale where goods are sold to the person who offers the most money for them. **auctioneer** *(n).*

audience
1 *(n)* the people who watch or listen to a performance, speech, or show.
2 *(n)* a formal meeting with an important or powerful person.

audiovisual *(adj)* **Audiovisual** equipment uses sound and pictures, often to teach people something.

audition *(n)* a short performance by an actor, singer, etc., to see whether they are suitable for a part in a play, concert, etc.

aunt *(n)* the sister of your father or mother, or the wife of your uncle.

au pair *(oh-pair) (n)*
a young person from another country who lives with a family and helps them, in order to learn a language.

aural *(or-al) (adj)*
related to listening. *My piano exam includes an aural test.*

author *(n)* the writer of a book, play, or poem. **authorship** *(n).*

authority authorities
1 *(n)* the right to do something or to tell other people what to do. *The detectives have the authority to search our house.*
2 *(n)* a group of people with power in a certain area. *The Transportation Authority is planning new bus routes.*
3 *(n)* someone who knows a lot about a particular subject. *Sam is an authority on computers.*

authorize authorizing authorized *(v)* to give permission for something to happen. **authorization** *(n).*

autistic *(adj)* Someone who is **autistic** has a condition that can cause problems with social interaction and language skills.

autobiography autobiographies *(n)* a book that tells the story of the writer's life. **autobiographical** *(adj).*

autograph *(n)*
a famous person's signature.

automatic
1 *(adj)* An **automatic** machine can perform some actions without anyone operating it. **automatically** *(adv).*
2 *(adj)* An **automatic** action happens without your thinking about it. **automatically** *(adv).*

automation *(n)* the use of machines rather than people to do jobs, especially in factories. **automate** *(v).*

automobile a type of passenger motor vehicle. *See* **car**.

autumn *(n)* the season between summer and winter, when it gets colder and the leaves fall from the trees. It is also called **fall**. **autumnal** *(adj).*

available
1 *(adj)* ready to be used or bought. **availability** *(n).*
2 *(adj)* not busy, and so free to talk to people. **availability** *(n).*

avalanche *(av-uh-lanch) (n)* a large mass of snow and ice that suddenly moves down the side of a mountain.

avenue *(n)* a road in a town or city, often with trees on either side.

average
1 *(n)* In math, you find an **average** by adding a group of figures together and then dividing the total by the number of figures you have added. *The average of 2, 4, and 6 is 4.*
2 *(adj)* usual, or ordinary.

aviary aviaries *(n)* a large cage or other enclosed area for birds.

aviation *(n)* the science of building and flying aircraft. *The great age of aviation began in 1903, when Orville Wright first left the ground in the* Flyer, *shown below.* **aviator** *(n).*

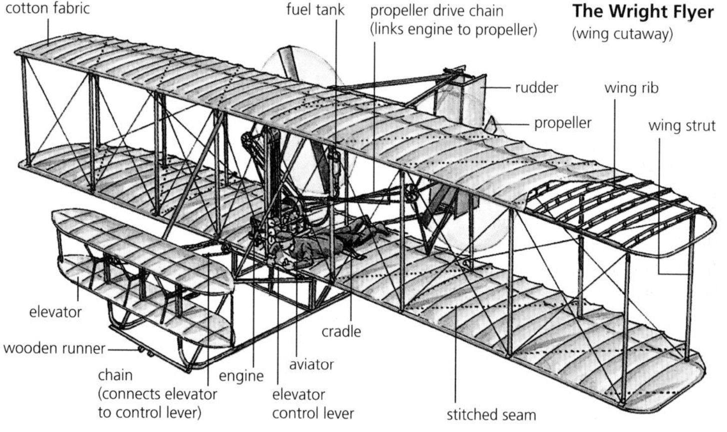

The Wright Flyer
(wing cutaway)

avoid avoiding avoided
1 *(v)* to keep away from a person or place. **avoidance** *(n).*
2 *(v)* to try to prevent something from happening. *We must avoid making that mistake again.* **avoidance** *(n),* **avoidable** *(adj).*

await awaiting awaited *(v)* to wait for or expect someone or something.

awake awaking awoke awoken
1 *(adj)* not asleep. *I'm wide awake.*
2 *(v)* to wake up. **awakening** *(n).*

award awarding awarded *(v)* to give something to someone officially, often as a prize. **award** *(n).*

aware *(adj)* If you are **aware** of something, you know that it exists. **awareness** *(n).*

away
1 *(adv)* moving from a place, person, or thing. *Rosie ran away from me.*
2 *(adv)* distant from a place. *We live three miles away.*
3 *(adj)* not at home, or not present.
4 *(adv)* in a safe place. *Put your money away.*

awe *(n)* a feeling of admiration and respect, mixed with a little fear. **awesome** *(adj).*

awful
1 *(adj)* terrible or horrible.
2 *(adj) (informal)* very great. *I spent an awful lot of money.* **awfully** *(adv).*

awkward
1 *(adj)* causing difficulties. *An awkward catch.* **awkwardness** *(n),* **awkwardly** *(adv).*
2 *(adj)* not able to relax and talk to people easily. **awkwardness** *(n),* **awkwardly** *(adv).*

ax axing axed
1 *(n)* a tool with a sharp blade fixed to a long handle, used for chopping wood.
2 *(v)* to bring something to an end, usually to save money. *200 jobs will be axed.*

axis axes
1 *(n)* an imaginary line through the middle of an object, around which that object spins. *The Earth's axis.*
2 *(n)* a line at the side or the bottom of a graph.

axle *(n)* a rod in the center of a wheel around which the wheel turns.

Aztec *(n)* a member of a Mexican Native American people who had a great civilization before the conquest of Mexico in the 16th century. **Aztec** *(adj).*

Bb

babble babbling babbled
1 *(v)* to talk in an excited way, without making any sense.
2 *(v)* to make sounds like a baby.

baboon *(n)* a large monkey that lives in Africa. Baboons have long, dog-like snouts and large teeth.

olive baboons

baby babies *(n)* a newly born or very young child or animal. **babyish** *(adj).*

babysitter *(n)* someone who is paid to stay in the house and look after children while their parents are out.

bachelor *(n)* a man who has never been married.

back backing backed
1 *(n)* the rear part of your body between your neck and your bottom.
2 *(n)* the opposite end or side from the front. **back** *(adj).*
3 *(adv)* to where someone or something was before. *Ed came back.*
4 *(v)* to support someone.
5 **back down** *(v)* to admit that you were wrong.
6 **back out** *(v)* to decide not to do something that you had agreed to do.

backfire backfiring backfired
1 *(v)* If a car **backfires**, there is a small explosion inside its exhaust pipe.
2 *(v)* If an action **backfires**, it does not work out as you planned it.

background
1 *(n)* the part of a picture that is behind the main subject.
2 *(n)* the facts or events that surround something and help to explain why it happened.

backhand *(n)* a stroke in tennis that you play with the back of your hand facing outward and your arm across your body. *The sequence below shows how to play a backhand.*

backhand drive

backpack
1 *(n)* a bag that you carry on your back when you are walking or climbing.
2 If you **go backpacking,** you go on a long walk or hike.

backstroke *(n)* a style of swimming in which you swim lying on your back.

backward
1 *(adv)* in the direction that your back is facing. *Joe stepped backward.*
2 *(adv)* in the opposite to the usual way. *Say the alphabet backward.*

bacon *(n)* smoked or salted meat from the belly of a pig.

bacteria *(plural n)* microscopic living things that exist all around you and inside you. Many bacteria are useful, but some cause disease. *The diagram shows a simplified bacteria cell, magnified millions of times.*

bacteria cell (magnified)

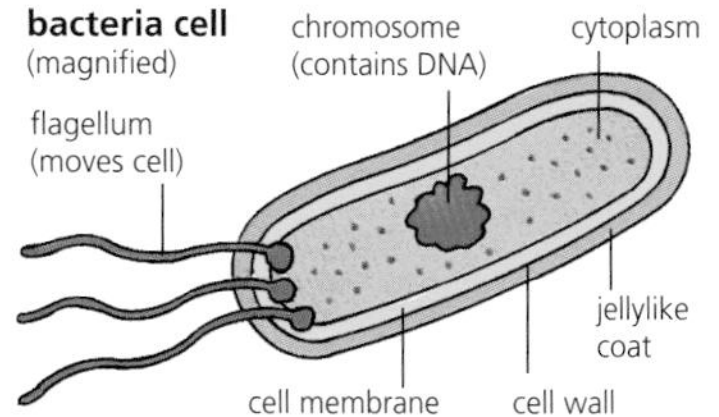

bad worse worst
1 *(adj)* not good.
2 *(adj)* serious. *A bad mistake.*
3 *(adj)* not fit to eat. *The fish has gone bad.*

badge *(n)* a small sign with a picture or message on it that you pin to your clothes.

badger badgering badgered
1 *(n)* a mammal with a gray body and a black and white head that lives in a burrow under the ground and comes out at night to feed.
2 *(v)* to keep asking someone to do something. *Fran kept badgering me to let her come with us.*

European badger's burrow (cutaway)

badly
1 *(adv)* not well or not skillfully.
2 *(adv)* urgently. *I want it badly.*

badminton *(n)* a game like tennis in which players use rackets to hit a shuttlecock over a high net.

badminton racket and shuttlecocks

baffle baffling baffled *(v)* to puzzle or confuse someone. **baffling** *(adj).*

bag *(n)* a container used for carrying things.

baggage *(n)* suitcases and bags.

baggy baggier baggiest *(adj)* hanging in loose folds. *Baggy shorts.*

bagpipes *(plural n)* a musical instrument. To play the bagpipes, you blow air through the blowstick into a bag, and squeeze it out through the drones and the chanter.

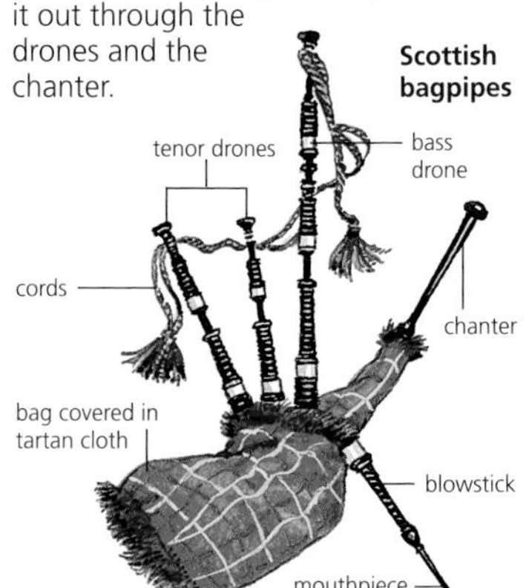

Scottish bagpipes

bail
1 *(n)* a sum of money paid to a court to allow someone accused of a crime to be set free until their trial.
2 *(v)* to scoop water out of a boat or ship.

bailiff *(n)* a law officer who makes sure that a court's decision is carried out, especially by taking someone's property when they owe money.

bail out bailing out bailed out
1 *(v)* to jump out of an aircraft, using a parachute.
2 *(v)* If you **bail someone out**, you help them out of a difficult situation.

bait *(n)* a small amount of food used to attract a fish or an animal, so that you can catch it. *See* **angling**.

baize *(n)* a felt-like material used for covering card tables, pool tables, etc.

bake baking baked
1 *(v)* to cook food in an oven, especially bread or cakes. **baker** *(n),* **bakery** *(n).*
2 *(v)* to heat something to make it hard. *Bake the clay in a kiln before glazing it.*

balaclava *(n)* a woolen hat that covers your head and neck, like a helmet.

balance balancing balanced
1 *(n)* an instrument used for weighing things.
2 *(v)* When two things **balance** on a pair of scales, they weigh the same and do not tip the scales either way.
3 *(n)* Your **balance** is your ability to keep steady and not fall over.
4 *(v)* If you **balance** something, you keep it steady and do not let it fall.
5 *(n)* When you subtract an amount from another amount, what you have left is the **balance**.

balcony
1 *(n)* a platform with railings on the outside of a building, usually on an upper level.
2 *(n)* the upstairs seating in a theater.

bald balder baldest
1 *(adj)* Someone who is **bald** has very little or no hair on their head. **baldness** *(n),* **balding** *(adj).*
2 *(adj)* A **bald** fact or statement is stated simply, without any attempt to make it more pleasant. **baldly** *(adv).*

baldfaced *(adj)* open and undisguised. *A baldfaced lie.*

ball
1 *(n)* a round object used in games.
2 *(n)* something made into a round shape. *A ball of wool.*
3 *(n)* a very formal party where people dance.
4 *(informal)* If you **have a ball**, you really enjoy yourself.

ballad *(n)* a song or a poem that tells a story.

ballast
1 *(n)* heavy material, such as water or sand, that is carried by a ship to make it more stable.
2 **ballast tank** *(n)* a large tank in a submarine that is filled with water to make the submarine sink, and with air to make it come to the surface.

ball bearings *(n)* small metal balls used to help parts of machinery move more smoothly against each other.

ballerina *(n)* a female ballet dancer.

ballet *(bal-ay)*
1 *(n)* a style of dance with set movements.

ballet movements

2 *(n)* a performance using dance and music, often to tell a story. *The picture above shows three ballet movements.*

ballistics *(singular n)* the science and study of missiles that are fired from guns. **ballistic** *(adj).*

balloon
1 *(n)* a small bag made of thin rubber that is blown up and used as a decoration.
2 *See* **hot-air balloon**.

ballot
1 *(n)* a special piece of paper used for marking a vote.
2 **ballot box** *(n)* a box with a slit in the top into which ballots are put.

ballpoint pen *(n)* a pen with a tiny ball at its tip that lets ink flow as you write.

balsa *(n)* a very light wood used to make models.

bamboo *(n)* a tropical grass with a hard, hollow stem, often used for making furniture.

ban banning banned *(v)* to forbid something. *Ball games are banned in this park.* **ban** *(n).*

banana tree

banana *(n)* a tropical fruit that is long, curved, and yellow.

band banding banded
1 *(n)* a narrow ring of rubber, paper, or other material that is put around something to hold it together.
2 *(n)* a group of people who play music together. *Stephanie plays in the school jazz band.*

3 *(n)* a group of people who do something together. *A band of robbers.*
4 *(v)* When people **band together**, they join together in a group in order to do something.

bandage *(n)*
a long piece of cloth that is wrapped around an injured part of the body to protect it. **bandage** *(v)*.

bandit *(n)*
an armed robber, usually one of a gang, who attacks travelers.

bang banging banged
1 *(n)* a sudden loud noise.
2 *(v)* to knock hard against something. **bang** *(n)*.

bangle *(n)*
a band of metal, plastic, etc. worn around the wrist.

bangs *(plural n)*
the hair that hangs over your forehead.

banish
banishes banishing banished *(v)*
to send someone away from a place and order them not to return. **banishment** *(n)*.

banister *(n)*
a rail that runs along the side of a flight of stairs.

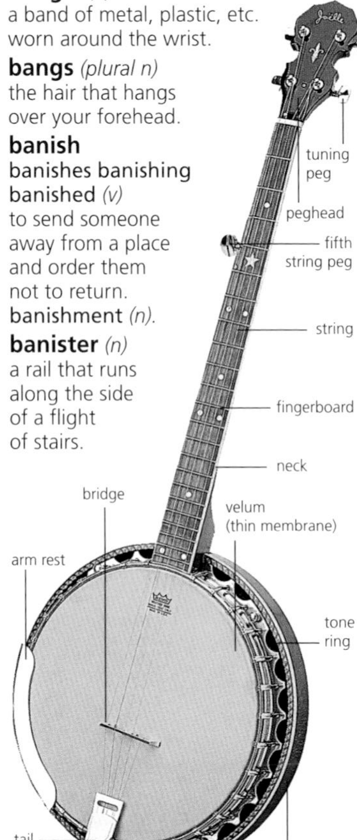

banjo

banjo *(n)* a musical instrument like a small, round guitar with a long neck.

bank banking banked
1 *(n)* a place where people keep their money. Banks also lend money and offer other financial services.
2 *(n)* the land along the sides of a river or a canal.
3 *(n)* a place where something is stored and collected. *A blood bank.*
4 *(v)* If you **bank on** something, you rely on it. *He was banking on the store being open.*

bankrupt *(adj)*
If a person or company is **bankrupt**, they cannot pay their debts. **bankruptcy** *(n)*, **bankrupt** *(v)*.

banner *(n)*
a long piece of material with writing on it, often carried in sports crowds and processions.

banquet *(n)*
a formal meal for a large number of people, usually on a special occasion.

banter *(n)* conversation that sounds mean-spirited but is actually good-natured. **banter** *(v)*.

baptize baptizing baptized *(v)*
to pour water on someone's head, or to immerse someone in water, as a sign that they have become a Christian. **baptism** *(n)*.

bar
1 *(n)* a long stick of metal. *An iron bar.*
2 *(n)* a long, flat block of something hard. *A chocolate bar.*
3 *(n)* one of the groups of notes into which a piece of music is divided.
4 *(v)* to block someone, or keep someone out. *Tom's mom barred him from the kitchen while she was cooking.*

barbarian *(n)*
a member of a wild and uncivilized tribe that lived in the past.

barbaric *(adj)* very cruel. *The animals were kept in barbaric conditions.*

barbecue
(n) an outdoor meal or party in which food is cooked using a grill. **barbecue** *(v)*.

barbed wire *(n)* wire with small spikes along it, used for fences.

barbell *(n)* a long rod with weights on each end used for weight-lifting exercises and competitons.

barber *(n)* someone who cuts men's and boys' hair.

bar code *(n)* a band of thick and thin lines printed on goods sold in stores that gives information about the goods.

bare
baring bared; barer barest
1 *(adj)* wearing no clothes.
2 *(adj)* empty. *The pantry was bare.*
3 *(v)* to uncover or reveal something. *The dog bared its teeth.*
4 *(adj)* plain and simple. *Just give me the bare facts.*

bareback *(adv)*
If you ride a horse **bareback**, you do not use a saddle.

barely *(adv)* only just. *Tina was so scared she could barely speak.*

bargain bargaining bargained
1 *(n)* something that you buy for less than the usual price.
2 *(v)* When you **bargain** with someone, you agree to do something if the other person will do something else in exchange. **bargain** *(n)*.

barge barging barged
1 *(n)* a long, flat-bottomed boat, used on canals.
2 *(v)* If you **barge** into someone, you knock against them roughly or push them out of the way.

baritone
1 *(n)* the second lowest singing voice for a man. **baritone** *(adj)*.
2 *(n)* a singer with a baritone voice.

bark barking barked
1 *(v)* When a dog **barks**, it makes a loud sound in its throat. **bark** *(n)*.
2 *(n)* the hard covering on a tree.
3 *(v)* to shout at someone gruffly. *"Attention!" barked the sergeant.*

barley *(n)*
a common cereal plant. *See* **grain**.

bar *or* **bat mitzvah** *(n)*
a celebration that takes place on a Jewish boy or girl's 13th birthday, after which he or she can take part in their religion as an adult.

barn *(n)* a farm building where crops or animals are kept.

barnacle *(n)* a small shellfish that sticks itself firmly to the sides of boats, rocks, and other shellfish. *See* **scallop**.

19th-century barometer

barometer *(n)*
an instrument that measures changes in air pressure and shows how the weather is going to change. *In the simple barometer shown here, liquid rises in the spout for stormy weather and falls for fine weather.*

baron *(n)*
a nobleman. In Britain, a baron is a male peer of the lowest rank. **baronial** *(adj)*.

baroness baronesses *(n)*
a noblewoman. In Britain, a baroness is a female peer of the lowest rank, or the wife of a baron.

barracks barracks *(n)*
the buildings where soldiers live.

barrage
1 *(n)* a dam built across a river to control the level of the water.
2 *(n)* a large amount of something that all comes at the same time. *A barrage of complaints.*

barrel
1 *(n)* a container for liquids, such as water or gasoline, which has curved sides and a flat top and bottom.
2 *(n)* the long part of a gun that looks like a tube. *See* **blunderbuss**.
3 *(n)* the part of a dart that you hold.
4 If someone has you **over a barrel**, they have made you powerless.

barren
1 *(adj)* If land is **barren**, farmers cannot grow crops on it.
2 *(adj) (old-fashioned)* A woman who is **barren** is not able to have children.

barricade barricading barricaded
1 *(n)* a wall built in a hurry to stop people from getting past.
2 *(v)* If people **barricade** themselves into a place, they build walls to stop other people from reaching them.

barrier
1 *(n)* a bar, fence, or wall that prevents people, traffic, water, etc. from going past it. *The Thames Barrier is made up of a series of linked gates across the River Thames that can be opened to let water through or closed to prevent flooding. The picture below shows a gate in the closed position.*
2 *(n)* something that prevents you from communicating properly with someone else. *A language barrier.*

barring
(prep)
except for. *We'll be there, barring an emergency.*

barrow *(n)*
a mound of earth made to cover a grave in prehistoric times.

barter bartering bartered *(v)*
to trade by exchanging food and other goods rather than by using money. **barter** *(n).*

base basing based; baser basest
1 *(n)* the lowest part of something, or the part that it stands on. **basal** *(adj).*
2 *(v)* to use something as the starting point for something else. *I based my story on a real event.* **basis** *(n).*
3 *(n)* the place from which a business, army, etc. is controlled. **base** *(v).*
4 *(n)* In baseball, a **base** is one of the four points to which you have to run in order to score a run. *See* **baseball**.
5 *(n)* In chemistry, a **base** is a substance that will neutralize an acid. Bases react with acids to form salts.
6 *(n)* In math, a **base** is the starting point for a counting system. For example, ten is the base of the decimal system.
7 *(adj)* selfish or mean. *A base trick.*
8 *(v)* If you **touch base**, you make brief contact with your family, friends, colleagues, etc.

left field
second base
diamond
pitcher's mound
infield
first base
third base
home plate
batter's box
catcher's box
baseball field

aircraft aluminum
rubber grip
baseball bat

webbed pocket
fingers laced together
leather ball with cork center
flexible leather
hand-stitching
fielder's glove and baseball

baseball *(n)*
an American game, played with a bat and ball and two teams of nine players. *The picture above shows the infield of a baseball field, beyond which is the outfield, a large fielding area. Some baseball equipment is also shown.*

basement *(n)* an area or room in a building below ground level.

bash bashes bashing bashed *(v) (informal)* to hit something hard.

bashful *(adj)* shy. **bashfully** *(adv).*

basic
1 *(adj)* simple and straightforward. **basically** *(adv).*
2 **basics** *(plural n)* the most important things to know about a subject.

basin
1 *(n)* a large bowl filled with water used for washing.
2 *(n)* an area of land around a river, from which water drains into the river.

basis *(n)* the idea or reason behind something. *The basis of a plan.*

bask basking basked
1 *(v)* to lie or sit in the sunshine and enjoy it.
2 *(v)* If you **bask in** someone's praise, admiration, etc., you enjoy it.

basket *(n)* a container, usually with handles, made of cane, wire, etc.

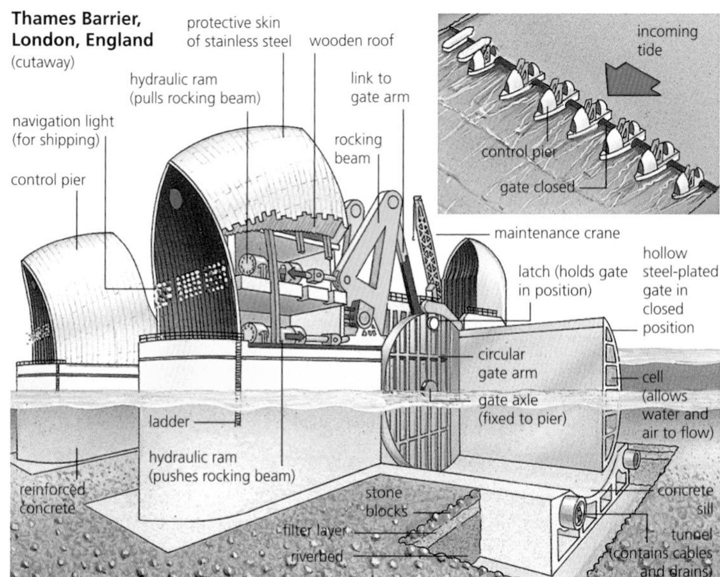

Thames Barrier, London, England (cutaway)

basketball *(n)*
a game played by two teams who try to score points by throwing a ball into a high net at the end of a court.
The picture sequence shows making a basket in basketball.

basketball

bass *(rhymes with lace)* **basses**
1 *(n)* the lowest singing voice for a man.
2 *(n)* a stringed instrument that makes a low sound.

bat **batting batted**
1 *(n)* a small, flying mammal that comes out at night to feed. *Bats find their way around by making high-pitched squeaks that send back echoes, which are then picked up by their sensitive ears.*
2 *(n)* a piece of wood used for hitting the ball in games such as baseball or cricket. *See* **baseball**.
3 *(v)* to take a turn at hitting the ball and scoring runs in games such as cricket and baseball. *It's Barry's turn at bat.*

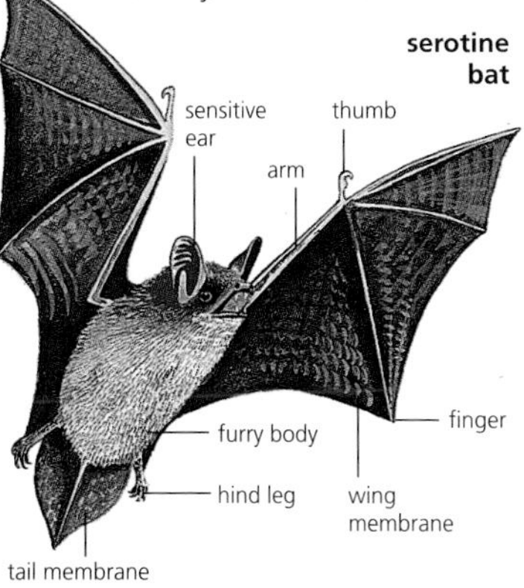

serotine bat

batch **batches** *(n)* a group of things that arrive together or are made together. *A batch of cookies.*

bathe **bathes bathing bathed** *(v)*
to clean yourself using water.

bathroom
1 *(n)* a room that contains a bathtub and a shower, and often a sink and toilet.
2 *(v) (informal)* If you **go to the bathroom** it means you need to use the toilet.

bathtub *(n)* a large, open container for water in which you sit and wash your whole body.

batik *(ba-teek) (n)* an Eastern method of printing designs on cloth. Parts of the cloth are covered with wax so that when it is put into the dye these parts are not colored.

baton
1 *(n)* a short, thin stick used by a conductor to beat time for an orchestra.
2 *(n)* a short stick passed from one runner to another in a relay race.

battalion *(n)*
a large number of soldiers.

batten *(n)*
a light strip of wood, used to support or strengthen something.

batter **battering battered**
1 *(v)* to hit someone or something many times. **battering** *(n)*.
2 *(v)* If someone **batters down** a door, they break through it by hitting it many times.
3 *(n)* a mixture of milk, eggs, and flour that can be cooked to make pancakes or used to coat food that you fry.

battering ram *(n)*
a heavy wooden beam, sometimes protected by a hut on wheels, that is rammed against an enemy's walls or gates. *Battering rams were used in ancient times and in the Middle Ages.*

medieval battering ram

battery
batteries
1 *(n)* a group of machines or heavy guns that are all used together.
2 *(n)* a container that stores chemicals that produce electrical power.
Also see **car**.

battery
(cutaway)

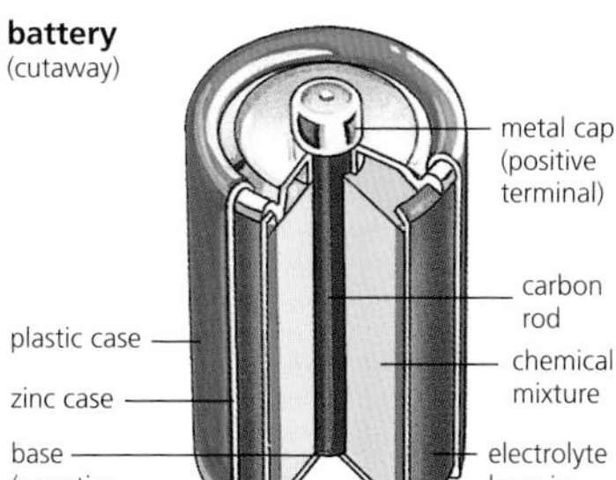

battle
1 *(n)* a fight between two armies.
2 *(n)* a struggle with someone.

battleship *(n)*
a warship armed with powerful guns.

bawl **bawling bawled**
1 *(v)* to cry loudly like a baby.
2 *(v)* to shout loudly in a harsh voice. *"Get off my roses!" bawled Mr. Jones.*

bay
1 *(n)* a part of the coast that curves inward.
2 If you keep something or someone **at bay**, you fight them off. *Anna managed to keep her fears at bay.*
3 **bay window** *(n)* a window that sticks out from the wall of a house. *See* **building**.

bayonet *(n)* a long knife that can be fitted to the end of a rifle.

bazaar
1 *(n)* a street market, especially one held in Middle Eastern countries.
2 *(n)* a sale held to raise money for charity.

B.C. the initials of the phrase "before Christ." B.C. are used to show that a date comes before the birth of Jesus Christ. *Julius Caesar died in 44 B.C.*

beach **beaches** *(n)* a strip of sand or pebbles where land meets water.

beacon *(n)* a light or fire used as a signal or warning.

bead
1 *(n)* a small piece of glass, wood, or plastic with a hole through the middle that can be threaded onto a string.
2 *(n)* a drop of liquid.
A bead of sweat.

beak *(n)* the hard, horn-like part of a bird's mouth. *See* **bird**.

beaker *(n)*
a plastic or glass jar used in chemistry. *See* **apparatus**.

beam **beaming beamed**
1 *(n)* a thick ray of light from a flashlight, car headlight, etc.
beam *(v)*.
2 *(n)* a long, thick piece of wood, concrete, or metal, used to support the roof or floors of a building.
3 *(v)* to smile widely. **beam** *(n)*.

bean **beaning beaned**
1 *(n)* **Beans** are large seeds that you can eat or that can be used to make a drink. *Baked beans. Coffee beans.*
2 *(v)* to hit someone on the head with something you throw.

bear bearing bore borne
1 *(v)* to support or carry something. *Is the ice thick enough to bear my weight?*
2 *(v)* When a tree or plant **bears** fruit, flowers, or leaves, it produces them.
3 *(v)* If you cannot **bear** something, you cannot put up with it, either because it upsets you or because you do not like it at all. *My mom can't bear rap music.* **bearable** *(adj).*
4 *(n)* a large, heavy mammal with thick fur. *The picture shows a young male grizzly bear catching a salmon.*

grizzly bear

beard *(n)* the hair on a man's chin.

beast
1 *(n)* a wild animal.
2 *(n)* a horrible or unkind person. **beastliness** *(n),* **beastly** *(adj).*

beat
beating beat beaten
1 *(v)* to hit someone or something many times. **beating** *(n).*
2 *(v)* to defeat someone in a game or contest. *George beat me at chess.*
3 *(n)* the regular rhythm of a piece of music or of your heart.
4 *(v)* If you **beat** a mixture, you stir it up quickly with a whisk or fork.

beautiful *(adj)* very pleasant to look at or listen to. **beauty** *(n),* **beautify** *(v),* **beautifully** *(adv).*

beaver beavering beavered
1 *(n)* an animal resembling a large rat with a wide, flat tail, that lives both on land and in water. Beavers build dams across streams to create safe areas for their lodges.

beaver's dam and lodge
(cutaway)

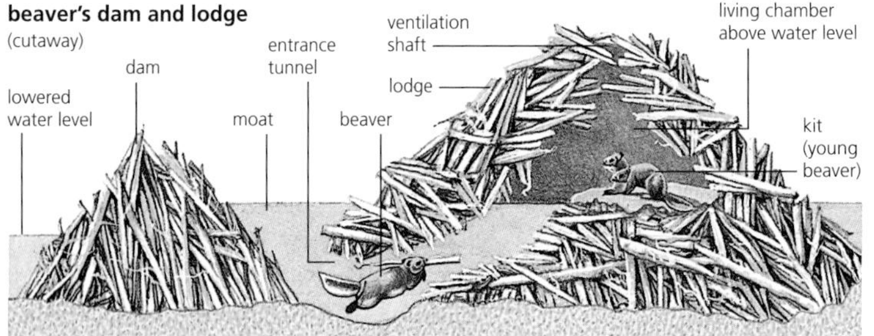

because *(conj)* for the reason that. *I came because I wanted to see you.*

beckon beckoning beckoned *(v)* to gesture to someone, asking them to come. *Jack beckoned us to come after him.*

become becoming became *(v)* to start to be. *When did you become suspicious?*

bed
1 *(n)* a piece of furniture that you sleep on.
2 *(n)* a place in a garden where flowers are planted.
3 *(n)* the bottom of an ocean or river.

bedding *(n)* sheets, quilts, comforters, blankets, etc.

bedridden *(adj)*
If you are **bedridden**, you are so ill that you cannot get out of bed.

bedroom *(n)*
a room used for sleeping.

bee *(n)* a flying insect with yellow and black stripes that makes honey. *A bee lets other bees know where food is by performing a "dance" in which it waggles its abdomen a certain number of times. Also see* **hive**, **honeycomb**, **insect**.

bee dance

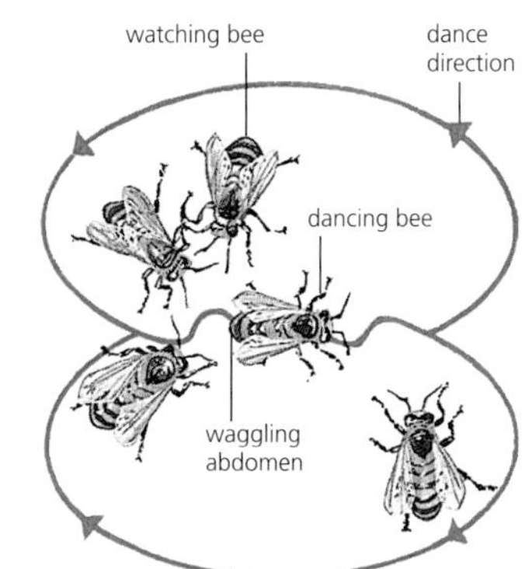

beech beeches *(n)*
a tree with a smooth gray bark and leaves that spread outward.

beef *(n)* the meat from a cow, a bull, or an ox.

beefy beefier beefiest *(adj)* *(informal)* big and muscular.

beehive *(n)* a nest or house where bees live. *Also see* **hive**.

beet *(n)* a purple-red root vegetable. *See* **vegetable**.

beetle *(n)* a flying insect with hard wing covers. *The goliath beetle weighs as much as a sparrow.*

goliath beetle

befall befalling befell *(v)* to occur or happen. *The captive had no idea what fate was to befall him.*

before
1 *(prep)* sooner or earlier than. *The time before last.*
2 *(adv)* earlier. *I've been here before.*

beg begging begged
1 *(v)* to ask someone in the street for help, especially for money or food. **beggar** *(n).*
2 *(v)* to plead with someone to do something. *Emily begged Tom to go to her party.*

begin beginning began begun *(v)* to start. **beginner** *(n),* **beginning** *(n).*

begrudge begrudging begrudged *(v)* to be jealous or resentful.

behalf If you do something **on behalf** of someone else, you do it for them or in their place.

behave behaving behaved
1 *(v)* to do and say things in a particular way. *Matthew behaved very strangely.* **behavior** *(n).*
2 *(v)* to act properly, and avoid being noisy or causing trouble. *I wish you would behave yourself!*

behind
1 *(prep)* on the other side, or toward the back of something. *Look behind the curtain!*
2 *(prep)* further back or in a lower position. *Al finished the race behind me.*

3 *(adv)* not making good progress. *I'm behind with my work.*

beige *(bayjh) (n)*
a pale brown color. **beige** *(adj).*

belch belches belching belched
1 *(v)* to let out gases from your stomach through your mouth with a loud noise. **belch** *(n).*
2 *(v)* to send out fire and smoke.

believe believing believed
1 *(v)* to feel that something is true. **belief** *(n),* **believer** *(n).*
2 *(v)* to support someone or something. *I believe in rights for children.* **believer** *(n).*

bell
1 *(n)* an instrument that makes a ringing sound. Bells are often cup-shaped and have a clapper hanging down inside them.
2 *(informal)* If something **rings a bell,** you think you have heard it somewhere before.
3 *(n)* a bell-shaped object, especially on a musical instrument. *See* **brass**.

bell (cutaway)
crown
shoulder
waist
lip
mouth
clapper

bellow bellowing bellowed
1 *(v)* to shout or roar. **bellow** *(n).*
2 **bellows** *(n)* an instrument used for pumping air into something like an organ or a fire.

belly bellies
1 *(n)* the stomach, or the part of a human's or animal's body that contains their stomach and bowels.
2 **belly flop** *(n)* a dive into water in which you hit the water hard with the front of your body.

belong belonging belonged
1 *(v)* If something **belongs** to you, you own it. **belongings** *(plural n).*
2 *(v)* If you **belong** to a group, you are a member of it.
3 *(v)* If something **belongs** somewhere, that is its proper place.

below
1 *(prep)* lower than. *The temperature is below freezing.*
2 *(prep)* at or to a lower place. *We hid below the stairs.*

belt belting belted
1 *(n)* a strip of leather or other material that you wear around your waist.
2 *(n)* a moving band of rubber, used for transporting objects or for driving machinery. *Conveyor belt.*
3 *(v) (informal)* to hit someone hard.

bench benches
1 *(n)* a long, narrow seat for several people, usually made of wood.
2 *(n)* a worktable in a workshop or laboratory.

bend bending bent
1 *(v)* If you **bend**, **bend down**, or **bend over**, you lean forward from your waist.
2 *(v)* If something **bends**, it changes direction by turning to one side. *The road bends to the left.* **bend** *(n).*
3 *(v)* to change the shape of something so that it is no longer straight.

beneath
1 *(prep)* underneath. *We hid beneath the covers.*
2 *(prep)* lower than, or not worthy. *It's beneath my dignity to talk to her.*

beneficial *(adj)* Something that is **beneficial** is good for you.

benefit benefiting benefited
1 *(v)* If you **benefit** from something, you gain an advantage from it or are helped by it. *We really benefited from our vacation.* **benefit** *(n).*
2 *(n)* money paid by the government to people who need it, such as people who are poor, ill, disabled, or unemployed.

Bengali *(ben-gol-lee) (n)*
a language spoken in Bangladesh and the Indian state of West Bengal.

benign *(adj)* harmless. *The tests showed that the lump was benign.*

bent
1 *(adj)* crooked or curved.
2 *(adj) (slang)* dishonest.

bequeath
bequeathing bequeathed *(v)*
to leave something to somebody in a will. **bequest** *(n).*

bereaved *(adj)* A person is **bereaved** if a friend or relative of theirs has died. **bereavement** *(n).*

berry berries *(n)*
a small, often brightly colored, fruit found on bushes or trees.

berth berthing berthed
1 *(n)* a bed in a ship, train, or caravan.
2 *(n)* a place in a harbor where a boat is tied up.
3 *(v)* When a boat **berths**, it comes into harbor and is tied up.

beside
1 *(prep)* next to.
2 If you are **beside yourself**, you are overcome with emotion. *John is beside himself with rage.*

besides
1 *(prep)* as well as, or apart from. *Who went to the match besides Jim?*
2 *(adv)* also, or in addition to this. *I hate boats; besides, I can't swim.*

besiege besieging besieged *(v)*
to surround a place to make it surrender. *Enemy troops are besieging the castle!*

best
1 *(adj)* better than everything else.
2 When you **do your best**, you try as hard as you can to do something.
3 **best man** *(n)* the friend of the bridegroom who helps him at his wedding.

bet betting bet
1 *(v)* to risk a sum of money on the result of something, such as a horse race. If you guess the result correctly, you win some money; if not, you lose money. **betting** *(n).*
2 *(v)* If you **bet** someone that they cannot do something, you dare them to do it. *I bet you can't climb that tree!*
3 *(v) (informal)* If you **bet** that someone does something, you predict that they will do it. *I bet Mona trips over that cat.*

betray betraying betrayed
1 *(v)* If you **betray** someone, you deliberately let them down or do something to hurt them. **betrayal** *(n).*
2 *(v)* If you **betray** your feelings, you are not able to keep them hidden.

better
1 *(adj)* more suitable or higher in quality.
2 *(adj)* no longer ill or hurting.
3 **better off** *(adj)* richer.

between
1 *(prep)* If something is **between** two things, it has them on either side. *Dan stood between two trees.*
2 *(prep)* from one to the other. *We threw the ball between us.*
3 *(prep)* somewhere within two limits. *Nadya left between three and four o'clock.*

beverage *(n)* a drink.

beware *(v)* If a person or sign tells you to **beware of** something, they warn you to look out for something dangerous or harmful.

bewilder bewildering bewildered
(v) to confuse or perplex someone. **bewilderment** *(n),* **bewildered** *(adj).*

beyond
1 *(prep)* on the far side of something. *We couldn't see beyond the bushes.*
2 *(prep)* If something is **beyond you**, you cannot understand it.

biased

biased *(by-ust) (adj)* prejudiced, or favoring one person or point of view more than another. *Tim thinks that the referee is biased against our team.* **bias** *(n).*

Bible *(n)*
the holy book of the Christian religion.

bibliography **bibliographies** *(n)*
a list of books on a subject. **bibliographical** *(adj).*

bicycle *(n)* a two-wheeled vehicle that you ride by steering with handlebars, and pedaling. *The mountain bike shown below is a type of bicycle that has been specially developed for off-road cycling.*

bid **bidding bid**
1 *(v)* to offer to buy something at an auction for a certain amount of money. **bid** *(n),* **bidder** *(n).*
2 *(v)* to order someone to do something. *Bid the prince to come here!*
3 *(n)* an attempt to do or win something. *Elvis made a bid for fame.*

biennial *(by-en-ee-ul)*
1 *(adj)* happening every two years or over a period of two years.
2 *(n)* a plant that lives for two years.

big **bigger biggest** *(adj)*
large or important.

bigot *(n)*
someone who has a strong and unreasonable dislike of certain other people, especially people of a different religion, race or nationality. **bigotry** *(n),* **bigoted** *(adj).*

bike **biking biked**
1 *(n)* a bicycle or a motorcycle.
2 *(v)* to ride a bicycle or motorcycle. **biker** *(n).*

bikini *(n)*
a two-piece bathing suit worn by women and girls.

bile *(n)*
a green liquid that is made by the liver and that helps to digest food.

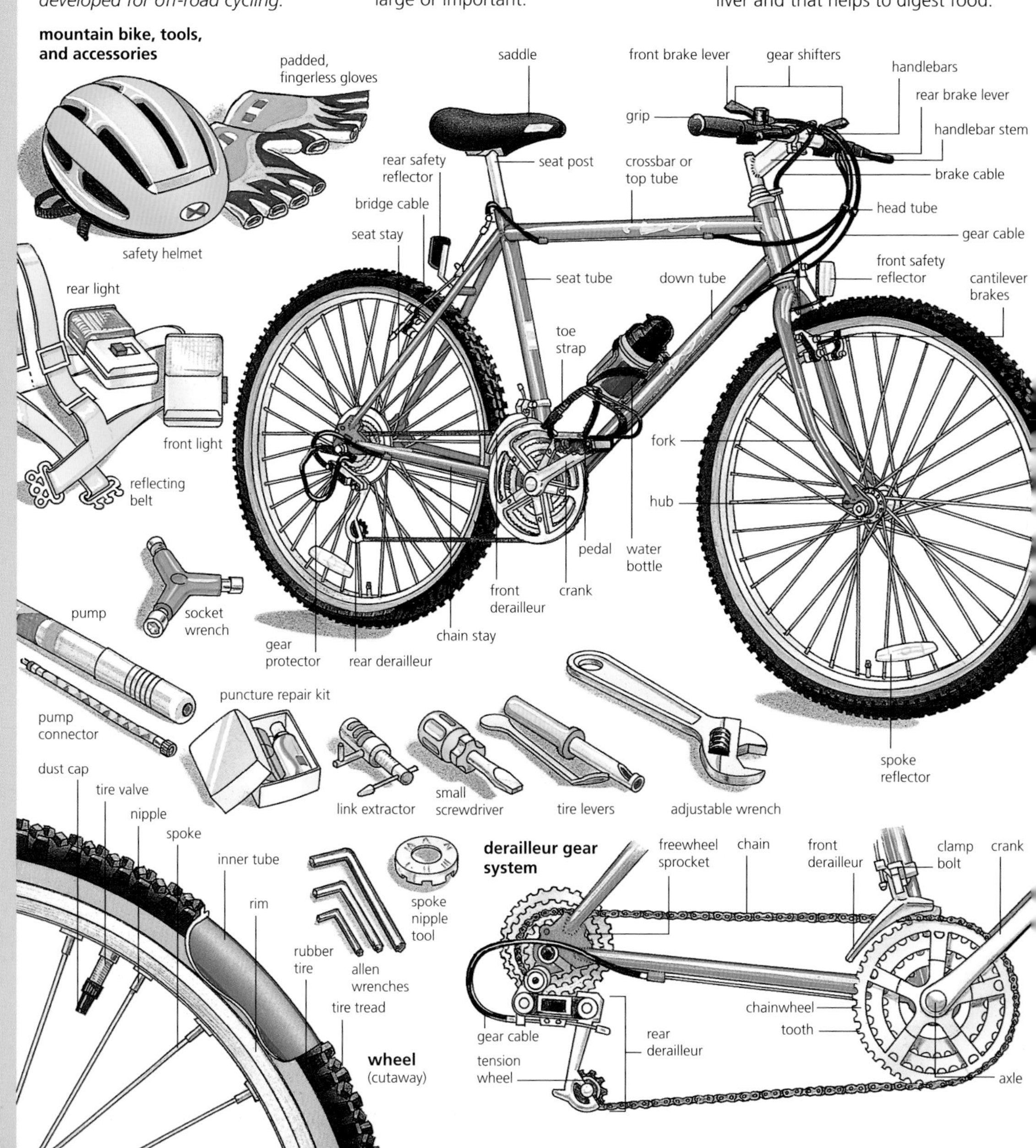

bilingual *(adj)*
If someone is **bilingual**, they can speak two languages very well.

bill
1 *(n)* a piece of paper telling you how much money you owe for something that you have bought.
2 *(n)* a written plan for a new law, to be discussed in Congress.
3 *(n)* the beak of a bird, especially a duck's beak.
4 *(n)* a piece of paper money.

billabong *(n) (Australian)*
a pond that used to be part of a river.

billiards *(singular n)*
a game in which you use a stick, called a cue, to hit balls around a table and into pockets.

billow **billowing billowed**
1 *(v)* When a curtain, sail, sheet, etc. **billows**, it is pushed outward by the wind.
2 *(v)* If smoke or fog **billows**, it rises up in large clouds.
3 *(n)* a large ocean wave.

binary
1 *(adj)* made up of two parts or units.
2 *(adj)* **Binary** arithmetic uses only two digits, 1 and 0.

bind **binding bound**
1 *(v)* to tie something up.
2 *(v)* to wrap a piece of material tightly around something.
3 *(v)* to fasten the pages of a book together and put a cover on them.

binder *(n)*
a hard folder with metal rings inside it, used for holding papers.

bingo *(n)* a game in which you cross out numbers on a card as they are called out.

binoculars *(plural n)* an instrument that you look through with both eyes to make distant things seem nearer.

biodegradable *(adj)*
Something that is **biodegradable** can be destroyed naturally by bacteria. *Biodegradable packaging helps to reduce waste and pollution.*

biography biographies *(n)*
a book that tells someone's life story. **biographer** *(n)*, **biographical** *(adj)*.

biology *(n)* the scientific study of living things. **biologist** *(n)*, **biological** *(adj)*, **biologically** *(adv)*.

biplane *(n)* an airplane with two sets of wings, one above the other. *See* **aviation**.

bird *(n)* a two-legged creature with wings, feathers, and a beak. All birds lay eggs, and most birds can fly. *Birds can be grouped according to their characteristics and behavior into 23 orders, or types, and an example of each order is shown below. The picture of an orange chat on the right shows the main parts of a bird's body.*

Some words that begin with a "bi" sound are spelled "by."

birth
1 *(n)* the event of being born.
2 *(n)* the beginning of something. *The birth of the internet.*
3 When a woman **gives birth**, she has a baby.

birthday *(n)* a yearly celebration of the day that someone was born.

birthmark *(n)* a discolored patch of skin that was there from birth or very soon after.

biscuit *(n)* a small bread roll made from dough.

bisect bisecting bisected *(v)* to divide a line, angle, or shape into two equal parts.

bishop
1 *(n)* a senior priest in the Christian church who is in charge of priests and churches in a large area called a diocese.
2 *(n)* a chess piece that can move diagonally across the board. *The picture shows a bishop from a 12th-century Viking chess set.* *Also see* **chess**.

bishop chess piece

bison bison *(n)* a large animal with a big shaggy head, humped back, and short horns, found in North America; a buffalo.

bit
1 *(n)* a small amount of something.
2 *(n)* the smallest unit of information in a computer's memory.
3 *(n)* the metal bar that goes in a horse's mouth and is attached to the reins. *See* **tack**.
4 *(n)* the end part of a drill. *See* **drill**.

bite biting bit bitten
1 *(v)* to close your teeth around something. *Lindsay bit into the apple and found a maggot!* **bite** *(n)*.
2 *(v)* If an insect or snake **bites** you, it pricks your skin and injects venom into your body. **bite** *(n)*.

bitter bitterest
1 *(adj)* tasting sharp and slightly sour, often in an unpleasant way.
2 *(adj)* If you feel **bitter**, you are upset and angry about something.
3 *(adj)* If the weather is **bitter**, it is very cold indeed.

black
1 *(n)* the color of coal, or of the sky at night. **black** *(adj)*.
2 *(adj)* **Black** people have naturally dark skin, or are descended from people with dark skin.

blackberry blackberries *(n)* a small, black fruit that grows on blackberry bushes. *See* **fruit**.

blackboard *(n)* a dark surface that you can write on with chalk.

black hole *(n)* the area in space around a collapsed star that sucks in everything around it, even light.

blackmail *(n)* the crime of threatening to reveal a secret about someone unless they pay a sum of money. **blackmail** *(v)*.

blackout *(n)* If someone has a **blackout**, they become unconscious for a short time. **black out** *(v)*.

blacksmith *(n)* someone who makes and fits horseshoes and mends things made of iron.

bladder *(n)* the organ in your body where waste liquid is stored before it leaves your body. *See* **organ**.

blade
1 *(n)* a sharp edge on a knife, sword, dagger, etc.
2 *(n)* the long, flat part of an oar or propeller.
3 *(n)* a single piece of grass.

blame blaming blamed *(v)* If you **blame** someone for something, you say that it is their fault. **blame** *(n)*.

bland blander blandest *(adj)* mild and rather dull. *Bland food.*

blank blanker blankest
1 *(adj)* If something is **blank**, it has nothing on it. *A blank disc.*
2 *(n)* a cartridge for a gun that makes a noise but does not fire a bullet.
3 if you **go blank** you suddenly cannot think of something.

blanket
1 *(n)* a cover for a bed.
2 *(n)* a thick covering of something, such as snow or flowers.

blare blaring blared *(v)* to make a very loud and unpleasant noise. *His radio has been blaring all day.*

blaspheme blaspheming blasphemed *(v)* to say offensive things about God or a religion. **blasphemy** *(n)*, **blasphemous** *(adj)*.

blast blasting blasted
1 *(n)* a loud noise or explosion.
2 *(n)* a sudden rush of air.
3 *(v)* to fire a gun.
4 *(v)* When a rocket or a spaceship **blasts off**, it leaves the ground.

blatant *(adj)* obvious and shameless. *Horace grinned as he told a blatant lie.* **blatantly** *(adv)*.

blaze blazing blazed
1 *(v)* to burn fiercely.
2 *(n)* a large fire.

blazer *(n)* an informal jacket.

bleach
bleaches bleaching bleached
1 *(n)* a chemical substance used to kill germs or to make things white.
2 *(v)* to make something white or very light. *The sun had bleached Jan's hair.*

bleak bleaker bleakest
1 *(adj)* A **bleak** place is cold, empty, and depressing.
2 *(adj)* without hope. *The future looks really bleak.*

bleat *(n)* the cry made by a sheep or goat. **bleat** *(v)*.

bleed bleeding bled *(v)* to lose blood. **bleeding** *(adj)*.

bleep bleeping bleeped *(v)* to make a short, high-pitched sound. **bleep** *(n)*.

blend blending blended *(v)* to mix two or more things together. **blend** *(n)*.

blender *(n)* an electrical machine that chops and mixes food.

bless blesses blessing blessed
1 *(v)* to ask God to look after someone or something. **blessing** *(n)*.
2 You say **bless you** when a person sneezes, or as a way of thanking someone.

blind
1 *(adj)* Someone who is **blind** cannot see. **blindness** *(n)*.
2 *(adj)* A **blind bend** or **blind corner** is so sharp that drivers cannot see around it.
3 *(n)* a covering for a window that can be pulled over it.
4 *(n)* A **blind spot** is the area slightly behind a driver that he or she cannot see in the rearview mirror or side-view mirror.

blink blinking blinked *(v)* to move your eyelids down and then up very quickly. *You blink all the time without realizing it.* **blink** *(n)*.

blinkers *(plural n)* leather flaps worn by racehorses on both sides of their head so that they can see only straight ahead.

bliss *(n)* great happiness. *It was bliss to be home again.* **blissful** *(adj)*, **blissfully** *(adv)*.

blister *(n)* a sore bubble of skin filled with liquid, that is caused by something burning your skin or rubbing against it.

blitz
1 *(n)* a sudden attack in which bombs are dropped from the air.
2 *(v)* *(informal)* to attack suddenly. If you blitz the quarterback, you try to tackle him before he can throw the ball.

Some words that begin with a "bi" sound are spelled "by."

blizzard *(n)* a heavy snowstorm.

bloated *(adj)* fat and swollen, often as a result of eating too much.

block blocking blocked
1 *(n)* a large lump of something hard. *A block of wood.*
2 *(v)* to stop something from getting past or from happening. **block** *(n).*
3 *(n)* the distance or area from one street to another.
4 *(n)* the area or section in a city surrounded by four streets.

blond or **blonde**
blonder blondest *(adj)*
Blond men and boys or **blonde** woman and girls have pale yellow hair.

blood
1 *(n)* the red liquid that is pumped around your body by your heart. *Blood is made up of red cells, white cells, and platelets, all floating in plasma.* **bloody** *(adj).*
2 **blood donor** *(n)* a person who lets some blood be taken out of their body to be stored and given to someone else.

red blood cell
white blood cell
plasma
nucleus
platelet

human blood
(magnified)

3 **blood vessel** *(n)*
one of the narrow tubes in your body through which your blood flows.

bloodshed *(n)*
all the killing that happens in a battle or war. *We must try to prevent further bloodshed.*

bloodthirsty *(adj)*
Someone who is **bloodthirsty** really enjoys violence and killing. **bloodthirstiness** *(n),* **bloodthirstily** *(adv).*

bloom blooming bloomed
1 *(n)* a flower on a plant.
2 *(v)* When a plant **blooms**, its flowers come out.
3 *(adj)* If someone is **blooming**, they look very healthy.

blossom blossoming blossomed
1 *(n)* the small flowers that appear on plants and trees in the spring.
2 *(v)* to grow or improve. *Francesca has blossomed into a first-rate dancer.*

blot blotting blotted
1 *(n)* a stain caused by spilled ink or paint.
2 *(v)* to dry ink on a page using a piece of soft paper.

blotch blotches *(n)*
an area of reddened skin, or a stain. **blotchy** *(adj).*

blouse *(n)* a piece of clothing, like a loose shirt, worn by women and girls.

blow blowing blew blown
1 *(v)* to make air come out of your mouth.
2 *(v)* to move in the wind. *The leaves were blowing around.*
3 *(n)* a punch or hit to the body.
4 *(n)* a disappointment.
5 **blow up** *(v)* to destroy something with an explosion.

blubber blubbering blubbered
1 *(n)* the fat under the skin of a whale or seal.
2 *(v)* to cry noisily.

blue bluer bluest
1 *(n)* the color of the sky on a sunny day. **blue** *(adj).*
2 *(adj)* sad and depressed.
3 **out of the blue** suddenly.

blueprint *(n)* a detailed plan for a project or an idea.

blues *(singular n)*
a type of slow, sad jazz music, first sung by African Americans.

bluff bluffing bluffed
1 *(v)* to pretend to be in a stronger position than you really are, or to know more about something than you really do. *Nat says he's going to win, but I think he's bluffing.* **bluff** *(n).*
2 If you **call someone's bluff**, you challenge them to do what they say they can do, because you think that they are bluffing.

blunder blundering blundered
1 *(n)* a stupid mistake. **blunder** *(v).*
2 *(v)* to move in an awkward and clumsy way, usually because you cannot see where you are going.

blunderbuss blunderbusses *(n)*
an old-fashioned gun with a wide-mouthed barrel that fires several lead balls at once. *When the trigger of a blunderbuss is released, the flint strikes against the frizzen, making the gunpowder explode and shoot the lead balls out of the barrel.*

blunt blunter bluntest
1 *(adj)* not sharp.
2 *(adj)* direct and straightforward in what you say. **bluntly** *(adv).*

blur blurring blurred
1 *(v)* to make something smeared and unclear.
2 *(n)* a shape that is unclear because it has no outline or is moving too fast. **blurred** *(adj).*

blurb *(n)*
writing on or about a product intended to get people interested in it.

blurt blurting blurted *(v)*
If you **blurt** something out, you say it suddenly, without thinking.

blush blushes blushing blushed *(v)*
When you **blush**, your face turns red because you are embarrassed or ashamed. **blush** *(n).*

bluster blustering blustered
1 *(v)* to blow in gusts. *The wind blustered round the chimney pots.* **blustery** *(adj).*
2 *(v)* to act or speak in an aggressive and over-confident way.

boar
1 *(n)* a male pig.
2 *(n)* a type of wild pig.

wild boar

board boarding boarded
1 *(n)* a flat piece of wood or cardboard. *A chess board.*
2 *(v)* to get on a train, an airplane, or a ship.
3 *(n)* The **board** of a company is the group of people who manage it.

boarder *(n)* a person who pays to live somewhere and receive meals.

boarding school *(n)*
a school that students live in during the school year.

boast boasting boasted
1 *(v)* to talk proudly about what you can do or what you own to impress people. **boast** *(n),* **boastful** *(adj),* **boastfully** *(adv).*
2 *(v)* If a place **boasts** something good, it possesses it. *Paris boasts many fine restaurants.*

18th-century blunderbuss

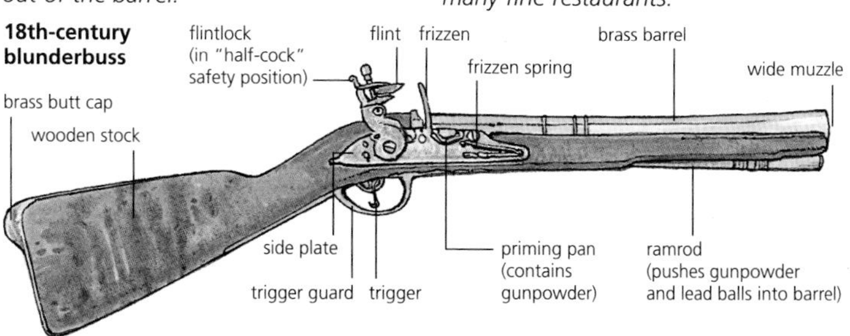

a b c d e f g h i j k l m n o p q r s t u v w x y z

boat

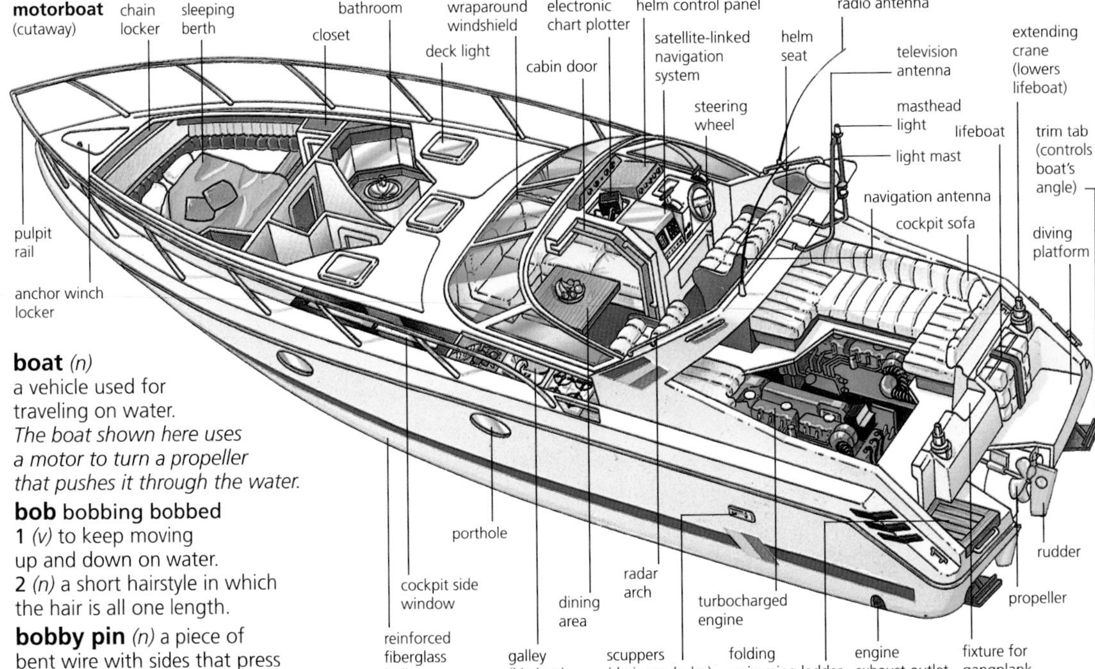

boat *(n)*
a vehicle used for traveling on water. *The boat shown here uses a motor to turn a propeller that pushes it through the water.*

bob bobbing bobbed
1 *(v)* to keep moving up and down on water.
2 *(n)* a short hairstyle in which the hair is all one length.

bobby pin *(n)* a piece of bent wire with sides that press together to hold your hair in place.

bobsled (n) a sled with mechanical steering and brakes, used for racing down a steep, ice-covered run. *A bobsled team consists of a driver, at the front and a brakeman at the back. Four-person bobsleds also have two pushers to help build up speed.*

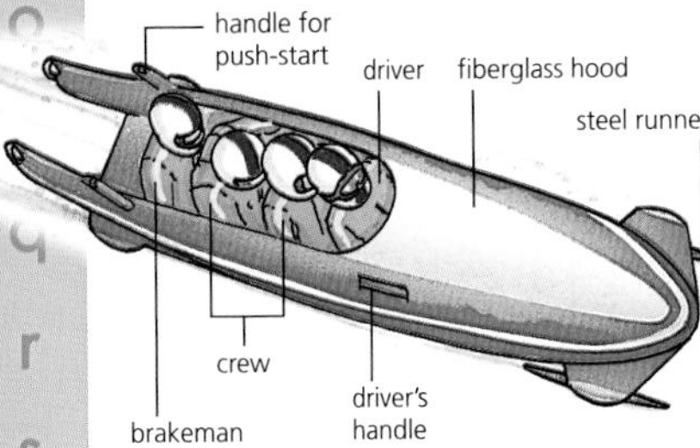

four-person bobsled

body bodies
1 *(n)* all the parts that a person or an animal is made of. *The human body.*
2 *(n)* the main part of something, especially a car or an aircraft.
3 *(n)* a dead person. *The detectives have found another body.*

bodyguard *(n)*
someone who protects an important person from attacks.

bog *(n)*
an area of wet spongy land. **boggy** *(adj)*.

bogus *(adj)* false. *Bill gave a bogus name to the police.*

boil boiling boiled
1 *(v)* to heat a liquid until it starts to bubble and give off vapor. **boiling** *(adj)*.
2 *(v)* to cook something in boiling water.
3 *(n)* an infected lump under the skin.

boiler *(n)* a tank that heats water for a house or other building.

boiling point *(n)*
the temperature at which a liquid that has been heated turns to gas.

boisterous *(adj)*
If you are **boisterous**, you behave in a rough and noisy way. **boisterousness** *(n)*, **boisterously** *(adv)*.

bold bolder boldest
1 *(adj)* Someone who is **bold** is very confident and shows no fear of danger. **boldness** *(n)*, **boldly** *(adv)*.
2 *(adj)* **Bold** colors stand out clearly.

bolster bolstering bolstered
1 *(v)* to support someone or something.
2 *(n)* a long pillow.

bolt bolting bolted
1 *(n)* a metal bar that slides into place and locks something. **bolt** *(v)*.
2 *(n)* a strong metal pin, used with a metal nut to hold things together.
3 *(v)* to run away suddenly.

bomb bombing bombed
1 *(n)* a container filled with explosives, used in war or to blow up buildings, vehicles, etc.
2 *(v)* to attack a place with bombs.

bombard
bombarding bombarded
1 *(v)* to attack a place with heavy gunfire. **bombardment** *(n)*.
2 *(v)* If you **bombard** someone with questions, you ask them a lot of questions in a short time.

bombshell
1 *(n)* a bomb.
2 *(n)* something that makes you shocked and surprised.

bond bonding bonded
1 *(n)* a close friendship or connection with someone. *A special bond developed between the boys.*
2 *(v)* When two things **bond**, they stick together. **bond** *(n)*.
3 **bonds** *(plural n)* ropes, chains, etc. used to tie someone up.

bone *(n)*
one of the hard, white parts that make up the skeleton of a person or an animal.

bonfire *(n)*
a large, outdoor fire, often used to burn yard debris.

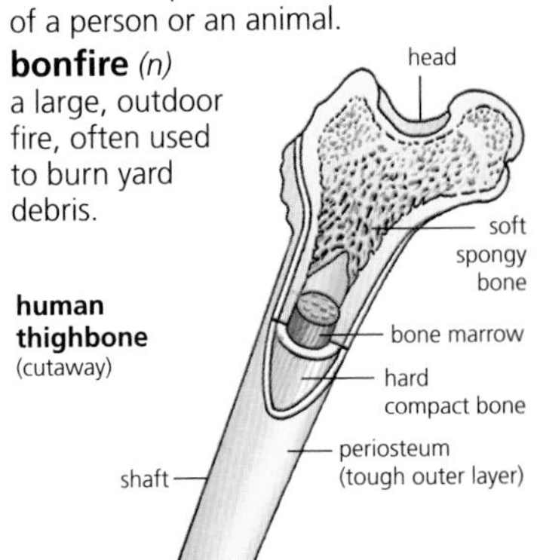

human thighbone (cutaway)

bonnet *(n)* a baby's or woman's hat, tied with strings under the chin.

bonsai *(bonz-eye)*
bonsai *(n)* a miniature tree or shrub often grown in a pot for decoration.

bonsai (needle juniper)

bonus bonuses
1 *(n)* an extra reward that you get for doing something well. bonus *(adj)*.
2 *(n)* a good thing that is more than you expected. *It's a bonus to have a library so close to our new house.*

booby trap *(n)*
a hidden trap or trick, which is set off when someone or something touches it.

book booking booked
1 *(n)* a set of pages that are bound together in a cover. *The picture below shows a book bound in a hardback cover.*
2 *(v)* to arrange for something to be kept for you to have or use later. *We've booked a vacation in Hawaii.*

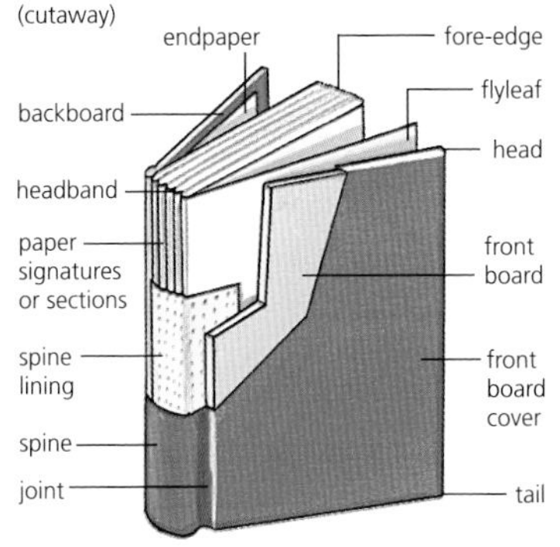

bookkeeper *(n)*
someone who keeps financial records for a business. **bookkeeping** *(n)*.

booklet *(n)*
a book with a paper cover and a small number of pages.

bookworm *(n)*
someone who loves reading books.

boom
booming boomed
1 *(n)* a very loud, deep sound, like an explosion. **boom** *(v)*.
2 *(v)* to speak in a loud, deep voice. *"Sit down!" the guard boomed at us.*
3 *(n)* a rapid increase in something. *A housing boom.*

boomerang *(n)*
a curved stick that is thrown through the air and returns to the thrower if it misses its target. *Boomerangs were used by Aboriginal hunters in Australia.*

Aboriginal boomerang

boost boosting boosted
1 *(v)* to lift someone or something by pushing from below.
2 *(v)* to increase the power or amount of something. **boost** *(n)*.
3 *(n)* If something gives you a **boost**, it cheers you up.

booster
1 *(n)* a rocket that gives extra power to a spacecraft.
2 **booster shot** *(n)* an injection of a vaccine, given to increase the effect of an earlier injection.

boot booting booted
1 *(n)* a heavy shoe that covers your ankle and sometimes part of your leg.
2 *(v)* When you **boot up** a computer, you turn it on and get it ready to work.

booty
1 *(singular n)* valuable objects that are taken by force by an army after a battle.
2 *(n)* a knitted sock for a baby.

border bordering bordered
1 *(n)* the dividing line between one country or region and another.
2 *(v)* If one country **borders** another, their boundaries meet.
3 *(n)* a decorative strip around the edge of something.

bore boring bored
1 *(v)* If something or someone **bores** you, you find them very dull and uninteresting. **bore** *(n)*, **boredom** *(n)*.
2 *(v)* to make a hole in something with a drill. *This machine can bore into solid rock.*
3 *(n)* the hole inside a gun barrel.

borough *(burr-roh)*
1 *(n)* in some states, a town or a village that has its own local government.
2 *(n)* one of the five political divisions of New York City.

borrow borrowing borrowed *(v)*
to use someone else's belongings for a short time, with their permission.

bosom
1 *(n)* the front part of someone's chest.
2 *(adj)* close and dear. *Joe and Jack are bosom buddies.*

boss bosses bossing bossed
1 *(n)* someone in charge of a company or someone for whom people work.
2 **boss around** *(v)* to keep telling somebody what to do.

bossy bossier bossiest *(adj)*
A **bossy** person likes telling other people what to do. **bossiness** *(n)*.

botany *(singular n)*
the study of plants. *The picture shows a watercolor painting of a Christmas rose, from an 18th-century book on botany.* **botanist** *(n)*, **botanical** *(adj)*.

botanical drawing

bother
bothering
bothered
1 *(v)* If something **bothers** you, it disturbs or annoys you.
2 *(n)* Something that annoys you. *Cleaning is such a bother.*
3 *(v)* to make an effort to do something. *At least Jane bothered to come to the meeting.*

bottle bottling bottled
1 *(n)* a glass or plastic container for liquids.
2 *(v)* to put things into bottles.
3 *(v)* If you **bottle up** your feelings, you keep them to yourself.

bottleneck *(n)* a narrow part of a road that causes traffic jams.

bottom
1 *(n)* the lowest part of something. *The bottom of the sea.* **bottom** *(adj)*.
2 *(n)* the part of your body that you sit on.
3 *(n)* the most basic part of something. *He'll get to the bottom of this.*

bough *(n)* a thick branch on a tree.

boulder *(n)* a large, rounded rock.

bounce bouncing bounced
1 *(v)* to spring back after hitting something. **bounce** *(n)*, **bouncy** *(adj)*.
2 *(n)* If someone has a lot of **bounce**, they are very cheerful. **bouncy** *(adj)*.

bound bounding bounded
1 *(v)* to move forward quickly with leaps and jumps. **bound** *(n)*.
2 *(adj)* If something is **bound** to happen, it will definitely take place.
3 If a place is **out of bounds**, you are not allowed to go there.

boundary boundaries *(n)*
the line that separates one area from another.

bouquet *(boh-kay or boo-kay) (n)* a bunch of flowers.

bow bowing bowed
1 *(rhymes with cow) (v)* to bend low as a sign of respect or to accept applause. **bow** *(n)*.
2 *(rhymes with low) (n)* a knot with loops.
3 **bow** *or* **bows** *(rhymes with cow) (n)* the front of a ship.
4 *(rhymes with low) (n)* a long flat piece of wood with strings stretched along it, used for playing stringed instruments. *See* **strings**.
5 *(rhymes with low) (n)* a curved piece of wood with a stretched string attached to it, used for shooting arrows. *This archer from the Bayeux tapestry draws his bow, ready to shoot, and holds some spare arrows in his hand.*

medieval archer

bowels *(plural n)* the part of your body that carries solids away from your stomach; intestines.

bowl bowling bowled
1 *(n)* a deep dish. *This porcelain dragon bowl was made in China in the 16th century.*

Chinese dragon bowl

2 *(v)* When you **bowl** a ball, you roll it along a lane to knock over pins. **bowling** *(n)*
3 *(v)* When something **bowls you over**, it greatly surprises you.

bow tie *(n)* a necktie in the shape of a bow.

box boxes boxing boxed
1 *(n)* a container, especially one with six flat sides.
2 *(v)* to fight with your fists as a sport. **boxer** *(n)*, **boxing** *(n)*.
3 If you **box someone into a corner**, you surround them so that they cannot escape.

box office *(n)* the place in a theater where you buy tickets.

boy *(n)* a male child. **boyish** *(adj)*.

boycott boycotting boycotted *(v)* to refuse to take part in something or buy something as a way of making a protest. **boycott** *(n)*.

boyfriend *(n)*
1 *(n)* the man or boy with whom someone is having a romantic relationship.
2 *(n)* a male friend.

bra *(n)* a piece of underwear that supports a woman's breasts. Bra is short for brassière.

brace bracing braced
1 *(n)* an object that supports another object or holds it in place. **brace** *(v)*.
2 **braces** *(plural n)* a device with wires worn inside your mouth to straighten your teeth.
3 *(v)* If you **brace yourself**, you prepare yourself for a shock or for the force of something hitting you.

bracelet *(n)* a band worn around the wrist as a piece of jewelry.

bracket
1 *(n)* a support, made of metal or wood, used to hold up a shelf.
2 *(n)* a grouping. *This game is intended for your age bracket and is in my price bracket.*

brag bragging bragged *(v)* to talk in a boastful way about how good you are at something.

braid *(n)* a piece of hair that has been divided into sections and twisted together.

Braille *(brayl) (n)* a system of printing for blind people. Braille uses raised dots that are read by feeling with the fingertips. *This picture shows what the word "Braille" looks like when it is printed in Braille.*

B R A I L L E

brain
1 *(n)* the organ inside your head that controls your body and allows you to think and have feelings.
2 *(n)* your mind or intelligence.

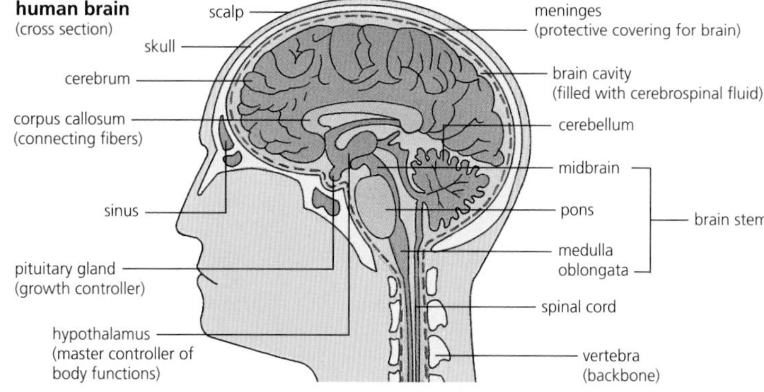

brainstorm
brainstorming brainstormed
1 *(v)* If people **brainstorm**, they get together to share ideas on a topic or to solve a problem.
2 *(n)* a sudden idea.

brainwash brainwashes brainwashing brainwashed *(v)* to make someone accept and believe something by saying it to them over and over again. **brainwashing** *(n)*.

brainwave *(n)* a sudden good idea.

brainy brainier brainiest *(adj)* *(informal)* clever, or intelligent.

brake braking braked
1 *(n)* You use **brakes** to slow down or stop a vehicle. The brakes press against a wheel and stop from it turning.
2 *(v)* to slow down or stop by using brakes.

bran *(n)* the outer covering of wheat or other grains that is sifted out when flour is made. Bran is used in baked goods and cereals.

branch
branches branching branched
1 *(n)* a part of a tree that grows out of its trunk like an arm.
2 *(v)* When a road, river, etc. **branches**, it splits into two parts that go in different directions. **branch** *(n)*.
3 *(n)* A **branch** of a company or organization is one of its stores, offices, etc., in a particular area.

brand branding branded
1 *(n)* a particular make of a product. *A brand of toothpaste.*
2 *(v)* If someone **brands** an animal, they burn a mark onto its skin to show that the animal belongs to them. **brand** *(n)*.
3 *(v)* to call by a shameful name. *The soldier was branded a coward.*

brash *(adj)* especially bold, tactless or reckless.

brass
1 *(n)* a yellow metal made from copper and zinc.
2 *(adj)* The **brass** section in an orchestra contains musical instruments that are made of brass and usually have a funnel-shaped mouthpiece.
The picture shows the main instruments in an orchestra's brass section.

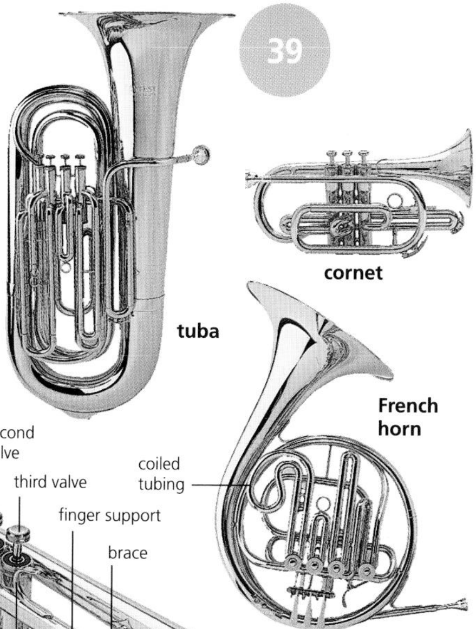

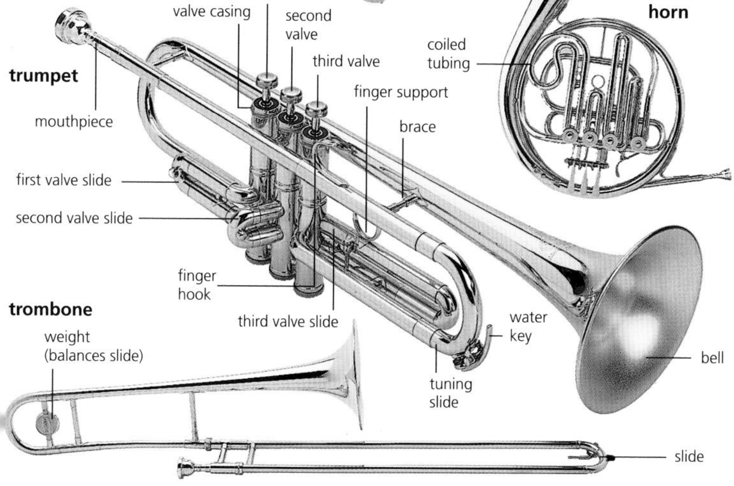

tuba

cornet

French horn

trumpet

first valve
valve casing
second valve
third valve
coiled tubing
finger support
brace
mouthpiece
first valve slide
second valve slide
finger hook
third valve slide
water key
bell
tuning slide

trombone

weight (balances slide)
slide

brassière *see* **bra**.

brass rubbing *(n)*
a copy of a picture carved on a brass plate. Brass rubbings are made by rubbing with a wax crayon, graphite, or chalk on a piece of paper placed over the plate.
This brass rubbing is taken from the tomb of a 15th-century knight.

brass rubbing

bravado *(n)* If you are full of **bravado**, you pretend to be braver and more confident than you really are.

brave
braving braved; braver bravest
1 *(adj)* If you are **brave**, you show courage and are willing to do difficult things. **bravery** *(n)*, **bravely** *(adv)*.
2 *(v)* If you **brave** something difficult, you face it deliberately.
3 *(n)* an American Indian warrior.

brawl *(n)* a rough fight. **brawl** *(v)*.

bray braying brayed
1 *(v)* When a donkey **brays**, it makes a loud, harsh noise in its throat. **bray** *(n)*.
2 *(v)* When a person **brays**, they make a harsh noise like a donkey.

brazen
1 *(adj)* shameless. **brazenly** *(adv)*.
2 *(adj)* made of brass.

brazier *(bray-zee-er) (n)*
a pan for holding burning coals, used for cooking or to keep people warm out of doors.

bread
1 *(n)* a baked food made from flour, water, and often yeast.
2 *(n) (slang)* money.

breadline *(n)* a line of people waiting to receive free food.

breadth
1 *(n)* the distance from one side of something to the other.
2 *(n)* a wide range. *Jack has a breadth of experience in caring for animals.*

breadwinner *(n)* someone who earns money for a family.

break breaking broke broken
1 *(v)* to damage something so that it is in pieces or it no longer works. **breakage** *(n)*, **breakable** *(adj)*.
2 *(n)* a rest from working or studying.
3 *(v)* If someone **breaks** the rules or the law, they do something that is not allowed.
4 **break in** *(v)*
to get into a building by force.
5 **break out** *(v)* to begin suddenly. *Fighting broke out on the streets.*

break dance *(n)* a very energetic and acrobatic form of dance.

breakdown
1 *(n)* If you have a **breakdown** while you are traveling, your car stops moving because its engine has stopped working.
2 *(n)* If someone has a **breakdown**, they are so worried or depressed that they become ill.

breaker *(n)* a big sea wave.

breakfast *(n)*
the first meal of the day.

breakthrough *(n)* an important step toward achieving something.

breakwater
1 *(n)* a wall built in the sea to protect a harbor from the force of the waves.
2 *(n)* a barrier built on a beach to reduce the force of the waves.

breaststroke *(n)*
a style of swimming on your front in which you move your arms forward and out from your chest and kick your legs like a frog.

breath
1 *(n)* the air that you take into your lungs and breathe out again.
2 If you are **out of breath**, you have difficulty breathing.
3 When you say something **under your breath**, you say it very quietly.

breathe breathing breathed *(v)*
to take air in and out of your lungs.

breather *(n) (informal)* a short rest.

breathless
1 *(adj)* out of breath.
breathlessly *(adv)*.
2 *(adj)* fast-paced and exciting. *The car chase in the spy movie was breathless.*

breathtaking *(adj)*
very beautiful or impressive. *The view from the cliff was breathtaking.* **breathtakingly** *(adv)*.

breathy *(adj)*
breathing heavily or noisy.

breed breeding bred
1 *(v)* to keep animals or plants so that you can produce more of them and control their quality. **breeder** *(n)*.
2 *(v)* When animals **breed**, they mate and produce babies.
3 *(n)* a particular type of animal. *A popular breed of dog.*

breeze *(n)*
a gentle wind. **breezy** *(adj)*.

brew brewing brewed
1 *((v)* to make tea or coffee.
2 *(v)* If something is **brewing**, it is about to start. *There's trouble brewing at home.*

briar *(n)*
a woody plant with a prickly stem.

bribe bribing bribed
1 *(n)* money or a gift that you offer to someone to persuade them to do something for you, especially something wrong.
2 *(v)* to offer someone a bribe. **bribery** *(n).*

bric-a-brac *(n)*
various objects, such as ornaments, that are not worth very much.

brick *(n)* a block of hard, baked clay, used for building.

bride *(n)* a woman who is about to be married or has just been married.

bridegroom *(n)*
a man who is about to be married or has just been married.

bridesmaid *(n)*
a girl or a woman who helps a bride on her wedding day.

bridge bridging bridged
1 *(n)* a structure built over a river, railway, etc. so that people or vehicles can get to the other side. *The picture below shows four types of bridges.*
2 *(n)* a card game for four players.
3 *(v)* If something **bridges a gap**, it provides a connection between two different things.
4 *(n)* an upright piece of wood on a guitar, violin, etc. over which the strings are stretched. *See* **guitar**, **strings**.

bridges

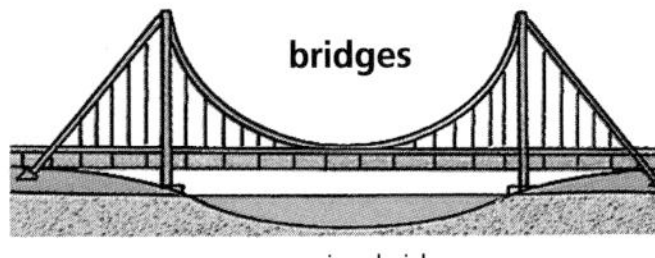

suspension bridge

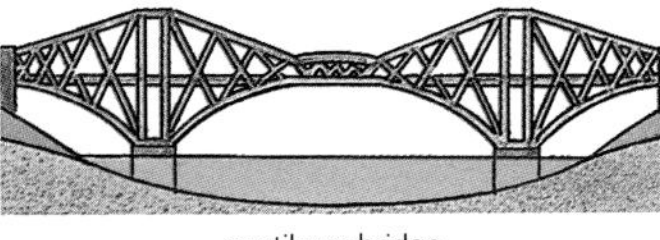

cantilever bridge

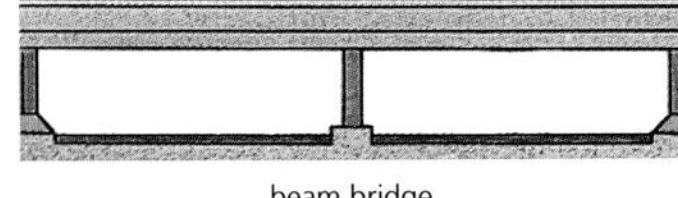

beam bridge

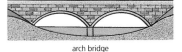

arch bridge

bridle *(n)* the straps that fit around a horse's head and mouth, and are used to control it. *See* **tack**.

bridle path *(n)* a track or path for horse riders or walkers.

brief
briefing briefed; briefer briefest
1 *(adj)* lasting only a short time. *A brief visit.* **briefly** *(adv).*
2 *(adj)* using only a few words. *Be as brief as you can.* **briefly** *(adv).*
3 *(v)* to give someone information so they can carry out a task. **brief** *(n).*
4 **briefs** *(plural n)* underpants.

briefcase *(n)* a bag with a handle, used for carrying papers.

brigade *(n)* a unit of an army.

bright brighter brightest
1 *(adj)* A **bright** light or color is strong and can be seen clearly. **brightness** *(n),* **brightly** *(adv).*
2 *(adj)* cheerful. **brightly** *(adv).*
3 *(adj) (informal)* clever.

brilliant
1 *(adj)* shining very brightly. *A brilliant diamond.* **brilliance** *(n).*
2 *(adj)* very clever. **brilliance** *(n),* **brilliantly** *(adv).*

brim *(n)* the wide part that sticks out around the bottom of a hat.

brine *(n)* salty water.

bring bringing brought
1 *(v)* to take something or someone with you. *Bring a friend.*
2 *(v)* to make something happen or appear. *Hooligans bring trouble.*
3 *(v)* If a company **brings out** a product, it starts selling it.
4 **bring up** *(v)* to look after and guide a child as it grows up.
5 **bring in** *(v)* If you **bring something in**, you introduce it.

brink
1 *(n)* the edge of something, such as a cliff or a riverbank.
2 If you are **on the brink** of something, you are just about to do it. *Jake is on the brink of leaving.*

brisk brisker briskest
1 *(adj)* quick and energetic. *A brisk walk.* **briskly** *(adv).*
2 *(adj)* fresh and invigorating. *Brisk weather.*

bristle
1 *(n)* one of the long, wiry hairs used to make brushes. **bristly** *(adj).*
2 **bristles** *(plural n)* the short, stiff hairs that start to grow on a man's chin if he does not shave. **bristly** *(adj).*
3 *(v)* to show anger. *Jack bristled when he saw his sister being teased.*

brittle *(adj)*
easily snapped or broken. *Dried flowers can be very brittle.*

broach broaches broaching broached *(v)* When you **broach** a subject with someone, you start to talk or ask about it.

broad broader broadest
1 *(adj)* wide. **broaden** *(v).* *The Mississippi is a broad river.*
2 *(adj)* covering the most important points, but not the details. *Give me a broad outline of the story.* **broadly** *(adv).*

broadcast broadcasting **broadcast** *or* **broadcasted**
1 *(v)* to send out a program on television, radio, the internet, etc. **broadcaster** *(n),* **broadcasting** *(n).*
2 *(n)* a television or radio program.

broccoli *(n)*
a green vegetable with rounded heads on stalks. *See* **vegetable**.

brochure *(broh-shur) (n)*
a booklet, usually with pictures, that gives information about a product or service. *These brochures advertise vacations.*

broiler *(n)*
an oven that heats food from above.

broke *(adj) (informal)*
If you are **broke**, you have no money.

broken
1 *(adj)* smashed or in pieces.
2 *(adj)* not working.

bronchitis *(bron-ky-tiss) (n)*
an illness of the throat and lungs that makes you cough a lot.

bronze
1 *(n)* a hard, reddish brown metal that is a mixture of copper and tin.
2 *(n)* a reddish brown color.

brooch
(rhymes with coach)
brooches *(n)*
a piece of jewelry that can be pinned to your clothes. *The Tara brooch, shown here, was made in 10th-century Ireland.*

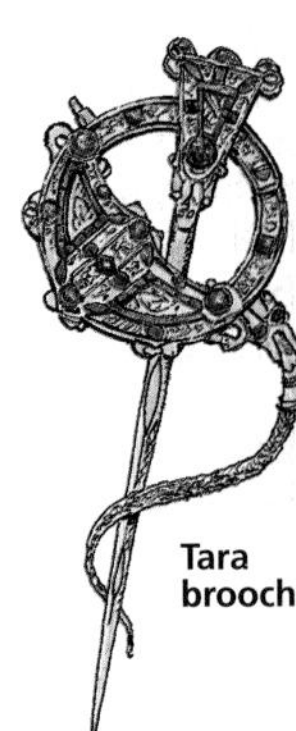

Tara brooch

brood
brooding brooded
1 *(n)* a family of young birds.
2 *(v)* to keep worrying or thinking about something. *Don't brood over your problems.*

brook *(n)* a small stream.

broom *(n)*
a large brush with a long handle, used for sweeping floors.

brother *(n)*
a boy or man with the same parents as you. **brotherly** *(adj).*

brow
1 *(n)* forehead. *A wrinkled brow.*
2 *(n)* the top of a hill.

brown *(n)* the color of wood, leather, and coffee. **brown** *(adj).*

brownie *(n)* a small, flat chocolate cake, usually with nuts.

browse browsing browsed *(v)*
to look at something in a casual way. *Max browsed the internet.*

browser *(n)* a computer program that allows you to use the internet.

bruise *(brewz) (n)* a dark mark that you get on your skin when you fall or are hit by something. **bruise** *(v).*

brunette *(adj)*
a dark color, especially of hair.

brush brushes brushing brushed
1 *(n)* an object with bristles and a handle, used for sweeping, painting, or smoothing hair.
2 *(v)* to use a brush. *Brush your hair before you go out.*
3 *(v)* to touch something lightly.

brutal *(adj)* cruel and violent. *A brutal murder.* **brutally** *(adv).*

brute
1 *(n)* a rough and violent person. *You brute!*
2 If you do something by **brute force**, you use a lot of strength instead of skill or intelligence.

bubble bubbling bubbled
1 *(n)* one of the tiny balls of gas in carbonated drinks, boiling water, etc.
2 *(v)* to make bubbles. *The water bubbled in the saucepan.*

bubbly
1 *(adj)* If a liquid is **bubbly**, it is full of balls of gas.
2 *(adj)* If a person is **bubbly**, they are very lively and talkative.

buccaneer

buccaneer *(n)*
(old-fashioned)
a pirate.

buck
bucking
bucked
1 *(n)*
a male deer, kangaroo, etc.
2 *(n) (slang)* a dollar.
3 *(v)* If a horse **bucks**, it jumps in the air with all four feet off the ground.
4 If you **pass the buck**, you pass the responsibility for something on to someone else.

bucket *(n)*
a plastic or metal container with a handle, used for carrying liquids.

buckle buckling buckled
1 *(n)* a metal fastening on shoes, belts, or straps. *The elaborate buckle shown here was made by Anglo-Saxon craftsmen in the 7th century A.D.* **buckle** *(v).*
2 *(v)* to crumple. *Hugh's legs buckled under him and he fell.*

buckle

bud *(n)*
a small shoot on a plant that grows into a leaf or flower.
See **plant**.

Buddha

Buddha
1 *(n)* the name given to Siddhartha Gautama, the teacher who founded the religion of Buddhism.
2 *(n)* a statue or picture of Buddha.

Buddhism *(n)*
a religion based on the teachings of Buddha and practiced mainly in eastern and central Asia. Buddhists believe that you should not become too attached to material things and that you live many lives in different bodies. **Buddhist** *(n),* **Buddhist** *(adj).*

budge budging budged *(v)*
If you cannot **budge** something, you are not able to move it.

budgerigar *(n)* a brightly colored Australian bird, often kept as a pet.

budget budgeting budgeted
1 *(n)* a plan for how money will be earned and spent. **budgetary** *(adj).*
2 *(v)* If you **budget** for something, you plan how to spend your money so that you can afford it.

buff
1 *(n)* a pale, yellow-brown color. **buff** *(adj).*
2 *(n) (informal)* someone who knows a lot about a particular subject. *Barry is a great movie buff.*

buffalo buffaloes *(n)*
a type of ox with heavy horns.

buffer *(n)* something that softens a blow, especially the springs fixed to the front and back of a railway car. *See* **steam locomotive**.

buffet buffeting buffeted
1 *(buff-et) (v)* to strike and shake something or someone. *The wind buffeted the trees.*
2 *(buh-fay) (n)* a meal in which many dishes are laid on a table and people serve themselves.

bug bugging bugged
1 *(n)* an insect.
2 *(n) (informal)* a minor illness caused by germs. *A stomach bug.*
3 *(n) (informal)* an error in a computer program or system that prevents it from working properly.
4 *(adj) (informal)* If a room is **bugged**, someone has hidden microphones there so that they can listen to what people are saying. **bug** *(n),* **bug** *(v).*
5 *(v) (informal)* If someone or something **bugs** you, they annoy you.

buggy buggies
1 *(n)* a baby carriage.
2 *(n) (old-fashioned)* a light, two-wheeled carriage pulled by a horse. *This buggy dates from the 1800s and has seats for three passengers.*

hooded buggy

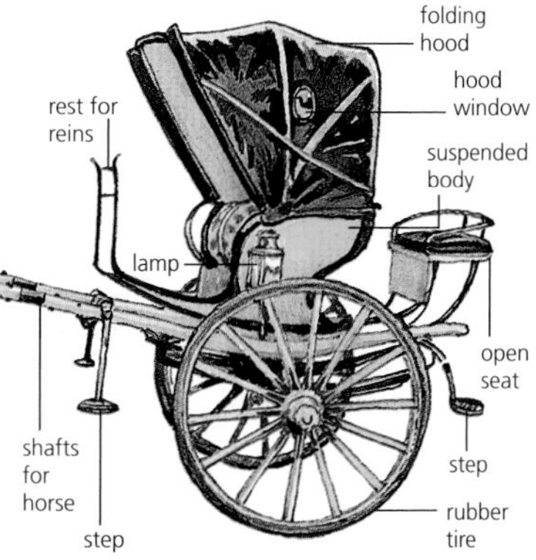

bugle *(n)* a musical instrument like a small trumpet, often used in the army to send signals to the troops. *The picture shows a 19th-century army bugle.*

bugle

build building built
1 *(v)* to make something by putting different parts together.
2 *(n)* the size and shape of a person's body. *Nick has quite a large build.*
3 **build up** *(v)* to increase or make stronger. *The traffic has built up. You must build yourself up for the race.*

building

building *(n)*
a structure with walls and a roof. *This cutaway picture of a modern house shows the different parts of a building.*

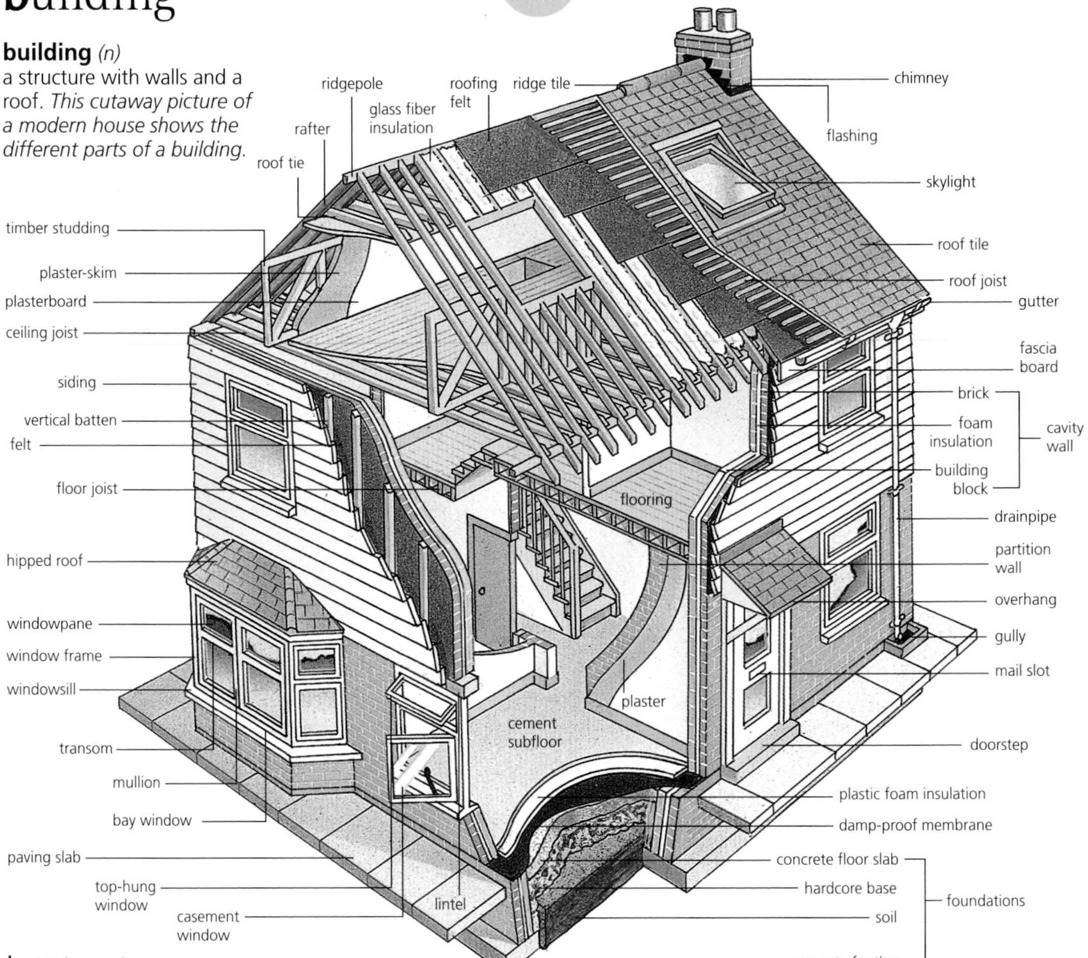

ridgepole
roofing felt
ridge tile
chimney
glass fiber insulation
rafter
flashing
roof tie
skylight
timber studding
roof tile
plaster-skim
roof joist
plasterboard
gutter
ceiling joist
fascia board
siding
brick
vertical batten
foam insulation
cavity wall
felt
building block
floor joist
flooring
drainpipe
partition wall
hipped roof
overhang
windowpane
gully
window frame
mail slot
windowsill
plaster
cement subfloor
transom
doorstep
mullion
plastic foam insulation
bay window
damp-proof membrane
paving slab
concrete floor slab
top-hung window
hardcore base
foundations
lintel
casement window
soil
concrete footing

house (cutaway)

bulb
1 *(n)* the onion-shaped root of some plants.
2 *(n)* the glass part of an electric light or flashlight that lights up when you switch it on.

bulge **bulging** **bulged** *(v)*
to swell out like a lump. *Ella's bag bulged with presents.* **bulge** *(n)*.

bulk
1 *(n)* large size. *We were surprised by the bulk of the dresser.*
2 *(n)* The **bulk** of something is the main part of it. *We have finished the bulk of the work.*
3 When you buy **in bulk**, you buy in large quantities.

bulky **bulkier** **bulkiest**
1 *(adj)* large and difficult to handle. *A bulky suitcase.*
2 *(adj)* very filling. *Bulky food.*

bull
1 *(n)* the male of the cattle family.
2 *(n)* a male elephant, seal, or whale.

bulldozer *(n)*
a powerful tractor with a wide blade at the front, used for moving earth and rocks.

bullet *(n)* a small, pointed metal object fired from a gun.

bulletin *(n)* a short news report on television or radio.

bulletproof *(adj)*
Something that is **bulletproof** is made to protect people from bullets. *Bulletproof glass.*

bullfight *(n)*
a public entertainment in which people fight against bulls.

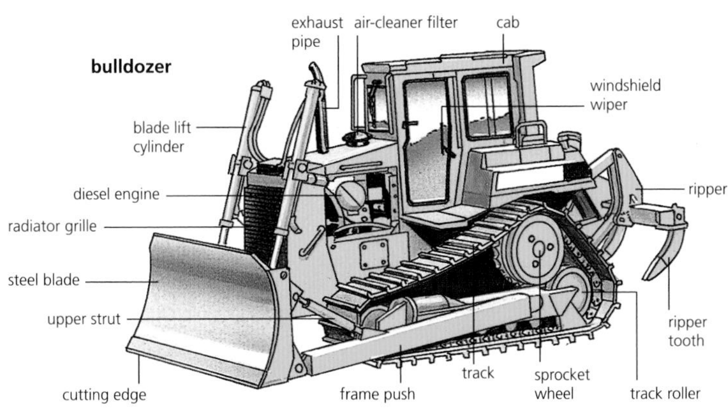

bulldozer

a b c d e f g h i j k l m n o p q r s t u v w x y z

bullion *(n)*
bars of gold or silver.

bully
bullies bullying bullied *(v)*
to frighten or hurt people who are weaker than you. **bully** *(n)*.

bump bumping bumped
1 *(v)* to knock into something by accident. **bump** *(n)*.
2 *(n)* the sound of one thing hitting something else. *I fell out of bed with a bump.*
3 *(n)* a round lump or swelling.
4 *(v) (informal)* If you **bump into** someone, you meet them by chance.
5 *(v)* to move with jolts and jerks. *The cart bumped along the dirt road.*
6 **speed bump** *(n)*
a ridge across a road designed to reduce the speed of vehicles.

bumptious *(adj)*
loud and conceited.

bumpy bumpier bumpiest *(adj)*
very uneven. *A bumpy road.*

bun
1 *(n)* a small, round cake or roll.
2 *(n)* hair fastened in a round shape at the back of the head.

bunch bunches *(n)*
a group of things or people. **bunch** *(v)*.

bundle bundling bundled
1 *(v)* to tie or wrap things together loosely. **bundle** *(n)*.
2 *(v)* to hurry someone. *We bundled the children off to the movies.*

bungalow *(n)*
a house with only one floor.

bungee jumping *(n)*
an extreme sport in which someone jumps from a high place and is stopped from hitting the ground by a long elastic cord attached to his or her legs.

bungle bungling bungled *(v)*
to do something badly or clumsily.

bunk
1 *(n)* a narrow bed.
2 *(n)* a bed stacked on top of or below another.

bunker
1 *(n)* an underground shelter from bomb attacks and gunfire.
2 *(n)* a large, sand-filled hollow on a golf course.

bunny *(n)* a rabbit.

bunting
1 *(n)* a light cloth used for making flags.
2 *(n)* small flags joined by a string and used for decoration.

buoy
*(**boo**-ee or boy) (n)*
a floating marker in the sea or in a river.

top mark
lantern
radar reflector
water line
float
shackle for mooring line
tail

buoy

buoyant
1 *(adj)* able to keep afloat. **buoyancy** *(n)*.
2 *(adj)* cheerful. **buoyantly** *(adv)*.

burden
burdening burdened
1 *(n)* a heavy load that someone has to carry.
2 *(v)* to weigh someone down with heavy things. *We burdened Dad with all our bags and cases.*
3 *(n)* a serious task or responsibility.

bureau *(**byoor**-oh)*
1 *(n)* a chest of drawers.
2 *(n)* an office that provides information or some other service.

burger *(n)* a round, flat piece of cooked meat, usually served on a bun.

burglar *(n)* someone who breaks into a house and steals things. **burglary** *(n)*, **burgle** *(v)*.

burlap *(n)* a tough, coarse material, used to make bags that will hold heavy objects during shipping.

burly *(adj)* strong and with large muscles. *The burly police officer was able to subdue the criminal.*

burn burning burned *or* burnt
1 *(v)* to hurt or damage someone or something with heat or fire.
2 *(n)* a sore area on the skin or a mark on something, caused by heat.

burp burping burped *(v)* to make a noise because gases have been forced up from your stomach, usually after eating or drinking. **burp** *(n)*.

burrow burrowing burrowed
1 *(n)* a tunnel or hole in the ground where a rabbit or other animal lives. *See* **badger**.
2 *(v)* to move along under the ground by digging.

burst bursting burst
1 *(v)* to explode or break apart suddenly. *The balloon burst.*
2 *(n)* a short, concentrated outbreak of something, such as speed, gunfire, or applause.
3 *(v)* to start doing something suddenly. *Kim burst into tears.*
4 *(v)* to be very full. *The suitcase is bursting with clothes.*

bury buries burying buried
1 *(v)* to put a dead body into a grave. **burial** *(n)*.
2 *(v)* to hide something in the ground or under a pile of things.

bus buses *(n)* a large vehicle used for carrying passengers.

bush bushes
1 *(n)* a large plant with many branches.
2 **the bush** *(n)* the wild areas of Australia and Africa.

bushy bushier bushiest *(adj)*
growing thickly. *Bushy eyebrows.*

business businesses
1 *(n)* the type of work that someone does. *Hank's in the music business.*
2 *(n)* the buying and selling of goods and services. *Our company does a lot of business with Japan.*
3 *(n)* a company or shop that makes or sells things or provides a service.
4 If something is **none of your business**, it is nothing to do with you.

businesslike *(adj)*
efficient and practical.

bust busting busted *or* bust
1 *(n)* a statue of a person's head and shoulders. *This bust is of the Ancient Greek scientist Galen.*
2 *(v)* to break something. **bust** *(adj)*.

marble bust

bustle
bustling bustled *(v)*
to rush around being busy. **bustle** *(n)*.

busy busier busiest
1 *(adj)* If you are **busy**, you have a lot of things to do. **busily** *(adv)*.
2 *(adj)* A **busy** place has a lot of people in it and is full of activity.

butcher *(n)*
someone who sells meat.

butler *(n)*
the chief male servant in a house.

butt butting butted
1 *(n)* a large barrel for water.
2 *(v)* to hit with the head or horns.
3 *(n)* the handle of a gun.

butter *(n)*
a yellow fat made from cream, used in cooking and for spreading on bread. *This picture shows a 19th-century dairymaid using a plunger churn to turn cream into butter.*

butter-making

buttercup *(n)*
a small, yellow wildflower. *See* **plant**.

butterfly
butterflies *(n)* a thin-bodied insect with large, brightly colored wings. *Also see* **caterpillar**.

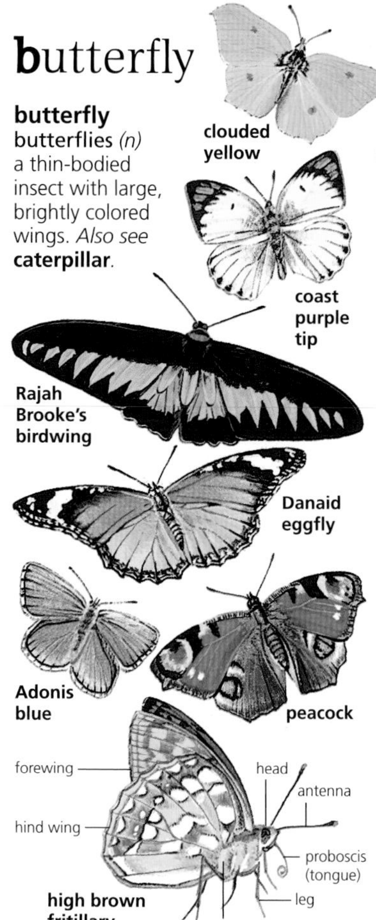

buttock *(n)* the back of your hip that forms the fleshy part on which you sit.

button
1 *(n)* a round piece of plastic, metal, etc. that is sewn onto clothing and used as a fastener. **button** *(v)*.
2 *(n)* a small knob on a machine that you press to switch it on or off.

buy buying bought *(v)* to get something by paying money for it.

buzz buzzes buzzing buzzed *(v)* to make a noise like a bee or a wasp. **buzz** *(n)*.

bypass
bypasses bypassing bypassed
1 *(n)* a main road that goes around a town rather than through it.
2 *(v)* to avoid something by going around it. **bypass** *(adj)*.

byte *(n)* a unit of information that is contained in a computer's memory.

Byzantine
1 *(adj)* having to do with Byzantium, the ancient eastern Roman empire.
2 *(adj)* in the style of art or architecture used in the Byzantine empire. Byzantine buildings have large domes and rounded arches, and are highly decorated. *See* **architecture**.

Cc

cabbage *(n)*
a large leafy vegetable. *See* **vegetable**.

cabin
1 *(n)* the driver's section of a vehicle.
2 *(n)* a room for passengers on a ship or plane.
3 *(n)* a small wooden house.

cabinet
1 *(n)* a cupboard with shelves or drawers.
2 *(n)* a group of top members of a government who advise the leader.

cable
1 *(n)* a thick wire or rope.
2 *(n)* a tight bundle of wires used for carrying electricity, television signals, etc.
3 **cable car** *(n)* a vehicle pulled along by a moving cable, used for carrying people up mountains and steep hills.
4 **cable television** *(n)* a television service received by cable with a wide choice of channels.

cactus
cacti *or* cactuses *(n)* a spiky plant that grows in hot, dry regions.

prickly pear cactus
barrel cactus
cacti

cadet *(n)*
a young person who is training to become a member of the army, navy, air force, or police force.

café *(kaf-ay) (n)* a small restaurant that serves snacks and hot drinks.

cafeteria *(n)* a kitchen or dining hall at school or in a place of work.

caffeine *(kaf-een) (n)* a chemical found in tea and coffee that makes your brain and body more active.

caftan *or* **kaftan** *(n)* a long, loose piece of clothing with long sleeves, worn by people in Arab countries.

cage *(n)* a container in which animals or birds are kept, made of wires or bars. **cage** *(v)*, **caged** *(adj)*.

cajole cajoling cajoled *(v)* to persuade someone to do something by flattering them.

cake caking caked
1 *(n)* a sweet food made by baking flour, butter, eggs, and sugar together.
2 *(v)* If you are **caked** in something, you are covered in it.

calamity calamities *(n)*
a terrible disaster. **calamitous** *(adj)*.

calcium *(n)* a soft, white element found in teeth and bones.

calculate
calculating calculated *(v)* to work out by arithmetic. *Andy calculated that it would take two hours to get there by car.* **calculation** *(n)*.

calculating *(adj)* A **calculating** person makes clever plans so that things work out the way they want.

calculator *(n)* a small electronic machine used for figuring out sums. *This picture shows the face, circuit board and case of a pocket calculator.*

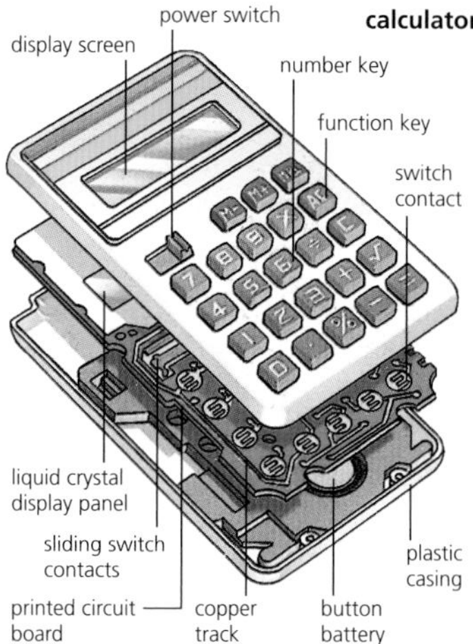

calculator

calendar *(n)*
a chart showing all the days in a year.

calf calves
1 *(n)* a young cow, seal, elephant, giraffe, or whale.
2 *(n)* the fleshy part at the back of your leg, below your knee.

call calling called
1 *(v)* to shout something out, especially someone's name.
2 *(v)* to give someone or something a name.
3 *(v)* to telephone someone. **call** *(n)*.
4 *(v)* If you **call on** someone, you visit them. **caller** *(n)*.
5 **call off** *(v)* If you **call something off**, you cancel it.
6 **call collect** *(v)* to reverse telephone charges from someone who is making the call to the person who is receiving it.

calligraphy *(n)* the art of beautiful handwriting. *The picture shows a dip pen and the word "calligraphy," written in this handwriting.*

calligraphy

Some words that begin with a "c" sound are spelled with a "k."

callous *(adj)* hard-hearted and cruel. **callousness** *(n)*, **callously** *(adv)*.

calm
calming calmed; calmer calmest
1 *(adj)* peaceful and untroubled. **calmness** *(n)*, **calmly** *(adv)*.
2 *(v)* to soothe an animal or a person.
3 *(n)* peacefulness.

calorie *(n)*
a measurement of the amount of energy that a food gives you.

calypso *(n)* a West Indian song with a strong rhythm.

camcorder *(n)* a video camera with a sound recorder, which you can carry around with you.

camel *(n)* a mammal with one or two humps on its back that is used for carrying people and goods across the desert. *The two types of camels are shown here.*

camels

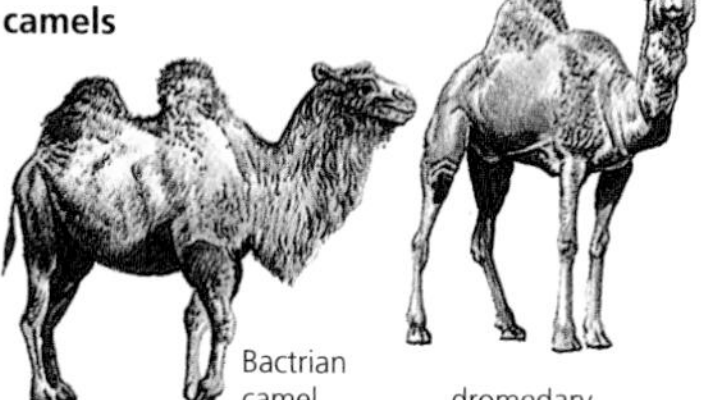

cameo *(kam-ee-oh)*
1 *(n)* a small medallion with a carved figure on it.
2 *(adj)* A **cameo** role is a small character part taken in a play or a movie, usually by a famous actor.

cameo

camera *(n)*
a machine for taking photographs or making movies.

cameraman *(n)*
someone whose job is to use a camera to make movies and television programs.

camouflage *(kam-ah-flaj)*
camouflaging camouflaged
1 *(n)* coloring or covering that makes animals, people, or objects look like their surroundings.
2 *(v)* to disguise something so that it blends in with its surroundings. *The picture below shows a stonefish, a sea creature that camouflages itself as a stone to hide on the seabed.*

stonefish

camp camping camped
1 *(n)* an outdoor area, usually with tents or cabins, where people stay for a while.
2 *(v)* to live or stay in a camp.

campaign *(n)*
a series of actions organized over a period of time to achieve or win something. *An election campaign.*

camper
1 *(n)* someone who stays or vacations in a tent.
2 *(n)* a large vehicle in which you can sleep and cook meals.

can could
1 *(v)* to be able to. *Natalie can speak fluent French.*
2 *(v) (informal)* to be allowed to do something. *You can stay out until dark.*
3 *(n)* a metal container. **canned** *(adj)*.

canal *(n)* a man-made waterway used by ships.

cancel canceling canceled
1 *(v)* If someone **cancels** something that has been arranged, they say that it is not going to happen. **cancellation** *(n)*.
2 **cancel out** *(v)* If two things **cancel each other out**, they stop the effect of one another. *If you eat all day, it will cancel out the benefit of all the exercise you've done.*

cancer *(n)*
a serious disease in which some cells in the body produce harmful growths. **cancerous** *(adj)*.

candid *(adj)* honest and open in what you are saying. **candidly** *(adv)*.

candidate *(n)*
someone taking an examination, applying for a job, or running for office in an election. **candidacy** *(n)*.

candle *(n)*
a stick of wax with a string or wick running through it, which you burn to give light. **candlelight** *(n)*.

candy candies *(n)*
a small piece of food, made with sugar or chocolate.

cane caning caned
1 *(n)* the hollow stem of a plant such as bamboo, used to make furniture.
2 *(n)* a stick, especially a walking stick.
3 *(v)* to beat someone with a cane as a punishment.

canine
1 *(adj)* having to do with dogs.
2 *(n)* the pointed tooth on each side of your upper and lower jaw. *See* **teeth**.

cannibal *(n)* someone who eats human flesh. **cannibalism** *(n)*.

cannon *(n)*
a heavy gun, which fires large metal balls. *The picture shows an 18th-century cannon.*

cannon
(cutaway)

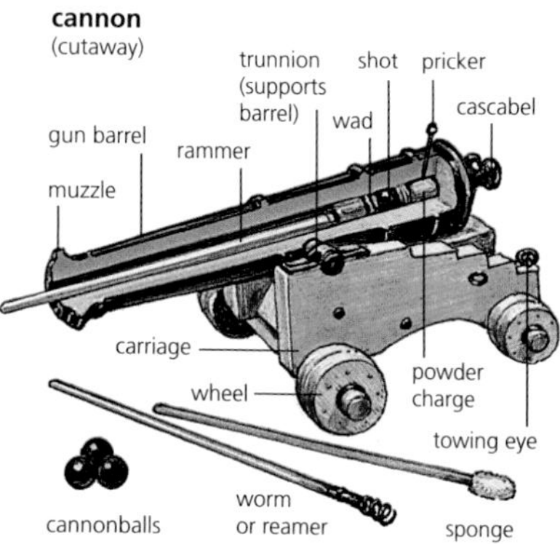

canoe *(n)*
a narrow boat that you move through the water by paddling.

canopy canopies
1 *(n)* a piece of cloth used as a cover over a doorway, bed, etc.
2 *(n)* a shelter over something. *Treetops formed a canopy over the forest floor.*
3 *(n)* a cover over a cockpit. *See* **glider**, **helicopter**.

canteen *(n)*
a small portable metal container for carrying liquids.

Some words that begin with a "c" sound are spelled with a "k."

canter cantering cantered *(v)* When a horse **canters**, it runs at a speed between a trot and a gallop. **canter** *(n)*.

canvas canvases
1 *(n)* a type of coarse, strong cloth used for tents, sails, and clothing.
2 *(n)* a surface for painting, made from canvas cloth stretched over a wooden frame. *Artists paint on canvases.*

canvass canvasses canvassing canvassed *(v)* to ask people for their opinions or votes. **canvasser** *(n)*.

canyon *(n)*
a deep, narrow river valley.

cap capping capped
1 *(n)* a soft, flat hat with a peak at the front.
2 *(n)* the top of a bottle, jar, or pen.
3 *(v)* If you **cap** someone's story, you tell an even better one.
4 *(n)* a small amount of explosive on a piece of paper that makes a bang when fired in a toy gun.

capable
1 *(adj)* If you are **capable** of doing something, you are able to do it. *Ingrid is capable of winning the competition.* **capability** *(n)*.
2 *(adj)* able to do something well and skillfully. *Danny is a capable tennis player.* **capably** *(adv)*.

capacity capacities
1 *(n)* the amount something can hold.
2 *(n)* an ability to do something. *Simon has the capacity to absorb facts very quickly.*

cape
1 *(n)* a sleeveless coat that you wear over your shoulders.
2 *(n)* a part of the coastline that sticks out into the sea. *The picture shows Cape Cod, on the east coast of North America.*

Cape Cod

cape

capillary capillaries
1 *(n)* a small tube in your body that carries blood between arteries and veins.
2 **capillary tube** *(n)* a very thin tube, made out of glass. *See* **thermometer**.

capital
1 *(n)* the main city of a country or state, where the government is based.
2 *(n)* a large letter. *You begin a sentence with a capital.*
3 *(singular n)* an amount of money used to start a business.
4 **capital punishment** *(n)* punishment by death.

capitalism *(n)* a way of organizing a country so that all the land, houses, factories, etc. belong to private individuals rather than the state. **capitalist** *(n)*, **capitalist** *(adj)*.

cappuccino *(kap-uh-cheen-oh) (n)* coffee made with frothy milk and often flavored with cinnamon.

capricious *(adj)* Someone who is **capricious** is unpredictable and tends to change their mind without any obvious reason.

capsize capsizing capsized *(v)* If a boat or ship **capsizes**, it turns over in the water.

capsule
1 *(n)* a small container of medicine that you can swallow.
2 *(n)* the part of a rocket or spacecraft in which the crew travel.

captain
1 *(n)* the person in charge of a ship or an aircraft.
2 *(n)* the leader of a sports team.
3 *(n)* an army officer.

caption *(n)* a short title or description printed below a cartoon, drawing, or photograph.

captivate captivating captivated *(v)* to delight someone. *Clara captivated us with her singing.*

captive *(n)* a person or animal who has been taken prisoner. **captivity** *(n)*, **captive** *(adj)*.

capture capturing captured *(v)* to take a person or a place by force.

car *(n)*
a type of passenger motor vehicle.

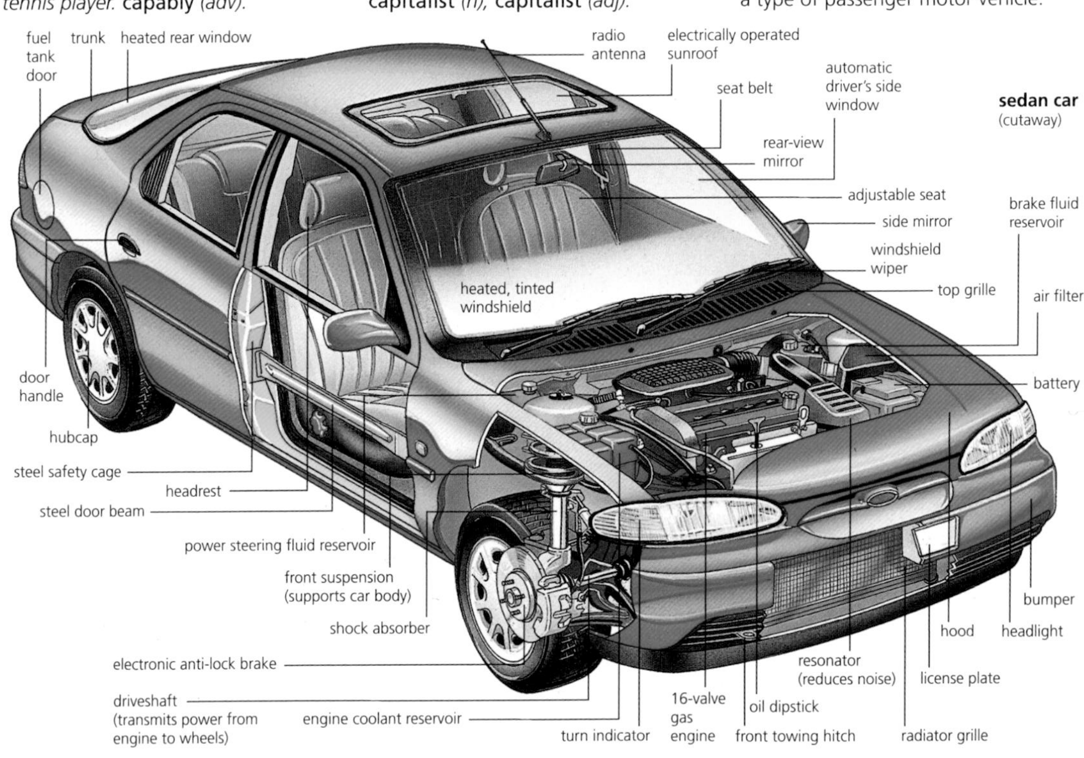

sedan car (cutaway)

caramel
1 *(n)* burned sugar.
2 *(n)* a candy made from burned sugar, butter, and milk.
3 *(n)* a light brown color. caramel *(adj).*

carat *(n)*
a unit for measuring the weight of precious metals.

caravan *(n)*
a group of people traveling, typically with vehicles, or with animals such as camels. *This picture shows part of a desert caravan.*

carbohydrate *(n)*
a substance in foods such as bread and potatoes that gives you energy.

carbon
1 *(n)* an element found in coal and diamonds and in all plants and animals.
2 **carbon dioxide** *(n)* a gas that is breathed out by people and animals, and is also used to make drinks fizzy.
3 **carbon fiber** *(n)* a light, strong material made from threads of carbon and used for fishing rods, race car bodies, etc.
4 **carbon footprint** *(n)* the amount of greenhouse gas generated by a person's or organization's energy use.

carburetor *(n)*
the part of a car's engine where air and gas mix.

carcass
carcasses *(n)*
the body of a dead animal.

card
1 *(n)* a folded piece of card sent on birthdays and special occasions.
2 *(n)* one of a set of rectangular pieces of cardstock used in games such as poker and bridge. *The cards shown were made in the 18th century.*

playing cards

cardboard *(n)* very thick cardstock, used for making boxes.

cardiac *(adj)*
having to do with the heart.

cardigan *(n)* a sweater or jacket that fastens down the front.

care caring cared
1 *(v)* If you **care** about someone or something, you are very concerned about what happens to them. caring *(adj).*
2 If you **take care of** someone, you look after them.
3 If you do something **with care**, you pay attention to what you are doing.

career *(n)* the series of jobs that a person has in their life, usually in the same profession. *A career in teaching.*

carefree *(adj)* Someone who is **carefree** has no worries.

careful *(adj)* Someone who is **careful** pays attention to what they are doing and does not take risks. **carefully** *(adv).*

caregiver *(n)*
someone who takes care of children, or sick, disabled or elderly people.

careless *(adj)* Someone who is **careless** does not look after things well. **carelessness** *(n),* **carelessly** *(adv).*

caress caresses caressing caressed
(v) to touch gently. **caress** *(n).*

caretaker *(n)*
someone whose job is to look after a school or some other public building.

cargo cargoes *(n)* goods that are carried by ship, train, truck, or aircraft.

caricature *(n)*
an exaggerated picture of someone.

carnival *(n)* a public celebration. People wear colorful costumes, walk in processions, and dance in the streets at carnival time.

carnivore *(n)* an animal that eats meat. **carnivorous** *(adj).*

carob
1 *(n)* an evergreen tree whose beans are used to make a food like chocolate.
2 *(n)* a chocolate-like food.

carol *(n)* a religious song that people sing at Christmas.

carpenter *(n)* someone who makes or repairs the wooden parts of buildings. **carpentry** *(n).*

carpet
1 *(n)* a thick floor covering. **carpet** *(v).*
2 *(n)* a thick layer of something. *A carpet of flowers.* **carpet** *(v).*

carriage
1 *(n)* a vehicle with wheels that is pulled by horses.
2 *(n)* Your **carriage** is the way that you stand, sit, and walk.

carrot
1 *(n)* a long root vegetable. *See* **vegetable**.
2 *(n)* If someone offers you a **carrot**, they promise you something nice in order to persuade you to do something.

carry carries carrying carried
1 *(v)* to hold on to something and take it somewhere. *Please carry this tray.*
2 *(v)* If a sound **carries**, it can be heard some distance away.
3 *(v)* If you **carry out** a plan or idea, you put it into practice.

cartilage *(n)* a strong, stretchy substance found around your joints.

cartography *(n)* the art of drawing maps. **cartographer** *(n).*

carton *(n)* a cardboard or plastic box, usually containing food or drink.

cartoon
1 *(n)* a short, animated movie.
2 *(n)* a funny drawing or series of drawings. **cartoonist** *(n).*
3 *(n)* a rough sketch for a finished piece of art.

cartridge
1 *(n)* a tube of ink used in a fountain pen.
2 *(n)* a container that holds a bullet or pellets and the explosive that fires them.

cartwheel *(n)*
a circular, sideways handstand.

carve carving carved
1 *(v)* to cut slices from a piece of meat.
2 *(v)* to cut a shape out of a piece of wood, stone, etc. **carver** *(n),* **carving** *(n).*

case
1 *(n)* a container for carrying clothes when you travel.
2 *(n)* an example of something. *This is a case of deliberate disobedience!*
3 *(n)* a trial in a court of law.
4 *(n)* a crime that the police are investigating.
5 *(n)* The **case** of a noun or pronoun is the form that it takes, depending on its relationship with other words in the sentence. *"I" is in the nominative case, "me" is in the accusative case, and "my" is in the possessive case.*

cash cashes cashing cashed
1 *(n)* money in the form of bills and coins.
2 *(v)* If you **cash in** on something, you take advantage of it.

Some words that begin with a "c" sound are spelled with a "k."

cashier

cashier *(n)* someone who takes or pays out money in a store or bank.

cash machine *(n)*
a machine from which people can take out money from their bank accounts, by using a plastic card. Also called an ATM, which stands for "automated teller machine."

casino *(n)* a place where people play gambling games such as roulette.

casket
1 *(n)* a jewelry box.
2 *(n)* a box that contains the body or the ashes of a dead person.

casserole
1 *(n)* a stew-like dish that is cooked slowly in the oven.
2 *(n)* a dish with a lid that is used for cooking casseroles.

cast casting cast
1 *(n)* the actors in a play or movie.
2 *(n)* a hard plaster covering that supports a broken arm or leg.
3 *(v)* When fishermen **cast** their fishing lines or nets, they throw them into the water.
4 *(v)* to form something by pouring soft material into a mold. *The sculptor cast the statue in bronze.*

castaway *(n)* someone left on a deserted island after a shipwreck.

castle
1 *(n)* a large strong building, often surrounded by a wall and a moat. In the Middle Ages, noble families stayed in castles and soldiers defended them from attack. *The picture shows a cutaway view of a medieval castle's keep, or tower, and a ground plan of the castle. Also see* **portcullis**.
2 *(n)* a chess piece, also known as a rook, that moves in straight lines across a chessboard. *See* **chess**.

asual
(adj) not planned.
casual meeting. **casually** (adv).
(adj) not formal.
asual dress. **casually** (adv).
(n) If a person is doing **casual work**,
means they don't have a full-time or
art-time job, but they take on small
eces of work when they come up.

asualty casualties (n)
omeone who is injured or killed
an accident, disaster, or war.

at
(n) any member of the cat family,
cluding
ons,
gers, and
heetahs.
(n) a small,
urry mammal
ften kept
s a pet.
*he picture
hows a
ange of
omestic
ats.*

silver Classic tabby
Chinchilla
ats
brown Abyssinian
ed Devon Rex
seal-point Siamese

:atalog
(n) a book listing things you can buy
rom a company or works of art on
how in an exhibition. **catalog** (v).
(n) a list of all the books in a library.

:atalyst
(n) a substance that causes or
peeds up a chemical reaction,
vithout changing itself.
2 (n) a person or thing that
auses something to happen.

:atamaran (n) a boat with
wo hulls joined together.

:atapult
1 (n) a simple, Y-shaped weapon,
vith elastic stretched over it,
sed for shooting small stones.
2 (n) a large weapon used in the
ast for firing rocks over castle walls.

:ataract
1 (n) a waterfall.
2 (n) an eye disease in which
he lens becomes cloudy and
vision becomes blurred.

catastrophe *(ka-tass-tro-fee) (n)* a sudden disaster. **catastrophic** *(kat-ass-trof-ik) (adj)*.

catch catches catching caught
1 *(v)* to grab hold of something moving through the air. **catch** *(n)*.
2 *(v)* to get someone whom you are chasing. *The police caught the thieves.*
3 *(v)* If you **catch** a bus or train, you get on it.
4 *(v)* If you **catch** someone doing something wrong, you see them doing it.
5 *(n)* a fastening on a door, box, etc.
6 *(v)* If something **catches on**, it becomes very popular.

categorical *(adj)* clear and plain. *Henry's reply was a categorical "No."* **categorically** *(adv)*.

category categories *(n)* a class or group of things that have something in common.

cater catering catered
1 *(v)* to provide food for a lot of people. **caterer** *(n)*, **catering** *(n)*.
2 *(v)* to provide people with the things that they need. *This restaurant caters to vegetarians.*

caterpillar *(n)* a larva that changes into a butterfly or moth. *The pictures below show the main parts of a swallowtail caterpillar and the lifecycle of a swallowtail butterfly.*

catfish *(n)* a freshwater fish with long tendrils around its mouth that look a little like cat whiskers.

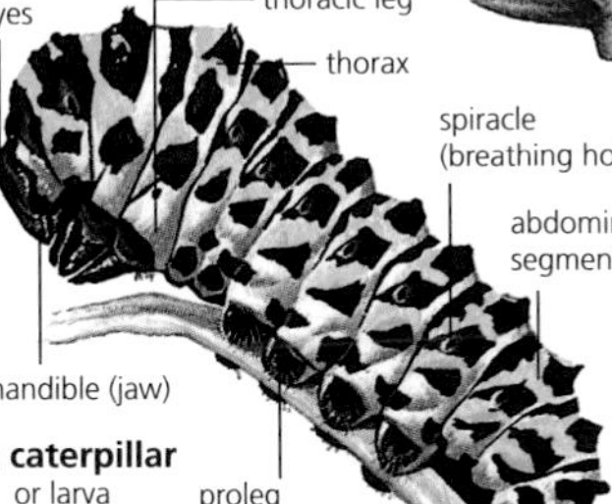

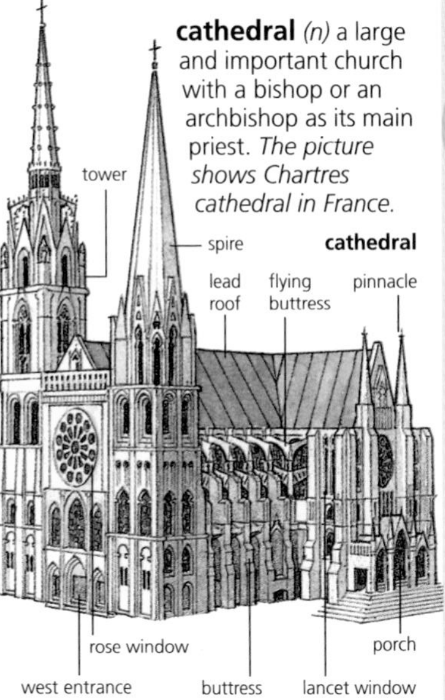

cathedral *(n)* a large and important church with a bishop or an archbishop as its main priest. *The picture shows Chartres cathedral in France.*

Catholic *(n)* a member of the Roman Catholic Church. **Catholic** *(adj)*, **Catholicism** *(n)*.

cattle *(plural n)* cows and bulls.

cauldron *(n)* a large, round cooking pot.

cauliflower *(n)* a vegetable with a large, round, white center, surrounded by leaves. *See* **vegetable**.

cause causing caused
1 *(v)* to make something happen.
2 *(n)* the reason that something happens.
3 *(n)* a goal or principle for which people fight.

cautious *(adj)* If you are **cautious**, you try hard to avoid mistakes or danger. **caution** *(n)*, **cautiously** *(adv)*.

cavalry
1 *(plural n)* soldiers who fight on horseback.
2 *(plural n)* soldiers who fight in armored vehicles.

cave *(n)* a large hole underground or in the side of a hill or cliff.

caveman cavemen *(n)* someone who lived in caves in prehistoric times.

cave painting *(n)* a picture painted on a cave wall in prehistoric times. *This cave painting of a bison was discovered in northern Spain.*

cave painting

cavern *(n)* a large cave.

cavity cavities *(n)* a hole or hollow space in something solid, such as a tooth.

cavort *(v)* to leap or dance around in a lively way. *Cavorting around town.*

CCTV *short for* **closed circuit television**.

CD *short for* **compact disc**.

cease ceasing ceased *(v)* to stop.

cease-fire *(n)* a period during a war when both sides agree to stop fighting.

ceaseless *(adj)* without stopping. **ceaselessly** *(adv)*.

cedar *(n)* a large evergreen tree with needle-like leaves.

ceiling
1 *(n)* the upper surface inside a room.
2 *(n)* the upper limit that something can reach. *A price ceiling.*

celebrate celebrating celebrated *(v)* to do something enjoyable on a special occasion, such as having a party. **celebration** *(n)*, **celebratory** *(adj)*.

celebrated *(adj)* famous.

celebrity celebrities *(n)* a famous person, especially an entertainer or a movie star.

celery *(n)* a vegetable with white or green crisp stalks, often eaten raw or in salads. *See* **vegetable**.

celestial *(adj)* having to do with the sky or the heavens. **celestially** *(adv)*.

cell
1 *(n)* a room in a prison or police station where someone is locked up.
2 *(n)* a basic, microscopic part of an animal or a plant.

plant cell
(magnified)

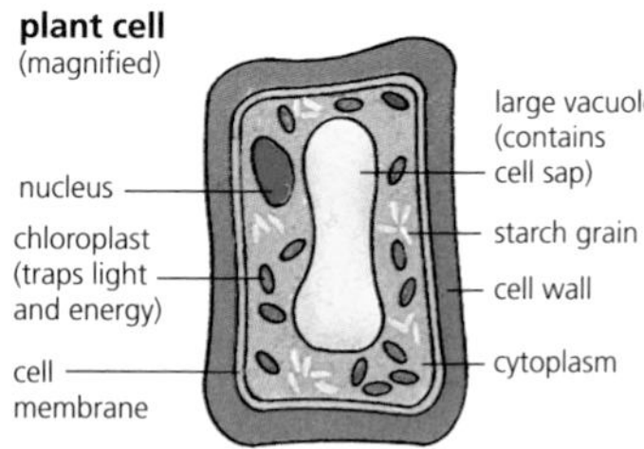

cellar *(n)* a room below ground level in a house, often used for storage.

cellophane *(n)* clear plastic material made from cellulose. It is used to wrap food and make clear tape.

cell phone *(n)* a portable telephone.

cellular *(adj)* made out of, or having to do with cells. *Cellular tissue.*

celluloid
1 *(n)* a type of plastic, once used to capture very early motion pictures.

cellulose *(n)* the substance from which the cell walls of plants are made.

Celsius *(adj)* measured on a temperature scale on which water boils at 100° and freezes at 0°. Celsius is also called centigrade.

cement
1 *(n)* a gray powder, used in building, that becomes hard when you mix it with water and let it dry.
2 *(n)* a substance that joins two things together. *See* **tooth**.

cemetery cemeteries *(n)* a place where dead people are buried.

censor censoring censored
1 *(v)* to remove parts of a book, movie, play, etc. that are thought to be harmful to the public. **censorship** *(n)*.
2 *(n)* someone whose job is to censor books, movies, plays, etc.

census *(n)* an official count of all the people living in a country.

cent *(n)* a coin in the United States, Canada, Australia, New Zealand and many countries in Europe. *One hundred cents make one dollar.*

centaur *(n)* a creature found in Greek and Roman myths that had the body and legs of a horse but the chest, arms, and head of a man.

centenary centenaries *(n)* the hundredth anniversary of something.

center centering centered
1 *(n)* the middle of something.
2 *(n)* a place where people go to do a particular activity. *An arts center.*
3 *(v)* to concentrate on something. *The campaign centers on the problems of the elderly.*
4 **center of gravity** *(n)* the point on an object at which it can balance.

centigrade *see* **Celsius**.

centipede *(n)* a small creature with a very long body and a lot of legs.

central
1 *(adj)* in the middle. **centrally** *(adv)*.
2 *(adj)* most important. *The central problem.*
3 **central heating** *(n)* a system for heating a building, where water or air is heated in one place and then carried in pipes or ducts all over the building.

centrifugal *(adj)* pulling away from the center. *You can feel the centrifugal effect when you swing an object in a circle.*

centripetal *(adj)* pulling toward the center. *When you swing an object around in a circle, you pull it inward and exert a centripetal force.*

centurion *(n)* an officer in the Roman Army in command of a company of soldiers.

century centuries *(n)* a period of 100 years.

ceramics
1 *(singular n)* the craft of making objects out of clay.
2 *(plural n)* objects made of clay. **ceramic** *(adj)*.

cereal
1 *(n)* a grain crop grown for food, such as wheat, corn, rice, oats, and barley.
2 *(n)* a breakfast food usually made from grain and eaten with milk.

ceremony ceremonies *(n)* formal actions, words, and often music, performed to mark an important occasion. *A wedding ceremony.* **ceremonial** *(adj)*, **ceremonially** *(adv)*.

certain
1 *(adj)* If you are **certain** about something, you are sure about it. *Alex was certain he had mailed the letter.* **certainty** *(n)*, **certainly** *(adv)*.
2 *(adj)* particular. *The store is closed at certain times.*

certificate *(n)* a piece of paper given to someone to prove that they have done something. *An examination certificate.*

chain
1 *(n)* a line of metal rings, called links, joined together.
2 *(n)* a series of connected things. *A chain of events.*
3 **chain store** *(n)* one of a group of stores in different towns that are owned by the same company and sell similar goods.

chair chairing chaired
1 *(n)* a piece of furniture that you sit on, with four legs and a back.
2 *(n)* the person in charge of a meeting, also called the chairman, chairwoman, or chairperson.
3 *(v)* to take charge of a meeting.

chairlift *(n)* a line of chairs attached to a moving cable, used for carrying people up mountains.

Some words that begin with a "c" sound are spelled with a "k."

chalet *(shall-ay) (n)* a small, wooden house with a sloping roof.

chalk
1 *(n)* a soft white rock.
2 *(n)* a stick of soft rock that can be used for drawing and writing. **chalk** *(v)*.

chalkboard *(n)*
a hard, smooth, dark surface on which chalk is used.

challenge challenging challenged
1 *(n)* something difficult that you try to do. **challenging** *(adj)*.
2 *(v)* If you **challenge** someone, you invite them to fight or to try to do something. **challenge** *(n)*.
3 *(v)* If you **challenge** something, you question whether it is right or not.

chamber
1 *(n)* a large room.
2 *(n)* a hollow place in something.
3 **chamber music** *(n)* classical music for a small number of instruments.

chameleon *(kam-ee-lee-un) (n)*
a lizard that can change color to match its surroundings.

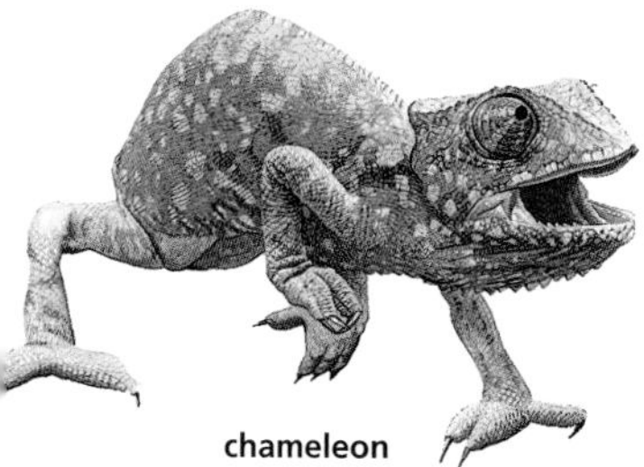
chameleon

chamomile *(n)*
a plant with a strong-smelling flower often used to make tea.

champion
championing championed
1 *(n)* the winner of a competition or a tournament. **championship** *(n)*.
2 *(v)* If someone **champions** a cause, they support it. **champion** *(n)*.

chance
1 *(n)* the possibility of something happening. *We have a chance of winning the cup.*
2 *(n)* an opportunity to do something. *Warren has the chance to learn to ski.*
3 If you **take a chance**, you try something even though it is risky.
4 If something happens **by chance**, it happens accidentally.

chancellor *(n)* a name for the leader of a university or a country. For example, the Chancellor of Germany is its elected leader.

change changing changed
1 *(v)* to become different or to make something different. **change** *(n)*.
2 *(n)* If you pay more money than something costs, the money you get back is called **change**.
3 *(n)* coins rather than bills.

channel
1 *(n)* a narrow stretch of sea between two areas of land.
2 *(n)* a television or radio station.

chant chanting chanted *(v)*
to say or sing a phrase over and over again. **chant** *(n)*.

Chanukah *see* **Hanukkah**.

chaos *(kay-oss) (n)*
total confusion. **chaotic** *(adj)*, **chaotically** *(adv)*.

chapel
1 *(n)* a small church.
2 *(n)* a side section of a large church.
3 *(n)* a place in a school, prison, hospital, etc. where Christian services are held.

chapter *(n)* one of the parts into which a book is divided.

character
1 *(n)* Your **character** is what sort of person you are.
2 *(n)* one of the people in a story, book, movie, or play.
3 *(n)* a letter, figure, or other mark used in printing.

characteristic
1 *(n)* a typical quality or feature. *Stubbornness is a characteristic of our family.* **characteristically** *(adv)*.
2 *(adj)* typical. *Sophie worked with characteristic efficiency.* **characteristically** *(adv)*.

charcoal *(n)*
a form of carbon made from burned wood. Charcoal is used for drawing and as a fuel for barbecue grills.

charge charging charged
1 *(v)* to ask someone to pay a particular price for something. **charge** *(n)*.
2 *(v)* to rush at someone to attack them. **charge** *(n)*.
3 *(v)* When you **charge** a battery, you pass an electric current through it so that it stores electricity.
4 If someone is **in charge** of something, they have to deal with it or take control of it.

chariot *(n)*
a small, horse-drawn vehicle, used in ancient times in battles or for racing. *The picture shows a Roman chariot.*

Roman chariot

charity charities
1 *(singular n)* money or other help given to people or animals in need.
2 *(n)* an organization that raises money for people or animals in need.

charm charming charmed
1 *(n)* If someone has **charm**, they behave in a pleasing and attractive way. **charmer** *(n)*, **charming** *(adj)*.
2 *(v)* to please someone and make them like you.
3 *(n)* a small object that some people believe will bring them good luck. *This ancient Egyptian charm represents a sacred eye.*

Egyptian charm

chart charting charted
1 *(n)* a drawing showing information in the form of a table or picture.
2 *(n)* a map of the stars or the sea.
3 *(v)* to show information in the form of a chart.

chase chasing chased *(v)*
to run after someone to catch them or make them go away. **chase** *(n)*.

chasm *(kaz-um) (n)* a deep crack in the surface of the Earth.

chassis *(cha-see)* chassis *(n)*
the frame onto which the body of a vehicle is built.

chat chatting chatted
1 *(v)* to talk to someone in a friendly and informal way. **chat** *(n)*.
2 *(v)* to communicate with other people through a website on the internet by typing messages on a computer or phone. **chat** *(n)*.
3 **chat room** *(n)* a website on the internet where people can communicate by typing messages to one another.

château *(shat-oh)* châteaux *(n)*
a castle or large country house in France.
The picture shows the Azay-le-Rideau château in the Loire valley in France.

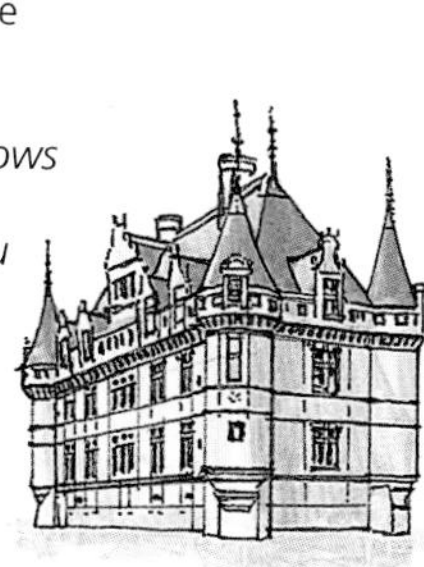
château

chatter
chattering
chattered
1 *(v)* to talk about unimportant things. **chatter** *(n)*.
2 *(v)* When your teeth **chatter**, they knock together because you are cold.

chauffeur *(show-fur) (n)*
someone whose job is to drive a car for somebody else. **chauffeur** *(v)*.

a b c d e f g h i j k l m n o p q r s t u v w x y z

chauvinist *(show-vin-ist)*
1 *(n)* a man who believes that women are inferior to men. **chauvinism** *(n)*, **chauvinistic** *(adj)*.
2 *(n)* someone who believes that no other country is as good or as important as their own. **chauvinism** *(n)*, **chauvinistic** *(adj)*.

cheap cheaper cheapest
1 *(adj)* not costing very much. **cheapness** *(n)*, **cheaply** *(adv)*.
2 *(adj)* unkind and mean. *That was a cheap trick you played on me!*

cheat cheating cheated
1 *(v)* to act dishonestly to win a game or get what you want.
2 *(n)* a person who acts dishonestly.

check checking checked
1 *(v)* to look at something to make sure that it is all right. **check** *(n)*.
2 *(v)* to stop something from moving or growing. *We must check inflation.*
3 *(n)* a pattern of differently colored squares. **checked** *(adj)*.
4 *(n)* a printed piece of paper on which someone writes to tell their bank to pay money from their account.

checkers *(plural n)*
a game played with black and white or red and white markers on a squared board.

checkout *(n)* the place in a store where you pay for your goods.

checkup *(n)*
a medical examination to make sure that there is nothing wrong with you.

cheek *(n)* the side of your face below your eyes.

cheer cheering cheered
1 *(v)* to shout encouragement or approval. **cheer** *(n)*.
2 *(v)* If you **cheer up**, you begin to feel better.
3 *(n)* happiness.

cheerful *(adj)* happy and lively. **cheerfulness** *(n)*, **cheerfully** *(adv)*.

cheese *(n)*
a food made from the solid parts of milk after it has turned sour.

cheetah *(n)*
a wild cat with a spotted coat that is found in Africa. Cheetahs can run faster than any other land animal.

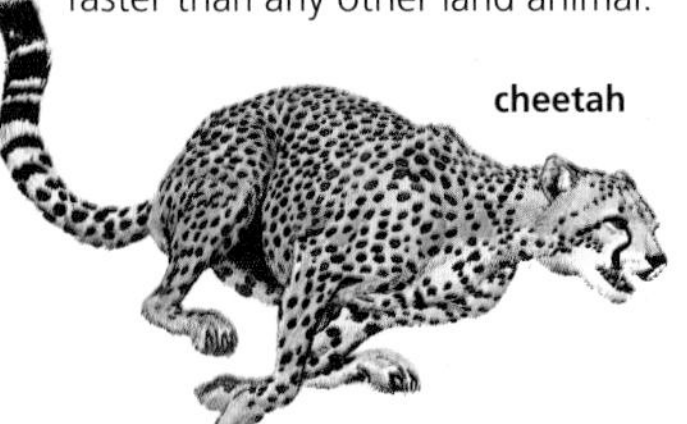
cheetah

chef *(sheff) (n)*
the chief cook in a restaurant.

chemical
1 *(n)* a substance used in chemistry. *Dangerous chemicals.*
2 *(adj)* having to do with, or made by chemistry. *A chemical reaction. Chemical fertilizers.* **chemically** *(adv)*.

chemist *(n)*
a person trained in chemistry.

chemistry *(n)*
the scientific study of substances and the ways in which they react with each other.

cherish
cherishes cherishing cherished *(v)*
to care for someone or something in a kind and loving way.

cherry cherries *(n)*
a small red or black fruit with a pit at its center. *See* **fruit**.

chess *(n)*
a game for two people with sixteen pieces each, played on a black and white board.

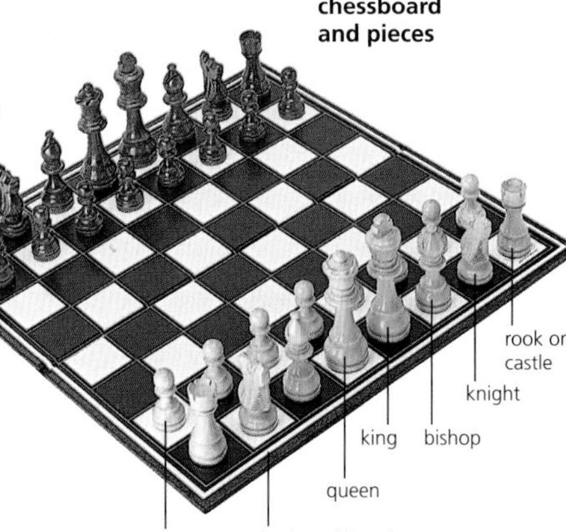

chessboard and pieces

chest
1 *(n)* the front part of your body between your neck and waist.
2 *(n)* a large, strong box.

chestnut
1 *(n)* a large red-brown nut that grows in a prickly case.
2 *(n)* a tree that produces chestnuts.
3 *(n)* a red-brown color. **chestnut** *(adj)*.

chest of drawers chests of drawers *(n)* a piece of furniture with drawers, used for storing clothes.

chew chewing chewed *(v)*
to crush food between your teeth.

chewing gum *(n)*
a kind of candy that you chew for a long time but do not swallow.

chick *(n)* a very young bird, especially a very young hen.

chicken
1 *(n)* a hen, usually a young one.
2 *(n)* the meat from a young hen. *Roast chicken.*
3 *(n) (slang)* someone who is too scared to do something

chicken (cross section)

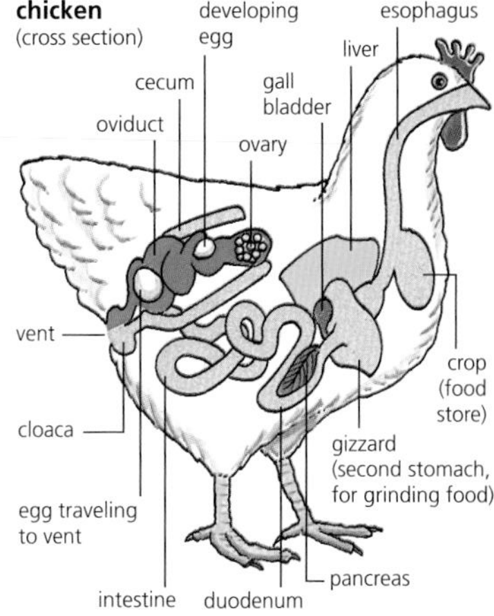

chickenpox *(n)*
a common disease that gives you red, itchy spots on your skin.

chide chiding chided *(v)*
to scold or find fault with someone.

chief
1 *(n)* the leader of a group of people. *The chief of police.*
2 *(adj)* main or most important. **chiefly** *(adv)*.

chigger *(n)*
a tiny insect that burrows under the skin, causing a rash and itching.

child children
1 *(n)* a young person who is not yet grown up.
2 *(n)* a son or daughter.

childhood *(n)*
the time when you are a child. *Marcus had a happy childhood.*

childish *(adj)* immature and thoughtless. *Childish behavior.* **childishness** *(n)*, **childishly** *(adv)*.

chill chilling chilled
1 *(v)* to make something cold.
2 *(n)* a feeling of slight coldness. *There is a chill in the air.* **chilly** *(adj)*.
3 *(n)* a cold. *Don't catch a chill.*
4 *(n)* a feeling of fear. **chilling** *(adj)*.

chime chiming chimed *(v)*
When a bell or clock **chimes**, it makes a ringing sound. **chime** *(n)*.

chimney *(n)* a vertical structure through which smoke escapes from a fire. *See* **building**.

chimpanzee *(n)*
a large ape with dark fur, which comes from Africa. Chimpanzees can be very intelligent. *See* **ape**.

chin *(n)* the part of your face below your mouth.

china
1 *(n)* very thin, delicate pottery.
2 *(n)* cups, plates, and dishes made out of china. *See* **bowl**.

chink
1 *(n)* a narrow opening.
2 *(n)* a gentle, jingling sound.

chip chipping chipped
1 *(v)* to break a small piece off something by accident. **chip** *(n)*.
2 *(n)* a very thin slice of potato, cooked in oil.
3 If you have a **chip on your shoulder**, you feel angry because you think you have been treated unfairly.
4 *(n)* a tiny piece of silicon, with electronic circuits printed on it, used in computers and other electronic equipment. *The magnified silicon chip shown above is small enough to fit on your fingernail.*

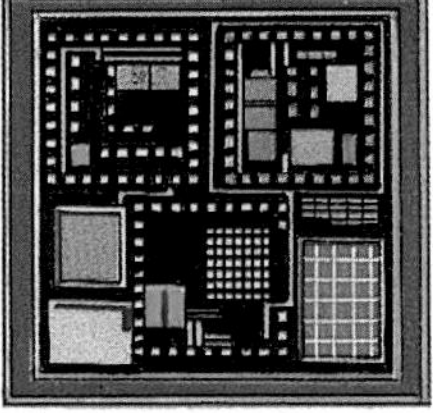

silicon chip (magnified)

chiropractor *(ky-ro-prak-tor) (n)*
someone who treats back pain and other illnesses by adjusting the spine.

chivalry *(shiv-ul-ree)*
1 *(n)* very polite and helpful behavior, especially by a man toward a woman. **chivalrous** *(adj)*.
2 *(n)* a way of behaving that a medieval knight was meant to practice.

chlorine *(klor-een) (n)* a strong-smelling gas that is added to water to kill harmful germs. **chlorinate** *(v)*.

chlorophyll *(klor-oh-fill) (n)*
the green substance in plants that allows them to use the Sun's energy.

chocolate *(n)* a sweet food made from beans that grow on the tropical cacao tree. *The picture shows a cacao pod and some dried and roasted beans that can be ground up to make chocolate.*
chocolaty *(adj)*.

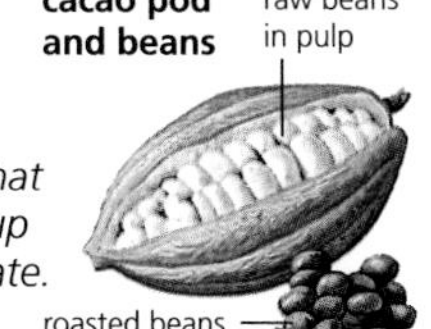

cacao pod and beans

choice
1 *(n)* the thing or person that you have selected. *Jake was a good choice as team captain.*
2 *(n)* all the things that you can choose from. *This menu offers a very wide choice.*
3 *(adj)* of very good quality. *Choice fruit and vegetables.*
4 *(n)* the chance to choose. *Alicia had the choice of going to Europe or South America during her summer vacation.*

choir *(kwire) (n)*
a group of people who sing together.

choke choking choked
1 *(v)* to struggle to breathe because something is blocking your breathing passages.
2 *(v)* to kill someone by squeezing their neck until they stop breathing.
3 *(v)* to block something. *Leaves had choked the stream.*

cholera *(kol-er-ah) (n)*
a dangerous disease that causes severe sickness and diarrhea.

cholesterol *(kol-est-er-ol) (n)*
a substance found in foods such as butter and cheese that is used to carry fats around your body.

choose choosing chose chosen
1 *(v)* to pick out one person or thing from several.
2 *(v)* If you **choose** to do something, you decide to do it.

chop chopping chopped
1 *(v)* to cut something with a knife or an ax. **chop** *(n)*.
2 *(n)* a small piece of lamb or pork on a bone.

choppy choppier choppiest *(adj)*
When the sea is **choppy**, it is quite rough.

chopstick *(n)* one of a pair of thin sticks for eating food, used by people in Far Eastern countries.

choral *(kor-al) (adj)*
sung by a choir. *Choral music.*

chord *(kord)*
1 *(n)* a combination of musical notes played at the same time. *See* **notation**.
2 *(n)* a straight line that joins two points on a curve. *See* **circle**.

chore *(chor) (n)* a job that has to be done many times, such as washing dishes or cleaning.

choreographer
(koh-ree-og-raf-er) (n)
someone who arranges dance steps and movements for a ballet or show. **choreography** *(n)*.

chorus *(kor-uss)*
choruses chorusing chorused
1 *(n)* the part of a song that is repeated after each verse.
2 *(n)* a large group of people who sing or speak together.
3 *(v)* to say something all together.

chowder *(n)*
a thick soup made with clams or fish and vegetables.

Christ *(n)*
the name given to Jesus, the man whom Christians believe is the Son of God and the Savior. *This mosaic of Christ was made in the 12th century.*

Christ

christening *(n)* a Christian ceremony in which a person is accepted into the Christian church and is given a name. **christen** *(v)*.

Christianity *(n)* the religion based on the life and teachings of Jesus Christ. Christians believe that Jesus is the Son of God, and that they will live with God after they die if they believe in him and follow his teachings. **Christian** *(n)*, **Christian** *(adj)*.

Christmas Christmases *(n)*
the Christian festival that celebrates the birth of Jesus Christ.

chromatography *(n)*
the process of separating parts of a mixture by letting it travel through a material that absorbs each part at a different rate. *You can use chromatography to separate the differently colored chemicals in ink.*

chromosome *(n)*
the part of a cell that carries the genes that give living things their special characteristics. You inherit your chromosomes from your parents.

chronic *(adj)* If something is **chronic**, it does not get better for a long time. *Chronic bronchitis.* **chronically** *(adv)*.

chronicle chronicling chronicled *(v)*
to record historical events in a careful, detailed way. **chronicle** *(n)*.

chronological *(adj)*
arranged in the order in which events happened. **chronology** *(n)*, **chronologically** *(adv)*.

chrysalis *(kriss-uh-liss)* chrysalises *(n)* a moth or butterfly at the stage of development between a caterpillar and an adult. A chrysalis is covered by a hard outer shell. *See* **caterpillar**.

chubby chubbier chubbiest *(adj)*
slightly fat or plump.

chuckle chuckling chuckled *(v)* to laugh quietly. **chuckle** *(n)*.

chug chugging chugged *(v)* to make a heavy, regular, thumping sound while moving along. *The truck chugged slowly up the hill.*

chunk *(n)* a thick piece of something.

church churches
1 *(n)* a building used by Christians for worship.
2 *(n)* a group of Christians.

churn churning churned
1 *(n)* a large metal container for milk.
2 *(n)* a machine in which milk is made into butter. *See* **butter**.
3 *(v)* to move around roughly. *The tractor churned through the mud.*

chute *(shoot) (n)* a narrow sloped surface that you can slide things along. *See* **castle**, **windmill**.

chutney *(n)* a mixture of vegetables, fruit, and spices, eaten with meat or cheese.

cider *(sy-der) (n)* a drink made from apples.

cinder *(n)* a small piece of wood or coal that has been partly burned.

cinema
1 *(n)* the movie industry.
2 *(n)* a movie theater.

cinnamon
1 *(n)* a red-brown spice taken from the bark of a tree. *See* **spice**.
2 *(adj)* a red-brown color.

circa *(prep)* the Latin word for "about." You can also write circa as "c." *Socrates was born circa 469 B.C.*

circle circling circled
1 *(n)* a flat, perfectly round shape. *The diagrams below show parts of a circle and other geometric terms connected with circles.* **circular** *(adj)*.
2 *(v)* to draw or make a circle around something. *Circle the correct answer. The plane circled the airport twice before coming in to land.*
3 *(n)* a group of people who all know one another. *Dominic has a wide circle of friends.*
4 *(n)* a curved upper area of seating in a theater.

parts of a circle

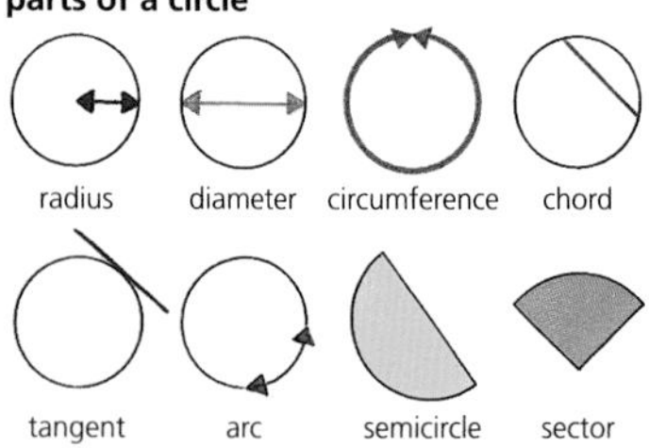

circuit *(sir-kit)*
1 *(n)* a circular route. *A race circuit.*
2 *(n)* the complete path that an electrical current can flow around.
3 **circuit diagram** *(n)* a diagram that shows an electrical circuit, using symbols recognized throughout the world. *The picture shows some symbols used in circuit diagrams.*

circuit symbols

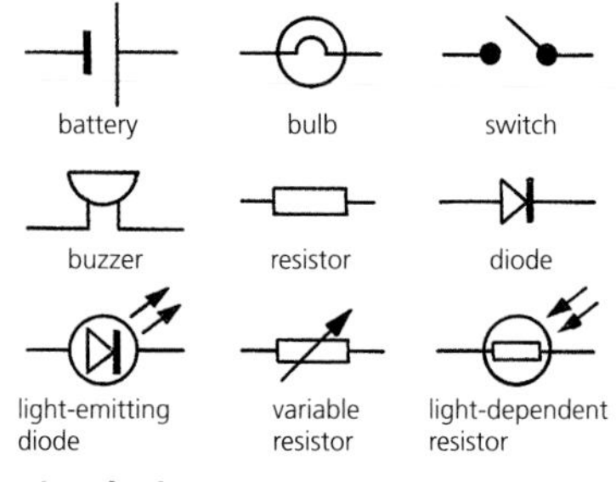

circulation
1 *(n)* the number of copies of a newspaper, magazine, etc. that are bought each day, week, etc.
2 *(n)* the movement of blood in blood vessels around the body. *Blood travels from the heart in arteries, and returns to the heart in veins. It then travels to the lungs to collect oxygen, before returning to the heart to be pumped around again.*

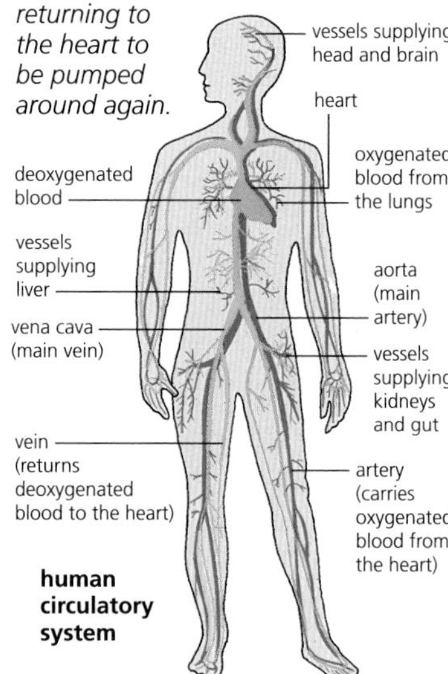

human circulatory system

circumference
1 *(n)* the outer edge of a circle. *See* **circle**.
2 *(n)* the distance around the edge of a circle.

circumspect *(adj)* cautious or careful. **circumspectly** *(adv)*.

circumstance *(n)* The **circumstances** of an event are the things that affect the way that it happens.

circus circuses *(n)* a traveling show in which clowns and acrobats perform.

cistern *(n)* a reservoir or tank for storing water.

citizen
1 *(n)* a member of a particular country who has the right to live there. *A United States citizen.*
2 *(n)* a person who lives in a particular town or city. *A citizen of New York.*

citizenship *(n)* the rights, privileges, and duties that come with being a citizen of a certain country. *Ben was granted U.S. citizenship.*

citrus fruit *(n)* a sharp-tasting, juicy fruit with a thick skin, such as an orange, a lemon, or a grapefruit.

city cities *(n)* a very large or important town.

civic *(adj)* having to do with a city or the people who live in it. *Civic center.*

civics *(n)* the study of being a good citizen of a community or country.

civil
1 *(adj)* having to do with the government or people of a country, rather than its army or religion. *The civil service.*
2 *(adj)* polite. *Please try to be civil to your great-aunt!* **civility** *(n)*.
3 **civil rights** *(plural n)* the claims that all members of a society have to equal treatment and freedom.
4 **civil servant** *(n)* someone who works in a government department, such as a tax office.
5 **civil war** *(n)* a war between different groups of people within the same country.

civilian *(n)* someone who is not a member of the armed forces.

civilization
1 *(n)* a highly developed and organized society, especially one in the past. *The ancient civilizations of Greece and Rome.*
2 *(n)* an advanced stage of human development, organization, and culture.

civilize civilizing civilized
1 *(v)* to improve a society, so that it is better organized and its people have a higher standard of living. **civilized** *(adj)*.
2 *(v)* to improve someone's manners and education. **civilized** *(adj)*.

Some words that begin with a "c" sound are spelled with a "k."
Some words that begin with a "ci" sound are spelled "sci," "psy," "si," or "scy."

claim claiming claimed
1 *(v)* to say that something belongs to you or that you have a right to have it. *My dad claims the best spot on the sofa.* **claim** *(n).*
2 *(v)* to say that something is true. *Ned claims he can beat me.* **claim** *(n).*

clam *(n)* a large shellfish with two tightly closed shells.

clamber clambering clambered *(v)* to climb up or over something with difficulty.

clammy clammier clammiest *(adj)* unpleasantly damp. *My hands get clammy when I'm nervous.*

clamor clamoring clamored *(v)* to demand something noisily. *The children all clamored for food.* **clamor** *(n).*

clamp clamping clamped
1 *(n)* a tool for holding things firmly in place.
2 *(v)* to fasten something with a clamp.
3 *(v)* When you **clamp down** on something, you control it more firmly. *The police have clamped down on illegal parking.*

clan *(n)* a large group of related families, especially in Scotland.

clap clapping clapped
1 *(v)* to hit your hands together in order to show that you have enjoyed something. **clap** *(n).*
2 *(n)* a loud bang of thunder.

clarify clarifies clarifying clarified *(v)* to make something clear. **clarification** *(n).*

clarity *(n)* clearness. *Ellie writes with great clarity.*

clash clashes clashing clashed
1 *(v)* to fight or argue violently. **clash** *(n).*
2 *(v)* If colors **clash**, they look unpleasant together.
3 *(v)* to make a loud, crashing noise.

clasp clasping clasped
1 *(v)* to hold on to something firmly and tightly. *Dawn clasped Gary's hand as they approached the cave.*
2 *(n)* a small fastener, for example on a purse.

class classes
1 *(n)* a group of people or things that are similar.
2 *(n)* a group of people who are taught together.
3 *(n)* a group of people in society. *The middle class.*
4 *(n) (informal)* attractiveness and stylishness. *That bike has class!* **classy** *(adj).*

classic
1 *(adj)* of very good quality and likely to remain popular for a long time.
2 *(adj)* typical. *A classic example of sixties style.*
3 **classics** *(plural n)* the languages and literature of ancient Greece and Rome.

classical
1 *(adj)* in the style of ancient Greece or Rome. *Classical architecture.*
2 *(adj)* traditional or accepted.
3 **classical music** *(n)* serious music that does not become out of date.

classify
classifies classifying classified *(v)* to put things into groups according to their characteristics. **classification** *(n).*

clatter clattering clattered *(v)* When things **clatter**, they bang together noisily. **clatter** *(n).*

clause
1 *(n)* a group of words that contain a verb and form one part of a sentence. *The sentence "She ran away when she saw the alien" is made up of two clauses: "She ran away" and "when she saw the alien."*
2 *(n)* one section of a formal legal document.

claustrophobia
*(klos-tro-**foh**-bee-yuh) (n)* the fear of being in small, enclosed places. **claustrophobic** *(adj).*

claw clawing clawed
1 *(n)* a hard, curved nail on the foot of an animal or a bird.
2 *(v)* If a person, animal, or bird **claws** something or someone, they scratch at it with their nails or claws.

clay *(n)* a kind of earth that is baked to make bricks or pottery.

clean
cleaning cleaned; cleaner cleanest
1 *(adj)* not dirty, or not messy. **cleanly** *(adv).*
2 *(v)* to remove the dirt from something. **cleaner** *(n).*

cleanse cleansing cleansed *(v)* to make something clean or pure.

clear
clearing cleared; clearer clearest
1 *(adj)* easy to see through. **clearly** *(adv).*
2 *(adj)* easy to understand. **clearly** *(adv).*
3 *(v)* to remove things that are covering or blocking a place. *Clear the table.* **clear** *(adj).*
4 *(v)* to jump over something without touching it. *The horse cleared all the jumps.* **clearance** *(n).*
5 *(v)* to declare that someone is not guilty of a crime.

clearing *(n)* an area of a forest or woods that has been cleared of trees.

clef *(n)* a symbol written at the beginning of a line of music, to show the pitch of the notes. *Bass clef. Treble clef. See* **notation**.

cleft *(n)* a split, or a division.

clench
clenches clenching clenched *(v)* to hold or squeeze something tightly.

clergy *(plural n)* priests in the Christian church.

clerical
1 *(adj)* **Clerical** work is general office work, for example, filing.
2 *(adj)* having to do with the clergy.

clerk *(rhymes with lurk)*
1 *(n)* a salesperson in a store.
2 *(n)* someone who keeps records in an office, a bank, or a law court.

clever cleverer cleverest
1 *(adj)* able to understand things or to do things quickly and easily. **cleverness** *(n),* **cleverly** *(adv).*
2 *(adj)* intelligently and carefully thought out. *A clever plan.* **cleverly** *(adv).*

cliché *(**klee**-shay) (n)* a phrase that is used so often that it no longer has very much meaning. *"Over the moon" is a cliché.*

click clicking clicked
1 *(v)* to make a short, sharp sound. *Click your tongue.* **click** *(n).*
2 *(v) (informal)* If an idea **clicks**, it suddenly becomes clear to you.

client *(n)* someone who uses the services of a professional person, such as a lawyer or an accountant.

cliff *(n)* a high, steep rock face on a coast.

cliff-hanger *(n)* a story, movie, etc. that is exciting because you do not know what is going to happen next.

climate
1 *(n)* the usual weather in a place. *A warm climate.* **climatic** *(adj).*
2 *(n)* the general situation or mood at a particular time. *A positive economic climate.*

climax climaxes *(n)* the most exciting part of a story or an event, which usually happens near the end.

climb climbing climbed
1 *(v)* to move upward. **climber** *(n).*
2 *(n)* an upward movement or slope.
3 *(v)* to get on or off something using your hands to support and help you.

clinch clinching clinched *(v)* to settle a matter once and for all.

cling clinging clung *(v)* to hold on to something very tightly.

clinic *(n)* a room or building where people can go for specialized medical treatment or advice. *A health clinic.*

clip clipping clipped
1 *(v)* to trim something. *Clip the hedge.*
2 *(v)* to attach things together with a small fastener.
3 *(n)* a small metal or plastic fastener.
4 *(n)* a short piece of a movie or television program shown by itself.

clip art *(n)* images stored on a computer for use in illustrating documents.

clipboard *(n)* a board with a clip at the top, for holding papers.

clique *(kleek) (n)* a small group of people who are very friendly with one another and do not easily accept others into their group. **cliquey** *(adj).*

cloak *(n)* a loose coat with no sleeves that you wrap around your shoulders and fasten at the neck.

cloakroom *(n)* a room where you can hang coats, and store umbrellas, hats, and bags.

clock *(n)* an instrument that tells the time. *The picture shows the main working parts of a spring-driven clock. When you wind the clock, you tighten the mainspring, which unwinds very slowly. Energy from the mainspring is transferred to the hour and minute hands by a series of wheels. The escape wheel keeps the clock ticking regularly.*

spring-driven clock

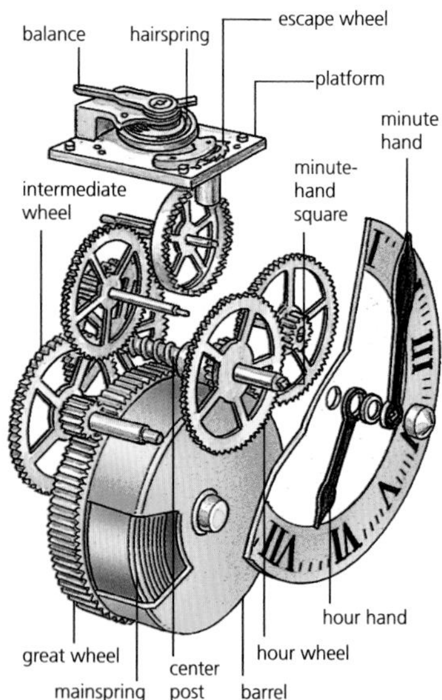

clockwise *(adv)* in the direction that the hands of a clock move. *We ran clockwise around the track.* **clockwise** *(adj).*

clockwork
1 *(n)* a mechanism that makes things such as clocks and toys work when they are wound up with a key. **clockwork** *(adj).*
2 If things go **like clockwork**, there are no problems.

clod *(n)* a lump of earth or clay.

wooden clogs

clog clogging clogged
1 *(v)* to block something. *Some leaves had clogged the drain.*
2 *(n)* a heavy slip-on shoe, traditionally made of wood.

clone cloning cloned *(v)* to grow a plant or animal from the cells of a parent plant or animal so that it is identical to the parent. **clone** *(n).*

close closing closed; closer closest
1 *(rhymes with nose) (v)* to shut something.
2 *(rhymes with nose) (v)* to end something. *The inquiry is closed.* **close** *(n).*
3 *(rhymes with dose) (adv)* near. *Stay close to me!* **close** *(adj).*
4 *(rhymes with dose) (adj)* careful. *Keep a close watch on the children.* **closely** *(adv).*
5 *(rhymes with nose) (v)* to fill or stop up. *James closed the hole with putty.*

closed-circuit television or **CCTV** *(n)* a television system that shows things happening nearby. It is often used to watch shoppers or people in banks.

closet *(n)* a small room used for storing things, especially clothes.

close-up *(n)* a very detailed view of something, especially a photograph taken from close to a person or thing. *The actress applied fresh makeup in preparation for her close-up.* **close-up** *(adj).*

clot clotting clotted *(v)* When a liquid, such as blood, **clots**, it becomes thicker and forms lumps. **clot** *(n).*

cloth
1 *(n)* material made from wool, cotton, etc.
2 *(n)* a small piece of material used for cleaning.

clothes *(plural n)* things that you wear, for example, shirts and pants. **clothe** *(v).*

cloud clouding clouded
1 *(n)* a white or gray mass of water drops or ice crystals suspended in the air. *The picture shows different types of clouds and their approximate levels in the sky.* **cloudy** *(adj).*
2 *(n)* a mass of smoke or dust. **cloudy** *(adj).*
3 *(v)* If something **clouds over**, it becomes less easy to see through.

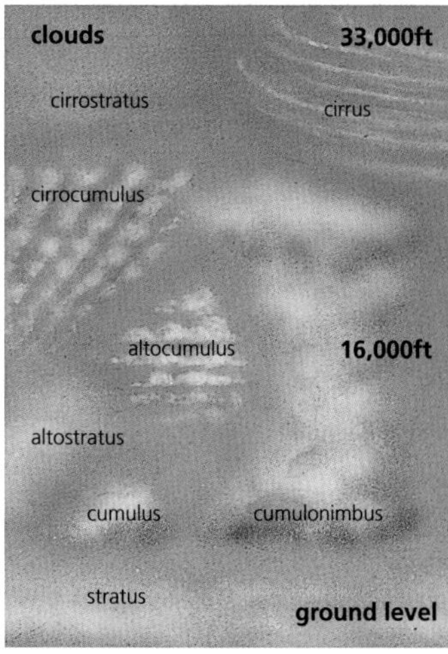

clover *(n)* a small plant with pink or white flowers, and leaves divided into three parts. *Four-leaf clovers are rare and are believed to be lucky.*

clown clowning clowned
1 *(n)* an entertainer who wears funny clothes, has a painted face, and tries to make people laugh.
2 *(n)* someone who does silly or foolish things.
3 *(v)* to do silly things to make people laugh. *Antonio is always clowning around.*

club
1 *(n)* a group of people who meet regularly to enjoy a common interest.
2 *(n)* a stick with a metal head used in the game of golf. See **golf**.
3 *(n)* a thick heavy stick used as a weapon. **club** *(v).*
4 **clubs** *(plural n)* one of the four suits in a pack of cards, with a black three-leaf symbol.

clue *(n)* something that helps you to find an answer to a question or a mystery.

clump clumping clumped
1 *(n)* a group of trees or other plants growing together.
2 *(v)* to walk slowly, with clumsy, noisy footsteps. *Ed clumped up the stairs and woke everyone up.*

clumsy clumsier clumsiest *(adj)* careless and awkward in the way that you move or behave. **clumsiness** *(n),* **clumsily** *(adv).*

cluster clustering clustered *(v)* to stand or grow close together. *The flowers clustered around the tree.* **cluster** *(n).*

clutch clutches clutching clutched
1 *(v)* to hold on to something tightly.
2 *(n)* the pedal of a car or motorcycle that you press to change gear.
3 *(n)* a number of eggs laid by a bird.

clutter cluttering cluttered *(v)* to fill up a place and make it messy. **clutter** *(n).*

co. *short for* **company**.

coach coaches coaching coached
1 *(n)* a bus used for long journeys.
2 *(n)* a large carriage pulled by horses. *See* **stagecoach**.
3 *(v)* to train someone in a subject or sport. **coach** *(n).*

coal
1 *(n)* a black mineral formed from the remains of ancient plants. Coal is mined from under the ground and burned as a fuel.
2 **coals** *(plural n)* small pieces of burning coal.

coalfield *(n)* an area where there is coal under the ground and where coal is mined.

coalition *(ko-al-ish-un) (n)* When two or more groups form a **coalition**, they join together for a common purpose.

coarse coarser coarsest
1 *(adj)* If something is **coarse**, it has a rough texture or surface. **coarseness** *(n),* **coarsely** *(adv).*
2 *(adj)* If a person is **coarse**, they are rude and have bad manners. **coarseness** *(n),* **coarsely** *(adv).*

coast coasting coasted
1 *(n)* the land that is next to the sea. **coastal** *(adj).*
2 *(v)* to move along in a car or other vehicle without using any power.
3 *(v)* to make progress without much effort. *Ben coasted through his exams.*

coast guard *(n)* someone who watches the sea for ships in danger and who looks out for smugglers.

coat coating coated
1 *(n)* a piece of clothing that you wear over other clothes to keep you warm.
2 *(n)* an animal's fur or wool.
3 *(v)* to cover a surface with a thin layer of something. **coat** *(n).*

coating *(n)* a covering of something. *The cake had a chocolate coating.*

coat of arms coats of arms *(n)* a design in the shape of a shield that is used as the special sign of a family, a city, or an organization.

Royal coat of arms

coax *(kokes)* **coaxes coaxing coaxed** *(v)* to persuade someone gently and patiently to do something.

cobbles *(plural n)* small, round stones used in the past for making road surfaces. **cobbled** *(adj).*

cobra *(n)* a snake with a venomous bite. Cobras can spread the skin of their neck so that it looks like a hood.

cobweb *(n)* a very fine net of sticky threads, made by a spider to catch flies and other insects.

coccyx *(n)* a small bone at the bottom of the spine. Also known as the tailbone. *See* **skeleton**.

cockpit *(n)* the area in the front of a plane where the pilot sits.

cockroach cockroaches *(n)* a large insect that lives in warm, dark places, especially where food is stored. *See* **insect**.

cochlea *(n)* part of the inner ear, shaped like a snail's shell. **cochlear** *(adj).*

cocoa
1 *(n)* a brown powder made from the roasted beans of the cacao tree and used to make chocolate.
2 *(n)* a hot, milky drink made with cocoa powder.

coconut *(n)* a very large nut with a hard, brown, hairy shell and sweet, white flesh.

cocoon *(n)* a covering made from threads or mucus, produced by some animals to protect themselves or their eggs.

lynx spider (female)

cocoon (contains eggs)

cod cod *(n)* a fish that is found in the Atlantic and Arctic oceans, which has white flesh that you can eat.

code
1 *(n)* a system of words, letters, or numbers used instead of ordinary words to send secret messages. **coded** *(adj),* **code** *(v).*
2 *(n)* a set of numbers or letters used to give information briefly.
3 *(n)* a set of rules. *A safety code.*

coeducation *(n)* the system of teaching boys and girls together in the same school. **coeducational** *(adj).*

coerce *(ko-erss)* **coercing coerced** *(v)* to force someone to do something. **coercion** *(n).*

coffee
1 *(n)* a hot drink made from the roasted and ground beans of the coffee shrub.
2 *(n)* a brown powder made from coffee beans and used to make the drink of coffee.

coffin *(n)* a box that contains the body or ashes of a dead person.

cog
1 *(n)* one of the teeth on the edge of a wheel that turns machinery.
2 **cog wheel** *(n)* a wheel with teeth that turns machinery. *See* **gear**.

coherent *(ko-hear-unt) (adj)* clear and logical. *A coherent argument.*

coil coiling coiled
1 *(v)* to wind something round and round into a series of loops. *The sailor coiled the rope neatly.* **coil** *(n).*
2 *(v)* to form loops. *The snake coiled around Jan's leg.*

coin coining coined
1 *(n)* a piece of money in the form of a metal disk. **coinage** *(n).*
2 *(v)* to invent a new word or a new meaning of a word. **coinage** *(n).*

Ancient Chinese coins

coincide *(ko-in-side)* **coinciding coincided** *(v)* If two things **coincide**, they happen at the same time.

coincidence *(ko-in-sid-enss) (n)* a chance happening or meeting. **coincidental** *(adj),* **coincidentally** *(adv).*

colander *(n)* a bowl with holes in it, used for draining liquid off food such as vegetables.

cold colder coldest
1 *(adj)* having a low temperature. **cold** *(n),* **coldness** *(n).*
2 *(adj)* unfriendly. **coldness** *(n),* **coldly** *(adv).*
3 *(n)* a common mild illness that causes sneezing, a sore throat, and sometimes a slight fever.

Some words that begin with a "c" sound are spelled with a "k."

cold-blooded
1 *(adj)* **Cold-blooded** animals have body temperatures that change according to the temperature of their surroundings. *Reptiles and fish are cold-blooded.*
2 *(adj)* A **cold-blooded** act is done deliberately and cruelly.

collaborate
collaborating collaborated *(v)* to work with someone and help them to do something. **collaboration** *(n)*, **collaborator** *(n)*.

collage *(kol-**arj**)* *(n)*
a picture made by sticking different things on to a surface, for example gluing pieces of cloth on to paper.

collapse **collapsing collapsed**
1 *(v)* to fall down suddenly from weakness or illness. **collapse** *(n)*.
2 *(v)* to fail suddenly and completely. *The company collapsed after only six months.* **collapse** *(n)*.

collar **collaring collared**
1 *(n)* the part of a shirt, blouse, coat, etc., that fits around your neck and is usually folded down.
2 *(n)* a thin band of leather worn around the neck of a dog or a cat.
3 *(n)* band-shaped markings around an animal's neck.

colleague *(n)*
someone who works with you.

collect **collecting collected**
1 *(v)* to gather things together.
2 *(v)* to ask payment for something bought and delivered.

collection
1 *(n)* a group of things gathered over a long time. *A shell collection.*
2 *(n)* If you hold a **collection** for something, you take money for it.

college *(n)* an institution of higher education where students can study for a bachelor's degree.

collide **colliding collided** *(v)*
to crash into something violently, often at high speed. **collision** *(n)*.

colloquial *(kol-**oh**-kwee-al)* *(adj)*
Colloquial language is used in everyday, informal conversation.

colon
1 *(n)* the punctuation mark (:) used to introduce a list of things, an explanation, or a quotation. *See p5.*
2 *(n)* the part of your large intestine where remaining food is broken down by bacteria, and has water removed from it.

colonel *(n)*
an army, air force or Marine Corps officer, ranking below a general.

colony **colonies**
1 *(n)* a country that has been settled by people from another country and is controlled by that country. **colonial** *(adj)*.
2 *(n)* a large group of insects that live together. *A colony of ants.*

color **coloring colored**
1 *(n)* When you say what **color** something is, you say whether it is red, yellow, black, etc. **colorful** *(adj)*, **colorless** *(adj)*.
2 *(v)* to make something a certain color, using pens, paints, dye, etc.
3 *(v)* the appearance of a person's skin. *You have good color since you returned from the beach.*
4 *(adj)* If you are **color-blind**, you are unable to see the difference between certain colors. *You may not be able to see the number in this pattern if you are color-blind.*

color-blindness test

colossal *(adj)*
extremely large.

colt *(n)* a young male horse.

column
1 *(n)* a tall, upright pillar that helps to support a building. *The picture below shows three styles of Roman columns.*
2 *(n)* a row of figures or words running down a page.
3 *(n)* a piece of writing by the same person, or on the same subject, that appears regularly in a newspaper or magazine. **columnist** *(n)*.

Roman columns

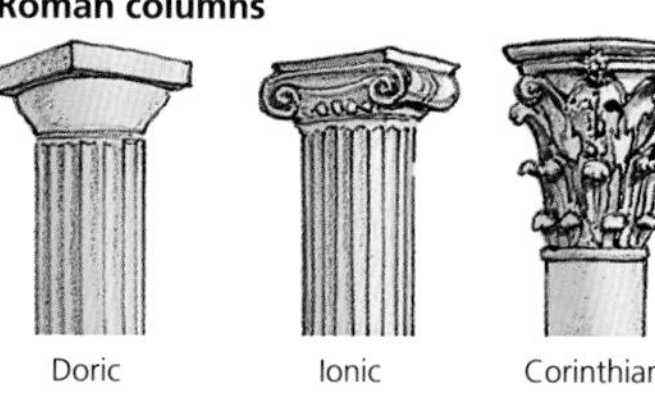

coma *(n)*
a state of deep unconsciousness from which it is very hard to wake up.

comb **combing combed**
1 *(n)* a flat piece of metal or plastic with a row of teeth used for making you hair smooth and neat.
2 *(v)* to use a comb to make your hair smooth and neat.
3 *(v)* to search a place thoroughly.

combat **combating combated**
1 *(v)* to fight against something. *Regular brushing helps combat tooth decay.*
2 *(n)* fighting between people or armies. **combatant** *(n)*.

combine **combining combined** *(v)*
to join or mix two or more things together. **combination** *(n)*. **combine harvester** *(n)*. *See* **harvest**.

combustion *(n)*
the process of catching fire and burning. **combust** *(v)*.

come **coming came come**
1 *(v)* to move toward a place. *Louise came into the house.*
2 *(v)* to arrive. *Barney was waiting for his friends to come.*
3 *(v)* If you **come from** a particular place, you were born in that place.
4 *(v)* If something **comes about**, it happens.
5 *(v)* If you **come across** something, you find it by chance.
6 *(v)* If you **come to**, you become conscious again.

comedian *(n)*
an entertainer who tells jokes and funny stories to make people laugh.

comedy **comedies**
1 *(n)* a funny play or movie.
2 *(n)* anything that makes people laugh. *Martha's first attempt at skating was a comedy.*

comet *(n)* a large orbiting piece of rock that travels around the Sun and leaves a trail of light behind it.

comfort **comforting comforted**
1 *(v)* to make someone feel less worried or upset. *We comforted the lost child.* **comforting** *(adj)*, **comfortingly** *(adv)*.
2 *(n)* the feeling of being relaxed and free from pain or worries.
3 *(n)* a luxury that makes your life more pleasant and enjoyable. *Home comforts.*

comfortable
1 *(adj)* If you are **comfortable**, you feel relaxed in your body or your mind. **comfortably** *(adv)*.
2 *(adj)* If something is **comfortable**, it allows you to relax and feel pleasure. *A comfortable chair.*

comic
1 *(n)* a magazine containing stories told with pictures.
2 *(n)* someone who tells jokes and funny stories.
3 *(adj)* funny or amusing. **comical** *(adj)*.

comma *(n)* the punctuation mark (,) used for separating different parts of a sentence or different words in a list.

command
commanding commanded
1 *(v)* to order someone to do something. **command** *(n)*.

2 (v) to have control over a group of people in the armed forces. **commander** (n).
3 (n) Your **command** of something is your knowledge of it and your skill in using it. *Alexia has a good command of Russian.*

commemorate commemorating commemorated (v) When you **commemorate** an event or the life of an important person, you do something special to remember them. **commemoration** (n), **commemorative** (adj).

commence commencing commenced (v) to begin something. **commencement** (n).

commend commending commended (v) to say that someone has done something very well. *The mayor commended our courage.* **commendation** (n), **commendable** (adj).

comment commenting commented (v) If you **comment** on something, you give an explanation or an opinion about it. **comment** (n).

commentary commentaries
1 (n) a description and comments about an event. *Political commentary.* **commentator** (n), **commentate** (v).
2 (n) a description of an event as it is happening, often broadcast on television or radio. *A race commentary.* **commentator** (n), **commentate** (v).

commerce (n) the buying and selling of goods in order to make money.

commercial
1 (adj) having to do with buying and selling goods. *Commercial activities.*
2 (adj) having profit as a main aim. *A commercial scheme.*
3 (n) a television or radio advertisement.

commercialized (adj) If something is **commercialized**, it has been changed, usually for the worse, in order to make a profit. **commercialization** (n).

commiserate commiserating commiserated (v) to share someone else's sadness or disappointment. *We commiserated with Alex over his bad luck.* **commiserations** (plural n).

commit committing committed
1 (v) to do something wrong or illegal. *To commit murder.*
2 (v) If you **commit** yourself to something, you promise that you will do it or support it. **commitment** (n), **committed** (adj).

committee (n) a group of people chosen to discuss things and make decisions for a larger group.

commodity commodities (n) a product that is bought and sold.

common
1 (adj) existing in large numbers.
2 (adj) happening often. *A common problem.*
3 (adj) ordinary and not special in any way.
4 (adj) shared by two or more people or things. *This feature is common to both cars.*

commonplace (adj) If something is commonplace, it happens frequently. *Traffic jams in city centers are commonplace events.*

common sense (n) the ability to think and behave sensibly.

commotion (n) a lot of noisy, excited activity.

communal (adj) shared by several people. *A communal bathroom.* **communally** (adv).

commune (n) a group of people who live together and share things with one another.

communicate communicating communicated (v) to share information, ideas, or feelings with another person by talking, writing, etc. **communication** (n), **communicative** (adj).

Communion (n) a Christian service in which people eat bread and drink wine in memory of the death and resurrection of Jesus Christ.

communiqué (kom-yoon-i-kay) (n) an official report or statement.

communism or **Communism** (n) a way of organizing a country so that all the land, houses, factories, etc. belong to the state and the profits are shared among everyone. **communist** (n), **communist** (adj).

community communities (n) a group of people who live in the same area or who have something in common with each other.

commuter (n) someone who travels a significant distance to work each day, usually by car or train. **commute** (v).

compact
1 (**kom**-pakt) (adj) designed to take up very little space. **compact** (v).
2 (**kom**-pakt) (n) a small, flat case containing face powder and a mirror.
3 (**kom**-pakt) (n) an agreement made between people or organizations.

compact disc or **disk** (n) a disc with music or information stored on it. *Also called a CD. The picture inset below shows the thin metal layer inside the plastic disc, with its pattern of pits and lands, which is read by a laser beam as the disc rotates.*

companion
1 (n) someone whom you spend time with; a friend.
2 (n) a person employed to spend time with another person.

compact disc

compact disc (magnified view from below)

land
laser beam
pit
aluminum layer

company companies
1 (n) a group of people who work together to produce or sell goods or services.
2 (n) a group of actors or dancers who work together.
3 (n) one or more guests. *We have company this weekend.*
4 (n) companionship. *I enjoyed her company this weekend.*
5 (n) an army unit under the command of a captain.

comparative
1 (adj) judged against other similar things. *This year's play was a comparative success.* **comparatively** (adv).
2 (adj) **Comparative** adjectives and adverbs are used when you compare two things or actions. *"Older" is the comparative of "old"; "more quickly" is the comparative of "quickly."* **comparative** (n).

compare comparing compared
1 (v) to judge one thing against another and notice similarities and differences. **comparison** (n).
2 (v) to be as good as something or somebody else. *Our team compares with any in the area.*

compartment (n) a separate part of a container, used for keeping certain things. *My wallet has a special compartment for stamps.*

compass compasses
1 *(n)* an instrument for finding directions, with a magnetic needle that always points north. *You can use a compass like the one shown below to follow a route on a map.*
2 **compasses** *(plural n)* an instrument used for drawing circles, which has two legs connected by a flexible joint. *See* **geometry**.

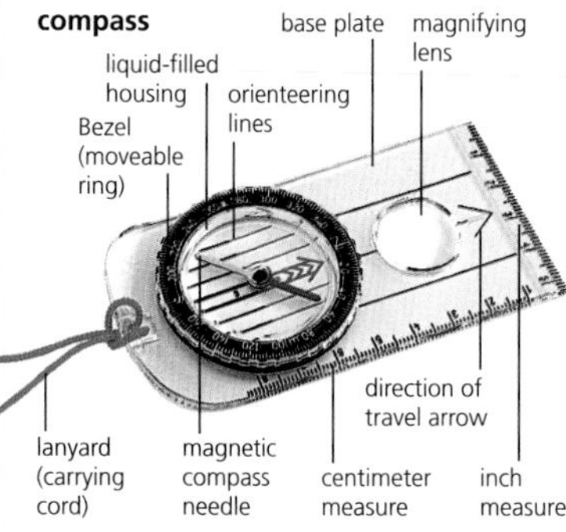

compassion *(n)* a feeling of sympathy for people who are suffering. **compassionate** *(adj)*, **compassionately** *(adv)*.

compatible *(adj)* If people or objects are **compatible**, they can live together or be used together without difficulty. **compatibility** *(n)*.

compel compelling compelled *(v)* to make someone do something by giving them orders or by using force.

compensate compensating compensated *(v)* to make up for something. *Nothing can compensate for my suffering.* **compensation** *(n)*.

competent *(adj)* If you are **competent** at something, you have the skill or ability to do it well. **competence** *(n)*, **competently** *(adv)*.

competition
1 *(n)* an event in which two or more people try to do something as well as they can, to see who is the best. **competitor** *(n)*, **compete** *(v)*.
2 *(n)* a situation in which two or more people are trying to get the same thing. *There was a lot of competition for awards at school.* **compete** *(v)*.

competitive
1 *(adj)* A **competitive** sport or game is one where the players try to win.
2 *(adj)* very eager to win.
3 *(adj)* If a store offers **competitive** prices, its prices are at least as low as in most other stores.

compile compiling compiled *(v)* to write a book or a report by bringing together many different pieces of information. **compilation** *(n)*.

complain complaining complained *(v)* to say that you are unhappy about something.

complaint
1 *(n)* a statement saying that you are unhappy about something.
2 *(n)* an illness. *A heart complaint.*

complete completing completed
1 *(adj)* If something is **complete**, it has all the parts that are needed or wanted. *A complete pack of cards.*
2 *(v)* to finish something. **completion** *(n)*.
3 *(adj)* in every way. *The news was a complete surprise.* **completely** *(adv)*.

complex complexes
1 *(adj)* very complicated. **complexity** *(n)*.
2 *(n)* a set of strong feelings that you cannot control or forget about and that causes problems for you. *Nathan has a complex about being short.*
3 *(n)* a group of buildings that are close together and are used for a particular purpose. *A leisure complex.*

complexion *(n)* the color and look of the skin on your face.

complicated *(adj)* Something that is **complicated** contains lots of different parts or ideas and so is difficult to use or understand. **complication** *(n)*, **complicate** *(v)*.

compliment complimenting complimented *(v)* When you **compliment** someone, you tell them that you admire them or think that they have done something well. **compliment** *(n)*.

complimentary
1 *(adj)* If someone is **complimentary** about a person or thing, they praise them. *Jason was complimentary about my new dress.*
2 *(adj)* free, or without cost. *Complimentary tickets.*

component *(n)* a part of a machine or system.

compose composing composed
1 *(v)* to write a piece of music, a poem, etc. **composer** *(n)*.
2 *(v)* If something is **composed of** certain things, it is made from those things.

compost *(n)* a mixture of rotted plants that is added to soil to make it richer.

comprehension *(n)* understanding. **comprehend** *(v)*.

comprehensive *(adj)* including everything that is necessary. *A comprehensive list.* **comprehensively** *(adv)*.

compress compresses compressing compressed *(v)* to press or squeeze something so that it will fit into a small space. **compression** *(n)*.

compromise compromising compromised
1 *(v)* to agree to accept something that is not exactly what you wanted. **compromise** *(n)*.
2 *(n)* an agreement that is halfway between two opposite views.

compulsory *(adj)* If something is **compulsory**, there is a law or rule that says you must do it.

computer *(n)* a machine that can store large amounts of information and do very quick and complicated calculations. **computing** *(n)*.

computer-aided design or **CAD** *(n)* plans and drawings made using a computer, especially product designs or architectural drawings.

comrade
1 *(n)* *(old-fashioned)* a good friend. **comradeship** *(n)*.
2 *(n)* a companion in battle.

concave *(adj)* curved inward, like the inside surface of a dish. *See* **lens**.

Wolfgang Amadeus Mozart (1756-1791) *began composing music at the age of five. He is shown here playing the piano.*

conceal concealing concealed *(v)* to hide something. **concealment** *(n)*.

concede conceding conceded *(v)* to admit something unwillingly. *Eventually, Natalie conceded that she was wrong.*

conceited *(adj)* If you are **conceited**, you are too proud of yourself and of what you can do. **conceit** *(n)*.

conceive conceiving conceived
1 *(v)* to form an idea in your mind. *Caspar conceived a cunning plan.*
2 *(v)* to become pregnant.

concentrate
concentrating concentrated
1 *(v)* to focus your thoughts and attention on something. **concentration** *(n)*.
2 *(v)* to make a liquid thicker and stronger by removing water from it. **concentrate** *(n)*, **concentration** *(n)*, **concentrated** *(adj)*.

concentric *(adj)* **Concentric** circles all have their center at the same point.

concept *(n)* a general idea or understanding of something. *Leo has a very vague concept of history.* **conceptual** *(adj)*.

conception
1 *(n)* a general idea that you have formed in your mind. *Do you have any conception of what it's like to be homeless?*
2 *(n)* the act of becoming pregnant.

concern concerning concerned
1 *(v)* to involve you, or to be of interest to you. *These plans concern you.* **concern** *(n)*.
2 *(v)* to be about a particular subject. *This project concerns local history.* **concerning** *(prep)*.

concerned *(adj)*
If you are **concerned** about something, you are anxious and worried about it. **concern** *(n)*.

concert *(n)* a performance given by musicians or singers.

concerto concertos *or* concerti *(n)* a piece of music for one or more solo instruments playing with an orchestra.

concession
1 *(n)* an agreement to allow something that would not normally be permitted. *As a special concession, you can stay up late.*
2 *(n)* permission to sell something granted by a government body to the seller. *My dad has the concession to sell snacks at the carnival this year.*

concise *(adj)* saying a lot in a few words. **concisely** *(adv)*.

conclude concluding concluded
1 *(v)* to decide that something is true because of the facts that you have. *I concluded that Bill must have stolen the jewels.* **conclusion** *(n)*.
2 *(v)* to finish or end something. **conclusion** *(n)*.

concoct concocting concocted
1 *(v)* to create something by mixing several different things together. **concoction** *(n)*.
2 *(v)* If you **concoct** an excuse, you invent it.

concrete
1 *(n)* a building material made from a mixture of sand, small stones, cement, and water. **concrete** *(v)*.
2 *(adj)* real or definite. *The detectives need some concrete evidence.*

concussion *(n)*
unconsciousness, dizziness or sickness caused by a heavy blow to your head. **concussed** *(adj)*.

condemn
condemning condemned
1 *(v)* to say very strongly that you do not approve of something. *Mahatma Gandhi condemned all violence.* **condemnation** *(n)*.
2 *(v)* to force someone to suffer something unpleasant. *The murderer was condemned to death.*

condense condensing condensed
1 *(v)* When a gas **condenses**, it turns into a liquid, usually as a result of cooling. **condensation** *(n)*.
2 *(v)* to make a piece of writing shorter by taking out unnecessary parts.

condescending *(adj)*
If you are **condescending**, you behave as though you are better or more important than other people. **condescension** *(n)*, **condescend** *(v)*.

condition
conditioning conditioned
1 *(n)* the general state of a person, an animal, or a thing. *My dog is in good condition. The hostages suffered terrible living conditions.*
2 *(n)* a medical problem that continues over a long period of time. *A lung condition.*
3 *(n)* something that is needed before another thing can happen or be allowed. *One condition of having a bike is that you always lock it up.*
4 *(v)* to train someone to believe certain things or to behave in certain ways. *Social conditioning.* **conditioning** *(n)*.

conditional *(adj)*
depending on something else. *My student aid is conditional on my keeping up at least a C average.* **conditionally** *(adv)*.

conditioner *(n)*
a thick liquid that you rub into your hair after washing it, to make it strong and shiny.

condolence *(n)*
an expression of sympathy for a person who is upset because a friend or relative has just died.

condominium *(n)* an apartment building or townhouse complex in which the apartment or townhouse is owned by the person who lives in it, but the gardens, swimming pool, etc. are shared by all the occupants.

conduct conducting conducted
1 *(kon-**dukt**)* *(v)* to organize something and carry it out. *The police conducted an investigation into the robbery.*
2 *(kon-**dukt**)* *(v)* to stand in front of a group of musicians and direct their playing.
3 *(kon-**dukt**)* *(v)* If something **conducts** heat, electricity, or sound, it allows them to pass through it. *Copper conducts electricity.* **conduction** *(n)*.
4 *(**kon**-dukt)* *(n)* behavior. *Your conduct at the party was unacceptable.*

conductor
1 *(n)* someone who stands in front of a group of musicians and directs their playing.
2 *(n)* someone who collects railroad fares.
3 *(n)* a substance that allows heat, electricity, or sound to travel through it. *Metal is a good conductor of heat.*

cone
1 *(n)* an object or shape with a round base and a point at the top. **conical** *(adj)*. *See* **shape**.
2 *(n)* the hard, woody fruit of a pine or fir tree.

confectionery *(n)* candy and chocolates. **confectioner** *(n)*.

confederation *(n)*
a union or confederacy.

conference *(n)* a formal meeting for discussing ideas and opinions.

confess
confesses confessing confessed *(v)* to admit that you have done something wrong. **confession** *(n)*.

a b c d e f g h i j k l m n o p q r s t u v w x y z

confetti *(plural n)* small pieces of colored paper that are thrown over the bride and groom after a wedding, or at parades.

confide confiding confided *(v)* If you **confide in** someone, you tell them a secret because you can trust them not to tell anyone else.

confident
1 *(adj)* having a strong belief in your own abilities. *Ella is a confident swimmer.* **confidence** *(n),* **confidently** *(adv).*
2 *(adj)* certain that things will happen in the way you want. *I am confident that it will be sunny tomorrow.* **confidence** *(n),* **confidently** *(adv).*

confidential *(adj)* secret. **confidentially** *(adv).*

confirm confirming confirmed
1 *(v)* to say that something is definitely true or will definitely happen. **confirmation** *(n).*
2 *(v)* When someone is **confirmed**, they are accepted as a full member of a church, in a special ceremony. **confirmation** *(n).*

confiscate confiscating confiscated *(v)* to take something away from someone as a punishment or because that thing is not allowed. **confiscation** *(n).*

conflict conflicting conflicted
1 *(kon-flikt) (n)* a serious disagreement.
2 *(kon-flikt) (n)* a war, or a period of fighting.
3 *(kon-**flikt**) (v)* When ideas or statements **conflict**, they are different. *Tom's ideas always conflict with mine.*

conform conforming conformed
1 *(v)* If you **conform**, you behave in the same way as everyone else, or in a way that is expected of you. **conformist** *(n),* **conformity** *(n).*
2 *(v)* If something **conforms** to a rule or law, it does what the rule or law requires. *All these toys conform to strict safety regulations.*

confront confronting confronted
1 *(v)* to meet or face someone in a threatening or accusing way. **confrontation** *(n).*
2 *(v)* If a problem **confronts** you, you have to deal with it.

confuse confusing confused
1 *(v)* If someone or something **confuses** you, you do not understand them or know what to do. **confusion** *(n),* **confusing** *(adj).*
2 *(v)* to mistake one thing for another. *I confused Alex with his twin brother.* **confusion** *(n),* **confused** *(adj).*

congeal congealing congealed *(v)* When a liquid **congeals**, it becomes thick or solid.

congested *(adj)* blocked-up and not allowing movement. *Congested roads. Congested sinuses.* **congestion** *(n).*

congratulate congratulating congratulated *(v)* to tell someone that you are pleased because something good has happened to them or they have done something well. **congratulations** *(plural n).*

congregation *(n)* a group of people gathered together for worship.

Congress *(n)* the lawmaking body of the United States. **Congressional** *(adj).*

conifer *(n)* an evergreen tree that produces cones. **coniferous** *(adj).*

conjunction *(n)* a word that connects two parts of a sentence or phrase. *"And," "but," and "if" are all conjunctions. See* page 3.

conjurer *or* **conjuror** *(n)* someone who performs magic tricks to entertain people. **conjuring** *(n).*

connect connecting connected *(v)* to join together two or more things, ideas, or places.

connection
1 *(n)* a link between objects or ideas.
2 *(n)* a train, plane, or bus arranged so that people getting off other trains, planes, or buses can use it to continue their journey.

connoisseur *(kon-uh-**soor**) (n)* someone who knows a lot about a subject, and appreciates things that are of good quality.

conquer conquering conquered *(v)* to defeat an enemy and take control of them by force. **conqueror** *(n).*

conscience *(**kon**-shenss) (n)* your knowledge of what is right and wrong, which makes you feel guilty when you have done something wrong.

conscientious
1 *(adj)* If you are **conscientious**, you make sure that you do things well and thoroughly. **conscientiously** *(adv).*
2 **conscientious objector** *(n)* someone who refuses to fight in a war because they believe that it is wrong to fight and kill.

conscious
1 *(adj)* awake and able to see, hear, think, etc. **consciousness** *(n).*
2 *(adj)* aware of something. *I slowly became conscious that everyone was looking at me.* **consciousness** *(n).*
3 *(adj)* deliberate. *I've made a conscious effort to improve.* **consciously** *(adv).*

consecutive *(adj)* happening or following one after the other. *Marcia was away for four consecutive days.* **consecutively** *(adv).*

consent consenting consented *(v)* If you **consent** to something, you agree to it. **consent** *(n).*

consequence *(n)* the result of an action. *If you steal, there will be consequences.* **consequent** *(adj),* **consequently** *(adv).*

conservation *(n)* the protection of nature, wildlife, and other valuable things, such as buildings and paintings. **conservationist** *(n).*

conservative *(adj)* moderate, cautious, and not extreme. *Marcus has a very conservative dress sense.* **conservatively** *(adv).*

conservatory conservatories *(n)*
1 a school for music or the arts.
2 a glass room attached to a house and used for growing plants.

consider considering considered
1 *(v)* to think about something carefully before deciding what to do.
2 *(v)* to believe that something is true. *Danny considers school to be a waste of time!*
3 *(v)* to take something into account. *We must consider Celia's feelings.*

considerable *(adj)* fairly large. *A considerable amount of money.* **considerably** *(adv).*

considerate *(adj)* If you are **considerate**, you think about other people's needs and feelings. **considerately** *(adv).*

consideration
1 *(n)* careful thought that you give to something before making a decision.
2 *(n)* a fact that needs to be taken into account before a decision can be made.
3 If you **show consideration**, you care about other people's needs and feelings.

considering *(conj)* taking into account certain things. *You got here very quickly, considering the weather.* **considering** *(prep).*

consignment *(n)* a number of things that are delivered together.

consist consisting consisted *(v)* If something **consists** of different things, it is made up of those things. *This dish consists of chicken, onions, peas and brown rice.*

consistent *(adj)*
If you are **consistent**, you always behave in the same way or support the same ideas or principles. **consistency** *(n)*, **consistently** *(adv)*.

console consoling consoled
1 *(kon-**sole**) (v)* to comfort someone in at a time of loss, grief, or sadness. **consolation** *(kon-soh-**lay**-shun) (n)*.
2 *(**kon**-sole) (n)* an electronic device connected to a television, on which you can play games.

consonant *(n)* any of the letters in the alphabet except the five vowels.

conspicuous *(adj)* Something that is **conspicuous** stands out and can be seen easily. **conspicuously** *(adv)*.

conspiracy conspiracies *(n)*
a secret, illegal plan made by two or more people. **conspirator** *(n)*, **conspire** *(v)*, **conspiratorial** *(adj)*.

constable *(n)* a low ranking officer of the British police force.

constant
1 *(adj)* happening all the time and never stopping. *The traffic creates a constant noise*. **constantly** *(adv)*.
2 *(adj)* staying at the same rate or level all the time. *A constant speed.*
3 *(adj)* If someone is **constant**, they continue to support a person or an idea without ever changing their mind. **constancy** *(n)*.

constellation *(n)* a group of stars that form a shape or pattern.

constipated *(adj)*
If you are **constipated**, you find it hard to pass solids from your body frequently or easily. **constipation** *(n)*.

constituent *(n)*
a voter represented by an elected official. *The senator went home to speak to his constituents.*

constitution
1 *(n)* the system of laws in a country that states the rights of the people and the powers of the government. **constitutional** *(adj)*.
2 *(n)* your general health and strength.

constraint *(n)*
something that limits what you are able or allowed to do. **constrain** *(v)*.

construct constructing constructed *(v)* to build or make something. **construction** *(n)*.

constructive *(adj)*
helpful and useful. *Constructive criticism.* **constructively** *(adv)*.

consult consulting consulted
1 *(v)* to go to a person for advice. *If you feel ill, you should consult a doctor.* **consultation** *(n)*.
2 *(v)* If you **consult** a book or a map, you use it to find information.

consultant *(n)*
a person with a lot of knowledge and experience of something, who gives professional advice to others.

consume consuming consumed
1 *(v)* to eat or drink something.
2 *(v)* to use something up. **consumption** *(n)*.
3 *(v)* If a fire **consumes** something, it destroys it.

consumer *(n)* someone who buys products, eats food, or uses services.

contact contacting contacted
1 When things are **in contact**, they touch each other.
2 If you are **in contact with** someone, you write or talk to them.
3 *(v)* to get in touch with someone. *I'll contact Janice about going to the beach on Saturday.*

contact lens contact lenses *(n)*
a small plastic lens that fits closely over your eyeball to improve your eyesight.

contagious *(adj)*
A **contagious** disease can be caught by touching someone or something already infected with it.

contain containing contained
1 *(v)* When an object **contains** something, it holds that thing inside itself or that thing forms a part of it. *The chest contained the treasure. This book contains many stories.* **container** *(n)*.
2 *(v)* to keep an emotion under control. *I tried to contain my excitement.*

contaminated *(adj)*
If something is **contaminated**, it has been made dirty or impure. *Contaminated drinking water.* **contamination** *(n)*.

contemplate
contemplating contemplated
1 *(v)* to think seriously about something. *Matthew contemplated leaving college.* **contemplation** *(n)*.
2 *(v)* to look at something thoughtfully. *Millie contemplated the view.* **contemplation** *(n)*.

contemporary contemporaries
1 *(adj)* up-to-date or modern.
2 *(adj)* If something is **contemporary** with something else, they both occurred at the same time.
3 *(n)* a person of about the same age as you. *A contemporary of mine from school.*

contempt *(n)* total lack of respect. **contemptuous** *(adj)*.

contend contending contended
1 *(v)* to compete. **contender** *(n)*.
2 *(v)* to try to deal with a difficulty. *Lucy has had a lot to contend with since her parents divorced.*

content contenting contented
1 *(adj)* happy and satisfied. **contented** *(adj)*, **contentedly** *(adv)*.
2 *(v)* If you **content yourself** with something, you are satisfied with it.

contents *(plural n)*
the things that are inside something or form part of something.

contest contesting contested
1 *(**kon**-test) (n)* a competition.
2 *(kon-**test**) (v)* to compete or fight for something. **contestant** *(n)*.
3 *(kon-**test**) (v)* to claim that something is wrong. *Thomas contested the judges' decision.*

context
1 *(n)* The **context** of a word or phrase is the writing around it, which helps you to understand its meaning.
2 If you put an event or an action **in context**, you take into account all the things that affect it.

continent
1 *(n)* one of the seven large landmasses of the Earth. **continental** *(adj)*.

continents

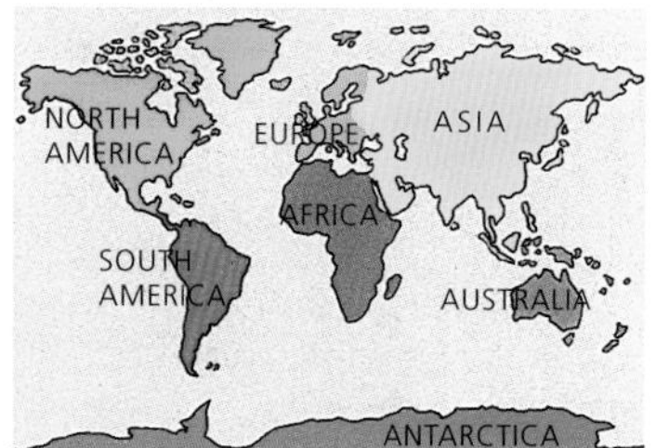

2 the Continent *(n)* colonies later forming the United States.

continual *(adj)* happening again and again. **continually** *(adv)*.

continue
continuing continued *(v)* to go on doing something. **continuation** *(n)*.

continuous *(adj)*
When something is **continuous**, it does not stop. *A continuous line.* **continuously** *(adv)*.

contort contorting contorted *(v)* to twist something out of its usual shape. *Rory contorted his face to show his disgust.* **contortion** *(n)*, **contorted** *(adj)*.

contour
1 *(n)* an outline.
2 *(n)* a line joining points of equal height on a map.

contract contracting contracted
1 *(kon-**trakt**)* *(v)* to become smaller.
2 *(**kon**-trakt)* *(n)* a legal agreement between people or companies, stating the terms on which one will work for the other or sell to the other.

contradict
contradicting contradicted *(v)* to say the opposite of what someone else has said. contradiction *(n).*

contraption *(n)* a strange and complicated-looking machine.

contrary
1 *(**kon**-trair-ee)* *(adj)* opposite.
2 *(kon-**trair**-ee)* *(adj)* deliberately awkward and difficult.

contrast contrasting contrasted
1 *(kon-**trast**)* *(v)* to be very different from something else. *Claude's views contrast strongly with mine.* contrast (**kon**-trast) *(n).*
2 *(kon-**trast**)* *(v)* to identify the difference between things.

contribute
contributing contributed
1 *(v)* to give help or money to a person or an organization. contribution *(n),* contributor *(n).*
2 *(v)* to write for a magazine or newspaper. contribution *(n),* contributor *(n).*

control controlling controlled
1 *(v)* to make something or someone do what you want. control *(n).*
2 *(plural n)* The controls of a machine are the levers and switches that make it work.

controversial *(adj)* If something is controversial, it causes a lot of argument. controversy *(n).*

convalescence *(n)*
a time during which someone recovers from an illness. convalesce *(v),* convalescent *(adj).*

convection *(n)* the movement of heat through liquids and gases. *The diagram shows how convection currents are created when a liquid is heated.*

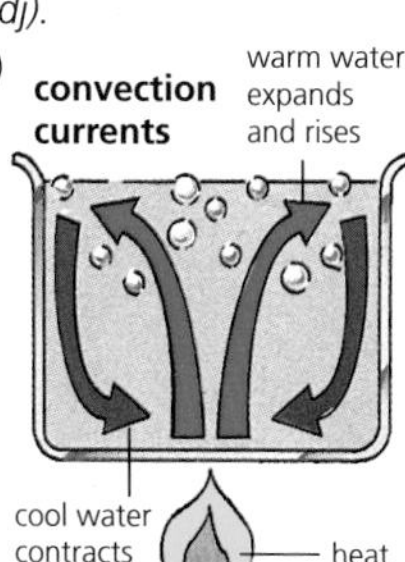

convenience
1 *(n)* something that is useful and easy to use. *This house has been fitted with modern conveniences.*
2 convenience foods *(plural n)* foods that are quick and easy to prepare, such as frozen meals.

convenient *(adj)*
If something is convenient, it is useful or easy to use. conveniently *(adv).*

convent *(n)*
a building where nuns live and work.

conventional *(adj)* A conventional person does things in a traditional or accepted way. conventionally *(adv).*

conversation *(n)* If you hold a conversation with someone, you talk with them for a while. converse *(v).*

convert converting converted *(v)* to make something into something else. *We've converted our loft into a bedroom.* conversion *(n).*

convex *(adj)* curving outward, like the side of a ball. *See* **lens**.

conveyor belt *(n)* a moving belt that carries objects in a factory.

convict convicting convicted
1 *(kon-**vikt**)* *(v)* to prove that someone is guilty of a crime.
2 *(**kon**-vikt)* *(n)* someone who is in prison because they have committed a crime.

conviction
1 *(n)* a strong belief in something.
2 *(n)* If you have a conviction for a crime, you have been found guilty of committing it.

convince convincing convinced *(v)*
If you convince somebody, you make them believe you. convincing *(adj),* convincingly *(adv).*

convoy *(n)* a group of trucks or other vehicles traveling together.

cook cooking cooked
1 *(v)* to prepare and heat food for a meal. cooking *(n).*
2 *(n)* someone whose job is to prepare food.

cookie
1 *(n)* a small flat cake, which has been baked until it is hard.
2 *(n)* a piece of information left on your computer after you have been using a webpage. Cookies are usually used to store information about the choices you have made on a webpage.

cool
cooling cooled; cooler coolest
1 *(adj)* rather cold. coolness *(n).*
2 *(v)* to lower the temperature of something.
3 *(adj)* unfriendly and distant. coolly *(adv).*
4 *(adj)* *(informal)* fashionable.

coop *(n)*
a small building used to house chickens and other small animals.

cooperate
cooperating cooperated *(v)* to work together. cooperation *(n).*

cooperative *(adj)* If you are cooperative, you work well with other people. cooperativeness *(n).*

coordinate
coordinating coordinated
1 *(v)* to organize activities or people so that they all work together. coordination *(n),* coordinator *(n).*
2 *(n)* a number used to show the position of a point on a line or map.

coordinated
1 *(adj)* If you are well coordinated, you have good control over how you move your arms and legs.
2 *(adj)* Coordinated clothes go well together.

cope coping coped *(v)*
to deal with something successfully.

copper
1 *(n)* a red-brown metal. *See* **mineral**.
2 *(n)* a red-brown color.
copper *(adj),* coppery *(adj).*

copy copies copying copied
1 *(v)* to do the same as someone else.
2 *(n)* A copy is made to look or sound exactly the same as something else.
3 *(v)* to make a copy of something.

copyright *(n)* If someone owns the copyright on a book, song, etc. people must ask for their permission before they copy or perform them.

coral *(singular n)*
sea creatures, closely related to sea anemones, whose skeletons remain after they die. Coral can be hard or soft. *Sea fans are not coral, but are closely related.*

cord *(n)* a length of string or rope.

cordial
1 *(n)* a sweet fruit drink. *Lime cordial.*
2 *(adj)* friendly. cordially *(adv).*

cordon *(n)* a line of people or objects used to control crowds. *A police cordon blocked the street.*

core *(n)* the center of something, such as the Earth or an apple.

cork *(n)* soft bark used as a stopper in bottles or to make mats, tiles, etc.

corkscrew
1 *(n)* a tool used for pulling corks out of bottles.
2 *(adj)* spiraling or turning in circles. *Corkscrew curls.*

Some words that begin with a "c" sound are spelled with a "k."

corn
1 *(n)* the sweet seeds that grow in large ears on tall grass plants that are eaten as a vegetable.
2 *(n)* a small patch of hard skin on your foot.

corner cornering cornered
1 *(n)* the place where two sides of something meet. *A square has four corners.*
2 *(v)* to get a person or animal into a situation where they are trapped.

cornet *(n)*
a brass musical instrument like a trumpet. See **brass**.

cornrow *(n)*
a flat braid close to the scalp.

coronary coronaries
1 *(adj)* having to do with the heart.
2 *(n)* a heart attack.

coronation *(n)* the ceremony when a king or queen is crowned.

coroner *(n)*
a medical official. If someone dies suddenly or in an unnatural way, a **coroner** investigates their death.

corporal *(n)*
a soldier of fairly low rank.

corporal punishment *(n)*
physical punishment, such as smacking.

corporation *(n)*
a group of people who work together to run a company, college, or town.

corpse *(n)* a dead body.

corpuscle *(kor-puss-ul) (n)*
a red or white blood cell. See **blood**.

correct correcting corrected
1 *(adj)* true or right. **correctly** *(adv)*.
2 *(v)* to make something right. **correction** *(n)*.

correspond
corresponding corresponded
1 *(v)* If two things **correspond**, they match in some way. **correspondence** *(n)*.
2 *(v)* When you **correspond** with someone, you write letters or emails to each other. **correspondence** *(n)*.

correspondent
1 *(n)* someone who writes letters.
2 *(n)* someone who reports for television, radio, or newspapers about a special subject or place.

corridor *(n)*
a long passage in a building or train.

corrode
corroding corroded *(v)*
to eat away at something. *Water corrodes metal and makes it rust.* **corrosion** *(n)*, **corrosive** *(adj)*.

corrugated *(adj)*
ridged or rippled. *Corrugated iron.*

corrupt corrupting corrupted
1 *(v)* to make someone bad or dishonest. **corrupt** *(adj)*.
2 *(adj)* If computer data is **corrupt**, it contains errors that make it useless. **corrupt** *(v)*.

cosmetic
1 **cosmetics** *(plural n)* beauty products such as lipstick or mascara.
2 *(adj)* changing the way that a person or a thing looks. *Cosmetic surgery.*

cosmic *(adj)* to do with the universe. *Cosmic laws.* **cosmically** *(adv)*.

cosmopolitan
1 *(adj)* someone who feels at home in more than one country.
2 *(adj)* containing elements of cultures from all around the world. *New York is a cosmopolitan city.*

cosmos *(n)* the universe.

cost costing cost *(v)* to make someone give up or lose something. *The battle cost many lives.* **cost** *(n)*.

co-star *(n)* an actor who appears in a movie with another actor of equal importance. **co-star** *(v)*.

costly costlier costliest *(adj)*
expensive. *Costly gifts.*

costume
1 *(n)* clothes worn by actors.
2 *(n)* clothes worn by people at a particular time in history. *The picture shows a selection of costumes from the 15th to the 19th centuries.*

European costume

cot *(n)* a small narrow bed that can be folded up and put away.

cottage *(n)* a small house, usually in the country. See **thatch**.

cottage cheese *(n)*
cheese made from curdled skimmed milk.

cotton
1 *(n)* soft, thin material made from the cotton plant and used to make clothes. **cotton** *(adj)*.
2 *(n)* thread used for sewing.

cotton plant
raw cotton
boll

cottontail *(n)*
a rabbit with a soft, fluffy white tail.

couch couches
1 *(n)* a long, soft seat with arms and a back, and room for two or more people.
2 **couch potato** *(n) (informal)* someone who spends most of their time watching television rather than being active.

cough *(koff)*
coughing coughed
1 *(v)* to make a sudden, harsh noise as you force air out of your lungs. **cough** *(n)*.
2 *(n)* an illness that makes you cough.

council *(n)*
a group of people chosen to look after the interests of a town, county, or an organization. *The city council.*

counsel counseling counseled *(v)*
to listen to people's problems and give advice. **counseling** *(n)*, **counselor** *(n)*.

count counting counted
1 *(v)* to say numbers in order.
2 *(v)* to work out how many there are of something. *I counted the planes as they took off.*
3 *(v)* If you can **count on** something or someone, you can rely on them.

Some words that begin with a "c" sound are spelled with a "k."

counter
1 *(n)* a small, flat, round playing piece used in some board games.
2 *(n)* a long, flat surface. *A counter in a department store.*

counteract counteracting counteracted *(v)* to act against something so that it is less effective. *You should get some exercise to counteract the effects of overeating.*

counterclockwise *(n)* in a direction opposite to the way the hands of a clock move.

counterfeit *(n)* a fake that has been made to look like the real thing.

countless *(adj)* so many that you cannot count them.

country countries
1 *(n)* a part of the world with its own borders and government.
2 *(n)* undeveloped land away from towns or cities. **country** *(adj)*.

countryside *(n)* undeveloped land away from towns or cities.

county counties *(n)* a division or part of a state that has its own local government.

couple
1 *(n)* two of something.
2 *(n)* two people. *A married couple.*

coupon *(n)* a small piece of paper which gives you a discount on something.

courage *(n)* bravery or fearlessness. **courageous** *(adj)*, **courageously** *(adv)*.

courier *(ku-ree-er)*
1 *(n)* someone who carries messages or packages for somebody else.
2 *(n)* someone who looks after a group of people on vacation.

course
1 *(n)* a series of classes.
2 *(n)* a part of a meal.
3 *(n)* a piece of ground where a sport is played. *A golf course.*

court
1 *(n)* a place where legal cases are heard.
2 *(n)* a place where games such as tennis or squash are played.
3 *(n)* a place where a king or queen meets visitors and advisors.

courteous *(kur-tee-us)* *(adj)* polite and respectful. **courtesy** *(n)*, **courteously** *(adv)*.

courtship
1 *(n)* attempts by an animal to attract a mate.
2 *(n)* attempts by one person to win the love and affection of another.

cousin *(n)* Your **cousin** is the child of your uncle or aunt.

cover covering covered
1 *(v)* to put something over something else. *Cover the table with a cloth.* **cover** *(n)*.
2 *(v)* to teach or study something thoroughly. *Have you covered that topic?* **coverage** *(n)*.
3 *(v)* to travel a certain distance. *We covered twenty miles before nightfall.*
4 *(v)* to include or provide for. *Does your insurance cover storm damage?*

cow
1 *(n)* an adult female farm animal that produces milk. *See* **cud**.
2 *(n)* an adult female seal or whale.

coward *(n)* someone who is easily scared and keeps away from frightening situations. **cowardice** *(n)*, **cowardly** *(adj)*.

cowboy *(n)* a man or boy who looks after cattle. *See* **rodeo**.

cozy cozier coziest *(adj)* comfortable, or snug. The house was small but cozy. **coziness** *(n)*, **cozily** *(adv)*.

crab *(n)* a creature with a hard shell, eight legs, and two pincers.

furrowed crab
carapace (shell)
eye on stalk
pincer
walking leg
abdomen
mouth

crack cracking cracked
1 *(v)* to break or split, often with a loud, sharp noise. **crack** *(n)*.
2 *(v)* to find the answer to something. *At last, we cracked the problem.*
3 *(informal)* When you **take a crack at something,** you try to do it.

cracker *(n)* a thin, plain biscuit or wafer.

crackle crackling crackled *(v)* to make a noise like lots of small bangs. *The dry leaves crackled.*

cradle cradling cradled
1 *(n)* a small bed for a young baby.
2 *(v)* to hold something or someone in your arms very gently. *Rachel cradled the kitten in her arms.*
3 *(n)* the place where something starts. *The cradle of democracy.*

craft
1 *(n)* work or a hobby where you make things with your hands. *Woodwork, pottery, and needlework are all crafts.*
2 *(n)* a vehicle, such as a boat, spaceship, or airplane.

craftsman craftsmen *(n)* someone skilled at making things with their hands. **craftsmanship** *(n)*.

crafty craftier craftiest *(adj)* A **crafty** person is clever at tricking other people. **craftily** *(adv)*.

crag *(n)* a steep, sharp rock. **craggy** *(adj)*.

cram cramming crammed *(v)* to fit things into a small space. *I crammed all my clothes into a backpack.*

cramp cramping cramped
1 *(n)* pain caused by a muscle tightening suddenly.
2 *(v)* *(informal)* If someone or something **cramps your style**, they do not allow you to express yourself freely.

cramped *(adj)* If a place is **cramped**, there is not enough room in it for everyone or everything.

crane craning craned
1 *(n)* a machine used for lifting heavy objects.
2 *(n)* a large wading bird.
3 *(v)* to stretch your neck so you can see better.

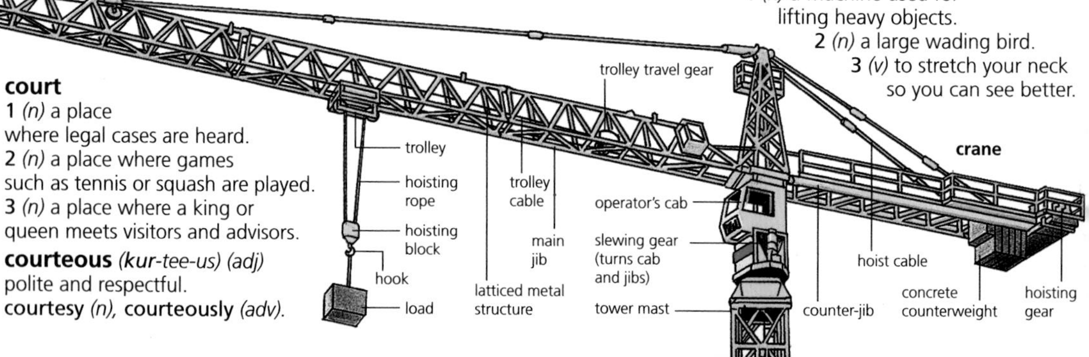

crane

crank cranking cranked
1 *(n)* a bent rod used for winding or lifting something. *See* **bicycle**.
2 *(n) (informal)* someone with strange ideas. *A health food crank.*

cranky *(adj)* acting in an annoyed or fretful way. *The baby is cranky because he is tired.*

crash crashes crashing crashed
1 *(v)* to make a loud noise like thunder.
2 *(n)* an accident in which a vehicle hits something at high speed. **crash** *(v)*.
3 *(v)* When a computer system or program **crashes**, it fails completely.

crate *(n)* a large, usually wooden, box. *A crate of oranges.*

crater
1 *(n)* a large hole in the ground caused by something, such as a bomb or a meteorite, falling on it.
2 *(n)* the mouth of a volcano. *See* **volcano**.

crave craving craved *(v)* to long for something desperately. **craving** *(n)*.

crawl crawling crawled
1 *(v)* to move on your hands and knees.
2 *(n)* a style of swimming on your front in which you use your arms in turn while kicking your legs.

crayon crayoning crayoned
1 *(n)* a colored pencil or wax stick used for drawing and coloring.
2 *(v)* to draw or color with a crayon.

craze *(n)*
a fashion that does not last very long.

crazy crazier craziest
1 *(adj)* mad, or foolish. **craziness** *(n)*, **crazily** *(adv)*.
2 *(adj) (informal)* very enthusiastic. *Josh is crazy about football.* **craziness** *(n)*.

creak creaking creaked *(v)* to make a squeaky, grating noise. **creak** *(n)*, **creaky** *(adj)*, **creakily** *(adv)*.

cream
1 *(n)* a thick liquid taken from the top of the milk. You eat cream with food. **creamy** *(adj)*.
2 *(n)* a thick, smooth substance like cream that you put on your skin. *Hand cream.*
3 *(n)* a yellowish-white color, or the color of cream. **cream** *(adj)*.

crease creasing creased *(v)* to make lines or folds in something, especially material or paper. **crease** *(n)*.

create creating created *(v)* to make or design something. **creator** *(n)*.

creation *(n)*
something that has been made.

creative *(adj)* If you are **creative**, you use your imagination and are good at thinking of new ideas. **creativity** *(n)*, **creatively** *(adv)*.

creature *(n)*
an animal, bird, or insect.

crèche *(rhymes with fresh) (n)*
a place where babies and young children can be looked after safely while their parents are busy.

credible *(adj)*
If something or someone is **credible**, you can believe in them or trust them. **credibility** *(n)*.

credit
1 If you or your bank account have **credit**, you have money.
2 *(n)* praise or acknowledgement. *No one gave me credit for my hard work.*
3 If you buy something **on credit**, you pay for it later.
4 *(plural n)* The **credits** at the end of a movie or television program tell you who acted in it and made it.

creek
1 *(n)* a narrow inlet where the sea flows inland for a long way.
2 *(n)* a small stream.

creep creeping crept
1 *(v)* to move very slowly and quietly.
2 *(v)* to crawl along the ground.
3 *(n) (slang)* an unpleasant person.
4 *(informal)* If something or someone **gives you the creeps**, they are unpleasant and frightening. **creepy** *(adj)*.

cremate cremating cremated *(v)* to burn a dead body. **cremation** *(n)*, **crematorium** *(n)*.

crescent *(n)* a curved shape.

crest
1 *(n)* a comb or tuft of feathers on a bird's head. **crested** *(adj)*.
2 *(n)* the top of something, such as a wave or a hill.
3 *(n)* a design that represents a noble family, a town, or an organization. *We have a dragon as our school crest.*
4 *(n)* part of a coat of arms. *See* **coat of arms**.

crevice *(n)* a crack or split in a rock.

crew *(n)* a team of people who work together, especially on a ship.

crib cribbing cribbed
1 *(n)* a small baby's bed.
2 *(v) (informal)* to copy someone else's work and pretend it is your own.
3 *(n)* a small farm building where grain is stored.

cricket
1 *(n)* a game played by two teams of eleven players, with two bats, a ball, and two sets of stumps. **cricketer** *(n)*.
2 *(n)* a jumping insect similar to a grasshopper.

crickets

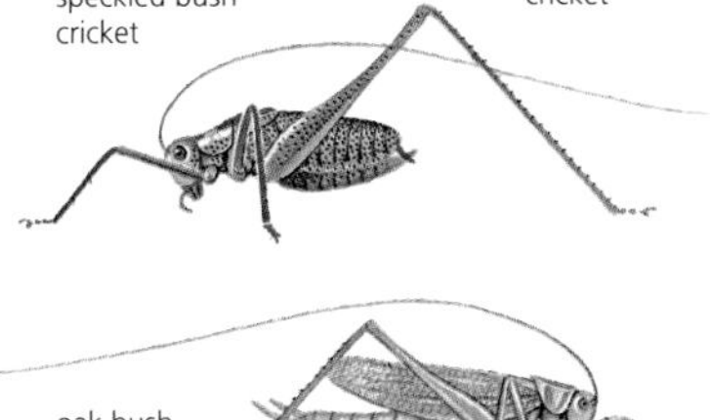

crime *(n)*
something that is against the law.

criminal
1 *(n)* someone who commits a crime. **criminally** *(adv)*.
2 *(adj)* to do with crime. *A criminal investigation.*

crimson *(n)*
a deep red color. **crimson** *(adj)*.

cripple crippling crippled
1 *(n) (old-fashioned)* someone who is lame or disabled. **crippled** *(adj)*.
2 *(v)* to stop someone or something from moving or working properly. *The company was crippled by strikes.*

crisis crises
1 *(n)* a time of danger and difficulty.
2 *(n)* a turning point or decision point.

crisp crisper crispest
1 *(adj)* firm and easily broken. *A crisp piece of toast.* **crispy** *(adj)*.
2 *(adj)* fresh, dry, and cool. *A crisp winter morning.* **crisply** *(adv)*.

critical
1 *(adj)* If you are **critical** of someone or something, you find faults in them. **critically** *(adv)*.
2 *(adj)* important, or serious. *A critical operation.* **critically** *(adv)*.

criticize criticizing criticized
1 *(v)* to tell someone what they have done wrong. **criticism** *(n)*.
2 *(v)* to point out the good and bad parts in a book, movie, etc. **critic** *(n)*, **criticism** *(n)*.

croak croaking croaked
1 *(v)* When a frog **croaks**, it makes a deep, hoarse sound. **croak** *(n)*.
2 *(v)* If you **croak**, you speak with a deep, hoarse voice. **croaky** *(adj)*.
3 *(v) (slang)* to die.

crochet *(crow-shay)* crocheting crocheted *(v)* to make a kind of lace from cotton thread or wool, using a hooked needle. **crochet** *(n)*.

crockery *(n)*
pottery that you use at home, such as plates, cups, and saucers.

crocodile *(n)*
a large, scaly reptile with short legs and strong jaws.

crocodile

crook
1 *(n)* a dishonest person or a criminal.
2 *(n)* a long stick with a hook at one end, used by shepherds.
3 *(adj) (Australian) (slang)* sick or ill.

crooked *(cruck-id)*
1 *(adj)* bent. *A crooked path.*
2 *(adj) (informal)* dishonest. *A crooked deal.*

crop cropping cropped
1 *(n)* a plant grown in large amounts, usually for food. *Potatoes and wheat are crops.*
2 *(v)* If an animal **crops** grass, it eats it.
3 *(v)* If something **crops up**, it happens unexpectedly.
4 *(n)* the pouch in a bird's gullet where food is stored and softened before being digested. *See* **chicken**.

cross crosses crossing crossed
1 *(v)* to go from one side to the other. *Columbus crossed the ocean.*
2 *(adj)* angry or not pleased.
3 *(n)* The shape "x" is a **cross**, as is "+."
4 *(n)* a wooden structure in the shape of a cross, on which criminals used to be crucified.
5 *(v)* If someone **crosses** you, they block your plans.

cross-country *(adj)*
A **cross-country** race is run through the countryside.

cross-examine
cross-examining cross-examined *(v)* to question somebody very closely. **cross-examination** *(n)*.

crossroads *(plural n)* a place where one road crosses another.

cross section
1 *(n)* a diagram that shows the inside of something, by cutting through it.
2 *(n)* A **cross section** of the public is a selection of different types of people.

crossword puzzle *(n)*
a puzzle in which you answer clues to fill blank spaces with words.

crouch crouches crouching crouched *(v)* When you **crouch**, you bend your legs and lower your body.

crow crowing crowed
1 *(n)* a large black bird.
2 *(v)* When a rooster **crows**, it makes a loud, crying noise.
3 *(v)* to boast about something.

crowd crowding crowded
1 *(n)* a lot of people packed together. **crowded** *(adj)*.
2 *(v)* If you **crowd** someone, you do not allow them enough room.

crown
1 *(n)* a headdress worn by a king or queen, made from precious metal and jewels.
2 *(n)* the top of something. *At last we reached the crown of the hill.*

crucial *(adj)* extremely important or vital. **crucially** *(adv)*.

crucify crucifies crucifying crucified *(v)* to put someone to death by fastening them to a cross and leaving them to die. **crucifixion** *(n)*.

crude cruder crudest
1 *(adj)* rough and poorly made. **crudely** *(adv)*.
2 *(adj)* A **crude** joke is rude and not very funny. **crudity** *(n)*, **crudely** *(adv)*.

cruel crueler cruelest *(adj)*
A **cruel** person deliberately causes pain to others or is happy to see them suffer. **cruelty** *(n)*, **cruelly** *(adv)*.

cruise cruising cruised
1 *(n)* If you go on a **cruise**, you take a vacation on a ship that calls at several places.
2 *(v)* to travel smoothly and easily. *We cruised down the river.*

cruiser
1 *(n)* a motorboat with a cabin. *See* **boat**.
2 *(n)* a large warship.

crumb *(n)*
a tiny piece of bread or cake.

crumble crumbling crumbled *(v)* to break into small pieces. **crumbly** *(adj)*.

crumple crumpling crumpled
1 *(v)* If you **crumple up** a piece of paper, you squash it into a ball.
2 *(v)* to collapse. **crumpled** *(adj)*.

crunch
crunches crunching crunched *(v)* If you **crunch** something, you crush it or chew noisily. *Ali crunched her carrot.* **crunchy** *(adj)*.

crush crushes crushing crushed
1 *(v)* to squash something under a heavy weight.
2 *(n) (slang)* If you have a **crush** on someone, you like them very much, but usually only for a short time.

crust
1 *(n)* the crisp outer case of bread or pastry. **crusty** *(adj)*.
2 *(n)* The Earth's **crust** is its thin outer layer of land and sea. *See* **Earth**.

crutch crutches *(n)*
one of two long sticks used to help support someone with injured legs.

cry cries crying cried
1 *(v)* to weep tears. **cry** *(n)*.
2 *(v)* to shout out. **cry** *(n)*.

crystal *(n)* a hard glassy piece of rock with many sides. Crystals are formed when minerals boil, then cool and solidify. **crystallize** *(v)*, **crystalline** *(adj)*. *See* **quartz**.

cub *(n)* a young lion, wolf, bear, etc.

cube cubing cubed
1 *(n)* a three-dimensional shape with six square faces. *Dice are cubes.* **cubic** *(adj)*. *See* **shape**.
2 *(v)* to multiply a number by itself twice. *3 cubed is 3 x 3 x 3 = 27.*

cubicle *(n)* a small office or area surrounded by partitions.

cucumber *(n)* a long green vegetable with a watery center. *See* **vegetable**.

cud *(n)* undigested food that cows bring up from the first part of their stomachs to chew again. *Grass is formed into cud balls in the rumen, returned to the mouth for chewing and passed into the reticulum where any stones are trapped. The pulp can then be digested.*

digestive system of a cow

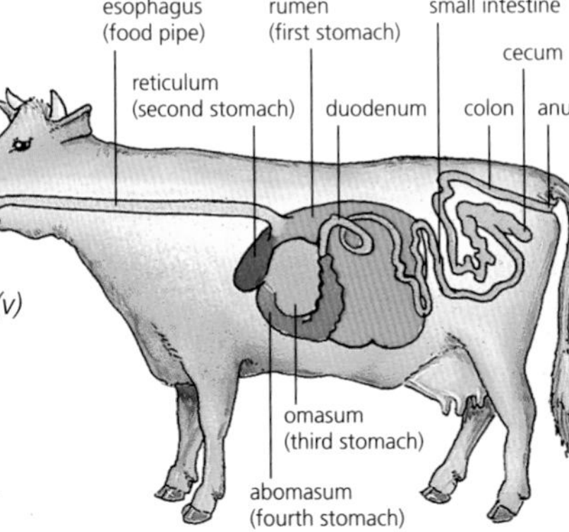

cuddle cuddling cuddled *(v)* to hold someone closely in your arms.

cue *(kyoo)*
1 *(n)* a long stick used to hit the ball in games such as billiards and pool.
2 *(n)* the signal to say some lines or take an action in a play.

cuff
1 *(n)* the end part of a shirt or blouse that goes around your wrist.
2 If you speak **off the cuff**, you give a speech or an answer without preparing it first.

culprit *(n)* someone who has done something wrong.

cult
1 *(n)* a religion with a small following.
2 *(n)* a strong, almost religious devotion to a person, an idea, or a way of life. *The hippie cult.*
3 *(n)* A **cult hero** is someone who is very popular with his or her followers.

cultivate cultivating cultivated *(v)* If you **cultivate** land, you grow crops on it. **cultivation** *(n).*

culture
1 *(n)* the arts, such as music, painting, literature, etc. **cultural** *(adj).*
2 *(n)* The **culture** of a group of people is their way of life, ideas, and traditions.

cultured *(adj)* well-educated.

cunning *(adj)* A **cunning** person is clever at tricking people. **cunning** *(n),* **cunningly** *(adv).*

cupboard *(n)* a piece of furniture or a built-in space used for storing things.

curator *(n)* the person in charge of a museum or art gallery.

curb curbing curbed *(v)* to control and hold back something. *I curbed my desire for another piece of cake.*

curd *(n)* the solid part of sour milk, often used to make cheese.

curdle curdling curdled *(v)* When milk **curdles**, it goes sour and breaks up into curds and whey.

cure curing cured
1 *(v)* to make someone better when they have been ill.
2 *(n)* a drug or course of treatment that makes someone better.

curfew *(n)* a rule or an order that prevents people from traveling around freely, especially after dark.

curious
1 *(adj)* eager to find out. **curiosity** *(n),* **curiously** *(adv).*
2 *(adj)* strange. *A curious creature.* **curiosity** *(n),* **curiously** *(adv).*

curl curling curled
1 *(n)* a curved lock of hair. **curly** *(adj).*
2 *(v)* to bend into a spiral shape.

currant *(n)* a dried grape.

currency *(n)* the money used in a country.

current
1 *(adj)* happening now. **currently** *(adv).*
2 *(n)* the movement of water in a river or an ocean, or of electricity through a wire.

current affairs *(plural n)* important events that are happening now and are often discussed on television, in newspapers or on the internet.

curriculum curricula *(n)* a program of study for a school or college.

curry curries *(n)* a spicy meal of meat or vegetables, often served with rice.

curse cursing cursed
1 *(n)* an evil spell intended to harm someone.
2 *(v)* to swear.

cursor *(n)* a small indicator that shows your position on a computer screen.

curtain *(n)* a piece of fabric that's pulled across a window or a stage to cover it.

curtsy *or* **curtsey** curtsies curtsying curtsied *(v)* to bend slightly at the knee, with one leg crossed behind the other. Women and girls curtsy to show respect or to accept applause. **curtsy** *(n).*

curve curving curved
1 *(v)* to bend or turn gently. *The path curved toward the cottage.*
2 *(n)* a bend in something. **curved** *(adj),* **curvy** *(adj).*

cushion cushioning cushioned
1 *(n)* a type of pillow used to make chairs or sofas more comfortable.
2 *(v)* to soften the effect of something. *The mattress cushioned her fall.*

custard *(n)* a sweet yellow dessert made from milk, eggs, and sugar.

custody
1 *(n)* If someone has **custody** of a child, they have the legal right to look after that child. **custodial** *(adj).*
2 If someone is **taken into custody**, they are arrested by the police. **custodial** *(adj).*

custom
1 *(n)* a tradition. **customary** *(adj).*
2 *(n)* something that you do regularly. *A family custom.* **customary** *(adj).*
3 **customs** *(n)* a checkpoint at country borders, ports, or airports where officials make sure that you are not carrying anything illegal.

customer *(n)* A store's **customers** are the people who buy things from it.

customize customizing customized *(v)* to change something to suit your needs and to make it look unusual. *Garth customized his car.*

cut cutting cut
1 *(v)* to use a sharp instrument, such as scissors or a knife, to divide, shorten, or shape something.
2 *(n)* a skin wound.
3 *(v)* to reduce something. *The store is cutting its prices.* **cut** *(n).*
4 *(v)* If you are **cut off** from other people, you cannot contact them.
5 *(v)* If you **cut down** on something, such as eating candies, you do it less often.
6 *(v)* If a person or an organization **cuts back**, they reduce the amount of money that they spend. **cutback** *(n).*

cute cuter cutest *(adj)* charming and attractive.

cutlery *(singular n)* knives, forks, and spoons.

cutting
1 *(n)* something cut off or cut out of something else. *A plant cutting. A newspaper cutting.*
2 *(adj)* If you make a **cutting** remark, you say something hurtful.

cycle *(sy-kul)* cycling cycled
1 *(n)* a series of events that are repeated over and over again. *The cycle of the seasons.*
2 *(n)* a bicycle. *See* **bicycle**.
3 *(v)* to ride a bicycle. **cyclist** *(n).*

cyclone *(sy-klone) (n)* a very strong wind that blows in a spiral.

cygnet *(sig-net) (n)* a young swan. *See* **swan**.

cylinder *(sill-in-der)*
1 *(n)* a shape with circular ends and curved walls. *Most drink cans are cylinders.* **cylindrical** *(adj). See* **shape**.
2 *(n)* a tube-shaped container in an engine. *See* **engine**.

cynical *(sin-ik-al) (adj)* Someone who is **cynical** always expects the worst to happen, and thinks that anything people do is for selfish reasons. **cynic** *(n),* **cynicism** *(n),* **cynically** *(adv).*

cytoplasm *(n)* the contents of a cell, apart from its nucleus. *See* **cell**.

czar *or* **tsar** *(zar) (n)* a Russian king. *The last czar was murdered in 1918.*

Some words that begin with a "cy" sound are spelled "ci," "psy," "si," or "scy."

Dd

dab dabbing dabbed *(v)* to touch a surface gently with something soft. *Amy dabbed some ointment on the wound.* **dab** *(n).*

dabble dabbling dabbled
1 *(v)* to dip something into water and splash it around. *Harvey dabbled his fingers in the stream.*
2 *(v)* If you **dabble** in something, you do it, but not very seriously or very well. **dabbler** *(n).*

dad *or* **daddy** *(n)* an informal name for your father.

daffodil *(n)* a spring plant with yellow, bell-like flowers.

dagger *(n)* a short pointed knife, used as a weapon. *The dagger shown below was made by the ancient Sumerians around 4,000 B.C.*

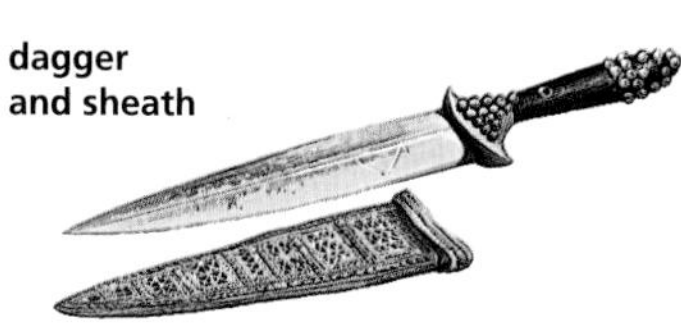

dagger and sheath

daily *(adj)* produced or happening every day. *A daily newspaper.*

dainty daintier daintiest *(adj)* small and delicate. **daintiness** *(n),* **daintily** *(adj).*

dairy **dairies** *(n)* a place where milk is bottled and milk products, such as cheese and yogurt, are made.

dais *(day-us) (n)* a raised platform at the end of a hall.

daisy **daisies** *(n)* a wild flower with white petals and a yellow center.

dam *(n)* a strong barrier built across a river to hold back water. *See* **beaver**.

damage damaging damaged
1 *(v)* to harm something.
2 *(n)* the harm that something does. *Flood damage.* **damaging** *(adj).*
3 **damages** *(plural n)* money given to someone by a court of law to try to make up for an injury or loss that they have suffered.

damp damper dampest *(adj)* slightly wet or moist. **dampness** *(n).*

damsel *(n) (old-fashioned)* a young woman.

dance dancing danced
1 *(v)* to move in time to music. **dancer** *(n),* **dancing** *(n).*
2 *(n)* a social event with music.
3 *(n)* the movements that go with a particular kind of music. *Square dance.*

dandruff *(n)* small white flakes of dead skin found in some people's hair.

danger
1 *(n)* a situation that is not safe. *The children are in danger.*
2 *(n)* something or someone that is not safe. *George's motorcycle is a danger on the road.* **dangerous** *(adj),* **dangerously** *(adv).*
3 **danger!** *(interject)* a warning word.

dangle dangling dangled *(v)* to swing or hang down. *Maurice dangled from the drainpipe.*

dank danker dankest *(adj)* unpleasantly wet or damp. *The cellar was cold and dank.*

dappled *(adj)* marked with spots, or with patches of light and dark. *A dappled pony.*

dare daring dared
1 *(v)* to challenge someone to do something. **dare** *(n).*
2 *(v)* to be brave enough to do something. *Do you dare to dive into the river?* **daring** *(adj),* **daringly** *(adv).*

daredevil *(n)* someone who takes risks and does dangerous things.

dark darker darkest
1 *(adj)* without light. *A dark room.*
2 *(adj)* containing more black than white. *Dark blue.*
3 *(n)* sunset. *I'm not allowed out after dark.*
4 *(n)* a place without light. *I can't see in the dark.*

darn darning darned *(v)* to mend a hole in a piece of clothing by sewing across it. **darning** *(n).*

dart darting darted
1 *(n)* a pointed object that you throw in the game of darts.
2 *(v)* to move forward suddenly. *Stefan darted out into the traffic.*
3 **darts** *(singular n)* a game in which players score points by throwing darts at a board with numbers on it.

dash dashes dashing dashed
1 *(n)* a small line (–) used as a punctuation mark or in Morse code.
2 *(v)* to move quickly. *I dashed to the store before it closed.*

data *(n)* information or facts. *The scientists examined all the data.*

database *(n)* a store of information held on a computer.

date dating dated
1 *(n)* a particular day, month, or year.
2 *(n)* an appointment to meet someone, especially a significant other.
3 *(v)* to go out with your boyfriend or girlfriend regularly.
4 *(v)* If something **dates from** a certain time, it was made then.
5 *(n)* a sticky brown fruit with a long thin pit inside it.
6 If something is **dated** or **out-of-date**, it is no longer fashionable.
7 If something is **up-to-date**, it is modern.

daughter *(n)* Someone's **daughter** is their female child.

daunt daunting daunted *(v)* If something **daunts** you, it frightens and discourages you. *We were a little daunted by the long climb ahead.*

dawdle dawdling dawdled
1 *(v)* to walk slowly. *The boys dawdled on their way to school.* **dawdler** *(n).*
2 *(v)* to do something slowly. *Jess dawdled over her breakfast.*

dawn dawning dawned
1 *(n)* sunrise or the beginning of the day. **dawn** *(v).*
2 *(n)* the start of something new. *The dawn of a new age.* **dawn** *(v).*
3 *(v)* If something **dawns on** you, you begin to understand it.

day
1 *(n)* a 24-hour period, from midnight to midnight.
2 *(n)* the light part of the day.

daydream daydreaming daydreamed
1 *(n)* a dream that you have while you are awake.
2 *(v)* to let your mind wander. **daydreamer** *(n).*

daze *(n)* If you are **in a daze**, you are stunned and unable to think clearly. **dazed** *(adj).*

dazzle dazzling dazzled
1 *(v)* to blind someone for a short time with a bright light. **dazzling** *(adj).*
2 *(v)* to amaze someone. *Tanya dazzled the audience with her playing.* **dazzling** *(adj).*

dead *(adj)* no longer alive.

deaden deadening deadened *(v)* to weaken or make less sharp.

dead end
1 *(n)* a street that is closed to traffic at one end.

a b c d e f g h i j k l m n o p q r s t u v w x y z

2 **dead-end** *(adj)* leading nowhere. *Pete had a dead-end job.*

deadline *(n)* a time by which a piece of work or a job must be finished.

deadlock *(n)* a situation where no decision can be reached.

deadly deadlier deadliest *(adj)* capable of killing or likely to kill.

deaf deafer deafest
1 *(adj)* If someone is **deaf**, they cannot hear anything, or they can hear very little. **deafness** *(n).*
2 *(adj)* If you are **deaf to** something, you choose not to hear it.

deafening *(adj)* very loud. *A deafening crash.* **deafeningly** *(adv).*

deal dealing dealt
1 *(v)* to do business. *Hugo deals in antiques.* **dealer** *(n).*
2 *(n)* a business agreement.
3 *(v)* When you **deal with** something, you sort it out.
4 *(v)* to give out cards to people playing a game. **dealer** *(n).*
5 *(v)* to cover a subject or an area. *Does that book deal with dogs?*

dear dearer dearest
1 *(adj)* highly valued or much loved. *A dear friend.* **dearly** *(adv).*
2 *(adj)* You use the word **Dear** when you write to someone. *Dear Sir.*
3 *(n)* a kind or sweet person.

death *(n)* the end of life.

deathly *(adj)* very pale, or very quiet. *His face went deathly white. There was a deathly hush.*

death trap *(n)* a place or a vehicle that is very dangerous.

debate debating debated
1 *(n)* a discussion between sides with different views, usually held in public.
2 *(v)* to consider or discuss something. *The family debated where to go on vacation.* **debatable** *(adj).*

debit debiting debited
1 *(n)* money that you owe. *My account shows a small debit.*
2 *(v)* If a bank account is **debited** with a sum of money, that money is taken out of the account.

debris *(deb-ree) (n)* the scattered remains of something.

debt *(rhymes with pet)*
1 *(n)* an amount of money that you owe.
2 If you are **in debt** to someone, you owe them money or a favor. **debtor** *(n).*

debug debugging debugged
1 *(v)* to remove the faults in a computer program.
2 *(v)* to remove secret listening devices from a place.

debut *(day-byoo) (n)* a first public appearance. *An acting debut.*

decade *(n)* a period of ten years.

decaffeinated *(adj)* If a drink, such as coffee or tea, is **decaffeinated**, it has had most of its caffeine removed.

decapitate decapitating decapitated *(v)* to remove the head of a person or creature.

decathlon *(n)* a competition made up of ten athletic events.

decay decaying decayed *(v)* to rot or break down. **decay** *(n).*

deceased *(adj)* dead.

deceive deceiving deceived *(v)* If someone **deceives** you, they trick you into believing something that is not true. **deceit** *(n),* **deceitful** *(adj),* **deceitfully** *(adv).*

decent
1 *(adj)* good or satisfactory. *Decent quality.* **decently** *(adv).*
2 *(adj)* respectable and proper. *Decent behavior.* **decency** *(n),* **decently** *(adv).*

deception *(n)* a trick that makes people believe something that is not true. **deceptive** *(adj),* **deceptively** *(adv).*

decibel *(n)* a unit for measuring the volume of sound.

decide deciding decided
1 *(v)* to make up your mind about something.
2 *(v)* to settle something. *The vote was decided by a show of hands.*

deciduous *(adj)* Trees that are **deciduous** shed their leaves every year.

decimal
1 *(adj)* A **decimal** system uses units of tens, hundreds, thousands, etc. *Decimal currency.*
2 **decimal point** *(n)* a dot separating whole numbers from tenths, hundredths, thousandths, etc. *The numbers 2.5, 3.75, and 4.624 all use decimal points.*
3 *(n)* a fraction, or a whole number and a fraction, written with a decimal point. *0.5, 6.37, and 82.54 are all decimals.*

decipher deciphering deciphered *(v)* to figure out something that is written in code or is hard to understand. *I can't decipher Jim's handwriting.* **decipherable** *(adj).*

decision *(n)* If you make a **decision**, you make up your mind about something.

decisive *(adj)* If you are **decisive**, you make choices quickly and easily. **decisively** *(adv).*

deck
1 *(n)* the floor of a boat or ship. *See* **ship**.
2 *(n)* a platform with railings on the outside of a building.
3 *(n)* a full set of playing cards

declare declaring declared
1 *(v)* to say something firmly. *Justin declared that he would never eat meat again.* **declaration** *(n).*
2 *(v)* to announce something formally. *The government declared that the war was over.* **declaration** *(n).*

decline declining declined
1 *(v)* to turn something down or to refuse something. *I'm afraid we must decline your invitation.*
2 *(v)* to get worse or to get smaller. *Ludwig's health began to decline. The population of our village is declining.* **decline** *(n).*

decode decoding decoded *(v)* to turn something that is written in code into ordinary language.

decompose decomposing decomposed *(v)* to rot or to decay. **decomposition** *(n).*

decongestant *(n)* a drug that unblocks your nose and chest when you have a cold. **decongestion** *(n).*

decontaminate decontaminating decontaminated *(v)* to remove radioactive or other harmful substances from something or some place. **decontamination** *(n).*

decorate decorating decorated
1 *(v)* If you **decorate** something, you add things to it to make it prettier. **decoration** *(n),* **decorative** *(adj).*
2 *(v)* to give a medal or badge to someone. *She was decorated for bravery in the war.* **decoration** *(n),* **decorator** *(n).*

decrease decreasing decreased
1 *(v)* to become less, smaller, or fewer. *I have noticed that enthusiasm for this project is rapidly decreasing.* **decreasing** *(adj),* **decreasingly** *(adv).*
2 *(n)* a loss or the amount by which something lessens.

decree decreeing decreed *(v)* to give an order that must be obeyed. *The teacher decreed that there should be no more cheating.* **decree** *(n).*

decrepit *(adj)* old and feeble.

dedicate dedicating dedicated
1 *(v)* If you **dedicate** yourself to something, you give a lot of time and energy to it. **dedication** *(n).*
2 *(v)* If you **dedicate** a book to someone, you put their name at the front of it to thank them or to show that you like and admire them. **dedication** *(n).*

deduce deducing deduced *(v)* to figure something out from clues or from what you know already.

deduct deducting deducted *(v)* to take away or subtract something, especially money. **deductible** *(adj).*

deduction
1 *(n)* something that is figured out from clues.
2 *(n)* an amount that is taken away or subtracted from a larger amount.

deed
1 *(n)* something that is done. *A good deed.*
2 *(n)* a legal document saying who owns a house or a piece of land.

deep deeper deepest
1 *(adj)* going a long way down. *A deep well.* **deepen** *(v).*
2 *(adj)* very intense and strong. *Deep sorrow.* **deepen** *(v),* **deeply** *(adv).*

deep-sea *(adj)* living or happening in the deeper part of an ocean. *Some deep-sea creatures, such as this viper fish, make their own light from luminous cells.*

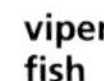
viper fish

deer deer *(n)* a fast-running wild animal with four legs. Male deer grow bony, branching antlers. *See* **antler**.

deface defacing defaced *(v)* to spoil the way something looks.

defeat defeating defeated
1 *(v)* to beat someone in a war or competition.
2 *(n)* If you suffer a **defeat**, you are beaten.

defect defecting defected
1 *(dee-fect) (n)* a fault or weakness in something or someone. **defective** *(adj).*
2 *(de-**fect**) (v)* to leave your country or political party and join another one.

defend defending defended
1 *(v)* to protect something or someone from harm. **defense** *(n).*
2 *(v)* to support someone or some idea by arguing. *The strikers defended their action.* **defense** *(n).*
3 *(v)* to try to stop goals from being scored in football, soccer, hockey, etc. **defense** *(n),* **defender** *(n).*

defendant *(n)* the person in a legal case who has been accused of a crime.

defensive
1 *(adj)* having to do with defending yourself or others. *The players took defensive action.*
2 *(adj)* If you are **defensive**, you feel and act as if someone is attacking or criticizing you. **defensiveness** *(n),* **defensively** *(adv).*

defer deferring deferred *(v)* to put something off until later. *The trip will be deferred until next year.*

defiant *(adj)* If you are **defiant**, you stand up to someone or to some organization and refuse to obey them. **defiance** *(n),* **defiantly** *(adv).*

deficient *(adj)* lacking something. *My diet is deficient in vitamin C.* **deficiency** *(n).*

deficit *(def-a-sit) (n)* If an account shows a **deficit**, more money has been spent than has come into it.

define defining defined *(v)* to explain or describe something exactly.

definite
1 *(adj)* certain. *Do we have a definite date for the test?* **definitely** *(adv).*
2 *(adj)* clear. *These drawings have a very definite outline.*
3 **definite article** *(n)* the grammatical term for "the." *See page 3.*

definition *(n)* an explanation of what a word or an idea means. *This dictionary has thousands of definitions.*

deflate deflating deflated
1 *(v)* to let the air out of something, such as a tire or balloon. **deflation** *(n).*
2 *(v)* to make someone feel less confident and important. *The teacher's comments deflated Don.*

deflect deflecting deflected *(v)* to make something go in a different direction. *The ball was deflected off the post into the goal.* **deflection** *(n).*

deforestation *(n)* the cutting down of forests.

deformed *(adj)* If something is **deformed**, it is a strange shape. *A deformed carrot.* **deformity** *(n).*

defraud defrauding defrauded *(v)* to cheat someone out of money, property, etc.

defrost defrosting defrosted
1 *(v)* to allow frozen food to thaw out completely.
2 *(v)* to remove ice from a refrigerator or freezer.

deft defter deftest *(adj)* skillful, quick, and neat. *Deft footwork.* **deftness** *(n),* **deftly** *(adv).*

defuse defusing defused
1 *(v)* When someone **defuses** a bomb, they make it safe so it cannot explode.
2 *(v)* If a situation is **defused**, it is made calmer.

defy defies defying defied
1 *(v)* If you **defy** a person or a rule, you refuse to obey them.
2 *(v)* to challenge someone, or to dare them to do something. *I defy you to eat all that cake!*

degenerate degenerating degenerated *(v)* to become worse. *The lesson degenerated into a riot.*

degrading *(adj)* If a situation or an activity is **degrading**, it makes you feel worthless or disgraced. **degradation** *(n),* **degrade** *(v).*

degree
1 *(n)* a unit for measuring temperature or angles. The symbol for a degree is °. *The temperature today reached 85° Fahrenheit. A 90° angle.*
2 *(n)* a qualification given by a college or university.

dehydrated
1 *(adj)* If you are **dehydrated**, you do not have enough water in your body. **dehydration** *(n),* **dehydrate** *(v).*
2 *(adj)* **Dehydrated** food has had the water removed from it. **dehydration** *(n),* **dehydrate** *(v).*

deity *(day-it-ee)* **deities** *(n)* a god or goddess.

dejected *(adj)* sad and depressed. **dejection** *(n),* **dejectedly** *(adv).*

delay delaying delayed
1 *(v)* to be late. *Don't delay or we'll miss the bus!* **delay** *(n).*
2 *(v)* to make someone late. *The accident delayed me.*
3 *(v)* to put something off until later. *Sara delayed doing her homework.*

delegate delegating delegated
1 *(del-e-gate) (v)* to give someone responsibility for doing a part of your job or task.

2 *(del-a-gut)* *(n)* someone who represents other people at a meeting.

delete deleting deleted *(v)* to remove something from a piece of writing or digital text. **deletion** *(n).*

deliberate deliberating deliberated
1 *(de-lib-er-ut)* *(adj)* planned, or intended. **deliberately** *(adv).*
2 *(de-lib-er-ate)* *(v)* to consider something carefully. **deliberation** *(n).*

delicate
1 *(adj)* finely made or sensitive. *A delicate instrument.* **delicately** *(adv).*
2 *(adj)* If a person is **delicate**, they are not very strong and easily become sick.

delicatessen *(n)* a store that sells different kinds of food already prepared.

delicious *(adj)* very pleasing to taste or smell. **deliciously** *(adv).*

delight delighting delighted
1 *(n)* great pleasure. **delightful** *(adj).*
2 *(v)* If something **delights** you, it pleases you very much. **delighted** *(adj).*

delinquent *(n)* a young person who is often in trouble with the police. **delinquency** *(n),* **delinquent** *(adj).*

delirious *(adj)* If you are **delirious**, you cannot think straight because you have a fever or you are extremely happy or tired. **deliriously** *(adv).*

deliver delivering delivered
1 *(v)* to take something to someone. **delivery** *(n).*
2 *(v)* When someone **delivers** a baby, they help it to be born. **delivery** *(n).*
3 *(v)* *(old-fashioned)* to rescue someone from something. *Deliver us from evil.* **deliverance** *(n).*

delta
1 *(n)* the fourth letter of the Greek alphabet. *See* **alphabet**.
2 *(n)* an area of land where a river deposits its sediment as it enters the sea, causing it to split into channels. *See* **river**.

deluge deluging deluged
1 *(n)* heavy rain or a flood.
2 *(v)* If a river or a storm **deluges** a place, it floods it.
3 *(v)* If people **deluge** you with letters, presents, etc., they send you a lot of them. **deluge** *(n).*

demand demanding demanded
1 *(v)* to claim something or to ask for something firmly. *We demand justice!*
2 *(n)* If there is a **demand** for something, many people want it.

demanding
1 *(adj)* If somebody is **demanding**, they are always wanting things and are hard to please.
2 *(adj)* A **demanding** job requires a lot of effort.

demeanor *(n)* the way that you behave.

demo *(n)* *(informal)* an example of a product not yet for sale.

democracy democracies
1 *(n)* a way of governing a country, in which the people choose their leaders in elections.
2 *(n)* a country that has an elected government.

democrat
1 *(n)* someone who agrees with the system of democracy.
2 **Democrat** *(n)* a supporter of the Democratic Party.

democratic
1 *(adj)* A **democratic** system is one where all people have equal rights. **democratically** *(adv).*
2 **Democratic Party** *(n)* the name of one of the main political parties in the United States.

demolish demolishes demolishing demolished
1 *(v)* to knock down something and break it up. *The builders demolished the old school.* **demolition** *(n).*
2 *(v)* *(informal)* to eat something quickly. *Will demolished his lunch in five minutes.*

demon *(n)* a devil or an evil spirit. **demonic** *(adj).*

demonstrate demonstrating demonstrated
1 *(v)* to show other people how to do something or how to use something. *Alice demonstrated how to use the computer.* **demonstration** *(n).*
2 *(v)* to join together with other people to protest against something. **demonstration** *(n),* **demonstrator** *(n).*
3 *(v)* to show something clearly. *Adam demonstrated how angry he felt by shouting loudly.* **demonstrative** *(adj).*

demoralized *(adj)* If you are **demoralized**, you feel depressed and hopeless.

den
1 *(n)* the home of a wild animal, such as a lion.
2 *(n)* a private place where you can work or play.

denim *(n)* strong cotton material used for making jeans and other articles of clothing. **denim** *(adj).*

denominator *(n)* In fractions, the **denominator** is the number under the line, which shows how many equal parts the whole number can be divided into. *In the fraction* $^7/_8$*, 8 is the denominator.*

denounce denouncing denounced *(v)* to say in public that someone has done something wrong.

dense denser densest
1 *(adj)* thick or crowded. *Dense fog.* **denseness** *(n),* **densely** *(adv).*
2 *(adj)* *(informal)* slow to understand. **denseness** *(n),* **densely** *(adv).*

density *(n)* The **density** of an object is how heavy or light it is for its size. Density is measured by dividing an object's mass by its volume.

dent denting dented *(v)* to damage something by making a hollow in it. **dent** *(n).*

dental *(adj)* having to do with your teeth. *Dental hygiene.*

dentist *(n)* someone who is trained to check and treat teeth.

denture
1 *(n)* a plate that fits into your mouth, with a false tooth or false teeth attached to it.
2 **dentures** *(plural n)* a set of false teeth.

deny denies denying denied
1 *(v)* to say that something is not true. *Laura denied that she had taken the money.* **denial** *(n).*
2 *(v)* to stop someone from having something or going somewhere. *The guards denied us entry to the hall.*

deodorant *(n)* a substance used to cover up or get rid of unpleasant smells.

depart departing departed *(v)* to leave, especially to go on a journey. **departure** *(n).*

department *(n)* a part of a store, hospital, university, etc. **departmental** *(adj).*

depend depending depended
1 *(v)* If something **depends on** something else, it is related to it or influenced by it in some way. *The result depends on the skill of our team.* **dependent** *(adj).*
2 *(v)* to rely on someone or something. *We're depending on your help.* **dependence** *(n),* **dependable** *(adj),* **dependent** *(adj).*

dependant *(n)* someone who is looked after and supported by somebody else.

depict depicting depicted *(v)* to show something in a picture, or by using words.

deplorable *(adj)* shockingly bad. *Louis has deplorable taste in clothes.* **deplore** *(v)*, **deplorably** *(adv)*.

deport deporting deported *(v)* to send someone back to their own country. *The terrorists were deported to face trial at home.* **deportation** *(n)*.

deportment *(n)* the way that you stand and move.

depose deposing deposed *(v)* If a king or queen is **deposed**, they have their power taken from them. **deposition** *(n)*.

deposit depositing deposited
1 *(n)* a sum of money given as the first part of a payment, or as a promise to pay for something. **deposit** *(v)*.
2 *(n)* a natural layer of rock, sand, or mineral found in the ground.
3 *(v)* to place, or to lay down. *Dad deposited the shopping bags on the table.*

depot *(deep-oh)* *(n)* a bus station or railroad station.

depreciate depreciating depreciated *(v)* to lose value. **depreciation** *(n)*.

depressed *(adj)* sad and gloomy. **depress** *(v)*, **depressing** *(adj)*.

depression
1 *(n)* a mental illness that makes a person feel very sad and unmotivated.
2 *(n)* an area of air at low pressure that may bring rain.
3 *(n)* a time when businesses do badly and many people are poor.
4 *(n)* a shallow dip in the ground.

deprive depriving deprived *(v)* to prevent someone from having something, or to take something away from someone. **deprivation** *(n)*, **deprived** *(adj)*.

depth
1 *(n)* deepness, or a measurement of deepness.
2 If you study something **in depth**, you study it thoroughly.
3 If you are **out of your depth**, you cannot understand what is going on.

deputy deputies *(n)* someone who helps somebody else in their job and takes their place when they are ill or absent. **deputize** *(v)*.

deranged *(adj)* insane.

derelict *(adj)* neglected and in ruins.

derive deriving derived
1 *(v)* to take or receive something. *Angelica derives a lot of pleasure from her work.*
2 *(v)* If a word is **derived** from another word, it has developed from it. *The word dictionary is derived from the Latin word "dictio," meaning word or phrase.* **derivation** *(n)*.

descant *(n)* a tune that is played or sung above the main tune.

descend descending descended
1 *(v)* to climb down or go down to a lower level. **descent** *(n)*.
2 *(v)* If you are **descended** from someone, you belong to a later generation of their family. **descendant** *(n)*

describe describing described *(v)* to say or write what something is like. **description** *(n)*, **descriptive** *(adj)*.

desert deserting deserted
1 *(dez-urt)* *(n)* a sandy or stony area where hardly any plants grow because there is so little rain. *The map shows some of the main deserts of the world and is surrounded by examples of desert wildlife.* **desert** *(adj)*.
2 *(de-zert)* *(v)* to abandon someone, or to run away from the army. **deserter** *(n)*.

deserve deserving deserved *(v)* to earn something because of the way that you behave. *Uma deserves a reward for her hard work.*

design designing designed
1 *(v)* to draw something that could be built or made. **designer** *(n)*.
2 *(n)* the shape or style of something.

desire *(n)* a strong wish or need for something or someone. **desire** *(v)*, **desirable** *(adj)*.

desk *(n)* a table, often with drawers, used for working at or writing on.

desktop *(n)* the main screen display on a computer, from which you can run programs and open windows.

desolate
1 *(adj)* deserted, or uninhabited. *A desolate village.* **desolation** *(n)*.
2 *(adj)* sad and lonely. *After my friend left, I felt really desolate.* **desolation** *(n)*, **desolately** *(adv)*.

deserts and desert wildlife

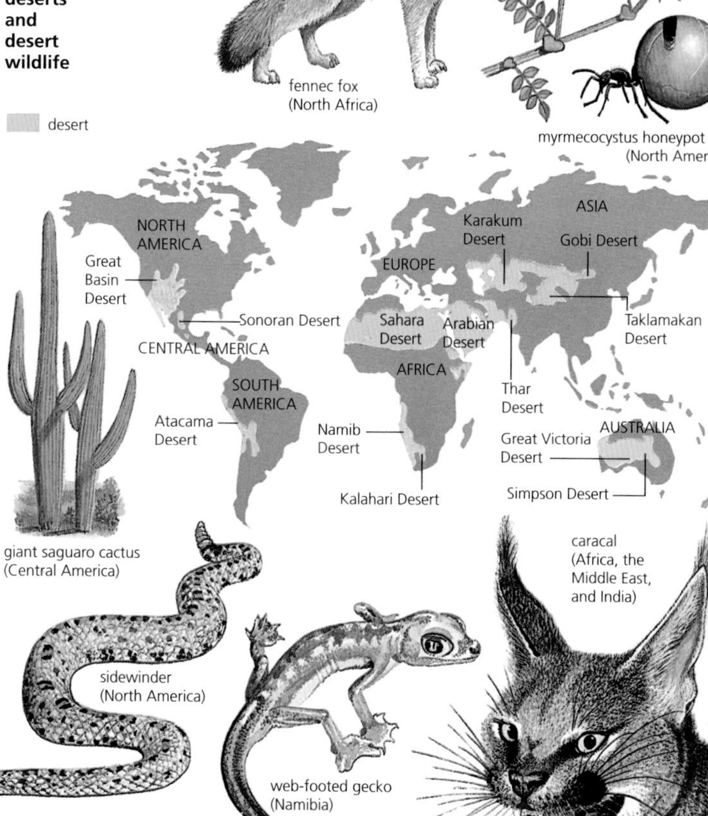

Sturt's desert pea (Australia)

fennec fox (North Africa)

myrmecocystus honeypot a (North Americ

giant saguaro cactus (Central America)

caracal (Africa, the Middle East, and India)

sidewinder (North America)

web-footed gecko (Namibia)

despair despairing despaired *(v)* to lose hope completely. *Harry despaired of getting home on time.* **despair** *(n)*, **despairing** *(adj)*.

desperate
1 *(adj)* If you are **desperate**, you will do anything to change your situation. **desperation** *(n)*, **desperately** *(adv)*.
2 *(adj)* dangerous or difficult. *A desperate shortage of medicine.* **desperately** *(adv)*.

despise despising despised *(v)* If you **despise** someone, you dislike them and have no respect for them.

despite *(prep)* in spite of. *Ralph won the race despite falling off his bike.*

dessert *(duh-**zert**)* *(n)* the sweet course of a meal.

destination *(n)* the place that someone or something is traveling to.

destiny destinies *(n)* Your **destiny** is your fate or the future events in your life. *Cinderella's destiny was to marry a handsome prince.*

destitute *(adj)* A **destitute** person has no money to live on.

destroy destroying destroyed *(v)* to ruin something or someone completely. **destruction** *(n)*.

destructive *(adj)* causing lots of damage and unhappiness. **destructively** *(adv)*.

detach
detaches detaching detached *(v)* to separate one part of something from the rest of it. **detachable** *(adj)*.

detached
1 *(adj)* A **detached** house stands by itself.
2 *(adj)* If you are **detached**, you are able to stand back from a situation and not get too involved in it. **detachment** *(n)*.

detail
1 *(n)* a small part of something larger.
2 *(n)* delicate work. *Iona's paintings are full of detail.* **detailed** *(adj)*.
3 *(plural n)* If you ask for **details** about something, you want information about it.

detain detaining detained *(v)* to keep somebody back when they want to go. *The police detained two men for questioning.*

detect detecting detected *(v)* to notice, or to discover something. *I detected a strange smell in the house.* **detection** *(n)*.

detective *(n)* someone who investigates crimes, usually for the police.

detention
1 *(n)* a punishment in which a student has to stay in school when other students are free.
2 *(n)* If someone is held **in detention**, they are kept prisoner.
3 **detention center** *(n)* a type of prison for young offenders.

deter deterring deterred *(v)* to prevent or discourage someone from doing something.

detergent *(n)* liquid or powder used for cleaning things.

deteriorate
deteriorating deteriorated *(v)* to get worse. **deterioration** *(n)*.

determined *(adj)* If you are **determined** to do something, you have made a firm decision to do it. **determination** *(n)*.

deterrent *(n)* something that stops you from doing something because you are afraid of the consequences. *Burglar alarms are effective deterrents against crime.*

detest detesting detested *(v)* If you **detest** something or someone, you dislike them very much. **detestable** *(adj)*.

detonate detonating detonated *(v)* to set off an explosion. **detonator** *(n)*, **detonation** *(n)*.

detour *(n)* a longer, alternative route to somewhere, usually taken to avoid an obstacle.

detract detracting detracted *(v)* to make something less enjoyable or valuable. *The rain detracted from the pleasure of our walk.*

detrimental *(adj)* harmful. *Smoking is detrimental to your health.*

deuce *(jooss)* *(n)* In tennis, the score of **deuce** means that both players have 40 points.

devalue devaluing devalued
1 *(v)* to reduce the value of a currency in relation to another currency or to gold. **devaluation** *(n)*.
2 *(v)* to make something worth less than it was. *Why do you always devalue my efforts?*

devastated
1 *(adj)* very badly damaged or destroyed. *The area was devastated by the floods.* **devastation** *(n)*, **devastate** *(v)*.
2 *(adj)* shocked and distressed. *I was devastated by the dreadful news.* **devastating** *(adj)*.

develop developing developed
1 *(v)* to grow. *The boys' friendship developed slowly.* **development** *(n)*.
2 *(v)* to build on something, or make something grow. *The farmer has decided to develop the field as a campsite.* **developer** *(n)*, **development** *(n)*.
3 *(v)* When photographic film was **developed**, it was treated with chemicals to bring out the pictures that had been taken.

deviate deviating deviated *(v)* to do something different from what is normal or acceptable. *The cyclist deviated from his usual route.* **deviation** *(n)*, **deviant** *(adj)*.

device
1 *(n)* a piece of equipment, which does a particular job. *This is a useful device for taking the tops off bottles.*
2 If you are **left to your own devices**, you can do what you want.

devil
1 *(n)* In many religions, **the Devil** is the main spirit of evil.
2 *(n)* If you call someone a **devil**, you mean that they are naughty or wicked.

devious *(adj)* A **devious** person keeps their thoughts and actions secret, and cannot be trusted. **deviousness** *(n)*, **deviously** *(adv)*.

devise devising devised *(v)* to think something up or invent something. *Let's devise a way to escape.*

devoid *(adj)* without something, or empty of something. *The house was devoid of furniture.*

devolution *(n)* the handing over of some power from a central government to a local government.

devoted *(adj)* loyal and loving. **devotion** *(n)*, **devotedly** *(adv)*.

devour devouring devoured *(v)* to eat something quickly and greedily.

devout *(adj)* deeply religious. **devoutness** *(n)*, **devoutly** *(adv)*.

dew *(n)* small drops of moisture that form overnight on cool surfaces outside. **dewy** *(adj)*.

dexterity *(n)* skill, especially in using your hands. *Simon showed great dexterity in modeling the clay.* **dexterous** *(adj)*.

diabetes *(dye-a-**bee**-tees)* *(n)* a disease in which you have too much sugar in your blood. **diabetic** *(dye-a-**bet**-ik)* *(adj)*.

diabolical
1 *(adj)* extremely wicked. *A diabolical plan.*
2 *(adj)* having to do with the devil. **diabolical** *(adj)* **diabolically** *(adv)*.

diagnose diagnosing diagnosed *(v)* to discover what disease a patient has or what the cause of a problem is. **diagnosis** *(n)*.

diagonal *(adj)* A **diagonal** line is a straight line joining opposite corners of a square or rectangle. **diagonally** *(adv)*.

diagram *(n)* a drawing or plan that explains something simply. **diagrammatic** *(adj)*.

dial dialing dialed
1 *(n)* the face on a clock, watch, or measuring instrument.
2 *(v)* to enter a telephone number by pressing buttons on a telephone.
3 **dial tone** *(n) (old fashioned)* the sound you should hear when you first pick up the telephone.

dialect *(n)* a way of speaking that belongs to a particular place.

dialogue *(n)* conversation, especially in a play, movie, or book.

diameter *(dye-**am**-it-er) (n)* a straight line through the center of a circle, from one side to another. *See* **circle**.

diamond
1 *(n)* a very hard, clear, precious stone. *See* **mineral**.
2 *(n)* a shape with four equal sides, like a square standing on one of its corners.
3 **diamonds** *(plural n)* one of the four suits in a pack of cards.

diaper *(n)* a piece of soft, absorbent clothing, worn as underwear by babies and young children.

diaphragm *(dye-a-fram)*
1 *(n)* the wall of muscle between your chest and your stomach. *See* **respiration**.
2 *(n)* the thin disk in a telephone or microphone that vibrates to change voice signals into electrical signals. *See* **microphone**.

diarrhea *(dye-a-ree-a) (n)* a stomach illness that causes normally solid waste to become runny.

diary diaries *(n)* a book in which people write down things that happen each day, either to use as a record or to plan ahead.

dice dicing diced
1 *(v)* to cut something, such as vegetables, into small cubes. *Dice the carrots.* **diced** *(adj)*.
2 *(plural n)* six-sided cubes with a different number of spots on each face, used in games. The singular of dice is die, although many people say dice.

dictate dictating dictated
1 *(v)* to talk aloud so that someone can write down what you say. **dictation** *(n)*.
2 *(v)* to control something. *Mom dictates our bedtimes.*

dictator *(n)* someone who has complete personal control of a country. **dictatorship** *(n)*.

dictionary dictionaries *(n)* a book like this one that explains what words mean and shows you how to spell them.

didgeridoo *or* **didjeridu** *(dij-er-ree-**doo**) (n)* a long decorated tube, made from a hollowed-out branch or tree trunk, which is played as a musical instrument by Aborigines.

didgeridoo

die dying died
1 *(v)* to stop living, or come to an end.
2 *(v)* If you are **dying** to do something, you really want to do it.
3 *(n)* the singular form of the word dice.

diesel *(dee-sull) (n)* a fuel used in diesel engines that is heavier than gasoline.

diesel engine *(n)* a type of engine used in trains and motor vehicles. In a diesel engine, the fuel is ignited by heat from compressed air rather than by a spark plug.

diet dieting dieted
1 *(n)* Your **diet** is what you eat. **dietary** *(adj)*.
2 *(v)* When you **diet**, you choose what you eat in order to lose weight.
3 *(n)* a controlled eating plan.

difference
1 *(n)* the way in which things are not like each other. *What's the difference between me and you?* **differ** *(v)*, **different** *(adj)*, **differently** *(adv)*.
2 *(n)* The **difference** between two numbers is the amount by which one is less or more than the other. *The difference between 5 and 2 is 3.*

difficult
1 *(adj)* not easy. *A difficult exam.*
2 *(adj)* A **difficult** person is not easy to get along with.

difficulty difficulties *(n)* a problem.

dig digging dug
1 *(v)* to use a shovel to move earth.
2 *(n)* a push or a poke.
3 *(n)* an unkind remark.
4 *(n)* an archaeological excavation.

digestion *(n)* the process of breaking down food in the stomach so that it can be absorbed into the blood. *This diagram shows the main organs used in human digestion.* **digest** *(v)*, **digestive** *(adj)*.

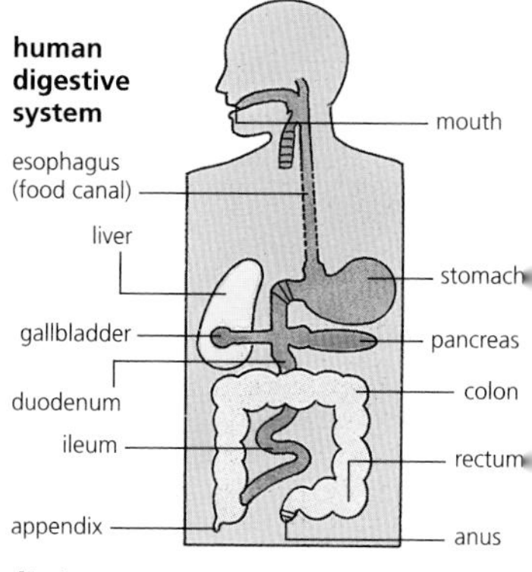

digit *(dij-it)*
1 *(n)* a finger.
2 *(n)* a single figure. *625 is a three digit number.*

digital
1 *(adj)* **Digital** information is represented as a series of ones and zeros. **digitize** *(v)*, **digitally** *(adv)*.
2 *(adj)* **Digital** equipment works by using information stored as a series of ones and zeros. *A digital camera.*
3 *(adj)* A **digital** display shows time, speed, etc. in numbers.

dignified *(adj)* calm, serious, and in control. **dignity** *(n)*.

dilapidated *(adj)* shabby and falling to pieces. **dilapidation** *(n)*.

dilemma *(n)* If you are **in a dilemma**, you have to choose between alternatives.

diligent *(adj)* hard-working. **diligence** *(n)*, **diligently** *(adv)*.

dilute diluting diluted *(v)* When you **dilute** a liquid, you make it weaker by adding water. **dilution** *(n)*.

dimension *(n)* The **dimensions** of an object are its measurements or its size. Objects have three dimensions: length, width, and height.

diminish diminishes diminishing diminished *(v)* If something **diminishes**, it becomes smaller or weaker. *A diminishing flame.*

dimple *(n)* a small dent in a person's cheek or chin. **dimpled** *(adj)*.

dine dining dined *(v)* to have a meal in a formal way. *Mr. and Mrs. Cartwright dined at eight.* **diner** *(n)*.

Some words that begin with a "di" sound are spelled "dy."

mast
kicking strap
mainsheet (controls the sail)
boom
spreader
centerboard
thwart (seat)
hiking strap
tiller
mainsheet traveler
rudder
tiller extension
transom
sailing dinghy

dinghy dinghies *(n)* a small open boat.

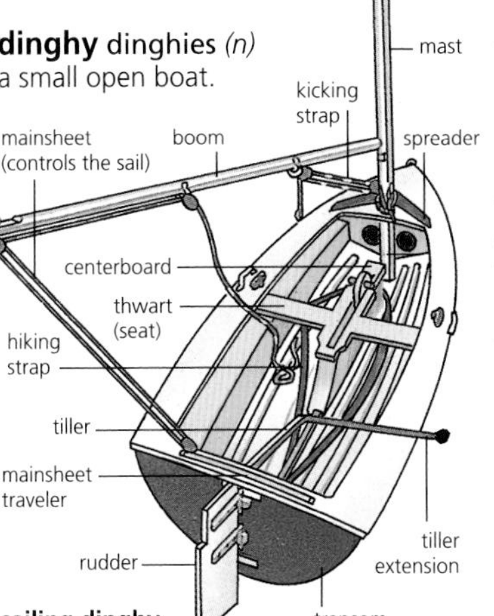

dingy *(din-jee)* **dingier dingiest** *(adj)* dull and shabby. *A dingy room.*

dinner
1 *(n)* the main meal of the day, eaten in the evening.
2 *(n)* a formal banquet.

dinosaur *(n)* the general name for the large, land-living reptiles that existed in prehistoric times. *The picture shows a range of dinosaurs and the periods when they existed.*

dip dipping dipped
1 *(v)* to push something briefly into a liquid. *Dip your brush in the water.*
2 *(v)* to slope downward. **dip** *(n).*
3 *(n)* If you take a **dip**, you have a short swim.
4 *(n)* a savory sauce into which you dip raw vegetables, chips, etc.

diploma *(n)* a certificate showing that you have gained a qualification in a particular academic subject.

diplomat *(n)* a person who represents their country's government in a foreign country. **diplomacy** *(n).*

diplomatic
1 *(adj)* If you are **diplomatic**, you are tactful and good at dealing with people. **diplomacy** *(n).*
2 *(adj)* having to do with being a diplomat. *The diplomatic service.*

dire direr direst *(adj)* disastrous. *Dire consequences.*

direct directing directed
1 *(adj)* in a straight line, or by the shortest route. **directly** *(adv).*
2 *(v)* to supervise people, especially in a play or movie.
3 *(v)* to tell someone the way to go. *Please direct me to the hotel.*
4 *(adj)* If someone is **direct**, they have a very straightforward manner. **directly** *(adv).*

direction
1 *(n)* the way that someone or something is moving or pointing. *We traveled in a westerly direction.*
2 **directions** *(plural n)* instructions. *Follow the directions carefully.*

director
1 *(n)* one of the senior people in charge of a company.
2 *(n)* the person in charge of making a movie or television program.

directory directories *(n)* a book that gives addresses, phone numbers, etc. in alphabetical order.

dirty dirtier dirtiest
1 *(adj)* not clean. **dirt** *(n).*
2 *(adj)* unfair. *A dirty trick.*
3 *(n)* **Dirty jokes** are rude jokes that may offend some people.

disabled *(adj)* People who are **disabled** are restricted in what they can do, usually because of an illness or injury. **disability** *(n).*

dinosaurs

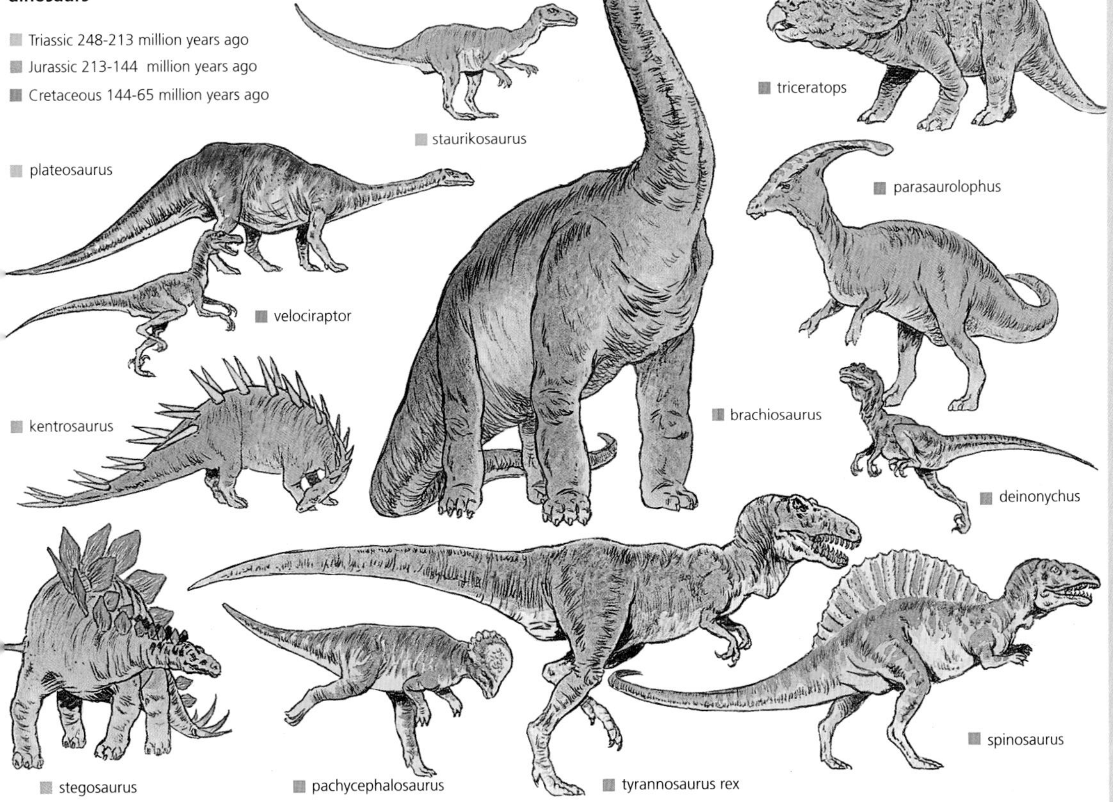

Triassic 248-213 million years ago
Jurassic 213-144 million years ago
Cretaceous 144-65 million years ago
staurikosaurus
triceratops
plateosaurus
parasaurolophus
velociraptor
kentrosaurus
brachiosaurus
deinonychus
stegosaurus
pachycephalosaurus
tyrannosaurus rex
spinosaurus

disadvantage
1 *(n)* something that causes a problem or makes life more difficult.
2 *(n)* loss or damage. *It is to your disadvantage if you turn up late for the meeting.* **disadvantaged** *(adj).*
3 *(adj)* People who are **disadvantaged** are poor and lack opportunities.

disagree disagreeing disagreed *(v)* If you **disagree** with someone, you do not think the same way as they do. **disagreement** *(n).*

disappear
disappearing disappeared *(v)* to go out of sight. **disappearance** *(n).*

disappoint
disappointing disappointed *(v)* to let someone down by failing to do what they expected. **disappointment** *(n),* **disappointed** *(adj).*

disapprove disapproving disapproved *(v)* If you **disapprove** of something, you do not think it is a good thing. **disapproval** *(n).*

disarm disarming disarmed
1 *(v)* to take weapons from somebody.
2 *(v)* If a country **disarms**, it gives up its weapons. **disarmament** *(n).*
3 *(v)* If someone **disarms** you, they stop you from feeling angry.

disaster
1 *(n)* a very serious accident, earthquake, etc. in which many die.
2 *(n)* If something is a **disaster**, it goes completely wrong. **disastrous** *(adj),* **disastrously** *(adv).*

disbelief *(n)* refusal to believe something. *My story was greeted with total disbelief.* **disbelieve** *(v).*

disc *(n)* another spelling of disk.

discard discarding discarded *(v)* to throw something away.

discharge discharging discharged
1 *(diss-**charge**)* *(v)* to tell someone officially that they can go.
2 *(diss-**charge**)* *(v)* to release a substance into the open. *The factory discharged chemicals into the river.* **discharge** *(**diss**-charge)* *(n).*

disciple *(n)* someone who follows the teachings of a leader or a set of ideas.

discipline *(n)* control over the way that you or other people behave. **discipline** *(v),* **disciplinary** *(adj).*

disc jockey *(n)* someone who plays music on the radio, at a disco, etc.

disco
1 *(n)* a nightclub in which music is played for dancing.
2 *(adj)* a type of music sometimes played at clubs.

disconnect
disconnecting disconnected
1 *(v)* to separate things that are joined together. **disconnection** *(n).*
2 *(v)* If something, such as an internet connection or electricity supply, is **disconnected**, it is cut off.

discontented *(adj)* not satisfied. **discontent** *(n),* **discontentedly** *(adv).*

discontinue
discontinuing discontinued *(v)* to stop doing something that you have been doing regularly.

discord
1 *(n)* disagreement between two or more people.
2 *(n)* a mixture of musical notes that sounds unpleasant. **discordant** *(adj).*

discount *(n)* a price cut.

discourage
discouraging discouraged *(v)* If you **discourage** someone from doing something, you persuade them not to do it. **discouragement** *(n).*

discouraged *(adj)* If you are **discouraged**, you lose your enthusiasm or confidence.

discover discovering discovered
1 *(v)* to find something. *We discovered the treasure.* **discovery** *(n).*
2 *(v)* to find out about something. *I soon discovered that Abigail was lying.* **discovery** *(n).*

discreet *(adj)* If you are **discreet**, you know the right thing to say and can be trusted to keep a secret. **discretion** *(n),* **discreetly** *(adv).*

discriminate
discriminating discriminated
1 *(v)* If you **discriminate** against someone, you are prejudiced against them and treat them unfairly. **discrimination** *(n).*
2 *(adj)* A **discriminating** person knows the difference between things of good and bad quality. **discrimination** *(n).*

discus *(**dis**-kuss)* discuses *or* disci *(n)* a large, weighted disk that is thrown in athletics events. *This statue shows an ancient Greek athlete throwing the discus. Also see* **track and field**.

discus thrower

discuss *(dis-**kuss**)* discusses discussing discussed *(v)* to talk something over. *Can we meet to discuss the new plans?* **discussion** *(n).*

disease
1 *(n)* an illness. *Measles is an infectious disease.*
2 *(n)* sickness. *Disease spread throughout the city.* **diseased** *(adj).*

disgrace disgracing disgraced
1 *(v)* If you **disgrace yourself**, you do something that other people disapprove of and that makes you feel ashamed.
2 *(n)* If something is a **disgrace**, it is very bad indeed. **disgraceful** *(adj).*

disguise disguising disguised
1 *(v)* to hide something. *Sebastian tried to disguise his boredom.*
2 *(n)* If you put on a **disguise**, you dress up to hide your identity.

disgusting *(adj)* very unpleasant and offensive to others. **disgust** *(n),* **disgustingly** *(adv).*

dish dishes dishing dished
1 *(n)* a bowl used for cooking or for serving food.
2 *(n)* one course of a meal. *A chicken dish.*
3 **dish out** *(v)* If you **dish something out**, you divide it among several people.

disheveled *(adj)* very untidy.

dishonest *(adj)* not truthful. **dishonesty** *(n),* **dishonestly** *(adv).*

disillusion
disillusioning disillusioned *(v)* If you **disillusion** someone, you destroy their ideas about something.

disinfectant *(n)* a household chemical used to kill germs. **disinfect** *(v).*

disintegrate
disintegrating disintegrated
1 *(v)* to break into small pieces. *The dirt mound disintegrated when Max stomped on it.* **disintegration** *(n).*
2 *(v)* to break up. *Emily is sad because her parents' marriage is disintegrating.*

disjointed *(adj)* unconnected or not flowing smoothly.

disk *or* **disc**
1 *(n)* a flat, circular shape.
2 *(n)* a piece of plastic, used for recording music or information. *See* **compact disc**.

dislike disliking disliked *(v)* If you **dislike** something or someone, you do not like them. **dislike** *(n).*

dislocate dislocating dislocated *(v)* If you **dislocate** a bone, it comes out of its usual place. **dislocation** *(n).*

dismal
1 *(adj)* gloomy and sad.
2 *(adj)* dreadful. *A dismal failure.*

dismantle dismantling dismantled *(v)* to take something apart.

Some words that begin with a "dis" sound are spelled "dys."

lismayed *(adj)* If you are lismayed, you are upset and vorried by something. **dismay** *(n)*.

lismiss
lismisses dismissing dismissed
(v) to allow people to leave. *Our teacher dismissed us early.*
(v) to fire someone from neir job. **dismissal** *(n)*.
(v) to put something out f your mind. *I've dismissed ne idea of having a party.*

lisobedient *(adj)*
you are **disobedient**, you do not o as you are told. **disobedience** *(n)*, **lisobediently** *(adv)*.

lisorderly
(adj) untidy and disorganized. *disorderly desk.*
(adj) A **disorderly** person is ncontrolled and possibly violent.

lisorganized *(adj)* mixed up nd not in order. **disorganization** *(n)*.

lisown disowning disowned *(v)*
you **disown** someone, you act s though you do not know them.

lispatch
lispatches dispatching dispatched
(v) to send something or omebody off. *We dispatched Incle Albert to catch his train.*
(n) a message or a report.

lispensary dispensaries *(n)*
place where medicines are repared and given out. **dispense** *(v)*.

lisperse
lispersing dispersed *(v)* to scatter. *he crowd dispersed.* **dispersal** *(n)*.

lisplace displacing displaced
(v) to take the place of something r somebody else. *When you sit n the bathtub, you displace some vater.* **displacement** *(n)*.
(v) to move someone or omething from their usual place.

lisplay displaying displayed
(v) to show something. *o displayed no emotion s she read my note.*
(n) a public show or exhibition.
(n) special behavior y an animal to attract mate. *This picture hows part of the ourtship display f a bird f paradise.*
(n) a screen r panel on lectronic quipment, howing nformation.

courtship display

disposable *(adj)*
suitable for throwing away after use. *Disposable plates.* **dispose** *(v)*.

disprove disproving disproved *(v)*
If you **disprove** something, you show that it cannot be true.

dispute disputing disputed
1 *(n)* a disagreement.
2 *(v)* If you **dispute** what someone says, you say that you think they are wrong.

disqualify disqualifies disqualifying disqualified *(v)*
to prevent someone from taking part in an activity, often because they have broken a rule. **disqualification** *(n)*.

disregard disregarding disregarded *(v)* to take no notice of someone or something. **disregard** *(n)*.

disreputable *(adj)*
If someone or something is **disreputable**, they are known for being bad in some way. **disrepute** *(n)*.

disrespect *(n)* lack of respect, or rudeness. **disrespectful** *(adj)*, **disrespectfully** *(adv)*.

disrupt disrupting disrupted *(v)*
to disturb or break up something that is happening. *Josh disrupted the class by shouting loudly.* **disruption** *(n)*, **disruptive** *(adj)*.

dissatisfied *(adj)* unhappy or discontented. **dissatisfaction** *(n)*.

dissect dissecting dissected *(v)*
to cut something up and examine it. **dissection** *(n)*.

dissident *(n)*
someone who disagrees with the laws of a country or other organization. *A political dissident.* **dissidence** *(n)*.

dissolve dissolving dissolved
1 *(v)* to mix with liquid. *Does this tablet dissolve in water?*
2 *(v)* If a partnership is **dissolved**, it is officially ended. **dissolution** *(n)*.

distance
1 *(n)* the amount of space between two places.
2 If you see something **in the distance**, it is a long way off. **distant** *(adj)*.

distill distilling distilled *(v)* to purify a liquid, by heating it until it turns into a gas and then letting it cool to form a liquid again. **distillation** *(n)*.

distinct
1 *(adj)* very clear. *Juliette has a distinct French accent.* **distinctly** *(adv)*.
2 *(adj)* clearly different. *The original recording is quite distinct from the cheap copies.* **distinctive** *(adj)*.

distinction
1 *(n)* a clear difference.
2 *(n)* something that makes a person or object different or unusual. *Jenny has the distinction of being the best player on the soccer team.*

distinguish distinguishes distinguishing distinguished *(v)*
to tell the difference between things. *Can you distinguish between a frog and a toad?* **distinguishable** *(adj)*.

distinguished *(adj)*
A **distinguished** person is famous for the important things they have done.

distort distorting distorted
1 *(v)* to twist something out of shape. **distortion** *(n)*, **distorted** *(adj)*.
2 *(v)* to try to twist the truth.

distract distracting distracted *(v)*
If something or someone **distracts** you, they draw your attention away from what you are doing. **distraction** *(n)*.

distress
1 *(n)* a feeling of great pain or sadness. **distressed** *(adj)*, **distressing** *(adj)*.
2 **distress signal** *(n)* a radio message, flare, etc. from a ship or aircraft to show that it is in trouble.

distribute distributing distributed
1 *(v)* to give things out. *Juan distributed the cookies among his friends.* **distribution** *(n)*.
2 *(v)* to deliver products to various places. **distribution** *(n)*.

distributor
1 *(n)* a person or company that delivers products to various places.
2 *(n)* the part of a car engine that revolves, sending electricity from the ignition system to fire each cylinder in turn.

district *(n)* an area or region.

distrust distrusting distrusted *(v)*
If you **distrust** someone, you think that they cannot be trusted. **distrust** *(n)*, **distrustful** *(adj)*, **distrustfully** *(adv)*.

disturb disturbing disturbed
1 *(v)* to interrupt somebody when they are doing something.
2 *(v)* to worry someone.

disturbed *(adj)* If someone is **disturbed**, they are unstable and have difficulty in controlling their behavior.

ditch ditches ditching ditched
1 *(n)* a long, narrow channel that drains water away.
2 *(v)* If a pilot **ditches** his plane, he makes an emergency landing in water.
3 *(v)* *(slang)* If one person **ditches** another, they leave them suddenly. *Jodie ditched her boyfriend last week.*

a b c d e f g h i j k l m n o p q r s t u v w x y z

ditto *(adj)* **Ditto** marks are used in lists to show that what is written above is repeated on the line below.

dive diving dived *or* dove
1 *(v)* to plunge headfirst into water with your arms stretched out in front of you. **dive** *(n)*.
2 *(v)* to drop down suddenly. *The kite dived to the ground.* **dive** *(n)*.

diver *(n)*
someone who uses a breathing apparatus to work or explore underwater. *See* **scuba diving**.

diverse *(adj)*
varied or assorted.
Hal has a diverse collection of friends.

diversion *(n)*
something that takes your mind off other things.

divert diverting diverted
1 *(v)* If someone **diverts** the traffic, they make it take a different route.
2 *(v)* When you **divert** someone's attention from something, you stop them from thinking about it.

divide dividing divided
1 *(v)* to split into parts.
2 *(v)* In math, if you **divide** one number by a second number, you work out how many times the second number will go into the first. *12 divided by 4 is 3* or $12 \div 4 = 3$.
3 *(v)* to share something out.
Let's divide the food between us.

divine divining divined
1 *(adj)* having to do with God, or like a god.
2 *(v)* to discover something by instinct, magic, or guesswork. **divination** *(n)*.
3 *(adj) (informal)* wonderful.

division
1 *(n)* the act of dividing one number by another.
2 *(n)* one of the parts into which something large has been divided. *The research division of the company.*
3 *(n)* something that separates.

divorce *(n)*
the ending of a marriage by a court of law. **divorce** *(v)*, **divorced** *(adj)*.

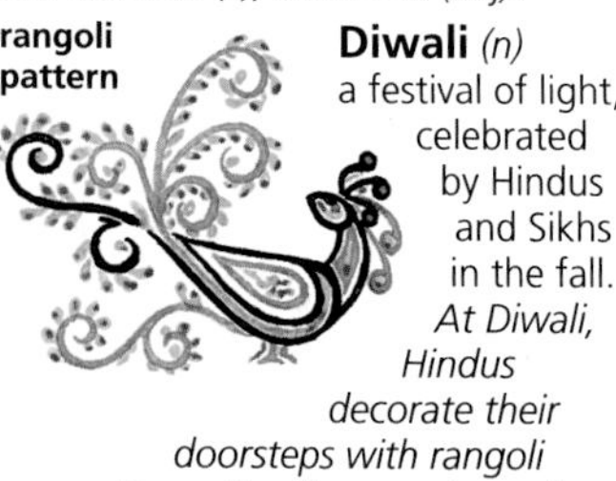
rangoli pattern

Diwali *(n)*
a festival of light, celebrated by Hindus and Sikhs in the fall. *At Diwali, Hindus decorate their doorsteps with rangoli patterns like the one shown here.*

dizzy dizzier dizziest
(adj) If you feel **dizzy**, you feel giddy and confused.

D.J. *short for* **disc jockey**.

DNA *(n)* the molecule that carries information, which gives living things their special characteristics. The letters stand for deoxyribonucleic acid. *The diagram shows the linked strands of DNA that separate, as a cell divides, to produce two identical new cells.*

DNA

do does doing did done
1 *(v)* to perform an action.
Dad was doing the dishes.
2 *(v)* to fix or arrange something.
Have you done your hair today?
3 *(v)* to be acceptable or suitable.
This bread will do until tomorrow.
4 *(v)* to get on. *Patty is doing well at college.*

dock docking docked
1 *(n)* a place where ships load and unload their cargo. **dock** *(v)*.
2 *(n)* In a court of law, the **dock** is where the accused person stands.

doctor *(n)*
someone trained to treat sick people.

document
documenting documented
1 *(n)* a piece of paper containing important or useful information.
2 *(n)* a file on a computer.
3 *(v)* to write down the facts about something.

documentary documentaries *(n)*
a movie or television program made about real situations and people.

dodge dodging dodged *(v)*
to avoid something or somebody by moving quickly. *Kirsty dodged the ball.*

doe *(n)* the female of animals such as rabbits, deer, or kangaroos.

dog dogging dogged
1 *(n)* a four-legged mammal that is often kept as a pet.
2 *(v)* to follow someone closely.

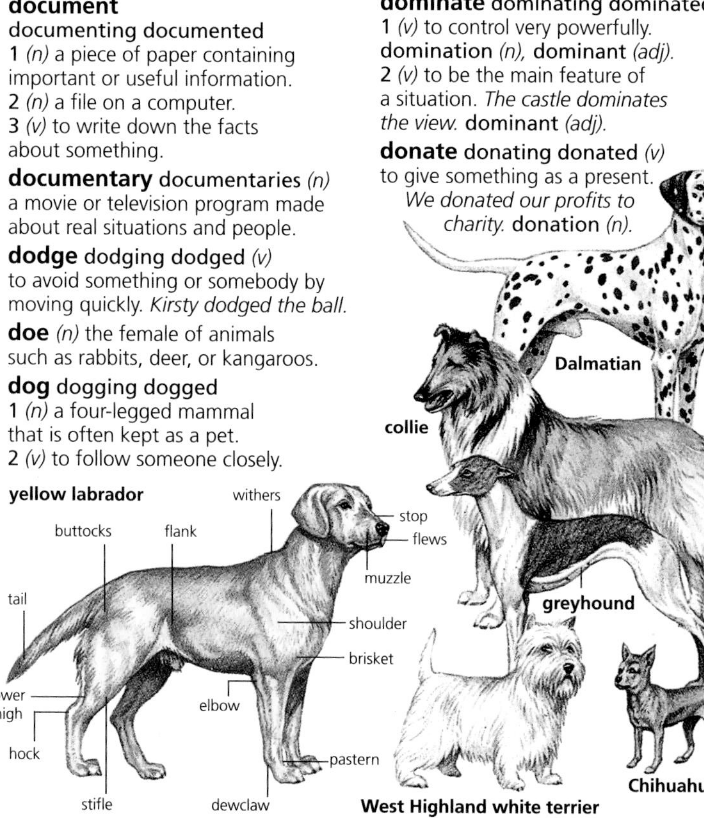

dole doling doled *(v)*
If you **dole out** something, such as food or money, you give it out in small quantities.

dollar *(n)* the main unit of money in many countries, such as the United States, Canada, and Australia.

dolphin *(n)* an intelligent water mammal with a long snout.

bottlenose dolphin
rostrum (beak)
forehead
dorsal fin
gape (lower jaw)
flipper
tail fluke

dome *(n)*
a rounded roof.

domestic
1 *(adj)* having to do with the home.
Domestic chores.
2 *(adj)* **Domestic** animals are kept by people in their homes as pets. **domesticated** *(adj)*.
3 *(adj)* having to do with your own country. *A domestic flight.*

dominate dominating dominated
1 *(v)* to control very powerfully. **domination** *(n)*, **dominant** *(adj)*.
2 *(v)* to be the main feature of a situation. *The castle dominates the view.* **dominant** *(adj)*.

donate donating donated *(v)*
to give something as a present.
We donated our profits to charity. **donation** *(n)*.

donkey *(n)*
a long-eared mammal,
related to the horse.

donor
1 *(n)* someone who gives something, usually to an organization or a charity.
2 *(n)* someone who gives part of their body, usually after they are dead, to help sick people. *A kidney donor.*

doodle **doodling doodled** *(v)*
to draw absent-mindedly while concentrating on something else.

doom *(n)*
If you meet your **doom**, you suffer a terrible fate, usually ending in death. **doomed** *(adj).*

door
1 *(n)* a barrier that opens and closes at the entrance of a building, room, etc.
2 *(n)* a house or a building. *My friend lives three doors away.*

dormant
1 *(adj)* Animals become **dormant** when they hibernate. They show no signs of action as if they were asleep.
2 *(adj)* A **dormant** volcano is not active at present but could still erupt.
3 *(adj)* If plants or seeds are **dormant**, they are alive but not growing.

dormitory **dormitories** *(n)*
a building with many separate sleeping rooms.

dose
1 *(n)* a measured amount of medicine.
2 *(n)* a brief experience of something unpleasant.

dot **dotting dotted**
1 *(n)* a small, round point.
2 *(v)* when you **dot** your 'i's, you put a point above the line.

double **doubling doubled**
1 *(v)* If you **double** something, you make it twice as big. **double** *(adj).*
2 *(n)* If you have a **double**, there is someone who looks just like you.
3 *(n)* When you play **doubles** in tennis, badminton, etc. there are two players on each side.

doubt *(dowt)* **doubting doubted**
1 *(v)* If you **doubt** something, you are uncertain about it. **doubtful** *(adj).*
2 *(n)* uncertainty.

dough *(doh) (n)*
a thick, sticky mixture of flour, water, etc., used to make bread, pastry and other baked goods.

doughnut *or* **donut** *(doh-nut)*
(n) a small cake, often with a hole in the center, that is made from dough, deep-fried and covered with sugar.

dove *(n)* a bird that makes a gentle cooing sound. *The dove is often used as a symbol of peace.*

down
1 *(prep)* from a higher to a lower place. *Emma ran down the hill.* **downward** *(adj),* **down** *(adv).*
2 *(n)* the soft feathers of a bird. **downy** *(adj).*
3 *(adj)* If you feel **down**, you feel sad or depressed.

download
downloading downloaded *(v)*
to copy information or pictures onto your computer from another computer or phone over a network or the internet. **downloadable** *(adj).*

dowry **dowries** *(n)*
the money or property that women in some cultures bring with them when they marry.

doze **dozing dozed** *(v)*
to sleep lightly for a short time. *Uncle Arthur has dozed off again.* **doze** *(n).*

dozen *(n)* a group of twelve.

Dr. *short for* **doctor**.

drab *(adj)*
very dull and dreary. *Gemma wore a drab gray dress.* **drabness** *(n).*

draft **drafting drafted**
1 *(v)* When you **draft** something, such as a letter, you make a first, rough copy of it. **draft** *(n).*
2 *(v)* If someone is **drafted**, they are made to join the armed forces. **draft** *(n)*
3 *(n)* a flow of cold air. **drafty** *(adj).*

drag **dragging dragged**
1 *(v)* to pull something heavy along the ground.
2 *(n) (informal)* If something is **a drag**, it is boring.
3 *(v)* If something **drags on**, it seems to go slowly. *The class dragged on and on.*

Chinese dragon

dragon *(n)*
a fire-breathing monster that appears in stories and legends. *In China, people create colorful dragons that dance in their New Year processions.*

drain **draining drained**
1 *(v)* to remove the liquid from something.
2 *(n)* a pipe or channel that takes away water or sewage. **drainage** *(n).*

drained *(adj)* If you feel **drained**, you have no energy left.

drama
1 *(n)* a play.
2 *(n)* If you study **drama**, you learn about acting and the theater.
3 *(n)* something that affects people seriously.

dramatic
1 *(adj)* having to do with acting and the theater.
2 *(adj)* very noticeable. *A dramatic change.* **dramatically** *(adv).*
3 *(adj)* If someone is being **dramatic**, they are making too much fuss about something.

dramatize
dramatizing dramatized
1 *(v)* to adapt a story into a play or movie. **dramatization** *(n).*
2 *(v)* If you **dramatize** an event, you make it seem very exciting.

drapes *(plural n)* pieces of material that are pulled across a window or a stage to cover it.

drastic *(adj)* If you do something **drastic**, you take action suddenly and violently. **drastically** *(adv).*

draw **drawing drew drawn**
1 *(v)* to make a picture with a pencil, pen, etc. **drawing** *(n).*
2 *(v)* to pull something. *The carriage was drawn by horses. The band drew enormous crowds.*
3 *(n)* If a competition ends in a **draw**, both sides are even.
4 *(n)* a competition where something is picked out. *A lucky draw.*

drawback *(n)*
a problem or a disadvantage.

drawer *(n)* a sliding box in a piece of furniture, used for storing things.

drawing room *(old-fashioned) (n)*
a formal room where guests are entertained.

drawl *(v)* to speak slowly with drawn-out vowel sounds. *A Southern drawl.*

dread **dreading dreaded** *(v)*
If you **dread** something, you are very afraid of it. **dread** *(n),* **dreaded** *(adj).*

dreadful
1 *(adj)* very unpleasant. *A dreadful accident.* **dreadfully** *(adv).*
2 *(adj)* very bad. *A dreadful movie.*

dreadlocks *(plural n)*
a hairstyle in which the hair is grown long and twisted into strands.

dream
dreaming dreamed *or* **dreamt**
1 *(v)* to imagine events while you are asleep. **dream** *(n).*
2 *(v)* If you **dream** of doing something, you really want to do it. **dream** *(n).*

Aboriginal bark painting

dreamtime *(n)* Aborigines believe that life began in the **dreamtime**, when the world was created by animal, plant, and human ancestors. *This painting shows the Rainbow Serpent giving birth to the Aboriginal people in the dreamtime.*

dreamy
dreamier dreamiest *(adj)* If you are **dreamy**, you are always daydreaming and imagining things. **dreamily** *(adv).*

dreary **drearier dreariest** *(adj)* dull and miserable. **drearily** *(adv).*

dredge **dredging dredged** *(v)* to scrape sand, mud, etc. from the bed of a river or harbor. **dredger** *(n).*

drench
drenches drenching drenched *(v)* to make something completely wet.

dress **dresses dressing dressed**
1 *(v)* to put clothes on.
2 *(n)* a piece of clothing worn by women and girls that covers their body from shoulders to legs.
3 *(n)* a general name for clothes. *Formal dress.*
4 *(v)* If you **dress a wound**, you clean it, put ointment on it, and cover it.

dresser
1 *(n)* a piece of furniture with shelves and cupboards.
2 *(n)* a piece of furniture with drawers, used for storing clothes, also called a chest of drawers.

dressing
1 *(n)* a covering for a wound.
2 *(n)* a type of sauce for salads.

dressing table *(n)* an item of bedroom furniture, often with a mirror and drawers.

dress rehearsal *(n)* the last rehearsal of a play, in full costume.

dribble **dribbling dribbled**
1 *(v)* to let saliva trickle from your mouth.
2 *(v)* When you **dribble** in basketball, you run with the ball, bouncing it and keeping it close to you.

drift **drifting drifted**
1 *(v)* When something **drifts**, it moves wherever the water or wind takes it.
2 *(n)* a pile of sand or snow, created by the wind.
3 *(v)* to move or act without any sense of purpose. *Ollie spent the whole day just drifting about.* **drifter** *(n).*

drill **drilling drilled**
1 *(n)* a tool used for making holes.
2 *(v)* to use a drill.
3 *(n)* a way of doing something that is governed by strict rules. *Fire drill.*

electric drill
(cutaway)

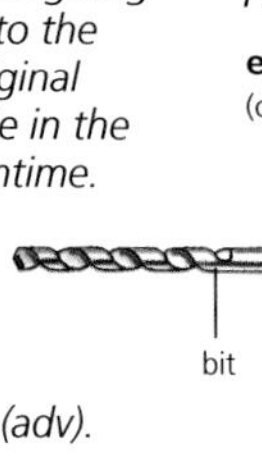

drink **drinking drank drunk**
1 *(n)* a liquid that you swallow.
2 *(v)* to swallow liquid.

drip **dripping dripped**
1 *(v)* When a liquid **drips**, it falls down slowly, drop by drop. **drip** *(n).*
2 *(n) (informal)* a silly and rather boring person.

drippings *(n)* fat and juice obtained from meat while it is cooking, which can often be used again.

drive **driving drove driven**
1 *(v)* to control a vehicle. **driver** *(n),* **driving** *(n).*
2 *(v)* to force someone into a desperate state. *Losing his passport drove Matt to despair.*
3 *(n)* energy. *Jenny will succeed, because she has a lot of drive.*

drivel *(n)* If someone talks **drivel**, what they say is nonsense.

driveway *(n)*
a private road leading to a house.

drizzle *(n)*
light rain. **drizzle** *(v).*

drone **droning droned**
1 *(v)* to make a steady, dull sound.
2 *(v)* to talk in a dull and monotonous way. *Hector droned on about baseball.*
3 *(n)* a bee that does not make honey and doesn't sting. *See* **honeycomb**.
4 *(n)* a pipe attached to a bagpipe. *See* **bagpipes**.

drool **drooling drooled**
1 *(v)* to let saliva trickle from your mouth.
2 *(v)* If you **drool over** something, you really like and want it.

droop **drooping drooped**
1 *(v)* to hang down, or to sag.
2 *(v)* When people **droop**, they run out of energy.

drop **dropping dropped**
1 *(v)* to let something fall. *Nancy dropped her bag on the couch.*
2 *(v)* to go downward. *The acrobat dropped to the floor.* **drop** *(n).*
3 *(n)* a small quantity of liquid. *A drop of water.*
4 *(v)* If you **drop out**, you stop doing something. **dropout** *(n).*
5 *(v)* When players are **dropped**, they are dismissed from a team.

drought
(rhymes with shout) (n)
a long spell of very dry weather.

drown
drowning drowned
1 *(v)* When someone **drowns**, they die because their lungs fill with water.
2 *(v)* to make a louder noise than something else. *The noise of the drill drowned out my singing.*

drowsy **drowsier drowsiest** *(adj)* sleepy. *This medicine may make you feel drowsy.* **drowsiness** *(n),* **drowse** *(v),* **drowsily** *(adv).*

drug
1 *(n)* a chemical substance used to treat illness.
2 *(n)* an illegal substance that people take because of its effect on them. Drugs are dangerous and usually cause addiction.
3 *(v)* to make someone unconscious by giving them a drug. **drugged** *(adj)*
4 **drug addict** *(n)* someone who cannot give up using drugs.

drugstore *(n)*
a store where medicines and various other items are sold.

drum drumming drummed
1 *(n)* a musical instrument, with a hollow body covered with a stretched skin, which makes a loud noise when you hit it.
2 *(v)* to beat a drum or other surface with drumsticks or your fingers. *Joe drummed his fingers on the table.* **drummer** *(n).*

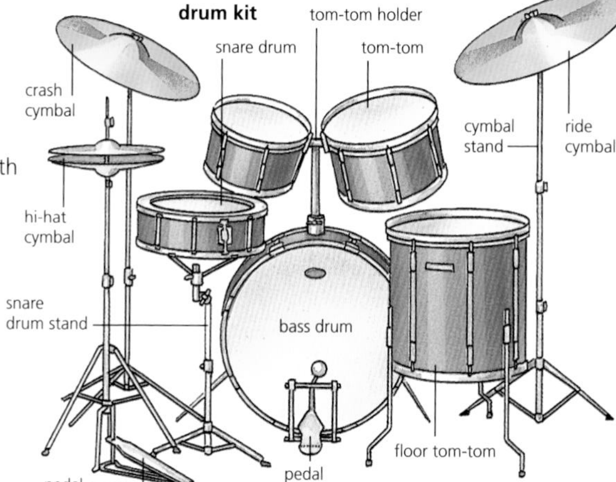

drumstick
1 *(n)* a stick used to hit a drum.
2 *(n)* the cooked leg of a chicken, turkey, etc.

druthers *(n)*
a personal preference. *If I had my druthers, I'd drive a monster truck to work.*

dry dries drying dried; drier driest
1 *(v)* to take the moisture out of something.
2 *(adj)* not wet.
3 *(adj)* dull or boring. *A dry speech.*

dry clean
dry cleaning dry cleaned *(v)* to clean clothes with special chemicals to remove stains. **dry cleaner** *(n).*

dual *(adj)* double.

dubious *(doo-bee-us) (adj)* If you are **dubious** about something, you are not sure about it. **dubiously** *(adv).*

duchess *(n)*
the wife or widow of a duke, or a woman with the rank that is equal to a duke.

duck ducking ducked
1 *(n)* a water bird.
2 *(v)* to bend low to avoid something.

due
1 *(adj)* If something is **due**, it is expected to arrive or happen. *When is your baby due?* **duly** *(adv).*
2 *(adj)* suitable. *Please handle these books with due care.* **duly** *(adv).*
3 If something happens **due to** something else, it happens because of it.

duel *(n) (old-fashioned)* a sword fight or gunfight between two people, fought according to strict rules.

duet *(n)* a piece of music or a song performed by two people.

duke *(n)* a nobleman. In Britain, a duke is the highest rank of male peer.

dull duller dullest
1 *(adj)* not bright.
2 *(adj)* not clever.
3 *(adj)* boring.

dumb dumber dumbest
1 *(adj)* temporarily not able to speak.
2 *(adj) (informal)* stupid.

dummy dummies
1 *(n)* an imitation person or object.
2 *(n) (informal)* a foolish person.

dump dumping dumped
1 *(v)* to leave something thoughtlessly or roughly. *Don't dump your bag there!*
2 *(n)* a place where unwanted things can be left. *A garbage dump.*

dune *(n)* a sand hill made by the wind, near the sea or in a desert.

dung *(n)* the solid waste products of large animals.

dungeon *(n)* a prison, usually underground. *See* **castle**.

duplicate duplicating duplicated *(v)* to make an exact copy of something. **duplicate** *(n).*

during *(prep)* within a particular time. *Please call during the morning.*

dusk *(n)* the time of day after sunset when it is nearly dark.

dust dusting dusted
1 *(n)* particles of dirt, fluff, etc. that gather on surfaces.
2 *(v)* to remove dust from surfaces with a cloth. **duster** *(n).*

duty *(doo-tee)* duties
1 *(n)* the things a person must do or ought to do. *A soldier's duty.*
2 *(n)* tax charged on goods brought into a country.
3 If you are **on duty**, you are at work.

duvet *(doo-vay) (n)*
a thick, padded cover for a bed, filled with feathers or other light material.

DVD *(n)* a disk that looks like a CD and stores sound, information and moving pictures. The initials DVD stand for Digital Versatile Disc. *Is that movie on DVD yet?* **DVD player** *(n).*

dwarf dwarfs *or* dwarves dwarfing dwarfed
1 *(n)* a very small person, animal, or plant. **dwarf** *(adj).*
2 *(v)* to make something else seem very small.

dwell dwelling dwelt *or* dwelled *(v) (old-fashioned)* to live in a place.

dwindle dwindling dwindled *(v)* to become smaller or less.

dye dyeing dyed
1 *(n)* a substance used to change the color of something.
2 *(v)* If someone **dyes** something, they change its color by soaking it in dye.

dynamic *(adj)* energetic and good at getting things done. **dynamism** *(n).*

dynamite *(n)* an explosive.

dynamo *(n)* a machine for converting the power of a turning wheel into electricity. Some bicycle lights are powered by a generator known as a dynamo. *As the bicycle wheel turns, the roller makes the magnet inside the dynamo rotate, creating a moving magnetic field. Electricity is produced as the magnetic field sweeps over the wire coil.*

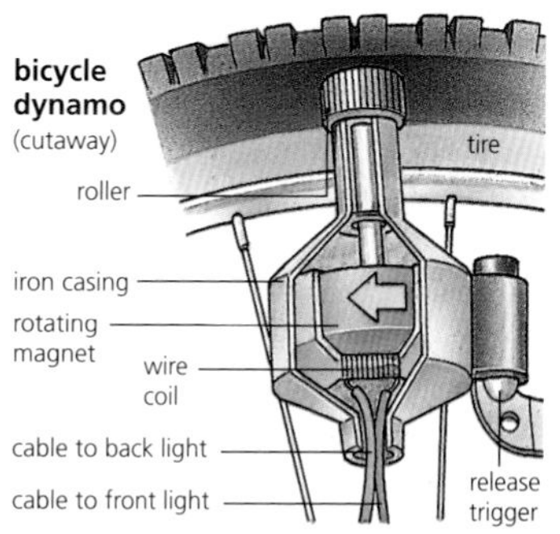

dyslexia *(dis-lex-ee-a) (n)* If you have **dyslexia**, you find reading and spelling difficult, often because you confuse the order of letters. **dyslexic** *(adj).*

Ee

eager *(adj)* keen and enthusiastic. **eagerness** *(n)*, **eagerly** *(adv)*.

eagle *(n)* a large bird of prey that often nests in mountainous areas.

Philippine eagle

ear *(n)* the part of the body used for hearing. *Sound waves travel down the ear canal and hit the eardrum, making it vibrate. These vibrations are transferred to the cochlea, where they are changed to electrical signals and sent to the brain.*

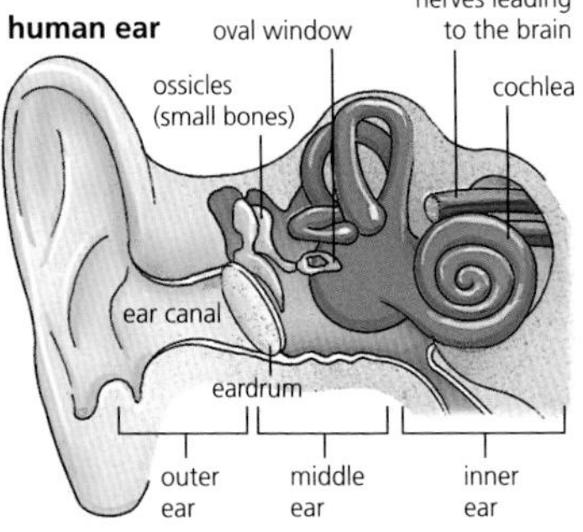

human ear

earache *(n)* a pain inside the ear.

earl *(n)* a nobleman. In Britain, an earl is a male peer of middle rank.

early earlier earliest
1 *(adj)* before the usual time. *An early start.* **earliness** *(n)*, **early** *(adv)*.
2 *(adj)* near the beginning of a period of time. *An early-20th-century house.*

earn earning earned
1 *(v)* to receive money for working. **earner** *(n)*, **earnings** *(plural n)*.
2 *(v)* to work to achieve a result. *You have earned your reward.*

earnest *(adj)* serious and eager. **earnestly** *(adv)*.

earth
1 Earth *(n)* the planet on which we live. *The diagram shows the different layers of the Earth.* **earthly** *(adj)*.
2 *(n)* soil. **earthy** *(adj)*.

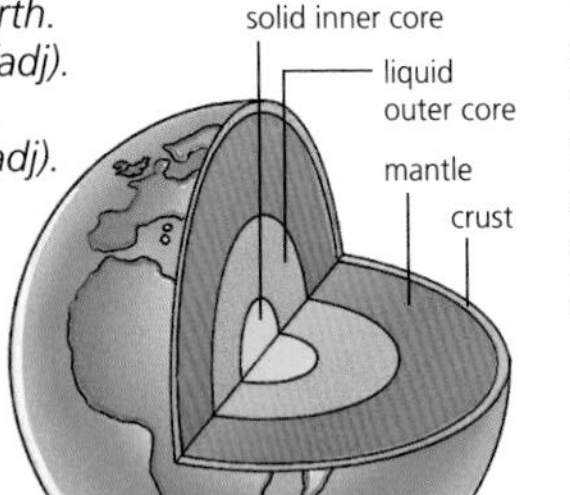

Earth (cutaway)

3 If someone is **down to earth**, he or she does not pretend to be someone important.

earthquake *(n)* a violent shaking of the Earth, caused by a movement of rock plates at the Earth's surface. *See* **fault**.

easel *(n)* a folding wooden stand for a painting.

east
1 *(n)* one of the four main points of the compass, the direction from which the Sun rises. **east** *(adj)*, **east** *(adv)*.
2 *(adj)* An **east wind** blows from the east. **easterly** *(adj* or *n)*.
3 *(adj)* having to do with or existing in the east. *The east coast.* **eastern** *(adj)*.

Easter *(n)* the Christian festival in which people celebrate the resurrection of Jesus Christ.

easy easier easiest
1 *(adj)* If something is **easy**, it does not require much effort or ability. **easiness** *(n)*, **easily** *(adv)*.
2 *(adj)* comfortable and relaxing. *An easy chair.* **ease** *(n)*.

eat eating ate eaten
1 *(v)* to take in food through your mouth.
2 If something is being **eaten away**, it is being destroyed slowly.

eavesdrop eavesdropping eavesdropped *(v)* to listen in secret to someone's conversation.

ebb ebbing ebbed
1 *(v)* When the tide **ebbs**, it goes out and the sea level goes down. **ebb** *(n)*.
2 *(v)* to get weaker. *The wounded tiger's strength ebbed away.*

ebony
1 *(n)* a very hard, black wood.
2 *(n)* a deep black color. **ebony** *(adj)*.

e-book *(n)* a book in electronic form.

eccentric *(ek-**sen**-trik)*
1 *(adj)* odd or strange. **eccentrically** *(adv)*.
2 *(n)* someone with odd habits. *He's a real eccentric.*

echo echoes echoing echoed *(v)* When a sound **echoes**, it repeats several times, because its sound waves have met a large surface and bounced back. **echo** *(n)*.

éclair *(ay-**klair**) (n)* a finger-shaped cake made from sweet pastry, filled with cream and usually covered with chocolate.

eclipse
1 *(n)* In an **eclipse of the Moon**, the Earth comes between the Sun and the Moon, so that all or part of the Moon's light is blocked out.
2 *(n)* In an **eclipse of the Sun**, the Moon comes between the Sun and the Earth so that all or part of the Sun's light is blocked out.
3 *(v)* to do much better than. *They eclipsed all the other teams.*

ecological *(adj)* causing little or no damage to the environment. *An ecological detergent.*

ecology
1 *(n)* the study of the relationship between plants, animals, and their environment. **ecologist** *(n)*.
2 *(n)* the study of how human activity affects the Earth. This is also known as human ecology. **ecologist** *(n)*, **ecological** *(adj)*, **ecologically** *(adv)*.

e-commerce *(ee-**kom**-urs) (n)* **e-commerce** is the general name for business carried out on the internet.

economical *(adj)* not wasteful. *Our car is very economical on gas.*

economics *(singular n)* the study of the way money is made and used in a society. **economist** *(n)*.

economy economies
1 *(n)* the way that a country runs its industry, trade, and finance.
2 When you **make economies**, you do things differently to save money. **economize** *(v)*.

ecosystem *(**ehk**-oh-sis-tem) (n)* a self-contained community of creatures, plants, and their environment. *If part of an ecosystem is destroyed, other parts may be affected.*

ecstasy ecstasies *(n)* a feeling of great happiness. **ecstatic** *(adj)*, **ecstatically** *(adv)*.

eczema *(**egg**-ze-mah) (n)* a skin condition that makes the skin dry, rough, and itchy.

eddy eddies *(n)* a circular current in a liquid. **eddy** *(v)*, **eddying** *(adj)*.

edge edging edged
1 *(n)* a boundary.
2 *(v)* to move very slowly and carefully. *We edged our way along the ledge.*
3 If you are **on edge**, you are nervous or anxious. **edgy** *(adj)*.

edgewise
1 *(adv)* sideways.
2 If you cannot **get a word in edgewise** in a discussion, people do not give you a chance to speak.

edible *(adj)* fit or safe to be eaten. *Pick only the edible mushrooms!*

edit editing edited
1 *(v)* to check a piece of writing for errors and cut it down if it is too long.
2 *(v)* to select, cut and arrange material for a movie, television program, etc.

edition *(n)* a version of a book or newspaper, published at a particular time. *A new e-book edition.*

editor
1 *(n)* the person in charge of a newspaper or magazine.
2 *(n)* someone who checks the contents of a book, etc. and gets it ready to be published.

educate educating educated *(v)* to give people knowledge or a skill.

education *(n)*
the process of gaining knowledge and skills. **educational** *(adj).*

eel *(n)* a long, thin, snake-like fish. *The electric eel stuns its prey with a strong electric shock.*

electric eel

eerie eerier eeriest *(adj)* strange and frightening. **eerily** *(adv).*

effect *(n)* the result or consequences of something.

effective *(adj)* If something or someone is **effective**, they do their job very well. **effectively** *(adv).*

effervescent
1 *(adj)* An effervescent liquid is fizzy. **effervescence** *(n).*
2 *(adj)* An effervescent person is lively.

efficient *(adj)* If someone or something is **efficient**, they work very well and do not waste time or energy. **efficiency** *(n),* **efficiently** *(adv).*

effluent *(eff-loo-ent) (n)*
waste water and sewage.

effort *(n)* If you make an **effort**, you try hard.

effortless *(adj)*
easy to do or needing little effort.

e.g. the initials of the Latin phrase *exempli gratia*, meaning "for example."

egg
1 *(n)* an oval or rounded object produced by female birds, reptiles, and fish, in which their young develop. *Also see* **chicken**.
2 *(n)* a cell created within a woman's body that, when fertilized, grows into a baby.

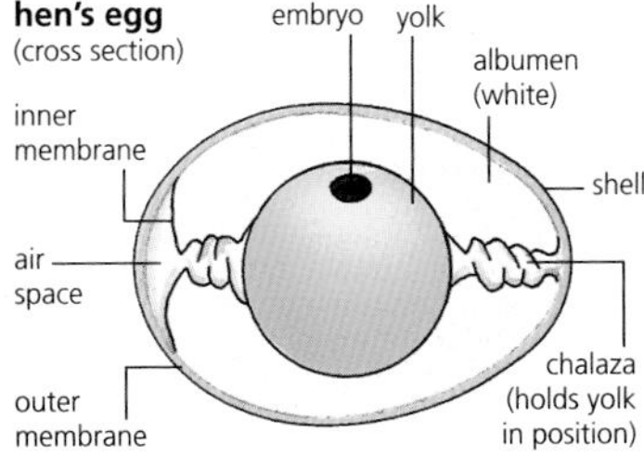

egocentric *(adj)*
If you are **egocentric**, you are far more interested in yourself than in others. **egocentricity** *(n).*

eiderdown *(eye-der-down) (n)*
a warm bed cover filled with feathers or some other stuffing.

Eid-ul-Adha *(n)*
a Muslim festival during the last month of the Islamic year when many Muslims make a pilgrimage to Mecca. Some Muslims celebrate the festival by sacrificing animals.

Eid-ul-Fitr *(n)*
the Muslim festival to celebrate the end of the Ramadan period of fasting.

either
1 *(conj)* **Either** can be used to indicate a choice. *You can either stay or go.*
2 *(pronoun)* one of two. *Take either of them.* **either** *(adj).*
3 *(adv)* also, or similarly. *If Tom's not going, I won't either.*

eject ejecting ejected
1 *(v)* to push something out. *Press this button to eject the CD.*
2 *(v)* to throw someone out. *We ejected the troublemakers from the meeting.*
3 *(v)* When pilots **eject** from their planes, they are thrown out of the cockpit by a special seat.

ejector seat

spur (breaks through plane canopy)
protective helmet with safety visor
oxygen mask
quick-release harness
lightweight seat (contains rocket motors, parachutes, and survival pack)
leg restraint line
life raft (inflates on contact with water)

elaborate elaborating elaborated
1 *(e-lab-or-ut) (adj)* complicated and detailed. *An elaborate pattern.* **elaborately** *(adv).*
2 *(e-lab-or-ate) (v)* to give more details. *Please elaborate on your plans.*

elapse elapsing elapsed *(v)*
When time **elapses**, it passes.

elastic *(n)* a rubbery material that stretches. **elasticity** *(n).*

elated *(adj)*
very pleased and excited. **elation** *(n).*

elbow *(n)*
the joint that connects the upper and lower parts of your arm.

elder *(adj)* older. *My elder sister.*

elderly *(adj)* old.

elect electing elected *(v)*
to choose someone or decide something by voting. **election** *(n).*

electrician *(n)* someone who installs electrical systems and repairs electrical machines.

electricity *(n)* a form of energy, caused by moving electrons, that is used for lighting, heating, and making machines work. **electric** *(adj),* **electrical** *(adj).*

electrocute electrocuting electrocuted *(v)* to kill or injure someone by giving them a severe electric shock. **electrocution** *(n).*

electrode *(n)*
a conductor through which an electric current can flow into or out of a gas or liquid. *See* **spark plug**.

electrolyte *(n)* a soluble substance that conducts electricity.

electromagnet *(n)*
a magnet that works by electricity.

electron *(n)* one of the microscopic parts of an atom. Electrons carry electrical energy. *See* **atom**.

electronic *(adj)*
Electronic machines contain transistors or silicon chips that control an electric current, which makes the machine work. *Computers, televisions, and radios are all electronic.* **electronically** *(adv).*

electronics
1 *(singular n)* the study of minute electrical currents, by creating circuits with electronic components.
2 *(singular n)* the technology that makes electronic machines work.

elegant *(adj)* graceful and stylish. *Molly is an elegant young woman.* **elegance** *(n),* **elegantly** *(adv).*

element
1 *(n)* In chemistry, an **element** is a substance that cannot be split into a simpler substance. *Oxygen, copper, and carbon are elements.*
2 *(n)* one of the simple, basic parts of something. *Claude taught me the elements of cooking.*
3 *(n)* a wire or coil in an electrical heater, toaster, etc. that heats up when electricity passes through it. *See* **iron**.
4 **the elements** *(plural n)* the weather.

elementary *(adj)* simple or basic.

elephant *(n)* a large mammal with a long trunk and ivory tusks, which lives in Africa or southern Asia.

elevate elevating elevated
1 *(v)* to lift something up.
2 *(v)* to promote someone to an important job or status. **elevation** *(n)*, **elevated** *(adj)*.

elevator
1 *(n)* a machine that carries people or goods between different levels of a building.
2 *(n)* the moveable part of a tail plane, used to alter the angle of flight of an aircraft. *See* **aircraft**.

elf elves *(n)* a small, magical, mischievous person described in legends and fairy tales. **elfin** *(adj)*.

eligible
1 *(adj)* If you are **eligible** for something, such as a job, you have the right qualifications for it. **eligibility** *(n)*.
2 *(adj)* An **eligible** man or woman is a suitable person for someone to marry.

eliminate eliminating eliminated
1 *(v)* to get rid of someone or something. **elimination** *(n)*.
2 *(v)* When a person or a team is **eliminated** from a competition, they cannot take part in it anymore. **elimination** *(n)*.

elite *(el-eet)* *(n)* a group of people who have special advantages and privileges. **elitism** *(n)*, **elite** *(adj)*.

ellipse *(n)* an oval shape. **elliptical** *(adj)*.

elocution *(n)* the art of speaking clearly.

elongate elongating elongated
1 *(v)* to make something longer or stretch it out.
2 **elongated** *(adj)* long and thin.

elope eloping eloped *(v)* When a young man and woman **elope**, they run away from their homes to get married. **elopement** *(n)*.

eloquent *(el-oh-kwent)* *(adj)* An **eloquent** person speaks easily and interestingly. **eloquence** *(n)*.

else
1 *(adv)* other or different. *They have gone somewhere else.*
2 *(adv)* more. *Tell me if you need anything else.*

elsewhere *(adv)* somewhere else.

elusive *(adj)* very hard to find or catch. **elusiveness** *(n)*, **elusively** *(adv)*.

email email *(n)* a message sent electronically.

embankment
1 *(n)* a long, low, earthen bank, built to carry a railway, road, etc.
2 *(n)* a high bank at the sides of a river, built to stop it from flooding.

embargo embargoes *(n)* an official order forbidding something from happening.

embark embarking embarked
1 *(v)* to go on board a ship or airplane, ready for a journey.
2 *(v)* to start something that will take a long time to finish. *Tanya has embarked on a massive art project.*

embarrass embarrasses embarrassing embarrassed *(v)* If something **embarrasses** you, it makes you feel awkward and uncomfortable. **embarrassment** *(n)*.

embezzle embezzling embezzled *(v)* to steal money secretly from the organization for which you work. **embezzlement** *(n)*.

emblem *(n)* a symbol or a sign. *The emblem of our club is a spider.*

embrace embracing embraced *(v)* to hug someone. **embrace** *(n)*.

embroider embroidering embroidered *(v)* to sew a picture or a design on to cloth. **embroidery** *(n)*.

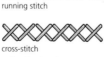

embroidery stitches

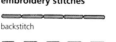

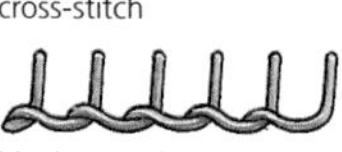

embryo *(em-bree-oh)* *(n)* an unborn baby in the very early stage of development in its mother's womb.

emerald
1 *(n)* a bright green precious stone.
2 *(n)* a bright green color. **emerald** *(adj)*.

emerge emerging emerged
1 *(v)* If you **emerge** from somewhere, you come out into the open. **emergence** *(n)*.
2 *(v)* to become known. *News is emerging of a serious traffic accident.*

emergency emergencies *(n)* a sudden and dangerous situation that must be dealt with quickly.

emigrate emigrating emigrated *(v)* to leave your own country to live in another one. **emigrant** *(n)*, **emigration** *(n)*.

eminent *(adj)* well-known and respected. *An eminent surgeon.* **eminence** *(n)*, **eminently** *(adv)*.

emir *(n)* a ruler in some Muslim countries, known as emirates.

emission
1 *(n)* the release of something, such as chemicals, into the air.
2 **emissions** *(plural n)* substances released into the air.

emit emitting emitted *(v)* to release or send out something, such as heat, light, or sound. *The spaceship emitted a strange beeping sound.*

emotion *(n)* a strong feeling, such as happiness, love, anger, or grief.

emotional
1 *(adj)* having to do with your feelings. *Emotional problems.*
2 *(adj)* When someone becomes **emotional**, they show their feelings, especially by crying. **emotionally** *(adv)*.

emperor *(n)* the male ruler of an empire.

emphasize emphasizing emphasized *(v)* If you **emphasize** something, you make it stand out clearly because you think it is important. **emphasis** *(n)*, **emphatic** *(adj)*.

empire
1 *(n)* a group of countries that all have the same ruler. *The Roman Empire.*
2 *(n)* a large group of companies controlled by one person.

employ employing employed
1 *(v)* to pay someone to work for you. **employer** *(n)*, **employment** *(n)*.
2 *(v)* to use something. *You can employ an electric whisk to beat the eggs.*

employee *(n)* a person who works for someone or for an organization and is paid by them.

empress empresses *(n)* the female ruler of an empire, or the wife of an emperor.

empty empties emptying emptied; emptier emptiest
1 *(adj)* If a container is **empty**, there is nothing inside it.
2 *(v)* to take the contents out of a container.
3 *(adj)* without meaning or purpose. *An empty promise.* **emptiness** *(n)*.
4 *(n)* an empty bottle or can.

emulsion *(n)* a mixture of two liquids in which the particles of one liquid spread out in the other liquid but do not dissolve. *When oil and vinegar are mixed, they form an emulsion.*

enable enabling enabled *(v)* to make it possible for someone to do something. *Telescopes enable people to see the stars more clearly.*

enamel
1 *(n)* a shiny, glass-like substance that is used to coat and protect metal, pottery, and glass. **enameled** *(adj)*.
2 *(n)* the hard, white surface of your teeth. *See* **tooth**.

enchanted *(adj)* A place or thing that is **enchanted** has been put under a magic spell or seems magical. *An enchanted castle.*

enchanting *(adj)* delightful and lovely. **enchanted** *(adj)*, **enchantingly** *(adv)*.

enclose enclosing enclosed
1 *(v)* to put a fence or wall around an area. **enclosure** *(n)*.
2 *(v)* to put something in an envelope or package with a letter. **enclosure** *(n)*.

encore *(on-kor) (n)* an extra item added to the end of a performance because the audience has been applauding so much.

encounter *(n)* an unexpected or difficult meeting. **encounter** *(v)*.

encourage encouraging encouraged *(v)* to give someone confidence by praising or supporting them. **encouragement** *(n)*, **encouraging** *(adj)*.

encyclopedia *(en-sy-klo-pee-dee-a) (n)* a book or online collection of information about many different subjects, arranged in alphabetical order. **encyclopedic** *(adj)*.

end ending ended
1 *(n)* the last part of something.
2 *(n)* one of the two points furthest from the middle of an object.
3 *(v)* to finish something.

endanger endangering endangered *(v)* to be dangerous to someone or something. *Pollution can endanger wildlife.* **endangered** *(adj)*.

endangered species *(n)* a type of animal that is in danger of becoming extinct. *The blue whale is an endangered species.*

endless *(adj)* Something **endless** has no end, or seems to have no end. **endlessly** *(adv)*.

endure
1 *(v)* If you **endure** something unpleasant or painful, you put up with it. **endurance** *(n)*.
2 *(v)* If something **endures**, it lasts for a long time. **enduring** *(adj)*.

enemy enemies
1 *(n)* someone who hates you and wants to harm you.
2 *(n)* the country or army that you are fighting against in a war.

energetic *(adj)* strong and active. **energetically** *(adv)*.

energy energies
1 *(n)* the strength to do active things without getting tired.
2 *(n)* power from gas, electricity, and other sources that makes machines work and produces heat.
3 *(n)* In physics, **energy** is the ability of something to do work. It is measured in joules.

engaged
1 *(adj)* If two people are **engaged**, they have decided that they will get married. **engagement** *(n)*.
2 *(adj)* If someone is **engaged** in doing something, they are busy and occupied doing it.

engine
1 *(n)* a machine that changes an energy source, such as gasoline, into movement. *In the gas engine shown here, electrical sparks from the spark plugs ignite the compressed gasoline and air mixture in the cylinders that burns rapidly and pushes the pistons down in turn. The fast-moving pistons turn the crankshaft, which produces a twisting effect that turns the wheels. Also see* **jet engine**.
2 *(n)* the front part of a train that pulls all the cars. *See* **steam locomotive**.

four-cylinder in-line gas engine (cutaway)

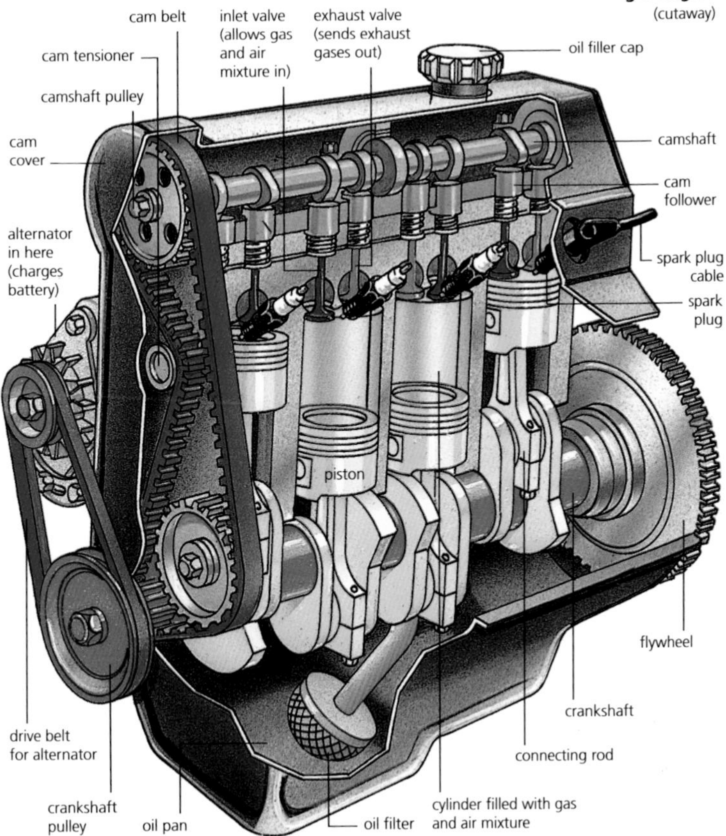

engineer engineering engineered
1 *(n)* someone who is trained to design and build machines, vehicles, bridges, roads, etc. **engineering** *(n).*
2 *(v)* to make something happen by using a clever plan. *Don engineered a meeting between the two rivals.*

English
1 *(adj)* from England or having to do with England.
2 *(n)* the main language spoken in Britain, the U.S., Australia, Canada, and many other countries.

engrave engraving engraved *(v)* to cut a design or letters into a metal or glass surface. **engraver** *(n),* **engraving** *(n).*

engrossed *(adj)* If you are **engrossed** in something, you give it all your attention. **engrossing** *(adj).*

engulf engulfing engulfed *(v)* to cover or swallow up. *A huge wave engulfed the swimmers.*

enigma *(n)* a mystery or a puzzle. **enigmatic** *(adj).*

enjoy enjoying enjoyed *(v)* to get pleasure from doing something. **enjoyment** *(n),* **enjoyable** *(adj),* **enjoyably** *(adv).*

enlarge enlarging enlarged *(v)* to make something bigger. *We want to enlarge this photo.* **enlargement** *(n).*

enlist enlisting enlisted
1 *(v)* to join the army, navy, or air force.
2 *(v)* If you **enlist** someone's help, you get them to help you.

enormity *(n)* a great evil or very wicked thing.

enormous *(adj)* extremely large. **enormousness** *(n),* **enormously** *(adv).*

enough *(n)* as much as is needed. **enough** *(adv).*

enrage enraging enraged *(v)* to make someone angry. *Lucinda's unhelpful comments enrage me!*

enrich enriches enriching enriched *(v)* to improve the quality of something by adding good things to it. *You can enrich soil with fertilizer.* **enrichment** *(n),* **enriching** *(adj).*

enroll enrolling enrolled *(v)* When you **enroll** in a club, class, or school, you put your name on a list because you want to join. **enrollment** *(n).*

ensemble *(on-som-bul) (n)* a group of musicians or actors who often perform together.

ensue ensuing ensued *(v)* to happen next. *A furious argument ensued.* **ensuing** *(adj).*

ensure ensuring ensured *(v)* to make certain that something happens. *Please ensure that you lock the door when you leave.*

enter entering entered
1 *(v)* to go into a place.
2 *(v)* to say that you want to take part in a competition, race, or exam.
3 *(v)* to type a small amount of information into a computer, or write it in a book. *Enter your name here.*

enterprise *(n)* something that you try to do that is new and difficult.

enterprising *(adj)* someone who is **enterprising** has a lot of good ideas and is brave enough to try things that are new and difficult.

entertain entertaining entertained
1 *(v)* to amuse and interest someone. **entertainer** *(n),* **entertainment** *(n),* **entertaining** *(adj).*
2 *(v)* to invite people to your home for a meal. *We're entertaining friends tonight.*

enthusiastic *(adj)* If you are **enthusiastic** about something, you are very eager to do it or like it very much. **enthusiasm** *(n),* **enthusiast** *(n).*

entice enticing enticed *(v)* to tempt someone to do something. **enticement** *(n),* **enticing** *(adj).*

entire *(adj)* whole. **entirely** *(adv).*

entrance entrancing entranced
1 *(en-trunss) (n)* the way into a place.
2 *(en-**trans**s) (v)* to give someone a feeling of wonder and pleasure. **entrancing** *(adj).*

entrant *(n)* someone who takes part in a competition, race, or exam.

entrepreneur *(n)* someone who starts businesses and is good at finding new ways to make money. **entrepreneurial** *(adj).*

entrust entrusting entrusted *(v)* If you **entrust** someone with something valuable or important, you give it to them to look after for you.

entry entries
1 *(n)* a way into a place.
2 *(n)* a picture, story, answer, etc. that you send into a competition.
3 *(n)* a small piece of information in a dictionary, diary, computer, etc.

envelop *(en-**vel**-up)* enveloping enveloped *(v)* to cover or surround something completely. *The house was soon enveloped in flames.*

envelope *(**en**-ve-lope or **on**-ve-lope) (n)* a paper cover for a letter or card.

enviable *(adj)* If someone has something **enviable,** you would like to have it yourself.

envious *(adj)* If you are **envious**, you wish that you could have something that someone else has. **enviously** *(adv).*

environment
1 *(n)* the natural world of the land, sea, and air. *We must protect the environment.* **environmentalist** *(n),* **environmental** *(adj),* **environmentally** *(adv).*
2 *(n)* all the things that influence your life, such as the area where you live, your family, and the things that happen to you. *Some children never have a secure home environment.*

environmentally friendly *(adj)* Products are **environmentally friendly** if they are made of substances that do not damage the natural environment.

envy envies envying envied *(v)* to wish that you could have something that someone else has. **envy** *(n).*

enzyme *(n)* a protein in the bodies of humans and animals that speeds up chemical reactions without being changed itself. *Enzymes help to digest food.*

epic
1 *(n)* a long story, poem, or movie about heroic adventures and great battles. **epic** *(adj).*
2 *(adj)* heroic or impressive.

epidemic *(n)* When there is an **epidemic**, an infectious disease spreads quickly to many people.

epigram *(n)* a short, sometimes witty, saying. **epigrammatic** *(adj).*

epilepsy *(n)* a disorder that causes sudden blackouts or convulsions. **epileptic** *(n),* **epileptic** *(adj).*

epilogue *(n)* a short speech or piece of writing added to the end of a play, story, or poem.

episode
1 *(n)* one of the programs in a television or radio series.
2 *(n)* an event or set of events in your life. *I don't want to talk about that embarrassing episode!*

epitaph *(n)* a short description of someone who has died, written on their gravestone.

equal equaling equaled
1 *(adj)* to be the same as something else in size, value, or amount. **equally** *(adv).*
2 *(v)* If you **equal** what someone else has done, you do as well as them.

equality *(n)* the same rights for everyone. *Racial equality.*

equation *(n)*
a mathematical statement that one set of numbers or values is equal to another set of numbers or values, for example, *4 x 4 = 16* or *3x + 2y = 13*.

equator *(n)*
an imaginary line around the middle of the Earth, halfway between the North and South Poles. *The equator is marked by a red line in the picture below.* **equatorial** *(adj)*.

equestrian *(adj)*
having to do with horseback riding. *Equestrian events.*

equilateral
(adj) An **equilateral** triangle has sides of equal length. *See* **shape**.

equator

equilibrium *(n)* balance.

equinox equinoxes *(n)*
one of the two days in the year when day and night last exactly the same length of time all over the world.

equip equipping equipped *(v)*
to provide someone with all the things that they need.

equipment *(n)*
the tools and machines that you need for a particular purpose.

equivalent *(adj)* If one thing is **equivalent** to another, it is the same as the other in amount, value, or importance. **equivalent** *(n)*.

era *(n)* a period of time in history or prehistory. *The Jurassic era.*

eradicate
eradicating eradicated *(v)* to get rid of something completely, especially something bad such as disease, crime, or poverty. **eradication** *(n)*.

erase erasing erased
1 *(v)* to rub a mark out with an eraser.
2 *(v)* to wipe out something stored in a computer, recorded on a CD, etc.

eraser *(n)* something used for rubbing off pencil marks from paper.

e-reader *(n)* an electronic device used for reading e-books.

erect erecting erected
1 *(adj)* standing upright. **erection** *(n)*, **erectly** *(adv)*.
2 *(v)* to put up a structure. *This building was erected in 2012.* **erection** *(n)*.

erode eroding eroded *(v)* When something is **eroded**, it is gradually worn away by water or wind.

erosion *(n)* the gradual wearing away of a substance by water or wind. *Soil erosion.*

errand *(n)*
If someone sends you on an **errand**, they ask you to go somewhere nearby to take a message or to deliver or collect something.

erratic *(adj)*
If something is **erratic**, it does not follow a regular pattern. *Erratic behavior.* **erratically** *(adv)*.

error *(n)* a mistake.

erupt erupting erupted
1 *(v)* When a volcano **erupts**, it throws out rocks, hot ash, and lava with great force. **eruption** *(n)*. *See* **volcano**.
2 *(v)* to start happening suddenly. *Fighting erupted on the streets.*
3 *(v)* If someone **erupts**, they suddenly become very angry.

escalator *(n)*
a moving staircase. *This diagram of an escalator shows how a moving belt of steps is controlled by a drive wheel.*

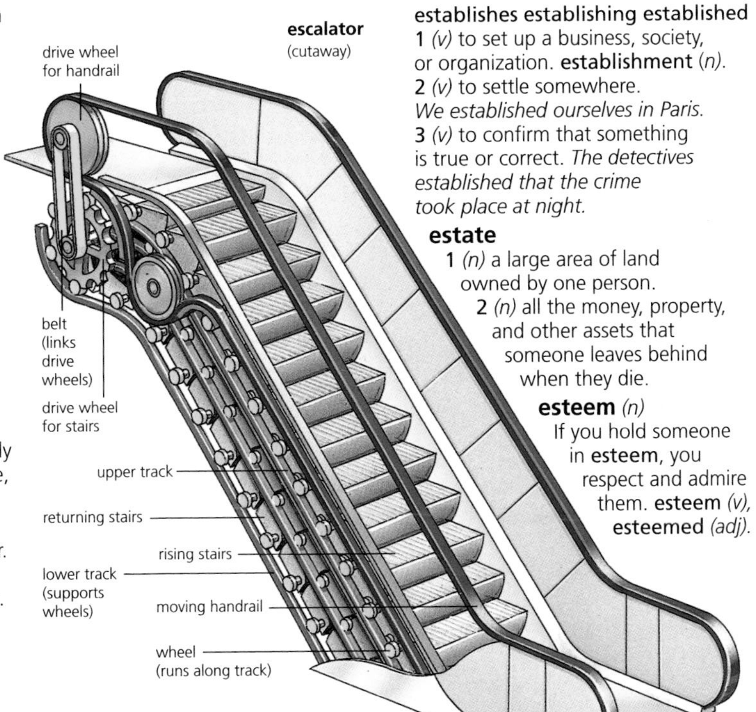

escalator (cutaway)

drive wheel for handrail
belt (links drive wheels)
drive wheel for stairs
upper track
returning stairs
rising stairs
lower track (supports wheels)
moving handrail
wheel (runs along track)

escape escaping escaped
1 *(v)* to break free from a place where you have been kept by force. **escape** *(n)*.
2 *(v)* to avoid something. *We escaped the rush hour traffic.*
3 *(v)* to leak out of a crack or hole in something. *Gas was escaping from the pipe.* **escape** *(n)*.

escort escorting escorted *(v)*
to go somewhere with someone, especially to protect them. **escort** *(n)*.

esophagus *(n)* the tube that carries food from the throat to the stomach.

especially *(adv)*
specially, or mainly. *Juan is especially good at singing. Alex loves sports, especially tennis.* **especial** *(adj)*.

Esperanto *(n)* an artificial language invented in the 19th century and intended to be a world language.

espionage *(n)* spying.

essay *(n)* a piece of writing about a particular subject.

essential
1 *(adj)* vital and important. *It is essential that you read the instructions before you begin.* **essentially** *(adv)*.
2 *(n)* something you really need and cannot do without. *Make sure that you bring the essentials listed below.*

establish
establishes establishing established
1 *(v)* to set up a business, society, or organization. **establishment** *(n)*.
2 *(v)* to settle somewhere. *We established ourselves in Paris.*
3 *(v)* to confirm that something is true or correct. *The detectives established that the crime took place at night.*

estate
1 *(n)* a large area of land owned by one person.
2 *(n)* all the money, property, and other assets that someone leaves behind when they die.

esteem *(n)*
If you hold someone in **esteem**, you respect and admire them. **esteem** *(v)*, **esteemed** *(adj)*.

estimate
estimating estimated
1 *(ess-tim-ate) (v)* to work something out roughly.
2 *(ess-tim-ut) (n)* a rough guess or calculation about an amount, distance, cost, etc.

estuary *(est-yu-air-ee)* **estuaries** *(n)* the wide part of a river where it joins the sea.

etc. an abbreviated form of the Latin phrase *et cetera*, which means "and the rest." Etc. is used at the end of lists.

eternal *(adj)* lasting forever. **eternally** *(adv)*.

ethnic *(adj)* having to do with different racial groups. **ethnically** *(adv)*.

E.U. *(n)* a group of countries in Europe, which have special trade and political agreements with each other. E.U. stands for European Union.

euro *(yoor-oh)* *(n)* the currency of some of the countries in the E.U.

European *(adj)* from Europe, or having to do with Europe. **European** *(n)*.

euthanasia *(yooth-an-ay-zhuh)* *(n)* the painless killing of someone who is suffering from an incurable or painful disease.

evacuate **evacuating evacuated** *(v)* to move away from an area because it is dangerous. *Will everybody evacuate the building, please!* **evacuation** *(n)*.

evade **evading evaded**
1 *(v)* to keep away from someone, or to keep out of their way.
2 *(v)* to avoid something you should do or respond to. *Shauna keeps evading the question.* **evasive** *(adj)*.

evaluate **evaluating evaluated** *(v)* to decide how good or how valuable something is, after thinking carefully about it. **evaluation** *(n)*.

evangelical *(adj)* An **evangelical** Christian tells people about the Christian gospel.

evaporate **evaporating evaporated**
1 *(v)* When a liquid **evaporates**, it changes into a vapor. **evaporation** *(n)*.
2 *(v)* to become less and then completely disappear. *Neal's confidence evaporated when he walked into the crowded room.*

even **evening evened**
1 *(adj)* An **even** number can be divided exactly by two.
2 *(adj)* equal. *An even score.* **evenly** *(adv)*.
3 *(adj)* smooth and level. *An even surface.*
4 *(adv)* in spite of. *Even if it takes all day, I'll complete the class.*
5 *(adv)* surprisingly. *We all enjoyed the movie, even Sarah.*
6 **even out** *(v)* If you **even things out**, you make them more equal.

evening *(n)* the time of day between the late afternoon and the early part of the night.

event
1 *(n)* something that happens, especially something interesting or important. **eventful** *(adj)*.
2 *(n)* one of the activities, such as a race, that is held during a sports competition.

eventually *(adv)* finally or at last. **eventual** *(adj)*.

ever
1 *(adv)* at any time. *Have you ever tried hang-gliding?*
2 *(adv)* all the time. *Ever grateful.*

evergreen *(n)* a bush or tree that has green leaves all the year round. **evergreen** *(adj)*.

everlasting *(adj)* never-ending.

every *(adj)* all the people or things in a group. *Every day of the week.*

everybody *(pronoun)* all people.

everyday *(adj)* usual or normal. *An everyday event.*

everyone *(pronoun)* all people.

everything *(pronoun)* all things.

everywhere *(adv)* in all places.

evict **evicting evicted** *(v)* to force someone to move out of their home. **eviction** *(n)*.

evidence *(n)* information and facts that help to prove something or make you believe that something is true.

evident *(adj)* clear and obvious. **evidently** *(adv)*.

evil *(adj)* wicked and cruel. **evil** *(n)*.

evolution
1 *(n)* the gradual development of animals and plants over millions of years to fit in better with their environment. **evolve** *(v)*, **evolutionary** *(adj)*.
2 *(n)* a gradual change into a different form. **evolve** *(v)*.

ewe *(n)* a female sheep.

exact *(adj)* perfectly correct and accurate. **exactness** *(n)*, **exactly** *(adv)*.

exaggerate **exaggerating exaggerated** *(v)* to make something seem bigger, better, more important, etc. than it really is. **exaggeration** *(n)* **exaggerated** *(adj)*.

exam *(n)* an official test that you take to show how much you know about a subject. Exam is short for examination.

examination
1 *(n)* See **exam**.
2 *(n)* a careful check or an inspection. *A medical examination.*

examine **examining examined**
1 *(v)* to look carefully at something. *The detectives examined the evidence.*
2 *(v)* When doctors **examine** you, they check your body carefully to see what is wrong with you.
3 *(v)* to test someone in an exam. **examiner** *(n)*.

example
1 *(n)* something typical of a larger group of things. *The wallaby is an example of a marsupial.*
2 *(n)* a model for others to follow. *Felicity is an example to the rest of the class.*
3 If you **make an example** of someone, you punish them as a warning to other people.

exasperate **exasperating exasperated** *(v)* If someone or something **exasperates** you, they make you very annoyed. **exasperation** *(n)*, **exasperating** *(adj)*.

excavate **excavating excavated** *(v)* to dig in the earth, either to put up a building or to discover ancient remains. **excavation** *(n)*, **excavator** *(n)*.

exceed **exceeding exceeded**
1 *(v)* to be greater or better than something else. *The vacation exceeded my wildest dreams.*
2 *(v)* to do more than is allowed or expected. *Drivers who exceed the speed limit will be fined.*

excel *(ex-sel)* **excelling excelled** *(v)* If you **excel** at something, you do it extremely well. *Gaby excels at sport.*

excellent *(adj)* very good. **excellence** *(n)*, **excellently** *(adv)*.

except *(prep)* apart from. *Everyone except Hannah went home.* **except** *(conj)*.

exception
1 *(n)* something that is not included in a general rule or statement. *Jasper hates girls, with just a few exceptions.*
2 If someone **takes exception** to something, they are offended or annoyed by it.

exceptional *(adj)* outstanding or rare. *James shows exceptional talent for drawing.*

excerpt *(n)* a short piece taken from a longer book, movie, or piece of music.

excess excesses
1 *(n)* too much of something. **excess** *(adj)*.
2 **in excess of** more than.
3 If you do something **to excess**, you do it too much.

excessive *(adj)* too much. *Gus always eats an excessive amount.* **excessively** *(adv)*.

exchange exchanging exchanged
1 *(v)* to give one thing and receive another. *We exchanged presents. They exchanged glances.* **exchange** *(n)*.
2 *(n)* a place where people meet to buy and sell things. *The Stock Exchange.*
3 **exchange rate** *(n)* a comparison of currencies throughout the world. You use the exchange rate to calculate how much money you will receive when you exchange one currency for another.

excite exciting excited *(v)* If something **excites** you, it makes you eager and interested. **excitement** *(n)*, **excited** *(adj)*, **exciting** *(adj)*.

exclaim exclaiming exclaimed *(v)* to say something loudly, especially because you are surprised or excited. **exclamation** *(n)*.

exclamation mark *(n)* the punctuation mark (!) used after an expression of surprise, excitement, or other strong feeling.

exclude excluding excluded
1 *(v)* If you **exclude** something, you leave it out. *The list excludes prices.* **excluding** *(prep)*.
2 *(v)* to stop someone from joining or taking part in something. **exclusion** *(n)*.

excrete excreting excreted *(v)* to pass solid waste matter out of your body. **excretion** *(n)*, **excretory** *(adj)*.

excruciating *(adj)* extremely painful. **excruciatingly** *(adv)*.

excursion *(n)* a short journey, often to a place of interest.

excuse excusing excused
1 *(ex-**kuze**)* *(v)* If you **excuse** someone for doing something, you forgive them. **excusable** *(adj)*.
2 *(ex-**kuse**)* *(n)* a reason you give to explain why you have done something wrong.
3 *(ex-**kuze**)* *(v)* to give someone permission not to do something. *The instructor excused Lydia from gym class because of her injured toe.*

execute executing executed
1 *(v)* to kill someone as a punishment for a crime. **execution** *(n)*.
2 *(v)* If you **execute** a plan or order, you put it into action.

executive *(n)* someone who has a senior job in a company and is involved in planning its future.

exempt *(adj)* If you are **exempt** from something, you do not have to take part in it. **exemption** *(n)*, **exempt** *(v)*.

exercise exercising exercised
1 *(n)* physical activity that you do to keep fit and healthy.
2 *(v)* to make your body work hard, for example, by playing sports to keep fit and healthy.
3 *(n)* a piece of work that you do to practice a skill. *Piano exercises.*

exhale exhaling exhaled *(v)* to breathe out. **exhalation** *(n)*.

exhaust exhausting exhausted
1 *(v)* If something **exhausts** you, it makes you very tired. **exhaustion** *(n)*, **exhausted** *(adj)*, **exhausting** *(adj)*.
2 *(v)* to use something up completely. *The explorers had almost exhausted their food supplies.*
3 *(n)* the exhaust fumes produced by the engine of a motor vehicle.
4 *(n)* the pipe at the back of a motor vehicle from which exhaust fumes from the engine are sent out.

exhibit exhibiting exhibited *(v)* to show something to the public. **exhibit** *(n)*, **exhibitor** *(n)*.

exhibition *(n)* a public display of works of art, historical objects, etc.

exhilarating *(adj)* very exciting and thrilling. **exhilaration** *(n)*.

exile exiling exiled *(v)* to send someone away from their own country and order them not to return. **exile** *(n)*.

exist existing existed
1 *(v)* to live or to be real. *Did King Arthur exist?* **existence** *(n)*.
2 *(v)* to have just enough food to stay alive. *We existed on berries and water.*

exit exiting exited
1 *(v)* to leave or to go out. **exit** *(n)*.
2 *(n)* the way out of a place.

exodus *(n)* a departure of a large number of people all at once.

exorcize exorcizing exorcized *(v)* to make an evil spirit leave a person or a place. **exorcism** *(n)*, **exorcist** *(n)*.

exotic
1 *(adj)* from a foreign, tropical country. *An exotic plant.*
2 *(adj)* strange and fascinating. *An exotic perfume.*

expand expanding expanded *(v)* to increase in size. **expansion** *(n)*.

expanse *(n)* a very large area. *A vast expanse of desert stretched ahead.*

expect expecting expected
1 *(v)* to think that something will happen. *I expect it will rain.*
2 *(v)* to wait for someone to arrive. *We're expecting visitors.*
3 *(v)* to think that something should happen. *Aunt Jane expects you to behave perfectly.* **expectation** *(n)*.
4 *(informal)* If a woman is **expecting**, she is pregnant.

expedition
1 *(n)* a long journey for a special purpose, such as exploring.
2 *(n)* a short trip to do something enjoyable. *A shopping expedition.*

expel expelling expelled
1 *(v)* If someone is **expelled** from a school, they have to leave because they have behaved badly. **expulsion** *(n)*.
2 *(v)* to send or force something out. *You expel air from your lungs.*

expenditure *(n)* the amount of money that a person, a company, or a country spends.

expense
1 *(n)* the spending of money, time, energy, etc. *Never mind the expense!*
2 **expenses** *(plural n)* money spent on something to do with a job, which is paid back later. *Business expenses.*

expensive *(adj)* costing a lot of money. **expensively** *(adv)*.

experience experiencing experienced
1 *(v)* If you **experience** something, it happens to you.
2 *(n)* something that happens to you.
3 *(n)* the knowledge and skill that you gain by doing something. *Do you have any experience of sailing?* **experienced** *(adj)*.

experiment experimenting experimented
1 *(n)* a scientific test to try out a theory or to see the effect of something. **experiment** *(v)*.
2 *(v)* to try something new. **experiment** *(n)*.

expert *(n)* someone who is very skilled at something or knows a lot about a particular subject. **expertise** *(n)*, **expert** *(adj)*.

expire expiring expired
1 *(v)* When a ticket, license, etc. **expires**, it reaches the end of the time when it can be used. **expiration** *(n)*.
2 *(v)* to die.

a b c d e f g h i j k l m n o p q r s t u v w x y z

explain explaining explained
1 *(v)* to make something clear so that it is easier to understand. **explanation** *(n)*, **explanatory** *(adj)*.
2 *(v)* to give a reason for something. *Please explain why you are so late.* **explanation** *(n)*.

explode exploding exploded *(v)*
If something **explodes**, it blows apart with a loud bang and great force.

exploit exploiting exploited
1 *(ex-**ployt**)* *(v)* to treat someone unfairly, usually by not paying them enough for their work. **exploitation** *(n)*.
2 *(**ex**-ployt)* *(n)* a brave or daring deed.

explore exploring explored
1 *(v)* to travel around a place to discover what it is like. **exploration** *(n)*, **explorer** *(n)*.
2 *(v)* If you **explore** an idea or possibility, you discuss it or think about it carefully. **exploratory** *(adj)*.

explosion
1 *(n)* a sudden and noisy release of energy.
2 *(n)* a sudden increase or growth. *A population explosion.*

explosive
1 *(n)* a substance that can blow up.
2 *(adj)* able or likely to explode. **explosively** *(adv)*.
3 *(adj)* If a situation is **explosive**, it is very dangerous.

export exporting exported *(v)*
to send goods to another country to be sold there. **export** *(n)*.

expose exposing exposed
1 *(v)* to uncover something so that people can see it.
2 *(v)* to reveal the truth about someone or something.
3 *(v)* *(old-fashioned)* to let light fall onto a photographic film.

exposure
1 *(n)* the harmful effect of very cold weather or water on someone's body. *The survivors from the shipwreck were suffering from exposure.*
2 *(n)* a piece of film, which produces a photograph when it is exposed to the light. *This film has 36 exposures.*
3 *(n)* the length of time that a photographic film is exposed to light.

express
expresses expressing expressed
1 *(v)* to show what you feel or think by saying, doing, or writing something. *Harriet expressed her happiness in a little dance.*
2 *(n)* a fast train that stops at only a few stations.
3 *(adj)* very fast. *Express delivery.*

expression
1 *(n)* the act of showing your feelings. *Self-expression.*
2 *(n)* the look on someone's face. *A puzzled expression.*
3 *(n)* a phrase that has a particular meaning. *Where does the expression "lock, stock, and barrel" come from?*

exquisite *(adj)* very beautiful and delicate. *An exquisite piece of embroidery.* **exquisitely** *(adv)*.

extend extending extended
1 *(v)* to make something longer or bigger. *We are going to extend our house at the back.* **extension** *(n)*.
2 *(v)* to stretch out. *Our garden extends right down to the stream.*

extensive
1 *(adj)* spreading over a wide area.
2 *(adj)* including a lot of things. *An extensive choice of desserts.*

extent *(n)*
the size, level, or scale of something. *What is the extent of the damage?*

exterior *(n)*
the outside of something, especially a building. **exterior** *(adj)*.

exterminate
exterminating exterminated *(v)*
to kill large numbers of people or animals. **extermination** *(n)*.

external *(adj)*
on the outside. **externally** *(adv)*.

extinct
1 *(adj)* If a type of animal or flower is **extinct**, it has died out. *The dodo was a large flightless bird that lived on the island of Mauritius and became extinct in the 17th century.* **extinction** *(n)*.
2 *(adj)* If a volcano is **extinct**, it has stopped erupting.

dodo

extinguish extinguishes
extinguishing extinguished
1 *(v)* to put out a flame, fire, or light.
2 *(v)* to put an end to a feeling or belief. *Nothing could extinguish Romeo's love for Juliet.*

extra
1 *(adj)* more than the usual amount. *An extra helping of fries.* **extra** *(adv)*.
2 *(n)* someone with a very small part in a movie, usually in a crowd scene.

extract extracting extracted
1 *(ex-**trakt**)* *(v)* to take or pull something out. **extraction** *(n)*.
2 *(**ex**-trakt)* *(n)* a short section taken from a book, piece of music, etc.

extraordinary *(adj)* very unusual or remarkable. **extraordinarily** *(adv)*.

extraterrestrial
1 *(adj)* having to do with, or coming from outer space. *Extraterrestrial messages.*
2 *(n)* a creature from outer space.

extravagant *(adj)*
If you are **extravagant**, you spend too much money, or are wasteful in the way you use things. **extravagance** *(n)*, **extravagantly** *(adv)*.

extreme
1 *(adj)* very great. *Extreme happiness.* **extremely** *(adv)*.
2 *(adj)* furthest, or outermost. *We reached the extreme edge of the woods.* **extremity** *(n)*.

extrovert *(n)* someone who enjoys being with other people and is lively and talkative. **extrovert** *(adj)*.

exuberant *(ex-**oo**-ber-ent)* *(adj)*
very cheerful and lively. **exuberance** *(n)*, **exuberantly** *(adv)*.

eye eyeing eyed
1 *(n)* one of the two organs in your head that you use for seeing.
2 *(n)* the small hole in a needle.
3 *(v)* to look carefully at someone or something. *Bart eyed the parrot suspiciously.*
4 *(n)* the calm, clear zone at the very center of a storm.

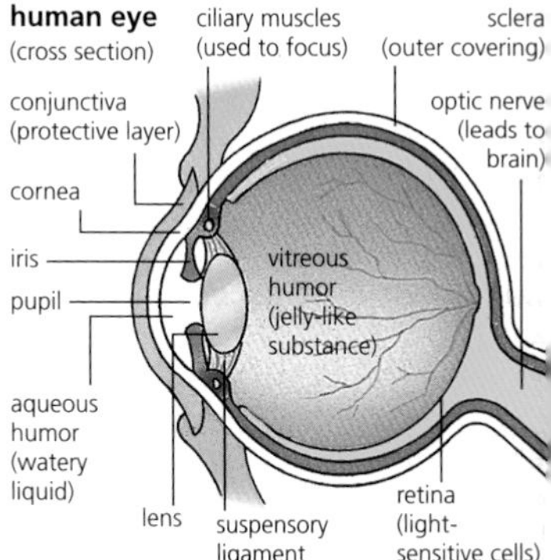

5 If you have an **eye for something**, you can judge how good it is. *Sue has an eye for a bargain.*

eyebrow *(n)* the line of hair that grows above each of your eyes.

eyelash eyelashes *(n)*
one of the short, curved hairs that grow on the edge of your eyelids.

eyelid *(n)*
the upper or lower fold of skin that covers your eye when it is closed.

eyesight *(n)* the ability to see.

eyewitness eyewitnesses *(n)*
someone who has seen something take place and can describe what happened.

Ff

fable *(n)* a story that teaches a lesson. Fables are often about animals.

fabric *(n)* cloth or material.

fabulous
1 *(adj)* wonderful or marvelous.
2 *(adj)* existing only in stories and legends. *Fabulous creatures.* **fabulously** *(adv).*

facade *(fuh-sahd)*
1 *(n)* the front of a building.
2 *(n)* a person's **facade** is the way he or she wants to be thought of or seen.

face facing faced
1 *(n)* the front of your head, from your forehead to your chin. **facial** *(adj).*
2 *(n)* a side or surface of something. *A mountain face. A clock face.*
3 *(v)* to look toward something. *Our apartment faces the park.* **facing** *(adj).*
4 *(v)* to meet or tackle something. *Robin faced many dangers.*

facility facilities
1 *(n)* a service provided for people to use and enjoy, such as a park, library, etc.
2 *(n)* the ability to do something easily. *Daisy has a facility for drawing.*

fact
1 *(n)* a piece of information that is true. **factual** *(adj),* **factually** *(adv).*
2 **in fact** *(adv)* actually.

factor
1 *(n)* one of the things that helps to produce a result. *Charlie's speed was a factor in his success.*
2 *(n)* a whole number that can be divided exactly into a larger number. *2, 3, 4, and 6 are factors of 12.*

factory factories *(n)*
a building where things are made in large numbers, using machines.

fad *(n) (informal)*
a temporary fashion or interest.

fade fading faded
1 *(v)* to become paler in color.
2 *(v)* to become gradually weaker. *Hope is fading among the survivors.*

Fahrenheit *(adj)* measured on a temperature scale on which water boils at 212° and freezes at 32°. *See* **thermometer**.

fail failing failed
1 *(v)* If you **fail** an exam or test, you do not pass it. **fail** *(n).*
2 *(v)* If you **fail** to do something, you do not do it. **failure** *(n).*
3 **without fail** *(adv)*
definitely, or every single time.

failing *(n)* a fault or weakness in someone or something.

faint
fainting fainted; fainter faintest
1 *(adj)* weak. *A faint sound.* **faintness** *(n),* **faintly** *(adv).*
2 *(v)* to become dizzy and lose consciousness for a short time.
3 *(adj)* A **faint** chance or idea is a very slight one.
4 **faint-hearted** *(adj)*
timid and not at all confident.

fair fairer fairest
1 *(adj)* reasonable and equal. *Fair treatment.* **fairness** *(n),* **fairly** *(adv).*
2 *(adj)* **Fair** hair is light in color.
3 *(adj)* quite good. **fairly** *(adv).*
4 *(n)* an outdoor entertainment with rides, amusements, and stalls. **fairground** *(n).*

fairy fairies
1 *(n)* a mythical, magical creature, such as a tiny person with wings, found in fairy tales.
2 **fairy tale** *(n)* a children's story about magic, fairies, giants, dwarves, etc.

faith
1 *(n)* trust and confidence in someone or something. *Our coach has a lot of faith in our team.*
2 *(n)* a religion.

faithful *(adj)* loyal and trustworthy. **faithfulness** *(n),* **faithfully** *(adv).*

fake faking faked
1 *(v)* to make a copy of something and pretend that it is genuine. *Mia faked her boss's signature.*
2 *(n)* a copy of something that is made to fool people. *This painting is not by Raphael, but it's a clever fake.* **fake** *(adj).*

falcon *(n)* a bird of prey that has long, tapered wings and hooked claws that catches small birds in flight. Traditionally, falcons are trained to return with their prey to their owner, or falconer.

falcon

fall
falling fell fallen
1 *(v)* to drop downward to the ground. **fall** *(n).*
2 *(v)* to decrease, or to become lower. *The temperature has fallen.* **fall** *(n).*
3 *(v)* to become. *After a while, Eve fell asleep.*
4 *(v)* to happen. *Night fell.*
5 *(n)* the season between summer and winter, when it gets colder, the days get shorter, and the leaves fall from the trees.
6 *(v)* If two people **fall out**, they quarrel with each other.
7 *(v)* If something **falls through**, it fails to happen.

fallow *(adj)*
Land that is **fallow** has been plowed, but not planted with crops so that it can improve in quality.

false
1 *(adj)* not true or not correct. *False information.* **falsely** *(adv).*
2 *(adj)* not real. *False eyelashes.*

fame *(n)* being famous. *Terry longs for fame.* **famed** *(adj).*

familiar
1 *(adj)* If something is **familiar**, it is well known or easily recognized. *A familiar saying.*
2 *(adj)* If you are **familiar** with something, you know it well. *Stu is familiar with all Shakespeare's plays.* **familiarity** *(n).*

family families
1 *(n)* a group of people related to each other, especially parents and their children.
2 *(n)* a group of related animals or plants. *The leopard and the jaguar are members of the cat family.*
3 **family tree** *(n)* a chart that shows how the members of a family are related over many generations.

famine *(n)* a serious shortage of food in a country.

famished *(adj)* If you are **famished**, you are very hungry.

famous *(adj)*
If someone is **famous**, they are well known to many people.

fan
1 *(n)* an enthusiastic supporter of something.
2 *(n)* a machine or an object that you use to blow or wave air onto yourself, to keep cool. **fan** *(v).*

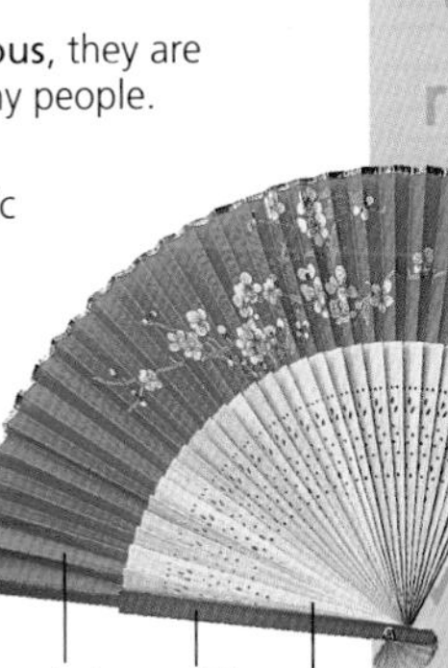

Japanese fan

fanatic *(n)*
someone who is wildly enthusiastic about a belief, a cause, or an interest. *Lee is a football fanatic.* **fanatical** *(adj),* **fanatically** *(adv).*

fancy fancier fanciest *(adj)* highly decorated or elaborate.

fang *(n)* a long, pointed tooth.

fantastic
1 *(adj)* too strange to be believable. **fantastically** *(adv).*
2 *(adj)* extremely good. **fantastically** *(adv).*

fantasy fantasies
1 *(n)* something that you imagine happening, but which is not likely to happen in real life. **fantasize** *(v).*
2 *(n)* a very imaginative story, often involving magic and fantastic animals.

far farther farthest
1 *(adv)* at or to a great distance. *Have you traveled far?*
2 *(adv)* very much. *I far prefer cycling to walking.*
3 *(adj)* opposite or distant. *Kim was waving on the far side of the river.*

farce
1 *(n)* a funny play in which there are many silly misunderstandings.
2 *(n)* a ridiculous situation. **farcical** *(adj).*

fare
1 *(n)* the cost of traveling on a bus, train, plane, etc.
2 *(v)* to get along. *How did James fare on his trip?*

Far East *(n)* the countries of eastern Asia, such as China and Japan.

farewell *(interject) (old-fashioned)* good-bye. **farewell** *(n).*

far-fetched *(adj)* hard to believe.

farm farming farmed
1 *(v)* to grow crops and raise animals. **farmer** *(n),* **farming** *(n).*
2 *(n)* land and buildings used for growing crops or raising animals. *The picture below shows a range of machinery used on a farm.* **farm** *(adj).*

farsighted *(adj)* If you are **farsighted**, you can see things more clearly when they are far away.

fascinate fascinating fascinated *(v)* If something **fascinates** you, you are really interested and excited by it. **fascination** *(n).*

fascism *(fash-izm) (n)* a way of organizing a country according to extreme right-wing and nationalist principles, with a powerful dictator and only one political party. **fascist** *(n).*

fashion
1 *(n)* a style of clothing that is popular at a certain time. **fashionable** *(adj).*
2 *(n)* a way of doing things.

fast food *(n)* food, such as burgers and pizzas, that is prepared and served quickly by restaurants.

fat fatter fattest
1 *(adj)* overweight or plump. **fatness** *(n),* **fatten** *(v).*
2 *(n)* the soft substance in the body of a person or animal that helps to keep them warm. **fatty** *(adj).*
3 *(n)* **Fats** are found in foods such as meat, milk, and cheese. They give you energy and are stored in your body to keep you warm.
4 *(adj)* big or thick. *A fat dictionary.*

20th-century fashions

fast fasting fasted; faster fastest
1 *(adj)* quick. **fast** *(adv).*
2 *(v)* to give up eating food for a time. *Muslims fast during Ramadan.* **fast** *(n).*
3 *(adv)* firmly or tightly. *Kitty's head was stuck fast between the railings.*
4 *(adj)* ahead of the right time. *My watch is five minutes fast.*
5 *(adj)* **Fast** colors or dyes do not run or fade when you wash them.

fasten fastening fastened *(v)* to tie or join something firmly. **fastener** *(n),* **fastening** *(n).*

fatal
1 *(adj)* causing death. *A fatal accident.* **fatally** *(adv).*
2 *(adj)* likely to have important, and usually bad, results. *A fatal decision.*

fatality fatalities *(n)* a death caused by an accident, a war, or another form of violence.

fate
1 *(n)* the force that some people believe controls events and decides what happens to people.
2 *(n)* Your **fate** is what will happen to you.

farm machinery

Some words that begin with an "f" sound are spelled "ph."

fateful *(adj)* important because it has a strong, usually unpleasant effect on future events. *I remember the fateful day I first met Archie.* **fatefully** *(adv).*

father *(n)* a male parent. **fatherhood** *(n),* **fatherly** *(adj).*

fathom fathoming fathomed
1 *(v)* If you cannot **fathom** something, you cannot understand it.
2 *(n)* a unit for measuring the depth of water. 1 fathom = 6ft or 1.8m.

fatigue *(fuh-teeg) (n)* great tiredness.

faucet *(faw-set) (n)* a piece of equipment used to control the flow of a liquid.

fault faulting faulted
1 *(n)* something wrong. *A mechanical fault.* **faulty** *(adj).*
2 *(n)* a weakness in someone's character. *Everyone has faults.*
3 *(n)* If something is your **fault**, you are to blame for it.
4 *(v)* to criticize or to find a mistake in something. *I can't fault your plan.*
5 *(n)* a large crack in the Earth's surface that can cause earthquakes. *The picture shows a tear fault, like the San Andreas fault in California, where parts of the Earth's crust have pulled in opposite directions.*

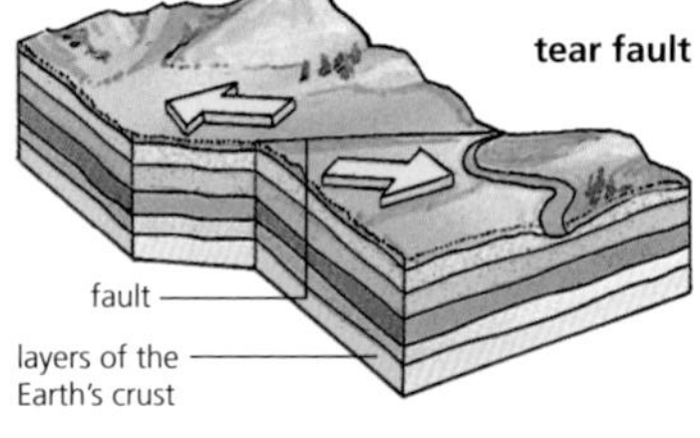

fauna *(n)* the animal life of a particular area. *Woodland fauna.*

favor favoring favored
1 *(n)* something helpful or kind that you do for someone.
2 *(v)* to like one thing or person best. *Dad always favors Johnny!*
3 If you are **in favor of** something, you agree with it or support it.

favorite
1 *(n)* the person or thing that you like best. **favorite** *(adj).*
2 *(n)* the person, team, or animal that is expected to win a race.

favoritism *(n)* unfair kindness shown to one person more than others.

fawn
1 *(n)* a young deer.
2 *(n)* a light brown color. **fawn** *(adj).*

fax faxes *(n)* a copy of a letter, document, etc. sent along a telephone line, using a special machine. **fax** *(v).*

fear fearing feared
1 *(n)* the feeling you have when you are in danger or you expect something bad to happen. **fearful** *(adj).*
2 *(v)* to be afraid of something or someone. *John feared no man.*
3 *(v)* to be worried about something. *I fear we're going to be late again.*

fearless *(adj)* very brave and not afraid. **fearlessly** *(adv).*

fearsome *(adj)* frightening. *A fearsome monster.*

feasible *(adj)* If something is **feasible**, it can be done. **feasibility** *(n),* **feasibly** *(adv).*

feast *(n)* a large meal for a lot of people on a special occasion. **feast** *(v).*

feat *(n)* an amazing achievement.

feather *(n)* one of the light, fluffy parts that cover a bird's body. **feathered** *(adj).*
Also see **bird**

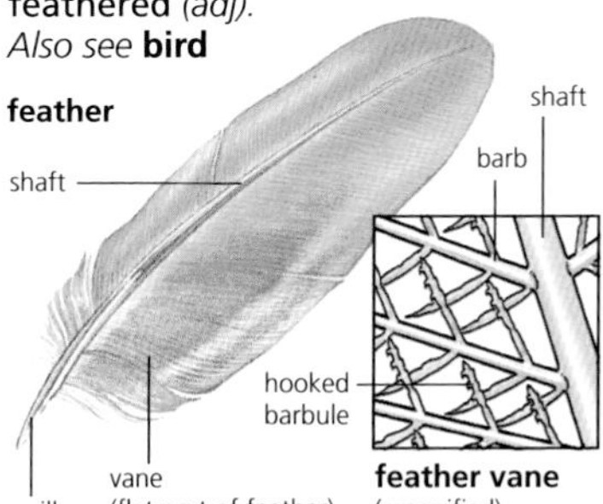

feature featuring featured
1 *(n)* Your **features** are the different parts of your face.
2 *(n)* an important part or quality of something. *My new laptop has several useful features.* **feature** *(v).*
3 *(v)* to use someone as one of the main stars in a movie.
4 *(n)* a newspaper article or part of a television program that deals with a particular subject. *A music feature.*

federal *(adj)* If a country has a **federal** government, it is made up of several states that are controlled by a central government but also have their own governments and make their own laws. **federalism** *(n),* **federalist** *(n).*

fed up *(adj) (informal)* If you are **fed up**, you are bored or unhappy about something.

fee *(n)* the amount of money that someone charges for a service.

feeble feebler feeblest *(adj)* very weak. **feebly** *(adv).*

feed feeding fed
1 *(v)* to give food to a person or an animal.
2 *(v)* When animals **feed**, they eat.
3 *(n)* food for animals.
4 *(v)* to put something, for example coins or information, into a machine. *Jan fed all the data into her computer.*

feedback
1 *(n)* comments and reactions to something. *I'd like some feedback on these ideas.*
2 *(n)* the loud, piercing noise made when the sound produced by an amplifier goes back into it.

feel feeling felt
1 *(v)* to touch something with your fingers, or to experience something touching you. *Jess felt the sun on her face.*
2 *(v)* to have a certain emotion or sensation. *Maddy felt angry.* **feeling** *(n).*
3 *(v)* to think, or to have an opinion. *Barney felt that he had been badly treated.* **feeling** *(n).*

feign *(rhymes with pain)* **feigning feigned** *(v)* to pretend. *Sam feigned illness so that he could miss the test.*

feisty *(fy-stee) (adj) (informal)* If you are **feisty**, you are lively and able to stand up for yourself.

feline *(adj)* having to do with cats.

fell felling felled *(v)* to cut something down or make something fall. *The gardener felled the tree. The wrestler felled his opponent.*

fellow
1 *(n) (old-fashioned)* a man or a boy.
2 *(adj)* belonging to the same class or group. *I like my fellow students.*

felon *(n)* someone who has committed a serious crime. **felony** *(n).*

felt *(n)* a thick cloth made of wool or other fibers pressed together.

female *(n)* a person or animal of the sex that can give birth to babies or lay eggs. **female** *(adj).*

feminine
1 *(adj)* having to do with women.
2 *(adj)* Someone who is **feminine** has qualities that are supposed to be typical of women. **femininity** *(n).*
3 *(adj)* belonging to one of the main classes or genders of nouns in French, Latin, and other languages.

feminist *(n)* someone who believes strongly that women should have the same opportunities and rights that men have. **feminism** *(n),* **feminist** *(adj).*

fen *(n)* an area of flat, low, marshy land.

Some words that begin with an "f" sound are spelled "ph."

a b c d e f g h i j k l m n o p q r s t u v w x y z

fence fencing fenced
1 *(n)* a wooden or wire barrier built to separate two areas of land. **fencing** *(n),* **fence** *(v).*
2 *(v)* to fight with long, thin swords or foils, as a sport. **fencer** *(n),* **fencing** *(n).*
3 If you **sit on the fence**, you are undecided and so avoid taking either side in an argument.

fend fending fended
1 *(v)* If you **fend for yourself**, you take care of yourself.
2 *(v)* If you **fend off** someone who is attacking you, you defend yourself.

fender
1 *(n)* a cover for the wheel of a car.
2 **fender bender** (n) (*informal*) a traffic accident.

feral *(adj)* wild or fierce.

fer-de-lance *(n)*
a type of venomous pit viper found in South and Central America.

fern *(n)* a plant with feathery leaves, or fronds, and no flowers, that usually grows in damp places.

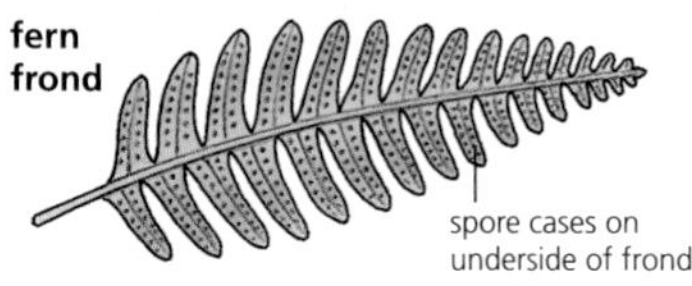

ferocious *(adj)*
very fierce and savage. **ferocity** *(n),* **ferociously** *(adv).*

ferret *(n)* a small, fierce mammal often used for catching rabbits.

ferry ferries ferrying ferried
1 *(n)* a boat or ship that regularly carries people across a stretch of water.
2 *(v)* to carry people or things from one place to another.

fertile
1 *(adj)* able to have babies. **fertility** *(n).*
2 *(adj)* Land that is **fertile** is good for growing a lot of crops and plants. **fertility** *(n).*

fertilize fertilizing fertilized
1 *(v)* When an egg or a plant is **fertilized**, sperm joins with the egg, or pollen comes into contact with the reproductive part of the plant, so that reproduction begins. **fertilization** *(n).*
2 *(v)* to put a substance, such as manure, on land to make it richer and make crops grow better. **fertilizer** *(n).*

fervent *(adj)* If someone is **fervent** about something, they believe in it passionately. **fervently** *(adv).*

festival
1 *(n)* a time when people celebrate something, such as a holiday.
2 *(n)* an organized set of events, often held at the same time each year. *A food festival.*

festive *(adj)* cheerful and lively because there is something to celebrate. *A festive mood.*

festoon
festooning festooned *(v)*
to cover something with decorations.

fetch fetches fetching fetched
1 *(v)* to go after and get something or someone.
2 *(v)* to be sold for a particular price. *That lamp should fetch a good price.*

fetching *(adj)* attractive or pretty.

fetus *(feet-uss)* fetuses *(n)*
a baby or animal before it is born, at the stage when it is developing in its mother's womb. *See* **pregnant**.

feud *(rhymes with chewed) (n)*
a bitter quarrel between two people or families that lasts for a long time. **feud** *(v).*

feudalism *(n)*
the medieval system in which people were given land and protection by the landowner, and, in return, worked and fought for him.
This diagram shows how feudalism worked, with the king at the head of the system and people at every level of society owing loyalty to the lord above them. **feudal** *(adj).*

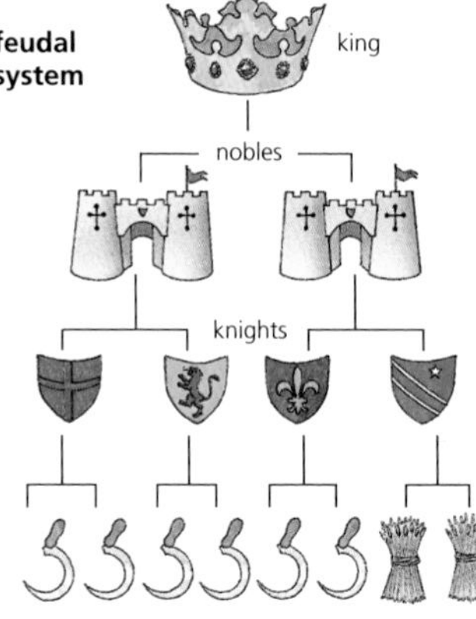

fever
1 *(n)* If someone has a **fever**, they have a high temperature. **feverish** *(adj).*
2 *(n)* great excitement or agitation. **feverish** *(adj).*

few fewer fewest *(adj)*
not many. **few** *(n).*

fez fezzes *(n)* a round flat-topped red hat worn by some Muslim men.

fiancé *(fee-on-say) (n)*
If a man and woman are engaged to be married, he is her **fiancé**.

fiancée *(fee-on-say) (n)*
If a man and woman are engaged to be married, she is his **fiancée**.

fiasco *(n)* a complete failure.

fib fibbing fibbed *(v)*
to tell a small lie. **fib** *(n),* **fibber** *(n).*

fiber
1 *(n)* a fine thread of cloth.
2 *(n)* a part of foods such as cereals and vegetables, which passes through the body, but is not digested. Fiber helps you to digest food. **fibrous** (adj).

fiberglass *(n)* material made from fine threads of glass, used in buildings, cars, boats, etc.

fiber optics *(singular n)*
the passing of light through extremely thin glass or plastic tubes, or fibers. Fiber optics is used in surgery and for sending communications signals.

fickle *(adj)*
Someone who is **fickle** changes their mind very often. **fickleness** *(n).*

fiction *(n)* stories that are made up. **fictional** *(adj).*

fiddle fiddling fiddled
1 *(v)* to keep touching or playing about with something.
2 *(n) (informal)* a violin. **fiddler** *(n).*

fiddly *(adj)* If something is **fiddly**, it is awkward to do because it is very small or very complicated.

fidget fidgeting fidgeted *(v)*
to keep moving because you are bored or uneasy. **fidgety** *(adj).*

field fielding fielded
1 *(n)* a piece of land, sometimes used for growing crops or playing sports.
2 *(v)* In games such as softball and baseball, the team that is **fielding** tries to catch the ball and get the batting team out.
3 *(n)* an area of study or interest. *Robin is an expert in the field of ornithology.*

fielder *(n)* someone who fetches or catches the ball in games such as baseball and softball.

Some words that begin with an "f" sound are spelled "ph."

field trip *(n)*
If you go on a **field trip**, you travel somewhere to study something.

fiend *(rhymes with leaned) (n)*
a wicked person or a devil. **fiendish** *(adj)*, **fiendishly** *(adv)*.

fierce fiercer fiercest *(adj)*
violent or aggressive. **fierceness** *(n)*, **fiercely** *(adv)*.

fiery fierier fieriest
1 *(adj)* like fire, or having to do with fire.
2 *(adj)* very emotional. *A fiery temper.*

fiesta *(fee-est-uh) (n)*
a holiday or religious festival, especially in Spain and Latin America.

fight fighting fought
1 *(v)* to attack someone and try to hurt them. **fight** *(n)*.
2 *(v)* to have an argument. **fight** *(n)*.
3 *(n)* a determined attempt to achieve something. *The speaker invited us to join the fight against poverty.*

figure figuring figured
1 *(n)* a written number.
2 *(n)* a person's shape. *Marilyn has a wonderful figure.*
3 *(n)* a person. *A well-known figure.*
4 **figure out** *(v)* to understand or solve something.

file filing filed
1 *(n)* a set of data held in a computer.
2 *(n)* a box or folder for papers or documents.
3 *(v)* to put data or documents in a file.
4 *(n)* a tool used to make things smooth. **file** *(v)*.

fill filling filled
1 *(v)* to make something full.
2 *(v)* If you **fill in a form**, you answer all the questions on it.
3 *(v)* If you **fill in** for someone, you do their job while they are away.

fillet *(fill-ay) (n)*
a piece of meat or fish with the bones taken out. **fillet** *(v)*.

filling
1 *(n)* a substance that a dentist puts into holes in your teeth to prevent more decay.
2 *(n)* the food inside a sandwich, pie, cake, etc.

filly fillies *(n)* a young female horse.

film filming filmed
1 *(n)* light-sensitive material that was used in a film-camera to take photographs.
2 *(v)* to record something with a camera.
3 *(n)* a very thin layer of something. *A film of dirt.*

filter filtering filtered
1 *(n)* a device that cleans liquids or gases as they pass through it. *See* **aquarium**.
2 *(v)* to put something through a filter.

filth
1 *(n)* dirt. **filthiness** *(n)*, **filthy** *(adj)*.
2 *(n)* foul or obscene language.

fin
1 *(n)* a flap-like shape on the body of a fish, used for steering it through the water. *See* **fish**.
2 *(n)* a small triangular-shaped structure on an aircraft, boat, etc., used to help with steering. *See* **aircraft**.
3 **fins** *(plural n)* long, flat attachments that you fit on your feet to help you swim underwater. *See* **scuba diving**.

final
1 *(adj)* last. **finally** *(adv)*.
2 *(n)* the last and usually most important examination in a school term.

finalize finalizing finalized *(v)*
to finish making arrangements. *Have you finalized the dates of your vacation?*

finance financing financed
1 *(n)* money or the management of money. *An expert in finance.* **financial** *(adj)*, **financially** *(adv)*.
2 *(v)* to provide money for something.
3 **finances** *(plural n)* the amount of money that an individual or a company has. *Our finances are in a mess at the moment.*

find finding found
1 *(v)* to discover or to come across something.
2 **find out** *(v)* to learn about something or someone.
3 *(n)* a valuable or important discovery. *This restaurant is a real find!*

findings *(plural n)* the results of an inquiry or a court case.

fine fining fined; finer finest
1 *(adj)* very good or excellent. *A fine painting.*
2 *(adj)* okay or all right.
3 *(adj)* not rainy. *A fine day.*
4 *(adj)* thin or delicate.
5 *(v)* to demand some money as a punishment for doing something wrong. **fine** *(n)*.

finger fingering fingered
1 *(n)* one of the long parts of your hand that you can move.
2 *(n)* an object shaped like a finger. *A chocolate finger.*
3 *(v)* to touch something lightly with your fingers. *Ted fingered the ornament carefully.*

fingerprint *(n)*
the print made by the pattern of curved lines on your fingertip.

finicky *(adj)* fussy, especially about food. *A finicky eater.*

finish finishes finishing finished
1 *(v)* to end or complete something.
2 *(n)* the end of something, such as a race.

finite *(fy-nyte) (adj)*
limited, or with an end. **finitely** *(adv)*.

fir *(n)* a pointed evergreen tree with needle-like leaves and cones.

fire firing fired
1 *(n)* flames, heat, and light produced by burning.
2 *(v)* to shoot a gun or other weapon.
3 *(v)* to force someone out of their job.

firecracker *(n)*
a firework that makes a loud noise.

fire extinguisher *(n)*
a metal case containing chemicals and water that you use to put out a fire. *When you squeeze the handle of a foam-and-water fire extinguisher, the piercer punctures the canister, which releases carbon dioxide gas. The gas pushes on the surface of the water and detergent mixture, forcing it up the tube, through the hose and out of the spray nozzle, in a jet of foam and water.*

foam-and-water fire extinguisher
(cross section)

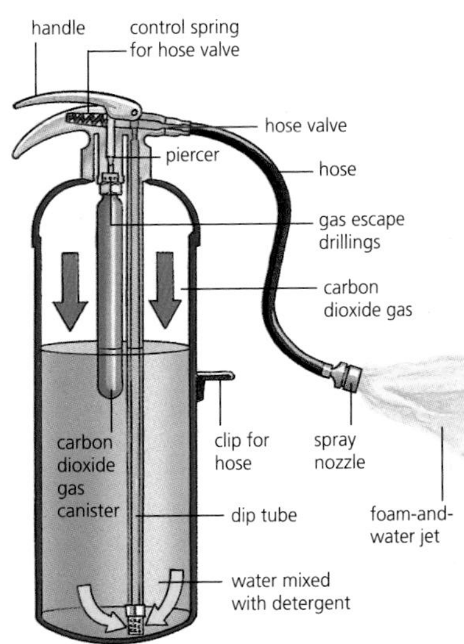

Some words that begin with an "f" sound are spelled "ph."

fireproof *(adj)* If something is **fireproof**, it is made from materials that will not catch on fire.

firetrap *(n)* a building that would be hard to escape from if it caught fire.

fireworks *(n)*
containers, filled with gunpowder and other chemicals, that make bangs and colored sparks when they are lit.

firm firmer firmest
1 *(adj)* strong and solid. *A firm bed.*
2 *(adj)* definite and not easily altered. *A firm manner.* **firmly** *(adv).*
3 *(n)* a business or a company.

first
1 *(n)* a person or a thing that acts or happens earliest. *Adam was the first to leave the party.*
2 *(adj)* earliest in time. *Michaela took the first bus.*
3 *(adv)* before something else. *Guy always gets to school first.*
4 *(adj)* most important. *The first team.* **firstly** *(adv).*

first aid *(n)*
medical help that is given to someone immediately after an accident.

fish
fish *or* **fishes; fishes fishing fished**
1 *(n)* an animal that lives in water and has scales, fins, and gills. *The fish shown below is a female perch. Also see* **gill**.
2 *(v)* to try to catch fish. **fishing** *(n). See* **angling**.
3 *(v)* If you **fish** for information, you try to discover something in an indirect way.

fit fitting fitted; fitter fittest
1 *(adj)* healthy and strong. **fitness** *(n).*
2 *(v)* to be the right size or shape. *This skirt doesn't fit.*
3 *(n)* a sudden uncontrollable attack of something. *A fit of giggles.*
4 *(adj)* good enough. *Fit for the job.*
5 *(n)* If someone has an epileptic **fit**, they suddenly become unconscious and their muscles become tense.

fitting
1 *(adj)* right or suitable. *Some people think it is fitting to wear dark colors at funerals.*
2 *(n)* a small metal or plastic part that connects things.

fix fixes fixing fixed
1 *(v)* to mend something.
2 *(v)* to decide on something. *Shall we fix a date for the party?*
3 *(v)* to attach something to another thing. *Fix the photograph to the wall.*
4 *(n) (informal)* If you are **in a fix**, you are in an awkward situation.
5 *(v)* to get something ready to eat.

fixation *(n)*
an obsession or something that you think about a great deal. *Jonathan has a fixation about his height.*

fixture *(n)*
an object that is fitted firmly and permanently into place.

fizz fizzes fizzing fizzed *(v)*
to bubble and hiss. **fizzy** *(adj).*

fizzle fizzling fizzled *(v)*
(informal) If something **fizzles out**, it gradually fails after a good start.

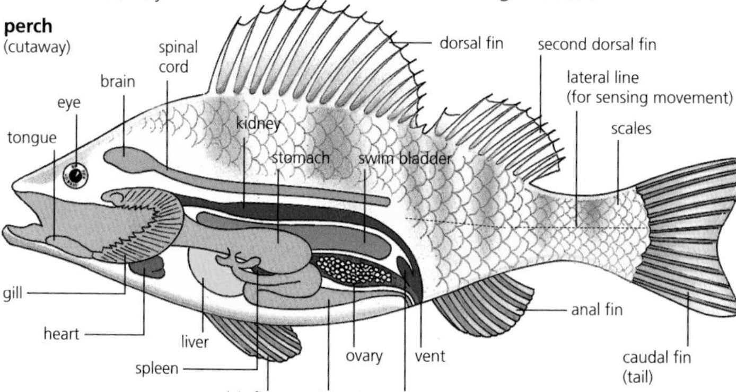

fisherman fishermen *(n)*
someone who catches fish for a job or as a sport.

fishy fishier fishiest
1 *(adj)* tasting or smelling of fish.
2 *(adj) (informal)* strange and suspicious. *A fishy story.*

fist *(n)* a tightly closed hand.

fjord *(fee-ord) (n)*
a narrow channel of sea that runs inland between high cliffs. Fjords were formed in the Ice Age by glaciers.

flab *(n)* extra fat on your body. **flabbiness** *(n),* **flabby** *(adj).*

flabbergasted *(adj) (informal)*
stunned and surprised.

flaccid *(flass-id) (adj)* soft and limp.

flag *(n)* a piece of cloth with a pattern on it, that is a symbol of a country, organization, etc.

international flags

United Nations

Olympic Games

International Red Cross

European Union

flair *(n)* natural skill or ability. *Jamie has a flair for cooking.*

flak
1 *(n)* anti-aircraft fire.
2 *(n) (informal)* opposition and criticism.

flake flaking flaked
1 *(n)* a small, thin piece of something. *Large flakes of paint fell off the door.*
2 *(v)* If something **flakes**, small, thin pieces of it peel off. **flaky** *(adj).*
3 **flake out** *(v) (informal)* to act in an unreliable, or childish way.
4 *(adj) (informal)* If someone is **flaky**, they are a little eccentric.

flamboyant *(adj)*
bold, showy, and brightly colored.

flame
1 *(n)* a tongue of fire. **flaming** *(adj).*
2 **flame-colored** *(adj)* deep orange-red.

flamingo
flamingos *or* **flamingoes**
(n) a long-legged bird with webbed feet.

flamingos with young

flammable *(adj)* likely to catch fire. *Flammable material.*

flank flanking flanked
1 *(n)* the side of an animal between its ribs and hips.
2 *(v)* to be at the side of someone or something. *The king was flanked by attendants.*

flannel *(n)* woven woolen fabric.

flap flapping flapped
1 *(v)* to move up and down. *The bird flapped its wings.*
2 *(v)* to swing loosely. *The sail flapped in the breeze.*

Some words that begin with an "f" sound are spelled "ph."

3 *(n)* something attached on one side only. *The flap of an envelope.*
4 *(n)* a hinged part on an aircraft wing, used to control the way that the aircraft rises and falls. *See* **aircraft**.

flapjack *(n)* a pancake.

flare flaring flared
1 *(n)* a bright flame used as an emergency signal.
2 *(v)* If something **flares up**, it suddenly becomes stronger or more violent.

flash flashes flashing flashed
1 *(n)* a short burst of light.
2 *(v)* to shine brightly in bursts.
3 *(n)* a short burst of something. *A flash of inspiration. A news flash.*
4 *(v)* to show something briefly. *Emily flashed a smile at Lou-Anne.*

flashback *(n)* a part of a book or movie that tells you what happened earlier.

flashlight *(n)* a portable light powered by a battery.

flashy flashier flashiest *(adj)* If something is **flashy**, it is showy and expensive. *Todd wears very flashy clothes.*

flask
1 *(n)* a narrow-necked bottle, used in a science laboratory. *See* **apparatus**.
2 *(n)* a small flat bottle made to be carried in the pocket.

flat flatter flattest
1 *(adj)* level or smooth. *A flat surface.*
2 *(adj)* not high. *Flat shoes.*
3 *(adj)* emptied of air. *A flat tire.*
4 *(adj)* very definite. *A flat refusal.*
5 *(adj)* In music, a **flat** note is lower in pitch than the usual note. *B flat is a semitone lower than B.*
6 *(adj)* In a musical score, a **flat** sign shows that the next note is flat. *See* **notation**.

flatter flattering flattered
1 *(v)* to praise someone, especially when you want a favor. **flatterer** *(n)*, **flattery** *(n)*.
2 *(adj)* If something, such as a piece of clothing, is **flattering**, it makes you look good.

flaunt flaunting flaunted *(v)* to show something off confidently. *The duchess flaunted her diamonds.*

flavor flavoring flavored
1 *(n)* taste. **flavored** *(adj)*, **flavorless** *(adj)*.
2 *(v)* to add taste to food. *Flavor the stew with herbs and pepper.* **flavoring** *(n)*.

flaw *(n)* a fault, or a weakness. **flawed** *(adj)*, **flawless** *(adj)*.

flea
1 *(n)* a small, jumping and biting insect that lives on the blood of people or animals.
2 **flea market** *(n)* an indoor or outdoor market selling old clothes and other secondhand items.

flea (magnified)

fleck *(n)* a spot, or a tiny patch of something. *A fleck of soot landed on Carl's white shirt.* **flecked** *(adj)*.

fledgling *(n)* a young bird.

flee fleeing fled *(v)* to run away from danger.

fleece *(n)* a sheep's woolly coat. **fleecy** *(adj)*.

fleet *(n)* a group of vehicles, such as ships or trucks.

fleeting *(adj)* not lasting long. *A fleeting glance.* **fleetingly** *(adv)*.

flesh
1 *(n)* the soft part of your body, made up of fat and muscle. **fleshy** *(adj)*.
2 *(n)* the meat of an animal, or the part of a fruit or vegetable that you can eat.

flex flexes flexing flexed *(v)* to bend or stretch something. *Tarzan flexed his muscles.*

flexible *(adj)* able to bend or change. *A flexible plastic ruler. Francis is flexible about Saturday's arrangements.* **flexibility** *(n)*, **flexibly** *(adv)*.

flick flicking flicked *(v)* to move with a quick, sudden movement. *Pete flicked a pea off the table.* **flick** *(n)*.

flicker flickering flickered *(v)* If something **flickers**, it moves unsteadily. *The flame flickered in the wind.* **flicker** *(n)*.

flight
1 *(n)* flying, or the ability to fly.
2 *(n)* a journey by aircraft.
3 If you **take flight**, you run away. **flight** *(n)*.

flimsy flimsier flimsiest *(adj)* thin or weak. *Flimsy material.* **flimsiness** *(n)*, **flimsily** *(adv)*.

flinch flinches flinching flinched *(v)* to make a quick movement away from a source of pain. *Di flinched as the nurse approached with a needle.*

fling flinging flung *(v)* to throw something violently.

flint *(n)* a hard gray stone, used in prehistoric times for making tools and weapons.

flip flipping flipped
1 *(v)* to turn over or move something quickly. *Ernesto flipped the pancakes.*
2 *(v) (informal)* If someone **flips**, they suddenly become angry or excited.
3 *(n)* a somersault. *A backflip.*

flippant *(adj)* careless and not serious. *A flippant comment.* **flippancy** *(n)*, **flippantly** *(adv)*.

flipper
1 *(n)* one of the broad flat limbs of a sea creature, such as a seal or dolphin, that help it to swim. *See* **dolphin**.
2 *(n)* one of the long flat attachments that you fit on your feet to help you swim.

flirt flirting flirted
1 *(v)* If you **flirt** with someone, you talk to them in a teasing, flattering way. **flirt** *(n)*, **flirtatious** *(adj)*.
2 *(v)* If you **flirt** with an idea, you consider it, but not very seriously.

float floating floated
1 *(v)* to rest on water or air.
2 *(v)* to move lightly and easily.
3 *(n)* a small object attached to the end of a fishing line, which shows when the fish is biting. Also called a **bobber**. *See* **angling**.
4 *(n)* a decorated truck that forms part of a procession.

flock flocking flocked
1 *(n)* a group of animals or birds. *A flock of sheep.*
2 *(v)* to gather in a crowd. *Hundreds of fans flocked to see the band.*

floe *(n)* a large sheet or block of floating ice in a lake, sea or river.

flog flogging flogged *(v)* to beat someone with a whip or stick. **flogging** *(n)*.

flood flooding flooded
1 *(v)* When something, such as a river, **floods**, it overflows with liquid beyond its normal limits. **flood** *(n)*.
2 *(v)* to overwhelm, or come in large amounts. *The charity was flooded with offers of help.*

floodlight *(n)* a strong light, used to light up buildings or athletic fields.

floor
1 *(n)* the flat surface that you walk on inside a building.
2 *(n)* a story in a building. *The skyscraper has more than 40 floors.*

flop flopping flopped
1 *(v)* to fall limply. **floppy** *(adj)*.
2 *(n) (informal)* a failure.

Some words that begin with a "f" sound are spelled "ph."

flora *(n)* the plant life of a particular area. *Desert flora.*

floral *(adj)* flowery. *Floral curtains.*

florist *(n)* someone who sells flowers.

flotsam *(n)* objects from a shipwreck found floating in the sea or washed up on the shore.

flounder floundering floundered
1 *(v)* to struggle through water, snow, mud, etc.
2 *(v)* to have difficulties in coping with something. *Luke is floundering with his math.*
3 *(n)* a flat fish.

flour *(n)* powder made from ground wheat, corn, etc., that you use for cooking and baking. **floury** *(adj).*

flourish
flourishes flourishing flourished
1 *(v)* to grow and succeed. *Our new computer club is flourishing.*
2 *(v)* to wave something around to show it off. **flourish** *(n).*

flout flouting flouted *(v)*
If you **flout** the rules, you break them deliberately.

flow flowing flowed *(v)* to move along smoothly like a river. **flow** *(n).*

flow chart *(n)*
a diagram that shows how something develops, stage by stage.

flower flowering flowered
1 *(n)* the colored part of a plant that produces seeds or fruit.
2 *(v)* to blossom or produce flowers.
3 *(n)* a plant that has flowers.

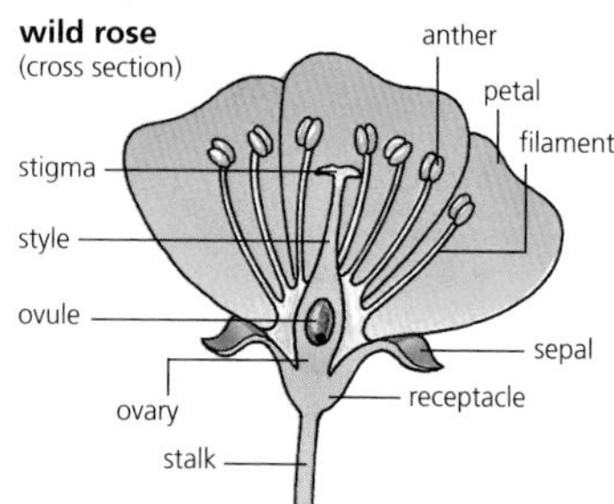

flu *(n)* an illness that gives you a high temperature and makes you feel weak. Flu is short for influenza.

fluctuate
fluctuating fluctuated *(v)*
to change all the time. *Gasoline prices keep fluctuating.* **fluctuation** *(n).*

fluent *(adj)* able to speak smoothly and clearly, especially in another language. **fluency** *(n),* **fluently** *(adv).*

fluff fluffing fluffed
1 *(n)* a light, soft downy substance.
2 *(v)* When a bird **fluffs** its feathers, it shakes them out.

fluid
1 *(n)* a flowing substance, either a liquid or gas.
2 *(adj)* flowing or liquid. **fluidity** *(n).*

fluke
1 *(n)* a lucky accident.
2 *(n)* part of the tail of a sea creature, such as a whale or dolphin. *See* **dolphin**.

fluorescent
1 *(adj)* giving off a bright light. *Fluorescent lighting.* **fluorescence** *(n).*
2 *(adj)* A **fluorescent** color is so bright that it seems to give off light when a light is shone on it.

fluoride *(n)*
a chemical put in toothpaste and water to prevent tooth decay.

flush flushes flushing flushed *(v)*
to flood something with water as a way of cleaning it. **flush** *(n).*

flushed *(adj)* If you are **flushed**, your face has become red. **flush** *(n).*

flustered *(adj)* If you are **flustered**, you are confused or rushed. **fluster** *(v).*

flutter fluttering fluttered
1 *(v)* to wave or flap rapidly. *The flag fluttered in the breeze.*
2 *(n)* If you are **in a flutter** about something, you are excited and nervous about it.

fly flies flying flew flown
1 *(v)* to travel through the air.
2 *(n)* an insect with wings. *See* **insect**.
3 *(n) (informal)* a flap on pants covering a zipper or buttons.
4 *(v)* to move fast, or to do something fast. *Time just flew by.*

fly fishing *(n)* a type of fishing using flies made from fur, feathers, etc. that are attached to a hook, which the fish swallows. *The picture shows examples of four types of fly used in fly fishing for trout: a dry fly, which represents an adult fly; a wet fly, which imitates a hatching fly; a nymph, which trout mistake for a fly larva; and a lure, which attracts the trout just by its color or brightness.*

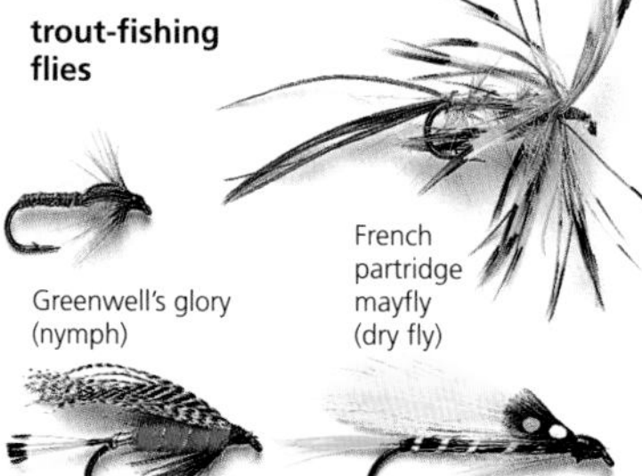

flying saucer *(n)* a saucer-shaped flying object, believed by some to be a spacecraft from another planet.

foal foaling foaled
1 *(n)* a young horse.
2 *(v)* to give birth to a young horse.

foam foaming foamed
1 *(n)* a mass of small bubbles.
2 *(v)* to make bubbles.

foam rubber *(n)*
a soft, spongy material often used to stuff toys or furniture.

focus focuses *or* foci;
focuses focusing focused
1 *(v)* to adjust your eyes or a camera lens so that you can see something clearly. *I focused my camera carefully before I took the picture.*
2 *(v)* to concentrate on something or somebody. *Let's focus on your problems.*
3 *(n)* the center of a picture or the center of attention. **focal** *(adj).*

fodder *(n)* food for cows and horses.

foe *(n)* an enemy.

fog *(n)* a very thick mist of water droplets in the air. **foggy** *(adj).*

foghorn *(n)* a loud siren used to warn ships in foggy weather.

foil foiling foiled
1 *(n)* thin, silvery sheets of metal.
2 *(v)* to prevent someone from carrying out a plan. *The police foiled the robbers' plot.*
3 *(n)* a sword used in fencing. *See* **fence**.

fold folding folded
1 *(v)* to bend something over on itself.
2 *(n)* a small fenced area for sheep.
3 *(v)* If a company **folds**, it collapses and stops trading.

folder
1 *(n)* a cardboard cover used for keeping papers.
2 *(n)* an electronic file used for storing computer documents.

foliage *(n)* leaves.

folk folk *or* folks
1 *(n)* people, especially your family.
2 *(adj)* traditional, and belonging to the ordinary people. *Folk music.*

folklore *(n)* the stories, customs, and knowledge of ordinary people that are passed down to their children.

follow following followed
1 *(v)* to go behind someone. *The patrol car followed us.*
2 *(v)* to come after. *December follows November.*
3 *(v)* to be guided by someone or something. *Harvey always follows the latest trends.* **follower** *(n).*

Some words that begin with an "f" sound are spelled "ph."

ollowing
 (prep) next or coming after omething. *Following drinks, we ate.*
 (adj) next or after. *The following day.*
 (n) If someone has **following**, they re very popular.

olly follies
 (n) foolishness.
 (n) a foolish act.
 (n) a building with o real purpose. *he folly in the icture is on the Isle f Wight, England.*

folly

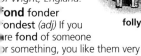

ond fonder ondest *(adj)* If you re **fond** of someone r something, you like them very nuch. **fondness** *(n)*, **fondly** *(adv)*.

ondle fondling fondled *(v)* o touch or stroke gently. *Nancy fondled the kitten's ears.*

ont
 (n) a style of typeface.
 (n) a large stone bowl used in a hurch to hold the water for baptisms.

ood *(n)* ubstances that people, animals, and lants take in to stay alive and grow.

ood chain *(n)* a group of animals nd plants that are dependent on ne another, since each one feeds on the one below them in the chain.

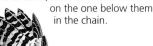

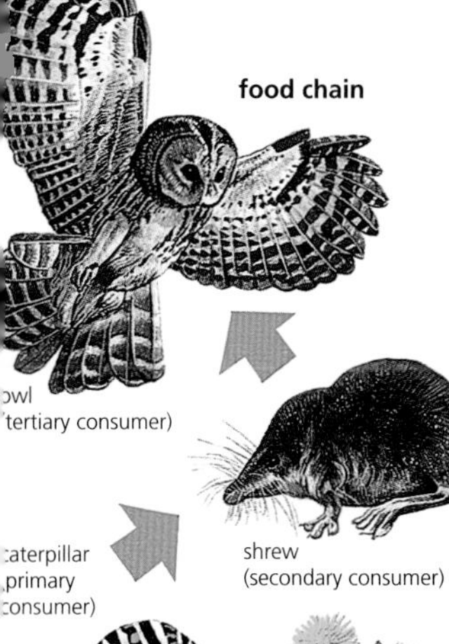

he food chain shown bove has one producer nd several levels of consumers.

food web *(n)* the complex network of food chains in an ecosystem.

fool fooling fooled
1 *(n)* a silly person. **foolishness** *(n)*, **foolish** *(adj)*.
2 *(v)* to trick someone. *The dealer fooled Josie into buying a fake watch.*

foolproof *(adj)* Something that is **foolproof** is very simple to use and cannot easily go wrong.

foot feet
1 *(n)* one of the two parts of your body that you walk on.
2 *(n)* the bottom or the lower end of something. *The foot of the bed.*
3 *(n)* a unit of length equal to 12 inches.

football
1 *(n)* an outdoor ball game in which two teams try to score by getting the ball across the opponent's goal line. *The picture shows a football player with part of his uniform cut away.*
2 *(n)* the ball used to play football.

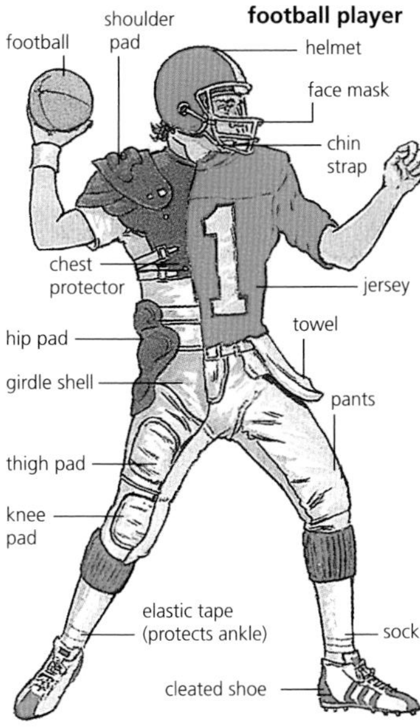

footnote *(n)* a note at the bottom of a page.

forage foraging foraged *(v)* to go in search of food. *We foraged for wild mushrooms.*

forbid forbidding forbade forbidden *(v)* to tell someone not to do something. **forbidden** *(adj)*.

forbidding *(adj)* unfriendly or off-putting. **forbiddingly** *(adv)*.

force forcing forced
1 *(v)* If you **force** someone to do something, you make them do it. **forceful** *(adj)*, **forcefully** *(adv)*.
2 *(n)* strength or power.
3 *(n)* In physics, a **force** is any action that alters the shape or the movement of an object.
4 *(n)* an army, or other team of people. *The police force.*

forceps *(plural n)* an instrument, similar to tongs, used for holding or lifting, especially in operations.

ford *(n)* a shallow part of a stream or river that you can cross on foot, on horseback, or in a vehicle. **ford** *(v)*.

forecast forecasting forecast *or* forecasted *(v)* to say what you think will happen in the future. *The weatherman forecasts rain for tomorrow.* **forecast** *(n)*, **forecaster** *(n)*.

foreground *(n)* the part of a picture that is in front of the main subject. *This painting has a cottage in the foreground.*

forehead *(n)* the top part of your face between your hair and your eyes.

foreign
1 *(adj)* having to do with, or coming from another country. **foreigner** *(n)*.
2 *(adj)* If something is **foreign** to you, it is strange or unnatural.

forensic *(adj)* A **forensic investigation** uses scientific information such as fingerprints, blood tests, handwriting analysis, etc. to help solve crimes.

foresee foreseeing foresaw foreseen *(v)* to expect or predict that something will happen. **foresight** *(n)*, **foreseeable** *(adj)*.

forest *(n)* a large area thickly covered with trees. **forested** *(adj)*.

forever *(adv)* always or continually. *Matt is forever asking questions.*

forfeit forfeiting forfeited
1 *(n)* a penalty. *If you lose the game, you have to pay a forfeit.*
2 *(v)* to give up the right to something. *If you are late, you will forfeit your place in the team.*

forge forging forged
1 *(v)* to make illegal copies of paintings, money, etc. **forger** *(n)*, **forgery** *(n)*.
2 *(v)* If you **forge ahead**, you move forward or make progress.
3 *(n)* a blacksmith's workshop.

forget forgetting forgot forgotten *(v)* If you **forget** something, you do not remember it. **forgetfulness** *(n)*, **forgetful** *(adj)*.

forgive forgiving forgave forgiven *(v)* to pardon someone or to stop blaming them for something. **forgiveness** *(n)*, **forgiving** *(adj)*.

Some words that begin with an "f" sound are spelled "ph."

fork forking forked
1 *(n)* an instrument with prongs, used for eating or for working in a garden.
2 *(n)* a place where a road, river, tree, etc., branches in two or more directions. **fork** *(v),* **forked** *(adj).*
3 *(v) (informal)* If you **fork over** for something, you pay for it reluctantly.

forklift *(n)*
a vehicle with two prongs, or forks, at the front, used for lifting and carrying loads. *When the driver operates the controls on this forklift, the cylinder rises and chains pull up the cage and the forks, which carry the load.*

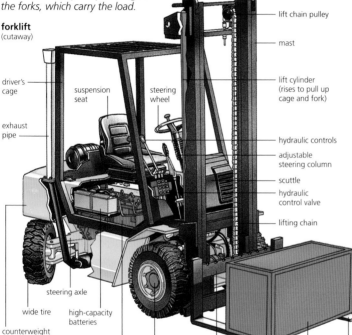

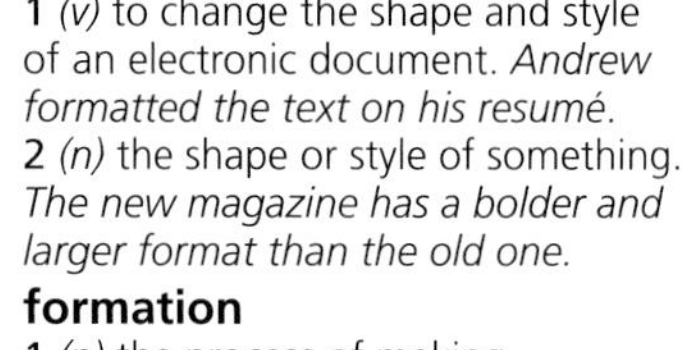

forklift
(cutaway)

forlorn *(adj)*
sad or lonely. **forlornly** *(adv).*

form forming formed
1 *(n)* shape. *The monster took on a human form.* **formless** *(adj).*
2 *(n)* a type or a kind. *Which form of travel do you prefer?*
3 *(v)* to make up or create something. *The lines formed a rectangle.*
4 *(n)* a piece of paper with questions to be filled in.
5 If you are **in good form**, you are fit and cheerful.

formal
1 *(adj)* official. *We're waiting for formal permission before we make any plans.* **formally** *(adv).*
2 *(adj)* proper and not casual. *Formal clothes.* **formally** *(adv).*

format formatting formatted
1 *(v)* to change the shape and style of an electronic document. *Andrew formatted the text on his resumé.*
2 *(n)* the shape or style of something. *The new magazine has a bolder and larger format than the old one.*

formation
1 *(n)* the process of making something. *We are studying the formation of crystals.*
2 *(n)* a pattern or a shape. *Look at that wonderful cloud formation!*

former
1 *(n)* the first of two things that you have been talking about. *I am fond of spiders and snakes but I really prefer the former.*
2 *(adj)* previous or earlier. *Our former house.* **formerly** *(adv).*

formidable *(adj)*
difficult or frightening. *A formidable challenge.* **formidably** *(adv).*

formula formulas *or* formulae
1 *(n)* a rule in science or math that is written with numbers and symbols.
2 *(n)* a suggested set of actions. *What's your formula for success?*

formulate
formulating formulated *(v)*
If you **formulate** a theory, you work out an idea and then state it clearly.

forsake forsaking forsook forsaken *(v)* to abandon or give up someone or something.

fort
1 *(n)* a building similar to a castle, which is strongly built to survive attacks.
2 If you **hold down the fort**, you look after things for someone else while they are away.

forte *(for-tay)*
1 *(n)* Your **forte** is your strong point.
2 *(adv)* loudly. **Forte** is an Italian word used as an instruction in music.

forthcoming
1 *(adj)* coming soon. *Forthcoming attractions.*
2 *(adj)* If someone is not very **forthcoming**, they do not say much.

fortify fortifies fortifying fortified
1 *(v)* to make a place stronger against attack. *The soldiers fortified the outpost's defenses.* **fortification** *(n).*
2 *(v)* If you **fortify** yourself, you make yourself feel better and stronger. *The climbers fortified themselves with hot soup.*

fortnight *(n)* a two-week period. **fortnightly** *(adj),* **fortnightly** *(adv).*

fortress fortresses *(n)*
a castle or town that is strengthened against attack.

fortunate *(adj)*
lucky. **fortunately** *(adv).*

fortune
1 *(n)* chance or good luck.
2 *(n)* a large amount of money.
3 *(n)* fate or destiny.

forward
1 *(adv)* toward the front, or ahead. *We crept forward cautiously.* **forward** *(adj).*
2 *(adv)* toward the future. *I am looking forward to the holidays.*
3 *(n)* a player in soccer, hockey, etc. who plays in an attacking position and tries to score goals.

fossil *(n)* the remains or trace of an animal or a plant from millions of years ago, preserved as rock. *Examples of different types of fossils are shown in this picture.* **fossilized** *(adj).*

fossils

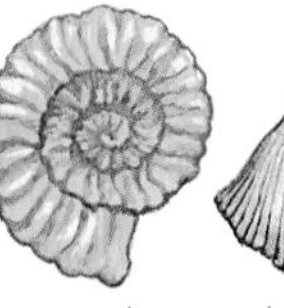

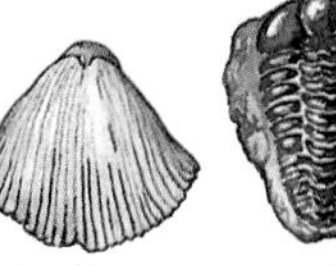

foster fostering fostered
1 *(v)* to encourage or develop something. *The new club fostered a sense of community.*
2 *(v)* to look after a child who is not your own, without becoming its legal parent.

foul fouling fouled; fouler foulest
1 *(adj)* very dirty or disgusting.
2 *(v)* to make something dirty or unpleasant.
3 *(n)* an action in sport that is against the rules. **foul** *(v).*

found founding founded *(v)* to set up or start something, such as a school. **founder** *(n).*

foundation
1 *(n)* the base or basis of something.
2 *(n)* the solid structure on which a building is built. *See* **building**.

foundry foundries *(n)* a workshop for melting and shaping metal.

fountain *(n)* a shower of water, pumped up into a pool, sometimes through an ornament or a statue.

fountain pen *(n)* a pen with a nib that is supplied with ink from a container inside the pen.

fowl fowl *or* fowls *(n)* a bird, such as a chicken or duck, that is kept for its eggs or meat.

fox foxes *(n)* a kind of wild dog, with large, pointed ears and a bushy tail.

red fox

foyer *(foy-ay) (n)* the entrance hall of a theater, an apartment building or a hotel.

fractal *(n)* a mathematically made pattern, the parts of which, when magnified, exactly resemble the whole.

fraction
1 *(n)* a part of a whole number. *$^1/_2$, $^3/_4$ and $^7/_8$ are all fractions.*
2 *(n)* a small amount. *Polly bought the painting for a fraction of its real value.* **fractional** *(adj),* **fractionally** *(adv).*

fracture fracturing fractured *(v)* to break or crack something, especially a bone. **fracture** *(n).*

fragile *(adj)* delicate or easily broken.

fragment *(frag-ment) (n)* a small piece of something. **fragment** *(frag-**ment**) (v).*

fragrant *(adj)* sweet-smelling. **fragrance** *(n).*

frail frailer frailest *(adj)* feeble and weak. **frailty** *(n).*

frame framing framed
1 *(n)* a basic structure over which something is built. *Our house has a timber frame.*
2 *(n)* a border that surrounds something. *A picture frame.*
3 *(v)* to put something in a frame.
4 *(v) (informal)* If someone **frames** an innocent person, they make them seem guilty by giving false information about them.

framework *(n)* the structure of a building or other object.

frank franker frankest *(adj)* open and honest. **frankness** *(n),* **frankly** *(adv).*

frantic *(adj)* wildly anxious or wildly excited. **frantically** *(adv).*

fraud
1 *(n)* If you practice **fraud**, you gain money by tricking people. **fraudulent** *(adj),* **fraudulently** *(adv).*
2 *(n)* If someone is a **fraud**, they pretend to be something they are not.

freak
1 *(adj)* very unusual. *Freak weather conditions.*
2 *(n)* an unnatural or strange person or animal.
3 *(n) (informal)* someone who is very enthusiastic about something. *A health freak.*

freckle *(n)* a small, light brown spot on your skin, caused by exposure to the sun. **freckled** *(adj),* **freckly** *(adj).*

free freeing freed; freer freest
1 *(adj)* If a person or animal is **free**, they can do what they like. **freely** *(adv).*
2 *(v)* If you **free** a person or animal, you let them go from a prison or cage.
3 *(adj)* If something is **free**, it does not cost anything.

freedom *(n)* the right to do and say what you like.

freelance *(adj)* If you are a **freelance** worker, you do not earn a salary but are paid for each job that you do. **freelancer** *(n).*

free-range *(adj)* Free-range animals are allowed to feed and wander freely outside cages or pens.

freeway *(n)* a main road with several lanes.

freeze freezing froze frozen
1 *(v)* to become solid or icy at a very low temperature. *Water freezes at 32°F.* **freezing** *(adj).*
2 *(v)* to stop still because you are frightened.

freezer *(n)* a large refrigerator that is kept very cold so that you can store food in it for several months.

freight *(frate) (n)* goods or cargo carried by trains, ships, planes, etc.

freighter *(**fray**-ter) (n)* a ship that carries goods.

French fries *(n)* sticks of fried potato.

frenzy frenzies *(n)* If you are in a **frenzy**, you are wildly excited or angry about something. **frenzied** *(adj).*

frequency frequencies
1 *(n)* the number of times that something happens. *The frequency of road accidents has increased.*
2 *(n)* the number of radio waves per second of a radio signal.

frequent frequenting frequented
1 *(**free**-kwent) (adj)* common or happening often. **frequently** *(adv).*
2 *(free-**kwent**) (v)* to visit somewhere often or regularly. *Mark frequents the local park.*

fresco frescos *or* frescoes *(n)* a painting made on a wall or ceiling while the plaster is still wet. *This ancient Minoan fresco shows a bull-leaping ritual.*

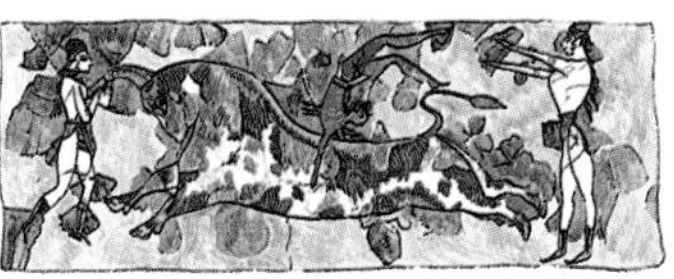

fresco

fresh fresher freshest
1 *(adj)* clean or new. **freshly** *(adv).*
2 *(adj)* not frozen or canned. *Fresh fruit.*
3 *(adj)* cool. *A fresh sea breeze.*

freshwater *(adj)* having to do with or living in water that does not contain salt. *Freshwater fish.*

fret fretting fretted
1 *(v)* to worry or get annoyed about something. **fretfulness** *(n),* **fretful** *(adj),* **fretfully** *(adv).*
2 *(n)* one of the bars on the fingerboard of a stringed musical instrument, such as a guitar. *See* **guitar**.

friction
1 *(n)* the force that slows objects down when they rub against each other.
2 *(n)* disagreement or arguing.

friend *(n)* someone whom you enjoy being with and know well. **friendship** *(n).*

friendly friendlier friendliest *(adj)* kind and helpful. **friendliness** *(n).*

fries *short for* **French fries**.

Some words that begin with an "f" sound are spelled "ph."

frieze *(freez)* *(n)* a decorated strip, usually along the top of a wall.

fright *(n)*
a sudden feeling of fear. *I had a fright when you jumped out on me.*

frighten
frightening frightened *(v)*
to scare someone. **frightening** *(adj).*

frightful *(adj)*
terrible or shocking. **frightfully** *(adv).*

frill *(n)*
a ruffled strip of material or paper, used as decoration. **frilly** *(adj).*

fringe fringing fringed
1 *(n)* a border or edge.
2 *(v)* to form an edge or border. *Tulips fringed the path.*
fringe *(n).*

frisk frisking frisked
1 *(v)* to play in a lively way. **frisky** *(adj),* **friskily** *(adv).*
2 *(v) (informal)* to search someone for weapons, drugs, etc.

frivolous *(adj)*
silly and light-hearted. **frivolously** *(adv).*

frog *(n)*
a small amphibian with long back legs that it uses for jumping. Frogs live on land but lay their eggs in water. *The pictures below show the life cycle of the common frog.* *Also see* **rain forest**.

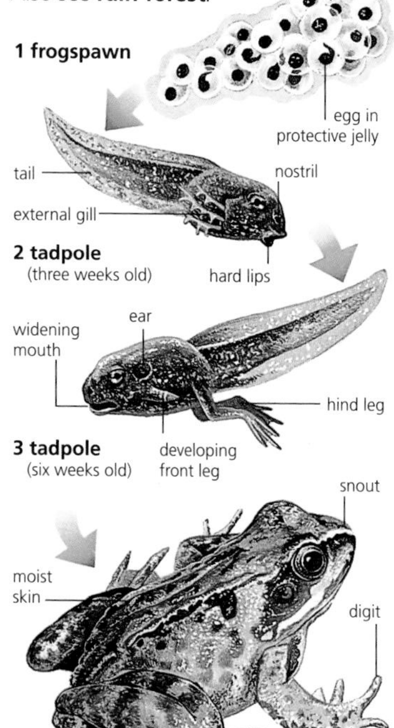

frogman frogmen *(n)*
someone who swims underwater using diving equipment, to investigate things. *A police frogman was called in to search the river.*

frolic frolicking frolicked *(v)*
to play happily. *The children frolicked in the sun.* **frolic** *(n).*

frond *(n)* a large, divided leaf on a plant such as a fern or palm. *See* **fern**.

front
1 *(n)* the part of something that faces forward. **front** *(adj).*
2 *(n)* the place where armies are fighting.
3 *(n)* the edge of a mass of cold or warm air.
4 If you **put up a front**, you pretend to feel or think something.

frontier *(n)*
the border between two countries.

frost frosting frosted
1 *(n)* powdery ice that forms on things in freezing weather.
2 *(v)* If something **frosts up**, it becomes covered with frost. *The windshield frosted up overnight.*
3 *(n)* weather with a temperature below freezing point.

frostbite *(n)*
If someone suffers from **frostbite**, parts of their body, such as their fingers, toes, or ears, are damaged by extreme cold. **frostbitten** *(adj).*

frosting *(n)* a sweet sugar coating used to decorate cakes.

frosty frostier frostiest
1 *(adj)* covered with frost.
2 *(adj)* cold weather caused by frost.
3 *(adj)* If someone is **frosty**, they are unfriendly.
frostiness *(n),* **frostily** *(adv).*

froth *(n)* a lot of small bubbles on top of a liquid. **froth** *(v),* **frothy** *(adj).*

frown frowning frowned *(v)*
to move your eyebrows together and wrinkle your forehead, usually as a sign that you are annoyed. **frown** *(n).*

frozen
1 *(adj)* If something, such as food, is **frozen**, it has been made so cold that all the water in it has turned into ice.
2 *(adj)* extremely cold. *My hands are frozen!*

frugal *(adj)*
If you are **frugal**, you are very careful not to waste anything. **frugality** *(n),* **frugally** *(adv).*

fruit fruit *or* **fruits**
1 *(n)* an edible part of a plant or tree, containing seeds. **fruity** *(adj).*
2 *(n)* the result of something. *This book is the fruit of many years' hard work.*

fruitful *(adj)* successful or useful. **fruitfulness** *(n),* **fruitfully** *(adv).*

fruitless *(adj)* unsuccessful or useless. **fruitlessly** *(adv).*

frustrate frustrating frustrated *(v)*
If something or someone **frustrates** you, they prevent you from doing something. **frustration** *(n),* **frustrated** *(adj),* **frustrating** *(adj).*

fry fries frying fried *(v)* to cook food in hot oil. **frying pan** *(n).*

fudge *(n)*
a sweet, rich candy made with butter, sugar, milk, and usually chocolate.

fuel *(n)*
something that is used as a source of energy, such as coal, wood, gasoline or natural gas. **fuel** *(v).*

fugitive *(n)*
someone who is fleeing or trying to escape. *The girl was a fugitive from an unhappy home.* **fugitive** *(adj).*

fulcrum fulcrums *or* fulcra *(n)*
the point at which something balances or turns.

fulfill fulfilling fulfilled
1 *(v)* to carry out something. *Toni fulfilled her promise by paying back all the money.* **fulfillment** *(n).*
2 *(v)* If you **fulfill** a need, a wish, or an ambition, you satisfy it. *The club fulfills a need for after-school activities.* **fulfillment** *(n).*

full fuller fullest
1 *(adj)* If something is **full**, there is no room left inside it. *The trunk is full of luggage.*
2 *(adj)* whole or complete. *I want a full explanation of what happened.* **fully** *(adv).*

fumble fumbling fumbled *(v)*
to handle something uncertainly or clumsily.

fume fuming fumed
1 *(v)* to be very angry. *Hector was fuming at Miguel's rudeness.*
2 **fumes** *(plural n)* strong-smelling or poisonous gas, smoke, or vapor given off by something burning or by chemicals.

function
functioning functioned
1 *(v)* If something **functions**, it works.
2 *(n)* a purpose, role, or job.

functional *(adj)* If something is **functional**, it is designed to work well rather than to look beautiful.

fund funding funded
1 *(n)* a store of money or other things. *A fund of jokes.*
2 *(v)* If someone **funds** something, they give money to support it.

fundamental *(adj)*
basic and necessary. *My father taught me the fundamental principles of physics.* **fundamentally** *(adv).*

funeral *(n)* the ceremony held after someone has died, at which the body is buried or cremated.

fungus fungi *(n)*
a type of plant that has no leaves, flowers, or roots. Mushrooms and toadstools are both fungi. *Many fungi are extremely poisonous.*

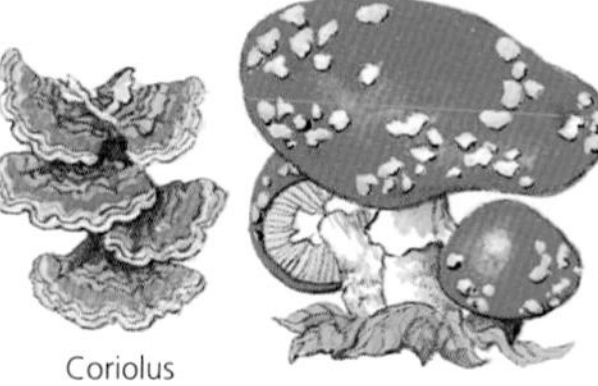

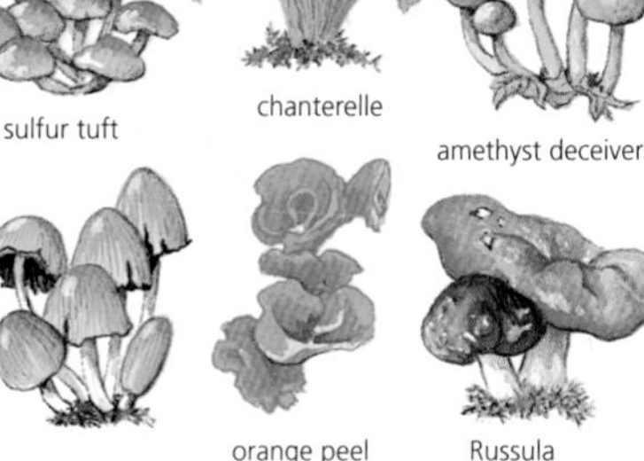

fungi

funnel funneling funneled
1 *(n)* an open cone that narrows to a tube, used for pouring liquids and powders into narrow-necked containers. *See* **apparatus**.
2 *(v)* to pour liquids and powders through a funnel.
3 *(n)* a chimney on a ship.

funny funnier funniest
1 *(adj)* amusing. **funnily** *(adv).*
2 *(adj)* strange. *There's a funny smell in the kitchen.* **funnily** *(adv).*

fur *(n)* the soft, hairy coat of an animal. **furry** *(adj).*

furious *(adj)*
extremely angry. **furiously** *(adv).*

furlong *(n)* a distance of 220 yards.

furnace *(n)* an extremely hot oven, used to melt metal, glass, etc. *The picture shows how pure iron is created from iron ore in a furnace. Blasts of hot air and burning coke raise the temperature of the iron mixture to melting point, when it separates into pure iron and waste products, or slag.*

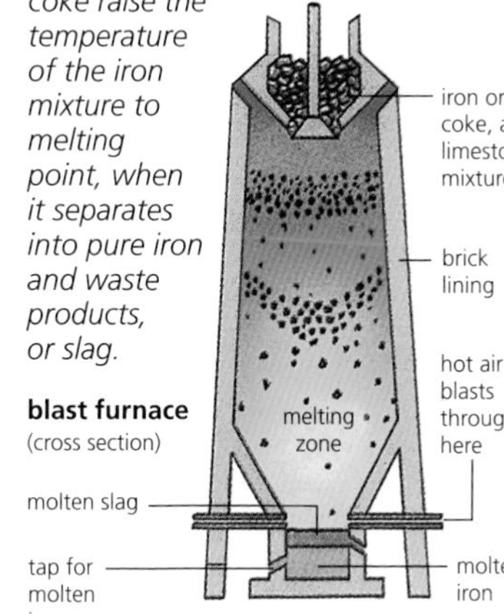

blast furnace
(cross section)

furnish
furnishes furnishing furnished
1 *(v)* to equip a room or house with carpets, drapes, and furniture. **furnishings** *(plural n).*
2 *(v)* to supply. *Can you furnish any proof of your age?*

furniture *(n)* large movable things such as chairs, tables and beds, which are needed in a home.

furrow *(n)* the groove cut by a plow when it turns over the soil.

furthermore *(adv)*
in addition or as well.

furtive *(adj)* sly and cautious. *A furtive glance.* **furtiveness** *(n).*

fury furies *(n)* violent anger.

fuse fusing fused
1 *(v)* to join two pieces of metal, plastic, etc. by heating them.
2 *(n)* a safety device in electrical equipment that cuts off the power in an emergency. If too much current is flowing in the circuit, the wire in the fuse melts, or blows, and the circuit is broken.
3 *(v)* If a piece of electrical equipment **fuses**, the fuse blows.
4 *(n)* a string or wick leading from a bomb, which is lit to make the bomb explode.

fuselage *(fyoo-sel-ahj) (n)* the body of an aircraft. *See* **aircraft**, **glider**.

fusion *(n)*
the joining together of two pieces of metal, plastic, etc., caused by heating.

fuss fusses fussing fussed
1 *(v)* to be unnecessarily worried or excited about something. **fussy** *(adj).*
2 *(n)* more talk or activity than is necessary. *Carla always makes a fuss about having visitors.*

futile *(adj)*
If an action is **futile**, it is useless and a waste of time. **futility** *(n).*

future *(n)*
the time to come. **future** *(adj).*

fuzz *(n)* short soft hair. **fuzzy** *(adj).*

Gg

gab gabbing gabbed *(v)* to chat or gossip.

gable *(n)* the triangular part of the outside wall of a building between the edges of a sloping roof.

gadget *(n)* a small machine that does a particular job.

Gaelic *(gay-lik* or *gal-ik)*
1 *(n)* the name of the traditional languages spoken by some people in Scotland, Ireland, and the Isle of Man.
2 **gaelic** *(adj)* having to do with Gaelic language and culture.

gag gagging gagged
1 *(v)* to tie something around someone's mouth to stop them from talking. **gag** *(n)*.
2 *(v)* to retch or feel like vomiting.
3 *(n) (informal)* a joke.

gain gaining gained
1 *(v)* to get or win something.
2 *(n)* a profit or an increase.
3 *(v)* If you **gain on** someone, you start to catch up with them.

gala *(n)* a special event or entertainment.

galaxy galaxies *(n)* a group of stars and planets. **galactic** *(adj)*.

gale *(n)* a very strong wind.

gallant *(adj)* brave and courteous. *A gallant knight.* **gallantly** *(adv)*.

gall bladder *(n)* the organ in your body that stores bile from the liver. *See* **anatomy**, **chicken**, **digestion**.

galleon *(n)* a sailing ship with three masts built from the 16th to 18th century.

gallery galleries
1 *(n)* a place where exhibitions of paintings, sculptures, photographs, etc. are displayed.
2 *(n)* an upstairs seating area, especially in large halls and theaters.

galley
1 *(n)* the kitchen on a boat or aircraft. *See* **aircraft**, **boat**.
2 *(n)* a long boat with oars, used in ancient times.

gallop galloping galloped *(v)* When a horse **gallops**, it runs as fast as it can. **gallop** *(n)*.

gallows *(singular* and *plural n)* a wooden frame used in the past for hanging criminals.

galore *(adj)* in large numbers. *There were rides galore at the fair.*

galoshes *(plural n)* waterproof shoes that fit over your ordinary shoes to protect them.

galvanize galvanizing galvanized
1 *(v)* to coat steel or iron with zinc to stop it from rusting.
2 *(v)* If you **galvanize** someone into action, you shock them into doing something.

gamble gambling gambled
1 *(v)* to bet money on a race, game, or something that might happen. **gambler** *(n)*.
2 *(v)* to take a risk. *We gambled on the weather staying fine all day.*

game
1 *(n)* an activity with rules that can be played by one or more people. *A game of tennis. A computer game.*
2 *(n)* wild animals, including birds, that are hunted for sport and for food. *Pheasants and hares are both types of game.*
3 *(adj)* If you are **game**, you are willing to try something new or adventurous.

gander *(n)* a male goose.

gang ganging ganged
1 *(n)* a group of people, usually with a leader.
2 *(n)* an organized group of criminals.
3 *(v)* If several people **gang up** on you, they all turn against you.

gangplank *(n)* a short bridge or piece of wood, used for walking on and off a boat.

gangrene *(n)* If someone has **gangrene**, their flesh rots, usually because the blood supply has been cut off.

gangster *(n)* a member of a criminal gang.

gangway
1 *(n)* a clear pathway between rows of seats, for people to walk.
2 *(n)* a gangplank.

gaol *see* **jail**.

gap *(n)* a space between things.

gape gaping gaped
1 *(v)* to open your mouth wide, usually with surprise. *The children gaped at all the presents.*
2 *(v)* to split or hang open. *My shirt is gaping at the seams.*
3 *(n)* the part of a beak that opens. *See* **dolphin**.

garage
1 *(n)* a building used for storing vehicles.
2 *(n)* a place where cars and other vehicles are repaired.

garbage
1 *(n)* unwanted things or waste material, usually from the home.
2 *(n)* nonsense.

garbled *(adj)* If you receive a **garbled** message, it is mixed up and does not make sense.

garden *(n)* a place where flowers, vegetables, shrubs, etc. are grown. **gardener** *(n)*, **gardening** *(n)*, **garden** *(v)*.

gargle gargling gargled *(v)* to move a liquid around your throat without swallowing it.

gargoyle *(n)* a grotesque stone head or figure carved below the roof of old buildings such as churches. *The image below shows a gargoyle that also functions as a waterspout.*

garish *(gair-ish) (adj)* brightly colored and over-decorated. **garishly** *(adv)*.

gargoyle

garland *(n)* a ring of flowers, often worn around the neck or on the head.

garlic
1 *(n)* a strong-smelling plant similar to an onion.
2 *(n)* the strong-tasting bulb of the garlic plant, used in cooking to add flavor to food.

garment *(n)* a piece of clothing.

garnish garnishes garnishing garnished *(v)* to decorate food with small amounts of other food or herbs. **garnish** *(n)*.

garrison *(n)* a group of soldiers based in a town and ready to defend it. **garrison** *(v)*.

garter *(n)* a piece of elastic worn around the top of socks or stockings to stop them from slipping down.

gas gases
1 *(n)* an air-like substance that will spread to fill any space that contains it. *Hydrogen gas.* **gaseous** *(adj)*. *See* **molecule**.
2 *(n)* a gas that is used as a fuel. Gas can be made from coal and can also be found underground.
3 *(n)* a liquid fuel used in many vehicles. Gas is short for **gasoline**.

gash gashes *(n)* a long, deep cut. *I've got a nasty gash on my knee.*

gasoline *(n)* a liquid fuel made from oil, which is used in many vehicles. Also called **gas**.

gasp gasping gasped *(v)* to take in breath suddenly because you are surprised or in pain. *Tyler gasped when he saw the spider.* **gasp** *(n).*

gastric *(adj)* having to do with the stomach. *Gastric juices.*

gate
1 *(n)* a frame or barrier that can be opened and closed.
2 *(n)* the number of people entering a sports arena for a match or event.

gate-crash gate-crashes gate-crashing gate-crashed *(v)* to go to an event without a ticket. **gate-crasher** *(n).*

gather gathering gathered
1 *(v)* to collect or pick things. *We gathered blackberries from the bushes beside the road.*
2 *(v)* to come together in a group. *A large crowd gathered.*
3 *(v)* to discover or learn something. *I gather we're not welcome here.*
4 **gathers** *(plural n)* small folds in material. **gather** *(v),* **gathered** *(adj).*

gaudy *(gaw-dee)* **gaudier gaudiest** *(adj)* very brightly colored and tasteless.

gauge *(rhymes with page)* **gauging gauged**
1 *(v)* to judge something or make a guess about it. *We've tried to gauge people's reactions to the plan.*
2 *(n)* an instrument for measuring something. *A pressure gauge.*
3 *(n)* the distance between the two rails of a railway track.

gaunt *(adj)* unnaturally thin and bony. *A gaunt face.*

gauntlet *(n)* a long protective glove. In the past, gauntlets were worn by soldiers to prevent injury from weapons. *This pair of leather gauntlets was worn by a cavalryman in the 17th century.*

gauntlets

gauze *(gawz)*
1 *(n)* a very thin woven cloth, used as a bandage.
2 *(n)* a thin mesh of wire. *See* **apparatus**.

gaze gazing gazed *(v)* to stare at something steadily. **gaze** *(n).*

gazetteer *(n)* an index of places at the back of a map or atlas.

gear
1 **gears** *(plural n)* a set of toothed wheels that fit together and pass on or change the movement of a machine. *The diagram below shows how gears work. The arrows show the direction of movement.*
2 *(n)* equipment or clothing.

gel *(jel) (n)* a thick, jelly-like substance. *Hair gel.*

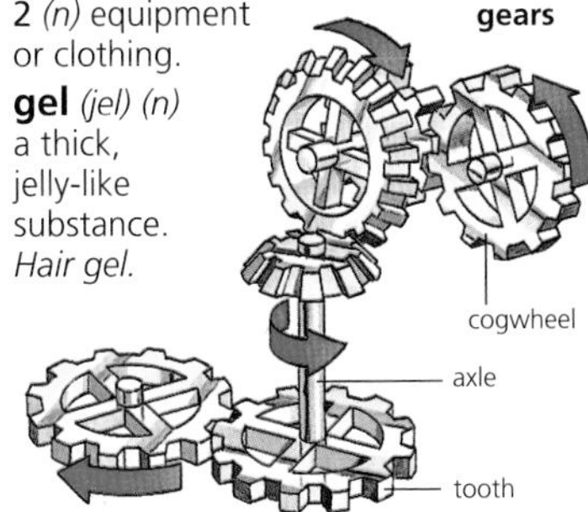

gelatin *(n)* a clear, tasteless substance that you add to liquids to make them become solid.

gem *(n)* a precious stone, such as a diamond, ruby, or emerald.

gender
1 *(n)* the sex of a person or creature.
2 *(n)* All nouns have genders. The four genders are masculine, feminine, neuter (neither masculine nor feminine), and common (either masculine or feminine). In some languages, such as French and German, the **gender** of a noun changes with the way in which it is used.

gene *(jeen) (n)* one of the parts of the cells of all living things. Genes are passed from parents to children and determine how you look and the way in which you grow. **genetic** *(adj).*

genealogy *(jeen-ee-ol-uh-jee)* **genealogies**
1 *(singular n)* the study of family history. **genealogist** *(n).*
2 *(n)* the history of a family.

general
1 *(adj)* to do with everybody or everything. *General knowledge.* **generally** *(adv).*
2 *(adj)* not detailed or not specialized.
3 *(n)* a very high-ranking army officer.

generation *(n)* all the people born around the same time.

generator *(n)* a machine that produces electricity.

generous *(adj)* People who are **generous** are happy to use their time and money to help others. **generosity** *(n),* **generously** *(adv).*

genetics *(singular n)* the study of the ways in which personal characteristics are passed from one generation to another through genes. **genetic** *(adj),* **genetically** *(adv).*

genius *(jee-nee-us)* **geniuses** *(n)* an unusually smart or talented person.

genome *(jee-nome) (n)* all the DNA making up a living plant or animal. *Scientists are studying the human genome to help them learn more about human diseases.*

gentle gentler gentlest
1 *(adj)* not rough. **gentleness** *(n),* **gently** *(adv).*
2 *(adj)* kind and sensitive. **gentleness** *(n),* **gently** *(adv).*
3 *(adj)* not extreme. *A gentle slope.*

gentleman gentlemen
1 *(n)* a polite name for a man.
2 *(n)* a man with good manners.

genuine *(jen-yoo-in)*
1 *(adj)* real and not fake.
2 *(adj)* If someone is **genuine**, they behave in a natural way and do not pretend. **genuinely** *(adv).*

geography *(n)* the study of the Earth, including its people, resources, climate, and physical features. **geographer** *(n),* **geographical** *(adj).*

geology *(n)* the study of the Earth's layers of soil and rock. **geologist** *(n),* **geological** *(adj).*

geometric
1 *(adj)* having to do with geometry.
2 *(adj)* A **geometric** shape is a regular shape, such as a circle, triangle, rectangle, or square.

geometry *(n)* the branch of mathematics that deals with lines, angles, shapes, etc. *The picture below shows a range of instruments used in geometry.*

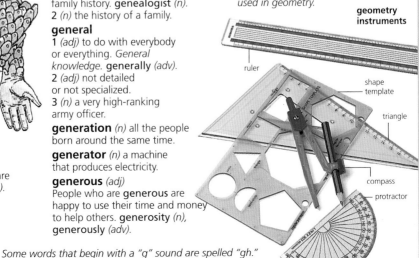

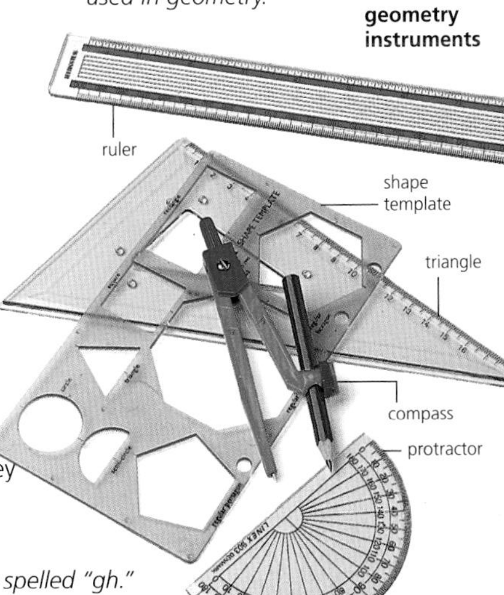

Some words that begin with a "g" sound are spelled "gh."

geranium *(n)* a common garden plant with thick stems and red, pink, white, or purple flowers.

gerbil *(n)* a small furry rodent with long feet and a long tufted tail. Gerbils are often kept as pets.

gerbil with babies

geriatric *(adj)* having to do with very old people. *A geriatric ward.*

germ *(n)* a very small living organism that can cause disease.

German measles *(singular n)* a contagious illness that gives you a rash and a slight fever. It is not usually serious, except for pregnant women.

germinate germinating germinated *(v)* When seeds or beans **germinate**, they start to grow shoots and roots.

germinating bean

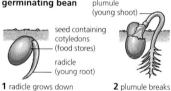

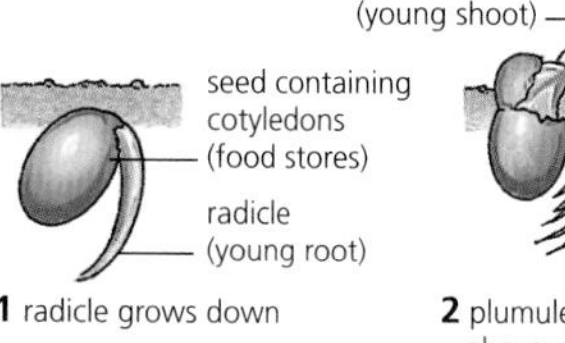

gesticulate *(jes-tik-yoo-late)* gesticulating gesticulated *(v)* to indicate something by waving your hands around in an excited or angry way. *The chef was gesticulating wildly from the kitchen.* **gesticulation** *(n).*

gesture gesturing gestured
1 *(v)* to move your head or hands to communicate a feeling.
The teacher gestured to Nikki that she should sit down. **gesture** *(n).*
2 *(n)* an action that shows a feeling. *I sent her flowers as a gesture of friendship.*

get getting got *or* gotten
1 *(v)* to obtain something.
Please get me a sheet of paper.
2 *(v)* to own something.
Have you got a pet?
3 *(v)* to become. *The pond got bigger.*
4 *(v)* to arrive somewhere.
At last we got home.
5 **get by** *(v)* to manage with very little money.
6 **get at** *(v)* to attack or annoy someone.
7 **get off with** *(v)* to escape a harsh sentence after committing a crime.
8 **get over** *(v)* to recover from something.

getaway *(n)* a fast escape from a situation, especially a crime.

geyser *(guy-zer) (n)* a hole in the ground through which hot water and steam shoots up in bursts. *Geysers are found in volcanic areas, where water is heated to boiling point underground and then is forced upward.*

geyser

geyser
hot spring
crater-shaped nozzle
collecting chamber
narrow passageway
hot cracked rocks

ghastly ghastlier ghastliest
1 *(adj) (informal)* very bad or unpleasant. *A ghastly mistake.*
2 *(adj)* If you feel or look **ghastly**, you feel or look very ill.

ghetto ghettos *or* ghettoes *(n)* an area of a city where a group of poor people of the same minority group live together.

ghost *(n)* a spirit of a dead person, believed to haunt people or places. **ghostly** *(adj).*

GI *(n)* a soldier. GI is short for Government Issue.

giant
1 *(n)* In stories, a **giant** is a very large and strong creature.
2 *(adj)* very large. *Giant size.*

giddy giddier giddiest *(adj)* If you feel **giddy**, you feel dizzy and unsteady, because you are ill or excited. **giddiness** *(n),* **giddily** *(adv).*

gift
1 *(n)* a present.
2 *(n)* a special talent. *Vincent has a gift for painting.* **gifted** *(adj).*

gig *(n) (informal)* a booking for a musician or band to play in public.

gigabyte *(n)* a unit used to measure the capacity of a computer's memory.

gigantic *(jy-gan-tik) (adj)* huge or enormous. **gigantically** *(adv).*

giggle giggling giggled *(v)* to laugh with quick catches of breath. **giggle** *(n),* **giggly** *(adj).*

gill *(n)* one of the two organs on the sides of a fish, through which the fish breathes. *The gill filaments are filled with blood. As water flows over them, oxygen from the water passes into the blood and carbon dioxide from the blood passes into the water.* *Also see* **fish**.

fish's gill

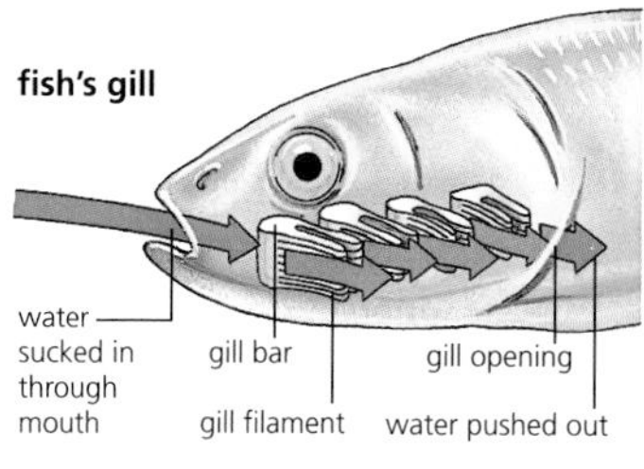

gilt *(adj)* A **gilt** object is decorated with a thin coating of gold leaf or gold paint. **gild** *(v).*

gimmick *(n)* something unusual, used to get people's attention. *The entertainer's gimmick was a flashing bow tie.* **gimmicky** *(adj).*

gin *(n)* machinery. A **cotton gin** separates cotton seeds from the fibers.

ginger
1 *(n)* a plant root used to give a hot, spicy flavor to food and drink.
2 *(n)* a red-brown color.
ginger *(adj),* **gingery** *(adj).*

gingerly *(adv)* cautiously and carefully.

gingham *(n)* checked cotton cloth.

giraffe *(n)* an African mammal with a very long neck and legs and dark blotches on its skin. The giraffe is the tallest animal in the world.

giraffes

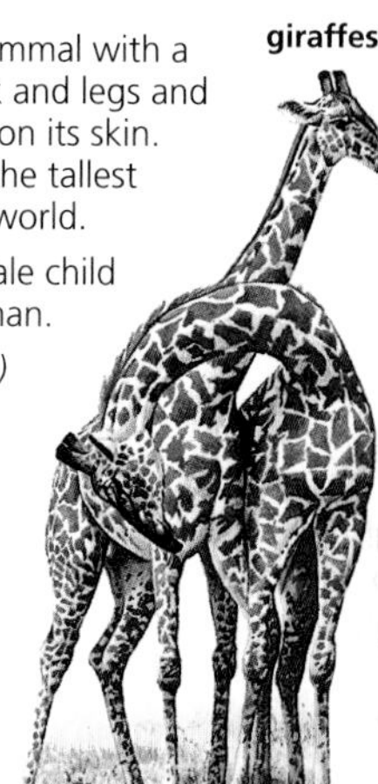

girl *(n)* a female child or young woman.

girlfriend *(n)* the girl or woman with whom a person is having a romantic relationship.

girth *(n)* the measurement around something.

Some words that begin with a "g" sound are spelled "gh."
Some words that begin with a "gi" sound are spelled "gy" or "gui."

jive giving gave given
 (v) to hand over something
o someone. *Give me that book!*
. (v) to pay. *What will you give
ne for this beautiful vase?*
give way (v) to let someone
lse go in front of you.
give in *or* **give up** (v)
o surrender or stop trying.

lacier *(glay-shur) (n)* a huge mass
f ice that flows down a mountain
alley. As the glacier moves,
t erodes rocks
nd deposits
noraines.

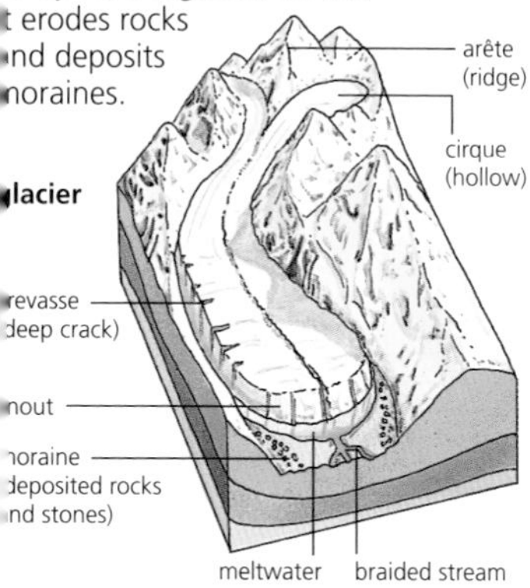

lacier

lad gladder gladdest *(adj)*
leased or happy. **gladness** *(n)*,
ladden *(v)*, **gladly** *(adv)*.

ladiator *(n)*
n ancient Roman warrior who
ought against other gladiators or
erce animals to entertain the public.
*he picture shows a fight between
wo types of gladiators, a retiarius,
rmed with a net and trident, and
 murmillo, fighting with a dagger
nd shield. Also see* **amphitheater**.

gladiators

lamorous *(adj)* attractive and
xciting. **glamour** *or* **glamor** *(n)*.

lance glancing glanced
 (v) to look at something
ery briefly. **glance** *(n)*.
 (v) to hit something and slide off
t an angle. *The ball glanced off the
oalpost into the net.* **glancing** *(adj)*.

gland *(n)* an organ in the body that either produces natural chemicals or allows substances to leave the body. *Sweat glands.* **glandular** *(adj)*.

glare glaring glared
1 *(v)* to look at someone in a very angry way. **glare** *(n)*.
2 *(n)* very bright light that dazzles.

glaring *(adj)* very obvious. *A glaring error.* **glaringly** *(adv)*.

glass glasses
1 *(n)* a transparent material used in windows, bottles, etc. *The picture below shows two 16th-century craftsmen blowing glass.*
2 *(n)* a container for drinking, made from glass.

glass-blowing

glasses *(plural n)* lenses set in frames, worn to improve your eyesight.

glaze glazing glazed
1 *(v)* to fit glass into a window.
2 *(v)* to apply a thin coat of a substance to pottery, paint, or pastry to give it a shiny finish. **glaze** *(n)*.
3 *(v)* If your eyes **glaze over**, they look fixed and glass-like because you are tired or bored. **glazed** *(adj)*.

glazier *(n)* a person who fits glass into windows.

gleam gleaming gleamed *(v)* to shine. **gleam** *(n)*.

glee *(n)* enjoyment and delight. **gleeful** *(adj)*, **gleefully** *(adv)*.

glee club *(n)* a choir that specializes in short sections of songs, called glees, usually with no accompanying music.

glen *(n)* a narrow valley, usually in Scotland.

glide gliding glided *(v)* to move smoothly and easily. *The swan glided down the stream.*

glider *(n)* a very light aircraft that flies by floating and rising on air currents instead of by engine power.

glimmer glimmering glimmered *(v)* to shine faintly. **glimmer** *(n)*.

glimpse glimpsing glimpsed *(v)* to see something briefly. **glimpse** *(n)*.

glint glinting glinted *(v)* to sparkle or to flash. **glint** *(n)*.

glisten glistening glistened *(v)* to shine in a sparkling way.

glitter glittering glittered *(v)* to sparkle with many tiny lights or reflections.

gloat gloating gloated *(v)* to delight in your own good luck or in someone else's bad luck.

global warming *(n)* a gradual rise in the temperature of the Earth's atmosphere, caused by an increase in the greenhouse effect. *See* **greenhouse effect**.

globe
1 *(n)* a round model of the world.
2 *(n)* the world. **global** *(adj)*.
3 *(n)* anything shaped like a round ball. **globular** *(adj)*.

gloomy gloomier gloomiest
1 *(adj)* dull and dark. *A gloomy dungeon.* **gloom** *(n)*.
2 *(adj)* If you are **gloomy**, you feel sad and pessimistic. **gloom** *(n)*.

glory glories
1 *(n)* fame and admiration. *After the victory, the team enjoyed their glory.* **glorious** *(adj)*.
2 *(n)* a beautiful and impressive sight. *The glories of Venice.* **glorious** *(adj)*.

gloss *(n)* a shine on a surface. **glossy** *(adj)*.

glossary glossaries *(n)* A **glossary** explains the meaning of technical words and phrases used in a book.

glove *(n)* a warm or protective hand covering.

glow glowing glowed *(v)* If something **glows**, it gives off a steady light, often because it is hot. **glow** *(n)*, **glowing** *(adj)*.

glow worm *(n)* a young fly or beetle, the tail of which gives off a green glow in the dark. *See* **insect**.

glucose *(n)* a natural sugar found in plants, which gives energy to living things.

glider

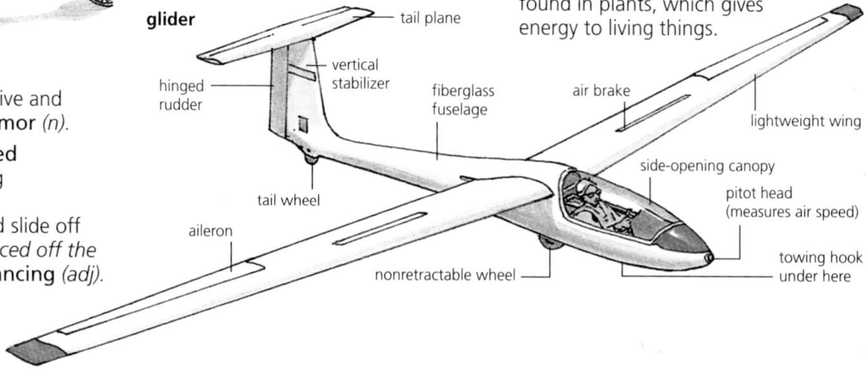

glue *(n)* a substance used to make one surface stick to another. **glue** *(v)*.

glum glummer glummest *(adj)* gloomy and miserable. **glumly** *(adv)*.

glutton *(n)* a very greedy person. **gluttony** *(n)*, **gluttonous** *(adj)*.

GM *(adj)* The initials **GM** stand for Genetically Modified. When plants or food are **genetically modified**, some of their genes are treated by scientists to change them in some way, such as making crops more resistant to pests.

gnarled *(narld) (adj)* twisted and lumpy with age. *A gnarled oak tree.*

gnash *(nash)* gnashing gnashed *(v)* If you **gnash** your teeth, you grind them together in anger or grief.

gnat *(nat) (n)* a small, winged insect that bites.

gnaw *(naw)* gnawing gnawed *or* gnawn *(v)* to keep biting something. *The dog gnawed at the bone.*

gnome *(nome) (n)* In folk and fairy tales, **gnomes** are dwarf-like old men.

go goes going went gone
1 *(v)* to move away from or move toward a place. *I'm going home.*
2 *(v)* to work properly. *This machine won't go.*
3 *(v)* to become. *The class went quiet.*
4 *(v)* If you are **going** to do something, you will do it in the future.
5 *(v)* to have a place or to belong. *Where do the plates go?*
6 *(n)* a turn. *It's my go at batting.*

goal
1 *(n)* something that you aim for.
2 *(n)* a frame with a net into which you aim a ball in sports such as soccer and lacrosse.
3 *(n)* When you score a **goal** in a game, you send the ball into or through a net, and win points.

goalkeeper *(n)* a player who defends the goal in various sports. *See* **ice hockey**, **soccer**.

goat *(n)* a farm animal with horns and a beard, reared mainly for its milk.

gobble gobbling gobbled
1 *(v)* to eat food quickly and greedily.
2 *(v)* to make the sound a turkey makes.

goblet *(n)* an old-fashioned drinking container with a stem and a base, usually made from pottery or metal.

goblin *(n)* In fairy tales, **goblins** are small, unpleasant, ugly creatures.

go-cart *(n)* a very low, small, open vehicle, built for racing.

God *(n)* In Christianity, Islam, and Judaism, **God** is the creator and ruler of the universe.

god *(n)* a supernatural being that is worshipped.

goddess goddesses *(n)* a female supernatural being that is worshipped.

Egyptian gods and goddesses

godparent *(n)* someone who promises their support for a child when the child is baptized into the Christian religion.

goggles *(plural n)* special glasses that fit tightly around your eyes to protect them. *Swimming goggles.*

gold
1 *(n)* a precious metal used to make jewelry, and sometimes for money. *See* **mummy**.
2 *(n)* a warm yellow color.
gold *(adj)*, **golden** *(adj)*.

goldfish goldfish *(n)* an orange-colored fish, often kept in ponds and aquariums.

golf *(n)* a game in which players use clubs to hit a small white ball around a special course. *This picture shows four types of clubs used for playing golf: a wood for striking the ball long distances; an iron for medium to short-range shots; a wedge for lifting the ball high in the air; and a putter for tapping the ball into the hole on the green.*
golfer *(n)*, **golfing** *(n)*.

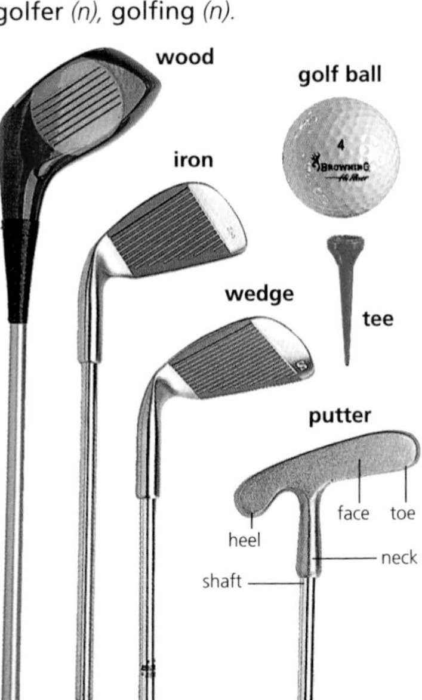

gondola
1 *(n)* a light boat with high pointed ends, used on the canals of Venice. Gondolas are moved through the water by a gondolier using a single oar.
2 *(n)* a cable car, such as those used to ascend mountains.

gondola

gong *(n)* a disk of metal that makes a hollow, echoing sound when it is hit with a hammer.

good better best
1 *(adj)* of high quality or deserving of praise. *A good teacher. A good book.*
2 *(adj)* kind or virtuous. *A good deed.*
3 *(adj)* suitable. *A good fit.*
4 *(adj)* well-behaved. *Mary is such a good girl!*
5 *(adj)* fit and well. *I'm feeling good.*
6 *(adj)* If something is **good** for you, it improves your health or behavior.

good-bye *(interject)* a word said to someone who is leaving.

goods *(plural n)* a general name for things that are sold or things that someone owns. *Leather goods.*

gooey gooier gooiest *(adj)* *(informal)* sticky. **gooeyness** *(n)*.

goose geese *(n)* a large long-necked bird with webbed feet. *See* **bird**.

goose bumps *(plural n)* tiny bumps on your skin that appear when you are cold or frightened.

gore goring gored
1 *(n)* blood and guts. **gory** *(adj)*.
2 *(v)* If someone is **gored** by a bull, they are pierced by its horns.

gorge gorging gorged
1 *(n)* a deep valley with steep
ocky sides. *See* **river**.
2 *(v)* If you **gorge** yourself,
ou stuff yourself with food.

gorgeous *(adj)*
eally beautiful or attractive.

gorilla *(n)* a large strong ape with
dark fur, which comes from Africa.

gory gorier goriest *(adj)*
f something is **gory**, it involves
a lot of blood. *A gory movie.*

gospel
1 *(n)* the teachings of Jesus.
2 *(n)* A **Gospel** is one of the first four
books in the New Testament
of the Bible, which describe
the life and teachings of Jesus.
3 If you **take something as gospel**,
ou believe it to be completely true.

gossip gossiping gossiped *(v)*
o talk with enjoyment about
other people's personal lives.
gossip *(n)*, gossipy *(adj)*.

Gothic *(adj)* in the style of the art or
architecture used in Western Europe
between the 12th and 16th centuries.
Gothic buildings have pointed arches
and windows. *See* **arch**.

govern governing governed *(v)*
o control a country, organization,
etc. using laws or rules. **governor** *(n)*.

government
1 *(n)* the people who rule
or govern a country or state.
2 *(n)* the control and administration
of a country, state or organization.
governmental *(adj)*.

gown
1 *(n)* *(old-fashioned)* a woman's dress.
2 *(n)* a loose robe worn by judges,
awyers, university teachers, etc.

GP *(n)* a family doctor who
reats common illnesses. GP
s short for General Practitioner.

grab grabbing grabbed *(v)*
o take hold of something suddenly
and roughly. *I grabbed the handrail
as I tripped on the stairs.*

grace
1 *(n)* an elegant way of moving.
graceful *(adj)*, **gracefully** *(adv)*.
2 *(n)* pleasant behavior. *Edward
accepted my apology with grace.*
gracious *(adj)*, **graciously** *(adv)*.
3 *(n)* a short prayer of thanks
poken before or after a meal.

grade
1 *(n)* a mark given for work done in
school, college, etc. **grade** *(v)*.
2 *(n)* quality. *The best grade cotton.*
3 *(n)* a class or year in a school.

grade school *(n)*
a school for the first five grades, as well as kindergarten.

gradient *(n)*
a slope or the steepness of a slope.

gradual *(adj)*
If something is **gradual**, it takes place slowly but steadily. **gradually** *(adv)*.

graffiti *(singular or plural n)*
things that people write or draw on the walls of public buildings.

graft grafting grafted
1 *(v)* to plant a shoot from one plant into a slit in another, so that they grow as one. **graft** *(n)*.
2 *(v)* to take the skin from one part of the body to help repair an injury to another part. *Surgeons grafted skin from Dean's leg onto his face, which had been badly burned.*

grain
1 *(n)* the seed of a cereal plant.
2 *(n)* a general name for the product of cereal crops.
3 *(n)* a very small particle of salt, sand, sugar, etc.

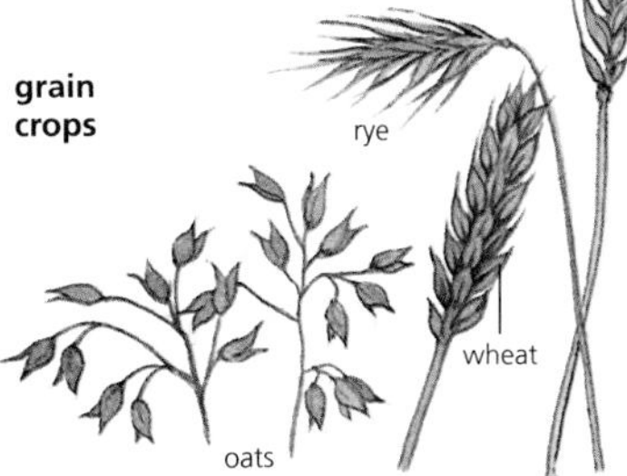

grain crops

grammar *(n)*
the rules of writing or speaking a language. **grammatical** *(adj)*.

grand grander grandest *(adj)*
large and impressive. **grandly** *(adv)*.

grandchild grandchildren *(n)*
You are the **grandchild** of your parents' parents.

grandparent *(n)* Your **grandparent** is the parent of one of your parents.

grandstand *(n)*
a covered structure at a sports ground with seats for spectators.

grant granting granted
1 *(v)* to give something or allow something. *We were granted permission to leave.*
2 *(n)* a sum of money given by the government or other organization for a special purpose. *A study grant.*
3 If you take something **for granted**, you do not appreciate it, or you assume that you will get it.

granulated sugar *(n)* sugar that is in the form of grains or tiny particles.

grape *(n)* the small fruit that grows on a vine that can be eaten as it is, dried to make currants, raisins, etc., or crushed to make juice. *See* **fruit**.

grapefruit
grapefruit *or* **grapefruits** *(n)* a large yellow or pink citrus fruit. *See* **fruit**.

grapevine
1 *(n)* a climbing plant on which grapes grow.
2 If you hear something **on the grapevine**, you hear news before most other people hear about it.

graph *(rhymes with laugh)* *(n)*
a diagram that shows how two sets of numbers are related.

graphic
1 *(adj)* very realistic. *Sonia told the story in graphic detail.*
2 *(adj)* having to do with art and design.

graphics
1 *(plural n)* the layout and pictures of a book or magazine.
2 *(plural n)* the pictures in a computer game. *This game has terrible graphics.*

grapple grappling grappled
1 *(v)* to wrestle with someone.
2 *(v)* If you **grapple** with a problem, you think hard about all the ways that it could be solved.

grasp grasping grasped
1 *(v)* to seize something and hold it tightly. **grasp** *(n)*.
2 *(v)* to understand something. *Have you grasped what I'm telling you?*

grass grasses *(n)*
a green plant with long, thin, leaves that grows wild and is used for lawns. **grassy** *(adj)*.

grasshopper *(n)*
a jumping insect with long back legs. *A grasshopper sings to other grasshoppers by rubbing the hard veins on its front wings over the tiny teeth inside its back legs.*

European grasshopper
hard vein
pronotum (protective shield)
teeth
wing
antenna
thorax
compound eye
ear on side of body
abdomen

grassland *(n)*
a large open area of grass, often used for animals to graze on.

Some words that begin with a "g" sound are spelled "gh."

a b c d e f g h i j k l m n o p q r s t u v w x y z

grate grating grated
1 *(v)* to shred food, such as cheese, into small, thin pieces.
2 *(v)* If something **grates** on you, it annoys you.
3 *(n)* a grid of metal bars in a fireplace.

grateful *(adj)*
If you are **grateful** for something that you are given, you appreciate it and are thankful for it. **gratefully** *(adv).*

gratitude *(n)*
a feeling of being glad and thankful.

grave graver gravest
1 *(n)* a place where a dead person or animal is buried.
2 *(adj)* very serious. *Grave danger.* **gravely** *(adv).*
3 **gravestone** *(n)* a piece of carved stone that marks a grave.
4 **graveyard** *(n)* a piece of land, often near a church, where dead people are buried; a cemetery.

gravel *(n)* small, loose stones used for paths and roads.

gravity
1 *(n)* the force that pulls things down toward the surface of the Earth and stops them from floating away into space.
2 *(n)* seriousness.

gravy *(n)* a hot, savory sauce served with meat and usually made from the juices of cooked meat.

gray *(n)* the color between black and white, like the color of the sky on a rainy day. **gray** *(adj).*

graze grazing grazed
1 *(v)* to scrape the surface off your skin. **graze** *(n).*
2 *(v)* When animals **graze**, they eat grass and other plants.

grease
1 *(n)* an oily substance found in animal fat and in hair and skin. **greasy** *(adj).*
2 *(n)* a thick oily substance used on machines to help the parts move easily. **grease** *(v),* **greasy** *(adj).*

great greater greatest
1 *(adj)* very big or large. **greatly** *(adv).*
2 *(adj)* very important and famous. *A great man.* **greatness** *(n).*
3 *(adj)* very good or wonderful. *We had a great time.*

greedy greedier greediest *(adj)*
If you are **greedy**, you want more of something than you need. **greed** *(n),* **greedily** *(adv).*

green greener greenest
1 *(n)* the color of grass or leaves. **green** *(adj).*
2 *(adj)* having to do with protecting the environment. *Green issues.*

greenhouse *(n)* a glass building used for growing plants.

greenhouse effect *(n)*
the warming of the atmosphere around the Earth, caused by gases such as carbon dioxide, which collect in the atmosphere and prevent the Sun's heat from escaping.

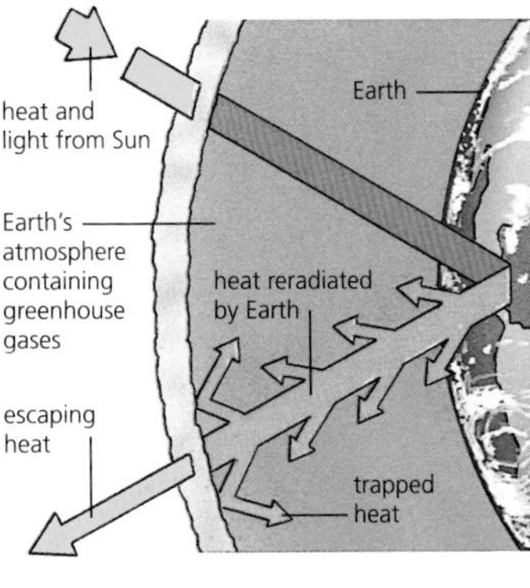

greenhouse effect

greenhouse gases *(plural n)*
gases such as carbon dioxide and methane that are found in the Earth's atmosphere and help to hold in heat.

greet greeting greeted
1 *(v)* to say something friendly or welcoming to someone when you meet them. **greeting** *(n).*
2 *(v)* to react to something in a particular way. *Harriet greeted the news with horror.*

grenade *(n)* a small bomb that is thrown by hand or fired from a rifle.

grid *(n)* a set of straight lines that cross each other at right angles to form a regular pattern of squares.

gridiron
1 *(n)* a playing field marked out for football.
2 *(n)* a griddle.

grief *(n)* a feeling of great sadness.

grievance *(n)*
If you have a **grievance**, you have a real or imagined reason to feel angry or annoyed about something.

grieve grieving grieved *(v)*
to feel very sad, usually because someone whom you love has died.

grill grilling grilled
1 *(n)* a cooking utensil used outdoors that cooks or heats food.
2 *(v)* to cook food on a grill.
3 *(v) (informal)* to ask someone a lot of detailed questions to find out information.

grim grimmer grimmest *(adj)*
gloomy, stern, and unpleasant. *A grim expression.* **grimly** *(adv).*

grime *(n)* thick dirt. **grimy** *(adj).*

grin grinning grinned *(v)* to give a large, cheerful smile. **grin** *(n).*

grind grinding ground *(v)*
to crush something into a powder.

grip gripping gripped
1 *(v)* to hold something very tightly. *Josh gripped the handlebars.* **grip** *(n).*
2 *(v)* If something **grips** you, it holds your attention completely because it is so exciting. **gripping** *(adj).*

gristle *(n)* a tough substance, sometimes found in meat.

grizzly bear *(n)* a large brown bear of western North America.

groan groaning groaned *(v)*
to make a long low sound, showing that you are in pain or are unhappy. *Amanda groaned when her teacher announced the pop quiz.* **groan** *(n).*

grocer *(n)*
someone who owns a store selling food and household goods.

groin *(n)* the area between the top of your leg and your stomach.

groom grooming groomed
1 *(n)* someone who looks after horses.
2 *(v)* to brush and clean an animal, such as a horse. **grooming** *(n).*
3 *(n)* a man who is about to get married or has just gotten married.

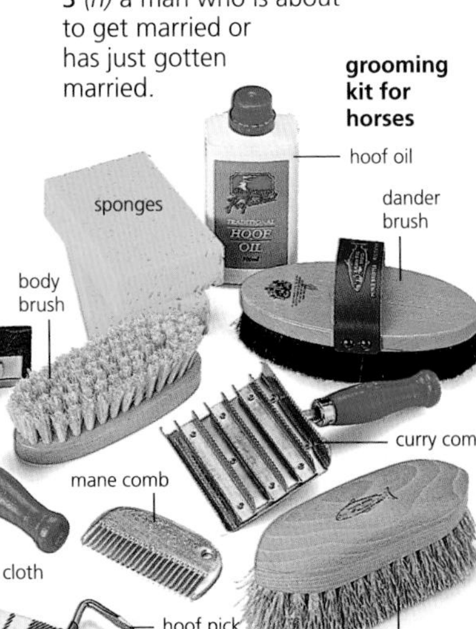

grooming kit for horses

roove *(n)* a long cut
ı the surface of something.

rope **groping groped** *(v)*
ɔ feel around with your hands
ɔr something that you cannot see.

ross **grosser grossest**
(adj) unpleasantly big and ugly.
(adj) The **gross** amount is the total
mount, with nothing taken away.
ross income. **gross** *(n).*
(adj) very rude and bad-mannered.
(adj) very bad. *A gross error.*
rossly *(adv).*
(singular or plural n)
group of 144 things.

rotesque *(grow-tesk) (adj)*
nnatural and horrible.
rotesquely *(adv).*

round
(n) the surface of the Earth.
(n) a piece of land used
ɔr playing a game or sport.
grounds *(plural n)*
eason or cause. *What grounds*
o you have for accusing me?
grounds *(plural n)*
ıe land surrounding a large
uilding or group of buildings.

rounded
(adj) If an aircraft is **grounded**,
cannot fly.
(adj) (informal) If you are **grounded**,
ou are not allowed to go out.

roup **grouping grouped**
(n) a number of things that go
ɔgether or are similar in some way.
(v) to put things into
roups, or to make a group.
(n) a number of musicians
/ho play or sing together.

rove *(n) (poetic)*
small group of trees. *An olive grove.*

rovel **groveling groveled** *(v)*
ɔ be unnaturally humble and
olite to someone because you
re afraid of them or because you
ıink that they are very important.

row **growing grew grown**
(v) to increase in size, length,
r amount. *The tree grew fast.*
(v) to plant something and look
fter it so that it lives and gets bigger.
nthony grows mint in his garden.
(v) to become.
imon grew lazier and lazier.
(v) If something **grows on you**,
ou gradually start to like it.

rowl **growling growled** *(v)* When
n animal **growls**, it makes a low,
eep noise, usually because it is angry.

rown-up *(n)*
n adult. **grown-up** *(adj).*

growth
1 *(n)* the process of growing. *Here's a chart to measure your growth.*
2 *(n)* a lump of body tissue either on or inside someone's body.

grub
1 *(n)* the young form of some insects, resembling a short white worm.
2 *(n) (slang)* food.

grubby **grubbier grubbiest** *(adj)* dirty. **grubbiness** *(n).*

grudge *(n)*
a feeling of anger toward someone who has hurt or insulted you in the past. *Jon bore a grudge against Daniel for months.*

grueling *(adj)* very demanding and tiring. *A grueling job.*

gruesome *(adj)* Something that is **gruesome** is disgusting and horrible. *A gruesome injury.*

gruff **gruffer gruffest** *(adj)* rough and bad-tempered. *A gruff voice.* **gruffly** *(adv).*

grumble **grumbling grumbled** *(v)* to complain about something in a bad-tempered way.

grumpy **grumpier grumpiest** *(adj)* bad-tempered. **grumpily** *(adv).*

grunge *(n)* a type of American music and a way of dressing. Grunge music features loud guitar playing and is influenced by heavy metal and punk. Grunge clothing is scruffy, and usually includes jeans and work boots.

grunt **grunting grunted** *(v)* to make a deep, gruff sound, like a pig. **grunt** *(n).*

guarantee
1 *(n)* a promise made by the makers of something that if it breaks or goes wrong within a certain time, they will mend or replace it for you. **guarantee** *(v).*
2 *(n)* a promise that something will definitely happen. **guarantee** *(v).*

guard **guarding guarded**
1 *(v)* to protect a person or place from attack.
2 *(v)* to watch a person carefully to prevent them from escaping.
3 *(n)* someone who protects or keeps watch over a person or place.
4 *(n)* a football player whose job is often to protect the quarterback or tackle the opposition's quarterback.
5 *(n)* an object placed near another object to provide protection.
6 *(v)* If you **guard against** something, you try to stop it from happening.

guardian
1 *(n)* someone who is not the biological parent of a child but who has the legal responsibility to look after them.
2 *(n)* someone who guards or protects something. **guardian** *(adj).*

guerrilla *(ger-il-uh) (n)*
a member of a small army that fights an official army by launching surprise attacks. **guerrilla** *(adj).*

guess *(gess)*
guesses guessing guessed
1 *(v)* to give an answer that may be right but that you cannot be sure about. *I guessed at the answer instead of figuring it out.* **guess** *(n).*
2 *(v)* to think or believe something. *I guess Karen will arrive shortly.*

guest
1 *(n)* someone who has been invited to visit you or to stay in your home.
2 *(n)* someone staying in a hotel.

guide **guiding guided**
1 *(v)* to help someone, usually by showing them around a place, or by leading them across difficult country. **guide** *(n).*
2 *(n)* a book containing maps and information about a place. **guidebook** *(n).*
3 **guide dog** *(n)* a dog trained to lead a blind person.

guillotine *(gil-oh-teen)*
1 *(n)* a large machine with a sharp blade, used in the past to behead criminals.
2 *(n)* an instrument with a sharp blade, used for cutting paper.

guilty **guiltier guiltiest**
1 *(adj)* If you are **guilty**, you have committed a crime or done something wrong. **guilt** *(n).*
2 *(adj)* If you feel **guilty**, you feel bad because you have done something wrong or have failed to do something. **guilt** *(n),* **guiltily** *(adv).*

guinea pig *(gin-ee pig)*
1 *(n)* a small mammal with smooth fur, short ears, and a very short tail. Guinea pigs are often kept as pets.
2 *(n)* a person who is used in an experiment.

guinea pig

guitar *(n)* a musical instrument with strings, which you pluck or strum. *The vibrations of the strings on this electric guitar are transformed by the pickups into electrical impulses which are then amplified through a loudspeaker. Also see* **acoustic guitar**.

electric guitar

Gujarati *(goo-jer-**ar**-tee) (n)* a language spoken in Gujarat, a state in Western India.

gulf
1 *(n)* a large area of sea that is partly surrounded by land. *The Persian Gulf.*
2 *(n)* a serious difference or disagreement between people.

gull *short for* **seagull**.

gullible *(adj)* If you are **gullible**, you believe anything that you are told and are easily tricked.

gully gullies *(n)* a long, narrow valley or ditch.

gulp gulping gulped
1 *(v)* to swallow something quickly and noisily.
2 *(n)* a large mouthful of drink.

gum
1 *(plural n)* Your **gums** are the areas of firm, pink flesh around the base of your teeth. *See* **tooth**.
2 *(n)* a thick liquid from various plants.
3 *(n) See* **chewing gum**.

gun gunning gunned
1 *(n)* a weapon that fires bullets through a long metal tube.
2 **gun down** *(v)* to shoot someone with a gun.

gunfire *(n)* the firing of guns.

gunpowder *(n)* a powder that explodes easily, used in fireworks and to fire some guns.

gunsmith *(n)* someone who makes and repairs guns.

guppy *(n)* a tiny freshwater fish popular in home aquariums.

gurgle gurgling gurgled
1 *(v)* When water **gurgles**, it makes a low, bubbling sound. **gurgle** *(n)*.
2 *(v)* to make a low, bubbling sound like gurgling water. *The baby gurgled happily.* **gurgle** *(n)*.

gush gushes gushing gushed
1 *(v)* When liquid **gushes**, it flows fast in large amounts. **gush** *(n)*.
2 *(v)* When a person **gushes**, they are embarrassingly sentimental or emotional. **gushing** *(adj)*.

gust *(n)* a sudden, strong blast of wind. **gusty** *(adj)*.

gut gutting gutted
1 *(plural n)* Your **guts** are the organs inside your body, especially your stomach and intestines.
2 *(v)* If a fire **guts** a building, it destroys the inside of it.
3 **guts** *(plural n) (informal)* courage.

gutter *(n)* a channel or length of tubing through which rain is drained away from a road or from the roof of a building. *See* **building**.

guzzle guzzling guzzled *(v)* to eat or drink something quickly and noisily.

gym
1 *(n)* a large room with special equipment for doing exercises and physical training. Gym is short for gymnasium.
2 *(n)* a class or course in physical education.

gymnasium *see* **gym**.

gymnastics *(singular n)* physical exercises, often on bars or ropes, which involve difficult and carefully controlled body movements. **gymnast** *(n)*, **gymnastic** *(adj)*.

Gypsy *(**jip**-see)* gypsies *(n)* a term sometimes used for the Romany people.

gyrate *(**jy**-rate)* gyrating gyrated *(v)* to move around and around in a circle. **gyratory** *(adj)*.

gyroscope *(n)* a wheel that spins inside a frame and causes the frame to balance in any position. Gyroscopes are used to help keep ships and aircraft steady.

gyroscope

Hh

habit
1 *(n)* something that you do regularly, often without thinking about it.
2 *(n)* a piece of clothing, such as a long, loose dress, worn by monks and nuns.

habitable *(adj)* If a building is **habitable**, it is safe, warm, and clean enough to live in.

habitat *(n)* the place and conditions in which a plant or an animal lives naturally.

habitually *(adv)* usually or normally. *Annie is habitually optimistic.* **habitual** *(adj)*.

hack hacking hacked
1 *(v)* to chop or cut something roughly.
2 *(v)* If you **hack** into a computer system, you manage to get information from it illegally. **hacker** *(n)*.
3 *(n)* a long, steady ride on horseback.

haggard *(adj)* Someone who is **haggard** looks thin, tired, and worried.

haggle haggling haggled *(v)* to argue, usually about the price of something.

haiku *(**hy**-koo) (n)* a short Japanese poem in three parts.

hail hailing hailed
1 *(v)* When it **hails**, small pieces of frozen rain fall from the sky. **hail** *(n)*.
2 *(v)* to attract someone's attention. *Travis hailed a taxi.*

hair *(n)* the mass of fine, soft strands that grow on your head or body, or on the body of an animal.

haircut *(n)* When you have a **haircut**, someone cuts and styles your hair.

hairdresser *(n)* someone who cuts and styles people's hair.

hair pin *(n)* a piece of bent wire with sides that press together to hold your hair in place.

hair-raising *(adj)* very frightening.

hairy hairier hairiest
1 *(adj)* covered in hair.
2 *(adj) (slang)* dangerous and frightening.

halal *(n)*
meat that has been produced and prepared according to the rules of the Muslim religion. **halal** *(adj).*

half halves
1 *(n)* one of two equal parts of something.
2 *(adv)* partly, or not completely. *The meal was only half-cooked.*

half-brother *(n)* a boy who shares only one parent with someone else.

half-sister *(n)* a girl who shares only one parent with someone else.

halftime *(n)*
a short break in the middle of a game such as football, or basketball.

hall
1 *(n)* an area of a house just inside the front door.
2 *(n)* a large room used for meetings or other public events.

hallelujah *(hal-ay-**loo**-ya) (interject)*
a word used to express joy and thanks to God.

Halloween *(n)*
the evening before All Saints' Day, believed in the past to be the night when witches and ghosts were active.

hallucinate *(hal-**oo**-sin-ate)*
hallucinating hallucinated *(v)*
to see something in your mind that is not really there.
hallucination *(n).*

halo *(hay-low)* haloes *(n)*
a circle of light around the heads of angels and holy people in paintings.

halt halting halted *(v)*
to stop. *Halt right there!* **halt** *(n).*

halve halving halved
1 *(v)* to cut or divide something into two equal parts.
2 *(v)* to reduce something so that there is only half as much as there was.

ham *(n)* the meat from the upper part of a pig's leg, that has been salted and sometimes smoked.

hamburger
1 *(n)* a round flat piece of ground meat, usually served on a bun.
2 *(n)* ground beef.

hamlet *(n)* a very small village.

hammer hammering hammered
1 *(n)* a tool with a metal head on a handle, used for hitting things such as nails. **hammer** *(v).*
2 *(v)* to hit something hard. *Elsa hammered at the door.*

hammock *(n)* a piece of strong cloth or net that is hung up by each end and used as a bed.

hamper hampering hampered
1 *(n)* a large box or basket used for carrying food, or for storing dirty clothes. *A picnic hamper. A laundry hamper.*
2 *(v)* to make it difficult for someone to do something. *Nina's high-heeled shoes hampered her running.*

hamster *(n)*
a small animal like a mouse, with a tiny tail, often kept as a pet. *Hamsters have pouches in their cheeks for storing food.*

hamster

hand
handing handed
1 *(n)* the part of your body on the end of your arm that you use for picking things up, writing, eating, etc.
2 *(v)* to pass or give something to someone. *Hand me the salt, please.*
3 *(n)* a set of cards that you hold in your hand during a game of cards.
4 *(n)* one of the pointers on a clock. *The minute hand.*
5 If you **give someone a hand**, you help them. *Do you need a hand with your bags?*

handbag *(n)*
a bag in which people carry their money and other small things.

handbook *(n)* a book that gives you information or advice.

handcuffs *(plural n)*
metal rings joined by a chain that are fixed around prisoners' wrists to prevent them from escaping. **handcuff** *(v).*

handful
1 *(n)* the amount of something that you can hold in your hand.
2 *(n)* a small number of people or things.
3 *(n) (informal)* If someone is a **handful**, they are difficult to cope with.

handicap
1 *(n)* If someone has a **handicap**, they are disabled in some way. **handicapped** *(adj).*
2 *(n)* something that makes it difficult for you to do something. *Laurie's platform shoes were a great handicap in the race.*
3 *(n)* a disadvantage given to the more skillful competitors in a sport, to make the competition more equal. *A golf handicap.*

handicraft *(n)* a skill, such as pottery or sewing, that involves making things with your hands.

handkerchief *(n)*
a small square of cloth that you use for blowing your nose.

handle handling handled
1 *(n)* the part of an object that you use to carry, move, or hold that object. *A door handle.*
2 *(v)* to pick something up and hold it in your hands to look at it carefully. *Please handle the goods with care, as they are very delicate.*
3 *(v)* to deal with someone or something. *Katy is very good at handling tricky situations.*

handlebars *(plural n)*
the bar at the front of a bicycle or motorcycle that you use to steer. *See* **bicycle**.

handshake *(n)*
a way of greeting someone by taking their hand and shaking it.

handsome *(adj)*
attractive or good looking.

handstand *(n)* When you do a **handstand**, you balance on your hands with your feet up in the air.

handwriting *(n)*
the style you use for forming letters and words when you write. *Archie has very neat handwriting.*

handy handier handiest
1 *(adj)* useful and easy to use.
2 *(adj)* skillful. *Sasha is handy with a power drill.*
3 *(adj)* close by. *Is there a cloth handy?*

hang hanging hung *or* hanged
1 *(v)* to fasten something somewhere by attaching the top of it and leaving the bottom free. *Hang your coat on this hook.*
2 *(v)* to kill someone by putting a rope around their neck and then taking the support from under their feet. The past tense and past participle of this sense of the verb is "hanged."
3 **hang up** *(v)* to end a telephone conversation abruptly and suddenly.
4 **hang out** *(v) (informal)* to spend a lot of time in a place.

hangar *(n)* a large building where aircraft are kept.

hanger *(n)* a piece of specially shaped wood, metal, or plastic used for hanging up clothes.

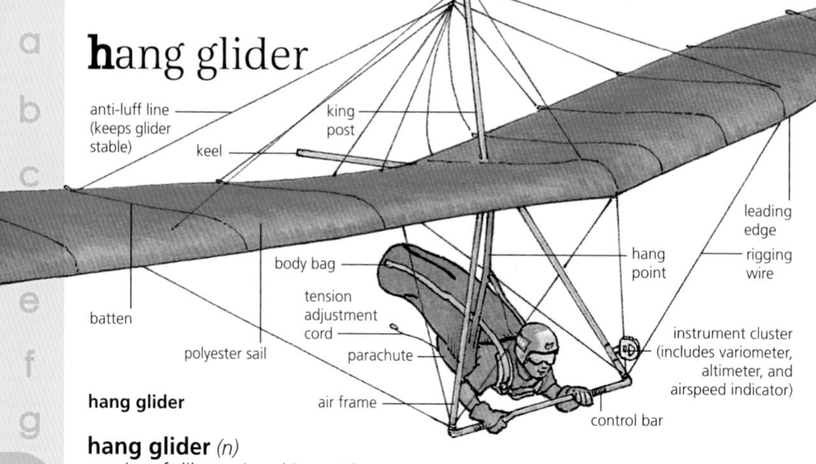

hang glider

hang glider *(n)*
an aircraft like a giant kite, with a harness for a pilot hanging below it. *The pilot controls the hang glider by moving his body.* **hang gliding** *(n).*

hang ten *(v)* a surfing maneuver, in which all ten of the the surfer's toes reach over the front of their board.

hang-up *(n) (informal)* If you have a **hang-up** about something, you worry about it all the time.

hanker hankering hankered *(v)* to wish or long for something. **hankering** *(n).*

Hanukkah *or* **Chanukah** *(hah-nuh-kah) (n)* the Jewish festival of lights, when Jews remember the purification of the Temple. *At Hanukkah, Jews light candles on a menorah, or branched candlestick.*

menorah

haphazard *(adj)*
disorganized and random. *Josh's attendance at school was hapahzard.* **haphazardly** *(adv).*

happen happening happened
1 *(v)* to take place or to occur.
2 *(v)* If you **happen** to do something, you have the chance or luck to do it. *Ned happened to arrive just as the bus was leaving.*

happy happier happiest
1 *(adj)* pleased and contented. **happiness** *(n),* **happily** *(adv).*
2 *(adj)* lucky, or fortunate. *Meeting Bob in town was a happy coincidence.*

harangue *(huh-rang)* haranguing harangued *(v)* to talk loudly or crossly to someone. **harangue** *(n).*

harass harasses harassing harassed *(v)* to pester or annoy someone. **harassment** *(n).*

harbor harboring harbored
1 *(n)* a place where ships shelter or unload their cargo.
2 *(v)* to look after someone secretly.

hard harder hardest
1 *(adj)* firm and solid. *A hard bed.* **hardness** *(n).*
2 *(adj)* difficult. *A hard exam.* **hardness** *(n).*
3 *(adj)* strong or powerful.
4 *(adj)* tough and brave.

hardboard *(n)* stiff board made from pressed wood pulp.

hard copy *(n)*
a printed version of a document.

hard disk *(n)* a disk inside a computer, used for storing large amounts of data.

harden hardening hardened
1 *(v)* to become harder, or to make something harder.
2 *(v)* to become tough and unfeeling. *The emperor hardened himself against the complaints of his subjects.* **hardened** *(adj).*

hardly *(adv)* scarcely or only just. *I could hardly wait to open my gifts.*

hardship *(n)* difficulty, or suffering.

hardware
1 *(n)* tools and other household equipment.
2 *(n)* computer equipment, such as a printer or a monitor.

hardwood *(n)*
strong, hard wood from deciduous trees, such as oak, beech, or ash.

hardy hardier hardiest *(adj)*
If a person, an animal, or a plant is **hardy**, they are tough and can survive in very difficult conditions.

hare *(n)* a mammal like a large rabbit, with long strong back legs. *Male and female hares often box together before they mate.*

hares boxing

harm harming harmed *(v)*
to injure or hurt someone or something. **harm** *(n),* **harmful** *(adj).*

harmonica *(n)* a small musical instrument, played by blowing out and drawing in your breath through the mouthpiece. *Harmonicas contain two sets of reeds fixed to reed plates above and below the mouthpiece. The reeds are left free at one end so that they can vibrate and produce notes when air passes over them.*

harmonica

cover plate
metal reed (fixed below plate)
metal reed (fixed above plate)
hole
mouthpiece
lower reed plate inside here
upper reed plate
slide (changes notes)

harmony harmonies
1 *(n)* agreement. *The team worked in harmony.* **harmonious** *(adj).*
2 *(n)* a pleasant-sounding set of musical notes played at the same time. **harmonious** *(adj).*

harness
harnesses harnessing harnessed
1 *(n)* a set of leather straps used to hitch a horse to a vehicle.
2 *(n)* an arrangement of straps, used to keep someone safe. *A climbing harness. See* **rock climbing**.
3 *(v)* to control and use something. *We can now create electricity by harnessing the Sun's energy.*

harp
harping harped
1 *(n)*
a large triangular musical instrument with strings that you play by plucking. **harpist** *(n).*
2 *(v)* If you **harp on** about something, you keep talking about it.

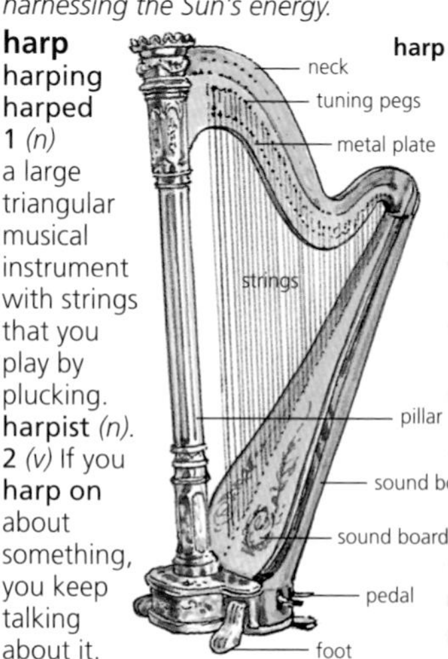

harp

harsh
harsher harshest
1 *(adj)* unpleasant or cruel. *A harsh punishment.* **harshly** *(adv).*

2 *(adj)* A **harsh** noise sounds rough and loud. **harshly** *(adv).*

harvest harvesting harvested *(v)* to collect or gather up crops. *The picture shows the main parts of a combine harvester, which is used to harvest crops such as wheat, barley, and peas. Wheat is gathered and cut by the header, and carried to the threshing drum and beater to separate the grain from the straw. The straw then travels along straw walkers, where more grain is collected and the waste is unloaded. The grain is cleaned in the cleaning shoe and stored in the grain tank, ready for unloading.* **harvest** *(n).*

hatch hatches hatching hatched
1 *(v)* When an egg **hatches**, a baby animal such as a bird or reptile breaks out of it.
2 *(n)* a covered hole in a floor, door, wall, or ceiling. *A serving hatch.*

turtles hatching

hatchback *(n)* a car with a rear door that opens upward.

2 *(v)* If something **haunts** you, you keep worrying about it. *Laura was haunted by the memory of the child's face.* **haunting** *(adj).*
3 *(n)* a place you have visited often.

have having had
1 *(v)* to own or possess something. *I have a new bicycle.*
2 *(v)* to experience or enjoy something. *Let's have some fun!*
3 *(v)* to receive or get something. *Did you have some lunch?*

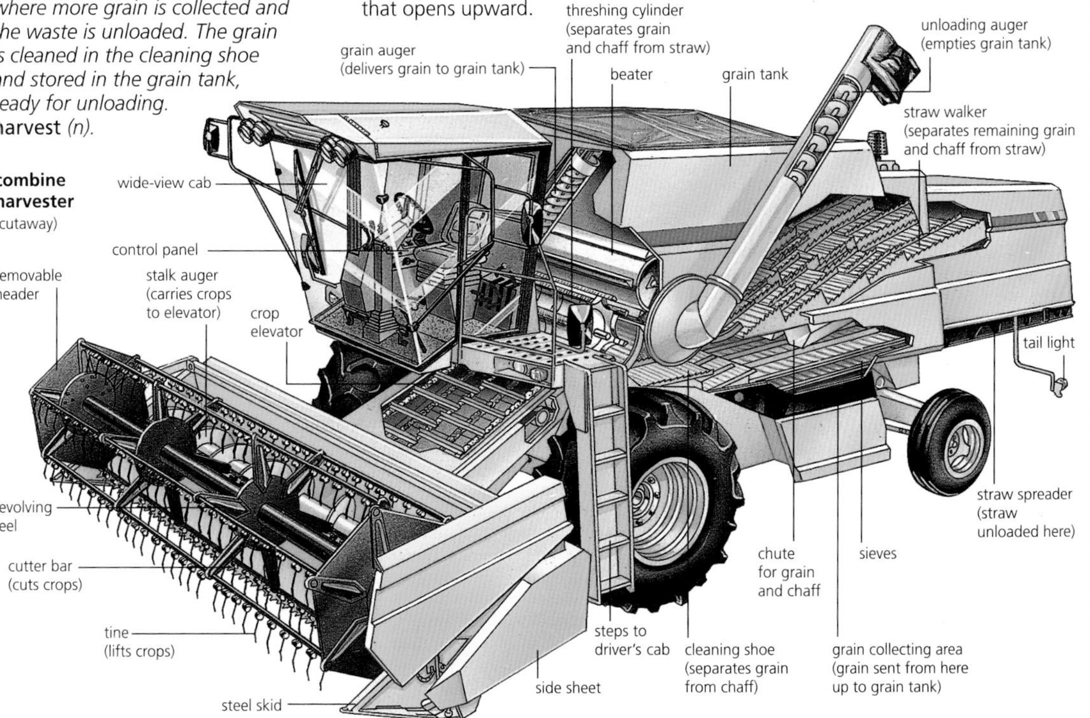

hash hashing hashed
1 *(v)* to chop food such as meat and potatoes into small pieces. **hash** *(n).*
2 *(v)* to confuse or mix up.
3 *(v)* If you **hash out** or **hash over** something, you talk about it or review it. *We hashed out a plan for our trip.*

hassle hassling hassled
1 *(v) (informal)* If someone **hassles** you, they annoy you by going on about something.
2 *(n) (informal)* a nuisance. *It was a real hassle to get up so early.*

hasty hastier hastiest *(adj)* quick or hurried. *A hasty decision.* **haste** *(n),* **hasten** *(v),* **hastily** *(adv).*

hat
1 *(n)* an item of clothing that you wear on your head.
2 **hat trick** *(n)* three successes in a row, such as three goals in a single game by a hockey player.

hatchet *(n)* a small ax.

hate hating hated *(v)* to dislike or detest someone or something. **hate** *(n),* **hatred** *(n).*

hateful *(adj)* horrible.

haughty haughtier haughtiest *(adj)* If you are **haughty**, you are very proud and look down on other people. **haughtily** *(adv).*

haul hauling hauled
1 *(v)* to pull something with difficulty. *Pat hauled the sack of potatoes into the shed.*
2 *(n)* a distance to be traveled. *The flight between London and Sydney is a long haul.*
3 *(n)* a quantity of something that is caught. *A big haul of fish.*

haunt haunting haunted
1 *(v)* If a ghost **haunts** a place, it visits it often. **haunted** *(adj).*

haven
1 *(n)* a harbor.
2 *(n)* a safe place.

havoc *(n)* great damage and chaos. *The floods have wreaked havoc.*

hawk *(n)* a bird of prey, with a hooked beak and sharp claws, that eats other birds and small animals.

hay *(n)* grass that is dried and fed to farm animals.

hay fever *(n)* an allergy to pollen or grass that makes you sneeze, makes your eyes water, and can make you wheeze.

haystack *(n)* a large pile of hay.

hazard hazarding hazarded
1 *(n)* a danger or a risk. *A fire hazard.* **hazardous** *(adj).*
2 *(v)* to risk or take a chance on something. *I'll hazard a guess at the answer.*

haze *(n)*
tiny specks of smoke, dust, or moisture in the air that prevent you from seeing a long way.

hazel
1 *(n)* a tree that produces hazelnuts.
2 *(n)* a green-brown color. **hazel** *(adj).*

hazy **hazier haziest**
1 *(adj)* misty. **hazily** *(adv).*
2 *(adj)* If you have a **hazy** memory of something, it is vague and unclear.

head **heading headed**
1 *(n)* the top part of your body where your brain, eyes, and mouth are.
2 *(n)* the person in charge. **head** *(adj).*
3 *(n)* the top or the front of something. *The head of the line.*
4 *(v)* to lead something. *Homer headed the expedition.*
5 *(v)* to move toward something. *We headed for the exit.*

headache *(n)* a pain in your head.

headdress **headdresses** *(n)*
a head covering. *This headdress was worn by Native Americans as a sign of their bravery in wars and raids.*

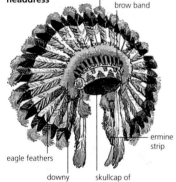

American Indian headdress
tufts of dyed horsehair
brow band
ermine strip
eagle feathers
downy feathers
skullcap of buffalo skin

heading *(n)* words written as a title above a section of writing.

head lice *(plural n)* tiny insects that live and breed in human hair.

headline
1 *(n)* the title of a newspaper article, printed in large type.
2 **headlines** *(plural n)* the most important items in a news broadcast.

headmaster *(n)* a man who is in charge of a private school.

headmistress **headmistresses** *(n)*
a woman who is in charge of a private school.

headphones *(plural n)*
speakers that you wear over your ears.

headquarters **headquarters** *(n)*
the place from which an organization is run.

headway *(n)* If you make **headway**, you go forward or make progress.

heal **healing healed** *(v)*
to cure someone, or make them healthy. **healer** *(n),* **healing** *(n).*

health
1 *(n)* strength and fitness.
2 *(n)* the state or condition of your body. *Aunt Agnes is in poor health.*

health food *(n)*
food that is natural and good for you.

healthy **healthier healthiest**
1 *(adj)* If you are **healthy**, you are fit and well. **healthiness** *(n).*
2 *(adj)* Something that is **healthy** keeps you fit and well. *A healthy diet.*

heap **heaping heaped**
1 *(n)* a pile. **heaped** *(adj).*
2 *(v)* to pile up.
3 *(n)* a great deal of something.

hear **hearing heard** *(v)*
to sense sounds through your ears. **hearing** *(n).*

hearing aid *(n)* a small piece of equipment that people wear in or behind their ears to help them hear.

hearsay *(n)* things you are told but have not actually seen or experienced.

hearse *(rhymes with curse) (n)*
a car that carries a coffin to a funeral.

heart
1 *(n)* the organ in your chest that pumps blood around your body.
2 *(n)* courage or enthusiasm.
3 *(n)* love and affection. *You have won my heart.*
4 *(n)* the center of something. *The heart of the city.*
5 If you learn something **by heart**, you memorize it.
6 **hearts** *(plural n)* one of the four suits in a pack of cards, with a red heart-shaped symbol. *See* **card**.

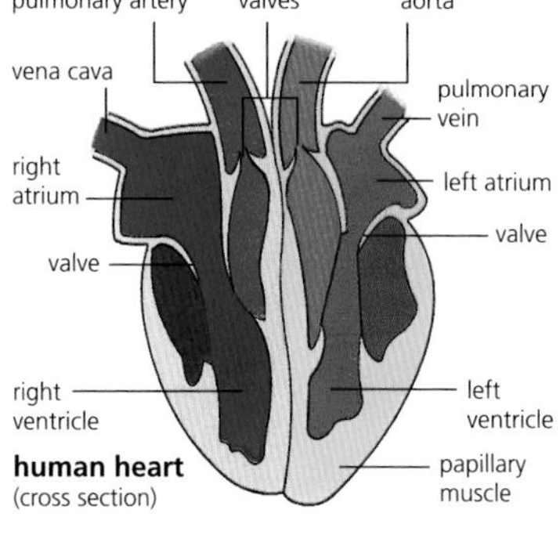

human heart (cross section)

heart attack *(n)*
If someone has a **heart attack**, they collapse because their heart has started to beat irregularly.

heartbroken *(adj)* If you are **heartbroken**, you are extremely sad.

hearth *(n)*
the area in front of a fireplace.

heartless *(adj)* cruel and unkind. **heartlessness** *(n),* **heartlessly** *(adv).*

hearty **heartier heartiest**
1 *(adj)* cheerful and enthusiastic. **heartiness** *(n),* **heartily** *(adv).*
2 *(adj)* A **hearty** meal is large and filling. *A hearty breakfast.*

heat **heating heated**
1 *(n)* great warmth.
2 *(v)* to warm or cook something.
3 *(n)* passion. *In the heat of the argument, I lost my self-control.* **heated** *(adj),* **heatedly** *(adv).*
4 *(n)* a stage in a competition. *Callum got through to the third heat.*
5 **heat wave** *(n)* unusually hot weather that lasts for a few days.

heath *(n)* a large wild area of grasses, ferns, and heather.

heathen
1 *(n)* someone who does not believe in any religion.
2 *(n) (old-fashioned)* someone who is uncivilized.

heather *(n)* a small spiky bush with pink, purple, or white flowers.

heave **heaving heaved**
1 *(v)* to lift, pull, push, or throw something with great effort.
2 *(v)* to go up and down. *Gloria's chest heaved with emotion.*

heaven
1 *(n)* a wonderful place where God is believed to live and where good people are believed to go after they die.
2 *(n)* a marvelous place, thing, or state. *It was heaven to be on vacation.* **heavenly** *(adj).*
3 **the heavens** *(plural n)* the sky.

heavy **heavier heaviest**
1 *(adj)* weighing a lot. **heaviness** *(n),* **heavily** *(adv).*
2 *(adj)* great in amount or force. *Heavy fighting. Heavy rain.* **heaviness** *(n),* **heavily** *(adv).*
3 *(adj) (slang)* serious and hard to cope with. *A heavy movie.*

heavy metal *(n)* a type of music with a strong beat, featuring loud electric guitars and drums.

heckle **heckling heckled** *(v)*
to interrupt a speaker by making rude comments. **heckler** *(n).*

hectic *(adj)*
very busy. **hectically** *(adv).*

hedge *(n)*
a border made from bushes.

hedgerow *(n)* a row of bushes.

heel
1 *(n)* the back part of your foot.
2 *(n)* something that supports the back part of your foot. *Sukie loves shoes with high heels.*

hefty **heftier heftiest** *(adj)* *(informal)* large or powerful. *Nathan used to be slim, but now he's really hefty.* **heftily** *(adv).*

heifer *(heff-er) (n)* a young cow that has not had a calf.

height
1 *(n)* a measurement of how high something is.
2 *(n)* the most important or greatest point of something. *Sadie thinks that her new hat is the height of fashion.*

heighten **heightening heightened** *(v)* to make something higher or stronger. *The painting looked wonderful after Pablo had heightened its colors.*

heir *(air) (n)* someone who has been, or will be, left money, property, or a title. *The heir to the throne.*

heiress *(air-ess)* **heiresses** *(n)* a girl or woman who has been, or will be, left money, property, or a title.

heirloom *(air-loom) (n)* something precious that is owned by a family and handed down from one generation to the next.

helicopter *(n)* an aircraft with large rotating blades on top, which can take off and land vertically. *The picture below shows a Schweizer 300C helicopter.*

hell
1 *(n)* a place of suffering and misery, where evil people are believed to go after they die.
2 *(n)* a very unpleasant place, thing, or state. **hellish** *(adj).*

hello *(interject)* a word said to somebody when you meet them.

helm
1 *(n)* the wheel or handle used to steer a boat. **helmsman** *(n).*
2 If someone is **at the helm** of something, they are in charge of it.

helmet *(n)* a hard hat that protects your head.

help **helping helped**
1 *(v)* to assist.
2 *(n)* assistance. **helper** *(n).*

helpful *(adj)* friendly and willing to help. **helpfulness** *(n),* **helpfully** *(adv).*

helping *(n)* a portion of food.

helpless *(adj)* If you are **helpless**, you cannot take care of yourself. **helplessness** *(n),* **helplessly** *(adv).*

hem **hemming hemmed**
1 *(v)* to fold over an edge of material and sew it down. **hem** *(n).*
2 *(v)* If you are **hemmed in**, you are surrounded and cannot get out.

hemisphere *(n)* one half of a sphere, especially of the Earth. *France is in the Earth's northern hemisphere.*

hemoglobin *(hee-muh-**glow**-bin) (n)* a substance found in your red blood cells, which contains iron and carries oxygen around your body.

hemophilia *(hee-moe-**fil**-ee-a) (n)* If someone suffers from **hemophilia**, their blood does not clot, so they bleed severely when they cut themselves. **hemophiliac** *(n).*

hemorrhage *(**hem**-er-ij) (n)* severe bleeding, usually inside someone's body.

hemp *(n)* a plant, the fibers of which are used to make rope and sacks.

hen
1 *(n)* a bird kept for its eggs and its meat. *See* **chicken.**
2 *(n)* a female bird.

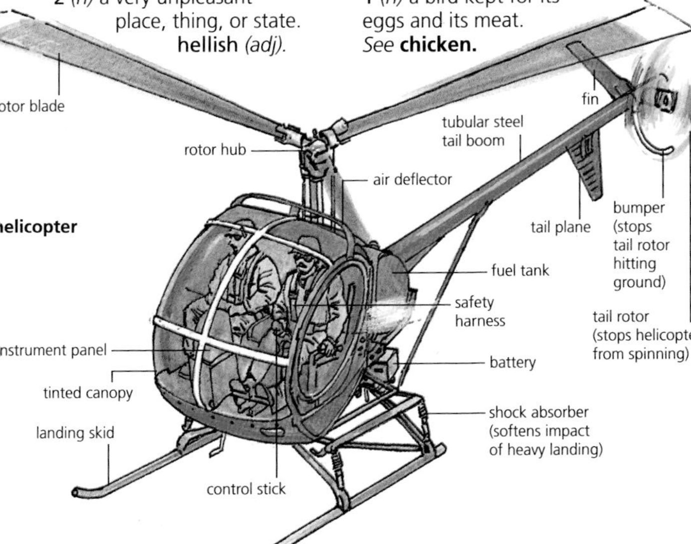

helicopter

heptathlon *(n)* a competition for women, made up of seven outdoor athletic events.

heraldry *(n)* the study of coats of arms and family histories. *The picture below shows some patterns and symbols used in heraldry.*

heraldry

cross

chevron

bend

fleur-de-lys

lion rampant

lion passant

herb *(n)* a plant used in cooking or medicine. **herbalist** *(n),* **herbal** *(adj).*

herbs

herbivore *(n)* an animal that eats plants rather than meat. *Rabbits are herbivores.* **herbivorous** *(adj).*

herd **herding herded**
1 *(n)* a large group of animals.
2 *(v)* to make people or animals move together as a group. *We were all herded into a tiny room.*

here
1 *(adv)* to, at or in this place. *Please come here.*
2 *(adv)* at this point in time. *Here the music gets louder.*

hereditary *(adj)* If something is **hereditary**, it is passed from parent to child. *A hereditary disease.*

heretic *(n)* someone whose views are unacceptable to religious leaders or to people in authority. **heresy** *(n).*

heritage *(n)* valuable or important traditions, buildings, etc. that belong to a country or a family.

hermit *(n)* someone who has chosen to live totally alone.

hero heroes
1 *(n)* a brave or good person. **heroism** *(n),* **heroic** *(adj).*
2 *(n)* the main character in a book, play, movie, etc.

heroine
1 *(n)* a brave or good girl or woman.
2 *(n)* the main female character in a book, play, movie, etc.

heron *(n)* a long-legged bird with a long thin beak, which lives near water.

herself *(pronoun)* her and nobody else. *Emily has hurt herself.*

hesitate hesitating hesitated *(v)* to pause before you do something. *Zoë hesitated before diving into the river.* **hesitation** *(n),* **hesitant** *(adj).*

hew hewing hewed *or* hewn *(v)* to chop or cut with an ax or knife. **hewn** *(adj).*

hexagon *(n)* a shape with six straight sides. **hexagonal** *(adj). See* **shape**.

heyday *(n)* Someone's **heyday** is the best or most successful period in their life.

hibernate
hibernating hibernated *(v)* When animals **hibernate**, they spend the winter in a deep sleep in which their heartbeat, temperature, and breathing rate sink to very low levels. Animals hibernate to survive low temperatures and lack of food. **hibernation** *(n).*

hiccup *(n)* a sudden sound in your throat, caused by a spasm in your chest.

hide hiding hid hidden
1 *(v)* to go where you cannot be seen.
2 *(v)* to keep something secret or concealed. *Julia managed to hide her disappointment.*
3 *(n)* an animal's skin that is used to make leather.

hideous *(adj)* ugly or horrible. **hideousness** *(n),* **hideously** *(adv).*

hieroglyphics *(hi-ro-glif-iks) (plural n)* writing used by ancient Egyptians, made up of pictures and symbols. *The hieroglyphics shown below were used to represent both objects and letters or sounds.*

hieroglyphics

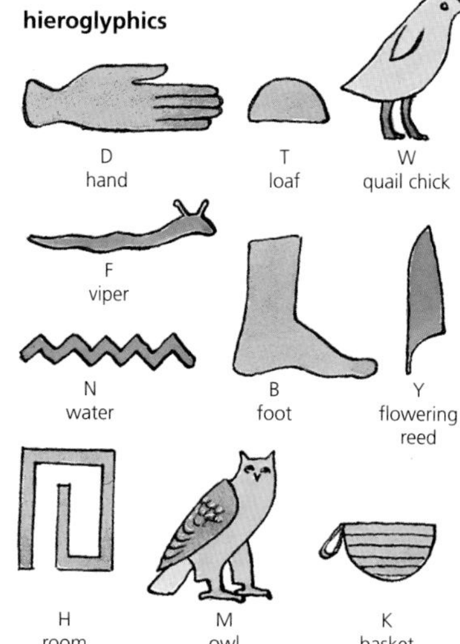

high higher highest
1 *(adj)* Something that is **high** is a great distance from the ground. *A high mountain.* **high** *(adv).*
2 *(adj)* measuring from top to bottom. *The tree was 75 feet high.*
3 *(adj)* more than the normal level or amount. *High prices.* **highly** *(adv).*
4 *(adj) (informal)* If you feel **high**, you are very excited.
5 **high tide** *(n)* the time when the sea is farthest up the beach.

higher education *(n)* education at college or university.

highland *(n)* an area with mountains or hills. **highland** *(adj).*

highlight
highlighting highlighted
1 *(v)* to draw attention to something.
2 *(n)* the best or most interesting part of something.
3 *(v)* to mark important words using a pen with brightly colored ink.
4 **highlights** *(plural n)* streaks of light color in your hair.

highway *(n)* a main public road.

hijack hijacking hijacked *(v)* If someone **hijacks** a plane or other vehicle, they take control of it and force its pilot or driver to go somewhere. **hijacker** *(n),* **hijacking** *(n).*

hike *(n)* a long walk in the country. **hiker** *(n),* **hiking** *(n),* **hike** *(v).*

hiker

hilarious *(adj)* very funny. **hilarity** *(n).*

hill *(n)* a raised area of land that is smaller than a mountain. **hilly** *(adj).*

himself *(pronoun)* him and nobody else. *Justin has hurt himself.*

hinder hindering hindered *(v)* If someone or something **hinders** you they make things difficult for you. **hindrance** *(n).*

Hindi *(n)* a language spoken in northern India.

Hinduism *(n)* the main religion of India. Hindus have a lot of gods, and believe that they live many lives in different bodies. *This is a statue of Shiva, one of the main gods in Hinduism.* **Hindu** *(n),* **Hindu** *(adj).*

Shiva

hinge hinging hinged
1 *(n)* a movable metal joint on a window or door. **hinged** *(adj).*
2 *(v)* to depend on something. *My future hinges on your decision.*

hint
1 *(n)* a clue or a helpful tip. **hint** *(v).*
2 *(n)* a trace or a tiny amount. *There's a hint of garlic in this soup.*

hip *(n)* the area at the side of your body between your thighs and your waist.

hip-hop *(n)* a style of dancing, art, music and dress that originated in urban areas and became popular through break dancing, graffiti, and rap music.

hippie *or* **hippy** hippies *(n)* a name for someone who does not live or dress in a conventional way. Hippies often live in groups.

Some words that begin with a "hi" sound are spelled "hy."

hippopotamus
hippopotamuses
or **hippopotami** *(n)*
a large African mammal, with short legs and thick skin, which lives near water.

hire **hiring hired** *(v)*
to rent something for a short time or employ someone. *We hired a driver for the day.*

Hispanic *(adj)*
coming from, or having to do with Spanish or Portuguese-speaking countries. **Hispanic** *(n).*

hiss **hisses hissing hissed** *(v)*
to make a "ssss" noise like a snake, especially to show that you do not like something or someone. *We hissed at the villains in the play.* **hiss** *(n).*

historic *(adj)*
important in history. *The historic first landing on the Moon.*

history **histories**
1 *(n)* the study of past events. **historian** *(n),* **historical** *(adj),* **historically** *(adv).*
2 *(n)* a description of past events. *I'm reading a history of the Wild West.*

hit **hitting hit**
1 *(v)* to smack or strike something with your hand, a bat, etc. **hit** *(n).*
2 *(v)* to knock or bump into something. *The stone hit the window.*
3 *(v)* to have a bad effect on someone or something. *The factory was hit by the recession.*
4 *(n)* a successful song, play, etc.
5 *(v) (informal)* If you **hit it off** with someone, you get along well with them.

hitch **hitches hitching hitched**
1 *(v)* to join something to a vehicle. *They hitched the trailer to the van.*
2 *(n)* a problem. *There's been a hitch in our plans, so we can't come.*
3 *(slang)* If you **get hitched,** you marry someone.

hitchhike **hitchhiking hitchhiked**
(v) to travel by getting lifts in other people's vehicles. *It can be very dangerous to hitchhike.* **hitchhiker** *(n).*

hither *(adv) (old-fashioned)*
to or toward this place. *Come hither!*

HIV
1 *(n)* a virus that can lead to AIDS. HIV stands for Human Immunodeficiency Virus.
2 *(adj)* If someone is **HIV positive,** they have the HIV virus and may develop AIDS.

hive *(n)*
a box for keeping bees so that their honey can be collected. *The queen bee lays her eggs in the brood box and honey is stored in the supers. The honey-filled supers are collected from the hive by beekeepers. Also see* **honeycomb**.

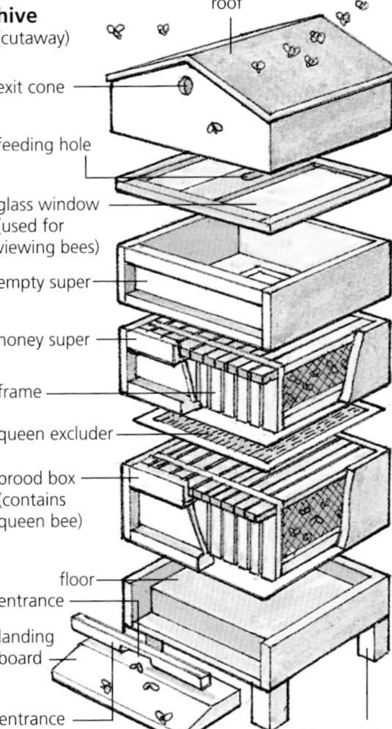

hoard **hoarding hoarded** *(v)*
to collect and store things. **hoard** *(n),* **hoarder** *(n).*

hoarse **hoarser hoarsest** *(adj)*
A **hoarse** voice is rough or croaky.

hoax *(rhymes with pokes)* **hoaxes** *(n)*
a trick or a practical joke.

hobble **hobbling hobbled** *(v)*
to walk with difficulty, because you are in pain or are injured.

hobby **hobbies** *(n)* something that you enjoy doing in your spare time.

hockey *(n)* a game played on an ice rink with sticks and a puck, by two teams aiming to score goals.

hoe *(n)* a gardening tool with a long handle and a thin blade, used for weeding and loosening earth. **hoe** *(v).*

hoist **hoisting hoisted**
1 *(v)* to lift something heavy, usually with a piece of equipment.
2 *(n)* a piece of equipment used for lifting heavy objects.

hold **holding held**
1 *(v)* to carry, support, or keep something. *Hold this cup.* **holder** *(n).*
2 *(v)* to contain something or be able to contain it. *This bottle holds a quart.*
3 *(v)* to organize or arrange something. *We are holding a party.*
4 *(n)* the part of a ship where the cargo is stored.

hole
1 *(n)* a hollow place or a gap. *My sock has a hole in it.*
2 *(n)* an animal's burrow.
3 *(n) (informal)* an unpleasant or dirty place. *Jeff's apartment is such a hole.*

holiday
1 *(n)* a day when school, work and other regular activities are suspended. Labor Day is a holiday.
2 *(n)* a religious festival or holy time such as Christmas, Passover, or the month of Ramadan.

hollow **hollowing hollowed**
1 *(adj)* If something is **hollow,** it has an empty space inside it. *This tree is hollow.* **hollow** *(n).*
2 **hollow out** *(v)* If you **hollow something out**, you take its insides out. *We need to hollow out the pumpkin before we carve it.*

holly *(n)* an evergreen tree or bush with prickly leaves and red berries.

hologram *(n)*
an image made by laser beams that looks three-dimensional.

holster *(n)*
a holder for a pistol, worn on a belt.

holy **holier holiest** *(adj)* having to do with or belonging to God or a god.

Holy Communion *(n)* a Christian service in which people eat bread and drink wine in memory of the death and resurrection of Jesus Christ.

home
1 *(n)* Your **home** is where you live or belong.
2 If you **feel at home** with something or someone, you feel comfortable with them.

homeopathy
*(home-ee-***op***-ath-ee) (n)*
a way of treating illness by giving people very small amounts of drugs that produce the same symptoms as the illness. **homeopathic** *(adj).*

homesick *(adj)* If you are **homesick**, you miss your home and family.

homicide *(n)* murder.

honest *(adj)* An **honest** person is truthful and will not lie or steal. **honesty** *(n),* **honestly** *(adv).*

honey *(n)* a sweet sticky golden-brown substance made by bees. *See* **hive, honeycomb**.

Some words that begin with a "hi" sound are spelled "hy."
Some words that begin with a "h" sound are spelled "wh."

a b c d e f g h i j k l m n o p q r s t u v w x y z

honeycomb *(n)*
a wax structure made by bees and used by them to store honey, pollen, and eggs. A honeycomb consists of many rows of six-sided cells. *The picture shows the different functions of the cells in a honeycomb. For the first six days, the brood cells are unsealed so the worker bees can feed the growing larvae. Then the bees seal the cells and the larvae change into pupae, which develop into bees.* *Also see* **hive**.

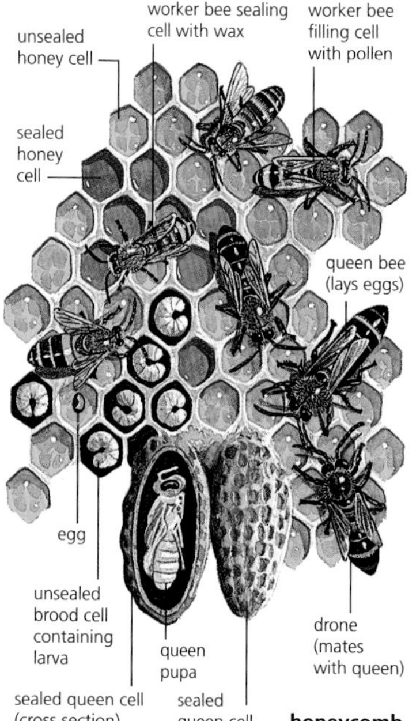

honeycomb

honeymoon *(n)*
a vacation that a husband and wife take together after their wedding.

honor honoring honored
1 *(n)* Someone's **honor** is their good reputation and the respect that other people have for them.
2 *(v)* to give praise or an award. *The mayor honored Kim for her bravery.*
3 *(v)* to keep an agreement. *Both parties must honor the contract.*

honorable
1 *(adj)* An **honorable** action is good and deserves praise. *It was very honorable of you to donate all that money to charity.*
2 *(adj)* If someone is **honorable**, they keep their promises.

hood
1 *(n)* the part of a jacket or coat that goes over your head. **hooded** *(adj).*
2 *(n)* the cover for a car's engine.

hoof hooves *or* hoofs *(n)*
the hard covering over the foot of a horse, deer, etc. *See* **horse**.

hook
1 *(n)* a curved piece of metal or plastic, used to catch or hold something.
2 *(n)* a punch in boxing, made with the elbow bent. *A right hook.*

hooked
1 *(adj)* curved. *A hooked nose.*
2 *(adj) (slang)* If you are **hooked** on something, you like it a lot, or are addicted to it.

hooligan *(n)*
a noisy, violent person who makes trouble. **hooliganism** *(n).*

hoop *(n)*
a large ring. **hooped** *(adj).*

hooray *see* **hurray**.

hoot hooting hooted *(v)*
to make a sound like an owl.

hop hopping hopped
1 *(v)* to jump, especially on one leg. **hop** *(n).*
2 *(v) (informal)* to get into or out of a vehicle. *Hop in the car!*

hope hoping hoped
1 *(v)* to wish for or expect something. **hopeful** *(adj),* **hopefully** *(adv).*
2 *(n)* a feeling of expectation or confidence. *I have plenty of hope for the future.* **hopefulness** *(n),* **hopeful** *(adj),* **hopefully** *(adv).*

hopeless
1 *(adj)* without hope. *A hopeless case.* **hopelessness** *(n),* **hopelessly** *(adv).*
2 *(adj)* bad or lacking in skill. *You're hopeless at map reading!* **hopelessness** *(n),* **hopelessly** *(adv).*

horde *(n)* a large, noisy, moving crowd of people.

horizon
1 *(n)* the line where the sky and the Earth or sea seem to meet.
2 *(n)* the limit of your experience or opportunities. *Travel broadens your horizons.*

horizontal *(adj)*
flat and parallel to the ground. *A horizontal line.* **horizontally** *(adv).*

hormone *(n)* Your **hormones** are chemicals made in your body that affect the way that you grow and develop. **hormonal** *(adj).*

horn
1 *(n)* a hard bony growth on the head of some animals. **horned** *(adj).*
2 *(n)* the hard, bony substance from which horns and hooves are made.
3 *(n)* a musical instrument that you blow. *A French horn. See* **brass**.
4 *(n)* a machine that gives a signal by making a honking sound. *A car horn.*

horoscope *(n)*
a prediction about your life, based on the position of the stars and planets when you were born.

horrible *(adj)*
very unpleasant. **horribly** *(adv).*

horrid *(adj)* nasty or unkind.

horrific *(adj)* shocking.

horrify
horrifies horrifying horrified *(v)*
If something **horrifies** you, you are shocked and disgusted by it. **horrifying** *(adj),* **horrifyingly** *(adv).*

horse
1 *(n)* a large strong animal with hooves, which people ride or use to pull coaches, carriages, plows, etc. *The picture shows a male Anglo-Arabian horse.*
2 *(n)* a piece of gymnastics apparatus that you jump over.

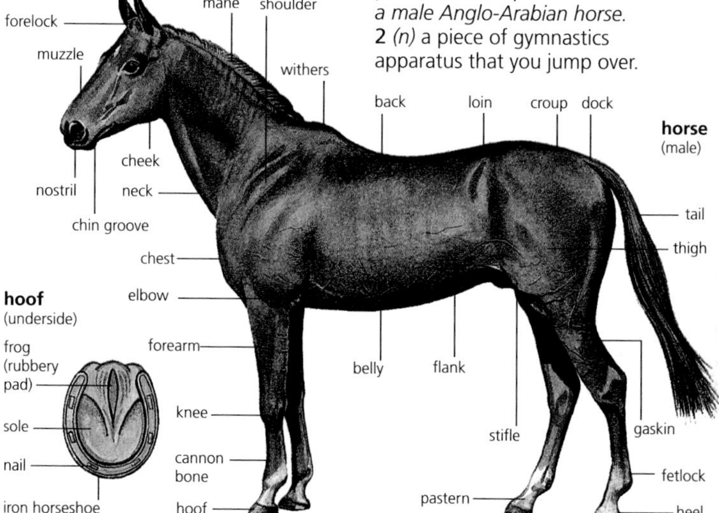

horse (male)

Some words that begin with a "h" sound are spelled "wh."

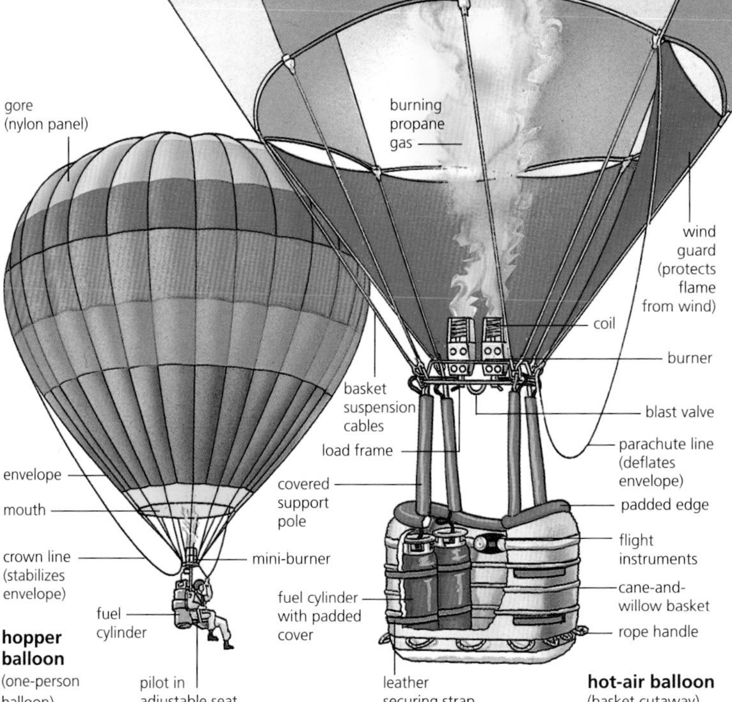

horsepower *(n)*
a unit for measuring engine power.

horticulture *(n)*
the growing of fruit, vegetables, and flowers. **horticultural** *(adj)*.

hose hosing hosed
1 *(n)* a long rubber or plastic tube through which liquids or gases travel.
2 *(v)* to wash or water something or someone with a hose.

hospice *(n)* a hospital that provides special care for people who are dying.

hospitable *(adj)* friendly and welcoming. **hospitality** *(n)*.

hospital *(n)* a place where you receive medical treatment and are looked after when you are ill.

host
1 *(n)* an organizer of an event, or a person who receives guests into their home. **host** *(v)*.
2 *(n)* a large number. *The audience asked a host of questions.*

hostage *(n)*
someone held prisoner and threatened by an enemy, as a way of demanding money or other conditions.

hostel *(n)* a building where people can stay, usually at low cost.

hostess hostesses *(n)*
a female organizer of an event.

hostile *(adj)* unfriendly or angry. *A hostile crowd.* **hostility** *(n)*.

hot hotter hottest
1 *(adj)* having a high temperature.
2 *(adj)* very spicy and strong-tasting.
3 *(adj)* recent or exciting. *Hot news.*

hot-air balloon *(n)*
an aircraft that consists of an enormous bag filled with hot air or gas, and a basket for carrying passengers.

hot dog *(n)*
a sausage eaten in a long bun.

hotel *(n)* a place where you pay to stay overnight and have meals.

hot-water bottle *(n)*
a container for hot water, used to warm a bed.

hound hounding hounded
1 *(n)* a dog. *A foxhound.*
2 *(v)* to chase or pester somebody. *Ziggy was hounded by journalists.*

hour *(n)* a unit of time equal to 60 minutes. **hourly** *(adv)*.

house housing housed
1 *(n)* a building where people live.
2 *(v)* If you **house** someone or something, you find a place for them to live or to be.
3 If something in a restaurant is **on the house**, it is free.

houseboat *(n)*
a boat that people live on, with cooking and sleeping areas.

household
1 *(n)* all the people who live together in a house. **householder** *(n)*.
2 *(adj)* belonging to or having to do with a house or family. *We all share the household chores.*

housework *(n)*
work done to keep a house clean and tidy.

hovel *(n)*
a small, dirty house or hut.

hover hovering hovered
1 *(v)* to stay in one place in the air.
2 *(v)* to linger or be uncertain. *Howie hovered in the doorway.*

hovercraft *(singular* and *plural n)*
a vehicle that can travel over land and water, supported by a cushion of air.

however
1 *(adv)* in whatever way, or to whatever extent. *You have to go, however much you hate it.*
2 *(adv* or *conj)* on the other hand. *We can't come on Friday. However, we could manage Saturday.*

howl howling howled
1 *(v)* to cry like a dog or wolf in pain.
2 *(v)* to yell out with laughter. *We howled at the joke.* **howl** *(n)*.

HQ *short for* **headquarters**.

hub
1 *(n)* the center of a wheel. *See* **bicycle**.
2 *(n)* the center of an organization or activity. *The kitchen was the hub of the party.*

huddle huddling huddled *(v)*
to crowd together in a tight group. *We huddled together against the cold.* **huddle** *(n)*.

hue *(n)* a color or a shade of a color.

huff *(n)*
If you are **in a huff**, you show that you are upset in a childish sulky way.

hug hugging hugged *(v)*
to hold someone tightly in a loving or caring way. **hug** *(n)*.

huge huger hugest *(adj)*
enormous or gigantic. *A huge amount of money.*

hulk
1 *(n)* the remains of a wrecked ship.
2 *(n)* a large clumsy person. **hulking** *(adj)*.

hum humming hummed
1 *(v)* to sing with your mouth closed. **hum** *(n)*.
2 *(v)* to make a steady, buzzing noise. **hum** *(n)*.

human
1 **human** *or* **human being** *(n)*
a person. **human** *(adj)*.
2 *(adj)* natural and understandable. *It was only human for Lucy to get angry when someone stole her new bike.*
3 *(plural n)* When people campaign for **human rights**, they fight for everyone's right to have justice, fair treatment, and free speech.

a b c d e f g h i j k l m n o p q r s t u v w x y z

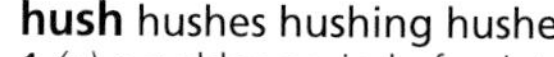

humane *(adj)*
kind and merciful. **humanely** *(adv).*

humanitarian *(adj)* having to do with helping people and relieving suffering. *Humanitarian aid.*

humanities *(plural n)*
non-science subjects, such as art, history, and literature.

humanity
1 *(n)* all human beings.
2 *(n)* kindness and sympathy.

humble humbler humblest *(adj)*
modest and not proud. **humbly** *(adv).*

humdrum *(adj)* A **humdrum** life is dull and filled with routine events.

humid *(adj)*
warm and damp. **humidity** *(n).*

humiliate
humiliating humiliated *(v)* to make someone look or feel totally foolish and undignified. **humiliation** *(n).*

humility *(n)* If you show **humility**, you are not proud and you recognize your own faults.

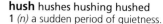

hummingbird *(n)* a very small, brightly colored tropical bird that makes a humming sound when it flaps its wings rapidly. *This Green Violetear hummingbird is sticking its long beak into a flower so that it can suck up nectar through its hollow tongue.*

hummingbird

humor humoring humored
1 *(n)* the general name for things that make people laugh or smile. **humorous** *(adj).*
2 *(n)* If you have a **sense of humor**, you are quick to appreciate the funny side of life. **humorous** *(adj).*
3 *(v)* If you **humor** someone, you keep them happy by agreeing with them or doing what they want.

hump humping humped *(n)*
a small hill or a large lump.

humus *(n)* rich earth made from rotting vegetable and animal matter.

hunch
hunches hunching hunched
1 *(v)* to lower your head into your shoulders and lean forward.
2 *(n)* an idea that is not backed by much reason or proof. *I had a hunch that I would hear some good news.*

hungry hungrier hungriest *(adj)*
wanting food. **hunger** *(n),* **hungrily** *(adv).*

hunk *(n)*
a large piece of bread, cheese, etc.

hunt hunting hunted
1 *(v)* to search for something. *Lisa hunted for her watch.*
2 *(v)* to chase deer or other wild animals for sport. **hunt** *(n),* **hunter** *(n),* **hunting** *(n).*

hurdle hurdling hurdled
1 *(n)* a small fence that you jump over in a running event. *The sequence below shows a hurdler clearing a hurdle.* **hurdler** *(n),* **hurdling** *(n).*
2 *(v)* to jump over something.
3 *(n)* an obstacle.

hurl hurling hurled *(v)*
to throw something with great effort.

hurdling

hurray *or* **hooray** *or* **hurrah** *(interject)* a word used when people cheer.

hurricane *(n)* a violent storm.

hurry hurries hurrying hurried
1 *(v)* to do things as fast as possible.
2 When you are **in a hurry**, you do everything very quickly and often impatiently. **hurried** *(adj).*

hurt hurting hurt
1 *(v)* to cause pain.
2 *(v)* to be in pain.
3 *(v)* to upset somebody by doing or saying something unkind. **hurtful** *(adj).*

hurtle hurtling hurtled *(v)*
to move at great speed.

husband *(n)*
the male partner in a marriage.

hush hushes hushing hushed
1 *(n)* a sudden period of quietness. *A hush fell on the audience as the curtain went up.*
2 *(interject)* be quiet! *Hush!*
3 **hush up** *(v)* to keep something secret. *The scandal was hushed up.*
4 **hush-hush** *(adj) (informal)* very secret and confidential.

husk *(n)*
the outer casing of seeds or grains.

husky huskies; huskier huskiest
1 *(adj)* A **husky** voice sounds low and hoarse. **huskiness** *(n),* **huskily** *(adv).*
2 *(n)* a strong dog with a furry coat, bred to pull sleds in arctic conditions.

hustle hustling hustled
1 *(v)* to push someone roughly to make them move. *The guard hustled the prisoners out of the room.*
2 *(v)* to work rapidly and energetically. *Simon hustled to finish the job by noon.*

hut
1 *(n)* a small primitive house.
2 *(n)* a wooden shed.

hutch hutches *(n)* a wooden cage for rabbits or other small pets.

hybrid *(n)*
a plant or an animal that has been bred from two different species.

hydrant *(n)* an outdoor water faucet for use in emergencies.

hydraulic *(hi-drawl-ik) (adj)* **Hydraulic** machines work by power that is created by liquid being forced through pipes under pressure. **hydraulics** *(singular n).*

hydroelectricity *(n)* electricity that is made from energy produced by running water. **hydroelectric** *(adj).*

hydrofoil *(n)* a boat with ski-like attachments at the front and back, which lift the hull out of the water once the boat is traveling fast.

radio antenna
flashlight
exhaust
radar antenna
control bridge
passenger cabin
hull (lifted out of water)
front steering flap
water forced out of engine
water sucked into engine
front strut
rear foil
jet engine
front foil

hydrofoil

hydrogen *(n)*
a colorless gas that is lighter than air and catches fire easily. *Hydrogen combines with oxygen to make water.*

hydrometer *(n)*
an instrument used to measure the density of a liquid.

hyena *(n)* a wild animal, similar to a dog, that eats the flesh of dead animals and has a shrieking howl.

hygienic *(hi-jen-ik) (adj)*
clean and free enough from germs not to be a health risk. **hygiene** *(n),* **hygienically** *(adv).*

hymn *(him) (n)*
a song of praise to God.

hymnal *(him-nuhl) (n)*
a book of religious songs used in religious services.

hype *(n)* extravagant claims made about something to promote it. *It won't live up to the hype.* **hype** *(v).*

hyperactive *(adj)* If someone is **hyperactive**, they are abnormally restless and lively. **hyperactivity** *(n).*

hyphen *(hi-fen) (n)*
the punctuation mark (-) used to separate the parts of a word made from two or more parts, for example, "middle-aged" and "ice-skate." **hyphenation** *(n),* **hyphenate** *(v).*

hypnotize hypnotizing hypnotized *(v)* to put someone into a trance. **hypnotism** *(n),* **hypnotist** *(n).*

hypochondriac
(hi-poe-kon-dree-ak) (n) someone who continually thinks that they are ill or will become ill. **hypochondria** *(n).*

hypocrite *(hip-oh-krit) (n)*
someone who pretends to believe or feel something that is different from their true beliefs or feelings. **hypocrisy** *(n),* **hypocritical** *(adj),* **hypocritically** *(adv).*

hypodermic *(n)* a hollow needle used for giving injections.

hypotenuse *(n)*
the side opposite the right angle of a right triangle.

hypothermia *(n)* If someone is suffering from **hypothermia**, they have become dangerously cold.

hypothesis hypotheses *(n)*
an idea about the way that a scientific investigation or experiment will turn out.

hysterical *(adj)* If someone is **hysterical**, they are very emotional and out of control, because they are very excited, frightened, or angry. **hysteria** *(n),* **hysterically** *(adv).*

Ii

ice icing iced
1 *(n)* frozen water. **ice** *(v),* **icy** *(adj).*
2 *(v)* If someone **ices** a cake, they cover it with a sweet coating.

Ice Age *(n)* a very early period of time when a large part of the world was covered with ice.

iceberg *(n)*
a huge mass of ice floating in the sea.

ice cream *(n)* a sweet, frozen food made from milk products.

ice hockey *(n)* a team game played with sticks and a flat disk called a puck by skaters aiming to score goals.

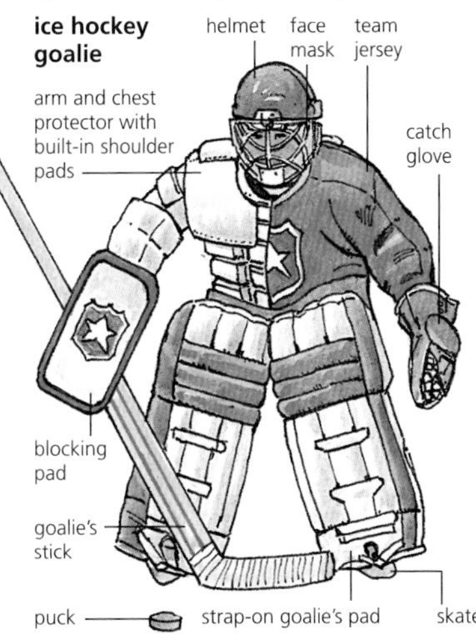

ice rink *(n)* a place where people skate on a prepared surface of ice.

ice-skate ice-skating ice-skated *(v)* to move around on ice, wearing boots with blades on the bottom. **ice skate** *(n).*

icicle *(n)*
a long, thin stem of ice, formed from dripping water that has frozen.

icing *(n)* a sugar coating used to decorate cakes; frosting.

icon *or* **ikon**
1 *(n)* a picture of Jesus or a saint found in some Eastern churches such as the Greek and Russian Orthodox churches. *This icon was painted by a Russian artist in the early 13th century.*
2 *(n)* one of several small pictures on a computer screen, phone, etc., representing programs or functions that you can use.

icon

icy icier iciest
1 *(adj)* very cold, or covered with ice.
2 *(adj)* unfriendly. *An icy stare.*

ID *short for* **identification**.

idea *(n)* a thought or a plan.

ideal
1 *(adj)* very suitable, or perfect. *Hamsters make ideal pets.*
2 *(n)* the situation you would most like to see. *My ideal is world peace.* **idealistic** *(adj).*

identical *(adj)*
exactly alike. **identically** *(adv).*

identification *(n)*
something that proves who you are.

identify identifies identifying identified *(v)* to recognize something or somebody.

identity identities *(n)*
Your **identity** is who you are.

idiom *(n)* a commonly used expression or phrase that means something different from what it appears to mean. For example, if you catch someone "red-handed," it does not mean that their hands are red.

idiot *(n)* a feeble-minded person. **idiotic** *(adj),* **idiotically** *(adv).*

idle idler idlest
1 *(adj)* lazy. **idleness** *(n),* **idly** *(adv).*
2 *(adj)* not active. *The factory stood idle during the strike.*

idol
1 *(n)* someone or something that is worshipped as a god.
2 *(n)* someone whom other people love and admire. *A pop idol.*

i.e. an abbreviation of the Latin phrase *id est*, which means "that is," and is used to explain something further. *It's the penultimate store, i.e. the one before last.*

if *(conj)* a word used to show that something will happen on the condition that another thing happens first. *I will pay you if you work hard.*

igloo *(n)*
the traditional dome-shaped shelter of the Inuit people, made of blocks of ice or hard snow.

ignite igniting ignited *(v)* to set fire to something, or to start burning.

ignition *(n)* the electrical system of a vehicle that uses power from a battery to start the engine.

ignorant
1 *(adj)* uneducated, or not knowing about many things. ignorance *(n)*, ignorantly *(adv)*.
2 *(adj)* not knowing about something. *I was completely ignorant of Barney's intentions.* ignorance *(n)*.

ignore ignoring ignored *(v)*
to take no notice of something. *Amy ignored their rude comments.*

ikon *see* **icon**.

ill
1 *(adj)* sick. illness *(n)*.
2 *(adj)* bad. *Did you suffer any ill effects after your accident?*

illegal *(adj)*
against the law. illegally *(adv)*.

illegible *(adj)* If your handwriting is illegible, it is very difficult to read.

illegitimate
1 *(adj)* An illegitimate child is born to parents who are not married. illegitimacy *(n)*.
2 *(adj)* against the law or unacceptable.

illiterate *(adj)* not able to read and write. illiteracy *(n)*.

illogical *(adj)* Something illogical is not reasonable and does not make sense. illogically *(adv)*.

illuminate
illuminating illuminated
1 *(v)* to light up something, such as a building. illuminated *(adj)*.
2 *(v)* to make something clearer and easier to understand. illuminating *(adj)*.
3 *(v)* In the Middle Ages, manuscripts were illuminated by adding pictures and decoration to the text. *The letter "L," shown here, comes from a manuscript that was illuminated by monks.* illumination *(n)*, illuminated *(adj)*.

illusion *(n)* something that appears to exist but does not. illusory *(adj)*.

illustration
1 *(n)* a picture in a book, magazine, etc. illustrator *(n)*, illustrate *(v)*, illustrative *(adj)*.
2 *(n)* an example. *Keri gave a lot of illustrations of her brother's stupidity.* illustrate *(v)*.

image
1 *(n)* a picture in a book, on a screen, etc.
2 *(n)* a picture that you have in your mind of something or someone. *I have an image of my ideal house.*
3 *(n)* Your **image** is the way that you appear to other people.
4 *(n)* When writers use an **image**, they describe something in terms of something else, for example, "The dragon's eyes were like pits of fire."

imagery *(n)*
descriptive language used by writers in poems, stories, etc. *Similes and metaphors are both types of imagery.*

imagine imagining imagined *(v)*
to picture something in your mind. imagination *(n)*, imaginary *(adj)*.

imbecile *(im-beh-sill)* *(n)* an idiot.

imitate imitating imitated *(v)*
to copy or mimic someone or something. imitation *(n)*.

immature
1 *(adj)* young and not fully developed. immaturity *(n)*.
2 *(adj)* If someone is immature, they behave in a silly, childish way. immaturity *(n)*, immaturely *(adv)*.

immediately *(adv)*
now or at once. immediate *(adj)*.

immense *(adj)* huge or enormous. immensity *(n)*, immensely *(adv)*.

immerse immersing immersed
1 *(v)* to cover something completely in a liquid. immersion *(n)*.
2 *(v)* If you are immersed in something, you are completely involved in it. immersion *(n)*.

immigrant *(n)*
someone who comes from abroad to live permanently in a country. immigration *(n)*, immigrate *(v)*.

imminent *(adj)* about to happen.

immobile
1 *(adj)* not moving.
2 *(adj)* unable to move. *Steve's accident left him immobile.*

immobilize
immobilizing immobilized *(v)*
to make it impossible for someone or something to move. *The accident immobilized Ella for weeks.*

immoral *(adj)* unfair, wrong, or wicked. immorality *(n)*.

immune *(adj)* protected against a disease. immunity *(n)*, immunize *(v)*.

impact
1 *(n)* the action of one thing hitting another with a lot of force.
2 *(n)* the effect that something has on people. *Our first visit to the theater had a great impact on me.*

impair impairing impaired *(v)*
to damage something, or to make something less effective. *The constant gunfire impaired the soldiers' hearing.* impairment *(n)*.

impartial *(adj)*
fair, or not favoring one person or point of view over another. impartiality *(n)*, impartially *(adv)*.

impatient
1 *(adj)* in a hurry or unable to wait. impatience *(n)*, impatiently *(adv)*.
2 *(adj)* easily annoyed. *Dad gets impatient with arguing children.* impatience *(n)*, impatiently *(adv)*.

imperfect
1 *(adj)* faulty or not perfect. imperfection *(n)*, imperfectly *(adv)*.
2 *(adj)* The **imperfect** form of a verb is used to describe actions that continue, for example, *"I was running"*, *"I am running"*, *"I will be running."*

imperial *(adj)*
having to do with an empire. *In the 19th century, Britain had strong imperial ambitions.*

impersonal
1 *(adj)* lacking in warmth and feeling. *The captain had a cold impersonal manner.*
2 *(adj)* having to do with people generally, rather than with one particular person.

impersonate
impersonating impersonated *(v)*
to pretend to be someone else, either seriously or for fun. impersonation *(n)*, impersonator *(n)*.

impertinent *(adj)*
rude and impudent. impertinence *(n)*.

impetuous *(adj)*
Someone who is impetuous does things suddenly, without thinking first. impetuously *(adv)*.

implement
implementing implemented
1 *(n)* a tool or utensil.
2 *(v)* to put something, such as a plan or an idea, into action. implementation *(n)*.

implication
1 *(n)* something that happens as a result of something else, and which is sometimes not foreseen.

2 *(n)* something suggested but not actually said. *Mom has not said "yes," but the implication is that we can go.*

imply implies implying implied *(v)* to suggest or mean something without actually saying it.

impolite *(adj)* If someone is **impolite**, they are rude and have bad manners. **impolitely** *(adv).*

import *(im-port)* **importing imported** *(v)* to bring foreign goods into your own country to be sold. **import** *(im-port) (n).*

important
1 *(adj)* Something **important** is worth taking seriously and can have a great effect. *An important choice.* **importance** *(n),* **importantly** *(adv).*
2 *(adj)* An **important** person is powerful and holds a high position.

impossible *(adj)* If something is **impossible**, it cannot be done or cannot happen. **impossibility** *(n),* **impossibly** *(adv).*

impostor *(n)* someone who pretends to be someone that they are not.

impractical *(adj)* not sensible or not useful. *An impractical plan.*

impress **impresses impressing impressed**
1 *(v)* to make people think highly of you. **impressive** *(adj).*
2 *(v)* If you **impress** something on someone, you make it very clear to them.

impression
1 *(n)* an idea or a feeling. *I had the impression that Sid didn't like me.*
2 *(n)* an imitation of someone or something. *Tom did his impression of a seal.*
3 If something or someone **makes an impression** on you, they have a strong effect on you.

impressionable *(adj)* If someone is **impressionable**, they are easily influenced by other people.

imprison imprisoning imprisoned *(v)* to put someone in prison or lock them up. **imprisonment** *(n).*

improve improving improved *(v)* to get better, or to make something better. **improvement** *(n).*

improvise improvising improvised
1 *(v)* to do the best you can with what is available. *We improvised a shelter from some old blankets.*
2 *(v)* When actors or musicians **improvise**, they make up words or music as they perform. **improvisation** *(n).*

impudent *(adj)* rude, cocky, and outspoken. *An impudent remark.* **impudence** *(n),* **impudently** *(adv).*

impulse *(n)* a sudden desire to do something. **impulsive** *(adj),* **impulsively** *(adv).*

inaccurate *(adj)* not very precise or not correct. **inaccuracy** *(n),* **inaccurately** *(adv).*

inadequate *(adj)* not enough or not good enough. **inadequately** *(adv).*

inappropriate *(adj)* unsuitable for the time, place, etc. *Sara's shoes are inappropriate for hiking.* **inappropriately** *(adv).*

inarticulate *(adj)* not able to express yourself very clearly in words.

inaudible *(adj)* not loud enough to be heard. **inaudibility** *(n),* **inaudibly** *(adv).*

inborn *(adj)* If a skill or quality is **inborn**, you inherit it from your parents and it is natural to you.

Inc. *short for* **incorporated company**. An incorporated company is one where, if the company goes bankrupt, the people who own shares in it only lose the value of those shares.

incapable *(adj)* If you are **incapable** of doing something, you are unable to do it.

incense incensing incensed
1 *(n)* a substance that is burned to give off a fragrant smell.
2 *(v)* to incite extreme anger.

incentive *(n)* something that encourages you to make an effort. *The prospect of winning a prize was an incentive to work hard.*

incessant *(adj)* nonstop or continuous. *Incessant noise.* **incessantly** *(adv).*

incident *(n)* an event, or something that happens.

incidentally *(adv)* by the way. **incidental** *(adj).*

incision *(n)* a neat cut made by a knife or blade.

incite inciting incited *(v)* If you **incite** someone to do something, you provoke them or urge them to do it.

incline inclining inclined
1 *(in-kline) (v)* to lean or to slope. **incline** *(in-kline) (n).*
2 If you are **inclined to** do something, you like to do it or you tend to do it. *Rowena is inclined to avoid exercise.* **inclination** *(n).*

include including included *(v)* to take in something or someone as part of something else. *The shopping list includes food for dinner. We included Abigail in our plans.*

inclusive *(adj)* including and covering everything. *The rent is inclusive of bills.*

incoherent *(adj)* unclear or not logical. **incoherently** *(adv).*

income
1 *(n)* the money that someone earns or receives regularly.
2 **income tax** *(n)* the portion of your earnings that is paid to the government to help run the country.

incompatible *(adj)* If people or objects are **incompatible**, they cannot live together or be used together. **incompatibility** *(n).*

incompetent *(adj)* If you are **incompetent** at something, you cannot do it very well or effectively. **incompetence** *(n),* **incompetently** *(adv).*

incomplete *(adj)* not finished or not complete. **incompletely** *(adv).*

incomprehensible *(adj)* impossible to understand. **incomprehensibly** *(adv).*

inconceivable *(adj)* impossible to believe or imagine. **inconceivably** *(adv).*

inconclusive *(adj)* not clear or not certain. *Inconclusive results.* **inconclusively** *(adv).*

inconsiderate *(adj)* Someone who is **inconsiderate** does not think about other people's needs and feelings. **inconsiderately** *(adv).*

inconspicuous *(adj)* Something that is **inconspicuous** cannot be seen easily. **inconspicuously** *(adv).*

inconvenient *(adj)* If something is **inconvenient**, it is awkward and causes difficulties. **inconvenience** *(n),* **inconveniently** *(adv).*

incorporate incorporating incorporated *(v)* When you **incorporate** something into another thing, you make it a part of that thing. *We've incorporated a new song into our show.* **incorporation** *(n).*

incorrect *(adj)* wrong. **incorrectly** *(adv).*

increase *(in-crease)* increasing increased *(v)* to grow in size or number. **increase** *(in-crease) (n),* **increasingly** *(adv).*

incredible *(adj)* unbelievable or amazing. *The beanstalk grew to an incredible height.* **incredibly** *(adv).*

incriminate
incriminating incriminated *(v)* to show that someone is guilty of a crime or other wrong action.

incubator
1 *(n)* a container in which premature babies are kept safe and warm while they grow larger and stronger.
2 *(n)* a container in which eggs are kept warm until they hatch. **incubation** *(n),* **incubate** *(v).*

incurable *(adj)*
A person with an **incurable** disease cannot be made better.

indecent *(adj)* rude or shocking. **indecency** *(n),* **indecently** *(adv).*

indeed *(adv)* certainly.

indefinite
1 *(adj)* not clear.
2 The **indefinite article** is the grammatical term for "a," "an," or "some," used before a noun.

indent *(in-dent)* **indenting indented** *(v)* to start a line of writing or typing a few spaces in from the margin. **indent** *(in-dent) (n).*

independent
1 *(adj)* free from the control of other people or things. **independence** *(n),* **independently** *(adv).*
2 *(adj)* If someone is **independent**, they do not want or need much help from other people. **independence** *(n),* **independently** *(adv).*

indestructible *(adj)* If something is **indestructible**, it cannot be destroyed. **indestructibly** *(adv).*

index indexes *or* indices
1 *(n)* an alphabetical list that shows you where to find words or pictures, for example, in a book.
2 *(n)* Your **index finger** is the one nearest to your thumb.

indicate **indicating indicated**
1 *(v)* to show or to prove something. *The report indicates that the company is losing money at a rapid rate.* **indication** *(n),* **indicative** *(adj).*
2 *(v)* to point something out. *The sign indicated the route to the beach.* **indication** *(n),* **indicator** *(n).*

indifferent
1 *(adj)* If someone is **indifferent** to something, they are not interested in it. *Amelia was indifferent to where we went.* **indifference** *(n).*
2 *(adj)* poor in quality. *Toby produced an indifferent piece of work.*

indigestion *(n)*
If you have **indigestion**, your stomach hurts because you are having difficulty in digesting food.

indignant *(adj)*
If you are **indignant**, you are upset and annoyed because you feel that something is not fair. **indignation** *(n),* **indignantly** *(adv).*

indirect *(adj)* not straightforward. *An indirect route.* **indirectly** *(adv).*

indispensable *(adj)*
If someone or something is **indispensable**, they are essential and cannot be replaced. **indispensably** *(adv).*

indistinguishable *(adj)* When two things are **indistinguishable**, you cannot tell them apart. *The twins are virtually indistinguishable.*

individual
1 *(adj)* single and separate. *Slowly, I got to know the individual members of the group.* **individually** *(adv).*
2 *(n)* a person. *A strange individual.*
3 *(adj)* unusual or different. *Ricky has a very individual hairstyle.* **individually** *(adv).*

indoors *(adv)* inside a building.

indulge **indulging indulged**
1 *(v)* to let someone have their own way. *Nathan's grandparents indulge him dreadfully.* **indulgence** *(n),* **indulgent** *(adj).*
2 *(v)* If you **indulge in** something, you allow yourself to enjoy it.

industrial *(adj)* having to do with businesses and factories. *The industrial area of the city.* **industrially** *(adv).*

industry **industries** *(n)* the business of making things or providing services in order to earn money.

inefficient *(adj)* If someone or something is **inefficient**, they do not work very well and they waste time and energy. **inefficiency** *(n),* **inefficiently** *(adv).*

inequality **inequalities** *(n)* the treatment of people in an unequal or unfair way.

inert
1 *(adj)* lifeless and unmoving.
2 *(adj)* An **inert** gas does not react with other chemicals.

inertia
1 *(n)* a lazy, tired feeling.
2 *(n)* The **inertia** of an object is its resistance to any change in motion. Inertia makes it hard to get something moving when it is still and hard to make something stop when it is moving.

inevitable *(adj)* If something is **inevitable**, it will certainly happen. **inevitability** *(n),* **inevitably** *(adv).*

inexpensive *(adj)*
cheap. **inexpensively** *(adv).*

inexperienced *(adj)*
An **inexperienced** person has had little practice in doing something.

inexplicable *(adj)*
If something is **inexplicable**, it cannot be explained. **inexplicably** *(adv).*

infamous *(in-fuh-muss) (adj)*
If someone or something is **infamous**, they have a very bad reputation.

infant *(n)*
a young child or baby. **infancy** *(n).*

infantry **infantries** *(n)*
the part of an army that fights on foot.

infatuated *(adj)*
If you are **infatuated** with someone, you like them so much that you stop thinking clearly and sensibly about your relationship. **infatuation** *(n).*

infection *(n)*
an illness caused by germs. **infect** *(v).*

infectious
1 *(adj)* An **infectious** disease is spread from one person to another by germs in the air or on objects.
2 *(adj)* If a mood is **infectious**, it spreads easily. *Infectious laughter.*

infectious mononucleosis *(n)*
an infectious illness which gives you a sore throat, swollen glands, and a high temperature. Often called **mono**.

infer **inferring inferred** *(v)*
to draw a conclusion from something that somebody says or does. *We inferred from Tim's tone of voice that he was being sarcastic.* **inference** *(n).*

inferior *(adj)*
If something is **inferior** to something else, it is not as good. **inferiority** *(n).*

infertile
1 *(adj)* unable to have babies. **infertility** *(n).*
2 *(adj)* Land that is **infertile** is useless for growing crops and plants. **infertility** *(n).*

infested *(adj)*
If an object or a building is **infested**, it is full of animal or insect pests. **infestation** *(n),* **infest** *(v).*

infiltrate
infiltrating infiltrated *(v)*
to join an organization secretly to spy on it or damage it in some way. **infiltration** *(n).*

infinite *(in-fin-it) (adj)* endless. *Infinite possibilities.* **infinitely** *(adv).*

infinitive *(n)*
the basic form of a verb, for example, "to run," "to be," "to write."

infirm *(adj)* weak or ill. **infirmity** *(n).*

infirmary **infirmaries** *(n)* a hospital.

inflammable *(adj)* An **inflammable** substance can catch fire easily.

inflatable *(adj)* An **inflatable** object can be filled with air or blown up. **inflatable** *(n)*.

inflate inflating inflated *(v)* to make something expand by blowing air into it.

inflation *(n)* a widespread rise in prices. **inflationary** *(adj)*.

inflexible *(adj)* not able to bend, or not able to change. **inflexibility** *(n)*, **inflexibly** *(adv)*.

inflict inflicting inflicted *(v)* to cause suffering to somebody or something. *The bombing inflicted severe damage on the town.*

influence influencing influenced *(v)* to have an effect on someone or something. **influence** *(n)*.

influenza *see* **flu**.

inform informing informed
1 *(v)* to tell someone something. *ee informed me that he was leaving.*
2 *(v)* If you **inform on** a criminal, you give the police information about them. **informer** *(n)*.

informal *(adj)* relaxed, easy-going, and casual. *An informal party.* **informality** *(n)*, **informally** *(adv)*.

information *(n)* facts and knowledge.

information technology *(n)* the use of computers and other electronic equipment to produce, store, or communicate information.

informative *(adj)* If something or someone is **informative**, they provide useful information.

infrequent *(adj)* not happening very often. **infrequently** *(adv)*.

infuriate infuriating infuriated *(v)* If someone or something **infuriates** you, they make you very angry. **infuriating** *(adj)*, **infuriatingly** *(adv)*.

ingenious *(in-jee-nee-us) (adj)* clever and original. *An ingenious plan.* **ingenuity** *(n)*, **ingeniously** *(adv)*.

ingredient *(n)* one of the items that something is made from, especially an item of food in a recipe.

inhabit inhabiting inhabited *(v)* If you **inhabit** a place, you live there. **inhabitant** *(n)*.

inhale inhaling inhaled *(v)* to breathe in. **inhalation** *(n)*.

inhaler *(n)* a container from which you take medicine by breathing it in through your mouth.

inherit inheriting inherited
1 *(v)* to receive money, property, or a title from someone who has just died. **inheritance** *(n)*.
2 *(v)* If you **inherit** a particular characteristic, it is passed down to you from one of your parents.

inhuman *(adj)* cruel and brutal. **inhumanity** *(n)*.

initial
1 *(adj)* first or at the beginning. *My initial reaction to seeing the ghost was to scream.* **initially** *(adv)*.
2 *(n)* the first letter of a name.

initiative *(in-ish-ee-uh-tiv) (n)* If you use your **initiative**, you do what is necessary without other people telling you what to do. **initiate** *(v)*.

inject injecting injected
1 *(v)* to use a needle and syringe to put medicine into someone's body. **injection** *(n)*.
2 *(v)* to add. *Please inject some humor into your writing.* **injection** *(n)*.

injure injuring injured *(v)* to hurt or harm someone.

injury injuries *(n)* damage or harm.

injustice
1 *(n)* unfairness.
2 *(n)* an unfair situation or action.

ink *(n)* a colored liquid used for writing and printing. **inky** *(adj)*.

inland *(adj)* away from the sea. *The hotel is five miles inland.*

inline skates *(plural n)* boots with wheels attacthed to the soles, in a straight line. **inline skating** *(v)*.

inmate *(n)* someone sentenced to live in a prison or other institution.

inner
1 *(adj)* inside or nearest the center. *A bicycle tire has an inner tube.*
2 *(adj)* private. *Inner thoughts.*

inning *(n)* a part of a baseball game in which each team gets a turn at bat.

innocent
1 *(adj)* not guilty. **innocence** *(n)*, **innocently** *(adv)*.
2 *(adj)* not knowing about something. **innocence** *(n)*, **innocently** *(adv)*.

a b c d e f g h i j k l m n o p q r s t u v w x y z

innovation *(n)*
a new idea, or an invention. **innovate** *(v)*, **innovative** *(adj)*.

inoculate inoculating inoculated *(v)* to inject a weak form of a disease into someone so that they become protected against it. **inoculation** *(n)*.

inpatient *(n)* someone who stays in the hospital while being treated.

input
1 *(n)* something that is contributed or put into something else. *Our team has benefited from George's input.*
2 *(n)* information fed into a computer. **input** *(v)*.

inquest *(n)*
an official investigation to find out why someone has died. *The police held an inquest after the accident.*

inquire inquiring inquired *(v)*
to ask about somebody or something. *Rudi inquired about the times of the trains.* **inquiring** *(adj)*, **inquiringly** *(adv)*.

inquiry inquiries *(n)*
a study or an investigation, especially an official one.

inquisitive *(adj)*
questioning or curious. **inquisitiveness** *(n)*, **inquisitively** *(adv)*.

insane *(adj)* mad or crazy. **insanity** *(n)*, **insanely** *(adv)*.

inscribe inscribing inscribed
1 *(v)* to carve or engrave letters on a surface. **inscribed** *(adj)*.
2 *(v)* to write a special message or dedication in a book.

inscription *(n)* a carved, engraved, or specially written message. *There are inscriptions under most statues.*

insect *(n)* a small creature, usually with three pairs of legs, two pairs of wings, three main sections to its body, and no backbone. *The picture below shows a selection of insects.*

insects

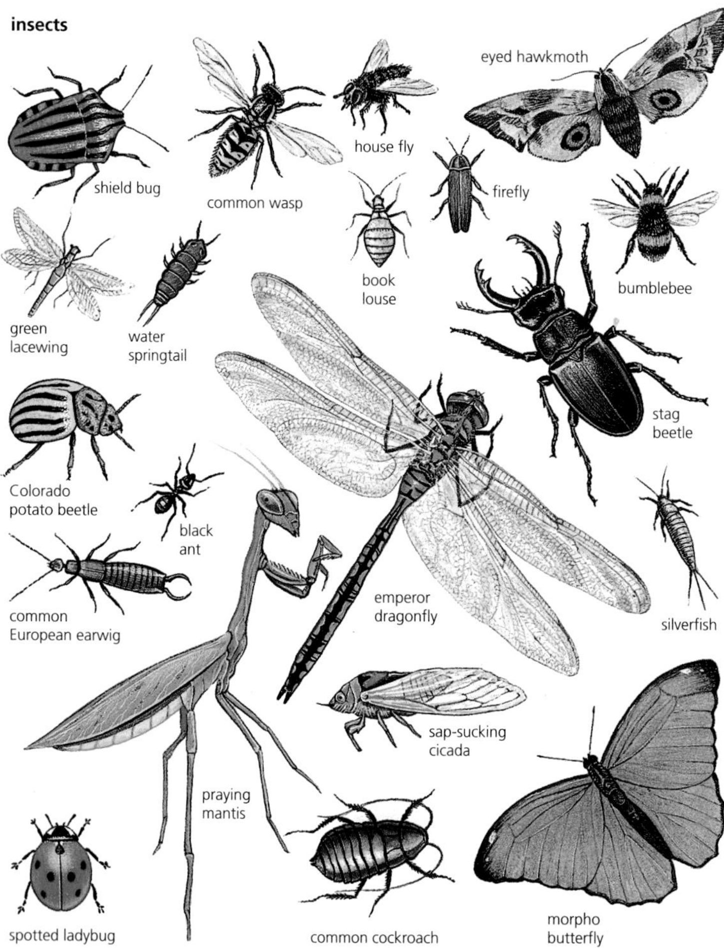

insecticide *(n)*
a chemical used to kill insects.

insecure
1 *(adj)* unsafe or not fastened properly. *These door locks are very insecure.* **insecurely** *(adv)*.
2 *(adj)* anxious and not confident. *Pam felt very insecure among so many strangers.* **insecurity** *(n)*.

insensitive *(adj)*
thoughtless and unsympathetic to other people's feelings. **insensitivity** *(n)*, **insensitively** *(adv)*.

insert inserting inserted
1 *(v) (in-**sert**)* to put something carefully inside something else. *Insert a coin in the slot.* **insertion** *(n)*.
2 *(n) (**in**-sert)* something that is put inside something else. *This magazine has an insert on mountain bikes.*

inside
1 *(n)* the interior or inner part of something. **inside** *(adj)*.
2 *(prep)* in less than. *We were back home inside an hour.*
3 *(prep)* within. *Put it inside the bag.*
4 *(adv)* in or into the inner part. *Look inside the house.*

insight *(n)* If you have **insight** into something or somebody, you understand something about them that is not obvious.

insignificant *(adj)*
not important. **insignificance** *(n)*, **insignificantly** *(adv)*.

insincere *(adj)*
Someone who is **insincere** is not genuine, or not honest. **insincerity** *(n)*, **insincerely** *(adv)*.

insipid *(adj)* dull or tasteless.

insist insisting insisted *(v)*
If you **insist** on something, you demand it very firmly. *Sally insisted on wearing her jeans.* **insistence** *(n)*, **insistent** *(adj)*.

insolent *(adj)* insulting and rude. **insolence** *(n)*, **insolently** *(adv)*.

insoluble
1 *(adj)* A substance that is **insoluble** will not dissolve.
2 *(adj)* A problem that is **insoluble** cannot be solved.

insomnia *(singular n)*
If you have **insomnia**, you often find it very hard to sleep. **insomniac** *(n)*.

inspect inspecting inspected *(v)*
to look at something very carefully. **inspection** *(n)*.

inspector
1 *(n)* someone who checks or examines things. *A ticket inspector.*
2 *(n)* a senior police officer.

nspire inspiring inspired *(v)*
o influence and encourage someone o do something. *The rock concert ıspired me to take guitar lessons.* ıspiration *(n)*, inspiring *(adj)*.

nstall installing installed *(v)*
o put something in place, eady to be used. *We have ad a new computer installed in ur classroom.* installation *(n)*.

nstallment
(n) If you pay for something by nstallments, you pay for it in regular, mall amounts over a period of time.
(n) one part of a serialized story.

nstance *(n)* an example. *lancy gave me several instances f when I had offended her.*

nstant
(n) a moment. *It was over in n instant.* instantaneous *(adj)*, nstantaneously *(adv)*.
(adj) happening immediately. *ıstant results.* instantly *(adv)*.

nstead *(adv)* in place of another erson or thing. *Bill couldn't o to the party, so I went instead.*

nstep *(n)* the top of your foot etween your toes and your ankle.

nstinct
(n) behavior that is natural rather han learned. *Ducks swim by instinct.*
(n) If you have an instinct about omething, you know or feel omething without being told bout it. *I had an instinct that he was not telling the truth.*
nstinctive *(adj)*, instinctively *(adv)*.

nstitute instituting instituted
(v) to begin, set up, or found. *he lawyer instituted an inquiry nto the missing money.*
(n) an organization set up to romote or represent the interests of particular cause or group of people.

nstitution
(n) a large organization where eople live or work together, such as a ospital or college. institutional *(adj)*.
(n) a well-established custom or radition. *Weekend barbecues have ecome an institution in our family.*

nstruct instructing instructed
(v) to give an order. *he captain instructed his rew to set sail.* instruction *(n)*.
(v) to teach a subject or skill. *Ginger instructed me in tap-dancing.* nstruction *(n)*, instructor *(n)*.

nstructions *(plural n)*
vritten or spoken words telling you vhat to do or how to do something.

instrument
1 *(n)* a tool used for delicate or scientific work. *Surgical instruments.*
2 *(n)* an object that you use to make music. *The picture shows a range of musical instruments from around the world.* instrumentalist *(n)*.

musical instruments

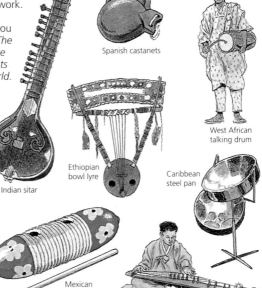

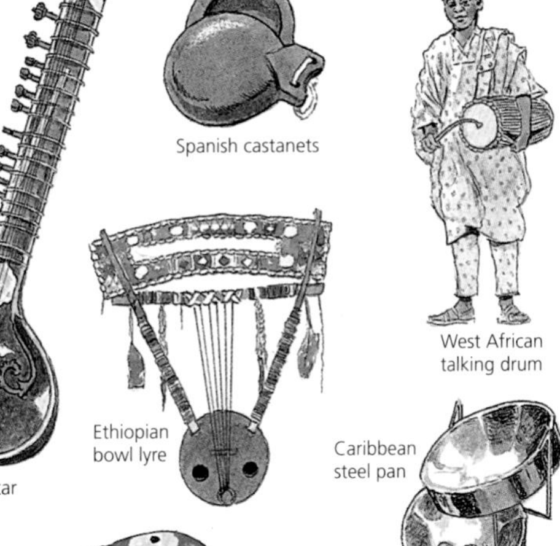

insufficient *(adj)* not enough or not adequate. insufficiently *(adv)*.

insulate insulating insulated *(v)* to cover something with material in order to stop heat or electricity from escaping from it. insulation *(n)*, insulating *(adj)*.

insulin *(n)* a hormone produced in your pancreas that regulates the amount of sugar that you have in your body. People who have diabetes need to be given insulin.

insult insulting insulted *(v)* to say or do something rude and upsetting to somebody. insult *(n)*, insulting *(adj)*.

insurance *(n)* When you take out **insurance**, you pay money to a company that agrees to pay you in the event of sickness, fire, accident, etc. insure *(v)*, insured *(adj)*.

intact *(adj)*
unharmed or complete. *Fortunately, our books survived the flood intact.*

intake
1 *(n)* the amount of people or things that are taken in. *Our college has a high intake of music students.*
2 *(n)* the act of taking in something. *A sharp intake of breath.*

integrate integrating integrated *(v)* to combine several things or people into one whole. *People of many nationalities have been integrated into our community.* integration *(n)*.

integrity *(n)*
If someone has **integrity**, they are honest and stick to their principles.

intellectual
1 *(adj)* involving thought and reason. *Bethany enjoys intellectual puzzles.*
2 *(n)* someone who spends most of their time thinking and studying.

intelligent *(adj)* Someone who is **intelligent** is clever and quick to understand, think, and learn. intelligence *(n)*, intelligently *(adv)*.

intelligible *(adj)*
If something is **intelligible**, it can be understood. intelligibly *(adv)*.

intend intending intended *(v)*
If you **intend** to do something, you mean to do it.

intense *(adj)* very strong. *Intense heat. Intense happiness.* intensity *(n)*, intensely *(adv)*.

intensify intensifies intensifying intensified *(v)* to make something more powerful or concentrated. *The police intensified their search.* intensification *(n)*.

intent
1 *(adj)* If you are **intent** on doing something, you are determined to do it. *Lance is intent on going to college.*
2 *(n)* an aim or a purpose.

intention *(n)* the thing that you mean to do. *It's my intention to win this race.* intentional *(adj)*.

a b c d e f g h i j k l m n o p q r s t u v w x y z

interactive *(adj)* If something such as a book or computer program is **interactive**, it allows users to make choices in order to control and change it in some ways. **interact** *(v)*.

intercept intercepting intercepted *(v)* to stop the movement of something or someone from one place to another. *The goalkeeper intercepted the ball.* **interception** *(n)*.

intercom *(n)* a microphone and speaker system that allows you to listen and talk to someone in another room or building.

interest interesting interested
1 *(v)* If something **interests** you, you want to know more about it. **interest** *(n)*, **interesting** *(adj)*.
2 *(n)* an additional amount of money paid by someone who borrows money, or paid to someone who invests money. Interest is usually an agreed percentage of the amount borrowed or invested.

interfere interfering interfered *(v)* to involve yourself in a situation that has nothing to do with you. **interfering** *(adj)*.

interference
1 *(n)* involvement in something that has nothing to do with you. *I can't stand any more interference from our neighbors!*
2 *(n)* When you get **interference** on your television or radio, something interrupts the signal so that you cannot see or hear it properly.

intergalactic *(adj)* between galaxies. *Intergalactic space travel.*

interior *(n)* the inside of something, especially a building. **interior** *(adj)*.

interjection *(n)* a word used as a greeting, or to express surprise, pain, or delight. *"Ah!", "oh!", and "hello!"* are all interjections. *See* page 3.

intermediate *(adj)* in between two things, or in the middle. *There are three swimming classes: beginners, intermediate, and advanced.*

intermission *(n)* a short break in a movie, play, or concert.

intermittent *(adj)* stopping and starting. *Intermittent rain.* **intermittently** *(adv)*.

internal *(adj)* happening or existing inside someone or something. *An internal examination.* **internally** *(adv)*.

international *(adj)* involving different countries. *International trade.* **internationally** *(adv)*.

internet *(n)* a network that connects millions of computers around the world.

interpret interpreting interpreted
1 *(v)* to decide what something means. *I interpreted Jim's wave as a sign of friendship.* **interpretation** *(n)*.
2 *(v)* If someone **interprets** for two people who each speak a different language, they translate for them. **interpreter** *(n)*.

interrogate interrogating interrogated *(v)* to question someone thoroughly. **interrogation** *(n)*.

interrupt interrupting interrupted
1 *(v)* to stop something from happening for a short time. *Vicky interrupted our game.* **interruption** *(n)*.
2 *(v)* to start talking before someone else has finished talking. *Don't interrupt me!* **interruption** *(n)*.

interval
1 *(n)* a time between events or parts of a play, concert, show, etc.
2 *(n)* a space between two things.

intervene intervening intervened
1 *(v)* If you **intervene** in a situation, you get involved in it to change what is happening. **intervention** *(n)*.
2 *(v)* If a period of time **intervenes** between events, it comes between them. **intervening** *(adj)*.

interview *(n)* a meeting when someone is asked questions. *A job interview.* **interview** *(v)*.

intestines *(plural n)* the very long tube through which food passes when it is digested after it leaves your stomach. **intestinal** *(adj)*. *See* **digestion**.

intimate *(adj)* Friends who are **intimate** are very close and share their feelings with one another. **intimacy** *(n)*, **intimately** *(adv)*.

intimidate intimidating intimidated *(v)* to frighten someone into doing something. **intimidation** *(n)*.

intolerable *(adj)* If something is **intolerable**, you cannot bear it. **intolerably** *(adv)*.

intolerant *(adj)* People who are **intolerant** get unreasonably angry when other people think or behave in a different way from them. **intolerance** *(n)*, **intolerantly** *(adv)*.

intransitive *(adj)* **Intransitive** verbs stand on their own and do not need an object. The verbs *"to laugh"*, *"to sneeze"*, and *"to frown"* are all intransitive.

intrepid *(adj)* An intrepid person is courageous and bold.

intricate *(adj)* detailed and complicated. *An intricate pattern.* **intricacy** *(n)*, **intricately** *(adv)*.

intrigue intriguing intrigued
1 *(v)* to fascinate or puzzle someone. *Kit's story intrigued me.* **intriguing** *(adj)*.
2 *(n)* a secret plot.

introduce introducing introduced
1 *(v)* to bring people together for the first time and tell each one the other's name.
2 *(v)* to bring in something new. *The company is introducing a new product.*

introduction
1 *(n)* Your **introduction** to something is your first experience of it. *I can still remember my introduction to rock climbing.*
2 *(n)* the act of introducing one person to another.
3 *(n)* the opening words of a book, speech, etc. **introductory** *(adj)*.

introvert *(n)* someone who keeps their thoughts and feelings to themselves and is shy. **introverted** *(adj)*.

intrude intruding intruded *(v)* to force your way into a place or situation where you are not wanted or invited. **intruder** *(n)*, **intrusion** *(n)*.

intuition *(n)* a feeling about something that cannot be explained logically. *My intuition tells me you will win this race.* **intuitive** *(adj)*.

Inuit *(plural n)* a group of peoples from the Arctic regions of Canada, Alaska, Russia, and Greenland. *This Inuit man is fishing through a hole in the ice.* **Inuit** *(adj)*.

Inuit

inundate inundating inundated
1 *(v)* to flood. *The village was inundated by flood water.*
2 *(v)* to overwhelm someone with a large quantity of something. *We were inundated with presents.*

invade invading invaded *(v)* to send armed forces into another country to take it over. **invader** *(n)*, **invasion** *(n)*.

nvalid
1 *(in-va-lid) (n)* someone who
s disabled or who is seriously ill.
2 *(in-**val**-id) (adj)* If a ticket, library
card, etc. is **invalid**, it cannot be used.

nvaluable *(adj)* very useful indeed.

nvent inventing invented
1 *(v)* to think of an original
machine, device, idea, etc.
nvention *(n)*, **inventor** *(n)*.
2 *(v)* to make something up.
*Leon invented a story to explain why
he was soaking wet.* **invention** *(n)*.

nventive *(adj)* good at thinking up
new ideas or ways of doing things.

nventory inventories
1 *(n)* a complete list of all
the items someone owns.
2 *(n)* all the items available
for sale in a store.

nvertebrate *(n)* a creature without
a backbone. **invertebrate** *(adj)*.

nvest investing invested
1 *(v)* to give or lend money to
something, such as a company, in the
belief that you will be rewarded in the
future. **investment** *(n)*, **investor** *(n)*.
2 *(v)* to give time or effort to
something. *I've invested a lot
of time in practicing the trumpet.*

nvestigate investigating
nvestigated *(v)* If you **investigate**
something, such as a crime, you find
out as much as possible about it.
nvestigation *(n)*, **investigative** *(adj)*.

nvincible *(adj)* unbeatable.

nvisible *(adj)*
Something that is **invisible** cannot be
seen. **invisibility** *(n)*, **invisibly** *(adv)*.

nvite inviting invited *(v)*
to ask someone to do something or to
go somewhere. *We've invited Howard
home for dinner.* **invitation** *(n)*.

nvoice *(n)* a written request
for payment after you have
done a job or sold something.

nvolve involving involved *(v)*
to include something as a necessary
part. *The project involves fieldwork.*

nvolved
1 *(adj)* If you are **involved** in
something, you take a part in it. *I was
one of the people involved in the play.*
2 *(adj)* complicated. *Involved work.*

nward *(adv)* toward the inside.

on *(n)*
an electrically charged atomic particle.

.Q. *(n)* a measure of a person's
intelligence. The initials I.Q. stand
for Intelligence Quotient.

rate *(adj)* angry or very annoyed.

iron
1 *(n)* a strong, hard metal used to make things such as gates and railings. Iron is also found in some foods and is used by your body to make blood.
2 *(n)* a piece of electrical equipment with a handle and a heated surface, used to smooth creases out of clothing. *This picture shows the main parts inside a steam iron.* **iron** *(v)*.

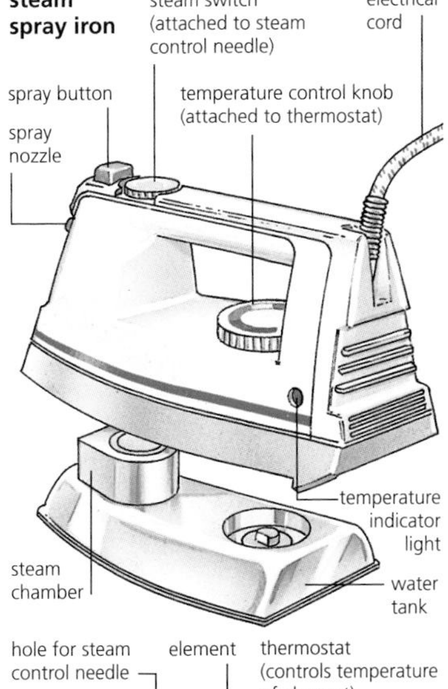

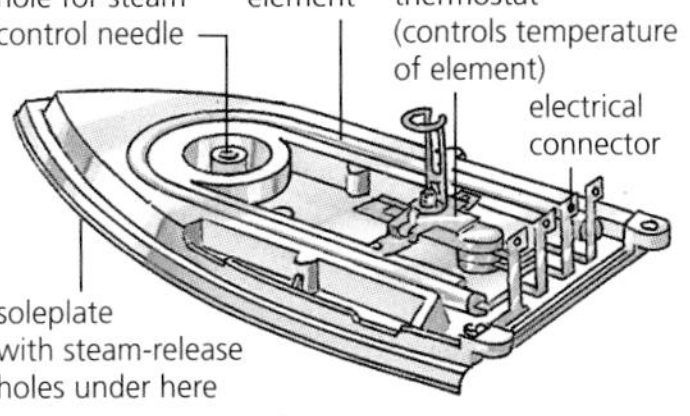

Iron Age *(n)* a period of history that began about 1,000 B.C., when iron was first used to make tools and weapons. *In the Iron Age, most people in Western Europe were farmers living in small settlements, like the one reconstructed in this picture.*

ironic
1 *(adj)* If a situation is **ironic**, the opposite happens to what you would expect. *It was ironic that the clumsiest boy in the class should become a famous ballet dancer.* **irony** *(n)*, **ironically** *(adv)*.
2 *(adj)* mildly sarcastic. *"A fine job you made of that!" said Rosa, with an ironic smile.* **irony** *(n)*.

irrational
1 *(adj)* not sensible or not logical. **irrationally** *(adv)*.
2 *(adj)* unreasonable or insane. **irrationally** *(adv)*.

irregular
1 *(adj)* not regular in shape, timing, or size, etc. *An irregular hexagon. An irregular bus service.* **irregularly** *(adv)*.
2 *(adj)* not following the normal pattern. *It's most irregular to come to school in slippers!* **irregularity** *(n)*.

irrelevant *(adj)* If something is **irrelevant**, it has nothing to do with a particular subject. *The story contained many irrelevant details.* **irrelevance** *(n)*, **irrelevantly** *(adv)*.

irresistible *(adj)*
too tempting to resist. *The fudge cake was irresistible.* **irresistibly** *(adv)*.

irresponsible *(adj)*
reckless and not capable of taking responsibility. **irresponsibly** *(adv)*.

irrigate irrigating irrigated *(v)*
to supply water to crops by digging channels and laying pipes. **irrigation** *(n)*.

irritable *(adj)*
Someone who is **irritable** is a little mad and grumpy. **irritably** *(adv)*.

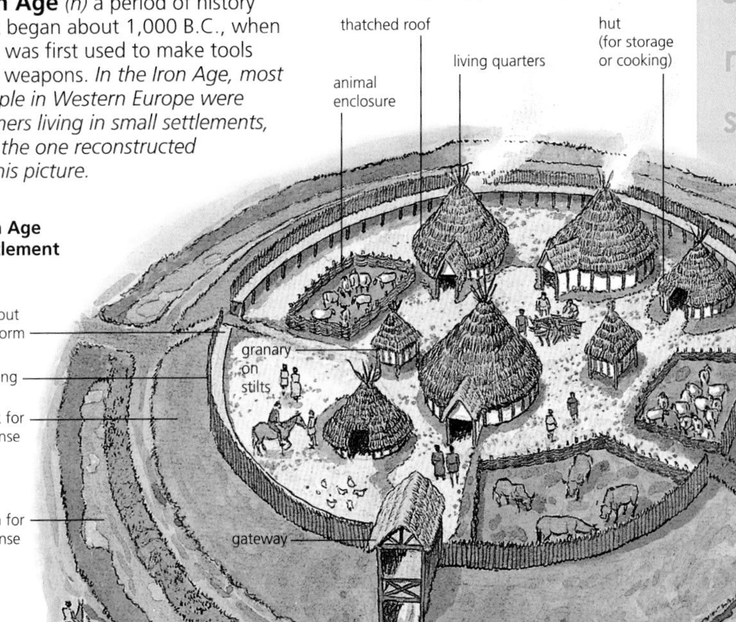

irritate irritating irritated *(v)* If something or someone **irritates** you, they make you annoyed. **irritation** *(n)*, **irritating** *(adj)*, **irritatingly** *(adv)*.

Islam *(n)* the religion based on the teachings of Mohammed. Muslims believe that Allah is God and that Mohammed is his prophet. Islam is based on prayer, fasting, charity and pilgrimage. **Islamic** *(adj)*.

island *(n)* land surrounded on all sides by water.

isolate isolating isolated
1 *(v)* to keep someone or something separate, or on their own. *Jessica was isolated because she had a highly infectious illness.* **isolation** *(n)*.
2 *(v)* to discover and identify something. *We've isolated the fault in your computer program.*

isosceles *(eye-soss-uh-leez)* *(adj)* Two of the sides of an **isosceles** triangle are the same length. *See* **shape**.

ISP *(n)* An **ISP** is a company that provides a service linking individual computers to the internet. ISP stands for Internet Service Provider.

issue issuing issued
1 *(v)* to send out or to give out. *Our group has issued a leaflet.*
2 *(n)* an edition of a newspaper or magazine.
3 *(n)* the main topic for discussion.
4 *(n)* a problem or concern.

IT *short for* **Information Technology**.

italic *(n)* a sloping form of print used to emphasize certain words or to make them stand out. The word *italic* is printed in italic. **italic** *(adj)*.

itch itches itching itched *(v)* If your skin **itches**, it is uncomfortable and you want to scratch it. **itch** *(n)*, **itchy** *(adj)*.

item *(n)* one of a number of things. *An item of clothing.*

itinerary itineraries *(n)* a detailed plan of a journey.

itself *(pronoun)* it and nothing else. *This machine works by itself.*

ivory
1 *(n)* the natural substance from which elephants' tusks are made.
2 *(n)* a creamy-white color. **ivory** *(adj)*.

ivy ivies *(n)* an evergreen climbing or trailing plant, which has pointed leaves.

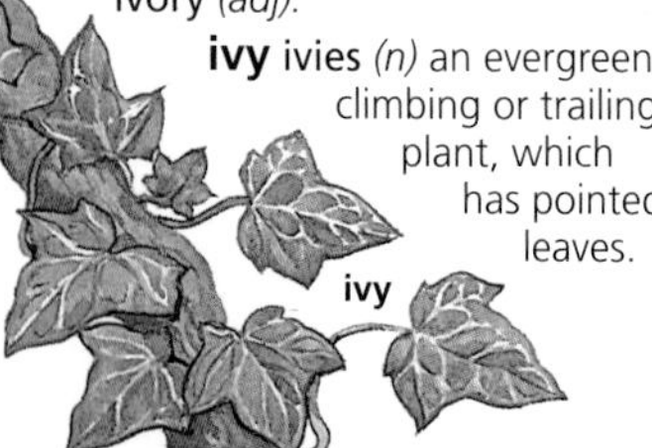

ivy

Jj

jab jabbing jabbed *(v)* to punch somebody, or poke them with something sharp. *Katy jabbed her elbow into my ribs.*

jabber jabbering jabbered *(v)* to talk in a fast and excitable way that is hard to understand.

jack
1 *(n)* a tool used to raise a vehicle off the ground for repair.
2 *(n)* a picture playing card with a value between that of a ten and a queen. The jack is sometimes called the knave.

jackal *(n)* a kind of wild dog, found in Africa and Asia, that feeds off the dead carcasses of other animals.

jacket
1 *(n)* a piece of clothing worn on the top half of your body, with a front opening and long sleeves.
2 *(n)* a covering. *A book jacket.*

jackknife jackknifing jackknifed *(v)* When a semitruck **jackknifes**, the trailer swings around at right angles to the direction of travel and the driver loses control.

Jacuzzi *(ja-koo-zee)* *(n)* Trademark name for a large bath with underwater jets of water, which massage your skin.

jade
1 *(n)* a green, semiprecious stone, used for making ornaments and jewelry. *The picture shows a jade death mask, made by the Mayas, an ancient civilization of Central America.*
2 *(n)* a green color. **jade** *(adj)*.

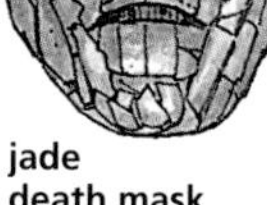

jade death mask

jaded *(adj)* If you are **jaded**, you are tired, bored and lacking in enthusiasm.

jagged *(jag-ed)* *(adj)* uneven and sharp. *A jagged edge.*

jaguar *(n)* a large wild cat, similar to a leopard, found in South and Central America.

jaguar

jail
1 *(n)* a prison. **jailer** *(n)*.
2 *(v)* to put someone in jail. *The murderer was jailed for life.*

jam jamming jammed
1 *(n)* a sweet, sticky food, made from boiled fruit and sugar.
2 *(n)* a situation in which things cannot move. *A traffic jam.*
3 *(v)* to squeeze or wedge something into place. *Alvin jammed his bag into the locker.*
4 *(n)* *(informal)* a difficult situation.
5 *(v)* *(informal)* When musicians **jam**, they make up music as they play together. **jam** *(n)*.

jangle jangling jangled *(v)* to make a loud, unpleasant, ringing sound.

janitor *(n)* someone whose job is to look after a school or some other public building.

jar jarring jarred
1 *(n)* a small, glass container with an airtight lid.
2 *(v)* to jolt or shake something or someone. *The fall jarred my knee.*
3 *(v)* If something **jars on you**, it makes you feel uncomfortable or annoyed.

jargon *(n)* words used by people in a particular business or activity, that other people cannot easily understand. *Computer jargon.*

jaundice *(n)* If you have **jaundice**, your skin turns yellow, often due to problems with your liver.

jaunt *(n)* a short pleasure trip or outing.

jaunty jauntier jauntiest *(adj)* giving a carefree and self-confident impression. *Sophie wore her cap at a jaunty angle.* **jauntily** *(adv)*.

javelin *(n)* a pointed, light, metal spear, thrown in an athletics event. *See* **track and field**.

jaw
1 *(n)* one of the two bones between your nose and your chin that hold your teeth. *See* **skeleton**.
2 *(n)* the lower part of your face.
3 *(n)* *(slang)* a friendly chat. **jaw** *(v)*.

jaywalk jaywalking jaywalked *(v)* to cross a street carelessly, taking no notice of traffic or signals. **jaywalker** *(n)*.

jazz *(n)* a lively, rhythmical type of music in which players often make up their own tunes, and add new notes in unexpected places. Jazz was started by African Americans between 1900 and 1905 in New Orleans, Louisiana.

jazzy jazzier jazziest *(adj) (informal)* Something that is **jazzy** is very noticeable, and often has bright colors and a strong pattern. *Jeff wore a very jazzy shirt.*

jealous *(adj)* If you are **jealous** of someone, you want what they have. **jealousy** *(n),* **jealously** *(adv).*

jeans *(plural n)* casual pants made of denim, or similar strong cloth, worn by both sexes.

Jeep *(n)* Trademark name for an open vehicle, used for driving over rough country.

jeer jeering jeered *(v)* to make fun of someone in a loud, unpleasant way. **jeeringly** *(adv).*

Jehovah *(n)* a name for God in the Old Testament.

Jell-O *(n)* Trademark name for a fruit-flavored dessert made with gelatin, that is boiled and then allowed to set.

jelly jellies *(n)* a sweet, sticky food, made from boiled fruit and sugar.

jellyfish jellyfish *or* jellyfishes *(n)* a sea creature with a soft, jelly-like body and trailing tentacles. *The picture shows how a jellyfish has arms stretching out from its mouth.*

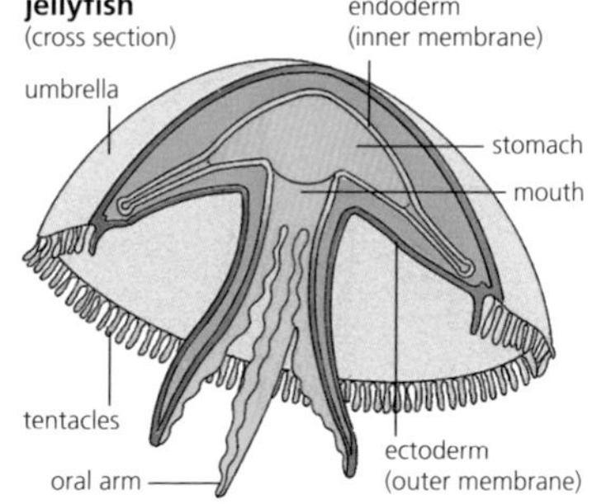

jeopardy *(jep-er-dee) (n)* If someone's job or life is **in jeopardy**, it is in danger or is threatened in some way. **jeopardize** *(v).*

jerk jerking jerked *(v)* to move suddenly, or to pull something suddenly and sharply. **jerky** *(adj).*

jest *(n)* a joke, or something said in fun. **jest** *(v).*

jester *(n)* an entertainer at a court in the Middle Ages.

jet
1 *(n)* a high-pressure stream of liquid or gas.
2 *(n)* an aircraft powered by jet engines.

jet engine *(n)* an engine that creates the forward thrust needed to move an aircraft, boat, etc. by sucking in air or water, and forcing it out at the rear. *The picture shows a jet turbofan engine, which is used on many aircraft. Air is sucked in by the fan, squeezed by the compressors, then mixed with fuel and burned in the combustion chamber. The gases produced in the chamber are forced out through a series of turbines, which drive the compressors and the fan. Also see* **hydrofoil**.

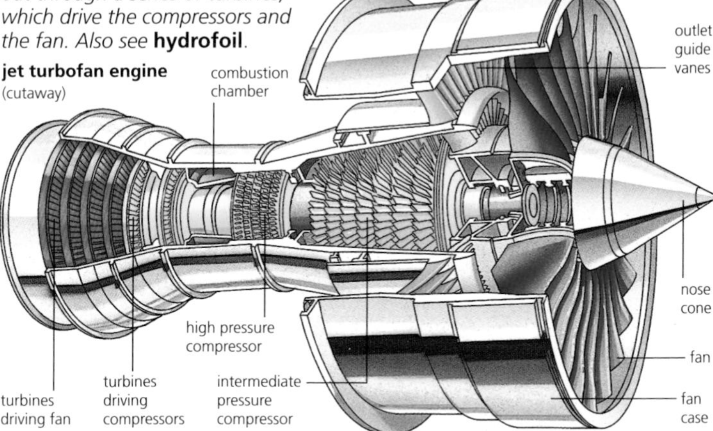

jet lag *(n)* a feeling of tiredness and confusion after a long flight from a different time zone.

jetsam *(n)* part of a ship's cargo that is thrown or lost overboard.

jettison jettisoning jettisoned *(v)* to throw overboard, or to throw out something that you no longer need.

jetty jetties *(n)* a structure built out into the sea to give shelter from the waves. Boats moor and unload beside jetties.

Jew
1 *(n)* someone who belongs to the race of people descended from the ancient tribes of Israel.
2 *(n)* someone who practices the religion of Judaism.

jewel *(n)* a precious stone, such as a diamond, ruby, or emerald.

jewelry *(n)* ornaments that you wear, such as rings, bracelets, and necklaces, made of jewels, gold, etc.

Jewish *(adj)* having to do with Jews or with the religion of Judaism.

jigsaw puzle *(n)* a wooden or cardboard puzzle made up of pieces of a picture that have been cut up and have to be put back together.

jingle
1 *(n)* a tinkling sound made by the movement of small bells, keys, etc. **jingle** *(v).*
2 *(n)* a simple song used to advertise a product.

jinx jinxes jinxing jinxed *(v)* to be hit by bad luck, supposedly because of a curse. *This project seems to be jinxed.* **jinx** *(n).*

job
1 *(n)* a task.
2 *(n)* the work that somebody does for a living.

jockey jockeying jockeyed
1 *(n)* someone who rides horses in races.
2 *(v)* If you **jockey for position** with someone, you try to beat them at something, often by unfair actions.

jocular *(adj)* cheerful and amusing. *Ray is a jocular fellow.*

joey *(n) (Australian) (informal)* a young kangaroo that is carried in its mother's pouch.

jog jogging jogged
1 *(v)* to run at a slow steady pace. *I jog to keep fit.* **jogger** *(n),* **jogging** *(n).*
2 *(v)* to knock something by accident.
3 *(v)* If something **jogs your memory**, it reminds you of something.

join joining joined
1 *(v)* to fasten or tie two things together. **join** *(n).*
2 *(v)* to come together with something or someone. *Please join us for supper.*
3 *(v)* to become a member of a club or group. *Hannah joined the marching band.*
4 **join up** *(v)* to become a member of the army, navy, or air force.

joiner *(n)* someone who makes wooden furniture and house fittings, such as door frames. **joinery** *(n).*

Some words that begin with a "j" sound are spelled with a "g."

joint
1 *(adj)* done or shared by two or more people. *A joint effort.* **jointly** *(adv).*
2 *(n)* a place where two bones meet, for example, your knee or elbow. There are four main types of joints in your body: pivot; gliding; hinge; and ball-and-socket. *This diagram of a human hip joint shows how the ball at the top of the femur fits into the socket of the pelvis.*

human hip joint
(ball-and-socket joint)
synovial fluid (lubricates bones)
pelvis (hip bone)
femur (thigh bone)
ball
socket
ligament (joins bones together)

3 *(n)* a cheap, unattractive place to eat, drink, or spend the night.

joke joking joked *(v)* to say funny things or play tricks on people to make them laugh. **joke** *(n).*

jolly jollier jolliest
1 *(adj)* happy and cheerful.
2 *(adv)* very. *Jolly good!*

jolt jolting jolted
1 *(v)* to move roughly. **jolt** *(n).*
2 *(v)* to bump into or knock someone or something. **jolt** *(n).*

jot jotting jotted *(v)* to write something down quickly. *I've jotted down some ideas.*

joule *(rhymes with fool) (n)* a unit for measuring energy or work done.

journal
1 *(n)* a diary in which you write what you have done each day.
2 *(n)* a serious magazine.

journalist *(n)* someone who collects information and writes articles for newspapers and magazines. **journalism** *(n),* **journalistic** *(adj).*

journey *(n)* a trip from one place to another. **journey** *(v).*

joust *(n)* a contest between two knights, riding horses and armed with lances. *The picture shows a medieval joust.* **joust** *(v).*

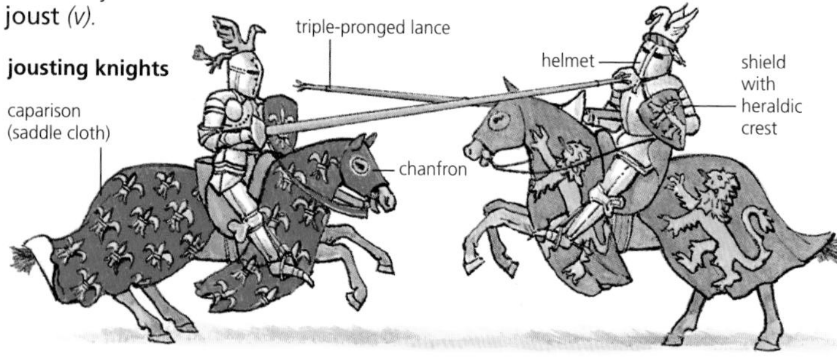

jousting knights

jovial *(adj)* Someone who is **jovial** is cheerful and enjoys talking and laughing with other people. **jovially** *(adv).*

joy
1 *(n)* a feeling of great happiness.
2 *(n) (informal)* good luck, or success. *I asked my dad for some money, but I didn't have any joy.*

joyful *(adj)* very happy. **joyfulness** *(n),* **joyfully** *(adv).*

joystick *(n)* a lever used to control movement in a computer game or in an aircraft.

jubilant *(adj)* very happy and delighted. *Josh was jubilant about winning the race.* **jubilation** *(n),* **jubilantly** *(adv).*

jubilee *(n)* a big celebration to mark the anniversary of a special event.

Judaism *(n)* the religion of the Jewish people, based on the law of Moses. Jews believe that they are God's chosen people. *The picture shows the symbol of Judaism, the six-pointed star of David.*

star of David

judge judging judged
1 *(v)* to hear cases in a law court and decide how a guilty person should be punished. **judge** *(n).*
2 *(v)* to decide who is the winner of a competition. **judge** *(n).*
3 *(v)* to form an opinion about someone or something. *After meeting Nat, I judged him to be honest.*

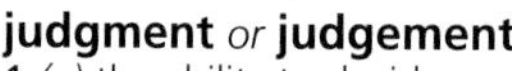

judgment *or* **judgement**
1 *(n)* the ability to decide or judge something.
2 *(n)* a decision made by a judge.
3 *(n)* an opinion of something or someone.

judicial *(joo-dish-uhl) (adj)* having to do with a court of law or a judge.

judicious *(joo-dish-uss) (adj)* sensible and wise. *A judicious decision.* **judiciously** *(adv).*

judo *(n)* a sport in which two people fight each other using controlled movements, and each tries to throw the other to the ground. *This sequence shows a basic forward throw in judo, called Harai goshi.*

judo
(forward throw)

jug *(n)* a container with a lip for pouring liquids.

juggernaut *(n)* a powerful force that can destroy anything in its path.

juggle juggling juggled *(v)* to keep a set of balls, clubs, or other objects moving through the air by repeatedly throwing them up and catching them again, one after another. **juggler** *(n).*

balls
clubs
juggling equipment

juice *(n)* liquid that comes out of fruit, vegetables, or meat. **juicy** *(adj).*

jukebox jukeboxes *(n)* a machine that plays songs when you put coins into it.

jumble jumbling jumbled *(v)* to mix things up so that they are untidy and not well organized.

jumbo
1 *(adj)* very large. *A jumbo packet.*
2 **jumbo jet** *(n) (informal)* a very large jet aircraft that can carry hundreds of passengers. *See* **aircraft**.

jump
jumping jumped
1 *(v)* to leap or to spring. **jump** *(n).*
2 *(n)* an object that you jump over. *The horse fell at the last jump.*
3 *(v)* If you **jump at** something, you accept it eagerly.

jumper *(n)* a sleeveless dress, usually worn over a shirt or sweater.

jumper cables *(n)* a set of wires that are used to connect the batteries of two cars so that one can be started using the other's battery.

jump rope *(n)* a length of rope used for skipping.

junction *(n)* a place where roads or railroad lines meet or join each other.

jungle *(n)* a thick, tropical forest.

junior
1 *(adj)* not very important in rank or position. *A junior manager.*
2 *(adj)* the younger of two. **Junior** is used after the name of a son who has the same name as his father, and may be written **Jr.** *John Smith, Jr.*
3 *(adj)* for young children. *A junior encyclopedia.*
4 *(n)* a third-year high school or college student.

junk
1 *(singular n)* things that are worthless or useless. *My room is full of junk!*
2 *(n)* a Chinese sailing boat with square sails and a flat bottom. *The picture below shows a Chinese junk. Junks have been used for trading for hundreds of years.*
3 **junk food** *(n)* food that is not good for you because it contains a lot of fat, sugar, and chemical additives.
4 **junk mail** *(n)* advertising leaflets and letters that you receive without having asked for them.

jury juries *(n)* a group of people at a trial who decide whether the person accused of a crime is innocent or guilty.

just
1 *(adj)* fair and right. *A just decision.* **justly** *(adv).*
2 *(adv)* exactly. *I'm sure I put the book just there.*
3 *(adv)* very recently. *I'm afraid that Brad has just left.*

justice
1 *(n)* fairness and rightness.
2 *(n)* the system of laws and punishments in a country.
3 **Justice of the Peace** *(n)* someone who hears cases in local courts of law and marries couples.

justify justifies justifying justified *(v)* If you **justify** an action, you give a reason or explanation to show that it is necessary and acceptable. *How can you justify stealing my pen?* **justification** *(n).*

jut jutting jutted *(v)* to stick out. *The cliff jutted into the sea.*

juvenile
1 *(n)* a young person who is not yet an adult, according to the law.
2 *(adj)* involving or concerning young people who are not yet adults, according to the law.
3 *(adj)* childish. *Juvenile behavior.*
4 **juvenile delinquent** *(n)* a young person who breaks the law. **juvenile delinquency** *(n).*

juxtapose juxtaposing juxtaposed *(v)* to place things side by side. **juxtaposition** *(n).*

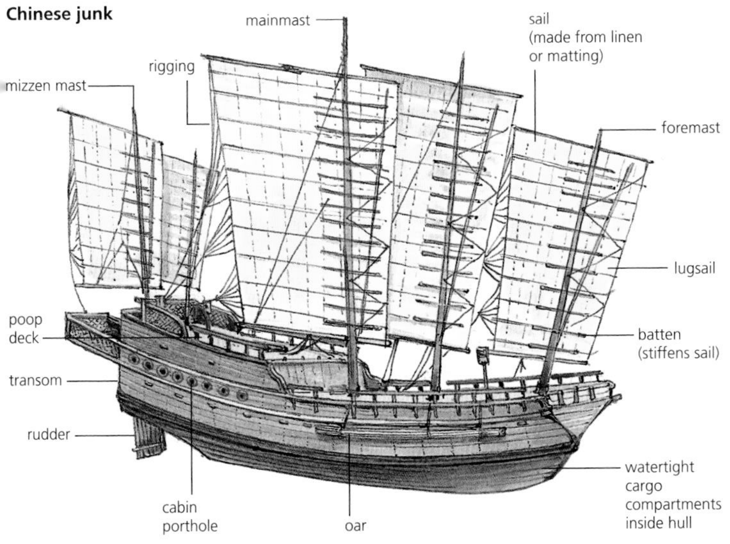

Kk

kaleidoscope *(n)* a tube through which you see changing patterns made by mirrors and pieces of colored glass. **kaleidoscopic** *(adj).*

kangaroo *(n)* a large Australian marsupial that carries its young in a pouch.

karaoke *(kare-ee-**oh**-kee) (n)* an entertainment in which people sing the words of popular songs while a machine plays the music.

karate *(ka-**rah**-tee) (n)* a sport in which two people fight each other using controlled movements, especially kicking with their feet and chopping with their hands.

kayak *(**ky**-ak) (n)* a covered, narrow boat in which you sit and move through the water by paddling with a double-bladed paddle.

kebob *(n)* small pieces of meat or vegetables, cooked on a skewer. *A lamb kebob.*

keel keeling keeled
1 *(n)* a long bar along the bottom of a boat that holds it together. *See* **ship**.
2 **keel over** *(v) (informal)* to fall over in one smooth, steady movement.

keen keener keenest
1 *(adj)* enthusiastic and eager. *Kim is keen to join the team.* **keenness** *(n).*
2 If you are **keen on** someone or something, you like them very much.
3 *(adj)* able to notice things easily. *A keen sense of smell.*

keep keeping kept
1 *(v)* to have something and not get rid of it. *Let's keep these books.*
2 *(v)* to stay the same. *We ran around to keep warm.*
3 *(v)* to continue doing something. *Dottie kept laughing at me.*
4 *(n)* a strong tower in a castle. *See* **castle**.

Some words that begin with a "k" sound are spelled with a "c."

keeper *(n)*
someone who looks after an animal, a park, or a museum collection.

keg *(n)* a small barrel.

kennel
1 *(n)* a small shelter for a dog to use for sleeping.
2 **kennels** *(plural n)* a place where dogs and cats are looked after while their owners are away.

kerosene *(n)* a liquid that is burned to give light or heat.

ketchup *(n)* a thick, puréed sauce, usually made from tomatoes.

kettle *(n)* a container with a handle and a spout, used for boiling water.

key
1 *(n)* a shaped piece of metal used for opening a lock, starting a car, etc.
2 *(n)* one of the buttons on a computer or typewriter.
3 *(n)* one of the black or white bars that you press on a piano.
4 *(n)* a scale of musical notes based around one particular note. *A tune in the key of F.*

keyboard
1 *(n)* the set of keys on a computer, typewriter, piano, etc.
2 *(n)* An **electronic keyboard** has keys like a piano, and controls to produce other sounds, and is worked by electricity.

khaki *(ka-kee) (n)*
a yellow-brown color, used especially for soldiers' uniforms. **khaki** *(adj).*

kibbutz *(kib-ootz)* **kibbutzim** *(n)*
a small community in Israel in which all the people live and work together.

kick **kicking kicked**
1 *(v)* to hit something with your foot. *Suzy accidentally kicked the chair as she went past.* **kick** *(n).*
2 *(n) (informal)* a feeling of excitement. *Dan gets a kick out of driving fast.*
3 **kick off** *(v)* to start a soccer match by kicking the ball. **kickoff** *(n).*

kid **kidding kidded**
1 *(n)* a young goat.
2 *(n) (informal)* a child.
3 *(v)* to make fun of or to tease someone. *I'm only kidding.*

kidnap **kidnapping kidnapped** *(v)*
to capture someone and keep them as a prisoner until certain demands are met. **kidnapper** *(n).*

kidney *(n)* Your **kidneys** are the organs in your body that remove waste matter from your blood and turn it into urine. *See* **organ**.

kill **killing killed** *(v)* to end the life of a person or animal.

kiln *(n)* a very hot oven, used to bake objects made of clay, glass and other materials.

kilohertz **kilohertz** *(n)*
a unit for measuring the frequency of radio signals.

kilojoule *(kil-uh-jool) (n)*
a unit for measuring energy or work done. 1 kilojoule = 1,000 joules.

kilowatt *(n)*
a unit for measuring electrical power. 1 kilowatt = 1,000 watts.

kilt *(n)*
a pleated plaid skirt worn by Scottish men as part of a traditional costume.

kimono *(n)*
a long loose dress with wide sleeves and a sash, worn by Japanese women.

kimono
tomoeri (over-collar)
eri (collar)
obijime (cord)
obi (sash)
kimono
tabi (split-toed socks)
zori (sandals)

kin
(plural n) people related to you.

kind
kinder
kindest
1 *(adj)* friendly, helpful, and generous. **kindness** *(n),* **kindly** *(adv).*
2 *(n)* a type or a sort.

kindergarten *(n)* a school or class for preschool children.

kindle **kindling kindled**
1 *(v)* to make something start to burn. *The campers quickly kindled a fire.*
2 *(v)* to get something started. *Our visit to the castle kindled my interest in history.*

kindling *(n)* small, thin pieces of wood used for starting fires.

kinetic *(adj)* having to do with movement, or caused by movement. *Kinetic energy.* **kinetically** *(adv).*

king
1 *(n)* a man from a royal family who is the ruler of his country.
2 *(n)* a chess piece that can move one square in any direction. *See* **chess**.
3 *(n)* a playing card with a picture of a king on it.

kingdom
1 *(n)* a country that has a king or queen as its ruler.
2 *(n)* a part of the natural world.

kingfisher

kingfisher *(n)*
a small, brightly colored bird that lives near water and catches fish for food. Kingfishers have a shrill whistle.

kiosk
(kee-osk) (n) a small stall from which snacks, newspapers, magazines, etc. are sold.

kiss **kisses kissing kissed** *(v)* to touch someone with your lips to greet them or to show affection for them. **kiss** *(n).*

kit
1 *(n)* a set of tools and materials for a certain purpose. *A sewing kit. A first-aid kit.*
2 *(n)* a collection of parts that you fix together to make something. *A model airplane kit.*

kitchen *(n)* a room in which food is prepared and cooked.

kite *(n)* a frame covered with paper or material that is flown in the wind, attached to a long piece of string. *The picture shows a stunt kite, which can be made to perform turns, dips, and loops.*

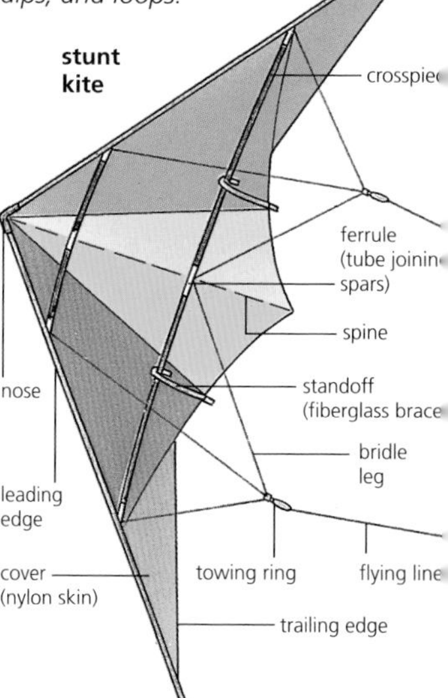

kitten *(n)* a young cat.

kitty **kitties** *(n)* an amount of money contributed by everyone in a group and then used to buy something. *We'll use the kitty to buy bread.*

kiwi *(kee-wee)*
1 *(n)* a bird from New Zealand that cannot fly.
2 *(n) (informal)* a name for someone who comes from New Zealand.

Some words that begin with a "k" sound are spelled with a "c."

knack *(nak) (n)* an ability to do something difficult or tricky.

knave *(nave) (old-fashioned)* a dishonest man or boy.

knead *(need)* **kneading kneaded** *(v)* When you **knead** dough, you punch it and stretch it to make it smooth.

knee *(nee) (n)* the joint between your upper and lower leg, that you bend when you walk.

kneel *(neel)* **kneeling knelt** *or* **kneeled** *(v)* to bend your legs and put your knees on the ground. *Please kneel down!*

knickers *(nik-ers) (plural n)* loose short pants that are fitted below the knee.

knife *(nife)* **knives; knifing knifed**
1 *(n)* a tool with a sharp blade, used for cutting things.
2 *(v)* to stab someone with a knife.

knight *(nite)*
1 *(n)* In medieval times, a **knight** was a warrior who fought on horseback. A king or noble would give a knight land and in return the knight would fight for him. **knightly** *(adj)*. *Also see* **feudalism**, **joust**.
2 *(n)* a man who has been given the title "Sir" as a reward for service to his country. **knighthood** *(n)*, **knight** *(v)*.
3 *(n)* a chess piece with a horse's head that can only move in an L-shape, three squares at a time. *See* **chess**.

mounted knight

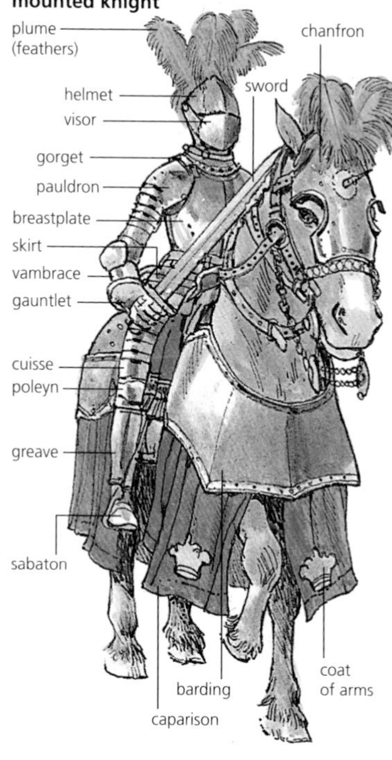

knit *(nit)* **knitting knitted**
1 *(v)* to make a piece of clothing out of wool, using a pair of long, pointed needles. **knitting** *(n)*.
2 *(v)* When a bone **knits**, it heals after it has been broken.

knob *(nob)*
1 *(n)* a small, round handle on a drawer or door.
2 *(n)* a control button on a machine.

knock *(nok)* **knocking knocked**
1 *(v)* to bang or hit something. *Knock the nails into the wall with a hammer.* **knock** *(n)*.
2 **knock out** *(v)* to make someone unconscious.

knocker *(nok-er) (n)* a piece of metal attached to a door that you use to knock on the door.

knot *(not)* **knotting knotted**
1 *(n)* a fastening made by looping and twisting string or rope together.
2 *(v)* to make a knot in a piece of string or rope.
3 *(n)* a hard spot in a piece of wood where a branch joined the main trunk.
4 *(n)* a unit for measuring the speed of a ship or aircraft.

knots
overhand knot or half hitch
figure-eight knot
reef knot or square knot
double carrick bend
sheet bend

know *(noh)* **knowing knew known** *(v)* to be familiar with a person, place, or piece of information.

knowledge *(nol-ij) (singular n)* the things that someone or everyone knows. *General knowledge.*

knowledgeable *(nol-ij-uh-bul) (adj)* If you are **knowledgeable**, you know a lot. *Al is knowledgeable about art.*

knuckle *(nuk-el) (n)* one of the joints where your fingers join your hand.

koala *(n)* an Australian mammal that looks like a small bear and lives in trees.

kookaburra *(n)* an Australian bird that makes a loud, cackling sound, like the sound of someone laughing.

Koran *or* **Qur'an** *(n)* the holy book of Islam.

kosher *(adj)* **Kosher** food is food that has been prepared according to the laws of the Jewish religion.

Ll

label **labeling labeled**
1 *(n)* a piece of paper, cloth, plastic, etc. that is attached to something and gives information about it.
2 *(n)* a word or phrase explaining something. *Picture labels.*
3 *(v)* to attach a label to something, or give something a label.

labor **laboring labored**
1 *(v)* to work hard. **labor** *(n)*.
2 *(n)* people employed to do work, especially physical work. *Part-time labor.*
3 *(n)* the work of giving birth to a baby.

laboratory **laboratories** *(n)* a room containing special equipment for people to use in scientific experiments.

Labor Day *(n)* a legal holiday in the United States to honor people who work. It is celebrated on the first Monday in September.

lace **lacing laced**
1 *(n)* thin material made from cotton or silk, with a pattern of small holes and delicate stitches. *This picture shows the equipment used to make lace.* **lacy** *(adj)*.
2 **laces** *(plural n)* long pieces of thin cord used to tie shoes.
3 *(v)* to tie something together with a lace. *Lace up your shoes.*

lace-making
pillow
lace
pins
bobbin
threads
pricking (pattern)

lack **lacking lacked**
1 *(v)* to be without something that you need. *The refugees lack food.*
2 *(n)* If there is a **lack** of something, people do not have enough of it.

lacrosse *(n)* a ball game for two teams, in which each player has a long stick with a small net on the end. The players run with the ball, pass it to each other, and aim to score goals.

lacrosse stick

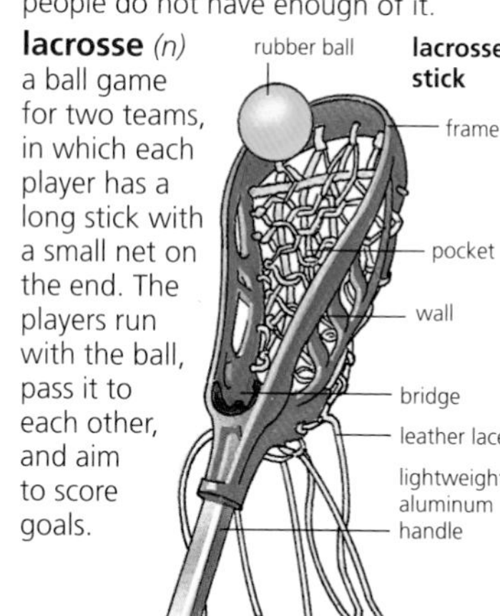

Some words that begin with a "k" sound are spelled with a "c."

lad *(n)* a boy or a young man.

ladder *(n)* a metal, wooden, or rope structure that you use to climb up and down. Ladders are made from two long side pieces linked by a series of cross-pieces called rungs.

laden *(adj)* carrying a lot of things. *Matt arrived laden with presents.*

ladle *(n)* a large deep spoon with a long handle, used for serving soup, casseroles, etc. **ladle** *(v).*

lady ladies
1 *(n)* a polite name for a woman.
2 **Lady** *(n)* In Great Britain, this title is used by a woman who has either earned the title herself, as a reward for service to her country, or who is married to a Lord or a man with the title "Sir."

ladybug *(n)* a small round beetle that has colorful wings with spots on them. Ladybugs eat small insects that are harmful to plants.

lag lagging lagged *(v)* If you **lag behind** other people, you do not keep up with them.

lagoon *(n)* a large pool of seawater separated from the sea by a bank of sand.

laid-back *(adj) (informal)* very relaxed and calm. *Jared is so laid-back, I'm surprised he gets anything done!*

lair *(n)* a place where a wild animal rests and sleeps.

lake *(n)* a large area of fresh water surrounded by land.

lamb
1 *(n)* a young sheep.
2 *(n)* meat from a young sheep.

lame lamer lamest
1 *(adj)* Someone who is **lame** has an injured leg and so is unable to walk properly. **lameness** *(n),* **lamely** *(adv).*
2 *(adj)* weak, or unconvincing. *A lame excuse.* **lamely** *(adv).*

lament lamenting lamented
1 *(n)* a sad song, especially one about someone's death.
2 *(v)* to feel or show great sadness.

lamp *(n)* a light that uses gas, oil, or electricity.

lance *(n)* a long spear used in the past by soldiers riding horses. *See* **joust**.

land landing landed
1 *(n)* the part of the Earth's surface that is not covered by water.
2 *(v)* to come down from the air to the ground. *The plane landed safely.*
3 *(v) (informal)* to succeed in getting something. *I've landed a place on the team.*
4 *(informal)* If you are **landed with** something, you have been given something difficult or unpleasant to deal with.

landfill *(n)* garbage and waste that is buried under the ground.

landing
1 *(n)* an area of floor at the top of a staircase.
2 *(n)* coming to land or to the shore after a flight or voyage.
3 **landing strip** *(n)* a strip of ground that aircraft use for taking off and landing.

landlady landladies *(n)* a woman who rents out a room, house, or apartment. *Robbie owes his landlady a lot of money.*

landlord *(n)* a man who rents out a room, house, or apartment.

landmark
1 *(n)* an object in a landscape that can be seen from a long way away.
2 *(n)* an important event in someone or something's development. *Leaving home was a landmark in Finn's life.*

landscape
1 *(n)* a large area of land that you can view from one place.
2 **landscape gardening** *(n)* the designing, shaping, and planting of a garden in an attractive way.

landslide
1 *(n)* a sudden fall of earth and rocks down the side of a mountain or hill.
2 *(n)* an election victory in which the winner gains many more votes than anyone else.

lane
1 *(n)* a narrow road or street.
2 *(n)* one of the strips marked on a main road, which is wide enough for a single line of vehicles.
3 *(n)* one of the strips, each wide enough for one person, into which a racetrack or swimming pool is divided. *Laura is running in lane eight.*

language
1 *(n)* the words that people use to talk and write to each other.
2 *(n)* a set of signs, symbols, or movements used to express meaning. *Sign language.*

lanky lankier lankiest *(adj)* Someone who is **lanky** is very tall and thin. **lankiness** *(n).*

Japanese lanterns

lantern *(n)* a candle with a protective frame around it. *Lanterns can be made from paper, like the ones shown here, or from glass and metal.*

lanyard *(n)* a cord worn around your neck to which you can attach a whistle, compass, etc. *See* **compass**.

lap lapping lapped
1 *(n)* the flat area formed by the top part of your legs when you are sitting down. *Why don't you sit on my lap?*
2 *(n)* the distance around a racetrack. *I can run a lap in 55 seconds.*
3 *(v)* When water **laps** against something, it moves gently against it.
4 *(v)* When an animal **laps up** a drink, it flicks the liquid up into its mouth with its tongue.

lapel *(n)* part of the collar of a coat or jacket that folds back over your chest.

lapse
1 *(n)* a small mistake or failure. *Kay has been dieting hard, with a slight lapse over Christmas.* **lapse** *(v).*
2 *(n)* the passing of time. *After a lapse of two years, Jo-Jo returned.*

laptop *(n)* a portable computer that is so small and light you can use it on your lap.

lard *(n)* solid white fat used in cooking.

large larger largest
1 *(adj)* big. **largeness** *(n).*
2 If a person or an animal is **at large**, they are free and dangerous. *There's a tiger at large in the town.*

largely *(adv)* mostly. *The crowd was largely made up of teenagers.*

lark
1 *(n)* a small brown bird that flies very high in the sky and has an attractive song.
2 *(n) (informal)* something silly that you do for fun or as a joke. **lark** *(v).*

larva larvae *(n)* an insect at the stage of development between an egg and a pupa. *See* **caterpillar**.

laryngitis *(la-rin-jy-tuss) (n)* a swelling of the throat caused by an infection.

larynx *(la-ringks) (n)* the top of your windpipe, which holds your vocal cords.

lasagna *(la-zahn-yuh) (n)* an Italian dish made from layers of pasta and meat or vegetables, covered with a cheese sauce.

aser
1 *(n)* a machine that makes a very narrow powerful beam of light that can be used for light shows, for cutting things, or for medical operations. The word laser stands for "light amplification by stimulated emission of radiation."
2 **laser beam** *(n)* a concentrated beam of light made by a laser. Laser beams are used to read compact discs. *See* **compact disc**.

ash lashes lashing lashed
1 *(n)* a stroke with a whip.
2 *(v)* to tie things together very firmly using rope.
3 *(n)* one of the small hairs growing around your eyes.
4 **lash out** *(v)* to hit someone suddenly and angrily.

ass lasses *(n)* a girl or young woman.

asso *(lass-oo)* lassos *or* lassoes *(n)* a length of rope with a large loop at one end, which can be thrown over an animal to catch it. **lasso** *(v)*.

ast lasting lasted
1 *(adj)* coming at the end or after everything else. *Jane was the last to leave.* **lastly** *(adv)*.
2 *(adj)* most recent. *I saw Dominic last week.*
3 *(v)* to go on for a particular length of time. *The movie lasts for 90 minutes.*
4 **last straw** *(n)* the final event in a series that leads to an emotional breakdown.
5 *(n)* If someone **has the last word**, it means they have put an end to an argument or discussion.

asting *(adj)* Something that is **lasting** keeps going for a long time.

atch latches latching latched
1 *(n)* a lock or fastening for a door. **latch** *(v)*.
2 *(v)* If you **latch on** to someone or something, you become very attached to them and dependent on them.

atchkey *(n)* a key that opens a door with a latch.

ate later latest
1 *(adj)* When someone or something is **late**, they come after the expected time. **lateness** *(n)*.
2 *(adj)* near the end of a period of time. *The late 20th century.*
3 *(adj)* no longer alive. *The late Elvis Presley.*

atecomer *(n)* someone who arrives late.

ately *(adv)* recently.

atent *(adj)* existing, but not yet very obvious or very strong. *A latent talent.*

lateral
1 *(adj)* on or toward the side. *A lateral root.* **laterally** *(adv)*.
2 **lateral thinking** *(n)* the ability to think about problems in an unusual and not obvious way.

lather *(n)*
a mass of white bubbles formed when soap is mixed with water.

Latin *(n)*
the language of the Ancient Romans.

latitude *(n)* the position of a place, measured in degrees north or south of the equator. **latitudinal** *(adj)*.

latter
1 *(n)* the second of two things just mentioned. *I like apples and pears, but I prefer the latter.*
2 *(adj)* later. *It snowed during the latter part of our vacation.*

lattice *(n)* a pattern of crossed lines with diamond-shaped spaces in between them. **latticed** *(adj)*.

laugh laughing laughed *(v)*
When you **laugh**, you make a sound to show that you think that something is funny. **laugh** *(n)*, **laughter** *(n)*.

laughable *(adj)* If something is **laughable**, it is ridiculous and cannot be taken seriously.

launch
launches launching launched
1 *(v)* to put a large ship into the water for the first time. **launch** *(n)*.
2 *(v)* to send a rocket up into space. **launch** *(n)*.
3 *(v)* to start or introduce something new. *The charity launched a new fundraising campaign.* **launch** *(n)*.
4 *(n)* a type of boat that is often used for sightseeing.
5 **launch pad** *(n)*
a place where rockets leave the ground to go into space.

Laundromat *(n)* Trademark name for a place where you pay to use washing machines and dryers.

laundry laundries
1 *(n)* clothes, towels, and sheets that are being washed or are about to be washed.
2 *(n)* a place where clothes are washed.

laurel
1 *(n)* an evergreen bush with smooth, shiny leaves.
2 *(n)* a wreath made from bay or laurel leaves, given to heroes and poets in Ancient Greece and Rome.
3 If you **rest on your laurels**, you rely on your past achievements and do not try any more.

lava *(n)* the hot liquid that pours out of a volcano when it erupts.

lavatory lavatories *(n)* a bathroom.

lavender
1 *(n)* a plant, usually with purple flowers that have a pleasant smell.
2 *(n)* a pale purple color, the color of most lavender flowers. **lavender** *(adj)*.

lavish lavishes lavishing lavished
1 *(adj)* generous or extravagant. *Lavish gifts.* **lavishly** *(adv)*.
2 *(v)* If you **lavish** attention, money, care, etc. on someone, you give them a lot of it.

law
1 *(n)* a rule made by the government that must be obeyed.
2 *(n)* a statement or principle in science, math, etc. *The law of gravity.*
3 *(n)* the profession and work of a lawyer. *A career in law.*

law-abiding *(adj)*
If you are **law-abiding**, you obey the laws of a country.

lawsuit *(n)*
a legal action brought against a person or group in a court of law.

lawful *(adj)* permitted by the law. **lawfulness** *(n)*, **lawfully** *(adv)*.

lawn *(n)* a piece of grass, usually next to a house.

lawn mower *(n)* a machine that people use to cut grass.

lawyer *(n)*
someone who advises people about the law and speaks for them in court.

lax *(adj)* relaxed or not strict. *He has a lax attitude toward the rules.*

laxative *(n)* a medicine or food that you eat to help you empty your bowels. **laxative** *(adj)*.

lay laying laid
1 *(v)* to put or to place. *Lay the clothes on the bed.*
2 *(v)* to produce an egg.
3 If you are **laid up**, you are in bed with an injury or illness.
4 If you have been **laid off**, you have been dismissed from a job.

layer *(n)* a thickness of something. *Layers of paint.* **layered** *(adj)*.

layoff *(n)* a situation in which people are fired from their job because there is not enough for them to do.

layout *(n)* the pattern or design of something. *The layout of a book.*

lazy lazier laziest *(adj)*
If you are **lazy**, you do not want to work or exercise. **laziness** *(n)*, **laze** *(v)*, **lazily** *(adv)*.

lead leading led
1 *(rhymes with bead) (v)* to show someone the way, usually by going in front of them. **leader** *(n).*
2 *(rhymes with bead) (v)* to be in charge. **leader** *(n),* **leadership** *(n).*
3 *(rhymes with bed) (n)* a soft gray metal.
4 *(rhymes with bead) (n)* a suggestion or a clue. *The police have been given several new leads.*

leaf leaves
1 *(n)* a flat and usually green part of a plant or tree, which grows out from a stem, twig, branch, etc. *The cross section of a leaf, below, shows the palisade cells, where light is converted to food in a process called photosynthesis, and the mesophyll cells, where respiration takes place.*
leafy *(adj).*
2 *(n)* a page of a book.

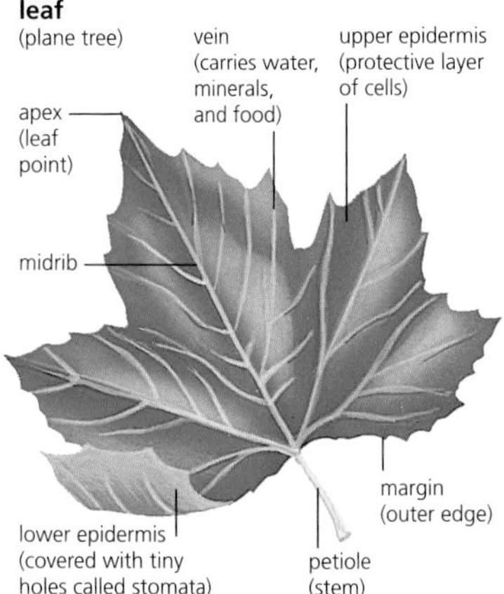

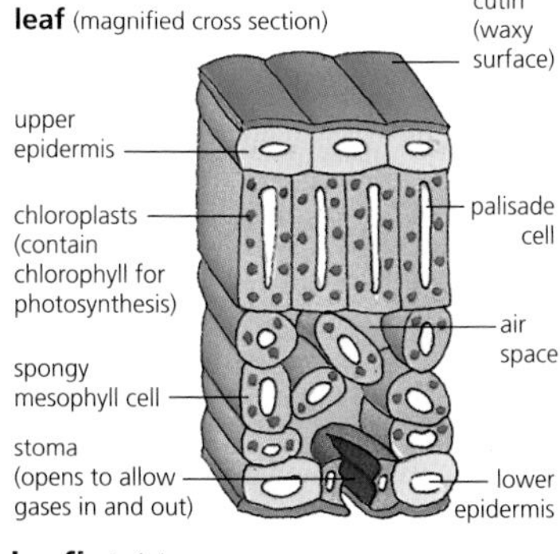

leaflet *(n)*
a printed, and usually folded, piece of paper that gives information or advertises something. **leaflet** *(v).*

league *(leeg) (n)* a group of people, countries, or teams who have a shared interest or activity. *A basketball league.*

leak leaking leaked
1 *(v)* If a container **leaks,** it lets liquid or gas escape from it.
leak *(n),* **leaky** *(adj).*
2 *(v)* If a liquid or gas **leaks,** it escapes through a hole or crack in a container. **leak** *(n).*
3 *(v)* If a story or information is **leaked,** somebody tells it to someone else who is not meant to know it. **leak** *(n).*

lean
leaning leaned; leaner leanest
1 *(v)* to bend toward or over something. *The mother leaned over her baby.*
2 *(v)* to slope.
Look how that wall leans!
3 *(v)* to rest your body against something for support.
4 *(adj)* slim and muscular.
5 *(adj)* If meat is **lean,** it has very little or no fat.

leaning *(n)* If you have a **leaning** toward something, you are interested in it or good at it.

leap leaping leaped *or* leapt *(v)* to jump, or to jump over something. **leap** *(n).*

leap year *(n)*
a year that has 366 days, caused by adding an extra day in February. A leap year comes every fourth year.

learn learning learned *or* learnt
1 *(v)* to gain knowledge or a skill.
2 *(v)* to discover some news. *I learned that Kevin was going away.*

lease *(n)* an agreement that you sign when you rent an apartment, land, etc.

leash leashes *(n)* a long strip attached to a collar, that you use to hold and control a dog.

least
1 *(n)* the smallest amount. *Of all the children, Sue eats the least.* **least** *(adj).*
2 *(adv)* less than anything else.
Turnip is my least favorite vegetable.
3 **at least** at a minimum. *We need at least another week's vacation.*

leather *(n)* animal skin that is treated and used to make shoes, bags, and other goods. **leathery** *(adj).*

leave leaving left
1 *(v)* to go away. *We're leaving for France tomorrow.*
2 *(v)* to let something stay or remain. *Leave the dishes, I'll do them later.*
3 *(n)* time away from work.
4 **leave behind** *(v)* If you **leave something behind,** you forget to bring it accidentally or deliberately.
5 **leave out** *(v)* If you **leave something out,** you do not include it.

lecture
1 *(n)* a talk given to a class or an audience to teach them something. **lecturer** *(n),* **lecture** *(v).*
2 *(n)* a scolding that lasts a long time. **lecture** *(v).*

ledge *(n)* a narrow shelf.
A window ledge. A mountain ledge.

leek *(n)* a long white vegetable with green leaves at one end.
See **vegetable**.

leer *(n)* an unpleasant grin. **leer** *(v).*

left
1 *(adj)* This page is on the **left-hand side** of the book. **left** *(n),* **left** *(adv).*
2 In politics, people **on the left** have liberal or radical views.

left-handed *(adj)* If you are **left-handed,** you use your left hand to write and draw. **left-hander** *(n).*

leftovers *(plural n)*
food that has not been eaten and can be used for another meal.

leg
1 *(n)* the part of your body between your hip and foot.
2 *(n)* one of the parts that supports a chair, table, etc.
3 *(n)* A **leg** of a journey is one part or stage of it.
4 *(informal)* If you **pull someone's leg,** you make fun of them by telling them something untrue.

legacy legacies *(n)*
money or property that has been left to someone in a will.

legal
1 *(adj)* having to do with the law.
Legal documents.
2 *(adj)* lawful or allowed by law. **legally** *(adv).*

legend
1 *(n)* an old and well-known story. **legendary** *(adj).*
2 *(n)* If someone is a **legend,** they are very famous. **legendary** *(adj).*

leggings *(plural n)* a covering for the legs that fit like tights.

legible *(adj)* If handwriting or print is **legible,** it can be read easily. **legibility** *(n),* **legibly** *(adv).*

legion
1 *(n)* part of the Roman army.
2 *(n)* a large body of soldiers or ex-soldiers. *The foreign legion.*
3 *(adj)* very many or numerous.
Melissa's faults are legion.

legislation *(singular n)* laws.
The government has introduced new traffic legislation. **legislate** *(v).*

egitimate
(adj) lawful or acceptable.
egitimately (adv).
(adj) A **legitimate** child is
orn to parents who are married.

gume (n)
plant with seeds that grow in
ods. *Peas, lentils, beans, and
eanuts are legumes.*

ei (lay) (n) a necklace of leaves
r flowers often given as a gift
f welcome in Hawaii.

eisure (n) free time when you do
ot have to work. **leisure** (adj).

eisurely (adj) unhurried. *We
njoyed a long leisurely breakfast.*

emon (n) a yellow citrus fruit
ith a thick skin. *See* **fruit**.

emonade (n)
sweet drink that is lemon-flavored.

end **lending** **lent** (v) to let someone
ave something for a short time.

ength
(n) the distance from one
nd of something to the other.
(n) the time that something
sts. *Do you know the length
f this movie?* **lengthy** (adj).

engthen
engthening **lengthened** (v)
o make something longer.

engthwise (adv)
the direction of the longest
de. *Fold the paper lengthwise.*

enient (lee-nee-ent) (adj)
entle and not strict. **leniently** (adv).

ens **lenses**
(n) the part of your eye
at focuses light. *See* **eye**.
(n) a piece of curved glass or
astic in a pair of glasses or in a
amera, telescope, etc. Lenses bend
ght rays so that you can focus a
amera or see things magnified
rough a telescope. *The diagram
hows how concave and convex lenses
ake light rays bend in different ways.
lso see* **telescope**.

enses

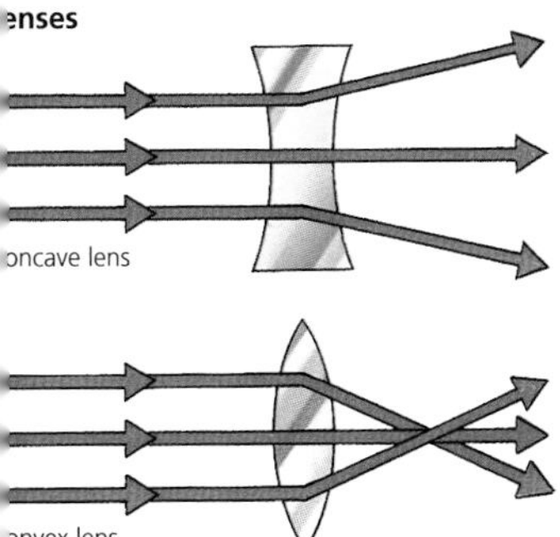

Lent (n)
the 40 days before Easter in the Christian church's year. Some people give up certain luxuries for Lent.

lentil (n) a small, dried seed that can be cooked and eaten. Lentils can be green, orange, or brown.

leopard (lep-erd) (n) a large wild cat with a spotted coat, found in Africa and Asia.

leopard

leprechaun
(lep-ri-kon or lep-ri-kawn) (n)
an annoying elf in Irish folklore.

leotard (lee-oh-tard) (n)
a tight one-piece garment worn for dancing or exercise.

less
1 (adj) smaller, or in smaller quantities. *There is less fat in margarine than in butter.* **less** (adv).
2 (prep) minus. *We bought it for the sale price, less ten percent discount.*

lessen **lessening** **lessened** (v)
to get smaller in size, strength, importance, etc. *The noise lessened as the teacher approached the classroom.*

lesson
1 (n) a set period in school when pupils are taught, or a session when a skill is taught.
2 (n) an experience that teaches you something.

let **letting** **let**
1 (v) to allow or permit something.
2 (v) to rent out a house, land, etc.
3 **let down** (v) If you **let someone down**, you disappoint them by not doing something that you promised.
4 (v) If you are **let off** a punishment or duty, you no longer have to undergo it or do it.

lethal (adj) If something is **lethal**, it can kill. **lethally** (adv).

letter
1 (n) a sign that is part of an alphabet and is used in writing. *The letter "a."*
2 (n) a message that you write to someone, or receive from someone.

lettering (n) letters written in a certain style. *Italic lettering.*

lettuce (n) a green leafy salad vegetable. *See* **vegetable**.

leukemia (loo-kee-mee-uh) (n)
a serious disease in which the blood makes too many white cells.

level **leveling** **leveled**
1 (adj) flat and smooth. **level** (v).
2 (adj) equal. *The scores are level.*
3 (n) a height. *Eye level. Sea level.*
4 (n) a standard or a grade. *Advanced-level study.*
5 (v) If something **levels out**, it stops rising or falling and stays the same.
6 (n) a tool used to show if a surface is flat.

lever (leh-ver)
1 (n) a bar that you use to lift an object by placing one end under the object and pushing down on the other end. **leverage** (n), **lever** (v).
2 (n) a handle that you use to make a machine work.

levitate **levitating** **levitated**
1 (v) to rise in the air and float, in seeming defiance of gravity.
2 (v) to cause to rise in the air and float.

liable
1 (adj) likely. *Judy is liable to get angry when she hears the news.*
2 (adj) If you are **liable** for something that you have done, you are responsible for it by law. **liability** (n).

liar (n) someone who tells lies. *Curtis says he has a hot tub, but he's a liar.*

libel (n) an untrue written statement about another person that is damaging to them. **libelous** (adj).

liberal
1 (adj) tolerant, especially of other people's ideas. **liberalism** (n).
2 (adj) generous. *A liberal helping of ice cream.*

liberate **liberating** **liberated** (v)
to set someone free. **liberation** (n).

liberated (adj) Someone who is **liberated** has been set free, or feels free. **liberation** (n).

liberty **liberties** (n) freedom.

library **libraries** (n)
a place where you can go to read or borrow books. **librarian** (n).

lice (plural n)
small insects without wings, which live on animals or people.

license
1 (n) a document giving permission for you to do something or own something. *A driving license.*
2 (v) If someone is **licensed** to do something, they have official permission to do it.

lichen
(lye-ken) (n)
a flat moss-like plant that grows on stones, trees, etc.

Himalayan lichen

lick licking licked
1 *(v)* to pass your tongue over something. **lick** *(n).*
2 *(v)* to touch something lightly. *Small waves licked the shore.*

lid *(n)* a top or a cover.

lie lying lied
1 *(v)* to say something that is not true.
2 *(n)* a statement that is untrue.

lie lying lay lain
1 *(v)* to get into, or to be in, a flat outstretched position.
2 *(v)* to be or to be placed somewhere. *The village lies in a deep valley.*

lieutenant *(loo-ten-uhnt) (n)* an officer of low rank in the armed forces.

life lives
1 *(n)* Your **life** is the time from your birth until your death.
2 *(n)* liveliness and cheerfulness. *I feel full of life today!*

lifeguard *(n)* someone who is trained to save swimmers in danger.

lifejacket *(n)* a jacket that will keep you afloat if you fall into water.

lifejacket

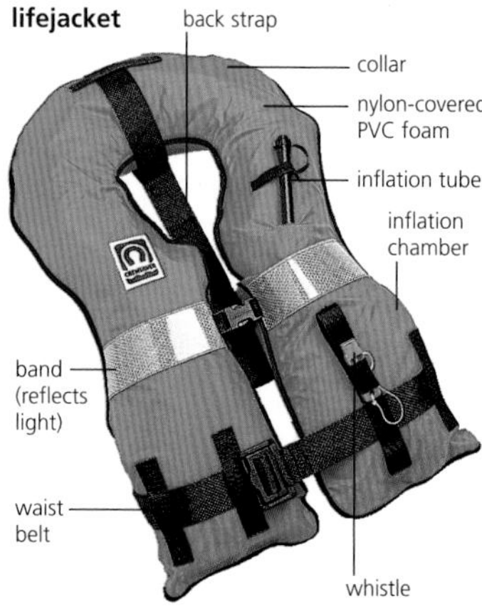

lifestyle *(n)* a way of living. *Alex has a very glamorous lifestyle.*

lift lifting lifted
1 *(v)* to raise something or someone.
2 *(v)* to rise into the air.
3 *(n)* a ride, especially in a car.

light lighting lit *or* lighted; lighter lightest
1 *(v)* to start something burning.
2 *(v)* to make something bright.
3 *(n)* brightness from the Sun, a lamp, etc.
4 *(adj)* not dark. *Light blue.*
5 *(n)* an object that gives out light, such as a flashlight or lamp.
6 *(adj)* weighing little. **lightness** *(n).*
7 *(adj)* gentle. **lightly** *(adv).*
8 **light up** *(v)* to make something bright. *A smile lit up Bill's face.*

lighthouse *(n)* a tower, set in or near the sea, with a flashing light that guides ships or warns them of danger.

lightning *(n)* flashes of electricity in the sky, usually with thunder.

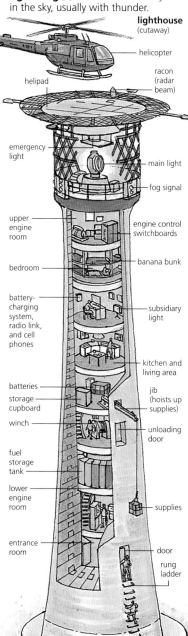

lighthouse (cutaway)

helicopter
helipad
racon (radar beam)
emergency light
main light
fog signal
upper engine room
engine control switchboards
banana bunk
bedroom
battery-charging system, radio link, and cell phones
subsidiary light
kitchen and living area
batteries
storage cupboard
jib (hoists up supplies)
winch
unloading door
fuel storage tank
lower engine room
supplies
entrance room
door
rung ladder

lightweight
1 *(adj)* not heavy. *A lightweight coat.*
2 *(adj)* not important or not serious.

light year *(n)*
a unit for measuring distance in space. A light year is the distance that light travels in one year.

like liking liked
1 *(v)* to enjoy or be pleased by something or someone. **liking** *(n).*
2 *(prep)* similar to. *I want a hat like yours.*
3 *(prep)* typical of. *It's just like Daisy to be late.*
4 *(adj)* similar or equal. *A like amount.*

likely likelier likeliest *(adj)* probable. **likelihood** *(n).*

likewise *(adv)*
also or in the same way. *I'll dance if you do likewise.*

lilac
1 *(n)* a plant, usually with light purple flowers that have a pleasant odor.
2 *(n)* a pale purple color, the color of lilac flowers. **lilac** *(adj).*

limb
1 *(n)* an arm or a leg.
2 *(n)* a branch of a tree.

limber limbering limbered
1 *(v)* When you **limber up**, you stretch your muscles before exercising.
2 *(adj)* supple and flexible.

lime
1 *(n)* a round green citrus fruit. *See* **fruit**.
2 *(n)* a white substance or powder, used to make cement and as a fertilizer on fields.

limelight *(n)*
If you are **in the limelight**, you are the center of attention.

limerick *(n)*
a nonsense verse made up of five lines that rhyme in a particular way.

limestone *(n)*
a rock that contains calcium carbonate and from which lime is made.

limit limiting limited
1 *(n)* an edge or a boundary. **limitless** *(adj),* **limitlessly** *(adv).*
2 *(v)* to keep within a certain area or amount. *I've limited myself to three cups of coffee a day.* **limitation** *(n).*

limited
1 *(adj)* small and unable to increase.
2 *(n)* A **limited edition** of a book, picture, etc. may be valuable because it is one of only a small number.

mp limping limped; limper limpest
(v) to walk in an uneven way,
sually because of an injury. **limp** *(n)*.
(adj) floppy and not firm.
limp handshake. **limply** *(adv)*.

ne lining lined
(n) a long narrow mark.
(n) a row of people or words.
(n) a piece of string, rope, etc.
(v) to make a lining for something.
(n) an attitude or an approach
) something.

nen *(n)* cloth made from the flax
'ant, used to make clothes and
ousehold items, such as sheets.

nesperson *(n)* an official who
ecides if the ball has gone over the
ne, in games such as football, soccer,
ockey, and tennis. *See* **soccer**.

nger lingering lingered *(v)* to stay,
to wait around. **lingering** *(adj)*.

nguist *(n)* someone who studies
oreign languages, or someone
ho speaks them well.

ning *(n)* a piece of material
ewn inside something. *A silk lining.*

nk linking linked
(n) one of the separate
ngs that make up a chain.
(n) a connection between
ings or people.
(v) to join objects, ideas,
people together.

nocut *(n)* a print made from
block of linoleum with a pattern
picture cut into it.

noleum *(n)* a smooth, shiny
aterial used as a floor covering.
ften called lino.

nt *(n)* tiny pieces of clothing
oer that gather together as wisps.

on *(n)* a large wild cat with
mane, found in Africa and Asia.

p
(n) Your **lips** are the pink
dges of your mouth.
(n) the edge or rim of a cup or hole.

p-read lip-reading lip-read *(v)*
/hen deaf people **lip-read**, they
atch someone's lips while they are
lking in order to understand what
ey are saying. **lip-reading** *(n)*.

quefy *(v)* to make something solid
to a liquid.

quid *(n)* a wet substance
at you can pour. **liquid** *(adj)*.

quid crystal display *(n)*
way of showing numbers and letters
n clocks, calculators, etc. Parts of a
id of liquid crystals reflect light as
ectronic signals are sent to them.
ften called LCD. *See* **calculator**.

liquidize liquidizing liquidized *(v)* to make solid food into a liquid. **liquidizer** *(n)*.

lira *(leer-a)* lire *(n)* the main unit of money in Turkey, and formerly in Italy.

lisp *(n)* a way of talking in which you say "th" instead of "s." **lisp** *(v)*.

list listing listed
1 *(v)* to set down numbers, words, etc. in a line. **list** *(n)*.
2 *(v)* When a ship **lists**, it leans to one side.

listen listening listened *(v)* to pay attention so that you can hear something. **listener** *(n)*.

literacy *(n)* the ability to read and write. **literate** *(adj)*.

literally *(adv)* If you take someone or something **literally**, you believe exactly what they say.

literature *(n)* books, especially novels, plays, and poems. *Nancy loves Spanish literature.* **literary** *(adj)*.

litmus *(n)* a substance that turns red when touched by an acid, and blue when touched by an alkali. Litmus comes in paper or liquid form.

litter
1 *(n)* garbage that is left scattered around. **litter** *(v)*.
2 *(n)* a group of kittens, piglets, puppies, etc. born at the same time to one mother.
3 **litter box** *(n)* an indoor toilet for a cat or other pet.

little littler littlest
1 *(adj)* small in size. *A little girl.*
2 *(n)* a small amount of something. *I'll have just a little.*
3 *(adj)* not much. *We have little time.*

live living lived
1 *(rhymes with give) (v)* to be alive. *Some cats live for 20 years.*
2 *(rhymes with five) (adj)* alive or living. *You can buy live chickens in the market.*
3 *(rhymes with give) (v)* to have your home somewhere. *Josie lives in Chicago.*
4 *(rhymes with five) (adj)* broadcast as it is happening. *Live music.*
5 *(rhymes with five) (adj)* If an electrical wire is **live**, it is carrying electricity which can give you a shock.
6 *(rhymes with five) (adj)* unexploded. *A live cartridge.*

livelihood *(n)* the way that you make money to support yourself. *Farming is my father's livelihood.*

lively livelier liveliest *(adj)* active and full of life. **liveliness** *(n)*.

liver
1 *(n)* the organ in your body that cleans your blood. Your liver also produces bile which helps to digest food. *See* **digestion**, **organ**.
2 *(n)* You can eat the **liver** of some animals, such as chickens.

livestock *(n)* animals kept on a farm, such as horses, sheep, and cows.

living
1 *(adj)* alive now.
2 *(n)* money to live. *Joe earns his living by painting.*

living room *(n)* a room in the house for the whole family.

lizard *(n)* a small reptile with a long body and a tail. *The picture shows parts of a lizard and a range of different lizards.*

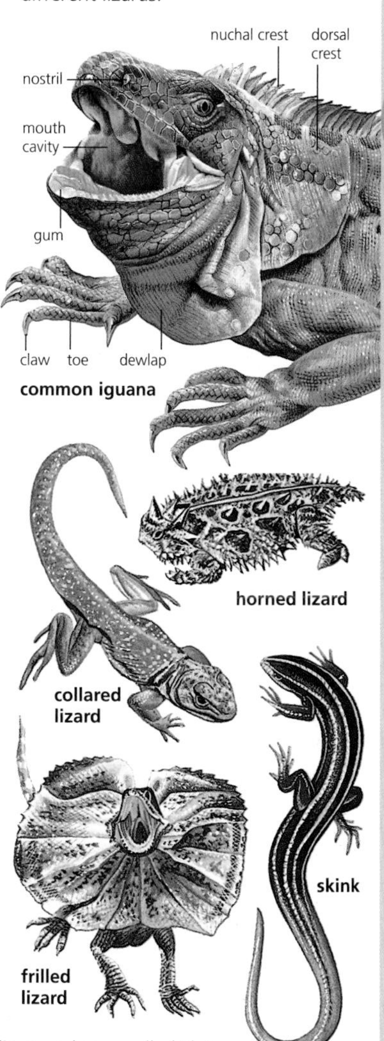

Some words that begin with a "li" sound are spelled "ly."

llama *(n)* a South American mammal kept for its wool and meat.

load loading loaded
1 *(n)* something that is carried, especially something heavy.
2 *(v)* to put things onto or into something. *Bobby loaded the car with camping equipment.*
3 *(v)* to put a bullet into a gun.
4 *(plural n) (informal)* If you have **loads** of something, you have a lot of it.
5 *(v)* If a computer, document or game is **loading**, it is starting up.

loaf loaves; loafing loafed
1 *(n)* bread baked in a shape.
2 *(n)* food that has been cooked in a loaf-shaped tin. *Meat loaf.*
3 *(v)* If you **loaf around**, you are lazy and do very little.

loafer
1 *(n)* someone who is lazy and does not do much.
2 **Loafer** *(n)* the Trademark name for a flat slip-on leather shoe.

loam *(n)* loose rich soil made of sand, clay, and rotted vegetable and animal material. **loamy** *(adj).*

loan loaning loaned
1 *(v)* to lend something to someone.
2 *(n)* an amount of money that you borrow. *A bank loan.*

loathe loathing loathed *(v)* to hate or dislike someone or something. **loathing** *(n).*

loathsome *(adj)* very unpleasant or disgusting. *A loathsome monster.*

lob lobbing lobbed *(v)* to throw or hit a ball high into the air. **lob** *(n).*

lobby lobbies
1 *(n)* a hall in a large building.
2 *(n)* a group of people who try to persuade politicians to act or vote in a certain way. **lobby** *(v).*

lobster *(n)* a sea creature with a shell, ten legs, and a long body. Lobsters can be eaten, and turn red or orange when they are cooked.

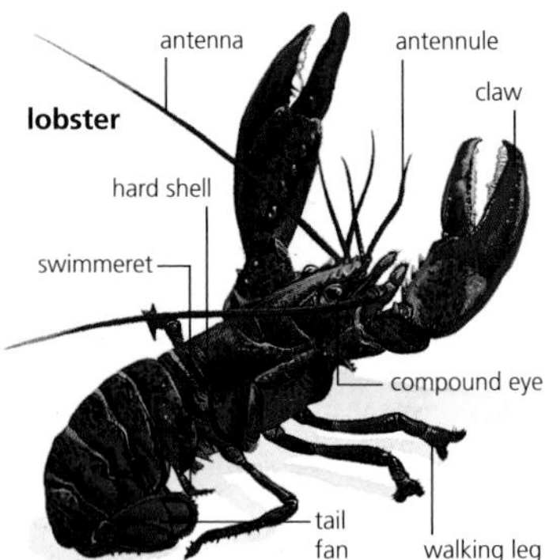

local
1 *(adj)* near your house, or having to do with the area where you live. *A local newspaper.* **locally** *(adv).*
2 *(n)* a train, subway, or bus that makes all the stops on a route.
3 *(adj)* affecting only a part of the body. *Local anesthetic.*

locality localities *(n)* an area, or a neighborhood.

locate locating located
1 *(v)* to find out where something is.
2 If something is **located** in a particular place, you will find it there.

location
1 *(n)* the place or position where someone or something is.
2 If a movie or television program is made **on location**, it is filmed out of the studio.

lock locking locked
1 *(n)* a part of a door, box, etc. that you can open and shut with a key.
2 *(v)* to fasten something with a key.
3 *(n)* a part of a canal with gates at each end where boats are raised or lowered to different water levels.
4 **locks** *(plural n) (poetic)* hair. *Curly locks.*

locker *(n)* a small closet that can be locked, where you can leave your belongings.

locket *(n)* a piece of jewelry that is worn on a chain around the neck and that often contains a photograph.

locksmith *(n)* someone who makes and repairs locks and keys.

locomotive *(n)* an engine used to push or pull railroad cars. *See* **steam locomotive**.

locust *(n)* an insect similar to a grasshopper, which eats and destroys crops. Locusts fly in swarms of up to 2,000 million.

locust

lodge lodging lodged
1 *(n)* a house, cottage, or cabin where you can stay.
2 *(v)* If you **lodge** with someone, you stay in their house and usually pay them money.
3 *(v)* If something **lodges** somewhere, it gets stuck there.
4 *(n)* a beaver's home. *See* **beaver**.

lodger *(n)* somebody who pays to live in a room in someone else's house. **lodgings** *(plural n).*

loft *(n)* a room in the roof of a building.

loft apartment *(n)* a large space in an old factory that has been converted into a living area.

lofty loftier loftiest
1 *(adj)* very high and imposing. *A lofty building.*
2 *(adj)* distant and haughty. **loftily** *(adv).*

log logging logged
1 *(n)* a part of a tree that has been chopped down or has fallen down.
2 *(n)* a record kept by the captain of a ship. **log** *(v).*
3 *(n)* a written record of something. *Liza kept a log of her progress.* **log** *(v).*
4 *(v)* When you **log on** or **log in** to a computer or website, you begin to use it by entering a name or a password.
5 *(v)* When you have finished using a computer or website, you **log off** or **log out**.

logic *(n)* careful and correct reasoning. **logical** *(adj),* **logically** *(adv).*

logo *(loh-go) (n)* a symbol that represents a particular company or organization.

loiter *(loy-ter)* loitering loitered *(v)* to stand around, usually because you have nothing to do.

loll lolling lolled
1 *(v)* to sit or stand in a lazy, sloppy way. *Wayne lolled on the couch.*
2 *(v)* to hang loosely. *The wolf's tongue lolled out of its mouth.*

lollipop *(n)* a piece of hard candy on a stick.

lonely lonelier loneliest
1 *(adj)* If you are **lonely**, you are sad because you are by yourself. **loneliness** *(n).*
2 *(adj)* far from other people or things. *A lonely farmhouse.*

long
longing longed; longer longest
1 *(adj)* more than the average length, distance, time, etc. *A long walk. A long shower.* **long** *(adv).*
2 *(adj)* from one end to the other. *The footpath was two miles long.*
3 *(adj)* taking a lot of time. *Is the movie very long?*
4 *(v)* If you **long for** something, you want it very much. **longing** *(n).*

longitude *(n)* the position of a place, measured in degrees east or west of a line that runs through the Greenwich Observatory in London, England. **longitudinal** *(adj).*

long-range
1 *(adj)* having to do with the future. *Long-range plans.*

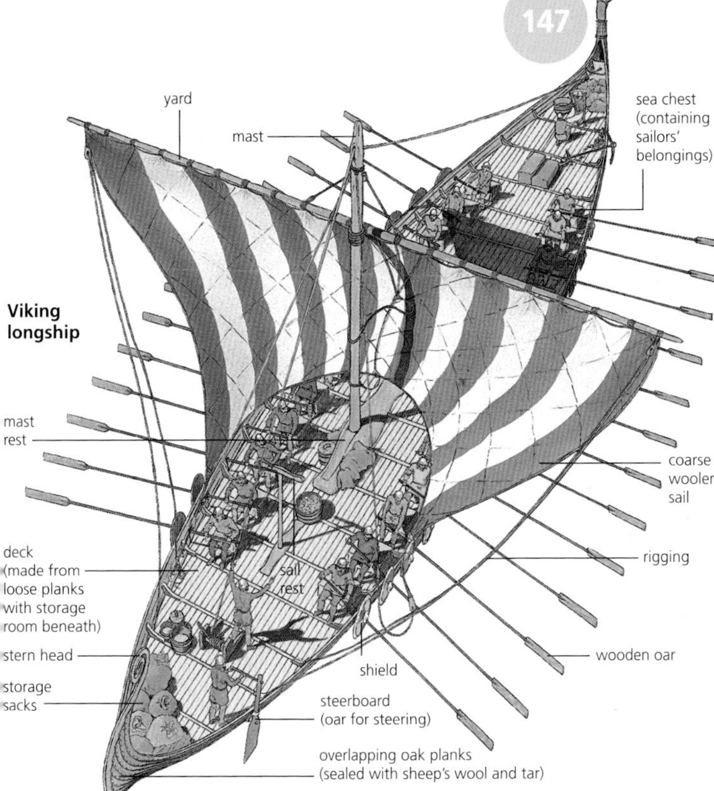

2 *(adj)* designed to travel a long way. *Long-range missiles.*

longship *(n)* a long narrow ship, with many oars and a sail, used especially by the Vikings. *The Vikings used longships such as the one shown above to carry warriors to new lands.*

long-term *(adj)* having to do with a long period of time. *Long-term plans.*

long-winded *(adj)* unnecessarily long and boring.

loofah *(n)* a rough sponge that you wash yourself with when bathing.

look looking looked
1 *(v)* to use your eyes to see things.
2 *(v)* to seem or to appear. *It looks as if the weather will be bad all week.*
3 *(n)* a glance or expression on someone's face. *An angry look.*
4 *(v)* If you **look after** something or someone, you take care of them.
5 *(v)* If you **look down on** someone, you think that you are better than they are.
6 *(v)* If you **look forward** to something, you wait for it eagerly.
7 *(v)* If you **look up** something, you try to find out about it in a book or on the internet.

lookout *(n)* someone who keeps watch for something. *We posted a lookout outside our den.*

loom looming loomed
1 *(v)* to appear in a sudden or frightening way. *Suddenly, a tall figure loomed out of the shadows.*
2 *(n)* a machine used for weaving cloth. *The picture shows a woman working on a traditional Bangladeshi backstrap loom.*

loom

loop *(n)* a curve or circle in a piece of string, rope, etc. **loop** *(v).*

loose *(looss)* looser loosest
1 *(adj)* not fitting tightly. *Loose pants.* **loosely** *(adv).*
2 *(adj)* not firm. *A loose tooth.* **loosely** *(adv).*
3 *(adj)* not contained, or not bound together. *Loose papers.* **loosely** *(adv).*

loosen loosening loosened
1 *(v)* to make something less tight.
2 *(v)* If you **loosen up**, you become less shy and more relaxed.

loot looting looted
1 *(v)* to steal from stores or houses in a riot or war. **looter** *(n).*
2 *(n)* stolen money or valuables.

lopsided *(adj)* unbalanced or with one side heavier than the other.

lord
1 *(n)* a nobleman. **lordly** *(adj).*
2 **Lord** *(n)* In Great Britain, a title used by a man who is a member of the aristocracy or who has earned the title as a reward for service to his country.
3 **Lord** *(n)* a title for God or Jesus.

lose *(looz)* losing lost
1 *(v)* If you **lose** something, you do not have it any more.
2 *(v)* to be beaten or defeated in a game, argument, etc.

loss losses
1 *(n)* the losing of something. *The loss of a friend.*
2 *(n)* something that is lost.

lot
1 *(n)* a large number or amount.
2 *(n)* a group of objects that are sold together at an auction.
3 If you **draw lots**, a group of you pick objects, such as straws, to decide who will do something.

lotion *(n)* a cream that you put on your skin or hair.

lottery lotteries *(n)* a competition in which you buy tickets, aiming to win a prize.

loud louder loudest
1 *(adj)* noisy or producing a lot of sound. **loud** *(adv),* **loudly** *(adv).*
2 *(adj)* very bright and colorful.

loudspeaker *(n)* a machine that turns electrical signals into sounds. *See* **speaker**.

lounge lounging lounged
1 *(v)* to sit around lazily.
2 *(n)* a room in a public building, such as a hotel, for sitting in.

love loving loved
1 *(v)* to like someone or something very much. **love** *(n).*
2 If you are **in love** with someone, you are passionately fond of them.
3 *(n)* in tennis, a score of no points.

lovely lovelier loveliest
1 *(adj)* If someone is **lovely**, they are beautiful to look at, or have a very attractive personality. **loveliness** *(n).*
2 *(adj)* enjoyable. *We had a lovely day.*

low lower lowest
1 *(adj)* not high. *A low table.*
2 *(adj)* A **low** sound is quiet and soft, or deep in pitch.
3 *(adj)* If someone feels **low**, they are depressed or ill.
4 **low tide** *(n)* the time when the sea is farthest down the beach.

lower lowering lowered
1 *(v)* to move something down.
2 *(adj)* not as high as something else.
3 *(adj)* **Lower case** letters are small, and not capital letters.

loyal *(adj)* Someone who is **loyal** supports their friends and does not betray or desert them. **loyalty** *(n),* **loyally** *(adv).*

luau *(loo-ow) (n)* a Hawaiian feast or party, often accompanied by music and other entertainment.

lubricate lubricating lubricated *(v)* to add oil or grease to the parts of a machine, so that it runs more smoothly. **lubricant** *(n),* **lubrication** *(n).*

luck
1 *(n)* something that happens to someone by chance. *This game is just a matter of luck.*
2 *(n)* good fortune, or good things that happen to you that have not been planned. *Wish me luck!*
3 *(v) (informal)* If you **luck out**, you are very lucky or successful.

lucky luckier luckiest
1 *(adj)* Someone who is **lucky** is fortunate and good things seem to happen to them.
2 *(adj)* Something that is **lucky** happens by chance and is fortunate. **luckily** *(adv).*
3 *(adj)* A **lucky** number, charm, etc. is one that you think will bring you luck.

ludicrous *(loo-dih-kruss) (adj)* ridiculous or foolish. **ludicrously** *(adv).*

lug lugging lugged *(v)* to move something heavy.

lukewarm
1 *(adj)* slightly warm.
2 *(adj)* not keen, or not enthusiastic.

lull lulling lulled
1 *(n)* a short pause or break during a period of fighting or activity.
2 *(v)* to make someone feel peaceful, safe, or sleepy. *The sound of the waves on the shore lulled Tara to sleep.*

lullaby lullabies *(n)* a gentle song sung to send a baby to sleep.

lumber lumbering lumbered
1 *(v)* to move around heavily and clumsily. *We could hear Tom lumbering around upstairs all evening.*
2 *(n)* sawn-up wood or timber.

luminous *(adj)* shining, or glowing in the dark. **luminously** *(adv).*

lump
1 *(n)* a mass of solid matter. *A lump of coal.*
2 *(n)* a swelling. *Look at this lump on my head!*

lunar *(adj)* having to do with the Moon. *A lunar eclipse.*

lunatic *(n) (informal)* a foolish and annoying person. **lunacy** *(n),* **lunatic** *(adj).*

lunch lunches *(n)* the meal that you eat in the middle of the day. **lunch** *(v).*

lung *(n)* Your **lungs** are the two organs inside your chest that you use to breathe. *See* **organ**, **respiration**.

lunge lunging lunged *(v)* to move forward quickly and suddenly. **lunge** *(n).*

lurch lurches lurching lurched
1 *(v)* to move in an unsteady, jerky way. *The train lurched to a halt.*
2 If someone **leaves you in the lurch**, they leave you in a difficult situation, without any help.

lure luring lured
1 *(v)* to attract someone or some creature and perhaps lead them into a trap.
2 *(n)* something that attracts you to a particular place. *I can never resist the lure of the sea.*

lurid
1 *(adj)* vivid and glowing. *A lurid yellow.*
2 *(adj)* sensational and shocking. *Lurid newspaper stories.*

lurk lurking lurked *(v)* to wait around secretly. *The robbers lurked behind the house.*

luscious *(lush-uss) (adj)* delicious and attractive. **lusciously** *(adv).*

lush *(adj)* growing thickly and healthily. *Lush vegetation.*

lust lusting lusted *(v)* To desire something or someone strongly. *Simon has always lusted after power.* **lust** *(n),* **lustful** *(adj).*

luxury luxuries
1 *(n)* something expensive which you do not really need, but which is enjoyable to have. **luxury** *(adj).*
2 If you live **in luxury**, you are surrounded by expensive and beautiful things that make your life very comfortable and pleasant. **luxurious** *(adj).*

lyric
1 *(n)* a short poem that expresses strong feelings, especially love. **lyrical** *(adj).*
2 **lyrics** *(plural n)* the words of a song.

Mm

macabre *(mak-ah-bruh) (adj)* gruesome and frightening. *This book is macabre.*

macaroni *(n)* short tubes of pasta. *See* **pasta**.

Mach *(mak) (n)* a unit for measuring an aircraft's speed. Mach 1 is the speed of sound.

machete *(ma-shett-ee) (n)* a heavy knife with a broad blade.

machine
1 *(n)* a piece of equipment made up of moving parts that is used to do a job.
2 **machine gun** *(n)* a gun that can fire bullets very quickly without needing to be reloaded.

machinery *(singular n)* a group of machines or the parts of a machine.

machinist *(n)* a person who operates or repairs machinery.

mackerel
mackerel *or* **mackerels** *(n)* a shiny, blue-gray sea fish that can be eaten.

mad madder maddest
1 *(adj)* insane. **madness** *(n).*
2 *(adj)* very foolish.
3 *(adj)* very angry.
4 *(adj) (informal)* If you are **mad about** someone or something, you like them very much. **madly** *(adv).*

madam *(n)* a formal name for a woman, used in speaking and writing. *Can I help you, madam? Dear Madam.*

magazine
1 *(n)* a thin book, that is published regularly, and contains news, articles, photographs, advertisements, etc.
2 *(n)* the part of a gun that holds the cartridges.

maggot *(n)* the larva of certain flies. Maggots are found in decaying animal matter.

magic
1 *(singular n)* In stories, **magic** is the power to make impossible things happen. **magical** *(adj),* **magically** *(adv).*
2 *(singular n)* clever tricks done to entertain people. **magician** *(n).*

magistrate *(n)* someone who acts as a judge in less serious law cases.

a b c d e f g h i j k l m n o p q r s t u v w x y z

magnet *(n)* a piece of metal that attracts iron or steel. Magnets have two ends, or poles, a north pole and a south pole. *The diagram illustrates a law of magnetism: the like poles of two magnets repel each other, while the unlike poles attract each other.* **magnetism** *(n)*, **magnetic** *(adj)*.

magnets

like poles repel

unlike poles attract

magnificent *(adj)* very impressive or beautiful. **magnificently** *(adv)*.

magnify
magnifies magnifying magnified
1 *(v)* to make something appear larger so that it can be seen more easily. **magnification** *(n)*, **magnified** *(adj)*.
2 *(v)* to make something seem greater or more important than it really is. *Sophie always magnifies her problems.*
3 **magnifying glass** *(n)* a glass lens that makes things look bigger.

magnitude *(n)*
the size or importance of something. *Once she had seen the mess, Cordelia realized the magnitude of her task.*

magpie *(n)*
a black and white bird with a large beak. Magpies often collect shiny objects.

mahogany *(n)*
a hard dark red-brown wood.

maid
1 *(n)* a female servant especially in a hotel.
2 *(n) (poetic)* a young unmarried woman.

maiden
1 *(n) (poetic)* a young unmarried woman.
2 *(n)* A woman's **maiden name** is the surname that she had before she married, if she took her husband's name.
3 *(n)* A **maiden voyage** or flight is the first one made by a particular ship or plane.

mail
1 *(n)* letters and packages sent by post. **mail** *(v)*.
2 *(n)* armor made by joining together small metal rings. *See* **centurion**.
3 *(n)* If you buy something by **mail order**, you order it and pay for it and then the item is mailed to you.

maim **maiming maimed** *(v)*
to injure someone so badly that part of their body is damaged for life.

main
1 *(adj)* largest or most important.
2 **mains** *(plural n)* the large pipes or wires that supply water, gas, or electricity to a building.

mainframe *(n)* a large and very powerful computer to which other, smaller computers are connected.

mainly
1 *(adv)* most importantly. *I mainly like swimming.*
2 *(adv)* almost completely. *The movie was mainly garbage.*
3 *(adv)* usually. *Mainly, I go straight home after school.*

maintain **maintaining maintained**
1 *(v)* to keep a machine or building in good condition. **maintenance** *(n)*.
2 *(v)* to continue to say that something is so. *Malcolm maintains that he is innocent.*
3 *(v)* to continue something and not let it come to an end. *We have always maintained a close friendship.*
4 *(v)* to give money to support somebody. **maintenance** *(n)*.

maize *(n)* Indian corn.

majesty
1 *(n)* dignity and grandeur. **majestic** *(adj)*, **majestically** *(adv)*.
2 *(n)* The formal title for a king or queen is **His Majesty** or **Her Majesty**.

major
1 *(adj)* important or serious. *A major disaster.*
2 *(n)* an army officer.
3 *(n)* In music, a **major scale** has a semitone between the third and fourth and the seventh and eighth notes.

majorette *(n)* a girl who leads a band or twirls a baton in a parade.

majority **majorities**
1 *(n)* more than half of a group of people or things. *The majority of students came by bike.*
2 *(n)* the number of votes by which someone wins an election.
3 *(n)* When someone reaches their **majority**, they become an adult by law.

make **making made**
1 *(v)* to build or produce something. *My mom makes great cakes.*
2 *(v)* to do something. *Wally made two phone calls.*
3 *(v)* to cause something to happen. *The view made Julie feel dizzy.*
4 *(v)* to add up to. *Six and five make eleven.*
5 *(v)* to earn. *He makes good money.*
6 *(n)* the name of the company that makes a particular type of product. *What make is your bicycle?*

makeshift *(adj)* A **makeshift** object is made from whatever is available and is only meant to be used for a short time.

makeup *(n)* the colored powders and creams that people put on their faces. *The picture shows two examples of the dramatic makeup used in Japanese Kabuki theater.*

Kabuki makeup

malaria *(mal-air-ee-a) (n)* a tropical disease that people get from mosquito bites. **malarial** *(adj)*.

male
1 *(n)* a man or boy.
2 *(n)* a person or animal of the sex that fertilizes the female. **male** *(adj)*.

malicious *(mal-ish-uss) (adj)* hurting other people deliberately. **malice** *(n)*, **maliciously** *(adv)*.

malignant
1 *(adj)* nasty and evil. *The villain gave a malignant grin.* **malignantly** *(adv)*.
2 *(adj)* A **malignant** growth or disease is dangerous because it tends to spread very fast.

mall *(rhymes with all)*
1 *(n)* a large, enclosed shopping center.
2 *(n)* a shaded public walk.

malleable *(mal-ee-uh-bul) (adj)* If a substance is **malleable**, it is easily molded into different shapes.

malnutrition *(n)* illness caused by not having enough food or by eating the wrong kind of food.

malt *(n)* dried grain, usually barley, used for making drinks. **malted** *(adj)*.

maltreat **maltreating maltreated** *(v)* to treat a person or an animal cruelly. **maltreatment** *(n)*.

mammal *(n)* an animal that feeds its young on its own milk. *Humans, cows, mice, and dolphins are all examples of mammals.*

mammoth
1 *(n)* an extinct animal that lived in the Ice Age and looked like a large elephant, with long curved tusks.
2 *(adj)* very large. *A mammoth task!*

woolly mammoth

man men; manning manned
1 *(n)* an adult male human being. **manhood** *(n)*, **manly** *(adj)*.
2 *(n)* the human race.
3 *(v)* to be in charge of equipment. *We need some people to man the phones.*

manage managing managed
1 *(v)* to be in charge of a store, business, people, etc. *Terry manages a small electrical company.* **management** *(n)*.
2 *(v)* to be able to do something that is difficult or awkward. *Can you manage to carry all those bags?*

manager *(n)* someone in charge of a store, business, etc. or in charge of a group of people at work. **managerial** *(adj)*.

mane *(n)* the long, thick hair on the head and neck of a lion or horse. *See* **horse**.

maneuver *(man-oo-ver)* maneuvering maneuvered
1 *(n)* a difficult movement that needs skill. *The pilots performed a series of breathtaking maneuvers.*
2 *(v)* to move something carefully into a particular position.
3 When an army is **on maneuvers**, a large number of soldiers, tanks, etc. are moved around an area in order to train them for battle.

manger *(n)* a container from which cattle and horses eat.

mangle mangling mangled *(v)* to crush and twist something. *The car was completely mangled in the crash.* **mangled** *(adj)*.

manhole *(n)* a covered hole in the ground leading to sewers or underground pipes.

maniac *(may-nee-ak) (n)* someone who is mad, or someone who acts in a wild or violent way. **maniacal** *(adj)*.

manicure *(n)* a treatment for your fingernails.

manipulate manipulating manipulated
1 *(v)* to use your hands in a skillful way. *Karen manipulated the plane's controls expertly.*
2 *(v)* to influence people in a clever way so that they do what you want them to do. **manipulation** *(n)*, **manipulative** *(adj)*.

mankind *(n)* the human race.

man-made *(adj)* Something that is **man-made** is made by people and not produced naturally. *Nylon is a man-made fiber.*

manner
1 *(n)* the way in which you do something. *Look at the manner in which Garth uses his paintbrush.*
2 *(n)* the way that someone behaves. *Kate has a very gentle manner.*
3 **manners** *(plural n)* polite behavior.

manor
1 *(n)* a lord's estate in the Middle Ages.
2 *(n)* a mansion.

mansion *(n)* a large grand house.

manslaughter *(n)* the crime of killing someone without planning it in advance.

mantel *(n)* a wooden or stone shelf above a fireplace.

manual
1 *(adj)* worked by hand. *A manual sewing machine.* **manually** *(adv)*.
2 *(n)* an instruction book that tells you how to do something.
3 **manual labor** *(n)* physical work.

manufacture manufacturing manufactured
1 *(v)* to make something with machines in a factory. **manufacture** *(n)*, **manufacturer** *(n)*.
2 *(v)* to invent something or make something up. *Eric manufactured a reason for his strange appearance.*

manure *(n)* animal waste put on land to improve the quality of the soil and to make crops grow better.

manuscript
1 *(n)* the original, handwritten or typed pages of a book, poem, piece of music, etc., before it is printed.
2 *(n)* a handwritten document. *A medieval manuscript.*

part of a page from a medieval manuscript

many more most
1 *(adj)* great in number. **many** *(pronoun)*.
2 **How many?** what number?

Maori *(mauw-ree)* **Maori** *or* **Maoris** *(n)* one of the native peoples of New Zealand who lived there before the Europeans arrived. **Maori** *(adj)*.

map mapping mapped
1 *(n)* a detailed plan of an area, showing features such as towns, roads, rivers, mountains, etc.
2 *(v)* to make a map of a place.
3 *(v)* If you **map out** something, you plan it.

maple *(n)* a tree with large, five-pointed leaves. Maples are grown for their wood and their sap, which is used to make syrup.

marathon
1 *(n)* a running race of approximately 26 miles, which is run along roads.
2 *(n)* something that lasts for a long time. *A movie marathon.*

marble
1 *(n)* a hard stone with colored patterns in it, used for building and making sculptures.
2 *(n)* a small glass ball used in a children's game.
3 **marbles** *(singular n)* a children's game in which small glass balls, called marbles, are rolled along the ground.

march marches marching marched
1 *(v)* When soldiers **march**, they walk together with regular steps.
2 *(n)* a piece of music to which you can march.
3 *(v)* to walk somewhere quickly and in a determined way. *Bravely, Cathy marched up to the principal.*
4 *(n)* a large group of people walking together in order to protest or express their opinion about something. **march** *(v)*.

mare *(n)* an adult female horse.

margarine *(n)* a yellow fat, similar to butter, that is usually made from vegetable oil.

margin
1 *(n)* the long, blank space that runs down the edge of a page.
2 *(n)* a difference between two amounts, especially a small one. *Ally won the election by a very narrow margin.* **marginal** *(adj)*.

marina *(n)* a small harbor where boats, yachts, etc. are kept.

marine
1 *(adj)* having to do with the sea. *Marine life.*
2 *(n)* a soldier trained to serve both at sea and on land.

mark marking marked
1 *(n)* a small scratch or stain on something. **mark** *(v)*.
2 *(v)* to put a mark on something, especially to show who something belongs to or where things are.
3 *(n)* a number or letter put on a piece of work to show how good it is. **mark** *(v)*.
4 *(v)* to keep very close to an opposing player, in games such as soccer, to prevent them from getting the ball.

market
1 *(n)* a group of stands, usually in the open air, where things are sold.
2 If a product is **on the market**, it is available and can be bought.

market research *(n)* When a person or company does **market research**, they collect information about the products that people buy and what people want and need.

marksman marksmen *(n)* someone who is an expert at shooting with a gun.

marmalade *(n)* a jam made from oranges or other citrus fruit and usually eaten on toast for breakfast.

maroon marooning marooned
1 *(v)* If someone is **marooned** somewhere, they are stuck and cannot leave. *The sailors were marooned on a desert island.*
2 *(n)* a dark, red-brown color. maroon *(adj).*

marquee *(mar-kee) (n)* a large sign over a building that displays featured attractions.

marriage *(n)* the relationship between a husband and wife.

married *(adj)* Someone who is **married** has a husband or wife.

marrow *(n)* the soft substance inside your bones. *See* **bone**.

marry marries marrying married
1 *(v)* When people **marry**, they go through a ceremony in which they promise to spend their lives together.
2 *(v)* to perform a marriage ceremony.

marsh marshes *(n)* an area of wet low-lying land. marshy *(adj).*

marshal marshaling marshaled
1 *(n)* an official who helps to organize a public event, such as a concert.
2 *(v)* to gather together a group of people or things and arrange them in a sensible order. *The general marshaled his troops.*
3 *(n)* an officer of a federal court who performs duties similar to those of a sheriff.

marshmallow *(n)* a soft spongy kind of candy.

marsupial *(mar-soo-pee-ul) (n)* a kind of mammal. Female marsupials carry their young in their pouches. *Kangaroos and koalas are marsupials.*

martial *(mar-shall)*
1 *(adj)* to do with war or soldiers.
2 **martial arts** *(plural n)* styles of fighting or self-defense that come from the Far East, for example, judo and karate.
3 **martial law** *(n)* government by the army.

martyr *(mar-ter) (n)* someone who is killed or made to suffer because of their beliefs. martyrdom *(n).*

marvel marveling marveled *(v)* If you **marvel** at something, you are filled with surprise and wonder.

marvelous *(adj)* very good indeed. marvelously *(adv).*

marzipan *(n)* a sweet, almond-flavored paste, used on cakes.

mascara *(n)* a substance put on eyelashes to color them and make them look thicker.

mascot *(n)* something that is supposed to bring good luck, such as an animal or a toy, especially something supposed to give good luck to a sports team.

masculine
1 *(adj)* having to do with men.
2 *(adj)* Someone who is **masculine** has qualities that are supposed to be typical of men. masculinity *(n).*
3 *(adj)* belonging to one of the main classes or genders of nouns in French, Latin, and other languages.

mash mashes mashing mashed *(v)* to crush food after it has been cooked.

mask masking masked
1 *(n)* a covering worn over the face to hide, protect, or disguise it. *This mask, made in Tami Island, New Guinea, would have been worn by a boy at a special ceremony to celebrate his coming of age.* masked *(adj).*
2 *(v)* to cover something up or disguise it. *The aniseed masked the taste of the poison.*

mask

mason *(n)* someone who cuts and carves stone for buildings, gravestones, etc.

masonry *(n)* stone used in a building.

mass masses
1 *(n)* a large number of people or things together.
2 *(n)* In physics, the **mass** of an object is the amount of physical matter that it contains. *Mass is measured in grams or ounces.*
3 **the masses** *(plural n)* the ordinary people. *This show is designed to appeal to the masses.*
4 *(adj)* **Mass-produced** things are made in very large quantities, usually by machine.

massacre *(mass-eh-ker) (n)* the killing of a very large number of people, often in battle. massacre *(v).*

massage *(mass-ahj)* massaging massaged *(v)* to rub someone's body with your fingers to loosen their muscles, or to help them relax. massage *(n).*

massive *(adj)* huge and bulky. massively *(adv).*

mass media *(plural n)* a general word for different forms of communication that reach a large number of people. Television, radio, and newspapers are all mass media.

mast *(n)* a tall pole that stands on the deck of a boat and supports its sails. *See* **dinghy**, **ship**.

master mastering mastered
1 *(v)* If you **master** a subject or skill, you become very good at it.
2 *(n)* a name for a male teacher, especially in a private school.

mastermind masterminding masterminded *(v)* If you **mastermind** a course of action, you plan it and control the way that it is carried out.

masterpiece *(n)* a brilliant piece of art, literature, music, etc.

mat *(n)* a thick pad of material, used for covering a floor, wiping your feet, protecting a table, etc.

matador *(n)* a bullfighter.

match matches matching matched
1 *(n)* a sports game in which one person or team plays another.
2 *(v)* If two things **match**, they go well together or look the same. matching *(adj).*
3 *(n)* a small, thin stick of wood with a chemical tip which is struck to produce a flame.
4 *(v)* to put two people or teams in opposition to each other. *The brothers are matched in the first round.*

mate mating mated
1 *(v)* When male and female animals **mate**, they reproduce. mating *(n).*
2 *(n)* the male or female partner of a couple or pair.

material
1 *(n)* the substances from which something is made. *What materials do you need to build a house?*
2 *(n)* cloth or fabric.
3 *(adj)* made from or having to do with matter. *The material world.*
4 *(adj)* having to do with the well-being of the body. *Good food and warm clothes are material needs.*

a b c d e f g h i j k l m n o p q r s t u v w x y z

materialistic *(adj)* People who are **materialistic** are concerned only with money and possessions. **materialism** *(n).*

maternal *(adj)* having to do with being a mother. *Maternal instinct.*

maternity
1 *(n)* motherhood.
2 **maternity leave** *(n)* time that a woman is allowed away from her job to have a baby.
3 **maternity ward** *(n)* an area in a hospital for women who have just had or are about to have a baby.

math *short for* **mathematics**.

mathematics *(singular n)* the study of numbers, quantities, and shapes. **mathematical** *(adj).*

matinee *(mat-i-nay) (n)* an afternoon performance of a play or showing of a movie.

matrimony *(n)* a general name for marriage. **matrimonial** *(adj).*

matrix *(may-trix)* **matrices** *(n)* In math, a **matrix** is a rectangular chart with figures set out in columns and rows.

matte *(adj)* not shiny. *A matte finish.*

matter **mattering mattered**
1 *(n)* things or materials. *Undigested matter. Printed matter.*
2 *(n)* something that needs to be dealt with. *Let's sort this matter out now.*
3 *(v)* If something **matters**, it is important.

mattress **mattresses** *(n)* a soft thick pad, usually containing springs, that you put on the base of a bed to sleep on.

mature **maturer maturest**
1 *(adj)* adult or fully grown. **maturity** *(n),* **mature** *(v).*
2 *(adj)* behaving in a sensible, adult way. *Ed is very mature for his age.* **maturity** *(n),* **maturely** *(adv).*
3 *(adj)* ripe. *Mature fruit.* **mature** *(v).*

maul **mauling mauled** *(v)* to handle someone or something in a rough and possibly damaging way.

mausoleum *(maw-zuh-lee-um) (n)* a large, often decorated, tomb.

mauve *(rhymes with stove) (n)* a light purple color. **mauve** *(adj).*

maximum *(n)* the greatest possible amount, or the upper limit. *Two hours is the maximum allowed for the test.* **maximum** *(adj).*

maybe *(adv)* perhaps.

mayhem *(n)* a situation of confusion or violent destruction.

mayonnaise *(n)* a creamy sauce made from egg yolks, oil, and vinegar.

mayor *(n)* the leader of a town or city government.

maze *(n)* a complicated network of paths or lines, made to be a puzzle to find your way through. *The picture shows the maze at Colonial Williamsburg, Virginia, which is based on a 17th-century maze at Hampton Court, England.*

maze (aerial view)

MB *short for* **megabyte**.

meadow *(n)* a piece of of grassland.

meal *(n)* food which is served and eaten, usually at a particular time of day. Breakfast and lunch are meals.

mean
meaning meant; meaner meanest
1 *(v)* to intend to do something. *I mean to go skating tomorrow.*
2 *(v)* to try to convey a message. *What does this poem mean?*
3 *(adj)* not generous. **meanness** *(n),* **meanly** *(adv).*
4 *(adj)* unkind or unfair. *A mean trick.* **meanness** *(n),* **meanly** *(adv).*
5 *(n)* an average. *The mean of 3, 5, and 10 is 6.*

meaning
1 *(n)* the idea behind something spoken or written.
2 *(n)* the importance or significance of something. *What is the meaning of life?*

meantime *(n)* the time in between. *We leave early tomorrow morning. In the meantime, let's get some sleep!*

meanwhile *(adv)* at the same time. *George went to explore. Meanwhile, Kate ate all the picnic.*

measles *(n)* an infectious disease causing a fever and a rash.

measure **measuring measured**
1 *(v)* to find out the size, capacity, weight, etc. of something. *Helen measured the fabric.* **measurement** *(n).*
2 *(n)* an action intended to achieve a result. *What measures can we take to fight crime?*

meat *(n)* the edible flesh of an animal. **meaty** *(adj).*

mechanic *(n)* someone who is skilled at operating or mending machinery.

mechanical *(adj)* operated by machinery. *A mechanical toy.* **mechanically** *(adv).*

mechanics *(singular n)* a part of physics that deals with the way that forces affect still or moving objects.

mechanism *(n)* the system of moving parts inside a machine.

medal *(n)* a piece of metal, shaped like a coin, star, or cross, which is given to someone for being brave, or for service to their country, or as a prize for an achievement in sports.

media *(plural n)* a general name for different forms of communication with people, such as television, radio, and newspapers.

medical
1 *(adj)* having to do with health treatment. **medically** *(adv).*
2 *(n) (informal)* an examination by a doctor. **Medical** is short for medical examination.

medicine
1 *(n)* a substance, usually liquid, used in treating illness. **medicinal** *(adj).*
2 *(singular n)* the treatment of illness. *You must study medicine to become a doctor.*

medieval *(adj)* having to do with the Middle Ages, the period of history between approximately A.D. 500 and A.D. 1450.

mediocre *(mee-dee-oh-ker) (adj)* of average or less than average quality. **mediocrity** *(n).*

meditate **meditating meditated**
1 *(v)* to think very deeply about something. *Fred meditated on the meaning of life.* **meditation** *(n).*
2 *(v)* to relax the mind and body by a regular program of mental exercise. **meditation** *(n).*

medium **media** *or* **mediums**
1 *(adj)* average or middle. *Kevin is of medium height.*
2 *(n)* the method by which something is communicated. *I will tell you my story through the medium of song.*
3 *(n)* **Mediums** claim to make contact with the spirits of the dead.

meek **meeker meekest** *(adj)* quiet, humble, and obedient. **meekly** *(adv).*

meet meeting met
1 *(v)* to come face-to-face with someone or something.
2 *(v)* to come together. *The paths met.*

meeting *(n)* an arranged event in which people come together, often to discuss something.

megabyte *(n)* a unit used to measure the capacity of a computer's memory.

melancholy *(adj)* very sad. **melancholy** *(n),* **melancholic** *(adj).*

mellow mellowing mellowed; mellower mellowest
1 *(adj)* soft, warm, and gentle. *Mellow colors.*
2 *(v)* If someone **mellows**, they become gentler and more relaxed.

melodramatic *(adj)*
If someone is **melodramatic**, they talk and behave in an exaggerated way and make a fuss about small things.

melody melodies *(n)*
a tune. **melodic** *(adj).*

melon *(n)*
a large rounded juicy fruit. *See* **fruit**.

melt melting melted *(v)*
When a substance **melts**, it changes from a solid to a liquid because it has become hotter.

member
1 *(n)* someone who belongs to a club, group, family, etc. **membership** *(n).*
2 *(n)* a part of a human or animal body, especially an arm or a leg.

membrane *(n)*
a very thin layer of tissue or skin, that lines or covers certain organs or cells. *See* **cell**, **egg**.

memo *(n)* a brief message sent by one person to another person in the same organization. **Memo** is short for memorandum.

memorable *(adj)* easily remembered or worth remembering.

memorize memorizing memorized *(v)* to learn something by heart.

memory memories
1 *(n)* the power to remember things.
2 *(n)* something that you remember from the past. *Happy memories.*
3 *(n)* the part of a computer in which information is stored.

menace
1 *(n)* a threat or a danger. **menacing** *(adj).*
2 *(n) (informal)* a nuisance.

mend mending mended *(v)*
to repair something that is broken.

meningitis *(men-in-**jeye**-tiss) (n)*
a serious disease that causes the membranes surrounding the brain to become very swollen.

mental *(adj)* having to do with the mind. *Mental powers.* **mentally** *(adv).*

mention mentioning mentioned *(v)* to speak briefly about something. **mention** *(n).*

menu
1 *(n)* a list of dishes served in a restaurant.
2 *(n)* a list of choices shown on a computer screen.

mercenary mercenaries
1 *(n)* a soldier who is paid to fight for a foreign army.
2 *(adj)* If someone is **mercenary**, they are mainly interested in making money.

merchandise *(singular n)* a general name for goods that are bought or sold, usually in large quantities.

merchant
1 *(n)* someone who sells goods for profit, especially someone who trades with foreign countries.
2 *(n)* A country's **merchant navy** is made up of the ships and crew that carry cargo for that country.

mercury *(n)*
a poisonous, silvery liquid metal.

mercy mercies *(n)* If you show **mercy** to someone, you are kind to them and do not punish them. **merciful** *(adj),* **mercifully** *(adv).*

merely *(adv)* only or simply. *Don't blame me, I'm merely the messenger.* **mere** *(adj).*

merge
merging merged *(v)*
When two things **merge**, they join together to form a whole.

merger *(n)* the act of making two businesses, teams, etc. into one.

merit
1 *(n)* If something has **merit,** it is good. **merit** *(v).*
2 *(n)* the good points or qualities of a person or thing.

mermaid *(n)* a mythical sea creature with the upper body of a woman and the tail of a fish.

merry merrier merriest *(adj)*
cheerful or joyful.

mesh meshes *(n)*
a network of wire, rope, etc.

mess messes messing messed
1 *(n)* a dirty or untidy state or thing. *My room is a mess!* **messy** *(adj),* **messily** *(adv).*
2 *(n)* a confused and disorganized state or thing. *My life is a mess!*
3 **mess around** *(v)* If you **mess around**, you spend time doing something unimportant.
4 **mess up** *(v)* If you **mess something up**, you make it dirty or untidy, or you make it go wrong.

message
1 *(n)* information sent to someone else. *A secret message.*
2 *(n)* the meaning of something, such as a book or movie.

messenger *(n)*
someone who carries a message.

metal *(n)* a chemical substance, such as iron, copper, or silver, which is usually hard and shiny, is a good conductor of heat and electricity, and can be melted and formed into shapes. **metallic** *(adj).*

metaphor *(n)* a way of describing something as though it were something else, for example, "The princess is a shining jewel, and her father is a raging bull."

meteorite *(n)* a remaining part of a meteoroid, which falls to Earth.

meteoroid *(n)* a small piece of rock from space that enters the Earth's atmosphere and burns up, giving a "shooting star" effect.

meteorology *(n)*
the study of the Earth's atmosphere and, in particular, its climate and weather. **meteorologist** *(n),* **meteorological** *(adj).*

meter
1 *(n)* a basic unit of length in the metric system. A meter is equivalent to 39.37 inches, or about 3 feet.
2 *(n)* an instrument for measuring the quantity of something, especially the amount of something that has been used. *An electricity meter.* **meter** *(v).*
3 *(n)* the pattern of rhythm in a line of poetry formed by stressing some syllables and not stressing others.

method *(n)*
a way of doing something.

methodical *(adj)*
careful, logical, and well-organized. **methodically** *(adv).*

meticulous *(adj)* very careful and precise. **meticulously** *(adv).*

metric *(adj)* The **metric** system of measurement is based on units of ten. Meters, liters, and kilograms are all metric measurements. *See* page 284.

metronome *(n)* a device that produces a regular beat which helps musicians to keep time as they play.

microbe *(n)* a germ or other living thing that is too small to be seen without a microscope.

microchip *(n)* a minute piece of silicon with electronic circuits printed on it, used in computers and other electronic equipment. *See* **chip**.

microcomputer *(n)* a very small computer, usually without an internal memory.

microorganism *(n)* a living thing that is too small to be seen without a microscope. *Bacteria and viruses are microorganisms. The illustration below shows groups of microorganisms known as plankton. These tiny plants and animals are found in water.*

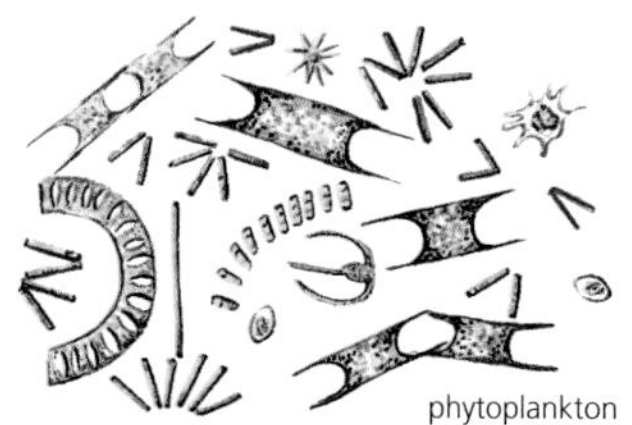

microorganisms

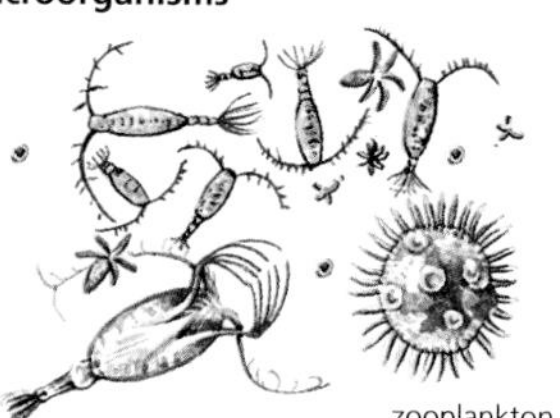

microphone *(n)* an instrument that changes sound into an electric current, to make the sound louder, record it, or transmit it to radio or television stations.

microprocessor *(n)* the central processing unit of a microcomputer.

microscope *(n)* an instrument with powerful lenses that magnifies very small things so that they look large enough to be seen and studied. *The illustration on the right shows a microscope with a revolving triple nosepiece. Each part of the nosepiece provides a different level of magnification. The eyepiece can be adjusted to focus the image seen through the nosepiece.*

microscopic *(adj)* too small to be seen without a microscope.

microwave
1 *(n)* a high frequency electromagnetic wave.
2 **microwave oven** *(n)* an oven that cooks food very quickly by beaming microwaves into it. The microwaves make the moisture in the food vibrate and become hot and this heat is passed through the food so that it cooks.

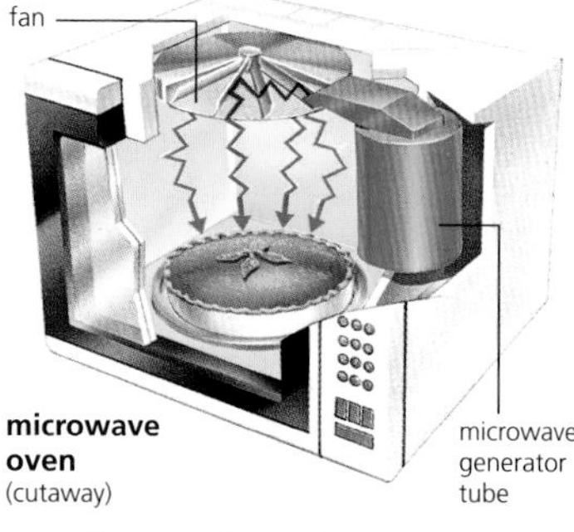

microwave oven (cutaway)

The diagram above shows a cutaway of a microwave oven, with microwave beams heating a dish in the center.

midday *(n)* noon, or 12 o'clock in the middle of the day. **midday** *(adj)*.

middle
1 *(adj)* central, or halfway between two extremes. **middle** *(n)*.
2 If you are **in the middle** of doing something, you are involved in doing it. *I'm in the middle of watching this program.*

middle-aged *(adj)* Someone who is **middle-aged** is between 40 and 60 years old.

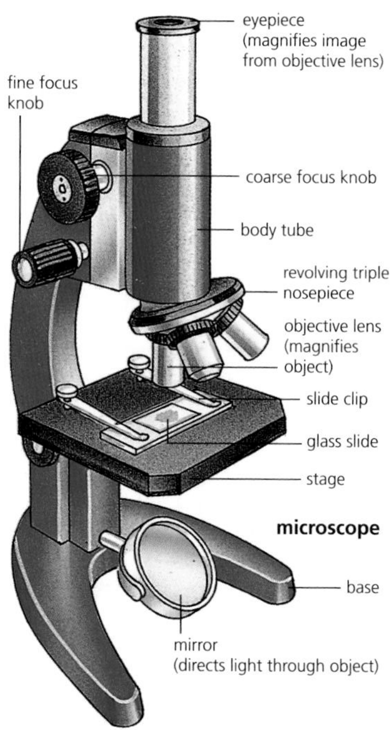

microscope

Middle Ages *(plural n)* the period of European history covering the 5th to the 15th centuries.

Middle East *(n)* the countries of Western Asia between the eastern end of the Mediterranean Sea and India. Israel, Iraq, and Iran are all in the Middle East. **Middle Eastern** *(adj)*.

midnight *(n)* 12 o'clock in the middle of the night. **midnight** *(adj)*.

midway *(adv)* halfway. *The car broke down midway between Sydney and Canberra.*

midwife **midwives** *(n)* a nurse trained to help when a baby is being born. **midwifery** *(n)*.

might *(n)* strength or force. **mighty** *(adj)*, **mightily** *(adv)*.

migraine *(n)* a very bad headache that makes you feel sick.

migrate **migrating** **migrated** *(v)* When birds **migrate**, they fly at a particular time of year to live in another region. **migration** *(n)*, **migratory** *(adj)*.

mild **milder** **mildest**
1 *(adj)* Someone who is **mild** is gentle and not aggressive. **mildness** *(n)*, **mildly** *(adv)*.
2 *(adj)* moderate and not too harsh. *Mild weather.* **mildness** *(n)*, **mildly** *(adv)*.

mildew *(n)* a thin coating of powdery fungus that can grow on damp cloth, paper, etc. **mildewed** *(adj)*.

mileage
1 *(n)* the total distance traveled or measured in miles.
2 *(n)* the average number of miles a vehicle travels on a gallon of fuel.

militant *(adj)* Someone who is **militant** is prepared to fight or to be very aggressive in support of a cause in which they believe. **militancy** *(n)*, **militantly** *(adv)*.

military *(adj)* having to do with soldiers and the armed forces.

militia *(mil-ish-uh)* *(n)* a group of soldiers recruited in an emergency.

milk **milking** **milked**
1 *(n)* the white liquid produced by female mammals to feed their young. People drink milk from cows and goats. **milky** *(adj)*.
2 *(v)* to take milk from a cow or other animal.

mill
1 *(n)* a building containing machinery for grinding grain into flour. **mill** *(v)*. *See* **windmill**.

2 *(n)* a large factory with machinery for processing textiles, wood, paper, etc. *A cotton mill.*
3 *(n)* a small machine used for grinding something into powder. *A pepper mill.* **mill** *(v).*

millennium millenniums *or* **millennia** *(n)* a period of a thousand years. **millennial** *(adj).*

millet *(n)* a cereal crop with tiny seeds, grown especially in India.

million
1 *(n)* a thousand thousands (1,000,000).
2 *(n) (informal)* a great many.

millionaire *(n)* someone whose money and property is worth at least a million dollars.

milometer *(n)* an instrument used for counting how many miles a vehicle has traveled.

mime *(n)* a form of acting in which actions are used instead of words. **mime** *(v).*

mimic mimicking mimicked *(v)* to imitate someone else's speech or actions. **mimic** *(n).*

mosque

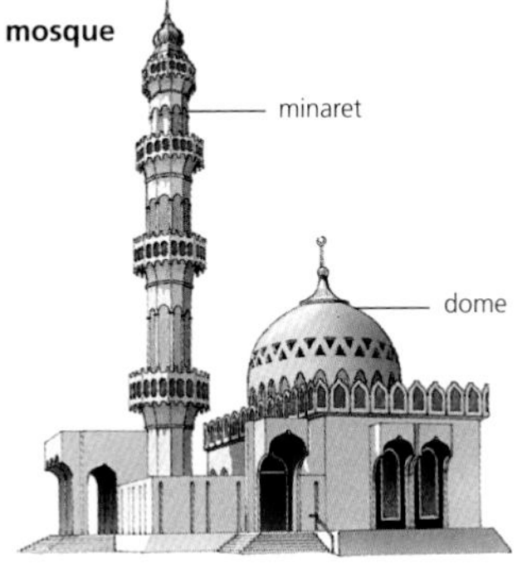

minaret *(n)* the tall, thin tower of a mosque, from which Muslims are called to prayer.

mince mincing minced *(v)* to cut or chop meat or similar substances into very small pieces.

mincemeat *(n)* a sweet mixture of dried fruit, spices, etc., used in pies and tarts.

mind minding minded
1 *(n)* the part of you that thinks, remembers, dreams, etc.
2 *(v)* to care or to be bothered about something. *Do you mind what she says about you?*
3 *(v)* to look after something or somebody. **minder** *(n).*
4 *(v)* to watch out for something. *Mind the step!*

mine mining mined
1 *(adj)* belonging to me.
2 *(v)* to dig up minerals from below the ground. **mine** *(n),* **miner** *(n).*
3 *(n)* a bomb placed in the ground or in the sea.

mineral
1 *(n)* a substance found in the ground, which can be obtained by mining. Iron, salt, and diamonds are all minerals. **mineral** *(adj).*
2 **mineral water** *(n)* water that has mineral salts and gases dissolved in it. Mineral water can be still or sparkling.

minerals

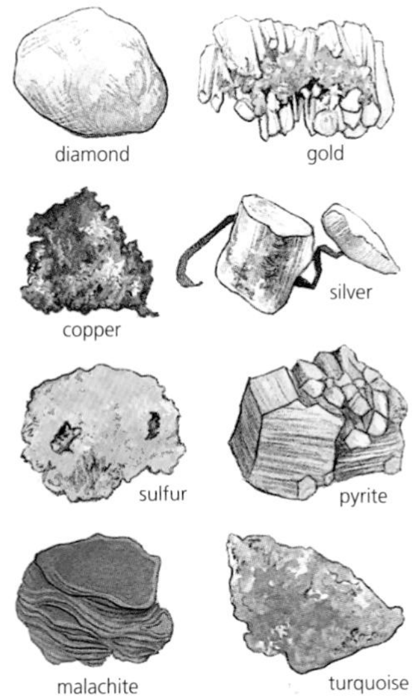

mingle mingling mingled *(v)* to mix together. *The guests mingled happily.*

miniature *(min-it-cher) (adj)* a small version of something bigger. *A miniature radio.* **miniaturize** *(v).*

minimize minimizing minimized
1 *(v)* to make something as small as possible. *Charlotte minimized the risk of getting lost by taking a map.*
2 *(v)* to make something seem as unimportant or insignificant as possible. *When we told Mom what had happened, we minimized the danger.*

minimum *(n)* the smallest possible amount or the lowest limit. *We need a minimum of six people to play this game.* **minimum** *(adj).*

miniskirt *(n)* a very short skirt.

minister
1 *(n)* a clergyman. **ministry** *(n).*
2 *(n)* someone sent by the government to represent it overseas. **ministerial** *(adj).*
3 *(v)* to help or serve someone.

mink *(n)* a small animal with dark brown fur, often raised for its pelt.

minnow *(n)* a tiny freshwater fish.

minor
1 *(adj)* less important or less serious. *We will deal with minor matters after the main issues have been discussed.*
2 *(n)* someone under adult age.
3 *(n)* In music, a **minor scale** has a semitone between the second and third notes.

minority minorities
1 *(n)* a small number or part within a bigger group. *Only a minority were against the proposal.*
2 *(n)* a group of people of a particular race or religion living among a larger group of a different race or religion.

minstrel *(n)* a medieval musician and poet.

mint
1 *(n)* a strongly scented plant with leaves that are used for flavoring. *See* **herb**.
2 *(n)* a peppermint-flavored candy.
3 *(n)* a place where coins are manufactured. **mint** *(v).*
4 *(n) (informal)* a very large amount of money. *His car must have cost a mint.*

minus
1 *(prep)* In math, a **minus** sign (–) is used in a subtraction sum. *6 minus 4 equals 2, or 6 – 4 = 2.*
2 *(prep) (informal)* without. *I went to school minus my sandwiches.*

minute minutest
1 *(min-it) (n)* a unit of time equal to 60 seconds.
2 *(my-newt) (adj)* very small indeed. **minutely** *(adv).*
3 **minutes** *(min-its) (plural n)* the written record of what was said at a meeting.

minuteman *(n)* a volunteer soldier in the American Revolutionary War who was ready to fight at a minute's notice.

miracle *(mir-ak-ul) (n)* a remarkable and unexpected event. **miraculous** *(adj),* **miraculously** *(adv).*

mirage *(mir-ahj) (n)* something that you think you see in the distance, such as water, which is not really there. Mirages are caused by light refracting off hot surfaces.

mirror *(n)* a very shiny surface that reflects the image of whatever is in front of it. **mirror** *(v)*.

misbehave misbehaving misbehaved *(v)* to behave badly.

miscalculate miscalculating miscalculated *(v)* to figure something out incorrectly or to judge a situation wrongly. **miscalculation** *(n)*.

miscarriage
1 *(n)* When a pregnant woman has a **miscarriage**, the baby dies in her womb, usually early in the pregnancy. **miscarry** *(v)*.
2 **miscarriage of justice** *(n)* a failure of the legal system to come to the right decision or verdict.

miscellaneous *(miss-el-ay-nee-uss) (adj)* assorted or of different types. *The drawer was full of miscellaneous socks, but I couldn't find a pair.* **miscellany** *(n)*.

mischief *(n)* playful, mildly naughty behavior that may cause annoyance to others. **mischievous** *(adj)*, **mischievously** *(adv)*.

misconduct *(n)* dishonest, irresponsible or immoral action by someone in a position of responsibility.

miser *(my-zer) (n)* a very stingy person who spends as little as possible in order to hoard money. **miserly** *(adj)*.

miserable *(adj)* sad, unhappy, or dejected. **misery** *(n)*, **miserably** *(adv)*.

misfit *(n)* someone or something not suited to the people or situation around them.

misfortune
1 *(n)* an unlucky event.
2 *(n)* bad luck.

misguided *(adj)* If you are **misguided**, you have the wrong idea about something. **misguidedly** *(adv)*.

mishap *(n)* an unfortunate accident.

mislay mislaying mislaid *(v)* to lose something for a short while because you have put it in a place where you cannot find it.

mislead misleading misled *(v)* to give someone the wrong idea about something. **misleading** *(adj)*, **misleadingly** *(adv)*.

misprint *(n)* a mistake in a book, newspaper, etc. where the letters have been printed wrongly.

miss misses missing missed
1 *(v)* to fail to hit something.
2 *(v)* to fail to catch, see, do, etc. *Charles missed the train by seconds.*
3 *(v)* to be unhappy because someone or something is not with you. *I missed my brother when he went away.*
4 **Miss** *(n)* a title given to a girl or an unmarried woman.

missile *(n)* a weapon that is thrown or shot at a target. *An atomic missile.*

misspell misspelling misspelled *(v)* to spell something wrongly.

mist *(n)* a cloud of water droplets in the air. **misty** *(adj)*.

mistake
mistaking mistook mistaken
1 *(n)* an error, or a misunderstanding.
2 *(v)* to believe that someone is somebody different. *I always mistake Tracy for her sister.*

mistletoe *(n)* an evergreen plant that grows as a parasite on trees. Mistletoe has white, yellow, or red berries and is often used as a Christmas decoration.

mistletoe

mistreat mistreating mistreated *(v)* to treat something or someone roughly or badly. **mistreatment** *(n)*.

mistress mistresses *(n)* a woman with power, responsibility, or control over something. *My mother is the mistress of this house.*

mistrust mistrusting mistrusted *(v)* to be suspicious of someone. **mistrust** *(n)*.

misunderstanding
1 *(n)* a failure to understand. **misunderstand** *(v)*.
2 *(n)* a disagreement between two people.

misuse *(miss-yooze)* misusing misused *(v)* to use something in the wrong way. **misuse** *(miss-yuce) (n)*.

mix mixes mixing mixed *(v)* to combine or blend different things. *Mix all the ingredients together.*

mixture *(n)* something made from things mixed together. *This suit is a mixture of wool and polyester.*

moan moaning moaned
1 *(v)* to complain in a dreary way. *Joan is always moaning about the weather.*
2 *(v)* to make a low, sad sound, usually because you are in pain or are unhappy. **moan** *(n)*.

mob *(n)* a large and dangerous crowd of people.

mobile
1 *(adj)* able to move or be moved. *A mobile crane.* **mobility** *(n)*.
2 *(n)* a decoration made of several things balanced at different heights and hung from a central thread.

mock mocking mocked
1 *(v)* to make fun of someone in an unpleasant way. **mockery** *(n)*.
2 *(adj)* false or imitation. *A mock battle.*

model
1 *(n)* a small version of a real-life object, made to scale. *A model railroad.*
2 *(adj)* perfect or ideal. *A model child.*
3 *(n)* someone who poses for an artist or a photographer. **model** *(v)*.
4 *(n)* a particular type of design or product. *This car is the very latest model.*

modem *(n)* a piece of electronic equipment used to send information between computers by telephone.

moderate
1 *(adj)* not extreme. *Moderate speed.* **moderation** *(n)*, **moderately** *(adv)*.
2 *(adj)* of average or below average quality. *My test scores were only moderate.*

modern *(adj)* up-to-date or new in style. *Modern architecture.*

modernize
modernizing modernized *(v)* to make something more modern or up-to-date. **modernization** *(n)*.

modest *(adj)* People who are **modest** are not boastful about their abilities or achievements. **modesty** *(n)*, **modestly** *(adv)*.

modify modifies modifying modified *(v)* to alter something slightly. **modification** *(n)*.

module *(n)* a separate, independent section that can be linked to other parts to make something larger.

Mohammed *see* **Muhammad**

moist *(adj)* damp and slightly wet. **moisture** *(n)*, **moisten** *(v)*.

mole
1 *(n)* a small, furry mammal that digs tunnels and lives underground.
2 *(n)* a small growth on the skin.

European mole

Some words that begin with a "mi" sound are spelled "my."

molecule *(n)* the smallest part of a substance that can exist on its own. Molecules are usually made of two or more atoms bonded together. *The diagrams show how molecules are tightly packed in solids, loosely linked in liquids, and widely spaced in gases. This means that solids usually keep their shape, liquids can flow, and gases can spread out easily.* **molecular** *(adj).*

molecules

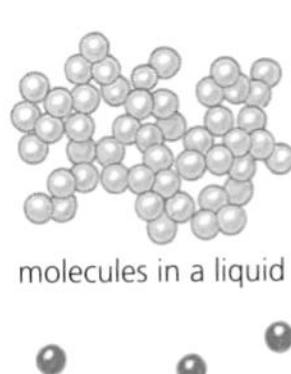
molecules in a solid

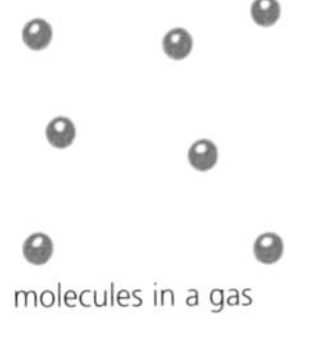
molecules in a liquid

molecules in a gas

molehill *(n)* a small mound of dirt pushed out of the ground by a mole.

molest molesting molested *(v)* to disturb, annoy, or interfere with someone.

mollusk *(n)* a creature with a soft body and no spine, usually protected by a shell. *Snails, clams, and oysters are all mollusks.*

molten *(adj)*
Molten metal is so hot that it has melted to become a liquid.

mom, mommy *(n)*
an informal name for your mother.

moment
1 *(n)* a very brief period of time. *I saw the rocket for only a moment.* **momentary** *(adj),* **momentarily** *(adv).*
2 If something is happening **at the moment**, it is happening now.

monarch *(n)*
a ruler, such as a king or queen, who has usually inherited his or her position. **monarchy** *(n).*

monastery monasteries *(n)*
a group of buildings where monks live and work. **monastic** *(adj).*

money monies or moneys *(n)*
the coins and notes that people use to buy things. **monetary** *(adj).*

mongrel *(n)*
a dog of mixed breed.

monitor
monitoring monitored
1 *(v)* to keep a check on something over a period of time.
2 *(n)* the visual display unit of a computer or television.

monk *(n)* a man who lives in a religious community and has promised to devote his life to God.

monkey *(n)* an animal like a small ape, usually with a tail.

mono
see **infectious mononucleosis**.

monocle *(n)* a glass lens worn to improve the eyesight of one eye.

monogram *(n)* a design made from two or more letters, usually someone's initials. **monogrammed** *(adj).*

monologue *(mon-ah-log) (n)*
a long speech by one person.

monopolize
monopolizing monopolized *(v)*
to keep something all to yourself.
Chris monopolized the conversation.

monopoly monopolies *(n)*
the complete control of something, especially a service or the supply of a product.

monorail *(n)* a railroad that runs on one rail, usually high off the ground.

monotonous *(adj)*
If something is **monotonous**, it goes on and on in a dull and boring way. **monotony** *(n),* **monotonously** *(adv).*

monsoon *(n)* a season of torrential rain and strong winds in India and other Asian countries.

monster
1 *(n)* In stories, a **monster** is a large, fierce, or horrible creature.
2 *(n)* a very wicked person.
3 *(adj) (informal)* huge. *Monster trucks.*

monstrous
1 *(adj)* extremely large, terrible, or strange. *A monstrous creature.* **monstrosity** *(n),* **monstrously** *(adv).*
2 *(adj)* wrong and wicked. *Monstrous behavior.* **monstrously** *(adv).*

month *(n)* one of the twelve parts that make up a year. **monthly** *(adj),* **monthly** *(adv).*

monument
1 *(n)* an old, important statue, building, etc. *An ancient monument.*
2 *(n)* a statue, building, etc. that is meant to remind people of an event or a person. *A war monument.*

monumental *(adj)*
very large or very important. **monumentally** *(adv).*

mood
1 *(n)* Your **mood** is the way that you are feeling.
2 If you are **in a mood**, you feel sulky or bad tempered.

moody moodier moodiest
1 *(adj)* cross, or unhappy. **moodily** *(adv).*
2 *(adj)* A **moody** person has frequent changes of mood or feelings. **moodiness** *(n).*

moon
1 *(n)* a satellite of a planet. *Mars has two moons.*
2 **Moon** *(n)* the satellite that moves around the Earth once each month and reflects light from the Sun. *The first diagram below shows how the Moon moves around the Earth, while the second identifies the different phases of the Moon as they are seen from the Earth during the course of a month.*

The Moon's motion

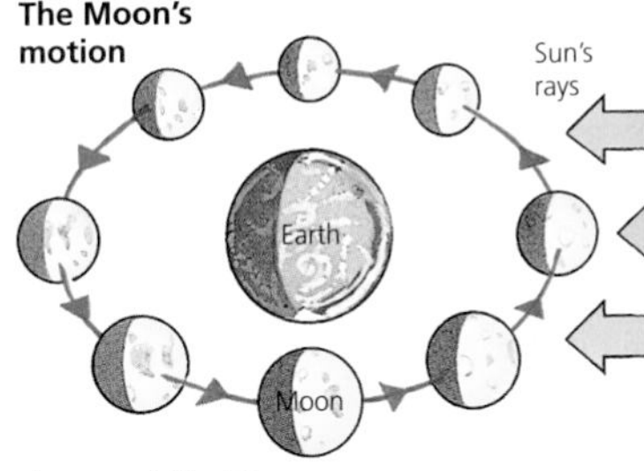

phases of the Moon

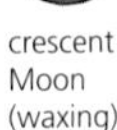

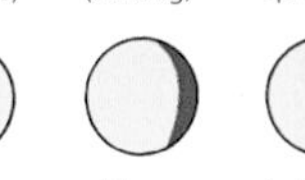

new Moon (invisible) | crescent Moon (waxing) | half-Moon (first quarter) | gibbous Moon (waxing)

full Moon | gibbous Moon (waning) | half-Moon (last quarter) | crescent Moon (old Moon)

moonlight
moonlighting moonlighted
1 *(n)* the light of the Earth's Moon that you can see at night. **moonlit** *(adj).*
2 *(v) (informal)* to work at a second job, usually at night, and often secretly.

moor mooring moored
1 *(n)* an open grassy area, often covered with heather.
2 *(v)* If you **moor** a boat, you tie it up or anchor it. **moorings** *(n).*

mop mopping mopped
1 *(n)* a long stick with a sponge or a bundle of cloth or string at one end, used to clean floors.
2 *(v)* to clean a floor, or soak up liquid with a mop, cloth, or sponge.

mope moping moped *(v)*
to be miserable and depressed.

moral
1 *(adj)* having to do with right and wrong. *Carl faced the moral dilemma of saying nothing or telling the truth.* **morality** *(n),* **morally** *(adv).*
2 *(plural n)* Your **morals** are your standards of behavior.
3 *(n)* the lesson taught by a story.

morale *(mor-**al**) (n)* hope or confidence. *The prisoners kept up their morale by telling jokes.*

morbid *(adj)* having to do with death and gruesome things. *A morbid sense of humor.* **morbidly** *(adv).*

more **most**
1 *(adj)* greater in number, size, etc. **more** *(n),* **more** *(adv).*
2 **more or less** roughly, or nearly.

morning *(n)* the time of day between dawn and noon.

morose *(adj)* gloomy and bad-tempered.

Morse code *(n)* a way of sending messages that uses light or sound in a pattern of dots and dashes to represent letters. *This picture shows the word "morse" in Morse code.*

M O R S E

morsel *(n)* a small piece of food.

mortal
1 *(adj)* unable to live forever. *All humans are mortal.* **mortality** *(n).*
2 *(n)* a human being.
3 *(adj)* deadly, or causing death. *A mortal wound.* **mortally** *(adv).*

mortar
1 *(n)* a mixture of sand, water, and cement or lime that is used for building.
2 *(n)* a deep bowl used, with a pestle, for crushing things.

mortgage *(n)* a loan from a bank to buy a house.

mortuary **mortuaries** *(n)* a room or building where dead bodies are kept until their funerals.

mosaic *(moh-**zay**-ik) (n)* a pattern or picture made up of small pieces of colored stone or glass. *This Ancient Roman mosaic represents a Byzantine empress.*

mosaic

Moslem *see* **Muslim**.

mosque *(mosk) (n)* a building used by Muslims for worship. *See* **architecture**.

mosquito *(moss-**kee**-toe)* **mosquitoes** *or* **mosquitos** *(n)* a small insect which sucks blood from animals and humans. Mosquitoes can spread diseases such as malaria.

mosquito

moss **mosses** *(n)* a small, furry, green plant that grows on wet soil or stone. Mosses do not have roots, flowers, or fruit, but reproduce by producing spores. **mossy** *(adj). See* **spore**.

mostly *(adv)* mainly or usually.

motel *(n)* a roadside hotel for motorists.

moth *(n)* an insect similar to a butterfly that usually flies at night. *The emperor moth is found in Europe and Asia.*

emperor moth (male)

mother *(n)* a female parent. **motherhood** *(n),* **motherly** *(adj).*

motion **motioning** **motioned**
1 *(n)* movement. *The motion of the boat made me feel sick.*
2 *(v)* to tell someone something through movement. *The teacher motioned Eliza to sit down.*
3 *(n)* a suggestion made at a meeting.

motivate **motivating** **motivated** *(v)* to encourage someone to do something. *The coach tried to motivate his team to win.* **motivation** *(n),* **motivated** *(adj).*

motive *(n)* a reason for doing something.

motocross *(n)* cross-country motorcycle racing.

motor **motoring** **motored**
1 *(n)* a machine that changes electrical energy into mechanical energy to produce movement. *See* **engine**.
2 *(adj)* having to do with cars or engines. *Motor mechanics.*
3 *(v)* to drive. **motoring** *(n).*

motorcycle *(n)* a two-wheeled vehicle with an engine. *The picture shows a Yamaha TDM850 motorcycle.*

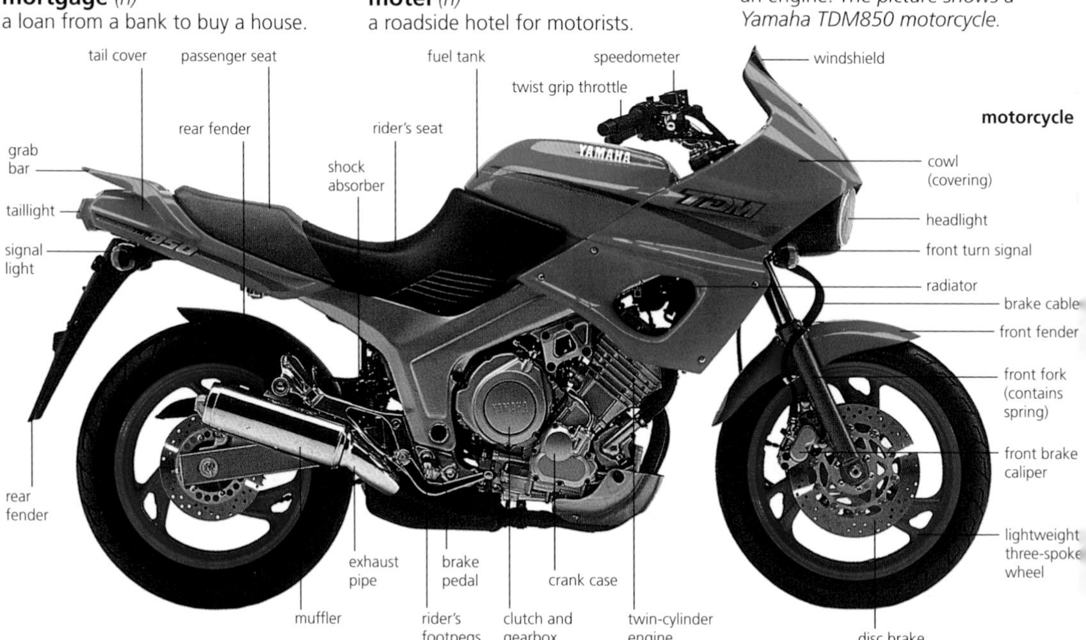

motorcycle

Some words that begin with a "mor" sound are spelled "mau."

motorist *(n)*
someone who travels by car.

mottled *(adj)*
If something is **mottled**, it is covered with patches of different colors.

motto mottos *or* mottoes *(n)*
a short sentence that is meant to guide your behavior. Some families have a motto as part of their coat of arms. *See* **coat of arms**.

mound
1 *(n)* a hill or pile. *A mound of garbage.*
2 *(n)* a slightly raised area for the pitcher in the center of a baseball diamond.

mount mounting mounted
1 *(v)* to get on, or to climb up. *Sheila mounted her horse.* **mount** *(n).*
2 *(v)* to rise, or to increase. *Excitement mounted as the great day drew near.*
3 *(v)* to put a picture or photograph in a frame. **mount** *(n).*
4 *(n)* a mountain. *Mount Everest.*
5 *(n)* a horse or other animal using for riding.

mountain
1 *(n)* a very high piece of land, higher than a hill.
2 *(n)* a large amount of something. *A mountain of work.*

mountain bike *(n)*
a strong bicycle with many gears and heavy tire treads that can be ridden on rough or hilly ground. *See* **bicycle**.

mountaineer *(n)*
someone who climbs mountains. **mountaineering** *(n).*

mourn mourning mourned *(v)*
to be very sad and grieve for someone who has died. **mourner** *(n),* **mourning** *(n).*

mournful *(adj)*
sad and miserable, filled with grief. *A mournful song.* **mournfully** *(adv).*

mouse mice
1 *(n)* a small, furry animal with a long tail. *The picture below shows a harvest mouse.*
2 *(n)* a small control box that you use to move the cursor on your computer screen.

harvest mouse

mousse
(rhymes with goose)
1 *(n)* a cold food made with beaten egg whites or whipped cream and gelatin, that is light and fluffy. *Chocolate mousse.*
2 *(n)* a substance that you use to style your hair.

moustache *See* **mustache**.

mousy
1 *(adj)* **Mousy** hair is light brown.
2 *(adj)* quiet and shy. **mousily** *(adv).*

mouth mouthing mouthed
1 *(n)* the part of your face that you use for eating and talking.
2 *(n)* the entrance to a cave or river.
3 *(v)* If you **mouth** words, you move your lips but do not make any sound.

mouthpiece
1 *(n)* a part of an instrument that goes in the mouth.
2 *(n)* a spokesperson.

move moving moved
1 *(v)* to change place or position.
2 *(n)* a step, or a movement.
3 *(v)* to put or keep in motion.
4 *(v)* to make someone do something.
5 *(n)* an action planned to bring about a result. *A smart move.*
6 *(v)* If you are **moved** by something, such as a movie or a piece of music, it makes you feel emotional. **moving** *(adj).*

movement
1 *(n)* a change from one place or position to another.
2 *(n)* a group of people who have joined together to support a cause. *The peace movement.*
3 *(n)* one of the main parts of a long piece of classical music.

movie *(n)* a motion picture.

mow mowing mowed mown *(v)*
to cut grass, corn, etc. **mower** *(n).*

mph
The initials **mph** stand for miles per hour. *This car's top speed is 130mph.*

Mr. *(miss-ter) (n)*
a title put in front of a man's name. *Mr. Mark Brown.*

Mrs. *(miss-iz) (n)*
a title put in front of a married woman's name. *Mrs. Clare White.*

Ms. *(miz) (n)*
a title put in front of a woman's name which does not indicate whether she is married or unmarried. *Ms. Isabella Stephenson.*

much
1 *(adv)* greatly. *It's much too expensive. Much to my surprise, Tom turned up for work on time this morning.* **much** *(adj).*
2 *(n)* a large amount of something. *I don't eat much.*

muck mucking mucked *(n)*
anything that is dirty, wet, sticky, or slimy. **mucky** *(adj).*

mucus *(mew-kuss) (n)*
a slimy substance made in some parts of your body, such as your nose. **mucous** *(mew-kuss) (adj).*

mud *(n)* earth that is wet and sticky. **muddy** *(v),* **muddy** *(adj).*

muddle muddling muddled
1 *(v)* to mix things up, or to confuse them. **muddled** *(adj).*
2 *(n)* a mess or confusion.

muffin *(n)* a small cake or bread shaped like a cupcake.

muffle muffling muffled *(v)*
to make a sound quieter or duller. *Hannah put a handkerchief to her mouth to muffle her laughter.*

mug mugging mugged
1 *(n)* a large cup with a handle. Mugs often have straight sides.
2 *(v) (informal)* to attack someone and try to steal their money. **mugger** *(n).*

muggy muggier muggiest *(adj)*
If the weather is **muggy**, it is warm and damp. **mugginess** *(n).*

Muhammad *or* **Mohammed**
the founder of the Islamic religion. Muslims believe that Muhammad is God's main prophet.

mule
1 *(n)* an animal produced by mating a female horse with a male donkey.
2 *(n)* a stubborn person.

multicultural *(adj)*
involving or made up of people from different races or religions. *A multicultural community.* **multiculturally** *(adv).*

multilingual *(adj)*
using several different languages. *A multilingual guidebook.* **multilingually** *(adv).*

multimedia *(adj)*
combining different media, such as sound, pictures, and text. *A multimedia presentation.* **multimedia** *(n).*

multiple
1 *(adj)* made up of many parts or things. *Multiple injuries.*
2 *(n)* a number into which a smaller number can go an exact number of times. *10 and 15 are multiples of 5.*
3 A **multiple-choice** test gives a number of answers for each question, from which you have to choose one.

multiple sclerosis *(n)*
a serious disease that causes loss of feeling in parts of the body.

multiply
multiplies multiplying multiplied
1 *(v)* to grow in number or amount. *The weeds keep multiplying.*
2 *(v)* to add the same number to itself several times. *If you multiply 3 by 4, you get 12.* **multiplication** *(n).*

multiracial *(adj)*
involving people of different races. *A multiracial community.* **multiracially** *(adv).*

multitude
1 *(n)* a crowd of people.
2 *(n)* a large number of things. *The new club offers a multitude of activities.* **multitudinous** *(adj).*

mummy mummies *(n)*
a dead body that has been preserved with special salts and resins and wrapped in cloth so that it will last for a very long time. The Ancient Egyptians placed the mummies of their rulers in elaborate coffins. *The illustration below shows Tutankhamun's mummy and the three coffins that surrounded it. The large picture shows the second coffin in more detail.* **mummify** *(v),* **mummified** *(adj).*

mumps *(n)*
an infectious illness that makes the glands in your neck swell up.

munch munches munching munched *(v)* to chew or crunch food.

mundane *(adj)* boring and ordinary.

mural *(n)* a wall painting.

murder murdering murdered *(v)* to kill someone. **murder** *(n),* **murderer** *(n).*

murky murkier murkiest *(adj)* dark, dirty, and gloomy.

murmur murmuring murmured
1 *(v)* to talk very quietly. **murmur** *(n).*
2 *(v)* to make a quiet, low, continuous sound. *The wind murmured in the trees.* **murmur** *(n).*

muscle
1 *(n)* one of the parts of your body that causes movement. Your muscles are attached to your skeleton and pull on your bones to make them move. *The diagram below shows the muscles that move your arm.*
2 *(n)* strength or power. *This job needs muscle.*

upper arm muscles
biceps (contract to bend arm)
tendons (attach muscle to bone)
triceps (contract to straighten arm)

museum *(n)*
a place where interesting objects are put on display.

mushroom mushrooming mushroomed
1 *(n)* a type of fungus that has no leaves, flowers, or roots. Many mushrooms can be eaten.
2 *(v)* to grow quickly or to spread. *New housing developments have mushroomed around the town.*

music
1 *(n)* a pleasant arrangement of sounds, played on instruments or sung. *Classical music.*
2 *(n)* printed or written signs or notes that represent musical sounds. *Can you read music? See* **notation**.

musical
1 *(adj)* If you are **musical**, you are very interested in music, or you can play an instrument well. **musically** *(adv).*
2 *(adj)* having to do with music. *Musical instruments.*
3 *(n)* a play or movie which includes singing and dancing.

musical instrument *(n)*
an instrument on which you can play music. *See* **brass**, **percussion**, **strings**, **woodwind**.

musician *(n)*
someone who plays or composes music.

musk *(n)*
a strong scent used in perfume.

musket *(n)*
an old-fashioned gun. **musketeer** *(n).*

Muslim *or* **Moslem** *(n)*
someone who follows the religion of Islam. **Muslim** *(adj).*

mussel *(n)*
a type of shellfish that you can eat. Mussels have hinged shells and soft bodies. *To feed, mussels pump seawater through their bodies.*

mussel
shell or valve
hinge
water passed out here
water drawn in here

must
1 *(v)* to have to do something. *I must go before the rain starts.*
2 *(v)* to be definitely doing something. *He must be lying.*
3 *(n)* something that you need. *This book is a must.*

mustache *or* **moustache** *(n)*
the hair that grows on a person's upper lip.

mustard *(n)* a hot and spicy food flavoring, usually eaten with meat.

muster mustering mustered
1 *(v)* to assemble in a group. *The passengers mustered on deck.*
2 *(v)* to gather something together. *Faith mustered all her strength for the final lap.*

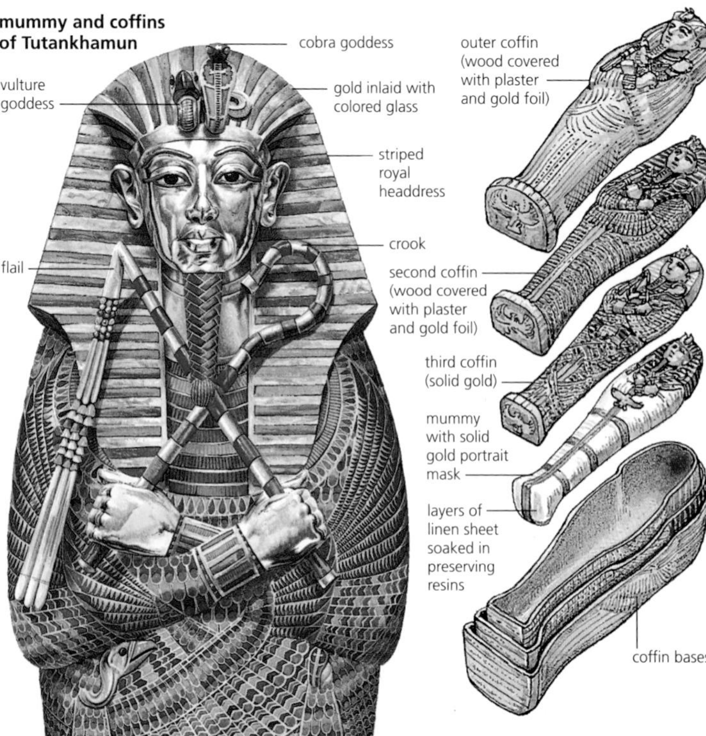

usty mustier mustiest *(adj)*
something or somewhere
musty, it smells of damp
ıd mold. **mustiness** *(n)*.

utant *(n)* a living thing that has
eveloped different characteristics
ecause of a change in its parents'
enes. **mutation** *(n)*, **mutate** *(v)*.

ute
(adj) silent or unable
speak. **mutely** *(adv)*.
(n) someone who cannot speak.
(n) something that can be
tted to a musical instrument
make it play less loudly.

ıutilate *(myoo-til-ate)*
utilating mutilated *(v)*
injure or damage someone
something. **mutilation** *(n)*.

utiny mutinies *(n)* a revolt
gainst someone in charge, especially
the army or navy. **mutineer** *(n)*,
utiny *(v)*, **mutinous** *(adj)*.

utter muttering muttered *(v)*
say something quietly so that
eople cannot hear you properly.

utton *(n)* meat from a sheep.

utual *(adj)* shared or joint.
mutual friend. **mutually** *(adv)*.

ıuzzle
(n) an animal's nose and
outh. *See* **dog**, **reindeer**.
(n) a cover for an animal's mouth
at keeps it from biting. **muzzle** *(v)*.
(n) the open end of a gun's
arrel. *See* **blunderbuss**.

ıyriad *(mir-ee-ad)* *(n)* a large
umber. *As we entered the hall, we
ere dazzled by a myriad of lights.*

ıyself *(pronoun)* me and
obody else. *I have hurt myself.*

ıysterious *(adj)*
uzzling and intriguing. *A mysterious
tranger.* **mysteriously** *(adv)*.

ıystery mysteries
(n) something that is puzzling
r hard to understand.
(n) a story containing a puzzle that
as to be solved. *A murder mystery.*

ıystify mystifies mystifying
ıystified *(v)* to puzzle or confuse
omeone. **mystification** *(n)*.

ıyth
(n) an old story or legend,
specially one about gods and
eroes. **mythology** *(n)*, **mythical** *(adj)*.
(n) a false idea that many
eople believe.

ıythology mythologies *(n)*
set of stories that has been made
p about such subjects as the ancient
ods and heroes. **mythological** *(adj)*.

Nn

nag nagging nagged *(v)* to try to persuade someone to do something by speaking about it constantly. **nag** *(n)*.

nail
1 *(n)* the hard covering at the end of your fingers and toes.
2 *(n)* a small piece of pointed metal that you hammer into something. **nail** *(v)*.

naive or **naïve** *(ny-eve)* *(adj)* If you are **naive**, you are not very experienced, and may believe or trust people too much. **naivety** *(n)*, **naively** *(adv)*.

naked *(adj)* bare or uncovered. **nakedness** *(n)*, **nakedly** *(adv)*.

name
1 *(n)* what a person or a thing is called. *What is your name?* **name** *(v)*.
2 *(n)* a reputation. *Wayne made his name as a singer.*

nanny nannies
1 *(n)* someone trained to look after young children in their home.
2 *(n)* an informal name for your grandmother.
3 **nanny goat** *(n)* a female goat.

nap napping napped *(v)* to sleep for a short time. **nap** *(n)*.

nape *(n)* the back of your neck.

napkin *(n)* a square piece of cloth or paper that you use to protect your clothes at mealtimes.

narrate narrating narrated *(v)* to tell a story. **narration** *(n)*, **narrator** *(n)*.

narrative
1 *(n)* a story, or an account of something that has happened.
2 *(adj)* telling a story. *Narrative verse.*

narrow
narrower narrowest
1 *(adj)* thin, or not wide. **narrowness** *(n)*, **narrow** *(v)*, **narrowly** *(adv)*.
2 *(adj)* If you have a **narrow** escape, you only just get away. **narrowly** *(adv)*.
3 If you are **narrow-minded**, you stick to your own ideas and do not want to listen to new ones.

narrow boat *(n)* a canal boat.

nasal *(adj)* having to do with your nose. *Nasal congestion.*

nasturtium *(n)* a plant with yellow, red, or orange flowers that can be eaten in salads.

nasty nastier nastiest
1 *(adj)* disgusting, or unpleasant. *A nasty taste.*
2 *(adj)* cruel, or unkind. **nastily** *(adv)*.

nation *(n)* a large group of people who live in the same part of the world and often share the same language, customs, etc. **national** *(adj)*, **nationally** *(adv)*.

nationalist *(n)* someone who is proud of their country, or who fights for its independence. **nationalism** *(n)*, **nationalistic** *(adj)*.

nationality nationalities *(n)* Your **nationality** is the nation or country to which you belong. *Sam has American nationality.*

nationalize
nationalizing nationalized *(v)* If an industry is **nationalized**, its ownership is transferred from a private company to the government. **nationalization** *(n)*.

native
1 *(n)* someone born in a particular place. *Barry is a native of Australia.* **native** *(adj)*.
2 **native country** *(n)* the country where you were born.

Nativity
1 *(n)* the birth of Jesus Christ.
2 **nativity play** *(n)* a play telling the story of the birth of Jesus Christ.

NATO *(n)* a group of countries, including the United States and Britain, which help each other to defend themselves. NATO stands for North Atlantic Treaty Organization.

natural
1 *(adj)* found in nature, or to do with nature. **naturally** *(adv)*.
2 *(adj)* normal or usual. *It's only natural to need a rest after a long run.* **naturally** *(adv)*.
3 *(adj)* In music, a **natural** note is one that is not sharp or flat. The natural notes on a piano are the white ones.
4 *(adj)* In a musical score, a **natural** sign shows that the next note is natural. *See* **notation**.

natural history *(n)* the study of animals and plants.

naturalist *(n)* someone who studies animals and plants.

nature
1 *(n)* everything in the world that is not made by people, such as plants, animals, the weather, etc.
2 *(n)* Your **nature** is your character.

naughty naughtier naughtiest *(adj)* badly-behaved or disobedient. **naughtiness** *(n)*, **naughtily** *(adv)*.

Some words that begin with a "na" sound are spelled "kna" or "gna."

nausea

nausea *(naw-zee-ah) (n)* a feeling of sickness. **nauseous** *(adj).*

nautical
1 *(adj)* having to do with ships and sailing.
2 **nautical mile** *(n)* a unit for measuring distance at sea. 1 nautical mile = 6,076 feet.

naval *(adj)* having to do with a navy or warships.

navel *(n)* the small, round hollow in your stomach, where your umbilical cord was attached when you were born.

navigate navigating navigated *(v)* to travel in a ship or other vehicle, using maps, satellites, compasses, etc. to guide you. *The sextant was used to navigate at sea in the 18th and 19th centuries. It helped the navigator to work out his position on a map by measuring the angle between the Sun and the horizon, or the angle between stars.* **navigation** *(n),* **navigator** *(n).*

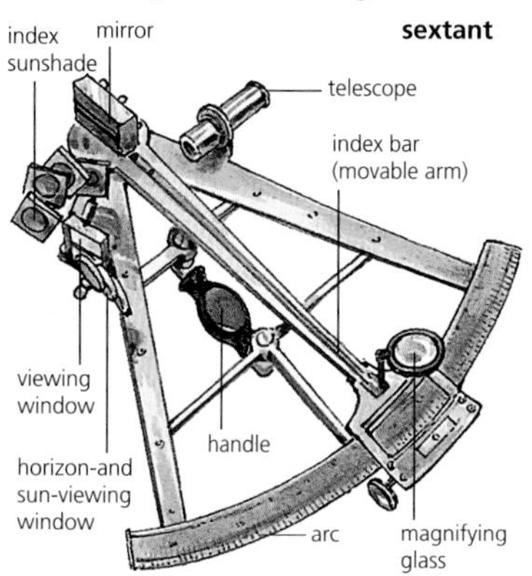

navy navies
1 *(n)* the ships and sailors that defend a country at sea.
2 **navy blue** *(n)* a very dark blue color. **navy blue** *(adj).*

n.b. the initials of the Latin phrase *nota bene*, which means "note well." The initials n.b. are used to make people take notice of something important.

near nearing neared
1 *(prep)* close to. *Alex lives near me.* **nearness** *(n),* **near** *(adj),* **near** *(adv).*
2 *(v)* to come closer to something. *The train neared the station.*

nearby *(adj)* near or close by. *The nearby store sells most basic household items.* **nearby** *(adv).*

nearly *(adv)* almost, or not quite. *We are nearly home.*

neat neater neatest
1 *(adj)* tidy and orderly. **neatness** *(n),* **neatly** *(adv).*
2 *(adj)* done in a clever or skillful way. *Peter taught the dog a neat trick.* **neatly** *(adv).*

necessary *(adj)* If something is **necessary**, you have to do it or have it. **necessity** *(n),* **necessarily** *(adv).*

neck necking necked
1 *(n)* the part of your body that joins your head to your shoulders.
2 *(n)* a narrow part of something. *The neck of the bottle.*
3 *(n)* the narrow part of a garment that fits around your neck.

necklace *(n)* a piece of jewelry worn around your neck.

nectar *(n)* a sweet liquid that bees collect from flowers and turn into honey.

need needing needed
1 *(v)* to want something urgently. *The refugees need food and shelter.*
2 *(n)* something that you must have. *I have few needs.*
3 *(v)* to have to do something. *I need to practice for the concert tomorrow.*

needle needling needled
1 *(n)* a thin pointed piece of metal with a hole for thread at one end, used for sewing.
2 *(n)* a long, thin, pointed rod used for knitting.
3 *(n)* a thin hollow tube with a sharp end that doctors use for giving injections or taking blood.
4 *(n)* a pointer on an instrument such as a compass. *See* **compass**.
5 *(v) (informal)* If someone **needles** you, they annoy you.

needless *(adj)* If something is **needless**, it is not necessary. **needlessly** *(adv).*

negative
1 *(adj)* giving the answer "no." *I asked James if he wanted to come, but his reply was negative.*
2 *(adj)* If someone is **negative**, they are against a lot of things and are unhelpful. **negatively** *(adv).*
3 *(n)* exposed film from an old-fashioned camera that shows light areas as dark and dark areas as light.
4 *(adj)* A **negative** number is less than zero.

neglect neglecting neglected
1 *(v)* to fail to look after someone or something. **neglectful** *(adj).*
2 *(n)* If a person, building, etc. is suffering from **neglect**, they have not been looked after properly.

negotiate negotiating negotiated *(v)* to bargain or discuss something, so that you can come to an agreement. **negotiation** *(n),* **negotiator** *(n).*

neigh *(nay)* neighing neighed *(v)* to make the sound that a horse makes. **neigh** *(n).*

neighbor *(n)* someone who lives next door to you or near to you.

neighborhood *(n)* Your **neighborhood** is the local area around your house.

neither *(adj)* not either. *Neither of my brothers likes coconut.* **neither** *(pronoun).*

neon *(n)* a gas that glows when an electric current is passed through it. Neon is used in lights and signs.

nephew *(n)* Someone's **nephew** is their brother's or sister's son.

nerve
1 *(n)* Your **nerves** are the thin fibers that send messages between your brain and other parts of your body, so that you can move and feel.
2 *(n)* courage and calmness. *You need a lot of nerve to be a lion tamer.*
3 *(n) (informal)* impudence or rudeness. *Harry's got a nerve, answering back like that!*
4 *(plural n) (informal)* If someone suffers from **nerves**, they are worried or frightened.

nervous
1 *(adj)* easily upset or frightened. **nervousness** *(n),* **nervously** *(adv).*
2 *(adj)* having to do with the nerves. *The human nervous system.*
3 *(n)* If someone has a **nervous breakdown**, they become very depressed and feel that they cannot cope with their problems.

nest nesting nested
1 *(n)* a place built by birds and many other animals to lay their eggs and bring up their young. *Wasps' nests are built by a queen wasp from chewed-up wood mixed with saliva. The queen lays her eggs in the cells and the eggs develop into worker wasps that enlarge and strengthen the nest.*
2 *(v)* to make a nest or home. *There are birds nesting in the tree outside my window.*

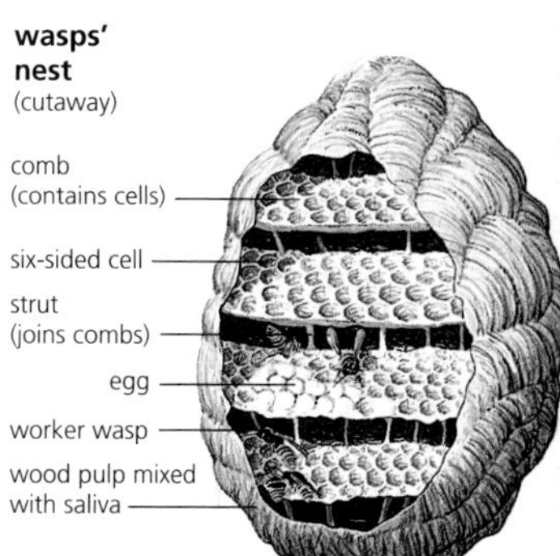

Some words that begin with an "n" sound are spelled "kn" or "gn."

nestle nestling nestled *(v)* to settle into a comfortable position. *The baby nestled against her mother's shoulder.*

net
1 *(n)* material made from fine threads or ropes that are knotted together with holes between them.
2 *(n)* a bag made from net material and attached to a pole, which you use to catch fish, butterflies, etc.
3 *(n)* A **net amount** of money is the amount left after everything necessary, such as tax, has been taken away.
4 *(n)* The **net weight** of something is its weight without packaging.
5 **the Net** *(n)* a network that connects millions of computers around the world. The Net is short for the internet.

nettle *(n)* a weed that stings you if you touch it.

network
1 *(n)* a large number of lines, forming a crisscross pattern.
2 *(n)* a system of things that are connected to one another. *A computer network.* **network** *(v).*
3 *(n)* a group of people who exchange professional or social information with each other. **networking** *(n).*

neurotic *(adj)* If someone is **neurotic**, they are very scared or worried, usually about something imaginary. **neurotically** *(adv).*

neuter neutering neutered
1 *(adj)* neither masculine nor feminine.
2 *(adj)* In some languages, such as German, nouns that are neither masculine nor feminine are **neuter**.
3 *(v)* If you **neuter** an animal, you perform surgery on it so that it cannot reproduce. **neutered** *(adj).*

neutral
1 *(adj)* If a country or a person is **neutral** in a war or an argument, they do not support either side. **neutrality** *(n),* **neutrally** *(adv).*
2 When a car is **in neutral**, the gears are not transmitting any power.
3 *(adj)* **Neutral** colors are pale and not bright. *Beige is a neutral color.*
4 *(adj)* In chemistry, a **neutral** substance, such as water, is neither an acid nor an alkali.

neutralize neutralizing neutralized *(v)* to stop something from working or from having an effect. *The medicine quickly neutralized the poison.*

neutron *(n)* one of the extremely small parts of an atom that has no electrical charge. *See* **atom**.

never *(adv)* at no time or not ever.

nevertheless *(adv)* in spite of that, or yet. *Tara was cold and hungry. Nevertheless, she kept on walking.*

new newer newest
1 *(adj)* just made or just begun.
2 *(adj)* different or strange. *New ideas.*
3 **New Age** *(adj)* having to do with spiritual and mystical ideas and beliefs.

news *(singular n)* fresh or recent information or facts.

newspaper *(n)* several sheets of folded paper containing news reports, articles, letters, etc. Newspapers are usually published daily.

newt *(n)* a small creature with short legs and a long tail that lives on land but lays its eggs in water.

marbled newt

newton *(n)* a unit for measuring force.

next
1 *(adj)* immediately following. *We'll catch the next train.* **next** *(adv).*
2 *(adj)* nearest. *Bruno's desk is next to mine.* **next** *(adv).*
3 **next door** *(adj)* in or at the nearest house, building, etc.

nib *(n)* the part of a pen through which ink flows.

nibble nibbling nibbled *(v)* to bite something gently, or to take small bites of something. **nibble** *(n).*

nice nicer nicest *(adj)* pleasant or good. **nicely** *(adv).*

niche *(nich)*
1 *(n)* a hollow place in a wall.
2 *(n)* the environment to which an animal or a plant has adapted, or to which it belongs.

nickname *(n)* a name that you give to a friend. **nickname** *(v).*

niece *(n)* Someone's **niece** is their brother's or sister's daughter.

night *(n)* the time between sunset and sunrise, when it is dark.

nightgown *(n)* a loose dress that girls or women wear in bed.

nightingale *(n)* a small bird that sings beautifully.

nightly *(adv)* happening every night. *The doctor visits nightly.* **nightly** *(adj).*

nightmare *(n)* a frightening or unpleasant dream or situation.

nil *(n)* nothing, or zero.

nimble nimbler nimblest *(adj)* If you are **nimble**, you move quickly and lightly. **nimbly** *(adv).*

nip *(n)* a sharp pinch or bite.

nipple *(n)* one of the two small, raised parts on a person's chest.

nitrogen *(n)* a colorless gas that makes up about four-fifths of the Earth's air.

nits *(plural n)* eggs laid by lice.

no
1 *(interject)* a word used to refuse something. *"No, I won't!"*
2 *(adj)* not any. *There was no hope.*

noble nobler noblest
1 *(adj)* A **noble** family is aristocratic and of high rank. **nobility** *(n),* **nobleman** *(n),* **noblewoman** *(n).*
2 *(adj)* If someone is **noble**, they act in a way that is good and unselfish. **nobility** *(n),* **nobly** *(adv).*

nobody nobodies
1 *(pronoun)* not a single person. *There was nobody there.*
2 *(n)* If a person is described as a **nobody**, they are not considered to be important.

nocturnal
1 *(adj)* having to do with the night, or happening at night. *A nocturnal journey.* **nocturnally** *(adv).*
2 *(adj)* A **nocturnal** animal is active at night. *Badgers and owls are nocturnal animals.*

nod nodding nodded *(v)* to move your head up and down, especially to say yes. **nod** *(n).*

noise *(n)* a sound, especially a loud or unpleasant one. **noisiness** *(n).*

noisy noisier noisiest *(adj)* loud. **noisily** *(adv).*

nomad *(n)* a member of a tribe that moves from place to place. *The picture shows the camp of some Bedouin nomads.* **nomadic** *(adj).*

nomads

Some words that begin with an "n" sound are spelled "kn," "gn," or "pn."
Some words that begin with a "ni" sound are spelled "ny."

nominate nominating nominated *(v)* to suggest that someone would be the right person to do a job. *I nominate George as our team leader.* **nomination** *(n).*

none *(pronoun)* not one, or not any. **none** *(adv).*

nonetheless *(adv)* in spite of that. *Harriet fell off her horse three times. Nonetheless, she completed the course.* **nonetheless** *(conj).*

nonfiction *(n)* writing that gives information about real things, people, and events, rather than made-up stories. **nonfiction** *(adj).*

nonsense *(n)* If something is **nonsense**, it is silly or has no meaning. **nonsensical** *(adj).*

nonstop *(adj)* without any stops or breaks. *A nonstop flight to Los Angeles.* **nonstop** *(adv).*

noodles *(plural n)* very thin pasta in long pieces that you can put in soups, Chinese dishes, etc.

noon *(n)* twelve o'clock in the middle of the day.

no one *(pronoun)* not a single person. *There was no one in the park this afternoon.*

noose *(n)* a large loop at the end of a piece of rope, which closes up as the rope is pulled.

normal *(adj)* usual and ordinary. **normality** *(n),* **normally** *(adv).*

north
1 *(n)* one of the four main points of the compass, the direction on your right when you face the setting Sun in the northern hemisphere. **north** *(adj),* **northern** *(adj),* **north** *(adv).*
2 *(adj)* A **north** wind blows from the north. **northerly** *(adv).*
3 **North Pole** *(n)* the very cold part of the Earth in the far north.

nose nosing nosed
1 *(n)* the part of your face that you use when you smell and breathe.
2 *(n)* the pointed part at the front of some aircraft. *See* **aircraft**.
3 *(v)* If a ship, car, etc. **noses** forward, it moves very slowly.

nostalgic *(adj)* People who are **nostalgic** like to think about the past and are sad because things have changed since then. **nostalgia** *(n).*

nostril *(n)* Your **nostrils** are the two holes in your nose through which you breathe and smell.

nosy nosier nosiest *(adj) (informal)* Someone who is **nosy** is too interested in things that do not concern them. **nosily** *(adv).*

notation *(n)* a series of signs or symbols used to represent elements in a system, such as music or math. *An example of music notation is shown below.*

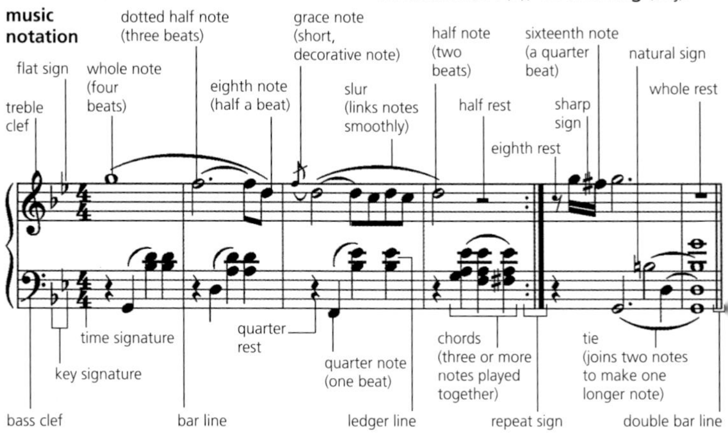

note noting noted
1 *(n)* a short letter or message.
2 *(n)* a piece of paper money.
3 *(n)* a musical sound or the symbol that represents it. *See* **notation**.
4 *(v)* to notice a fact and pay attention to it. *Please note the price increase.*
5 *(v)* to write something down. *I've noted your name in my book.*

notebook
1 *(n)* a small pad or book of paper, used for writing notes.
2 *(n)* a very small, portable computer.

nothing
1 *(pronoun)* not anything at all. *There was nothing in the pantry.*
2 *(pronoun)* not anything important. *I did nothing all weekend.*

notice noticing noticed
1 *(v)* to see or become aware of something. *Did you notice the smell?* **noticeable** *(adj),* **noticeably** *(adv).*
2 *(n)* a written message put in a public place to tell people about something.
3 If someone **gives notice**, they tell their employer that they will be leaving their job.

notify notifies notifying notified *(v)* to tell someone about something officially or formally. **notification** *(n).*

notorious *(adj)* If someone or something is **notorious**, they are well known for something bad. *The school is notorious for bullying.*

noun *(n)* a word that refers to a person or thing. *"Dog," "happiness," and "France" are all nouns. See* page 3.

nourish *(ner-rish)* nourishes nourishing nourished *(v)* to give a person, animal, or plant enough food to keep them strong and healthy. **nourishment** *(n),* **nourishing** *(adj).*

novel
1 *(n)* a book that tells a story. **novelist** *(n).*
2 *(adj)* new and interesting. *A novel idea.*

novelty novelties *(n)* something new, interesting, and unusual. **novelty** *(adj).*

novice *(n)* a beginner, or someone who is not very experienced.

nowhere *(adv)* not any place. *There was nowhere to hide.*

nuclear *(new-klee-ur)*
1 *(adj)* having to do with the splitting of atoms. *Nuclear physics.*
2 **nuclear power** *(n)* power created by the splitting of atoms.
3 **nuclear weapon** *(n)* a weapon that uses the power created by splitting atoms.
4 **nuclear reactor** *(n)* a large machine that produces nuclear power in a power station.

nucleus nuclei
1 *(n)* the central part of an atom, made up of neutrons and protons. *See* **atom**.
2 *(n)* the central part of a cell, that contains the chromosomes. *See* **cell**.

nude
1 *(adj)* naked. **nudist** *(n),* **nudity** *(n).*
2 *(n)* a naked human figure, especially one in a painting or sculpture.

nudge nudging nudged *(v)* to give someone or something a small push, often with your elbow. **nudge** *(n).*

nuisance *(new-sunss) (n)* someone or something that annoys you and causes problems for you.

Some words that begin with a "no" sound are spelled "kno" or "gno."

numb *(num) (adj)* unable to feel anything. **numbness** *(n)*, **numb** *(v)*.

number numbering numbered
1 *(n)* a word or sign used for counting and doing math.
2 *(v)* to give a number to something. *Isla numbered the cards from 1 to 10.*
3 *(v)* to amount to a number. *The crowd numbered at least 300.*

numeral *(n)* a written sign that represents a number. *Roman numerals.*

numerate *(adj)* If you are **numerate**, you can understand basic arithmetic. **numeracy** *(n)*.

numerator *(n)* In fractions, the **numerator** is the number above the line, which shows how many parts of the denominator are taken.

numerical *(adj)* having to do with numbers. *Numerical order.* **numerically** *(adv)*.

numerous *(adj)* many. *Tracy's DVDs are too numerous to count.*

nun *(n)* a woman who lives in a Christian religious community and has promised to devote her life to God.

nurse nursing nursed
1 *(n)* someone who cares for people who are ill, usually in a hospital.
2 *(v)* to care for someone who is ill.

nursery nurseries
1 *(n)* a place where very young children are cared for when their parents are at work or church.
2 *(n)* a baby's bedroom.
3 *(n)* a place where you can buy trees and plants.
4 **nursery rhyme** *(n)* a short poem for very young children.
5 **nursery school (preschool)** *(n)* a school for children aged three to five years old, before they go to kindergarten.

nut
1 *(n)* a fruit with a hard shell that grows on trees. **nutty** *(adj)*.
2 *(n)* a small piece of metal with a hole in the middle that screws onto a bolt and holds it in place.

nutritious *(noo-**trish**-uss) (adj)* Food that is **nutritious** contains substances that your body can use to help you stay healthy and strong. **nutrition** *(n)*, **nutritiously** *(adv)*.

nylon *(n)* a light, man-made fiber, used to make clothing, fishing line, etc.

nymph
1 *(n)* In ancient Greek and Roman stories, a **nymph** is a spirit of nature.
2 *(n)* a young form of an insect, such as a grasshopper, which changes into an adult by repeatedly shedding its skin.

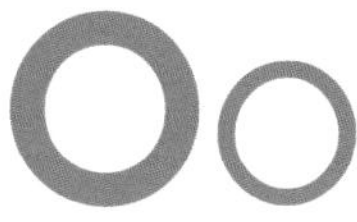

oak *(n)* a large hardwood tree that produces acorns.

oar *(n)* a wooden pole with a flat blade at one end, used for rowing a boat.

oasis *(oh-**ay**-siss)* **oases** *(n)* a place in a desert where there is water and where plants and trees grow.

oat *(n)* a cereal plant that is used as food for humans and animals. *See* **grain**.

oath
1 *(n)* a serious, formal promise.
2 *(n)* a swear word.

obedient *(adj)* If you are **obedient**, you do what you are told to do. **obedience** *(n)*, **obediently** *(adv)*.

obese *(adj)* very fat. **obesity** *(n)*.

obey obeying obeyed *(v)* to do the things that someone tells you to do.

object objecting objected
1 *(**ob**-jekt) (n)* something that you can see and touch, but is not alive.
2 *(**ob**-jekt) (n)* the thing that you are trying to achieve. *The object of this game is to get the ball into the net.*
3 *(**ob**-jekt) (n)* The **object** of a verb is the noun that receives the action of the verb and usually comes after it. *In the sentence "Jemima bumped the table," table is the object of the verb "to bump."*
4 *(ob-**jekt**) (v)* If you **object** to something, you dislike it or disagree with it. **objection** *(n)*, **objector** *(n)*.

objectionable *(adj)* unpleasant and likely to offend people.

objective
1 *(adj)* based on facts, not on feelings or opinions. *An objective report.* **objectivity** *(n)*, **objectively** *(adv)*.
2 *(n)* a goal that you are working toward. *Our objective is to produce a pollution-free car.*

obligation *(n)* something that it is your duty to do. *There's no obligation to stay.* **obligatory** *(adj)*.

oblige obliging obliged
1 *(v)* If you are **obliged** to do something, you have to do it.
2 *(v)* to do someone a favor. *We needed a ride, so our friends obliged by driving us there.* **obliging** *(adj)*, **obligingly** *(adv)*.

obliterate obliterating obliterated *(v)* to destroy something completely.

oblong *(n)* a shape with four straight sides and four right angles that is longer than it is wide.

obnoxious *(adj)* very unpleasant. **obnoxiously** *(adv)*.

obscene obscener obscenest *(adj)* indecent and shocking. **obscenity** *(n)*, **obscenely** *(adv)*.

obscure obscuring obscured; obscurer obscurest
1 *(adj)* not well known. **obscurity** *(n)*.
2 *(adj)* not easy to understand.
3 *(v)* to make it difficult to see something. *The pillar obscured our view of the stage.*

observant *(adj)* If you are **observant**, you are good at noticing things. **observantly** *(adv)*.

observatory observatories *(n)* a building containing telescopes and other scientific instruments for studying the sky and the stars.

observe observing observed
1 *(v)* to watch someone or something carefully. *The police have been observing the house all week.* **observation** *(n)*.
2 *(v)* to notice something by looking or watching. *I observed that Henry had torn his pants.* **observation** *(n)*.
3 *(v)* to make a remark. *Warren observed that the train was late again.* **observation** *(n)*.

obsess obsesses obsessing obsessed *(v)* If you are **obsessed with** something, you think about it all the time. **obsession** *(n)*, **obsessive** *(adj)*.

obsolete *(adj)* out of date and no longer used.

obstacle *(n)* something that gets in your way or prevents you from doing something.

obstinate *(adj)* If someone is **obstinate**, they are stubborn and unwilling to change their mind. **obstinacy** *(n)*, **obstinately** *(adv)*.

obstreperous *(adj)* If someone is **obstreperous**, they resist in a rough and noisy way. **obstreperously** *(adv)*.

obstruct obstructing obstructed
1 *(v)* to block a road or path. *Fallen trees obstructed the road.* **obstruction** *(n)*, **obstructive** *(adj)*.
2 *(v)* to prevent something from happening, or to make something difficult. *Max obstructed all attempts to make him clean his room.* **obstruction** *(n)*, **obstructive** *(adj)*.

obtain obtaining obtained *(v)* to get or to be given something.

obtuse
1 *(adj)* If someone is **obtuse**, they are slow to understand things.
2 *(adj)* An **obtuse** angle is an angle of between 90° and 180°.

obvious *(adj)* If something is **obvious**, it is easy to see or understand. **obviously** *(adv).*

occasion
1 *(n)* a time when something happens. *Lucas had been to London on several occasions.*
2 *(n)* a special or important event.

occasional *(adj)* happening sometimes. *Occasional visits.* **occasionally** *(adv).*

occupation
1 *(n)* a job. **occupational** *(adj).*
2 *(n)* something that you enjoy doing in your free time. *Football is Gary's favorite occupation.*
3 *(n)* the taking over and controlling of a country or an area by an army.

occupy
occupies occupying occupied
1 *(v)* to live in a building, room, etc. *Who occupies this house?* **occupant** *(n),* **occupier** *(n).*
2 *(v)* to keep someone busy and happy. *The boys were occupied for hours on the computer.*
3 *(v)* If an army **occupies** a country or an area, it captures it and takes control of it.

occur **occurring occurred**
1 *(v)* to happen. *When did the accident occur?* **occurrence** *(n).*
2 *(v)* If something **occurs to you**, you suddenly think of it.

ocean *(oh-shun) (n)* one of the large areas of water on the Earth's surface. *This map shows the five main oceans of the world.*

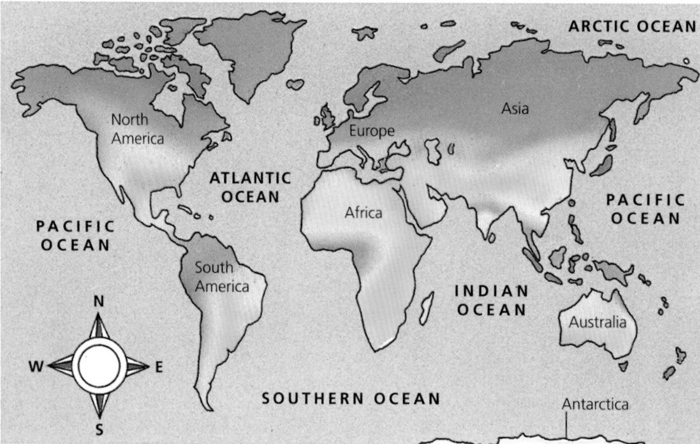

o'clock *(adv)* a word you use when saying what the time is. **O'clock** is short for **of the clock**. *It's 3 o'clock.*

octagon *(n)* a shape with eight straight sides. **octagonal** *(adj).* *See* **shape**.

octahedron *(n)* a solid shape with eight, usually triangular, faces. *See* **shape**.

octave *(n)* the eight-note gap in a musical scale between a note and the next note of the same name above or below it.

octopus **octopuses** *(n)* a sea creature with a soft body and eight long arms that it uses for catching its prey.

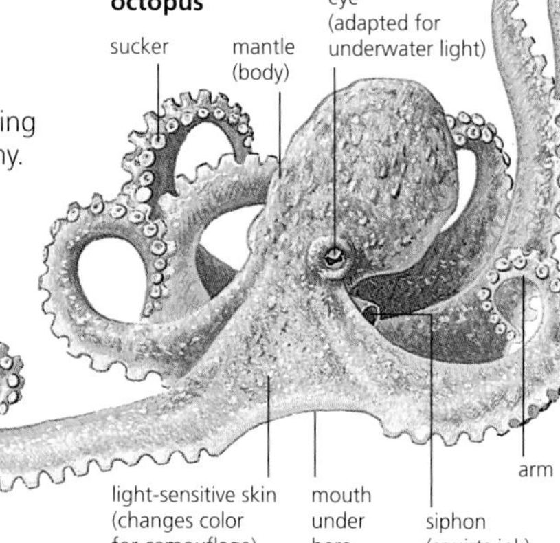

odd **odder oddest**
1 *(adj)* strange and difficult to explain or understand. **oddly** *(adv).*
2 *(adj)* An **odd** number cannot be divided exactly by two. *1, 13, 47, and 895 are all odd numbers.*
3 *(adj)* not matching. *Odd socks.*

odds *(plural n)* the probability of something happening. *The odds are that Abi will win the race.*

ode *(n)* a poem praising something. *Ode to a Nightingale.*

odor *(oh-der) (n)* a smell. *That cheese has a very strong odor.*

off
1 *(prep)* away from a place. *Take those books off the table.* **off** *(adv).*
2 *(adv)* not switched on. *Someone has turned off the computer.*

offend **offending offended**
1 *(v)* to upset someone. *I didn't mean to offend you.*
2 *(v)* to commit a crime. **offender** *(n).*

offense
1 *(n)* a crime.
2 If you **cause offense**, you upset someone. *Billy's play caused offense.*
3 If you **take offense**, you feel upset by something that someone has done or said.

offensive
1 *(adj)* If someone or something is **offensive**, they are unpleasant and upset people. **offensively** *(adv).*
2 *(n)* an attack, usually a military one.
3 *(adj)* attacking. *The army took offensive action.*

offer **offering offered**
1 *(v)* to ask someone if they would like something. *Can I offer you some cake?* **offer** *(n).*
2 *(v)* to say that you are willing to do something for someone. *I offered to take the message.* **offer** *(n).*

offering *(n)* something that is offered to God or to a god.

offhand
1 *(adj)* abrupt or casual.
2 *(adj)* without preparation. *I don't know the answer offhand.*

office
1 *(n)* a room or building in which people work, usually sitting at desks.
2 *(n)* an important, powerful position. *The office of governor.*

officer *(n)* someone who is in charge of other people, especially in the armed forces or the police.

official
1 *(adj)* If something is **official**, it has been approved by someone in authority. *There will be an official inquiry into the accident.* **officially** *(adv).*
2 *(n)* someone who holds an important position in an organization. *A government official.*

off-peak *(adj)* happening when there is less activity or demand. *Off-peak travel.*

off-putting *(adj) (informal)* discouraging or disturbing.

offside *(adj)* If a player is **offside** in a game such as soccer or hockey, they have broken the rules of the game by moving too far forward, ahead of the ball or puck. **offside** *(adv)*.

offspring *(plural n)* an animal's young or a human's children.

often *(adv)* many times.

ogre *(oh-ger) (n)* a fierce cruel giant in fairy tales.

oh *(interject)* a word used to express surprise, disappointment, or pain. *Oh no!*

ohm *(rhymes with dome) (n)* a unit for measuring how much resistance a substance gives to the flow of electricity through it.

oil oiling oiled
1 *(n)* a thick smooth liquid. Different types of oil are used for heating buildings, for cooking, and for making machines run smoothly. **oily** *(adj)*.
2 *(v)* to cover something with oil. *You should oil your bicycle chain regularly.*
3 **oils** *(plural n)* artists' paints containing oil. *See* **artist**.

oil platform *(n)* a large platform used as a base for drilling for oil under the sea or under the ground.
The picture shows an oil platform in the North Sea.

okay *or* **O.K.**
1 *(adj) (informal)* all right.
2 *(interject) (informal)* When you say **okay**, you mean that you agree.

old older oldest
1 *(adj)* Someone who is **old** has lived for a long time.
2 *(adj)* Something that is **old** has existed or been used for a long time.
3 *(adj)* from an earlier time. *A meeting of old pupils of the school.*

old age *(n)* the time when a person is old.

old-fashioned *(adj)* no longer fashionable or popular.

olive *(n)* a small black or green savory fruit that is eaten whole or crushed for its oil.

omelette *or* **omelet** *(n)* a dish made of fried, beaten egg.

omen *(n)* a sign or warning about something that will happen in the future.

ominous *(adj)* If something is **ominous**, it makes you feel that something bad is going to happen. *An ominous silence.* **ominously** *(adv)*.

omit omitting omitted
1 *(v)* to leave something out. *Ruth omitted a line from the song.* **omission** *(n)*.
2 *(v)* If you **omit** to do something, you do not do it. *Robert omitted to eat his breakfast.* **omission** *(n)*.

omnibus omnibuses *(n)* a collection of stories, books or television programs that were previously published or shown separately.

omnivore *(n)* an animal that eats plants and meat. **omnivorous** *(adj)*.

once
1 *(adv)* one time. *I've been to Boston only once.*
2 *(adv)* in the past. *This country was once covered by ice.*
3 *(conj)* after something has happened. *I'll tell you all about it once we get home.*
4 **at once** immediately. *Take those muddy shoes off at once!*

one-way
1 *(adj)* Traffic can travel in only one direction down a **one-way** street.
2 *(adj)* A **one-way** ticket allows you to travel to a place but not back again.

onion *(n)* a round vegetable with a strong smell and taste. *See* **vegetable**.

online
1 *(adj)* If you are **online**, you are connected to the internet.
2 *(adj)* having to do with the internet. *Online shopping.*

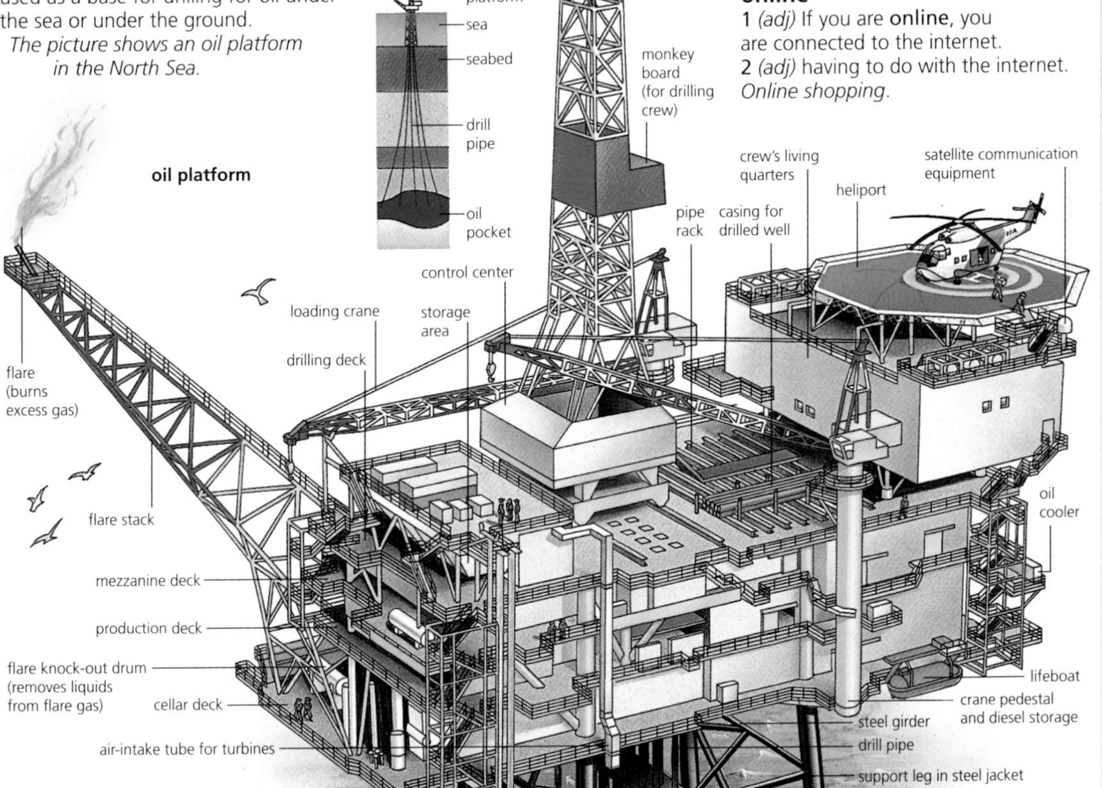

only
1 *(adv)* not more than, or just. *There were only three people in the shop.*
2 *(adj)* with nothing or no one else. *Maria was the only person there.*
3 *(conj)* but. *We would have gotten here earlier, only the car broke down.*
4 *(n)* An **only child** has no brothers or sisters.

onomatopoeia
*(on-oh-mat-ah-**pee**-ah) (n)* the use of a word that sounds like the thing it describes. *"Pop" and "sizzle" are examples of onomatopoeia.* **onomatopoeiac** *(adj).*

onward *(adv)* forward. *They lived there from 2011 onward.*

ooze **oozing oozed** *(v)* to flow out slowly. *Mud oozed from my shoes.*

opaque *(oh-**pake**) (adj)* not clear enough to see through. *The water in the stream was muddy and opaque.*

open **opening opened**
1 *(adj)* not shut. **open** *(v).*
2 *(adj)* not covered or not enclosed. *Open land. Open air.*
3 *(adj)* If you are **open** about something, you are honest about it. **openness** *(n),* **openly** *(adv).*
4 *(v)* to start or to begin. *The story opens in a wild forest.*
5 *(n)* If you have an **open mind**, you are able to accept new ideas.

opening
1 *(n)* a hole or a space in something. *A small opening in the hedge.*
2 *(adj)* coming at the beginning. *The opening lines of a play.* **opening** *(n).*
3 *(n)* a chance. *This part could give you an opening into show business.*

opera *(n)* a play in which the words are sung. **operatic** *(adj).*

operate **operating operated**
1 *(v)* to make something work. *Damian soon learned how to operate the machine.*
2 *(v)* to cut open someone's body to repair a damaged part or to remove a diseased part.
3 *(v)* to work. *Thieves operate in this area. I can't be expected to operate under these conditions!*

operation
1 *(n)* an event that has been carefully planned and involves a lot of people. *A massive security operation.*
2 If something is **in operation**, it is working.
3 *(n)* the cutting open of someone's body to repair a damaged part or to remove a diseased part.

operator *(n)* someone who works a machine.

opinion
1 *(n)* the ideas and beliefs that you have about something. *What's your opinion of our new teacher?*
2 **opinion poll** *(n)* a way of finding out what people in general think about something, by questioning a selection of people.

opponent *(n)* someone who is against you in a fight or a game.

opportunity **opportunities** *(n)* a chance to do something. *Carla's job gives her the opportunity to travel.*

oppose **opposing opposed** *(v)* to be against something and try to prevent it from happening. *James is opposed to hunting.*

opposite
1 *(prep)* If something is **opposite** you, it is facing you. **opposite** *(adj).*
2 *(adj)* completely different. *Sue ran off in the opposite direction when she saw me.* **opposite** *(n).*

opposition
1 *(n)* When there is **opposition** to something, people are against it. *There was a lot of opposition to the plans for a new supermarket.*
2 *(n)* the person or team that you play against in a match or competition.

oppress
oppresses oppressing oppressed
1 *(v)* to treat people in a cruel, unjust, and hard way. **oppression** *(n),* **oppressor** *(n),* **oppressive** *(adj).*
2 *(v)* If something **oppresses** you, it makes you feel worried or weighed down. **oppressive** *(adj).*

opt **opting opted**
1 *(v)* to choose to have or do something. *Lydia opted to learn German.*
2 **opt out** *(v)* to choose not to take part in something.

optical
1 *(adj)* having to do with eyes or eyesight.
2 **optical illusion** *(n)* something that you think you see that is not really there

optician *(n)* someone who tests your eyesight and supplies glasses and contact lenses.

optimistic *(adj)* People who are **optimistic** always believe that things will turn out well and successfully. **optimism** *(n),* **optimist** *(n).*

option *(n)* something that you can choose to do.

optional *(adj)* If something is **optional**, you can choose whether or not to have it or do it.

oral
1 *(adj)* having to do with your mouth. *Oral hygiene.* **orally** *(adv).*
2 *(n)* a spoken exam or test. *A French oral.*
3 *(adj)* having to do with speaking. **orally** *(adv).*

orange
1 *(n)* the color of most carrots, or a mixture of red and yellow. **orange** *(adj).*
2 *(n)* a round fruit with a thick, orange skin and sweet, juicy flesh. *See* **fruit**.

orbit **orbiting orbited**
1 *(n)* the invisible path followed by an object circling a planet or the Sun. **orbital** *(adj).*
2 *(v)* to travel around a planet or the Sun.

orchard *(n)* an area of land where fruit trees are grown.

orchestra *(n)* a large group of musicians who play their instruments together. *The diagram below shows the positions of the main instruments in a symphony orchestra, which usually plays classical music.*

symphony orchestra

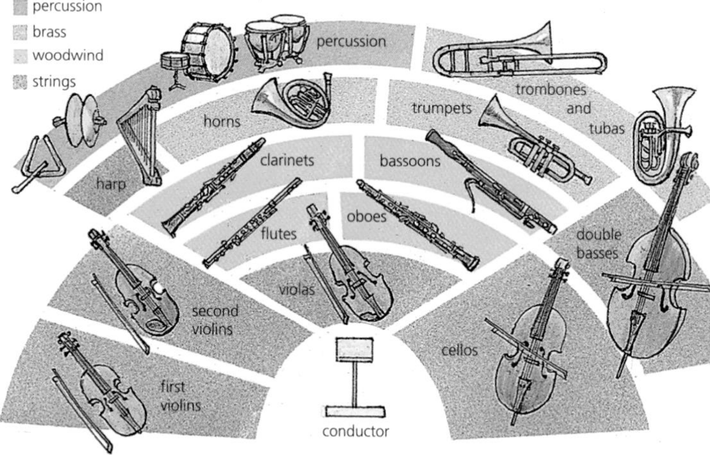

orchid *(or-kid) (n)* a plant with colorful and often unusually shaped flowers. *The Vanda tricolor orchid shown here grows in Southeast Asia.*

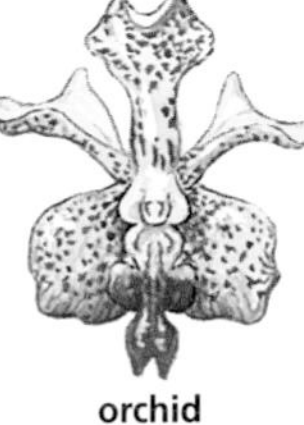

orchid

ordeal *(n)* a very difficult and testing experience.

order **ordering** **ordered**
1 *(v)* to tell someone that they have to do something. **order** *(n).*
2 *(v)* to ask for something in a restaurant. **order** *(n).*
3 *(v)* to ask a manufacturer, website or store to get you something. *I've ordered a new television.*
4 *(n)* neatness. *Penny loves order.* **orderly** *(adv).*
5 *(n)* good behavior. *Can we have some order in this classroom?*
6 If you put things **in order**, you arrange them so that each thing is in the right place.
7 If an object is **out of order**, it is broken and does not work.

ordinary *(adj)* normal or usual. **ordinarily** *(adv).*

ore *(n)* a rock that contains metal. *Iron ore.*

organ
1 *(n)* a large musical instrument with one or more keyboards and pipes of different lengths. **organist** *(n).*
2 *(n)* a part of the body that does a particular job. *The diagram shows the main human organs used for breathing, and for digesting and excreting food. The kidneys are shown separately because they are positioned behind the intestines.*

human organs

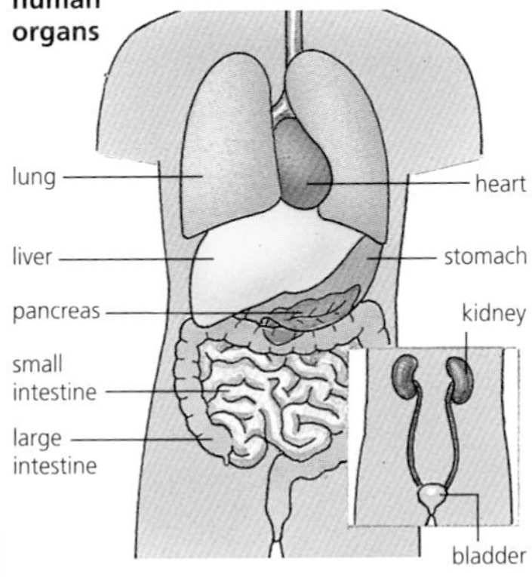

organic
1 *(adj)* using only natural products and no chemicals, pesticides, etc. *Organic farming.* **organically** *(adv).*
2 *(adj)* having to do with living things and their organs.

organism *(n)* a living plant or animal.

organization
1 *(n)* a large company, charity, or other group.
2 *(n)* the task of planning and running something. *We left the organization of the party to Jeff.*

organize **organizing** **organized**
1 *(v)* to plan and run an event. **organizer** *(n).*
2 *(v)* to arrange things neatly and in order. *Look how well Celia has organized the books on her shelves!*

oriental *(adj)* belonging to or coming from the countries of the Far East, especially Japan or China. **Orient** *(n).*

orienteering *(n)* a sport in which people have to find their way across rough country as fast as they can, using a map and compass.

origami *(singular n)* the Japanese art of paper folding. *This picture shows an example of origami.*

origami bird

origin *(n)* the point where something began. *What was the origin of this argument?*

original
1 *(adj)* first or earliest. *Who were the original settlers in Australia?* **originally** *(adv).*
2 *(adj)* new and imaginative. *What an original idea!* **originality** *(n).*
3 *(n)* a work of art that is not a copy. **original** *(adj).*

originate **originating** **originated** *(v)* to begin from somewhere or something. *This drawing originated from a doodle.* **origination** *(n).*

ornament *(n)* a small attractive object that you use to decorate a room. **ornamental** *(adj).*

ornate *(adj)* richly decorated. **ornately** *(adv).*

ornithology *(n)* the study of birds. **ornithologist** *(n).*

orphan *(n)* a child whose parents are both dead. **orphaned** *(adj).*

orphanage *(n)* a place where orphans live and are looked after.

orthodontist *(n)* someone who straightens uneven teeth.

orthodox
1 *(adj)* **Orthodox** views and beliefs are ones that are accepted by most people. **orthodoxy** *(n).*
2 *(adj)* Members of a religion are described as **orthodox** if they believe in its older, more traditional teachings.

orthopedic *(or-thoh-pee-dik) (adj)* having to do with the branch of medicine that deals with bones.

osmosis *(oss-moh-sis) (n)* the process by which a solvent passes through a membrane from a less concentrated solution to a more concentrated solution, until they reach the same level of concentration.

ostrich **ostriches** *(n)* a large African bird that cannot fly. *See* **bird**.

other
1 *(adj)* not the one that you have just mentioned. **other** *(pronoun).*
2 **others** *(pronoun)* the rest. *Where are the others?*

otherwise
1 *(conj)* or if not. *Catch a bus from the station. Otherwise, take a taxi.*
2 *(adv)* apart from that. *We didn't have very good seats, but otherwise the concert was excellent.*

otter *(n)* a furry mammal that lives in or near water and eats fish.

otter

ouch *(owch) (interject)* a cry of pain.

ought *(awt) (v)* If you **ought** to do something, you should do it.

our *(pronoun)* belonging to us.

ourselves *(pronoun)* us and no one else.

oust *(owst)* **ousting** **ousted** *(v)* to force someone out of a position or job. *Henry has been ousted as captain of the team.*

out
1 *(adj)* not in. *I came to see you but you were out.*
2 *(adv)* no longer burning or no longer alight. *The fire went out.*
3 *(adj)* no longer taking part in a game. *You will be out if you get a question wrong.*
4 *(adv)* aloud. *Meg called out for help.*
5 *(adv)* into the open or, in public view. *Is his latest book out yet?*

Some words that begin with a "or" sound are spelled "au" or "aw."

outback *(n)* the remote areas of Australia, away from the cities.

outbreak *(n)* a sudden start of something, such as disease or war.

outburst *(n)* a sudden pouring out of strong emotion. *An outburst of anger.*

outcast *(n)* someone who is not accepted by other people.

outcome *(n)* the result of something. *The outcome of the vote was a shock.*

outcry outcries *(n)* If there is an **outcry** about something, a lot of people complain loudly about it.

outdo outdoes outdoing outdid outdone *(v)* If you **outdo** someone, you do something better than they do. *Samantha's saxophone solo was good, but Larry outdid her.*

outdoors *(adv)* outside or in the open air. **outdoor** *(adj).*

outer
1 *(adj)* on the outside or furthest from the middle. *The outer edge.*
2 **outer space** *(n)* space beyond the Earth's atmosphere.

outfit
1 *(n)* a set of clothes.
2 *(n) (informal)* a group, company, or organization. *A printing outfit.*

outgoing *(adj)* Someone who is **outgoing** is very sociable and friendly.

outgrow outgrowing outgrew outgrown *(v)* to grow too big or too old for something.

outing *(n)* a short trip somewhere for pleasure.

outlaw outlawing outlawed
1 *(n) (old-fashioned)* a criminal, especially in the Wild West.
2 *(v)* to forbid something by law.

outlay *(n)* money spent on something.

outlet
1 *(n)* a pipe or hole that lets out liquid or gas.
2 *(n)* a store where a company's products can be bought.
3 *(n)* an activity that lets you express your feelings.

outline
1 *(n)* a line that shows the edge of something.
2 *(n)* the basic points or ideas about something. *Give me an outline of the movie's plot.*

outlook
1 *(n)* your general attitude to things. *Yasmin has a very positive outlook.*
2 *(n)* the way that something is likely to develop. *The weather outlook.*

outnumber
outnumbering outnumbered *(v)* to be larger in number than another group. *Girls outnumber boys in this class by four to one.*

outpatient *(n)* someone who goes to a hospital for treatment but does not stay there.

outpost *(n)* a remote fort or settlement.

output
1 *(n)* the amount produced by a person, machine, or business. *Our output has doubled this year.*
2 *(n)* information produced by a computer. **output** *(v).*

outrageous *(adj)* very shocking or offensive. **outrage** *(n),* **outrageously** *(adv).*

outright
1 *(adj)* total or complete. *The outright winner.*
2 *(adv)* instantly. *Kirk was dismissed outright for stealing.*

outset *(n)* the start or the beginning. *I knew from the outset that the show would be a success.*

outside
1 *(adv)* out of a building or in the open air. *Max waited outside while his friends went to buy a soda.* **outside** *(prep).*
2 *(n)* the surface of something or the part that surrounds the rest of it. *The outside of the box was painted pink.* **outside** *(adj).*
3 **outside chance** *(n)* a very small chance.

outskirts *(plural n)* the outer edges of a town or city.

outspoken *(adj)* If you are **outspoken**, you express your views strongly and clearly, especially when you are criticizing someone.

outstanding
1 *(adj)* extremely good. *An outstanding performance.*
2 *(adj)* not yet paid or not yet dealt with. *An outstanding bill.*

outward
1 *(adj)* appearing on the surface. *Phillip's outward appearance was calm, but really he was very nervous.* **outwardly** *(adv).*
2 *(adv)* toward the outside. *Stand facing outward.*

outwit outwitting outwitted *(v)* to gain an advantage over someone by being cleverer than them.

oval *(n)* a shape like an egg. **oval** *(adj).*

ovation *(n)* loud applause and cheering.

oven *(n)* an enclosed space where you cook food.

over
1 *(prep)* above or on top of something. *The shelf over the bed.*
2 *(prep)* across. *Rachel stepped over the line.*
3 *(prep)* more than. *Over 12 years old.*
4 *(adv)* leaning or falling down. *John fell over.*
5 *(adj)* finished. *The match was over in two hours.*
6 *(adv)* remaining. *I divided the candy among everyone, and still had three left over.*
7 If you **get over** an illness or an experience, you recover from it and are no longer ill or upset.

overall *(adv)* generally or considering everything. *Overall, I think the party was a success.* **overall** *(adj).*

overalls *(plural n)* loose pants with shoulder straps and a panel covering the chest.

overbearing *(adj)* very dominating or bossy.

overboard *(adv)* over the side of a boat. *The pirate fell overboard.*

overcast *(adj)* An **overcast** sky has dark clouds.

overcome
overcoming overcame overcome
1 *(v)* to defeat or deal with something, such as a feeling or problem. *I must overcome my fear of spiders.*
2 *(v)* If someone is **overcome** by smoke, emotion, guilt, etc. they are so strongly affected by it that they are made unconscious or helpless.

overdo overdoes overdoing overdid overdone *(v)* to do something too much.

overdraft *(n)* an amount of money that someone takes out of their bank when they do not have any money in their account. **overdrawn** *(adj).*

overdue *(adj)* late. *My library books are overdue.*

overflow
overflowing overflowed *(v)* to flow over the edges of something. *The bathtub overflowed.*

overgrown *(adj)* An **overgrown** garden is covered with weeds because it has not been looked after.

overhaul
overhauling overhauled *(v)* to examine carefully all the parts of a piece of equipment and make any repairs that are needed. **overhaul** *(n).*

overhead
1 *(adj)* above your head. *Overhead lighting.* **overhead** *(adv)*.
2 **overheads** *(plural n)* regular business costs, such as wages, rent, telephone, heating, and lighting.

overhear overhearing overheard *(v)* to hear what someone else is saying when they do not know that you are listening.

overjoyed *(adj)* If you are **overjoyed**, you are extremely happy. *Joel was overjoyed to win the race.*

overlap
overlapping overlapped *(v)* to cover part of something else. *Arrange the roof tiles so that they overlap. Our vacation dates overlap.*

overleaf *(adv)* on the next page.

overload overloading overloaded
1 *(v)* to give something or someone too much to carry or too much work to do. **overload** *(n)*.
2 *(v)* to send too much electricity through something so that it breaks down. **overload** *(n)*.

overlook overlooking overlooked
1 *(v)* to fail to notice something. *Daisy overlooked the extra costs.*
2 *(v)* to offer a view of something from above. *Our room overlooked the beach.*
3 *(v)* to choose to ignore something wrong that someone has done. *I overlooked Jude's rude remarks.*

overly *(adv)* very or excessively. *Oliver is always overly cautious.*

overnight
1 *(adv)* during the night. *We stayed overnight at a small hotel.* **overnight** *(adj)*.
2 *(adv)* suddenly. *Toby's fortunes changed overnight.*

overpass overpasses *(n)* a bridge that carries one road over another.

overpower
overpowering overpowered
1 *(v)* to defeat someone, because you are stronger than they are.
2 *(v)* If something **overpowers** you, it affects you very strongly. *I was overpowered by the disgusting smell.*

overrated *(adj)* If you think that something is **overrated**, you think that it is not really as good as many people say it is.

overrule overruling overruled *(v)* If someone in authority **overrules** a decision, they say that the decision was wrong and has to be changed.

overrun overrunning overran overrun
1 *(v)* to spread all over a place in large numbers. *The town was overrun with rats.*
2 *(v)* to flood beyond something. *The river overran its banks.*

overseas *(adj)* to or from other countries. *Overseas visitors.* **overseas** *(adv)*.

oversleep
oversleeping overslept *(v)* to sleep for longer than you intended.

oversight *(v)* a careless mistake. *It was an oversight not to call him.*

overtake overtaking overtook overtaken
1 *(v)* to come upon suddenly or by surprise. *A blizzard overtook the climber.*
2 *(v)* to catch up with someone.

overthrow overthrowing overthrew overthrown *(v)* to defeat a leader or ruler and remove them from power by force. **overthrow** *(n)*.

overtime *(n)*
time spent working beyond normal working hours.

overture *(n)*
a piece of music played at the start of a musical, opera, or ballet.

overturn
overturning overturned
1 *(v)* to turn something over so that it is upside down, or on its side.
2 *(v)* to reverse a decision that someone else has made.

overweight *(adj)*
too fat or too heavy.

overwhelm
overwhelming overwhelmed
1 *(v)* to defeat someone completely.
2 *(v)* to have a very strong effect. *I was overwhelmed by the applause.* **overwhelming** *(adj)*.

overwork
overworking overworked *(v)* to work too hard.

owe owing owed
1 *(v)* to have to pay money to someone, especially money that you have borrowed.
2 *(v)* to have a duty to do something for someone in return for something that they have done for you. *I owe you a favor.*
3 *(v)* to be grateful to someone for giving you something. *My sister owes her life to the brave firefighters.*

owl *(n)* a bird with large eyes, which hunts at night. *The tawny owl, shown below, is found throughout Europe.*

own owning owned
1 *(adj)* belonging to you. *My own pen.*
2 *(v)* to possess or to have something. **owner** *(n)*.
3 *(v)* If you **own up** to something, you confess that you have done something wrong.
4 **on your own** alone and by yourself.

ox oxen *(n)*
a large, horned mammal often used for carrying things or for pulling carts.

oxygen *(n)*
a colorless gas found in the air that humans and animals need to breathe.

oxymoron *(n)*
a short phrase in which the words seem to contradict each other, for example, "a wise fool."

oyster *(n)*
a flat, edible shellfish that occasionally contains a pearl. *See* **pearl**.

ozone
1 *(n)* a form of oxygen that can be poisonous in large quantities.
2 **ozone layer** *(n)* a layer of ozone high above the Earth's surface that blocks out some of the Sun's harmful rays. *In 1985, scientists discovered a hole in the ozone layer above Antarctica. Chemicals thought to cause the hole have been banned, and the hole has begun to shrink. In this satellite picture, the ozone hole is colored orange. Also see* **atmosphere**.

Pp

pace pacing paced
1 *(n)* a step or a stride.
2 *(n)* a rate of speed. *A rapid pace.*
3 *(v)* to walk backward and forward. *Archie paced up and down the hall.*

pacemaker *(n)* a machine put into someone's body to help their heart beat more regularly.

pacifier *(n)* a plastic or rubber teat given to a baby to suck on.

pacifist *(n)* someone who strongly believes that war and violence are wrong and who will not fight. **pacifism** *(n).*

pacify
pacifies pacifying pacified *(v)*
If you **pacify** someone, you make them feel calmer.

pack packing packed
1 *(v)* to put objects into a box, case, bag, etc. **packing** *(n).*
2 *(v)* to fill a space tightly. *A vast crowd packed the stadium.*
3 *(n)* a collection of objects. *A pack of cards.*
4 *(n)* a group of wild animals. *A pack of wolves.*
5 *(n)* a bundle or a load.
6 *(n)* a large quantity or amount. *A pack of lies.*

package
1 *(n)* a parcel or a bundle of something that is packed, wrapped, or put in a box. *I received a package in the mail.*
2 *(n)* a carton, box, or case that can be packed with something.

packaging *(n)* the wrapping on things that you buy.

packet *(n)* a small container or package. *A packet of seeds.*

pact *(n)* an agreement, often between two countries.

pad padding padded
1 *(n)* a wad of soft material used to absorb liquid, give protection, etc.
2 *(v)* to cover something with soft material.
3 *(v)* to walk around softly. *Barney padded along the corridor.*
4 *(n)* sheets of paper fastened together.

padding
1 *(n)* stuffing.
2 *(n)* extra words put into a speech or piece of writing to make it longer.

paddle paddling paddled
1 *(v)* to walk in shallow water.
2 *(n)* a short, wide oar used to propel some boats. **paddle** *(v).* *See* **inflatable, kayak.**

paddle steamer *(n)*
a boat that is propelled by large, revolving paddle wheels that are powered by a steam engine.

paddle steamer

paddock *(n)*
a small field where horses can be kept.

paddy *(n)*
a wet field where rice is grown.

paddy

padlock
(n) a lock with a U-shaped metal bar that you can put through an opening or link and snap shut.

page
1 *(n)* a sheet of paper in a book, newspaper, etc.
2 *(n)* In the past, **pages** were young, boy servants. Nowadays, a page is a boy attendant at a wedding.

pageant *(paj-ent) (n)*
a public show where people walk in processions or act out historical scenes. **pageantry** *(n).*

pager *(n)* a small electronic machine that people such as doctors carry so that they can be contacted easily.

pail *(n)* a bucket.

pain
1 *(n)* a feeling of physical hurt or of great unhappiness.
2 **pains** *(plural n)* effort or trouble. *John took great pains over his essay.*

painful *(adj)* If something is **painful**, it hurts you physically or makes you very unhappy. **painfully** *(adv).*

painkiller *(n)* a pill or other medicine that you take to stop pain.

painless *(adj)* free from pain.

painstaking *(adj)* careful and thorough. **painstakingly** *(adv).*

paint painting painted
1 *(n)* a liquid that you use to color surfaces.
2 *(v)* to use paint to make a picture or cover a surface. **painter** *(n),* **painting** *(n).*

pair *(n)* two things that match or go together. **pair** *(v).*

pal *(n)* a good friend or a buddy.

palace *(n)* a large splendid house or building. **palatial** *(adj).*

palate
1 *(n)* the roof of your mouth.
2 *(n)* a person's sense of taste.

pale paler palest *(adj)*
light or whitish in color. **paleness** *(n).*

palette
1 *(n)* a flat board that you use to mix paints on, with a hole for your thumb. *See* **artist.**
2 **palette knife** *(n)*
a thin rounded flexible knife used for painting or cooking. *See* **artist.**

palindrome *(n)*
a word or sentence that reads the same backward as forward. *The names Hannah, Bob and Otto are palindromes.*

pallid *(adj)* If you are **pallid**, you have a pale face or skin.

palm
1 *(n)* the flat surface on the inside of your hand.
2 *(n)* a tall tropical tree with large leaves at the top.

palmetto *(n)* a type of palm tree with fan-shaped leaves that grows in the southern United States.

palmistry *(n)* the practice of telling people's fortunes from the lines on their palms. **palmist** *(n).*

pampas
1 *(n)* a huge treeless plain in South America.
2 **pampas grass** *(n)*
a type of tall feathery grass.

pamper pampering pampered *(v)*
to spoil yourself or someone else with food, kindness, etc.

pamphlet *(n)* a small thin booklet.

pan panning panned
1 *(n)* a round metal container used for cooking.
2 *(v)* to look for gold by washing earth in a pan or sieve.
3 *(v)* to move a camera to follow an action. *The cameraman panned across the speeding car.*

pancake *(n)*
a round flat cake made from batter and cooked in a pan.

ancreas *(n)* a gland near your 'omach that makes a fluid that elps you to digest food. *ee* **digestion**.

anda *(n)* bear that ves in China. *he picture ıows a giant anda eating a amboo shoot.*

giant panda

ane *(n)* sheet f glass in window r door.

anel *(n)* a flat iece of wood r other material. **paneling** *(n)*. *(n)* a board with controls r instruments on it. *(n)* a group of people chosen ɔ do something, such as judge competition. **panelist** *(n)*.

ang *(n)* a brief pain or feeling f emotion. *A pang of regret.*

anic *(n)* a feeling of terror or fright. **anic** *(v)*, **panicky** *(adj)*. If you are **panic-stricken**, you 'e struck with a sudden fear.

annier *(n)* a basket hung on an ıimal, such as a donkey. *(n)* a bag hung beside ıe rear wheel of a bicycle.

anorama *(n)* wide view of an area. **anoramic** *(adj)*.

ansy **pansies** *(n)* small garden flower, usually ɔlored purple, yellow, or white.

ant **panting** **panted** *(v)* ɔ breathe in a quick and labored vay because you are out of breath.

anther *(n)* leopard, especially the black leopard.

antomime *(n)* the telling of a story r the acting out of a play using estures, facial expressions and body ıovements instead of words.

ants *(plural n)* piece of clothing with two legs that ɔvers the lower part of your body.

anty hose *(plural n)* close-fitting piece of clothing ıat covers the hips, legs, and feet.

aper **papering** **papered** *(n)* thin material usually ıade from wood pulp. *(n)* a newspaper. 3 *(n)* a written report for school. 4 *(v)* to put wallpaper up, or cover something with paper.

paperback *(n)* a book with a paper cover.

paperweight *(n)* a heavy, often decorative object used for holding down papers.

paperwork *(n)* writing, such as reports, that is part of someone's job.

papier-mâché *(pay-pur muh-shay) (n)* the art of making models, pots, etc. out of pieces of paper that have been soaked in glue.

papyrus *(puh-pye-russ)* **papyri** *(n)* paper made from the papyrus plant, which grows in northern Africa and southern Europe.

parable *(n)* a fable or story that has a moral or religious lesson. *The parable of the Good Samaritan.*

parachute *(pa-uh-shoot) (n)* a large piece of cloth fastened to thin ropes that is used to drop people or loads safely from airplanes. **parachutist** *(n)*, **parachute** *(v)*.

paradise *(n)* a wonderful place, or heaven.

paradox **paradoxes** *(n)* a statement that seems to contradict itself, but is true. **paradoxical** *(adj)*.

paraffin *(n)* a liquid that is burned to give light or heat in a lamp or stove.

paragliding *(n)* the sport of cross-country parachuting, using a special parachute shaped like flexible wings. **paraglider** *(n)*, **paraglide** *(v)*.

paragraph *(n)* a short passage in a piece of writing that begins on a new line.

parallel
1 *(adj)* If two lines are **parallel**, they stay the same distance from each other.
2 *(n)* If a situation has a **parallel**, there is another situation very similar to it. **parallel** *(v)*.
3 If electrical parts are connected **in parallel**, each one can receive power even when the others are not being used.

parallelogram *(n)* a flat four-sided shape with opposite sides that are equal and parallel. *See* **shape**.

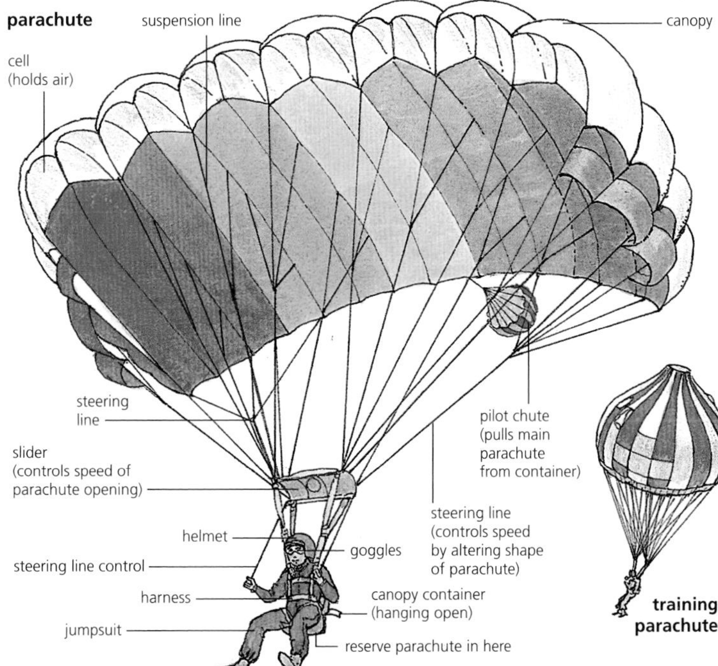

parade **parading** **paraded**
1 *(n)* a procession of people, decorated trucks, and musicians.
2 *(v)* If you **parade** something, you show it off.

paralyze **paralyzing** **paralyzed** *(v)* to make someone or something lose power, feeling, or movement. **paralysis** *(n)*.

paraphernalia *(n)* numerous pieces of equipment, belongings, etc.

paraphrase paraphrasing paraphrased *(v)* If you **paraphrase** speech or writing, you say or write it again in a different way, often to make it clearer. **paraphrase** *(n).*

paraplegic *(pair-uh-**plee**-jik) (n)* someone who has no feeling or movement in the lower part of their body. **paraplegic** *(adj).*

parasite
1 *(n)* an animal or plant that gets its food by living on or inside another animal or plant. *Leeches are parasites that use suckers to attach themselves to people or animals and then feed on their blood.* **parasitic** *(adj).*
2 *(n)* someone who lives on other people's money without doing anything to earn it.

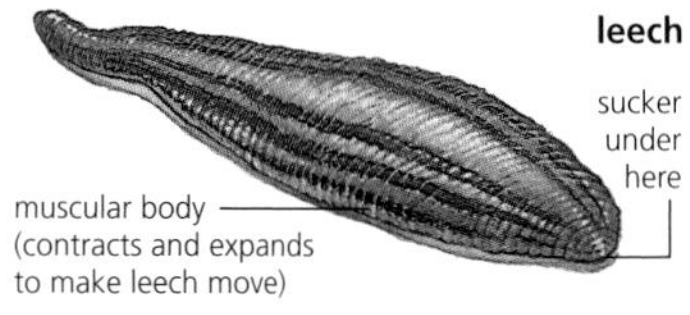

parasol *(n)* a type of umbrella that shades you from the sun.

paratroops *(plural n)* soldiers who are carried by airplane and dropped by parachute. **paratrooper** *(n).*

parcel *(n)* a package or something wrapped up in paper. **parcel** *(v).*

parched *(adj)* very dry or thirsty.

parchment
1 *(n)* heavy, paperlike material made from the skin of sheep or goats and used for writing on.
2 *(n)* very good quality writing paper.

pardon
pardoning pardoned
1 *(v)* to forgive or excuse someone, or to release them from punishment.
2 *(interject)* You say **I beg your pardon** as a polite way of asking someone to repeat what they have said, or to ask for forgiveness.

parent *(n)* a mother or father. **parenthood** *(n),* **parental** *(adj).*

parenthesis parentheses
1 *(n)* an extra phrase or explanation in brackets.
2 *(n)* one of a pair of round brackets ( ) used to mark off an extra phrase or explanation.

parish parishes
1 *(n)* an area that has its own church.
2 *(n)* the people who live in a parish.

parishioner *(n)* someone who lives in the parish of a church.

park parking parked
1 *(n)* a large garden or a piece of ground for public use.
2 *(v)* to leave a car in a parking place or on the side of a street.

parking meter *(n)* a machine that you put money into to pay for parking on the street.

parliament *(n)* the group of people who have been elected to make the laws in some countries, such as the United Kingdom and Canada. **parliamentary** *(adj).*

parody parodies *(n)* a funny imitation of a piece of writing, song, speech, etc. **parody** *(v).*

parole *(n)* the early release of a prisoner on condition that they behave well. **parole** *(v).*

paroxysm *(**par**-ox-ism) (n)* a sudden violent fit of something. *A paroxysm of laughter. A paroxysm of pain.*

parrot
1 *(n)* a tropical bird with a curved beak and brightly colored feathers. Parrots can learn to repeat things that are said to them. *The parrot shown here comes from the South American rain forest.*
2 *(n)* someone who repeats or imitates words without understanding what they mean. **parrot** *(v).*

scarlet macaw

parse parsing parsed *(v)* When you **parse** a sentence, you identify its subject and object, and, sometimes, the parts of speech of its words.

parsnip *(n)* a pale yellow root vegetable. *See* **vegetable**.

parson *(n)* a pastor or member of the clergy. **parsonage** *(n).*

part parting parted
1 *(n)* a portion or a piece.
2 *(n)* a character or role in a play or film. *Robert played the part of Hamlet.*
3 *(n)* an expected share of responsibility or work. *If everyone does their part, the show will be a success.*
4 *(n)* a line in your hair where it is combed in two directions.
5 *(v)* to separate or to divide. *We parted at the crossroads.*
6 *(v)* If you **part with** something, you give it away.

partial *(**par**-shul)*
1 *(adj)* Someone who is **partial** favors one person or side more than another. **partiality** *(n).*
2 *(adj)* not complete. *The vacation wa only a partial success.* **partially** *(adv).*
3 If you are **partial to** a particular food or drink, you are especially fond of it. **partiality** *(n).*

participate participating participated *(v)* to join in or share in an activity or event. **participant** *(n),* **participation** *(n).*

participle *(n)* a form of a verb. The English language has two participles, the present, for example "playing," and the past, for example "played." Participles can sometimes be used as adjectives, for example "shining," "crumpled," "swollen."

particle
1 *(n)* an extremely small thing or part of something.
2 **particle physics** *(singular n)* the study of the behavior of the minute parts of atoms.

particular
1 *(adj)* individual or special. *I want this particular painting.*
2 *(adj)* Someone who is **particular** is very fussy about small things.
3 *(n)* a fact or a detail. *Please send me some particulars about the course.*
4 **in particular** especially. *All the rides are fun, but there's one in particular that you must try.* **particularly** *(adv).*

parting *(n)* a separation. *An emotional parting.*

partly *(adv)* not completely.

partner
1 *(n)* one of two or more people who do something together. *Business partners. Dancing partners.* **partnership** *(n).*
2 *(n)* a husband, wife, or permanent companion.

part of speech parts of speech *(n,* a term, such as noun, verb, adjective, etc., that describes a word's type and function. *See* page 3.

part-time *(adj)* If you have a **part-time** job, you work for a few hours each day or a few days each week. **part-timer** *(n),* **part time** *(adv).*

party parties
1 *(n)* an organized occasion with music, games, entertainment, etc. when people enjoy themselves in a group. **party** *(v).*
2 *(n)* a group of people working together. *A search party.*
3 *(n)* an organized group of people with similar political beliefs who try to win elections. *The Democratic and Republican parties are the two largest political parties in the United States.*

ass passes passing passed
(v) to go past someone
r something. *Pass the*
ark and then turn left.
(v) to give something to
omebody. *Pass the salt, please.*
(v) to kick, throw, or hit a
all to someone in your team
a sport or game. **pass** *(n).*
(v) to succeed in a
est or course. **pass** *(n).*
(n) a free ticket. *Hall pass.*
pass away *(v)* to die.
pass out *(v)* to faint.

assage
(n) a corridor.
(n) a short section in
book or piece of music.
(n) a journey by ship or airplane.

assenger *(n)* someone who
avels in a car or other vehicle
nd is not the driver.

asserby passersby *(n)*
omeone who happens
be going past.

assion *(n)* a very strong
eeling of anger, love, hatred, etc.

assionate *(adj)* If you are
assionate about something
someone, you have strong
eelings about them.
assionately *(adv).*

assive
(adj) If you are **passive**,
ou let things happen to
ou and do not react when
ou are attacked. **passively** *(adv).*
(adj) A **passive** verb is one where
e verb's subject has something
one to it rather than doing the
ction itself. *In the sentence*
The ball was kicked," the verb is
assive, but in "I kicked the ball,"
e verb is active.

assover *(n)* an important
ewish holiday in the spring, in
emory of the way that God
scued the Israelites from slavery
Egypt.

assport *(n)* an official booklet
at proves who you are and
lows you to travel abroad.

assword *(n)* a secret word that
ou need to know to get into a
uilding or computer system.

ast
(n) the period of time before
e present. **past** *(adj).*
(adj) finished or ended.
(adj) previous. *I've drawn on my*
ast experience in my new job.
(prep) by, after, or beyond.
e went past us. **past** *(adv).*

5 *(n)* The **past participle** is the form of a verb used to show that something happened before the present. For example, "bought" is the past participle of "buy" and "played" is the past participle of "play."

pasta *(n)* a food made from flour, eggs, and water, which is made into shapes. *The picture shows a selection of different types of pasta.*

spaghetti
tagliatelle (ribbons)
farfalle (bows)
macaroni
rigatoni (tubes)
fusilli (twists)
conchiglie (shells)

pasta

paste pasting pasted
1 *(n)* a soft, sticky mixture that you can spread. *Tomato paste.*
2 *(v)* to stick with glue.

pastel
1 *(n)* a chalky crayon.
2 *(adj)* soft and light in color.
3 *(n)* a picture made with pastels.

pasteurized *(adj)* Milk that is **pasteurized** has been heated to kill bacteria. **pasteurize** *(v).*

pastor *(n)* a church minister or priest in charge of a congregation.

pastoral
1 *(adj)* having to do with the countryside.
2 *(adj)* **Pastoral** care is help with religious or personal matters.

pastry pastries
1 *(n)* a dough that is rolled out and used for pies.
2 *(n)* a small cake made from pastry.

pasture *(n)* grazing land for animals.

pasty pastier pastiest *(adj)* If you look **pasty**, you have a white or dull complexion.

pat patting patted
1 *(v)* to tap or stroke something gently with your hand. *Carrie patted the baby donkey.* **pat** *(n).*
2 If you give someone a **pat on the back**, you praise them and say that they have done well.

patch patches patching patched
1 *(v)* to put a piece of material on something in order to mend it. **patch** *(n).*
2 *(n)* a small, odd-shaped part of something, such as an area of white fur on a black dog.
3 *(n)* a piece of ground. *A vegetable patch.*
4 *(n)* a short period of time. *Rumer is going through a bad patch.*

patchwork *(n)* patterned fabric, made by sewing small patches of different material together.

patchy patchier patchiest *(adj)* uneven. *Patchy fog made the road dangerous.*

pâté *(pa-tay) (n)* a soft paste, usually made of meat or fish, that is spread on toast, crackers, etc.

patent patenting patented
1 *(v)* If you invent something, you can **patent** it to stop other people from copying your idea. **patent** *(n).*
2 *(adj)* obvious or open. *Leo told a patent lie.* **patently** *(adv).*
3 **patent leather** *(n)* very shiny leather used for shoes, bags, etc.

paternal *(adj)* having to do with being a father. **paternally** *(adv).*

path *(n)* a track or a route. **pathway** *(n).*

pathetic
1 *(adj)* feeble or useless.
2 *(adj)* causing pity, sorrow, or sympathy. **pathetically** *(adv).*

patience *(n)* If you have **patience**, you can put up with difficult things and are able to wait calmly.

patient
1 *(adj)* If you are **patient**, you are good at putting up with things and can wait calmly. **patiently** *(adv).*
2 *(n)* someone who is receiving medical treatment.

patio
1 *(n)* a paved area next to a house, used for sitting outside.
2 **patio doors** *(plural n)* glass doors that open out on to a patio.

patisserie *(n)* a store where you can buy cakes and pastries.

patriot *(n)* someone who loves their country and is prepared to fight for it. **patriotism** *(n),* **patriotic** *(adj).*

patrol patrolling patrolled
1 *(v)* to walk or travel around an area to protect it or to keep watch on people. *Police are patrolling the neighborhood carefully.*
2 *(n)* a group of soldiers, ships, etc., that protect and watch an area.

patron *(pay-trun)*
1 *(n)* a customer of a store, or someone who supports a theater, artist, writer, etc. **patronage** *(pay-tron-ij) (n).*
2 **patron saint** *(n)* a saint who is believed to look after a particular country or group of people.

patronize patronizing patronized
1 *(v)* to talk down to someone or act as though you are better than them.
2 *(v)* If you **patronize** a store, restaurant, etc. you go there regularly.

patter pattering pattered
1 *(v)* to make light, quick, patting sounds. *The rain pattered on my umbrella.* **patter** *(n).*
2 *(n)* fast talk. *A magician's patter.*

pattern
1 *(n)* an arrangement of colors, shapes, etc. on paper or fabric.
2 *(n)* a model that you can copy from. *A dress pattern.*
3 *(n)* If things follow a **pattern**, they happen in a similar way.

pause pausing paused *(v)* to stop for a short time. **pause** *(n).*

pavement
1 *(n)* a hard material, such as asphalt, used to cover roads or sidewalks.
2 *(n)* a paved road, or a sidewalk.

pavilion *(n)* a building that is used for shelter or recreation or for a show or exhibit, as in a park or a fair.

paw *(n)* the foot of an animal, such as a dog or cat.

pawn pawning pawned
1 *(v)* to leave a valuable item at a store called a pawnbroker's, in return for money. The item is returned to you if you repay your debt, or is sold if you fail to do so.
2 *(n)* the smallest piece on a chessboard. *See* **chess**.

pay paying paid
1 *(v)* to give money for something. **payment** *(n).*
2 *(v)* to be worthwhile, or to be advantageous. *It pays to be polite.*
3 *(v)* to give or offer something. *Hattie paid me a compliment.*
4 *(v)* to suffer. *Ed paid dearly for his mistake.*
5 *(n)* wages, or salary.

PC
1 *(n)* the initials for Personal Computer.
2 *(adj) (informal)* Someone who is **PC** makes a great effort not to offend minority groups, women, etc. The initials PC stand for Politically Correct.

PE *(n)* a class at school in which you do sports, gymnastics, etc. The initials PE stand for Physical Education.

pea *(n)* a small, green vegetable which grows in a pod. *See* **vegetable**.

peace
1 *(n)* calm and quiet. **peaceful** *(adj),* **peacefully** *(adv).*
2 *(n)* a period without war. **peacetime** *(n).*

peach peaches *(n)* a soft fruit with a furry skin and a pit at its center. *See* **fruit**.

peacock *(n)* a large, blue and green bird with long tail-feathers.

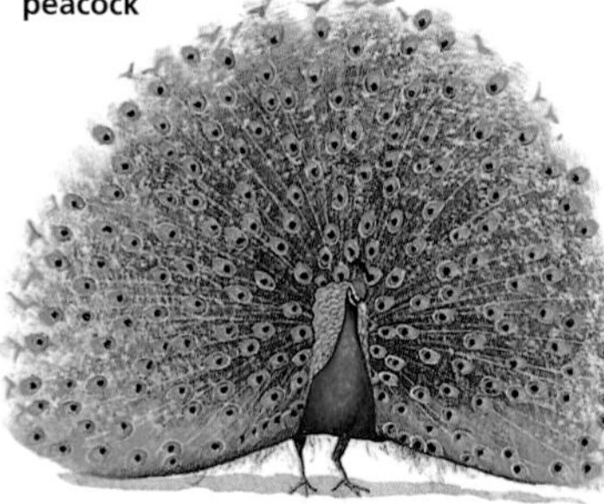
peacock

peak
1 *(n)* the top of something, such as a mountain.
2 *(n)* the highest or best point. *Carlton reached the peak of his career when he won the gold medal.* **peak** *(v).*
3 *(n)* the curved, front part of a cap.

peal pealing pealed *(v)* When bells **peal**, they ring.

pear *(n)* a juicy fruit that gets narrower towards its stalk. *See* **fruit**.

pearl *(n)* a small, round, whitish object that grows inside oysters and other shellfish and is used to make jewelry.

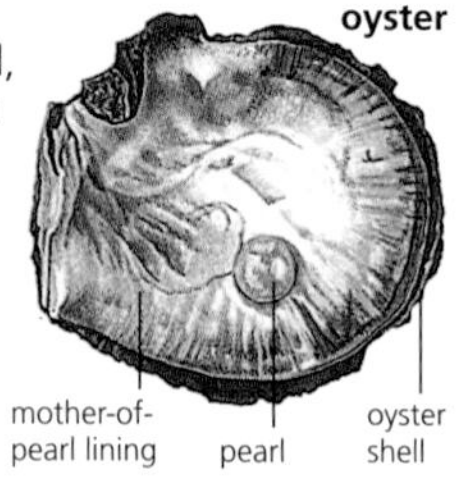

peasant
1 *(n)* someone who works on a small piece of land.
2 *(n)* In medieval times, **peasants** were agricultural laborers who worked for their local lord.

peat *(n)* dark brown, partly decayed vegetable matter that can be used as fuel or compost.

pebble *(n)* a small, round stone. **pebbly** *(adj).*

peck pecking pecked
1 *(v)* When a bird **pecks** at something, it strikes it or picks it up with its beak.
2 *(n) (informal)* a quick kiss. *Aunt Doris gave me a peck on the cheek.* **peck** *(v).*

peculiar
1 *(adj)* strange, or odd. **peculiarly** *(adv).*
2 **peculiar to** belonging to, or exclusive to. *Koalas are peculiar to Australia.* **peculiarity** *(n),* **peculiarly** *(adv).*

pedal pedaling pedaled
1 *(n)* a lever on a bicycle, car, piano, etc. that you push with your foot.
2 *(v)* to make something work or move by using a pedal or pedals.

peddle peddling peddled *(v)* to travel around selling things. **peddler** *(n).*

pedestal *(n)* a base for a statue.

pedestrian *(n)* someone who travels by foot.

pediatrician *(n)* a doctor who specializes in the care and treatment of children.

peek peeking peeked *(v)* to glance or look secretly at something. **peek** *(n).*

peel peeling peeled
1 *(n)* the tough outer skin of a fruit.
2 *(v)* to remove the peel of a fruit.
3 *(v)* to come off. *I got so sunburned that the skin on my back peeled.*

peer peering peered
1 *(v)* to look hard at something that is difficult to see.
2 *(n)* a nobleman. **peerage** *(n).*
3 *(plural n)* Your **peers** are people of similar age and type to you.

peg *(n)* a small piece of wood, metal, or plastic, used to hold things down or hang things up. **peg** *(v).*

pelican *(n)* a large water bird with a pouch below its beak where it holds the fish that it catches.

pelican

)ellet
ı *(n)* a small, rounded piece
of something, such as food
or balled-up paper.
2 *(n)* a small
ead ball fired
rom a gun.
3 *(n)* Many
birds make
pellets, which
are clumps of
things that they
cannot digest.
Pellets are
made in the
bird's stomach
and then
egurgitated,
or coughed up.

herring gull's pellet

bone
foil
plastic
string

pelt pelting pelted
ı *(v)* to strike or beat
again and again.
2 *(n)* an animal's skin or fur.

pen penning penned
ı *(n)* an instrument used
for writing with ink.
2 *(n)* a small, fenced area
for sheep, cattle, etc.
3 *(v)* to keep or shut up in a pen.

penalize penalizing penalized *(v)*
o make someone suffer
a punishment for something
hat they have done wrong.

penalty penalties
ı *(n)* a punishment.
2 *(n)* a disadvantage imposed
on a team or player in a game
when they break a rule.

pencil *(n)* an instrument
used for drawing and writing,
made from a stick of graphite
n a wood casing.

pendant *(n)*
a piece of jewelry that hangs
on a chain around the neck.

pendulum *(n)* a weight in
ome clocks that moves from
ide to side and helps to keep
he clock ticking regularly.

penetrate
penetrating penetrated *(v)*
o go inside something or through
omething. *The nail penetrated
Nick's shoe.* **penetration** *(n)*.

penguin *(n)*
large seabird that cannot fly,
nd that uses its wings as
lippers for underwater swimming.
See **polar**.

penicillin *(n)*
drug that kills bacteria and
elps to fight some diseases.

peninsula *(n)* a piece of land that sticks out into the sea, and is surrounded on three sides by water. *The map shows the state of Florida, which is a peninsula.* **peninsular** *(adj)*.

peninsula

penitent *(adj)* extremely sorry. **penitence** *(n)*.

pen name *(n)* a public name used by a writer.

penniless *(adj)* If you are **penniless**, you have absolutely no money.

penny pennies *or* pence *(n)* the smallest coin, in size and value.

pension *(n)* an amount of money paid regularly to someone who has retired from work. **pensioner** *(n)*.

pentagon
1 *(n)* a five-sided shape. **pentagonal** *(adj)*. *See* **shape**.
2 *(n)* **The Pentagon** is the Headquarters of the Department of Defense.

penultimate *(adj)* next to last. *"This" is the penultimate word in this sentence.*

people *(plural n)* human beings.

pepper
1 *(n)* a spicy powder used to flavor food. **peppery** *(adj)*.
2 *(n)* a hollow vegetable, usually red, green, or yellow. *See* **vegetable**.

peppermint
1 *(n)* a herb often used in flavoring.
2 *(n)* a peppermint-flavored candy.

per
1 *(prep)* in each, or for each. *There's enough for three candies per person.*
2 **per annum** *(adv)* each year.
3 **per capita** *(adj)* for each person.

perceive perceiving perceived *(v)* to notice something, or to understand a situation.

percent *(n)* one in every hundred. *Ten percent of a hundred is ten.*

percentage *(n)* a fraction or proportion of something, expressed as a number out of a hundred. The symbol for percentage is %.

perceptive *(adj)* If you are **perceptive**, you are quick to notice things or understand situations.

perch perches perching perched
1 *(n)* a place where a bird stands.
2 *(v)* to sit or stand on the edge of something, often high up.
3 *(n)* an edible, freshwater fish. *See* **fish**.

percussion *(n)* musical instruments that are played by being hit or shaken. *The picture shows some small percussion instruments.* **percussionist** *(n)*.

percussion instruments

perennial
1 *(n)* a flower that blooms every year.
2 *(adj)* happening repeatedly. *A perennial problem.* **perennially** *(adv)*.

perfect perfecting perfected
1 *(pur-fect) (adj)* without any faults. **perfection** *(n)*, **perfectly** *(adv)*.
2 *(pur-**fect**) (v)* to succeed, with effort, in making something work well. *After much practice, Callum perfected his juggling act.*

perforated *(adj)* **Perforated** paper has many small holes punched in it, usually so that a section can be torn off easily. **perforation** *(n)*.

perform performing performed
1 *(v)* to do something or to carry something out.
2 *(v)* to give a show in public.

performance *(n)* the public acting of a play, showing of a movie, etc.

perfume *(n)* a liquid you put on your skin to make yourself smell pleasant.

perhaps *(adv)* possibly.

peril *(n)* serious danger. **perilous** *(adj)*, **perilously** *(adv)*.

perimeter
1 *(n)* the outside edge of an area.
2 *(n)* the distance around the edge of a shape or an area.

period
1 *(n)* a length of time. *Ewan left the room for a short period.*
2 *(n)* the punctuation mark (.) used to show that a sentence has ended or that a word has been abbreviated.

periodical
1 *(adj)* happening at intervals. **periodically** *(adv)*.
2 *(n)* a journal or magazine that is published regularly.

periphery peripheries *(n)* the outside edge of something.

periscope *(n)* a vertical tube with prisms at each end that allows you to see something from a position a long way below it. Periscopes are used in submarines. *The diagram shows how a periscope works.*

periscope

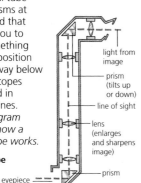

perish perishes perishing perished
1 *(v)* to die.
2 *(v)* If a substance, such as food or rubber, **perishes**, it becomes rotten.

perk perking perked
1 *(n) (informal)* an extra advantage that comes from doing a particular job. *One of the perks of working in this café is the free food.*
2 *(v)* If you **perk up**, you become more cheerful or alert. **perky** *(adj)*.

perm *(n)* a process in which hair is treated with chemicals to give it curls or waves that last for several months. Perm is short for permanent wave.

permanent *(adj)* lasting for a long time or forever. **permanence** *(n)*, **permanently** *(adv)*.

permeate permeating permeated *(v)* to spread or pass through something. *A delicious smell permeated the house.*

permissible *(adj)* If something is **permissible**, it is allowed.

permission *(n)* If you give **permission** for something, you say that it can happen.

permissive *(adj)* Someone who is **permissive** is very tolerant and allows freedom where others would not. **permissiveness** *(n)*.

permit permitting permitted
1 *(pur-**mit**) (v)* to allow something.
2 *(**pur**-mit) (n)* a written statement giving permission for something.

permutation *(n)* one of the ways in which a series of things can be arranged or put in order. *There are six permutations of the numbers 1, 2, and 3: 123, 132, 213, 231, 312, and 321.*

perpendicular *(n)* a line at right angles to another line, or vertical to the ground. **perpendicular** *(adj)*.

perpetual *(adj)* never-ending or unchanging. **perpetually** *(adv)*.

perplex perplexes perplexing perplexed *(v)* to make someone puzzled and slightly worried. **perplexity** *(n)*, **perplexed** *(adj)*.

persecute persecuting persecuted *(v)* to treat someone cruelly and unfairly because you are prejudiced against them. **persecution** *(n)*.

persevere persevering persevered *(v)* If you **persevere** at something, you keep on trying and do not give up. **perseverance** *(n)*.

persist persisting persisted *(v)* to keep on doing something. **persistence** *(n)*, **persistent** *(adj)*.

person people
1 *(n)* an individual human being.
2 If you do something **in person**, you do it yourself.
3 In grammar, the **first person** refers to "I" or "we," the **second person** refers to "you," the **third person** refers to "he," "she," "it," or "they."

personal *(adj)* having to do with one person only. *This letter is personal and private.* **personally** *(adv)*.

personal computer *(n)* a small computer that can stand on a desk or table and can be used at home.

personality personalities
1 *(n)* the type of character that someone has. *Florence has a very outgoing personality.*
2 *(n)* a famous person. *A show business personality.*

perspective
1 *(n)* a particular way of looking at a situation. *I enjoyed the trip, but from Guy's perspective it was a total disaster.*
2 If a picture is **in perspective**, distant objects are drawn smaller than nearer ones so that the view looks exactly as someone would see it.

perspire perspiring perspired *(v)* to sweat. **perspiration** *(n)*.

persuade persuading persuaded *(v)* to make someone do something by telling them reasons why they should do it. **persuasion** *(n)*, **persuasive** *(adj)*.

perturb perturbing perturbed *(v)* to worry or confuse somebody. *Harry's questions perturbed me.*

perverse *(adj)* deliberately unreasonable and stubborn. **perversity** *(n)*.

peso *(**peh**-soh) (n)* the main unit of money in Mexico, Argentina, the Philippines, etc.

pessimistic *(adj)* People who are **pessimistic** are gloomy and always think that the worst will happen. **pessimism** *(n)*, **pessimist** *(n)*, **pessimistically** *(adv)*.

pest
1 *(n)* an insect that destroys or damages flowers, fruit, or vegetables.
2 *(n)* any creature that causes serious interference with human activity.
3 *(n)* a persistently annoying person.

pester pestering pestered *(v)* to keep annoying other people, often by asking or telling them something again and again.

pesticide *(n)* a chemical used to kill pests, usually insects.

pestle *(pess-ul) (n)* a short stick with a thick rounded end, used to crush things in a bowl called a mortar.

pet petting petted
1 *(n)* a tame animal kept for company or pleasure.
2 *(n)* somebody's favorite person or thing. *Teacher's pet.*
3 *(v)* to stroke or pat an animal in a gentle, loving way.

petal *(n)* one of the colored, outer parts of a flower head. *See* **flower**.

petition *(n)* a letter, signed by many people, asking those in power to change their policy or actions.

petrified *(adj)* If you are **petrified**, you are unable to move because you are so frightened.

petroleum *(n)* a thick, oily liquid found beneath the Earth's surface. It is used to make gasoline, kerosene, heating oil, and many other products.

petticoat *(n)* a thin garment worn underneath a skirt or dress. *See* **underclothes**.

petty pettier pettiest *(adj)* trivial and unimportant. *Petty criticisms.*

pH *(n)* a measure of how acidic or alkaline a substance is. The initials pH stand for potential of hydrogen. *Acids have pH values under seven and alkalis have pH values over seven. The picture below shows strips of indicator paper. An indicator is a substance that changes color when it is placed in an acid or an alkali.*

phantom *(n)* a ghost.

Pharaoh *(fair-oh) (n)* one of the kings of ancient Egypt.

Pharaoh

pharmacist *(n)* a trained person who prepares and sells drugs and medicines. **pharmacy** *(n).*

phase phasing phased
1 *(n)* a stage in someone or something's growth or development. *Jack is going through a quarrelsome phase.*
2 **phase in** *(v)* to start something gradually.
3 **phase out** *(v)* to stop something gradually.

pheasant *(fez-ant) (n)* a large bird with a long tail. It is shot for sport and for food.

pheasant

phenomenal *(fuh-nom-in-al) (adj)* amazing or astonishing. *The group's first album was a phenomenal success.* **phenomenally** *(adv).*

phenomenon *(fuh-nom-in-on)* **phenomena** *(n)* something very unusual and remarkable.

philosophical *(fil-us-off-ik-al)*
1 *(adj)* having to do with philosophy.
2 *(adj)* If you are **philosophical**, you accept difficulties and problems calmly. **philosophically** *(adv).*

philosophy *(fil-oss-off-ee)*
1 *(n)* the study of ideas about human life. **philosopher** *(n).*
2 *(n)* A person's **philosophy** is their set of basic ideas and beliefs on how life should be lived.

phlegm *(flem) (n)* the thick substance that you cough up when you have a cold.

phobia *(n)* an overpowering fear of something. **phobic** *(adj).*

phone *short for* **telephone**.

phonetically *(adv)* If something is spelled **phonetically**, it is spelled using special symbols to represent the sounds it contains.

phonetics *(singular n)* the study of the sounds used in speaking.

photo *short for* **photograph**.

photocopier *(n)* a machine that copies documents instantly.

photocopy photocopies *(n)* a copy of a document made by a photocopier. **photocopy** *(v).*

photo finish photo finishes *(n)* a very close end to a race, so close that a photograph has to be studied to decide who has won.

photogenic *(foh-toh-jen-ik) (adj)* If someone is **photogenic**, they look very good in photographs. **photogenically** *(adv).*

photograph *(n)* an image recorded by a camera, and then printed or developed on paper, or stored digitally.

photography *(n)* the creation of pictures using a camera. **photographer** *(n),* **photographic** *(adj).*

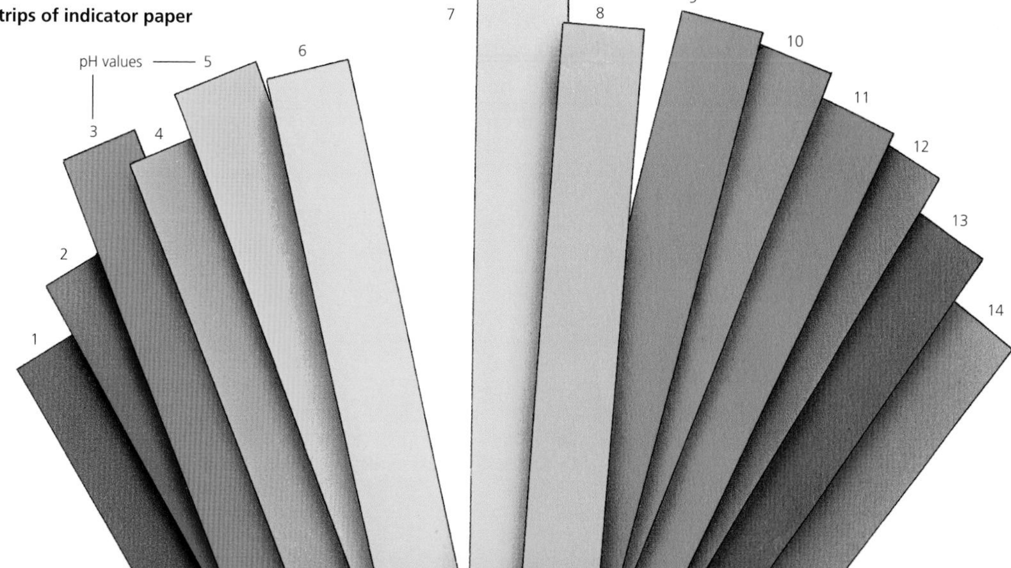

strips of indicator paper

a b c d e f g h i j k l m n o p q r s t u v w x y z

photosynthesis *(n)* a chemical process by which green plants make their food. Plants use energy from the Sun to turn water and carbon dioxide into food, and give off oxygen as a by-product. **photosynthesize** *(v)*.

phrase *(n)* a group of words that has a meaning but does not form a sentence.

physical
1 *(adj)* having to do with the body. *Physical education.* **physically** *(adv)*.
2 *(adj)* having to do with the shape and appearance of things. *Physical geography.* **physically** *(adv)*.

physical therapy *(n)* treatment for damaged muscles and joints, using exercise and massage. **physical therapist** *(n)*.

physics *(singular n)* the scientific study of energy, movement, heat, sound, light, etc. **physicist** *(n)*.

piano
1 *(n)* a large keyboard instrument that produces musical sounds when padded hammers strike tuned strings. **pianist** *(n)*.
2 *(adv)* softly. "Piano" is an Italian word, used as an instruction in music.

4 *(v)* If you **pick at** something, you take little bits off of it.
5 *(v)* If someone **picks on** you, they keep criticizing you.

picket picketing picketed *(v)* to stand outside a place of work, making a protest and sometimes trying to prevent people from entering. **picket** *(n)*, **picketer** *(n)*.

pickle pickling pickled
1 *(v)* to preserve food in vinegar or in salt water.
2 *(n)* a cucumber or other vegetable that has been preserved in vinegar.
3 *(n) (informal)* a difficult situation. *Jim was in a pickle.*

pickpocket *(n)* someone who steals from people's pockets or bags.

pickup *(n)* a small truck with an open back.

picky pickier pickiest *(adj) (informal)* fussy or choosy. *A picky eater.*

picnic picnicking picnicked
1 *(n)* a packed meal taken away from home to be eaten out of doors.
2 *(v)* to eat a picnic. **picnicker** *(n)*.

pictorial *(adj)* using pictures. *A pictorial guide.* **pictorially** *(adv)*.

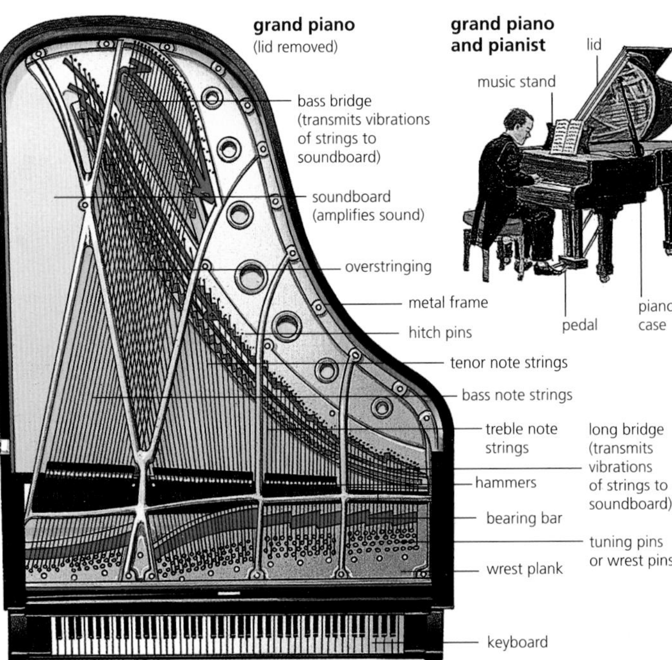

pick picking picked
1 *(v)* to choose or to select. *Pick a number.*
2 *(v)* to collect or to gather. *Have you picked all the strawberries?*
3 *(n)* a tool with pointed metal ends, used for breaking up earth or stones.

picture picturing pictured
1 *(n)* an image of something, for example a painting, photograph, or sketch.
2 *(v)* to imagine something. *I pictured Jim as tall, dark, and handsome.* **picture** *(n)*.

picturesque *(pik-chur-esk) (adj)* If a place or view is **picturesque**, it is beautiful to look at.

pie *(n)* a pastry shell filled with meat, fruit, etc. and baked in an oven.

piece piecing pieced
1 *(n)* a bit or section of something.
2 *(n)* something written or made. *A piece of embroidery.*
3 **piece together** *(v)* to put pieces together, or to put facts together.

pier
1 *(n)* a platform of metal and wood extending over the sea.
2 *(n)* a pillar supporting a bridge.

pierce piercing pierced *(v)* to make a hole in something. *Andy has had his ear pierced.*

piercing *(adj)* very loud and shrill. *A piercing scream.*

pig
1 *(n)* a farm animal with a blunt snout, which is kept for its meat.
2 *(n) (informal)* a greedy and disgusting person.

pigeon *(n)* a common, gray bird, sometimes used for racing or for carrying messages.

pigeon

piggy-back *(adv)* If someone carries you **piggy-back**, they carry you on their shoulders or on their back.

piggy bank *(n)* a container, often in the shape of a pig, used for saving coins.

pigment *(n)* a substance that gives color to something. There is pigment in paints and in your skin.

pigsty pigsties
1 *(n)* a shelter and yard where pigs are kept. Also called a pigpen.
2 *(n)* a very untidy and often dirty place. *Your bedroom is a pigsty!*

pigtail *(n)* a length of hair that has been divided into three and braided together.

pile
1 *(n)* a heap or mound of something. **pile** *(v)*.
2 **pileup** *(n) (informal)* a serious road crash involving several vehicles.

pilfer pilfering pilfered *(v)* to steal small things. **pilferer** *(n)*.

pilgrim *(n)* someone who goes on a journey to worship at a holy place. **pilgrimage** *(n)*.

pill *(n)* a small, solid tablet of medicine.

Some words that begin with a "pi" sound are spelled "py."

pillar *(n)* a column that supports part of a building. *See* **column**.

pillow *(n)* a large soft cushion on which you rest your head when you are lying in bed.

pillowcase *(n)* a fabric cover that you put over a pillow to keep it clean.

pilot **piloting piloted**
1 *(n)* someone who flies an aircraft.
2 *(n)* someone who steers a ship in and out of port.
3 *(v)* to control or guide something.
4 *(adj)* done as an experiment. *A pilot television program.* **pilot** *(n).*

pimple *(n)* a small raised acne spot on the skin. **pimply** *(adj).*

pin **pinning pinned**
1 *(n)* a thin pointed piece of metal usually used to join material together.
2 *(v)* to join things together with a pin. *Please can you pin up the hem of my dress?*
3 *(v)* to hold something or someone firmly in position. *I pinned a notice on the board. Sophia pinned me against the wall.*

pinball *(n)* a game in which you shoot small balls around a number of obstacles on a table.

pincer *(pin-ser)*
1 *(n)* the pinching claw of a shellfish, such as a crab. *See* **crab**.
2 **pincers** *(plural n)* a tool for gripping and pulling things, especially for pulling out nails.

pinch **pinches pinching pinched**
1 *(v)* to squeeze someone's skin painfully between your thumb and index finger. **pinch** *(n).*
2 *(n)* a small amount of something. *A pinch of salt.*

pine **pining pined**
1 *(n)* a tall, straight evergreen tree, with cones and needles rather than leaves.
2 *(v)* If you **pine** for someone, you feel very sad because you are separated from them.

pineapple *(n)* a large tropical fruit with yellow flesh and a tough skin. *See* **fruit**.

pink *(n)* a pale red color. **pink** *(adj).*

pins and needles
1 *(singular n) (informal)* a prickly, tingling feeling that you get when some of the blood supply to part of your body has been cut off.
2 *(singular n)* If you are **on pins and needles**, you are very nervous or jumpy about something that is going to happen.

pinstripe *(n)* a fabric with a very narrow stripe.

pioneer
1 *(n)* someone who explores unknown territory and settles there.
2 *(n)* one of the first people to work in a new and unknown area. *The Wright brothers were pioneers of flight.* **pioneer** *(v).*

pious *(py-uss) (adj)* Someone who is **pious** practices their religion faithfully and seriously. **piety** *(n),* **piously** *(adv).*

pipe **piping piped**
1 *(n)* a tube, usually used to carry liquids.
2 *(v)* to send something along pipes, tubes, or wires.
3 *(n)* a tube with holes in it used as a musical instrument or as part of an instrument. *The picture below shows some panpipes from Peru.*
4 **piped music** *(n)* music that is played all over a building.

pipeline
1 *(n)* a large pipe that carries water, gas, oil, etc. over long distances.
2 If something is **in the pipeline**, it is being planned.

panpipes

piping
1 *(n)* a system of pipes.
2 *(n)* a thin, pipe-like line of decoration on a cake, chair, etc.
3 *(adj)* very high or shrill.
4 If food is **piping hot**, it is very hot.

pirate **pirating pirated**
1 *(n)* someone who attacks and steals from ships at sea. **piracy** *(n).*
2 *(v)* If someone **pirates** a song, computer game, etc., they make illegal copies of the original version and sell them. **pirated** *(adj).*

pistachio *(n)* a small green nut with a hard shell.

pistol *(n)* a small handgun.

pit **pitting pitted**
1 *(n)* a hole in the ground.
2 *(n)* a small dip.
3 *(n)* the small hard seed of fruits such as plums, peaches, olives, etc.
4 *(v)* If two people are **pitted against** each other, they are made to compete with each other.
5 *(n)* When race cars **make a pit stop**, they pull in for fuel and repairs during a race.
6 **the pits** *(adj)* a very bad or the worst example of something. *This party is the pits.*

pitch **pitches pitching pitched**
1 *(n)* the level of a musical note.
2 *(v)* When you **pitch** a tent, you put it up.
3 *(v)* to throw something, especially a baseball.

pitcher
1 *(n)* an open-topped water container like a large jug.
2 *(n)* the person who throws the ball at the batter in a baseball game.

pitchfork *(n)* a long-handled fork with two prongs used for lifting hay.

pitfall *(n)* a hidden danger or difficulty.

pitiful
1 *(adj)* causing or deserving pity. *The lost children were in a pitiful state.* **pitifully** *(adv).*
2 *(adj)* useless or worthless. *This essay is a pitiful effort!* **pitifully** *(adv).*

pitiless *(adj)* If someone is **pitiless**, they show no pity or mercy. **pitilessly** *(adv).*

pity **pities pitying pitied** *(v)* If you **pity** someone, you feel sorry for them. **pity** *(n),* **pityingly** *(adv).*

pivot *(n)* the central point on which something turns or balances. **pivot** *(v).*

pixel *(n)* one of the tiny dots on a screen making up the visual image.

pixie *or* **pixy** *(n)* a small elf or fairy in legends and fairy tales.

pizza *(n)* a flat, round base of dough baked with toppings of cheese, tomato sauce, and other foods.

placard *(n)* a poster, nameplate, or notice.

placate **placating placated** *(v)* to make someone calm or happy, often by giving them something that they want.

place **placing placed**
1 *(n)* a particular area or position.
2 *(v)* to put something somewhere, deliberately and carefully. *Kim placed the goldfish bowl out of harm's way.*
3 *(v)* to identify by linking a person or object with a location. *I know I've met you before, but I can't place you.*
4 If something is **in place**, it is in its proper position.

Some words that begin with a "pi" sound are spelled "py."

placid *(plass-id) (adj)* Someone who is **placid** is calm and even-tempered. **placidly** *(adv).*

plague *(playg)* **plaguing plagued**
1 *(n)* a serious disease that spreads quickly to many people.
2 *(v)* If something **plagues** you, you are troubled and annoyed by it. *The explorers were plagued by flies.*

plaid *(rhymes with bad) (n)* cloth with a pattern of checks of different colors and sizes, usually made in Scotland.

plain **plainer plainest**
1 *(adj)* ordinary in appearance, and not fancy or beautiful.
2 *(n)* a large, level area of land.
3 *(adj)* simple and straightforward. *Just give me the plain facts.*
4 **plainclothes** *(n)* ordinary clothes, rather than a uniform. *The police wore plainclothes.* **plainclothes** *(adj).*

plaintive *(adj)* sad and mournful. *A plaintive cry.* **plaintively** *(adv).*

plan **planning planned**
1 *(v)* to figure out how you will do something. **plan** *(n).*
2 *(v)* If you **plan** to do something, you intend to do it. *I planned to go shopping today.*
3 *(n)* a diagram used in the construction of something.
4 *(n)* a map of a room, building, or small area.

plane
1 *(n)* a machine with wings and an engine that flies through the air. Plane is short for airplane. *See* **aircraft**.
2 *(n)* a tool used for smoothing wood. **plane** *(v). See* **woodwork**.
3 *(n)* a flat surface. *A die has six planes.*

planet *(n)* one of the round objects circling the Sun. *The picture below shows the planets of the solar system in their correct order, but not drawn to scale.* **planetary** *(adj).*

plank *(n)* a long flat strip of wood used, for example, for floorboards.

plankton *(n)* a general name for the minute animals and plants that live in water. *See* **microorganism**.

plant **planting planted**
1 *(n)* a living organism that often contains a green pigment called chlorophyll, which allows it to capture energy from the Sun. Many land plants have stems, roots, and leaves. *Also see* **flower**.
2 *(v)* to put plants or seeds in the ground so that they can grow.
3 *(v)* to put something in a secret place. *Terrorists planted a bomb in the store.*
4 *(n)* a factory, laboratory, or power station. *A chemical plant.*
5 *(n)* large industrial machinery or buildings.

buttercup
petal
flower
flower bud
auxiliary bud
lateral shoot
internode (area between two nodes)
leaf node
leaf
leaf stalk or petiole
stem
root
root hairs

plantation
1 *(n)* a farm in a hot country where coffee, tea, etc. are grown.
2 *(n)* a place where a large number of trees or bushes have been planted.

plaque *(plak)*
1 *(n)* a plate with words inscribed on it, usually on a wall in a public place.
2 *(n)* the coating made from food, bacteria, and saliva that forms on your teeth and can cause tooth decay.

plaster **plastering plastered**
1 *(n)* a substance made of lime, sand, and water used by builders to put a smooth finish on walls.
2 *(v)* to spread something thickly on a surface. *Joe plastered his hair with gel.*
3 **plaster cast** *(n)* a hard shell that holds the parts of a broken bone together until it mends.

plastic *(n)* a man-made substance that is light and strong and can be molded into different shapes.

plastic surgery *(singular n)* operations on skin and body tissue. Plastic surgery can be used to repair damage or to alter someone's appearance.

plate
1 *(n)* a flat dish for food.
2 *(n)* a flat sheet of glass or metal.
3 *(n)* an illustration in a book.
4 *(n)* one of the sheets of rock that make up the Earth's outer crust. *The map shows eight plates that make up the Earth's surface, sometimes known as the continental plates.*

continental plates

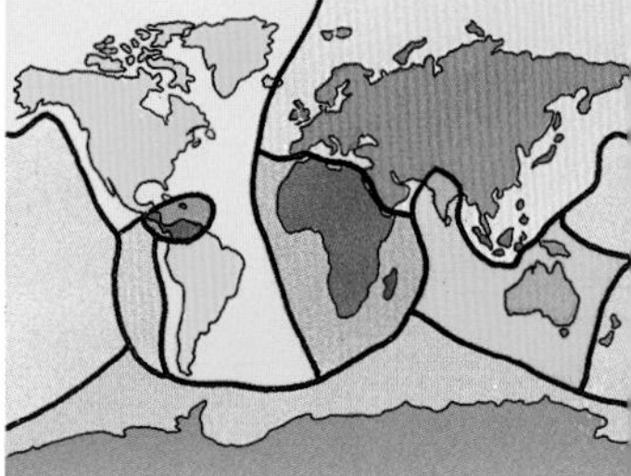

Eurasian plate
African plate
American plate
Caribbean plate
Nazca plate
Pacific plate
Antarctic plate
Indo-Australian plate

plateau *(plat-oh)* **plateaus** *or* **plateaux** *(n)* an area of high, flat land.

platform
1 *(n)* a flat, raised structure on which people or things can stand.
2 *(n)* a statement of beliefs of a group

planets

latinum *(n)*
very valuable silvery-white metal.

latypus platypuses *(n)*
n Australian mammal with
vebbed feet and a broad bill.

latypus

lausible
plaw-zib-ul) (adj) believable.
*Gus gave a plausible reason for
being so late.* **plausibly** *(adv)*.

lay playing played
(v) to take part in a game
r other enjoyable activity.
(n) a story that is acted,
usually in the theater.
(v) to make music on
n instrument. *Lesley
plays the saxophone.*
(v) to take part in a sport.
(v) to act a part in a play.

layground *(n)*
surfaced, fenced, outdoor
rea, often with swings, slides,
tc. where children can play.

layroom *(n)*
room in which children can play.

laywright *(n)*
omeone who writes plays.

lea *(n)* a strongly felt, emotional
equest. *A plea for mercy.*

lead pleading pleaded
(v) If you **plead** with someone,
ou beg them to do something.
(v) to say whether you are guilty
r not guilty in a court. *I plead guilty.*

leasant pleasanter
leasantest *(adj)* enjoyable and
kable. *We spent a pleasant day
by the river.* **pleasantly** *(adv)*.

lease pleasing pleased
(v) to satisfy or to give
leasure. *Your present
pleased me greatly.*
2 *(adv)* You say **please** when
you ask for something politely.
Please, may I have some cake?

leasure *(n)*
feeling of enjoyment or
atisfaction. **pleasurable** *(adj)*.

pleat *(n)* one of a series of
parallel folds in a piece of clothing,
such as a skirt. **pleated** *(adj)*.

pledge pledging pledged *(v)*
to make a firm promise. *The
school pledged to improve the
food in the cafeteria.* **pledge** *(n)*.

plentiful *(adj)*
existing in large amounts.
Food was plentiful at the feast.
plentifully *(adv)*.

plenty *(n)*
a great number, or a large
amount. *There's plenty of space.*

pliable *(ply-uh-bul)*
1 *(adj)* If an object or material
is **pliable**, it can be bent easily.
2 *(adj)* If a person is **pliable**,
they can be influenced easily.

plight *(n)*
a situation of great danger or
hardship. *Everyone is horrified by
the terrible plight of the refugees.*

plod plodding plodded *(v)*
to walk or work in a slow
and deliberate way.

plot plotting plotted
1 *(v)* to make a secret plan.
plot *(n)*.
2 *(n)* a small area of land.
A building plot.
3 *(n)* the story of a
novel, movie, play, etc.
4 *(v)* to mark out something, such
as a graph or a route, on a map.

plow *(rhymes with cow)*
plowing plowed
1 *(n)* a piece of farm equipment
pulled by an animal or a tractor
and used to turn over soil before
seeds are sown. *The picture
below shows a wooden model
of an ancient Egyptian plow.
Also see* **farm**.
2 *(v)* to turn over soil using a plow.
3 *(v)* If you **plow through**
something, you work hard
to get through it.

Egyptian plow

pluck plucking plucked
1 *(v)* to pick fruit or flowers.
2 *(v)* to play notes on a stringed
instrument by pulling on the strings.
3 *(v)* to pull feathers out of a dead bird.
4 *(n)* courage and bravery.
plucky *(adj)*, **pluckily** *(adv)*.

plug plugging plugged
1 *(n)* an object pushed into a hole
to block it. *A bath plug.* **plug** *(v)*.
2 *(n)* an electrical connector.
3 *(v) (informal)* to gain publicity
for something by talking about
it, usually on radio or television.

plum *(n)*
a small soft fruit with a purple,
yellow, or red skin. *See* **fruit**.

plumage *(plew-mij) (n)*
a bird's feathers. *Male peacocks
have blue-green plumage.*

plumbing *(plum-ing) (n)*
the system of water pipes
in a building. **plumber** *(n)*.

plump
plumper plumpest *(adj)*
slightly fat or rounded in shape.
My cat is getting plump in his old age.

plunder plundering
plundered *(v)* to use violence
to steal things, usually during
a battle. **plunder** *(n)*.

plunge plunging plunged
1 *(v)* to dive into water. **plunge** *(n)*.
2 *(v)* to push something into water.
Plunge the lettuce into ice-cold water.
3 *(v)* to slope steeply.
The cliffs plunged to the sea.
4 *(v)* to do something suddenly.
We plunged into action.

plural *(n)*
the form of a word that is used
for two or more of something.
The plural of 'child' is 'children.'

plus
1 In math, a **plus** sign (+) is
used in an addition sum. *6 plus
4 equals 10, or 6 + 4 = 10.*
2 *(prep)* in addition to.
*Celia has a husband plus
three children to feed.*

plywood *(n)*
board made from thin sheets
of wood glued together.

p.m.
the initials of the
Latin phrase *post meridiem,*
which means "after midday."
School finishes at 3 p.m.

pneumatic *(new-mat-ik)*
1 *(adj)* filled with air. *Pneumatic tires.*
2 *(adj)* operated by compressed
air. *A pneumatic drill.*

pneumonia *(ne-moan-yuh) (n)*
a serious lung disease that
makes breathing very difficult.

poach
poaches poaching poached
1 *(v)* to catch animals
illegally on someone else's land.
poacher *(n)*.
2 *(v)* to cook eggs, fish, etc.
by heating them gently in liquid.

a b c d e f g h i j k l m n o p q r s t u v w x y z

pocket pocketing pocketed
1 *(n)* a pouch sewn onto or into clothing and used for carrying things.
2 *(v)* to take something secretly. *Clive pocketed the money and ran.*
3 *(n)* a small area. *The army met pockets of resistance on their way.*

pod *(n)* a long shell that holds the seeds of certain plants. *A pea pod.*

poem *(n)* a piece of writing set out in lines, often with a noticeable rhythm and some words that rhyme.

poetry *(n)* a general word for poems. *Do you write poetry?* **poet** *(n).*

point pointing pointed
1 *(v)* to show where something is, especially by using your index finger.
2 *(n)* the sharp end of something. *A pencil point.*
3 *(n)* the main purpose behind something that is said or done. *The point of the presentation was to get people thinking.*
4 *(n)* a specific place or stage. *Don't go beyond this point.*
5 *(n)* a unit for scoring in a game.
6 *(v)* to aim at someone or something. *Don't point that gun at me!*
7 *(v)* If you **point out** something, you draw attention to it or explain it.

point-blank *(adj)* very close. *They shot at point-blank range.*

pointless *(adj)* If something is **pointless**, it has no realistic purpose. *It's pointless to take your bikini on an Arctic expedition.* **pointlessly** *(adv).*

poise *(rhymes with boys)* **poising poised** *(v)* to balance. *The glass was poised on the edge of the table.*

poised *(adj)* If you are **poised**, you are self-confident and carry yourself in a dignified way. **poise** *(n).*

poison *(n)* a substance that can kill or harm someone or something if it is swallowed or breathed in. **poison** *(v),* **poisonous** *(adj).*

poke poking poked
1 *(v)* to prod sharply with a finger or pointed object. **poke** *(n).*
2 *(v)* to move in a slow or lazy manner. *My little sister poked along behind me.*
3 *(v)* to stick out or thrust quickly. *The mouse poked its head out of the hole.*

poker *(n)* a long metal tool used for stirring up a fire.

poky pokier pokiest
1 *(adj) (informal)* very small and cramped. *A poky house.*
2 *(adj)* slow.

polar *(adj)* belonging to the icy regions, known as the Arctic and the Antarctic, around the North and South Poles.

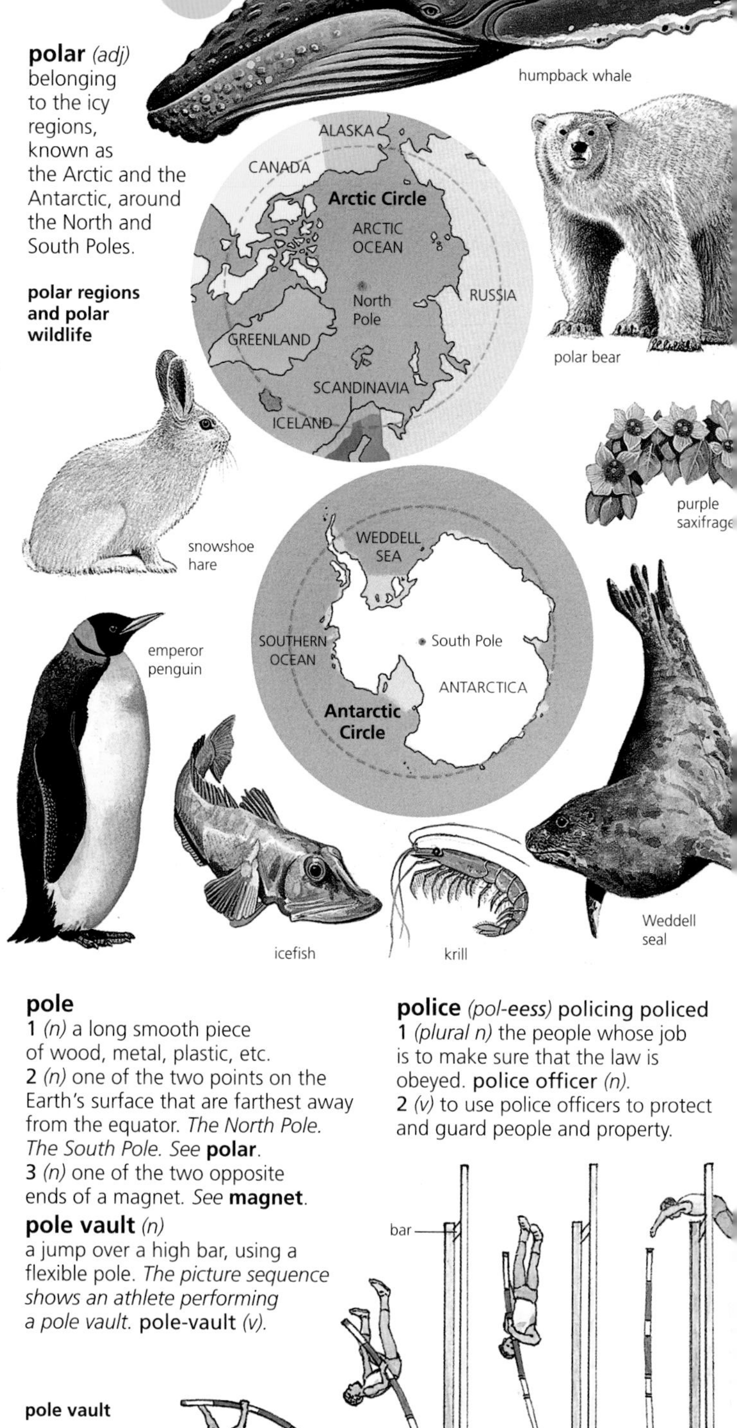

pole
1 *(n)* a long smooth piece of wood, metal, plastic, etc.
2 *(n)* one of the two points on the Earth's surface that are farthest away from the equator. *The North Pole. The South Pole. See* **polar**.
3 *(n)* one of the two opposite ends of a magnet. *See* **magnet**.

pole vault *(n)* a jump over a high bar, using a flexible pole. *The picture sequence shows an athlete performing a pole vault.* **pole-vault** *(v).*

police *(pol-eess)* **policing policed**
1 *(plural n)* the people whose job is to make sure that the law is obeyed. **police officer** *(n).*
2 *(v)* to use police officers to protect and guard people and property.

policy policies *(n)* a general plan of action. *A traffic policy.*

polio *(n)* an infectious virus that affects the brain and spine and that can cause paralysis. Polio is short for poliomyelitis.

polish polishes polishing polished
1 *(v)* to rub something to make it shine. **polish** *(n).*
2 *(n)* a cleaning substance used to make things shine.

polished *(adj)* If you give a **polished** performance, you are well rehearsed and perform confidently.

polite politer politest *(adj)* well-behaved and courteous to other people. **politeness** *(n),* **politely** *(adv).*

politician *(n)* someone involved in the government of a country, such as a congressman, senator, or governor.

politics *(n)* the debate and activity involved in governing a country. **political** *(adj),* **politically** *(adv).*

poll
1 *(n)* a counting of votes in an election.
2 *(n)* a place where people go to vote.
3 *(n)* a survey of people's opinions or beliefs.

pollen
1 *(singular n)* fine grains found inside flowers. Pollen contains fertilizing cells and is transferred to other plants by the wind or by insects.
2 **pollen count** *(n)* a measurement of the level of pollen in the air, which indicates how badly people with hay fever may be affected.

willow

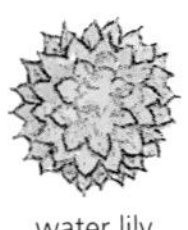
water lily

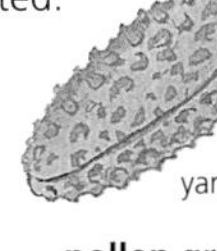
yarrow

pollen grains (magnified)

pollinate pollinating pollinated *(v)* to transfer pollen from one flower to another to fertilize the flower. **pollination** *(n).*

polling station *(n)* a building where people go to vote in elections.

pollution *(n)* damage to the environment caused by human activities. Pollution includes the harmful effects of noise and light. **pollute** *(v).*

polo *(n)* a game played on horseback by two teams of three or four players who try to hit a small ball through goal posts, using long wooden mallets.

polyester *(n)* a man-made substance used to make plastic products and fabric for clothes.

polygamy *(n)* If someone practices **polygamy**, they have several wives or husbands at once. **polygamous** *(adj).*

polygon *(n)* a flat shape with many sides.

polystyrene *(n)* a light, stiff plastic often used to make disposable cups and packing materials. *Styrofoam is a form of polystyrene.*

polythene *(n)* a light, flexible plastic used to make bags.

polyunsaturates *(plural n)* soft animal and vegetable fats and oils, thought to be healthier for you than other fats. **polyunsaturated** *(adj).*

pomegranate *(n)* a round red-yellow fruit with tough skin, red flesh, and many seeds.

pomp *(n)* an elaborate and stately display or ceremony.

pompous *(adj)* full of self-importance. **pompously** *(adv).*

pond *(n)* a pool of freshwater, usually smaller than a lake.

ponder pondering pondered *(v)* to think about things carefully.

ponderous
1 *(adj)* heavy and slow, or clumsy.
2 *(adj)* hard to understand and dull. *A ponderous speech.*

pondweed *(n)* a general name for plants that grow in freshwater ponds and slow streams.

pony ponies *(n)* a small horse.

ponytail *(n)* a bunch of hair that is tied with a band and hangs behind the head.

pony up *(v)* to pay, especially in settlement of an account.

poodle *(n)* a breed of dog with long curly hair.

pool pooling pooled
1 *(n)* a small area of still water.
2 *(n)* a swimming pool.
3 *(n)* a game in which you use a stick, called a cue, to hit colored balls into pockets on a table.
4 *(v)* If people **pool** their money, ideas, etc. they put them together to be shared.

poor poorer poorest
1 *(adj)* If you are **poor**, you do not have much money.
2 *(adj)* low in quality or standard. *Poor eyesight.*
3 *(adj)* unfortunate and provoking sympathy. *Poor Alex!*

poorly *(adv)* badly. *The room was poorly lit.*

pop popping popped
1 *(v)* to make a small bang or bursting sound. *The balloon popped when it got too close to the fire.* **pop** *(n).*
2 *(n) (informal)* a sweet, carbonated soft drink. *Soda pop.*
3 **pop music** *(n)* modern, popular music with a strong and, usually, fast beat. **pop** *(n).*
4 *(n) (informal)* father.
5 *(v) (informal)* to go somewhere or put something somewhere quickly. *Gary has just popped out. Laura popped a mint into her mouth.*

popcorn *(n)* kernels of corn that are heated until they swell up and burst open with a popping sound, eaten as a snack, especially in movie theaters.

pope *or* **Pope** *(n)* the head of the Roman Catholic Church.

poplar *(n)* a tall tree with wide leaves. *The aspen and the cottonwood are both poplar trees.*

poppy poppies *(n)* a flower with large colorful petals. Poppies have seedcases with tiny holes for the seeds to escape from when they are shaken by the wind.

popular *(adj)* liked or enjoyed by many people. *The soup is the most popular item on our menu.* **popularity** *(n),* **popularly** *(adv).*

common poppy

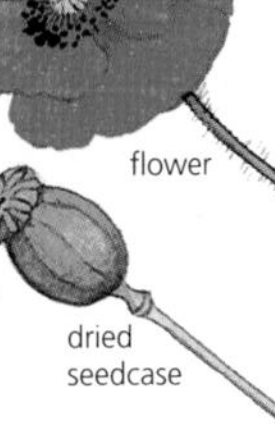

populated *(adj)* If a place is **populated**, it has people living there.

population
1 *(n)* the people who live in a place.
2 *(n)* the number of people who live in a place.

porcelain *(pors-lin) (n)* very fine china, often used to make ornaments or cups and saucers. *This 18th-century figure of Madame de Pompadour was made in porcelain at the Meissen factory in Germany.*

porcelain figure

a b c d e f g h i j k l m n o p

porch
porches *(n)*
a raised platform around the outside of a house.

porcupine *(n)*
a rodent covered with long sharp spines.

Malaysian porcupine

pore *(n)* one of the tiny holes in your skin through which you sweat. *See* **skin**.

pork *(n)*
meat from a pig.

porous *(adj)*
Something that is **porous** lets liquid or gas through it.

porridge *(n)*
a breakfast food made by cooking oats in milk or water.

port
1 *(n)* a town with a harbor.
2 *(n)* the left side of a ship or aircraft. **port** *(adj).*

portable *(adj)*
able to be carried easily.

portcullis portcullises *(n)*
a heavy grating in the entrance to a castle that was used as an extra defense.
This cutaway view of a castle gatehouse shows how the portcullis and drawbridge were raised and lowered.

castle gatehouse
(cutaway)

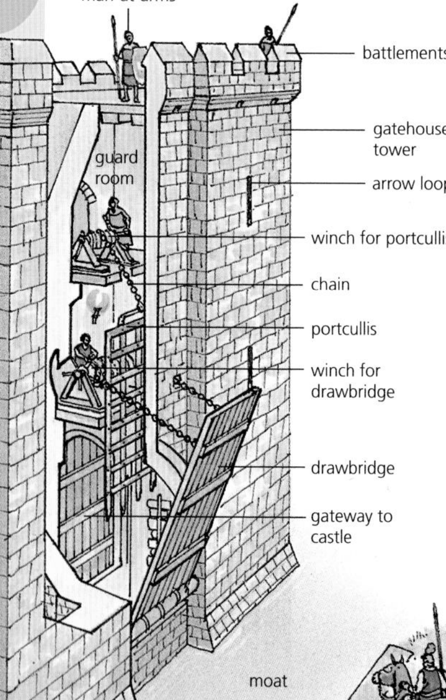

porter
1 *(n)* someone who carries luggage for people at a railway station or hotel.
2 *(n)* a person who waits on train passengers.

portion *(n)* a part or a piece.

portrait
1 *(n)* a drawing, painting, or photograph of a person.
2 *(n)* a description of something.

portray portraying portrayed
1 *(v)* to show or describe someone or something in a certain way. *The author portrays Abigail as an eccentric.* **portrayal** *(n).*
2 *(v)* to act a part in a play or movie. **portrayal** *(n).*

pose posing posed
1 *(v)* to keep your body in a particular position so that you can be photographed, painted, or drawn. **pose** *(n).*
2 *(v)* to pretend to be someone else to deceive people. *The thieves posed as police officers.*
3 *(v)* If you **pose a question**, you ask it.

position positioning positioned
1 *(n)* the place where something is.
2 *(v)* to put something in a particular place. *Position the pictures carefully.*
3 *(n)* the way in which someone is standing, sitting, or lying.
4 *(n)* your place in a race or competition.
5 *(n)* a particular job. *I'm applying for the position of nanny.*

positive
1 *(adj)* sure or certain. *I'm positive that I left my wallet here.* **positively** *(adv).*
2 *(adj)* hopeful and optimistic. *Dolly has a positive approach to life.*
3 *(adj)* A **positive** number is more than zero.

possession
1 *(n)* something that you own. **possess** *(v).*
2 If something is **in your possession**, you own it or have it.

possessive
1 *(adj)* If someone is **possessive**, they want to keep someone or something for themselves and do not want to share them with other people.
2 *(n)* the form of a noun or pronoun that shows that something belongs to it. *In "This ball is mine" and "Tom's bat," "mine" and "Tom's" are possessives.* **possessive** *(adj).*

possible *(adj)* If something is **possible**, it might happen or might be true. **possibility** *(n),* **possibly** *(adv).*

post posting posted
1 *(n)* a long thick piece of wood, concrete, or metal that is fixed in the ground.
2 *(n)* a particular job that someone has. *Mr. Jarvis holds the post of Principal.*
3 *(v)* to mail a letter or package from one place to another.
4 *(n)* a place where someone on duty is supposed to be. *The soldier was at his post.*
5 *(v)* to assign someone to a post.
6 **keep posted** *(v)* to keep someone up to date with the latest news or information. *Keep me posted about the latest developments on the project.*

postage *(n)* the cost of sending a letter or package in the mail.

postcard *(n)*
a card, usually with a picture on one side, that you send by mail.

poster *(n)* a large printed picture or notice that can be put up on a wall.

posthumous *(adj)*
coming or happening after death.

postmark *(n)*
an official mark on a letter to show when and where it was mailed. It also cancels the postage stamp.

postpone postponing postponed *(v)* to put something off until later. *We postponed the match because of rain.* **postponement** *(n).*

postscript *(n)*
a short message, beginning "p.s.," which you add to the end of a letter, after your signature.

posture *(n)*
the position of your body when you stand, sit, or walk. **postural** *(adj).*

posy posies *(n)*
a small bunch of flowers.

pot potting potted
1 *(n)* a round container used for cooking or storing food.
2 *(n)* a container made of clay, especially one used for growing plants.

potato potatoes *(n)* a round or oval root vegetable. *See* **vegetable**.

potent *(adj)* powerful or strong. *A potent smell.* **potency** *(n),* **potently** *(adv).*

potential
1 *(n)* Your **potential** is what you are capable of achieving in the future. **potential** *(adj),* **potentially** *(adv).*
2 *(n)* If an idea, place, etc. has **potential**, you think that you can develop it into something better.

othole *(n)*
hole in the surface of a road.

otion *(n)* a liquid drunk as a
nedicine or to bring about a magical
r mystical result. *In the story,
he hero drank a magic potion
o make himself invisible.*

otter *(n)*
omeone who makes objects
ut of clay, such as bowls, plates,
ases, etc. *The picture below shows
potter working at her wheel.*

ottery potteries
(n) objects made of baked
lay, such as bowls, plates,
ases, etc. Pottery can be used for
lecorative or practical purposes.
(n) a place where
lay objects are made.
(n) the craft or business
f making clay objects.

otter

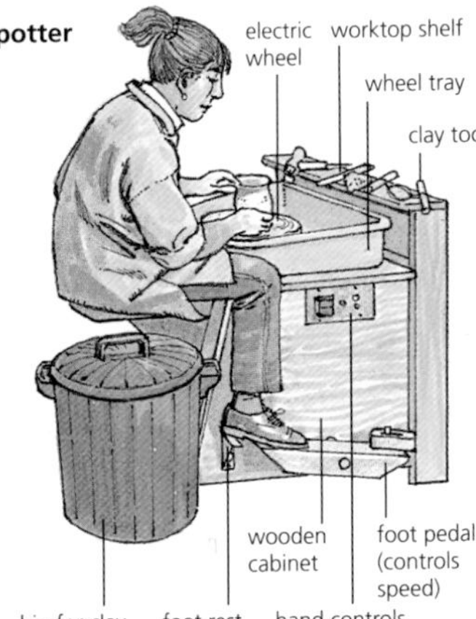

pouch pouches
1 *(n)* a small leather or fabric bag.
2 *(n)* a flap of skin in which kangaroos and other marsupials carry their young.

poultry *(plural n)*
farmyard birds kept for their eggs and meat. Chickens, turkeys, ducks, and geese are poultry.

pounce pouncing pounced *(v)*
to jump on something suddenly and grab hold of it. *The lion pounced on the antelope.*

pound pounding pounded
1 *(n)* the main unit of money in Britain.
2 *(n)* a unit of weight, equal to 16 ounces. See page 284.
3 *(v)* to keep hitting something noisily and with force. *The rain pounded on the roof.*
4 *(n)* an enclosure, especially one for stray dogs and other animals.
5 *(v)* to beat quickly or heavily. *My heart was pounding.*

pour pouring poured
1 *(v)* to make liquid flow out of a jug, bottle, etc.
2 *(v)* to rain heavily.
3 *(v)* to move somewhere quickly and in large numbers. *People poured out of the stadium into the street.*

pout pouting pouted *(v)*
to push out your lips because you are cross or disappointed about something. **pout** *(n)*.

poverty *(n)*
the state of being poor. *The refugees lived in dreadful poverty.*

powder powdering powdered
1 *(n)* tiny grains of a solid substance. **powdery** *(adj)*.
2 *(v)* to cover something with powder. *Gloria powdered her nose.*

power
1 *(n)* control over other people or things. **powerful** *(adj)*, **powerless** *(adj)*.
2 *(n)* the ability or authority to do something.
3 *(n)* great force or great strength. **powerful** *(adj)*, **powerfully** *(adv)*.
4 *(n)* electricity or other forms of energy.
5 **power of attorney** *(n)* a legal document that gives one person authority to act on another person's behalf.
6 **power outage** *(n)* a temporary stoppage in the electricity supply.
7 **power plant** *(n)* a place where electricity is produced.

practicable *(adj)* able to be done successfully. *Is it practicable to do all this work today?* **practicably** *(adv)*.

practical
1 *(adj)* having to do with experience or action rather than with theory and ideas. *Do you have any practical teaching experience?*
2 *(adj)* If someone is **practical**, they are good at making and doing things with their hands.
3 *(adj)* sensible and useful. *Brown is a practical color for a carpet.*

practical joke *(n)* a humorous trick played on someone.

practically
1 *(adv)* almost. *It's practically impossible to complete this level.*
2 *(adv)* in a sensible way. *Abby tackled the job very practically.*

practice practicing practiced
1 *(v)* to repeat an action regularly in order to improve it. *Practice the piano.* **practice** *(n)*.
2 *(n)* a custom or habit. *How old is the practice of sending birthday cards?*
3 *(n)* the business of a doctor or lawyer.
4 *(v)* If someone **practices** a religion, they follow its teachings and attend its services or ceremonies.
5 *(v)* to put something into action. *Practice what you preach.*
6 **in practice** *(adv)* what really happens when you do something rather than what is meant to happen. *The idea sounded fantastic, but in practice it didn't work.*

pragmatic *(adj)* having to do with the way things are actually done, not just the way they might be done in theory.

prairie *(n)* a large area of grassland with few or no trees.

praise praising praised
1 *(v)* to say good things about someone because you admire them or think that they have done something well. *The mayor praised the efforts of the fire department in his speech.* **praise** *(n)*.
2 *(v)* to thank and worship God. **praise** *(n)*.

prance prancing pranced
1 *(v)* to leap in a lively way.
2 *(v)* When a horse **prances**, it springs forward on its hind legs.

prank *(n)*
a trick played on someone.

pray praying prayed
1 *(v)* to talk to God, either out loud or silently. **prayer** *(n)*.
2 *(v)* to hope very much that something happens. *We're praying that it will be sunny tomorrow.*

preach
preaches preaching preached
1 *(v)* to give a religious talk to people, especially during a church service. **preacher** *(n)*.
2 *(v)* to tell other people what they should do. *I wish my mom would stop preaching at me!*

precarious *(adj)*
unsafe and risky. *The glass was perched in a precarious position on the edge of the table.* **precariously** *(adv)*.

precaution *(n)*
something that you do to prevent something dangerous or unpleasant from happening. *Let's take a first aid kit on the hike as a precaution.* **precautionary** *(adj)*.

precede *(pree-seed)* **preceding preceded** *(v)* If one thing **precedes** something else, it comes before it. *A short cartoon preceded the main movie.* **preceding** *(adj).*

precinct *(pree-sinkt) (n)* an area in a city that is the responsibility of a particular police station.

precious *(presh-uss)*
1 *(adj)* rare and valuable.
2 *(adj)* very special to you. *Precious memories.*
3 **precious stone** *(n)* a valuable mineral, often used in jewelry.

precipice *(n)* a steep cliff face.

precipitation *(n)* the falling of water from the sky in the form of rain, snow, hail, or sleet.

precise *(adj)* exact, accurate, and neat. *The precise time is 11:24 a.m.* **precision** *(n),* **precisely** *(adv).*

precocious *(pri-koh-shuss) (adj)* **Precocious** children are very advanced for their age.

predator *(n)* an animal that hunts and kills other animals. Tigers, sharks, and eagles are predators. **predatory** *(adj).*

predecessor
1 *(n)* someone who had your job or position before you.
2 *(n)* an ancestor.

predicament *(n)* an awkward or difficult situation.

predict predicting predicted *(v)* to say what you think will happen in the future. **prediction** *(n).*

predominate predominating predominated *(v)* to be greater in power or number than others. *Girls predominate in our class.* **predominance** *(n),* **predominant** *(adj).*

preen preening preened *(v)* When birds **preen** themselves, they clean and arrange their feathers with their beaks.

preface *(pref-uss) (n)* an introduction at the front of a book.

prefect *(n)* a school pupil, usually at a private school, who has special duties and responsibilities.

prefer preferring preferred *(v)* to like one thing better than another. *I prefer oranges over apples.* **preference** *(n).*

prefix prefixes *(n)* a part of a word added at its beginning that changes the word's meaning. "Sub," "un," and "re" are all prefixes. *The prefix "pre," which means "before," is used in "prehistoric" and "premeditated."*

pregnant *(adj)* A woman who is **pregnant** has a baby growing in her womb. *This diagram of a pregnant woman's womb shows a baby ready to be born.* **pregnancy** *(n).*

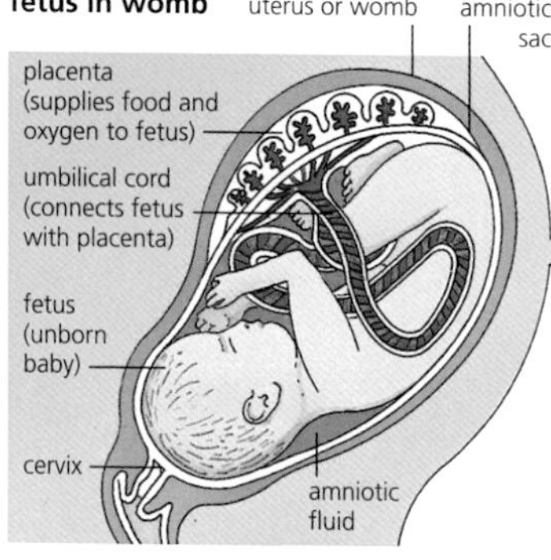

prehistoric *(adj)* belonging to a time very long ago before history was written. **prehistory** *(n).*

prejudice
1 *(n)* a fixed and unreasonable opinion. **prejudiced** *(adj).*
2 *(n)* unfair behavior that results from having fixed opinions about something or some people. *There are still too many cases of racial prejudice.*

preliminary *(adj)* preparing the way for what comes later. *We were given a preliminary talk before the class started.* **preliminary** *(n).*

premature *(adj)* happening or coming early. *A premature baby.* **prematurely** *(adv).*

premeditated *(adj)* planned in advance. *A premeditated attack.*

premier *(prem-eer)*
1 *(adj)* leading, top, or principal. *America's premier rock group.*
2 *(n)* the leader of a government.

premiere *(prem-ee-air) (n)* the first public performance of a movie or play.

premises *(plural n)* a building and the land that it belongs to.

premium
1 *(n)* money that is paid to take out an insurance policy.
2 If something is **at a premium**, it is rare and valued very highly.

premonition *(n)* a feeling that something is going to happen, especially something harmful or bad.

preoccupied *(adj)* If you are **preoccupied**, your thoughts are completely taken up with something. **preoccupation** *(n).*

prepare preparing prepared *(v)* to get ready. **preparation** *(n).*

preposition *(n)* a word showing the position of things or people in relation to each other. *"On," "beside" and "with" are prepositions.* See page 3.

preposterous *(adj)* ridiculous and absurd. *A preposterous idea.* **preposterously** *(adv).*

preschool
1 *(n)* a school, for example a nursery school, for children who are too young to go to elementary school.
2 *(adj)* having to do with children who are too young to go to elementary school. *Preschool education.*

prescribe prescribing prescribed
1 *(v)* to say what should be done. *Mom prescribed an early night.*
2 *(v)* When doctors **prescribe** medicine for a patient, they decide what drugs they should take and write a prescription for those drugs.

prescription *(n)* an order for drugs written by a doctor to a pharmacist.

presence
1 *(n)* being in a place. *We would appreciate your presence at our party.*
2 *(n)* the area immediately near a thing or person. *I'm shy in the presence of people I don't know.*

present presenting presented
1 *(prez-ent) (adj)* If someone is **present** in a place, they are there.
2 *(prez-ent) (n)* the time now.
3 *(priz-ent) (v)* to give someone a gift or prize in a formal way.
4 *(prez-ent) (n)* something that you buy or make to give to someone.
5 *(priz-ent) (v)* to introduce something, such as a television program. **presenter** *(n).*
6 *(n)* The **present participle** of a verb ends with "ing" and is used to form some tenses, for example "I am cooking" and "Harry will be cooking tomorrow." It can also be used as an adjective, as in "a thriving business," or as a noun, as in "their singing gave me a headache."

presentation
1 *(n)* the formal giving of a prize or present. *At the end of the year, we had a presentation for our teacher.*
2 *(n)* the way that something is produced and the way that it looks. *Your work is good but your presentation is atrocious!*

presently *(adv)* soon or shortly.

preserve preserving preserved
1 *(v)* to protect something so that it stays in its original state. **preservation** *(n).*
2 *(v)* to treat food so that it does not go bad. **preservative** *(n).*
3 **preserves** *(plural n)* jams and jellies.

ɔreside presiding presided *(v)*
ɔ be in charge of something.
Rodney presided over the meeting.

ɒresident
(n) the elected head of state
of a republic. *These portraits of*
American presidents are carved
out of rock at Mount Rushmore
in the U.S.A. **presidency** *(n)*,
ɒresidential *(adj)*.

(n) the head of a society
or organization.

ɒress presses pressing pressed
(v) to push firmly. *Press the button*
to open the door. **pressure** *(n)*.
(v) to smooth out the creases
in clothes with an iron.
3 *(n)* a machine for printing.
4 **the press** *(n)* a general name
for newspapers and the people
who produce them.

ɒressing *(adj)* urgent or needing
immediate attention. *I must run,*
I have a pressing appointment.

ɒressure
1 *(n)* the force with which
you press on something.
2 *(n)* the force with which
a liquid or gas pushes against
something. *Water pressure.*
3 *(n)* strong influence. *Crystal is*
under pressure to finish her work.
4 *(v)* to persuade strongly. *We*
pressured Eve into joining the band.

ɒressurize
pressurizing pressurized *(v)*
to seal off an aircraft cabin,
diving chamber, etc. so that the
air pressure inside stays the same as
the pressure at the Earth's surface.

ɒrestige *(press-teej) (n)*
the good reputation and high status
that comes from being successful,
powerful, rich, etc. **prestigious** *(adj)*.

ɒresumably *(adv)* probably.

ɒresume presuming presumed
(v) to think that something
is true without being certain.
I presume that you like chocolate.
2 *(v)* to dare. *Don't presume to tell*
me what to do! **presumption** *(n)*.

pretend pretending pretended
1 *(v)* to make believe.
The girls liked to pretend
that they were superheroes.
2 *(v)* to claim falsely. *Will pretended*
to know New York well, even
though he had never been there.
3 *(v)* to give a false show to
trick or deceive. *Sam pretended*
to be asleep. **pretense** *(n)*.

pretext *(n)* a false reason or excuse.
Joe went shopping on the pretext
of taking the dog for a walk.

pretty prettier prettiest
1 *(adj)* attractive and pleasing to
look at. **prettiness** *(n)*, **prettily** *(adv)*.
2 *(adv) (informal)* quite.
A pretty bad movie.

prevail prevailing prevailed
1 *(v)* to succeed despite difficulties.
2 *(v)* to be common or usual.
Poverty and crime prevail in
many inner cities. **prevalent** *(adj)*.

prevent preventing prevented *(v)*
to stop something from happening.
We hired night guards to prevent
robberies. **prevention** *(n)*.

preventive medicine *(n)*
health education or treatment
that is intended to stop people from
developing disease and illness.

preview *(n)*
a showing of a play or movie before
it is released for public viewing.

previous *(adj)* former or happening
before. *I like this school more than*
my previous one. **previously** *(adv)*.

prey *(rhymes with tray)*
prey; preying preyed
1 *(n)* a creature that is hunted and
eaten by other animals. **prey** *(v)*.
2 *(v)* When an animal **preys**
on another animal, it hunts
it and then eats it.

price pricing priced
1 *(n)* the amount that you
have to pay for something.
2 *(v)* to give something a price.

priceless *(adj)* If something
is **priceless**, it is too valuable for
anyone to say how much it is worth.

prick pricking pricked *(v)*
to make a small hole in something
with a sharp point. **prick** *(n)*.

prickle *(n)* a sharp point, for example
on the stalk of a rose. **prickly** *(adj)*.

pride
1 *(n)* a feeling of satisfaction
in something that you do.
Zara takes pride in her work.
2 *(n)* an opinion of your own
importance and cleverness
that is too high.

priest *(n)*
a religious leader who
leads services in a church, temple, etc.

prim primmer primmest *(adj)*
Someone who is **prim** is very formal
and hates anything rough or rude.

prima donna
1 *(n)* a female opera star.
2 *(n) (informal)* someone who is
demanding and often bad-tempered.

primarily *(adv)*
chiefly, or mainly.

primary
1 *(adj)* most important, chief,
or main. *The primary cause.*
2 *(adj)* first or earliest.
Primary education.

primary colors *(n)*
In painting, the **primary colors** are
red, yellow, and blue, which can be
mixed to make all the other colors.

primate
1 *(n)* any member of the group of
intelligent mammals that includes
humans, apes, and monkeys.
2 *(n)* the head bishop or archbishop
of a country or province.

prime *(adj)* of first importance or
quality. *Prime minister. Prime beef.*

prime minister *(n)* the leader
of a government in some countries.

prime number *(n)*
a number that can be divided
only by itself or by 1. *7, 13,*
and 29 are all prime numbers.

primeval *(pry-mee-vul) (adj)*
belonging to the earliest period
of the Earth.

primitive *(adj)*
uncivilized, basic, and crude.
Conditions at the campsite
were very primitive.

prince *(n)*
the son of a king or
queen, or the husband of a queen.

princess princesses *(n)*
the daughter of a king or
queen, or the wife of a prince.

principal
1 *(adj)* most important, chief,
or main. **principally** *(adv)*.
2 *(n)* the head of an elementary,
middle, or high school.

principle
1 *(n)* a scientific rule or truth.
2 *(n)* a basic rule that governs
your behavior. *It's against Sam's*
principles to eat meat.
3 If you agree to something
in principle, you are happy with
the general idea, but not necessarily
with the finer details.

print printing printed
1 *(v)* to produce words or pictures on a page with a machine that uses ink. *Color pictures are usually printed by combining four colors of ink on white paper. This is called four-color printing. The picture below has been magnified so that you can see how it is made up of millions of overlapping dots of black, yellow, cyan (blue), and magenta (pink).* **printer** *(n).*
2 *(v)* to write using letters that do not join up.
3 *(n)* a photograph or a printed copy of a painting.

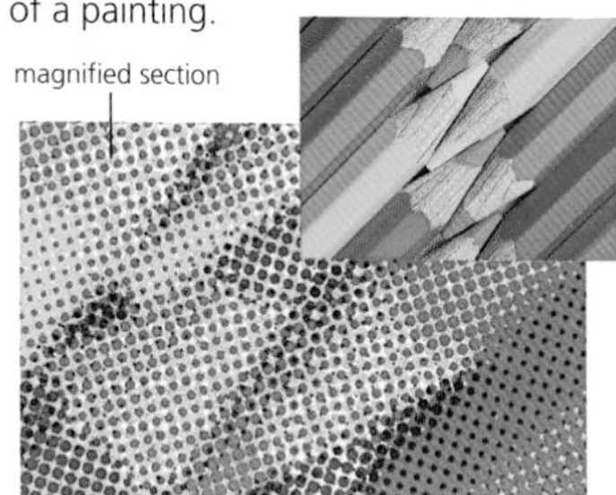

printout *(n)* a printed copy of information, often from a computer.

prior *(adj)* earlier. *Peter can't come because of a prior engagement.*

priority priorities *(n)* something that is more important than other things.

prism *(n)* a clear glass or plastic shape that bends light or breaks it up into the colors of the spectrum. Prisms usually have triangular ends. *See* **periscope**, **shape**, **spectrum**.

prison *(n)* a building where people are forced to stay, usually as punishment for a crime.

private
1 *(adj)* If something is **private**, it belongs to or concerns one person, organization, etc. and no one else. *Private possessions.* **privacy** *(n).*
2 *(adj)* secret. *Private thoughts.* **privately** *(adv).*
3 *(n)* a soldier of the lowest rank.

private school *(n)* a school where parents pay for their children's education.

privatize privatizing privatized *(v)* to sell or hand over a government-funded public industry or organization to private individuals or companies. **privatization** *(n).*

privilege *(n)* a special advantage given to a person or a group of people. **privileged** *(adj).*

prize prizing prized
1 *(n)* a reward for winning a game or competition.
2 *(v)* to value something very much. *I prize my freedom.*
3 **prize** or **pry** *(v)* to force something open, using a lever. **prized** *(adj).*

pro
1 *(adj)* If you are **pro** something, you are in favor of it. *Pro-democracy.*
2 *(n)* a shortened form of the word **professional**, often used in sports. *A golf pro.*
3 **pros and cons** advantages and disadvantages.

probable *(adj)* likely or expected to happen. *It's probable that Juan will win.* **probability** *(n),* **probably** *(adv).*

probation
1 *(n)* If someone is **on probation** at work, they are having a trial period. **probationary** *(adj).*
2 *(n)* If an offender is put **on probation** for a crime that they have committed, they are supervised for a certain time by a probation officer.

probe probing probed *(v)* to examine or explore something very carefully. **probe** *(n).*

problem
1 *(n)* a difficult situation that needs to be sorted out or overcome.
2 *(n)* a puzzle or question to be solved. *A math problem.*

procedure *(pro-see-jure) (n)* a way of doing something. *Follow the usual procedure for leaving the building.*

proceed proceeding proceeded
1 *(v)* to move forward or to carry on.
2 *(plural n)* The **proceeds** of an event are the sums of money that it raises.

process
processes processing processed
1 *(pross-ess) (n)* an organized series of actions that produce a result. *We studied the process of making rubber.* **processing** *(n).*
2 *(pross-ess) (v)* When food is **processed**, it is treated and changed from its original state. **processing** *(n),* **processed** *(adj).*
3 *(pro-sess) (v)* to take part in a procession.

procession *(n)* a number of people walking or driving along a route as part of a public festival, religious service, etc.

proclaim
proclaiming proclaimed *(v)* If someone **proclaims** something, they announce it publicly. **proclamation** *(n).*

procrastinate
procrastinating procrastinated *(v)* to put off something that you have to do. **procrastination** *(n).*

prod prodding prodded
1 *(v)* to poke something or someone. *I'll prod Max to wake him up.* **prod** *(n).*
2 *(v)* to push or urge someone into doing something. *My parents had to prod me to do my homework.*

prodigy *(prod-ij-ee)* **prodigies** *(n)* Child **prodigies** are extraordinarily intelligent or talented for their age.

produce producing produced
1 *(pro-doos) (v)* to make something. *This factory produces cars.*
2 *(pro-doos) (n)* things that are produced or grown for eating, especially fruit and vegetables.
3 *(pro-doos) (v)* to bring something out for people to see. *James produced a mouse from his pocket.*
4 *(pro-doos) (v)* to be in charge of putting on a play or making a movie. **producer** *(n).*

product
1 *(n)* something that is manufactured or made by a natural process.
2 *(n)* the result that you get when you multiply two numbers. *15 is the product of 3 and 5.*

production
1 *(n)* the process of manufacturing or growing something.
2 *(n)* a play, opera, show, etc.
3 **production line** *(n)* a system of manufacturing in which the product moves along while different things are added or done to it.

productive *(adj)* making a lot of products or producing good results. *A productive meeting.* **productivity** *(n).*

profession
1 *(n)* a job for which you need special training or study. *Medicine, teaching, and law are all professions.*
2 *(n)* something that you state openly. *A profession of love.* **profess** *(v).*

professional
1 *(n)* a member of a profession, for example a doctor, teacher, or lawyer. **professional** *(adj).*
2 *(n)* someone who is paid for doing something that many others do as amateurs. *A soccer professional.* **professional** *(adj).*
3 *(adj)* If somebody is **professional** at something, they are expert at it. **professionally** *(adv).*

professor *(n)* a teacher at a university or college.

proficient *(prof-ish-ent) (adj)* If you are **proficient** at doing something, you are able to do it properly and skillfully. **proficiency** *(n),* **proficiently** *(adv).*

profile
1 *(n)* the outline of someone's face, seen from the side.
2 *(n)* a brief account of someone's life or progress. *Pupil profiles.* **profile** *(v).*

profit *(n)* the money made by selling something, after the cost of making it or buying it has been taken away. **profit** *(v),* **profitable** *(adj).*

profound *(adj)*
very deeply felt or thought. *Profound sadness.* **profoundly** *(adv).*

profuse *(pro-**fyoos**) (adj)*
plentiful or more than enough.

program
programming programmed
1 *(n)* a series of instructions written in a special code that controls the way that a computer works.
2 *(v)* to give computers or other machines instructions to make them work. **programming** *(n).*
3 *(n)* a television or radio show.
4 *(n)* a schedule or a list of events.
5 *(n)* A theater or concert **program** is a pamphlet that gives you information about the performance.

programmer *(n)* someone whose job is to program a computer.

progress
progresses progressing progressed
1 *(v)* to move forward or to improve slowly. *How are you progressing with your fitness program?* **progress** *(n),* **progression** *(n).*
2 If something is **in progress**, it is happening. *Roadwork is in progress all this week.*

prohibit prohibiting prohibited *(v)* to stop or ban something officially. **prohibition** *(n).*

project projecting projected
1 *(**proj**-ekt) (n)* a scheme or a plan.
2 *(**proj**-ekt) (n)* a study of something worked on over a period of time. *We are starting a project on the Romans.*
3 *(pro-**jekt**) (v)* to stick out. *The branch projected into the road.* **projecting** *(adj).*
4 *(pro-**jekt**) (v)* to show an image on a screen. **projector** *(n).*
5 *(pro-**jekt**) (v)* to look ahead or to forecast. *The company has projected a loss for next year.*
6 *(pro-**jekt**) (v)* If you **project** your voice, you make it carry a long way.
7 *(**proj**-ekt) (n)* a group of apartment buildings planned and built as a unit.

projection
1 *(n)* something that sticks out. *We noticed a strange projection behind the curtain.*
2 *(n)* a forecast or a prediction.
3 *(n)* A **map projection** is a way of representing the globe on a flat page. *Mercator's projection.*

projector *(n)*
a piece of equipment that shows slides or movies on a screen.

prolific *(adj)*
very productive or producing a large quantity. *A prolific writer.*

prologue *(**pro**-log) (n)*
a short speech or piece of writing that introduces a play, story, or poem.

prolong prolonging prolonged *(v)* to make something last longer.

prom *short for* **promenade**.

promenade
1 *(n)* a formal ball or dance.
2 *(n)* a walk taken for pleasure.

prominent
1 *(adj)* very easily seen. *The windmill is a prominent landmark.*
2 *(adj)* famous or important. *A prominent politician.* **prominence** *(n).*

promise promising promised
1 *(v)* to say definitely that you will do something. **promise** *(n).*
2 *(n)* Someone who shows **promise** seems likely to do well in the future. **promising** *(adj).*

promote promoting promoted
1 *(v)* to move someone to a more important job. **promotion** *(n).*
2 *(v)* to make the public aware of something or someone. *Ronald is busy promoting his latest book.* **promotion** *(n).*

prompt prompting prompted; prompter promptest
1 *(adj)* very quick and without delay. *A prompt answer.* **promptly** *(adv).*
2 *(v)* to remind actors of their lines when they have forgotten them during a play. **prompt** *(n).*

prone
1 *(adj)* vulnerable or easily affected by something harmful. *Tara is prone to colds in the winter.*
2 *(adj)* lying flat or facedown.

prong *(n)*
one of the sharp points of a fork.

pronoun *(n)* a word that is used in place of a noun. "I," "me," "her," and "it" are all pronouns. *See* page 3.

pronounce
pronouncing pronounced
1 *(v)* to say words in a particular way. *How do you pronounce "psychic?"*
2 *(v)* to make a formal announcement. *The mayor pronounced the fair open.*

pronunciation
*(pro-nun-see-**ay**-shun) (n)* the way in which a word is pronounced.

proof *(n)* evidence that something is true. *Do you have proof of your age?*

prop propping propped
1 *(v)* to support something that would otherwise fall down. *Bob propped the ladder against the wall.* **prop** *(n).*
2 *(n)* In theater, movies, etc. a **prop** is any item that the actors need to carry or use. Prop is short for property.
3 *(n)* something used as a support.

propaganda *(singular n)*
biased information, used to present a certain viewpoint.

propel propelling propelled *(v)* to drive or push something forward. *The aircraft was propelled by twin jet engines.* **propulsion** *(n).*

propellant *(n)* a chemical or fuel that propels something. *See* **aerosol**.

propeller *(n)* a set of rotating blades that provide force to move a vehicle through water or air.

proper
1 *(adj)* accepted or right. *Is this the proper way to sit?* **properly** *(adv).*
2 *(adj)* correct in behavior. *Claudia is very prim and proper.* **properly** *(adv).*

proper noun *(n)* A **proper noun** is the name of a particular person, place, time, etc., such as "Jane," "New York," "Wednesday." Proper nouns start with a capital letter.

property properties
1 *(n)* the things that someone owns. *Lost property.*
2 *(n)* buildings and land belonging to someone. *Two fierce dogs guarded the property.*

prophesy *(**prof**-ess-eye)*
prophesies prophesying prophesied *(v)* to predict that something will happen in the future. **prophecy** *(**prof**-ess-ee) (n).*

prophet *(**prof**-it) (n)* someone who predicts what will happen in the future.

proportion
1 *(n)* a part of something. *A large proportion of the class supported me.*
2 *(n)* the amount of something in relation to other things. *The proportion of boys to girls in the school is growing.* **proportional** *(adj),* **proportionally** *(adv).*
3 If something is **in proportion** to something else, it is the correct size in relation to it. *Emily has a large nose, but it is in proportion to the rest of her features.*
4 *(plural n)* The **proportions** of something, such as a building, are its measurements or size.

propose proposing proposed
1 *(v)* to suggest a plan or an idea. *Candy proposed that we all go swimming.* **proposal** *(n).*
2 *(v)* to ask someone to marry you. **proposal** *(n).*

propulsion *(n)*
the force by which a plane, rocket, etc. is pushed along. *Jet propulsion.*

prose *(n)* writing that is in ordinary lines, not in verse.

prosecute prosecuting prosecuted *(v)* to accuse someone in a court of law. **prosecution** *(n).*

prospect
1 *(n)* something in the future that you look forward to or dread.
2 *(n)* a view or a scene.

prospectus prospectuses *(n)*
a brochure giving information about a school, company, etc.

prosper prospering prospered *(v)*
to be successful or to thrive. **prosperity** *(n),* **prosperous** *(adj).*

protect protecting protected *(v)*
to guard or shelter something. **protection** *(n),* **protective** *(adj).*

protein *(pro-teen) (n)* a substance found in foods such as meat, cheese, eggs, and lentils. Humans and animals need protein in their diet.

protest protesting protested
1 *(pro-test) (v)* to object to something strongly and publicly.
2 *(pro-test) (n)* a demonstration or a statement against something.

Protestant *(prah-tess-tent) (n)*
a Christian who does not belong to the Roman Catholic or Orthodox Church.

proton *(n)* one of the microscopic parts of an atom that carries a positive electrical charge. *See* **atom**.

protoplasm *(n)*
a jelly-like substance that makes up the living matter of all cells.

prototype *(n)* the first version of a new invention, used for experiment and development. **prototype** *(adj).*

protractor *(n)*
a semicircular instrument used for measuring angles and usually made of transparent plastic. *See* **geometry**.

protrude protruding protruded *(v)*
to stick out or to jut out. *The rocks protruded into the sea.*

proud prouder proudest
1 *(adj)* pleased with what you or someone else has achieved.
2 *(adj)* A **proud** person thinks too highly of their own importance or abilities.

prove proving proved *or* proven *(v)*
to show that something is true. *The experiment proved our hypothesis.*

proverb *(n)* a wise old saying.

provide providing provided
1 *(v)* to supply the things that someone needs. **provision** *(n).*
2 **provided** *(conj)*
on the condition that, or as long as. *I will go swimming provided that you come too.*

province *(n)*
a district, or a region of a country.

provision
1 *(n)* the act of providing something.
2 **provisions** *(plural n)* groceries and other household goods.

provisional *(adj)*
If something is **provisional**, it is temporary or not yet definite. *A provisional plan.* **provisionally** *(adv).*

provoke provoking provoked *(v)*
to annoy someone and make them angry. **provocation** *(n),* **provocative** *(adj).*

prowess *(n)*
skill or bravery. *Laura's prowess on the ski slopes is legendary.*

prowl prowling prowled *(v)*
to move around quietly and secretly, like an animal looking for food. *The cats prowled through the dark street.*

proximity *(n)* nearness.

prudent *(adj)*
If you are **prudent**, you are cautious and think carefully before you do something. **prudence** *(n),* **prudently** *(adv).*

prune pruning pruned
1 *(n)* a dried plum.
2 *(v)* to cut off branches from a tree or bush, to make it grow more strongly.

pry pries prying pried *(v)* If you **pry**, you look into other people's business in a nosy way. *Also see* **prize**.

P.S. *short for* **postscript** *or* **Public School**.

psalm *(salm) (n)*
a sacred song or poem, especially one from the Book of Psalms in the Bible.

pseudonym *(soo-doh-nim) (n)*
a name that you use that is not your own. Many writers use pseudonyms.

psychiatrist *(sy-ky-a-trist) (n)*
a doctor who is trained to treat mental illness. **psychiatry** *(n)* **psychiatric** *(adj).*

psychic *(sy-kik) (adj)* Someone who says they are **psychic** thinks they can use their mind in an unusual way, for example, to tell what other people are thinking. **psychic** *(n).*

psychologist *(sy-kol-oj-ist) (n)*
someone who studies people's minds and the ways that people behave. **psychology** *(n),* **psychological** *(adj).*

psychopath *(sy-koh-path) (n)*
someone who has something wrong with their character, so that they are violent or dangerous. **psychopathic** *(adj).*

psychotherapy *(sy-koh-ther-a-pee) (n)* a treatment that helps a person work through mental or emotional difficulties by talking. **psychotherapist** *(n).*

puberty *(pew-ber-tee) (n)*
the time when your body changes from a child's to an adult's.

public
1 *(adj)* having to do with people. *Public opinion.*
2 *(adj)* If something is **public**, it belongs to, or can be used by everybody. *Public transportation.* **publicly** *(adv).*
3 **the public** *(n)* people in general.

publication
1 *(n)* The **publication** of a book or magazine is the production and distribution of it, so people can buy it.
2 *(n)* a book or a magazine.

publicity *(n)* information that tells you about a person or an event. *The movie received a lot of publicity in the newspapers.*

publicize publicizing publicized *(v)* If you **publicize** an event, you make it known to as many people as possible. **publicist** *(n).*

public opinion *(singular n)*
the views or beliefs of people in general.

public school *(n)*
a school run by the state, providing free education.

publish publishes publishing published *(v)* to produce and distribute a book, magazine, etc., so that people can buy it. **publisher** *(n),* **publishing** *(n).*

pucker puckering puckered *(v)*
to wrinkle or to fold. **pucker** *(n).*

pudding *(n)* a sweet food served at the end of a meal. *Rice pudding. Chocolate pudding.*

puddle *(n)* a small pool of rainwater or other liquid.

a b c d e f g h i j k l m n o p q r s t u v w x y z

puff puffing puffed
1 *(v)* to blow or breathe out something, such as smoke or steam. **puff** *(n)*.
2 **puff up** *(v)*
to swell up. **puffy** *(adj)*.
3 **puff pastry** *(n)*
pastry made in thin layers, which puffs up when it is cooked.

puffin *(n)* a black-and-white seabird whose beak becomes brightly colored in the mating season. *The picture below shows an Atlantic Puffin.*

pugnacious *(adj)* If someone is **pugnacious**, they are fond of fighting or arguing. **pugnaciously** *(adv)*.

pull pulling pulled
1 *(v)* to move something toward you. **pull** *(n)*.
2 *(v)* to tug or pluck something. *Sally pulled up some of her plants.*
3 *(v)* If you **pull out** of something, you stop doing it. *Adam pulled out of the team because he had injured his knee.*
4 *(v)* If you **pull something off**, you do it with great success.

puffin

pulley
1 *(n)* a wheel with a grooved rim in which a rope or chain can run, used to lift loads more easily.
2 *(n)* a lifting machine made from a rope or chain and a set of linked pulleys. *The diagram below shows how a pulley is used to lift a heavy load.*

pulley
wheel
rope
load

pullover *(n)*
a shirt or sweater that you can pull over your head.

pulp *(n)* a soft crushed mass of something, such as fruit, vegetables, or wood. **pulp** *(v)*.

pulpit *(n)* a raised enclosed platform in a church where a priest stands to preach.

pulsate pulsating pulsated *(v)*
to beat or vibrate regularly. *Dance music pulsated through the house.*

pulse
1 *(n)* a bean, pea, or lentil seed.
2 *(n)* a steady beat or throb, especially the pumping of blood through your body. **pulse** *(v)*.

puma *(poo-ma)* *(n)*
a large wild cat in North and South America. Pumas are also called cougars or mountain lions.

pumice stone *(n)*
a piece of light gray rock, used for rubbing away hard skin.

pummel pummeling pummeled *(v)*
to punch someone or something repeatedly.

pump pumping pumped
1 *(n)* a machine that forces gases or liquids from one place or container into another. *A bicycle pump. A water pump.*
2 *(v)* to empty or fill a container using a pump.
3 *(v)* If you **pump** someone for information, you keep asking them questions.

pumpkin *(n)*
a very big round orange fruit that grows on the ground. People often carve faces in pumpkins at Halloween.

pumpkin

pun *(n)*
a joke based on a word that has two meanings. **pun** *(v)*.

punch
punches punching punched
1 *(v)* to hit something or someone with your fist. **punch** *(n)*.
2 *(n)* a drink made from fruit juice and spices.
3 *(n)* a metal tool used for making holes. **punch** *(v)*.
4 **punch line** *(n)*
the last line of a joke or story, which makes it funny or surprising.

punctual *(adj)*
If you are **punctual**, you arrive at the right time. **punctuality** *(n)*, **punctually** *(adv)*.

punctuation
1 *(singular n)* marks that you use in writing to divide sentences, to show that someone is speaking or to show questions, etc. **punctuate** *(v)*.
2 **punctuation mark** *(n)*
a written mark such as a comma, exclamation mark, period, etc.

puncture *(n)*
a hole in a ball, tire, etc., made by a sharp object. **puncture** *(v)*.

pungent *(adj)* If something is **pungent**, it tastes or smells strong or sharp. *A pungent drink.*

punish punishes punishing punished *(v)* If you **punish** someone, you make them suffer for committing a crime or for behaving badly. **punishment** *(n)*.

Punjabi *(poon-jah-bee)* *(n)* a language spoken in Punjab, a state of India.

punk
1 *(n)* a style of music and dress that was popular in the 1970s. Punks used razor blades and safety pins for decoration, and had brightly colored hair.
2 *(n)* a young person who is inexperienced or constantly getting into trouble.
3 **punk rock** *(n)* loud fast music played by punk bands, often with an anti-authoritarian message.

punt
1 *(v)* to kick a ball dropped from the hands before it reaches the ground.
2 *(n)* a boat used in shallow rivers, which you push along with a long pole. **punt** *(v)*.

puny punier puniest *(adj)* small and feeble. **puniness** *(n)*, **punily** *(adv)*.

pupa pupae *or* pupas *(n)*
an insect at the stage of development between a larva and an adult. *See* **caterpillar**.

pupil
1 *(n)* someone who is being taught, especially a schoolchild.
2 *(n)* the round black part of your eye, that lets light travel through it. *See* **eye**.

puppet *(n)* a toy in the shape of a person or an animal, which you control by pulling strings that are attached to it, or by moving your hand inside it.

puppy puppies *(n)* a young dog.

purchase purchasing purchased
1 *(v)* to buy something. **purchaser** *(n)*.
2 *(n)* something that has been bought.

pure purer purest *(adj)*
clean and not mixed with anything else. *Pure gold.* **purity** *(n)*.

puree *(pyoor-ay)* *(n)*
liquidized or sieved food. **puree** *(v)*.

purge purging purged *(v)*
to clean something out by getting rid of unwanted things. **purge** *(n)*.

purify purifies purifying purified *(v)* to make someone or something pure. **purification** *(n)*.

purple *(n)* the color of the skin of ripe eggplants. **purple** *(adj)*.

purpose
1 *(n)* a reason or an intention. **purposeful** *(adj)*, **purposely** *(adv)*.
2 **on purpose** deliberately.

purr purring purred
1 *(v)* When a cat **purrs**, it makes a low sound in its throat to show pleasure. **purr** *(n)*.
2 *(v)* to make a low sound like a cat. *The limousine purred up the drive.*

purse pursing pursed
1 *(n)* a handbag or a pocketbook.
2 *(v)* a sum of money given as a prize in an athletic competition.
3 If you **purse your lips**, you press them together.

pursue *(per-soo)* pursuing pursued
1 *(v)* to follow or chase something.
2 *(v)* to continue something. *We'll pursue this argument later.*

pursuit *(per-soot)*
1 *(n)* an activity or an occupation. *Leisure pursuits.*
2 If you are **in pursuit of** someone, you are trying to catch them.

pus *(n)* a thick, yellow liquid that comes out of an infected wound.

push pushes pushing pushed
1 *(v)* to move something away from you. **push** *(n)*.
2 *(v)* to press yourself forward. *We pushed through the crowd.*
3 *(v)* to try to force someone to do something. *Harry's father pushed him into a medical career.*

push-up *(n)* exercise in which you raise your body off the floor from a lying position by pushing up with your arms.

put putting put
1 *(v)* to place, lay, or move something.
2 *(v)* to express in words. *How can I put this so that you'll understand?*
3 **put off** *(v)* If you **put something off**, you delay doing it.
4 **put through** *(v)* If you **put someone through** something, you make them endure or suffer it. *How could you put me through this?*
5 **put up** *(v)* If you **put someone up**, you let them sleep overnight at your house.
6 **put up with** *(v)* If you **put up with** something, you allow it to continue.

putrid *(pyoo-trid) (adj)* decaying and foul-smelling.

putt *(rhymes with but)* putting putted *(v)* to tap a golf ball into the hole on a green. **putt** *(n)*, **putter** *(n)*.

putty putties *(n)* a paste that sets hard, used to fix windows into frames.

puzzle puzzling puzzled
1 *(n)* a game or activity for which you have to think hard to solve problems. *A crossword puzzle.*
2 *(n)* someone or something that is hard to understand.
3 *(v)* If something **puzzles** you, it makes you confused or unsure. **puzzled** *(adj)*.

pyramid
1 *(n)* a solid shape with triangular sides that meet at the top. Most pyramids have a square base and four sides. *See* **shape**.
2 *(n)* an ancient Egyptian stone monument where pharaohs and their treasure were buried.
The picture shows a reconstruction of how a pyramid was built and a cutaway view of the Great Pyramid at Giza in Egypt.

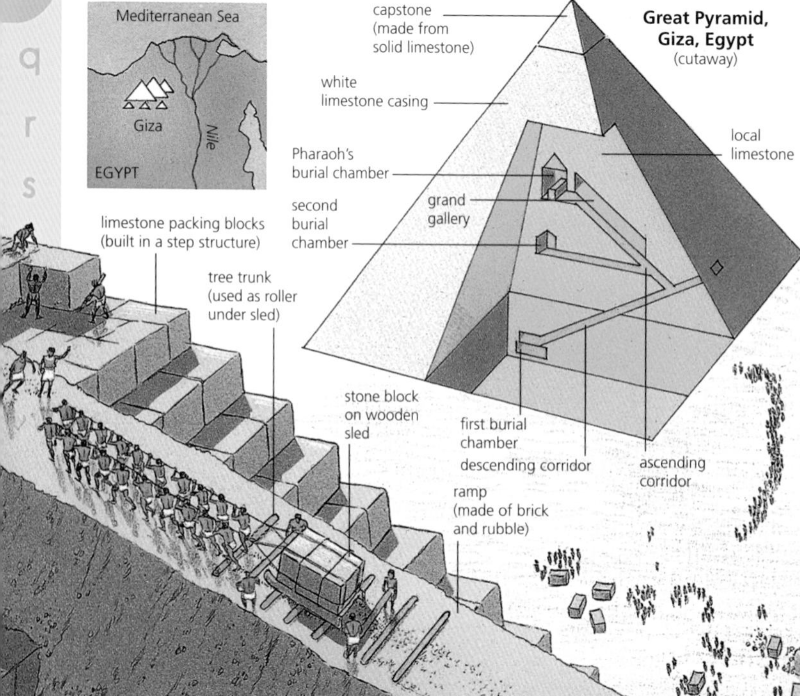

Qq

quack quacking quacked *(v)* When ducks **quack**, they make a sharp, loud sound. **quack** *(n)*.

quad
1 *(n)* one of four children born at almost the same time to one mother. Quad is short for quadruplet.
2 *(n)* an open square with buildings around it, in a school or college. Quad is short for quadrangle.

quadrant *(n)* a quarter of a circle or a quarter of the circumference of a circle.

quadrilateral *(n)* a flat shape with four straight sides. **quadrilateral** *(adj)*.

quadruped *(n)* a four-footed animal. *Horses are quadrupeds.*

quadruple
quadrupling quadrupled
1 *(v)* to multiply something by four.
2 *(adj)* four times as big, or four times as many.

quagmire *(n)* a wet and boggy area of ground.

quail quailing quailed *(n)* a small bird that is hunted for sport and for food.

quaint quainter quaintest *(adj)* charming and old-fashioned. *A quaint little fishing village.* **quaintness** *(n)*, **quaintly** *(adv)*.

quake quaking quaked
1 *(v)* to shake and tremble with fear.
2 *(n)* an earthquake.

qualification
1 *(n)* a skill or ability that makes you able to do something.
2 *(n)* a certificate that shows that you have certain skills or abilities.

qualify
qualifies qualifying qualified
1 *(v)* to reach a level or standard that allows you to do something. *Winning the match qualified us to play in the final.*
2 *(v)* to change or limit the meaning of something. *Victoria qualified the statement, "Boys are stupid," by adding the word "most."*

quality qualities
1 *(n)* The **quality** of something is how good or bad it is. *You can tell it is a cheap suit by its poor quality.*
2 *(n)* a special characteristic of someone or something. *Jody has all the right qualities to be a nurse.*

ualm *(kwalm) (n)*
feeling of worry or uneasiness.
had serious qualms about flying.

uandary *(kwon-dree)*
uandaries *(n)* If you are
n a quandary about something,
ou are confused and do not
now what to do about it.

uantity quantities *(n)*
n amount or number.

uarantine *(n)* When an animal
s put **in quarantine,** it is kept
way from other animals in case
: has a disease. **quarantine** *(v).*

uarrel quarreling quarreled
(v) to argue or to disagree.
uarrelsome *(adj).*
(n) an argument.

uarry quarries
(n) a place where stone,
ate, etc., is dug from the
round. **quarry** *(v).*
(n) a person or an animal
hat is being chased or hunted.

uarter
(n) one of four equal parts. **quarter** *(v).*
(n) a part of a town. *The Latin*
uarter in Paris is famous for its artists.
(n) a coin equal to 25 cents.
quarters *(plural n)* lodgings
r rooms where people live.

uarter note *(n)* a musical note.
ee **notation**.

uartet *(n)* a piece of music that
s played or sung by
our people.

uartz *(n)* a hard
nineral that comes
n many different
orms and colors.
Quartz is used to make
ery accurate clocks,
vatches, and electronic equipment.

quartz crystal

uash quashes quashing quashed
(v) to put down a rebellion.
(v) to reject an idea or a
lecision. *The appeal court*
quashed the conviction.

uaver quavering quavered
v) to shake or to tremble.
Desmond's voice quavered because
e was so nervous.

uay *(key) (n)* a place where
oats can stop to load or unload.

ueasy queasier queasiest *(adj)*
f you feel **queasy,** you feel sick
nd uneasy. **queasiness** *(n).*

ueen
(n) a woman from a royal family
vho is the ruler of her country.
(n) the wife of a king.
3 *(n)* a large female bee, wasp, or ant,
which can lay eggs. *See* **honeycomb**.
4 *(n)* a playing card with a picture of
a queen on it. *The queen of clubs.*
5 *(n)* the most powerful chess
piece, which can move in any
direction. *See* **chess**.

queer queerer queerest *(adj)*
odd or strange. **queerly** *(adv).*

quell quelling quelled *(v)* to stop
or to become calm. *My fears were*
quelled when I saw someone I knew.

quench
quenches quenching quenched
1 *(v)* If you **quench**
a fire, you put it out.
2 *(v)* If you **quench** your thirst, you
drink until you are no longer thirsty.

query *(kware-ee)*
queries querying queried
1 *(n)* a question or doubt
about something.
2 *(v)* to ask questions about
something because you think
there has been some mistake.
May I query that statement?

quest *(n)* a long search.

question questioning questioned
1 *(n)* a sentence that asks something.
2 *(n)* a problem or something that
needs to be talked about. *We need*
to tackle the question of bullying.
3 *(v)* to ask questions.
4 *(v)* to be doubtful about something.
I question the truth of that claim.

question mark *(n)* the punctuation
mark (?) used in writing to show
that a sentence is a question.

questionnaire *(n)*
a list of questions that someone
asks you to find out your opinions.

queue *(kyoo)* queuing queued
1 *(n)* a line of people waiting
for something.
2 *(v)* to wait in a line of people.

quibble quibbling quibbled *(v)*
to argue about unimportant
things. **quibble** *(n).*

quiche *(keesh) (n)* a savory dish
made of pastry and filled with
eggs, cheese, vegetables, etc.

quick quicker quickest
1 *(adj)* fast. **quicken** *(v),*
quick *(adv),* **quickly** *(adv).*
2 *(adj)* clever and lively.
3 *(n)* the skin under your nails.

quicksand *(n)*
loose, wet sand that you can sink into.

quiet quieter quietest
1 *(adj)* not loud. *Everyone spoke*
in quiet voices. **quietness** *(n),*
quiet *(v),* **quietly** *(adv).*
2 *(adj)* peaceful and calm.
We spent a quiet afternoon by the
river. **quietness** *(n),* **quietly** *(adv).*

quill
1 *(n)* the long, hollow,
central part of a bird's feather.
2 *(n)* one of the long,
pointed spines
on a porcupine.
See **porcupine**.
3 **quill pen** *(n)* a pen
made from a bird's
feather, with its quill
cut to form a nib.

quill pen
nib

quilt *(n)* a warm,
usually padded covering for a bed.

quilted *(adj)*
If material is **quilted**,
it is padded and sewn in lines.

quintet *(n)* a piece of music that
is played or sung by five people.

quip *(n)* a witty or clever remark.

quit quitting quit *or* quitted
1 *(v)* to stop doing something.
Dad has promised to quit smoking.
2 *(v)* to leave something. *Donovan*
decided to quit his job.

quite
1 *(adv)* rather, or fairly.
The concert was quite good.
2 *(adv)* completely. *I haven't*
quite finished.

quiver quivering quivered
1 *(v)* to tremble or vibrate. **quiver** *(n).*
2 *(n)* a case for arrows.

quiz quizzes quizzing quizzed
1 *(n)* a test or game where you
have to answer questions.
2 *(v)* to question someone closely.

quota *(n)* a fixed amount or
share of something. *Our class*
already has its quota of books.

quotation
1 *(n)* a sentence or short passage
from a book, play, speech, etc.,
that is repeated by someone else.
2 *(n)* a written estimate of how
much a job will cost.

quotation mark *(n)*
the punctuation mark (") or (')
used in writing to show where
speech begins and ends or used
to highlight certain words.

quote quoting quoted
1 *(v)* to repeat words that were spoken
or written by someone else. **quote** *(n).*
2 *(v)* to estimate or guess how
much a job will cost. **quote** *(n).*

quotient *(kwo-shent) (n)*
the number that you get when
you divide one number by another.
3 is the quotient of 12 and 4.

Qur'an *see* **Koran**.

Rr

rabbi *(rab-eye) (n)*
a Jewish religious leader.

rabbit *(n)* a small long-eared, furry mammal that lives in a burrow. *See* **angora**.

rabble *(n)* a noisy crowd of people.

rabies *(ray-beez) (n)* an often fatal disease that affects dogs, humans, and other animals. **rabid** *(rab-id) (adj)*.

raccoon *(n)* a mammal with a black-and-white face and a ringed tail.

race racing raced
1 *(n)* a test of speed. *A running race.* **race** *(v)*.
2 *(n)* one of the major groups into which human beings can be divided. People of the same race come from the same part of the world and share the same physical characteristics, such as skin color.
3 *(v)* to run or move very fast.

race car *(n)*
a car designed to race at very high speeds. *The picture below shows a cutaway view of a Camel Benetton Ford B193B Formula One race car, as used in 1993.*

race relations *(plural n)*
the way that people of different races get along together when they live in the same community.

racial
1 *(adj)* having to do with a person's race. *What is your racial origin?*
2 *(adj)* having to do with different races. *Racial harmony.*

racist *(ray-sist) (adj)* Someone who is **racist** thinks that some races are better than others, and treats people of other races unfairly or cruelly. **racism** *(n),* **racist** *(n).*

rack racking racked
1 *(n)* a framework for holding things, from which to hang things. *A plate rack. A clothes rack.*
2 *(n)* an instrument of torture used in the past to stretch the body of a victim.
3 *(v)* If you **rack your brains**, you think very hard. *I racked my brains to remember his name.*

racket
1 **racket** *or* **racquet** *(n)* a stringed bat that you use in tennis, squash, and badminton. *See* **badminton**.
2 *(n)* a very loud noise.
3 *(n)* a dishonest activity. *The police exposed a gambling racket.*

racquet *see* **racket**.

radar *(n)* Planes and ships use **radar** to find solid objects by reflecting radio waves off them. Radar stands for "radio detecting and ranging."

radial *(adj)*
spreading out from the center.

radiant
1 *(adj)* bright and shining. **radiance** *(n).*
2 *(adj)* Someone who is **radiant** looks very healthy and happy.

radiate radiating radiated
1 *(v)* to spread out from the center.
2 *(v)* to send out something strongly. *Mario radiates confidence.*

radiation
1 *(n)* the sending out of rays of light, heat, etc.
2 *(n)* particles that are sent out from a radioactive substance.

radiator
1 *(n)* a metal container through which hot water or steam circulates, sending out heat into a room.
2 *(n)* a metal device through which water circulates to cool a vehicle's engine. *See* **car**, **race car**.

radical
1 *(adj)* If a change is **radical**, it is thorough and has important and far-reaching effects. **radically** *(adv).*
2 *(adj)* Someone who is **radical** believes in extreme political change. **radical** *(n).*

radio radioing radioed
1 *(n)* a piece of equipment that you use to listen to sounds sent by electrical waves. **radio** *(adj).*
2 *(v)* to send a message using a radio.

radioactive *(adj)* If an object is **radioactive**, it gives off strong, usually harmful rays. **radioactivity** *(n).*

radiography *(n)* the process of taking X-ray photographs of people's bones, organs, etc. **radiographer** *(n).*

radish radishes *(n)*
a small red-and-white vegetable that you eat in salads. *See* **vegetable**.

radium *(n)* a radioactive element sometimes used to treat cancer.

radius *(ray-dee-uss)* **radii**
1 *(n)* a straight line drawn from the center of a circle to its outer edge. *See* **circle**.

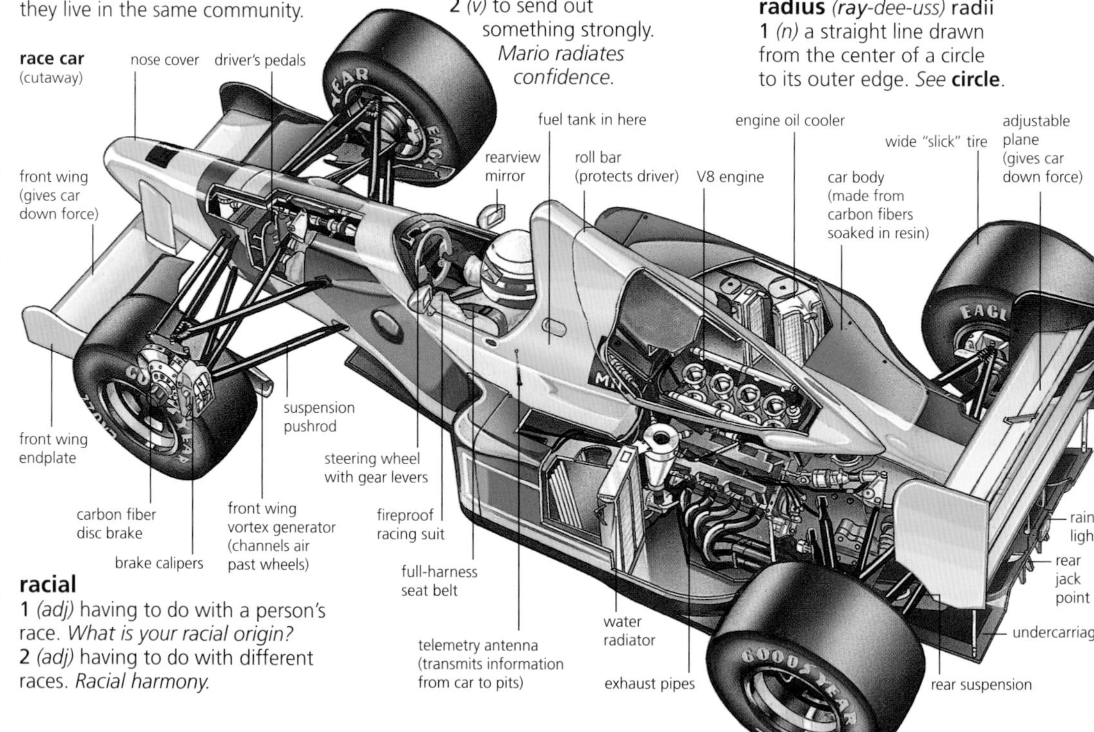

a b c d e f g h i j k l m n o p q r s t u v w x y z

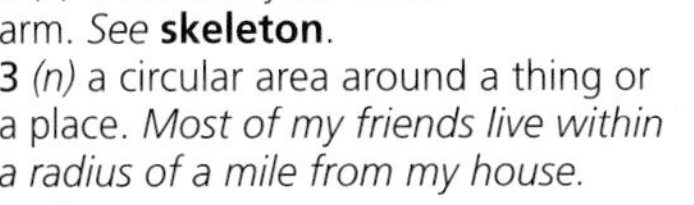

2 *(n)* a bone in your lower arm. *See* **skeleton**.
3 *(n)* a circular area around a thing or a place. *Most of my friends live within a radius of a mile from my house.*

raffle *(n)* a way of raising money by selling tickets and then giving prizes to people with winning tickets. **raffle** *(v)*.

raft rafting rafted
1 *(n)* a floating platform often made from logs tied together.
2 *(v)* to travel by raft. **rafting** *(n)*.
3 *(n)* an inflatable rubber craft with a flat bottom. *The picture shows an inflatable raft traveling through fast-moving water.*

inflatable raft

rag
1 *(n)* a piece of old cloth.
2 **rags** *(plural n)* very old, worn-out clothing.

rage raging raged
1 If you are **in a rage**, you are very angry.
2 *(v)* to be violent or noisy. *The bull raged through the town.*

ragged *(rag-ed) (adj)* old, torn, and scruffy. **raggedly** *(adv)*.

raid
1 *(n)* a sudden attack on a place. **raider** *(n)*, **raid** *(v)*.
2 *(n)* a sudden visit by the police to search for criminals, drugs, etc. **raid** *(v)*.

rail
1 *(n)* a fixed bar or metal track.
2 *(n)* the railroad. *Thomas loves traveling by rail.* **rail** *(adj)*.

railing *(n)* a metal bar that is a part of a fence.

railroad *(n)* a path made from metal tracks, which can support cars pulled by locomotives.

rain raining rained
1 *(n)* water that falls from clouds. **rain** *(v)*, **rainy** *(adj)*.
2 *(v)* to fall like rain.

rainbow *(n)* an arc of different colors caused by sunlight shining through raindrops. *See* **spectrum**.

rainfall *(n)* the amount of rain that falls in one place in a certain time.

rain forest *(n)* a thick tropical forest where a lot of rain falls. *The picture below shows the main rain forests of the world, and some examples of rain forest wildlife.* **rain forest** *(adj)*.

rain forests and rain forest wildlife

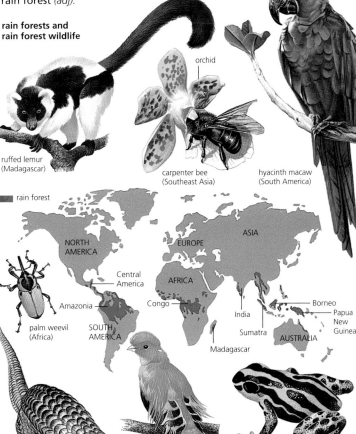

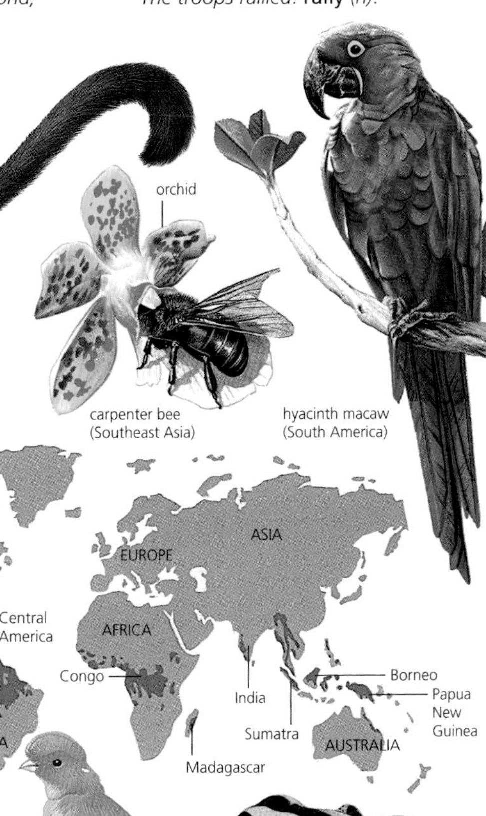

rally rallying rallied
1 *(v)* to come together as a group, often to achieve a common goal. *The troops rallied.* **rally** *(n)*.
2 *(n)* An exchange of shots during a racket sport such as tennis.

raise raising raised
1 *(v)* to lift something up. *Raise your glasses for a toast.*
2 *(v)* If you **raise** money, you collect it for a particular cause or charity.
3 *(v)* to look after children or young animals until they are adults. *Martha has raised five sons.*

raisin *(n)* a dried grape.

rake raking raked
1 *(n)* a garden tool with metal teeth used to level soil or to collect leaves, grass cuttings, etc.
2 *(v)* to use a rake. *Bernard is raking up leaves.*
3 *(v) (informal)* If you **rake it in**, you make a lot of money.

ram ramming rammed
1 *(n)* a male sheep.
2 *(v)* to crash into something deliberately.
3 *(v)* to push something into a space. *Kitty rammed her clothes into the bag.*

RAM *(n)* the part of a computer's memory that is lost when you switch the computer off. The initials RAM stand for random access memory.

Ramadan *(n)* the ninth month of the Islamic year when Muslims must not eat between sunrise and sunset.

Some words that begin with a "r" sound are spelled "wr."

ramble rambling rambled
1 *(v)* to wander about without purpose. **ramble** *(n)*, **rambler** *(n)*.
2 *(v)* to speak for a long time in a way that is hard to follow.

rambling *(adj)*
badly planned or out of control. *A rambling house. A rambling speech.*

ramp *(n)* a man-made slope linking one level with another.

rampage *(n)* If you go **on the rampage**, you rush about in a noisy and destructive way. **rampage** *(v)*.

rampant *(adj)* wild and unrestrained. *Rampant weeds.*

rampart *(n)* the surrounding wall or embankment of a fort or castle.

ramshackle *(adj)* rickety or likely to fall apart. *A ramshackle cottage.*

ranch ranches *(n)*
a large farm for cattle, sheep, or horses. **rancher** *(n)*.

rancid *(adj)* **Rancid** food tastes sour because it has gone bad.

rand *(n)* the main unit of money in South Africa, Lesotho, and Swaziland.

random
1 *(adj)* without any fixed plan or order. *Juan grabbed a random selection of clothes.* **randomly** *(adv)*.
2 If you do something **at random**, you do it without any plan or purpose.

range ranging ranged
1 *(n)* a collection or number of things.
2 *(v)* to vary between one extreme and the other. *The dogs ranged in size from tiny Chihuahuas to enormous St. Bernards.* **range** *(n)*.
3 *(n)* the distance that a bullet or rocket can travel.
4 *(n)* an area of open land used for a special purpose. *A cattle range.*
5 *(n)* a long chain of mountains.
6 *(v)* to wander over a large area. *Cattle ranged over the plains.*
7 *(n)* a cooking stove.

ranger *(n)* someone in charge of a wildlife park or forest.

rank
1 *(n)* an official position or job level. *Charles rose to the rank of colonel.*
2 *(n)* social class. *People of all ranks supported the cause.*
3 *(adj)* having a strong and unpleasant odor or taste.
4 *(adj)* complete or absolute. *Rank amateur.*

ransack ransacking ransacked *(v)*
to search a place wildly, usually looking for things to steal.

ransom *(n)* money that is demanded before someone can be set free.

rant ranting ranted *(v)* to talk or shout in a loud and angry manner.

rap rapping rapped
1 *(v)* to hit something sharply and quickly. **rap** *(n)*.
2 *(n)* a type of music where words are spoken in a rhythmical way with a musical backing. **rap** *(v)*.

rapacious
1 *(adj)* intent on gaining other's possessions.
2 *(adj)* ravenous.

rapid *(adj)* quick and speedy. **rapidity** *(n)*, **rapidly** *(adv)*.

rapier *(n)* a long double-edged sword often used in duels in the 16th and 17th centuries. *This rapier was made in Italy in the 16th century.*

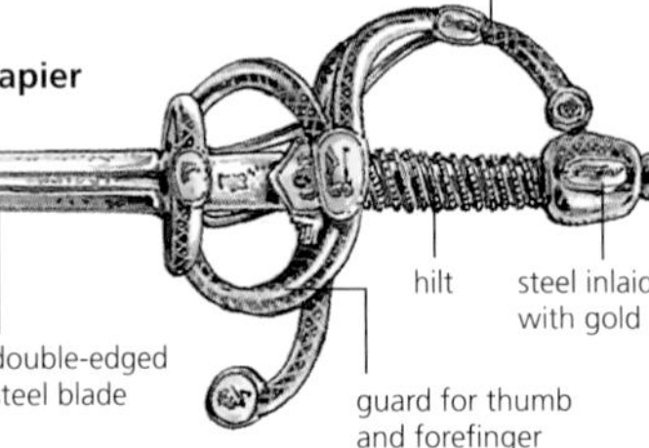

rare rarer rarest
1 *(adj)* not often seen or unusual. **rarity** *(n)*, **rarely** *(adv)*.
2 *(adj)* **Rare** meat is very lightly cooked. *I like my steak rare.*

rascal *(n)* a usually friendly name for someone who is very mischievous.

rash rashes; rasher rashest
1 *(n)* spots or red patches on your skin, caused by an allergy or illness.
2 *(adj)* If you are **rash**, you act quickly, without thinking first. **rashly** *(adv)*.

rasp rasping rasped
1 *(n)* a coarse file used for smoothing metal or wood. *See* **woodwork.**
2 *(v)* to speak in a harsh voice.

raspberry raspberries *(n)*
1 a small red, soft fruit. *See* **fruit**.
2 a dark purple-red color.

rat
1 *(n)* a long-tailed rodent like a large mouse. Rats sometimes spread disease.
2 *(n)* *(informal)* a disloyal or treacherous person.
3 **rat race** *(n)*
very stressful competition for success at work.

rat

rate rating rated
1 *(n)* the speed at which something happens. *Claire spends money at an alarming rate.*
2 *(n)* a charge, or a fee. *Mark charges very high rates for his work.*
3 *(n)* standard, or quality. *Ben gave a first-rate performance.*
4 *(v)* to value someone or something. *David's co-workers rate him highly.* **rating** *(n)*.

rather
1 *(adv)* fairly or quite. *It's rather a long way to walk.*
2 *(adv)* more willingly. *I'd rather be at the beach than at school.*

ratio *(ray-shee-oh)* *(n)*
the proportion of one thing to another, expressed in its simplest terms. *In a group with 15 girls and 5 boys, the ratio of girls to boys is 3 to 1.*

ration *(n)* a limited amount or a share. *No more chocolate for you today, you've already had your ration!* **rationing** *(n)*, **ration** *(v)*.

rational
1 *(adj)* sensible and logical. *We made a rational decision to turn the two small stores into one.* **rationally** *(adv)*.
2 *(adj)* calm, reasonable, and sane. *Rational behavior.* **rationally** *(adv)*.

rattle rattling rattled
1 *(v)* to make a rapid series of short sharp noises. **rattle** *(n)*.
2 *(n)* a baby's toy.

rattlesnake *(n)* a venomous snake from North and South America with a tail that rattles as it vibrates.

raucous *(raw-kus)*
1 *(adj)* harsh or loud. *A raucous voice.* **raucously** *(adv)*.
2 *(adj)* loud and rowdy. *A raucous party.*

rave raving raved
1 *(v)* to speak in a wild, uncontrolled way.
2 *(v)* *(informal)* to be very enthusiastic about something.

raven *(n)*
a large black bird of the crow family.

Some words that begin with a "r" sound are spelled "wr."

ravenous *(adj)* very hungry.

ravine *(n)* a deep, narrow valley with steep sides.

raw rawer rawest
1 *(adj)* Food that is **raw** has not been cooked or processed.
2 **raw materials** *(n)* the basic things used to make something.

ray
1 *(n)* a strong line of light, radiation, etc.
2 *(n)* a type of fish with a flat body, large wing-like fins, and a long tail.

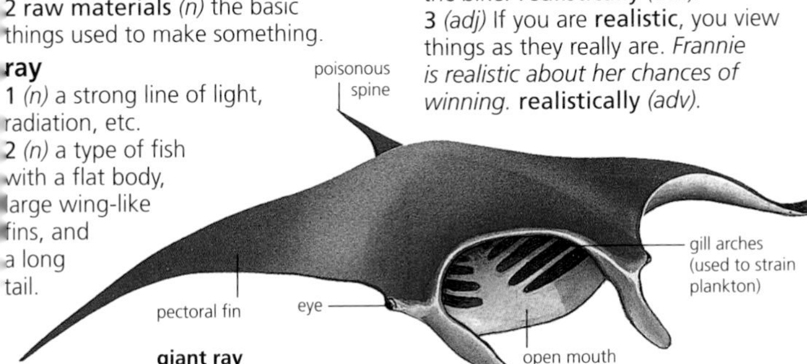

giant ray

razor *(n)* an instrument with a blade, used to shave hair from the skin.

reach reaches reaching reached
1 *(v)* to stretch out to something with your hand. *Can you reach the book on the top shelf?*
2 *(v)* to extend or to go as far as. *Our garden reaches down to the river.*
3 *(v)* to arrive somewhere. *We eventually reached the summit.*

react reacting reacted
1 *(v)* to respond to something that happens. *The firemen reacted quickly to the alarm.* **reaction** *(n).*
2 *(v)* If one substance **reacts** with another, a chemical change takes place in one or both of the substances as they are mixed together. **reaction** *(n).*

reactionary *(adj)* If someone is **reactionary**, they are against change and want to keep things as they are. **reactionary** *(n).*

reactor *(n)* a large machine in which nuclear energy is produced.

read reading read
1 *(v)* to look at written or printed words and understand what they mean.
2 *(v)* to understand some form of communication. *Hilary can read my mind.*

readily *(adv)* easily or willingly.

ready readier readiest *(adj)* If you are **ready**, you are prepared or you are in a position to start.

real
1 *(adj)* true and not imaginary. *The real story isn't quite so dramatic.* **reality** *(n).*
2 *(adj)* genuine and not artificial. *A real diamond.*

realistic
1 *(adj)* very like the real thing. *A realistic model.* **realism** *(n),* **realistically** *(adv).*
2 *(adj)* sensible, practical, or correct. *I will only pay a realistic price for the bike.* **realistically** *(adv).*
3 *(adj)* If you are **realistic**, you view things as they really are. *Frannie is realistic about her chances of winning.* **realistically** *(adv).*

reality realities
1 *(n)* truth or the actual situation. *Being a model looks glamorous, but the reality is not much fun.*
2 *(n)* a fact of life that must be faced. *After the vacation, we must return to the reality of work.*

realize realizing realized *(v)* to become aware that something is true. *Randall realized that he had been working too hard.* **realization** *(n).*

really
1 *(adv)* actually or in reality. *Are the rumors really true?*
2 *(adv)* very. *I'm really happy.*

reap reaping reaped
1 *(v)* to cut a crop for harvest.
2 *(v)* If you **reap the reward** for something you have done, you experience the results of it.

reappear
reappearing reappeared *(v)* to come into sight again. **reappearance** *(n).*

rear rearing reared
1 *(v)* to breed and bring up young animals.
2 *(v)* to care for and educate children.
3 *(n)* the back of something. **rear** *(adj).*
4 *(v)* If a horse **rears**, it rises up on its back legs.

rearrange rearranging rearranged *(v)* to arrange things differently.

reason reasoning reasoned
1 *(n)* the cause of something or the motive behind someone's action.
2 *(v)* to think in a logical way. *Aaron reasoned that it would be quicker to walk.* **reason** *(n).*
3 *(v)* If you **reason** with someone, you try to persuade them that what you suggest is sensible.

reasonable
1 *(adj)* fair. *Your offer seems reasonable to me.* **reasonably** *(adv).*
2 *(adj)* sensible. *Harry won't make a fuss, he's always very reasonable.* **reasonably** *(adv).*
3 *(adj)* moderate or quite good. *The weather was reasonable.* **reasonably** *(adv).*

reassure reassuring reassured *(v)* to calm someone and give them confidence. **reassurance** *(n).*

rebel *(reb-ell) (n)* someone who fights against a government or people in authority. **rebel** *(reb-**ell**) (v),* **rebellious** *(reb-**el**-yus) (adj).*

rebellion
1 *(n)* armed resistance against a government.
2 *(n)* an organized protest against people in authority.

rebuke rebuking rebuked *(v)* to tell someone off. **rebuke** *(n).*

recall recalling recalled
1 *(v)* to remember something. *I can still recall the day I met you.*
2 *(v)* to order someone to return. *The witness was recalled to the stand.*

recap recapping recapped *(v)* *(informal)* to repeat the main points of what has been said. Recap is short for recapitulate. **recap** *(n).*

recede receding receded
1 *(v)* to go back. *The tide receded.* **receding** *(adj).*
2 *(v)* to fade gradually. *Hopes of rescue receded as night fell.*
3 *(v)* When a man's hair **recedes**, he becomes more and more bald at the front. **receding** *(adj).*

receipt *(re-**seet**) (n)* a written acknowledgment that money or goods have been received.

receive receiving received *(v)* to get or to accept something.

receiver
1 *(n)* the part of a telephone that you hold in your hand.
2 *(n)* a piece of equipment for receiving radio or television signals.

recent *(adj)* happening, made, or done a short time ago. **recently** *(adv).*

reception
1 *(n)* the way in which something or someone is received. *The play was given a frosty reception. The reception on our television is very bad.*
2 *(n)* a formal party.

receptionist *(n)* a person whose job it is to greet people in an office, clinic, etc., or when they call on the telephone.

Some words that begin with a "r" sound are spelled "wr."

recess recesses
1 *(n)* a break from work or school for rest or relaxation.
2 *(n)* a part of a room set back from the main area.

recession *(n)* a time when a country produces fewer goods and more people become unemployed.

recipe *(ress-ip-ee) (n)* a set of instructions for preparing and cooking food.

recipient *(n)* a person who receives something. *The recipient of the first prize wins a trip to Barbados.*

recital *(n)* a musical performance by a single performer or by a small group of musicians.

recite reciting recited *(v)* to say aloud something that you have learned by heart. **recitation** *(n)*.

reckless *(adj)* If you are **reckless**, you are careless about your own and other people's safety. **recklessly** *(adv)*.

reckon reckoning reckoned
1 *(v)* to calculate or count. **reckoning** *(n)*.
2 *(v)* to think or to have an opinion. *I reckon that our team will win.*

reclaim reclaiming reclaimed
1 *(v)* to get back something that is yours. *Maud reclaimed her jewels from the safe.*
2 *(v)* to make land suitable for farming, etc., by clearing it or draining it. **reclamation** *(n)*.

recline reclining reclined *(v)* to lean or lie back.

recognize recognizing recognized *(v)* to see someone and know who they are. **recognition** *(n)*, **recognizable** *(adj)*, **recognizably** *(adv)*.

recollect recollecting recollected *(v)* to remember or to recall. **recollection** *(n)*.

recommend recommending recommended *(v)* to suggest something or someone because you think that they are good. *My uncle recommended my piano teacher.* **recommendation** *(n)*.

reconcile reconciling reconciled
1 *(v)* to make or become friendly again after an argument or fight. **reconciliation** *(n)*.
2 *(v)* to decide to put up with something. *I reconciled myself to working over the holidays.*

reconsider reconsidering reconsidered *(v)* to think again about a previous decision.

reconstruction
1 *(n)* the rebuilding of something that has been destroyed. **reconstruct** *(v)*.
2 *(n)* the careful piecing together of past events. **reconstruct** *(v)*.

record recording recorded
1 *(rek-**ord**) (v)* to write down information so that it can be kept. **record** *(**rek**-ord) (n)*.
2 *(rek-**ord**) (v)* to put music or other sounds onto a disk etc. so that it can be reproduced. **recording** *(n)*.
3 *(**rek**-ord) (n)*
If you set a **record** in something like a sport, you do it better than anyone has ever done before.

recorder
1 *(n)* a machine for recording sounds, music, speech etc.
2 *(n)* a woodwind musical instrument. You play the recorder by blowing into the mouthpiece and covering holes with your fingers to make different notes.

mouthpiece
window
ramp
head joint
finger hole
middle joint or barrel
double hole
foot joint

descant recorder

recover recovering recovered
1 *(v)* to get better after an illness or difficulty. **recovery** *(n)*.
2 *(v)* to get back something that has been lost or stolen. **recovery** *(n)*.

recreation *(rek-ree-ay-shun) (singular n)* the games, sports, hobbies, etc. that people do for pleasure in their spare time. *What do you do for recreation?* **recreational** *(adj)*.

recruit *(re-**kroot**) (n)* someone who has recently joined a business, or an organization such as the armed forces. **recruitment** *(n)*, **recruit** *(v)*.

rectangle *(n)* a four-sided shape with two pairs of equal, parallel sides and four right angles. **rectangular** *(adj)*. *See* **shape**.

rectify rectifies rectifying rectified *(v)* to make something right.

recuperate recuperating recuperated *(v)* to recover slowly from an illness or injury. **recuperation** *(n)*.

recur recurring recurred
1 *(v)* to happen again. *The same problem recurs every time I use the laptop.* **recurrence** *(n)*, **recurrent** *(adj)*.
2 *(v)* In a division problem, if a number in the answer **recurs**, it keeps occurring. For example, $10 \div 3 = 3.33333...$ or 3.3 recurring.

recycle recycling recycled *(v)* to process used items, such as glass bottles, newspapers, and cans, so that they can be reused to make new products. **recyclable** *(adj)*.

red *(n)* the color of blood. **red** *(adj)*.

redeem redeeming redeemed
1 *(v)* to save or to rescue. *Glen redeemed our reputation by scoring three goals.* **redemption** *(n)*.
2 *(v)* to claim back or exchange something. *Caroline redeemed her cans at the recycling center.*

red herring *(n)* something that diverts people unnecessarily from what they should be doing.

red tape *(n)* rules, regulations, and paperwork that make it difficult to get things done.

reduce reducing reduced *(v)* to make something smaller or less. *During the sale, all prices were reduced.* **reduction** *(n)*.

redundant *(adj)* too many words for what you mean to say or write. *Saying "round circle" is redundant.* **redundancy** *(n)*.

reed
1 *(n)* a plant with long, thin, hollow stems that grows in or near water.
2 *(n)* a piece of thin cane or metal in the mouthpiece of some musical instruments, such as a clarinet, oboe, or saxophone. When you blow over or through the reed, it vibrates and makes a sound. *See* **woodwind**.

reef
1 *(n)* a line of rocks or coral close to the surface of the sea. *The picture shows part of the Great Barrier Reef near Queensland, Australia.*
2 **reef knot** *(n)* a strong double knot. *See* **knot**.

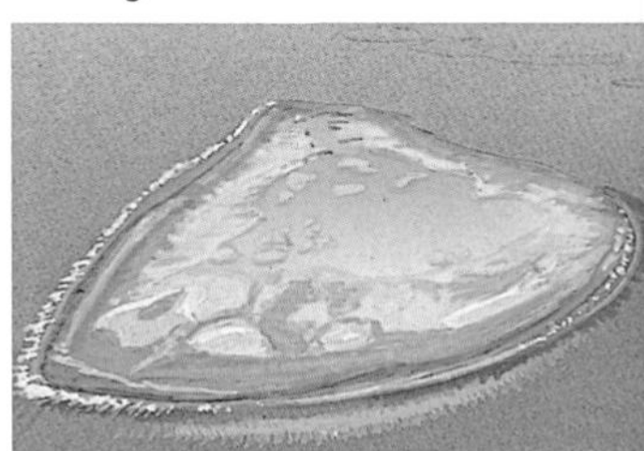

reef

Some words that begin with a "r" sound are spelled "wr."

reek reeking reeked *(v)* to smell strongly of something unpleasant. *The room reeked of cabbage.*

reel reeling reeled
1 *(n)* a cylinder on which thread, film, etc. is wound. *See* **angling**.
2 *(v)* to stagger around unsteadily. *The man reeled into a lamppost.*
3 *(n)* a type of folk dance.
4 *(v)* If you **reel off** something, you say it very fast.

ref *short for* **referee**.

refer referring referred
1 *(v)* If you **refer to** a book, you look in it for information.
2 *(v)* If you **refer to** something while talking or writing, you mention it.
3 *(v)* to pass a question or a problem on to someone else. *My doctor has referred me to a specialist.*

referee
1 *(n)* someone who supervises a sports match or game and makes sure that the players obey the rules.
2 *(n)* someone who provides a statement about a person's character and abilities.

reference
1 *(n)* a mention of someone or something. *There was a reference to you in the speech.*
2 *(n)* a written statement about someone's character and abilities. *You will need references for this job.*
3 *(n)* a book, magazine, website, etc. that you use to produce a piece of work. *Please list your references at the end of your essay.*

reference book *(n)* a book that you use to find information. *Encyclopedias and dictionaries are reference books.*

referendum
referendums *or* **referenda** *(n)* a vote by the people of a country on a very important question.

refill refilling refilled *(v)* to fill something again. **refill** *(n)*.

refine refining refined *(v)* to purify something, such as sugar.

refined *(adj)*
A **refined** person is very polite and has elegant manners and tastes.

refinery refineries *(n)*
a factory where raw materials are purified. *Oil refineries turn crude oil into gasoline and other products.*

refit refitting refitted *(v)*
to repair something or to supply it with new parts or equipment.

reflect reflecting reflected
1 *(v)* to show an image of something on a shiny surface. **reflection** *(n)*.
2 *(v)* When rays of light or heat are **reflected**, they bounce off an object. *The diagram below shows how a light ray is reflected when it hits a mirror.*
3 *(v)* to think carefully. *Arthur reflected on the meaning of life.* **reflection** *(n)*.

reflective
1 *(adj)* acting like a mirror.
2 *(adj)* thoughtful. **reflectively** *(adv)*.

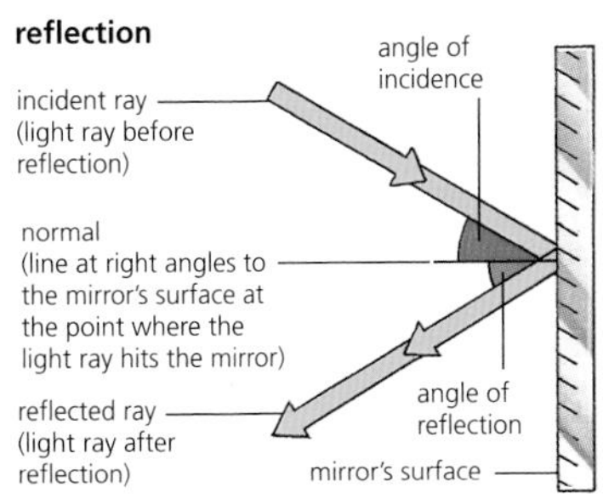

reflex reflexes
1 *(n)* an automatic and instinctive action. *Blinking is a reflex.* **reflex** *(adj)*.
2 *(adj)* A **reflex** angle is an angle between 180° and 360°.

reform reforming reformed *(v)*
to improve something that is unsatisfactory. *Buster is trying to reform his behavior.* **reform** *(n)*.

reformatory *(n)*
a school or institution for young people who have broken the law.

refract refracting refracted *(v)*
When a light ray or sound wave is **refracted**, it changes direction because it has traveled from one medium into another. *The diagram shows how a light ray is refracted as it moves from the air into glass and then back into the air.* **refraction** *(n)*.

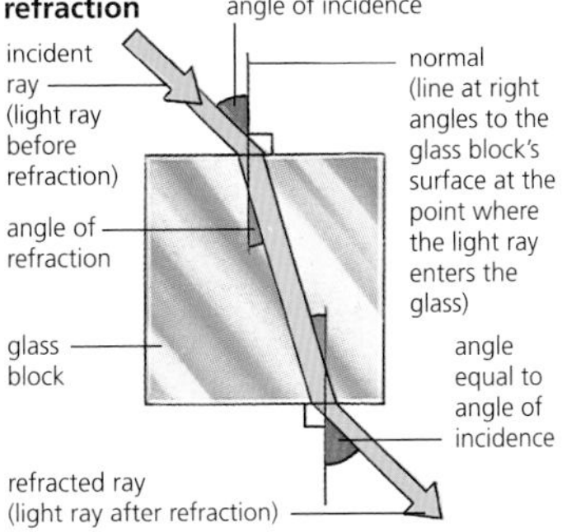

refrain refraining refrained
1 *(v)* to stop yourself from doing something. *Please refrain from standing on the seats.*
2 *(n)* a regularly repeated chorus or song.

refresh refreshes refreshing refreshed *(v)* If something **refreshes** you, it makes you feel fresh and strong again. **refreshing** *(adj)*.

refreshments *(plural n)*
drink and small amounts of food.

refrigerator *(n)* a very cold cabinet used for storing food and drink. *Refrigerators are kept cool by a special substance called refrigerant that circulates constantly. The diagram shows how refrigerant evaporates inside the refrigerator, drawing heat away from the food, and condenses outside it, sending out the heat that it has gained.* **refrigeration** *(n)*, **refrigerate** *(v)*.

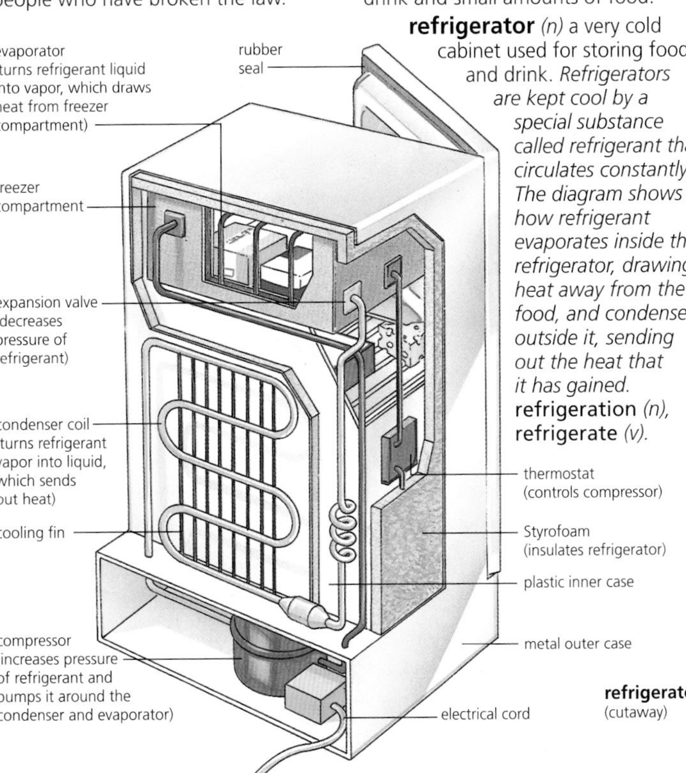

refrigerator (cutaway)

refuel refueling refueled *(v)* to take on more fuel.

refuge *(n)* a place of shelter and safety.

refugee *(n)* a homeless person who has been forced to leave their home because of war, persecution, or natural disaster.

refund refunding refunded *(v)* to give money back to the person who paid it. **refund** *(n).*

refuse refusing refused
1 *(ree-**fyooz**) (v)* to say you will not do something or accept something. **refusal** *(n).*
2 *(**ref**-yuce) (n)* trash or waste.

regal *(adj)* having to do with or fit for a king or queen. **regally** *(adv).*

regard regarding regarded
1 *(v)* to have an opinion about something. *Doug regards politicians with contempt.* **regard** *(n).*
2 *(v)* to look at closely. *The cats regarded each other with suspicion.*
3 *(v)* to respect or consider. *Melissa regards her sister's privacy.*
4 *(plural n)* If someone sends you their **regards**, they send you their best wishes.

regarding *(prep)* about or concerning.

regardless *(adj)* without considering anything or anyone else. *Nina drove at high speed, regardless of the other drivers.* **regardlessly** *(adv).*

regatta *(n)* a series of races for rowing or sailing boats.

reggae *(**reg**-ay) (n)* a type of rhythmic pop music that came from Jamaica.

regiment *(n)* a military unit usually made up of a number of battalions.

region *(n)* a large area or district. **regional** *(adj),* **regionally** *(adv).*

register registering registered
1 *(n)* a book in which names or official records are kept. *A class register.* **registration** *(n).*
2 *(v)* to enter something on an official list. *All cars must be registered.* **registration** *(n).*
3 *(n)* the range of notes produced by a musical instrument or a voice.
4 *(v)* to show an emotion. *Aaron's face registered dismay.*

regret regretting regretted *(v)* to be sad or sorry about something. **regret** *(n),* **regretful** *(adj).*

regrettable *(adj)* If something is **regrettable**, it is unfortunate and you wish that it had not happened.

regular
1 *(adj)* usual or normal. *This is my regular route home.* **regularly** *(adv).*
2 *(adj)* happening at predictable times. *Regular meals.* **regularity** *(n),* **regularly** *(adv).*
3 *(adj)* even or steady. *A regular pattern. A regular heartbeat.* **regularity** *(n),* **regularly** *(adv).*

regulate regulating regulated *(v)* to control or adjust something. *A thermostat regulates temperature.*

regulation
1 *(n)* an official rule.
2 *(n)* the act of controlling or adjusting something.

regurgitate *(re-**gurj**-it-ate)* regurgitating regurgitated *(v)* to bring food from the stomach back into the mouth. *Many birds regurgitate food to feed their young.*

rehearse *(re-**herss**)* rehearsing rehearsed *(v)* to practice for a public performance. **rehearsal** *(n).*

reign *(rain)* reigning reigned *(v)* to rule as a king or queen. **reign** *(n).*

reimburse *(re-im-**burss**)* reimbursing reimbursed *(v)* to pay someone back the money they have had to spend on your behalf. *The company will reimburse your train fare.* **reimbursement** *(n).*

reindeer reindeer *(n)* a deer that lives in Arctic areas. *Both the male and female reindeer have large, branching antlers.*

reindeer (male)

reinforce reinforcing reinforced *(v)* to strengthen something. *Concrete bridges are reinforced by metal rods.*

reinforcement
1 *(n)* something that strengthens something else.
2 **reinforcements** *(plural n)* extra troops sent to strengthen a fighting force.

reject rejecting rejected
1 *(re-**jekt**) (v)* to refuse to accept something. *Jim rejected all offers of help.* **rejection** *(n).*
2 *(**ree**-jekt) (n)* something or someone that is not wanted or accepted. *I've sorted out my collection of toys and given all the rejects away.*

rejoice rejoicing rejoiced *(v)* to be very happy about something.

relapse relapsing relapsed *(v)* to fall back or return to the position that you were in before. *Megan gave up chocolate for a month, but now she's relapsed.* **relapse** *(n).*

relate relating related
1 *(v)* If things **relate** to one another, there is a connection between them.
2 *(v)* If people **relate** to each other, they get along well together.
3 *(v)* to tell a story.

related *(adj)* If you are **related** to someone, you are part of their family.

relation
1 *(n)* a connection between things.
2 *(n)* a member of your family.

relationship
1 *(n)* the way in which two people get along together.
2 *(n)* the way in which things are connected.
3 *(n)* If you are **in a relationship** with someone, it means you are romantically involved with them.

relative
1 *(n)* a member of your family.
2 *(adj)* compared with others. *Poor people in the West live in relative luxury compared with many people in the world.*

relatively *(adv)* compared with others. *A 50-year-old seems relatively young in a room full of retirees.*

relax relaxes relaxing relaxed
1 *(v)* to rest and take things easy. **relaxation** *(n).*
2 *(v)* to become less tense and anxious. **relaxation** *(n).*
3 *(v)* to make something less strict. *The new principal has relaxed the discipline at our school.*

relay relaying relayed
1 *(**ree**-lay) (n)* a team race in which members of the team take turns to run, passing a baton.
2 *(re-**lay**) (v)* to pass a message on to someone else.

release releasing released
1 *(v)* to free something or someone. **release** *(n).*
2 *(v)* If a record, movie, etc. is **released**, it is issued for the first time. **release** *(n).*

relegate relegating relegated *(v)* to assign to a place or position of lesser importance.

relent relenting relented *(v)* to become less strict or more merciful. *I was supposed to stay in all day, but in the end, Mom relented.*

relentless *(adj)* endless and determined. *Alec practices the trumpet with relentless enthusiasm.* **relentlessly** *(adv).*

relevant *(adj)* If something is **relevant**, it is directly concerned with what is being discussed or dealt with. **relevance** *(n).*

reliable *(adj)* trustworthy or dependable. **reliability** *(n),* **reliably** *(adv).*

relic *(n)* something that has survived from the distant past.

relief
1 *(n)* a feeling of freedom from pain or worry. *It's such a relief to know that you're safe!*
2 *(n)* aid given to people in special need. *Famine relief.*
3 **relief map** *(n)* a map that shows the areas of high and low ground by shades of color.

relieve relieving relieved
1 *(v)* to ease someone's trouble or pain.
2 *(v)* If you **relieve** someone, you take over a duty from them.

religion
1 *(n)* belief in God or in gods and goddesses. **religious** *(adj).*
2 *(n)* the practice of your belief through worship, obedience, and prayer. **religious** *(adj).*

relish relishes relishing relished
1 *(v)* to enjoy something greatly.
2 *(n)* a sauce. *Tomato relish.*

reluctant *(adj)* If you are **reluctant**, you do not want to do something. **reluctance** *(n),* **reluctantly** *(adv).*

rely relies relying relied *(v)* If you **rely on** someone or something, you need and trust them. *I had to rely on my friends to help me.* **reliant** *(adj).*

remain remaining remained *(v)* to be left behind or left over.

remainder *(n)* the amount left over.

remains
1 *(plural n)* things left over. *What shall I do with the remains of my lunch?*
2 *(plural n)* a body after death.
3 *(plural n)* the ruins of ancient buildings. *Have you seen the remains of the Colosseum in Rome?*

remark remarking remarked *(v)* to make a comment about something. **remark** *(n).*

remarkable *(adj)* unusual and worth noticing. **remarkably** *(adv).*

remedial *(adj)* intended to help someone with a learning problem or physical difficulty. *Remedial math.*

remedy
remedies remedying remedied
1 *(n)* a cure for an illness.
2 *(n)* the answer to a problem.
3 *(v)* to put something right. *Bill remedied the problem with a phone call.*

remember
remembering remembered
1 *(v)* to keep something in your mind. *I'll always remember Marco.*
2 *(v)* to bring something to mind. *Try to remember the answer.*

remind reminding reminded *(v)* to make someone remember something. *Please remind me to lock the door.* **reminder** *(n).*

reminisce *(rem-in-**iss**)* reminiscing reminisced *(v)* to think or talk about the past and things that you remember. **reminiscence** *(n).*

remnant *(n)* a piece or part of something that is left over. *A remnant of material.*

remorse *(n)* a strong feeling of guilt and regret about something that you have done. **remorseful** *(adj),* **remorsefully** *(adv).*

remote remoter remotest *(adj)* far away, isolated, or distant. **remoteness** *(n),* **remotely** *(adv).*

remote control *(n)* a system by which machines can be operated from a distance, usually by radio signals or by an infrared beam. **remote-controlled** *(adj).*

remove removing removed *(v)* to take something away. **removal** *(n).*

Renaissance *(n)* the flowering of art and learning in Europe between the 14th and 17th centuries, inspired by a revival of interest in the ancient Greeks and Romans. *This picture is based on the pen-and-ink "Study for the Head of Leda," by Leonardo da Vinci, one of the leading Italian Renaissance artists.*

Italian Renaissance drawing

rendezvous *(**ron**-day-voo) (n)* an arranged place and time for a meeting. **rendezvous** *(v).*

renew renewing renewed
1 *(v)* to replace something old with something new. **renewal** *(n).*
2 *(v)* to start something again.
3 *(v)* to extend the period of a library loan, club membership, etc. **renewal** *(n).*

renewable energy *(n)* power from sources, such as wind, waves, and the Sun, that can never be used up.

renovate renovating renovated *(v)* to restore something to good condition or to make it more modern. **renovation** *(n).*

renowned *(adj)* famous or well-known. **renown** *(n).*

rent *(n)* money paid by a tenant to the owner of a property, in return for living in it or using it. **rent** *(v).*

rental *(n)* something that's on loan, such as a car, or a property. *I don't own an apartment; I live in a rental.*

repair repairing repaired *(v)* to make something work again or to put back together something that is broken. **repair** *(n).*

repay repaying repaid *(v)* to pay back money or something else. *Please repay the money you owe. I repaid her visit.* **repayment** *(n).*

repeat repeating repeated *(v)* to say or do something again. **repeat** *(n),* **repetition** *(n).*

repel repelling repelled
1 *(v)* to drive away. *The army repelled the enemy forces.*
2 *(v)* to disgust.

repellent
1 *(adj)* disgusting. *A repellent smell.*
2 *(n)* a chemical that keeps insects and other pests away.

repent repenting repented *(v)* to be deeply sorry for the bad things that you have done. **repentance** *(n),* **repentant** *(adj).*

repertoire *(**rep**-e-twah) (n)* the collection of songs, jokes, stories, etc. that an entertainer can perform.

repetition *(n)* the repeating of words or actions. **repetitious** *(adj),* **repetitive** *(adj).*

replace replacing replaced
1 *(v)* to put one thing or person in place of another. **replacement** *(n).*
2 *(v)* to put something back where it was.

replay replaying replayed
1 *(**re**-play) (n)* a second match between two teams or players when the first match has ended in a draw.
2 *(re-**play**) (v)* to play back a recording to see or hear something again. **replay** *(**re**-play) (n).*

replica *(n)* an exact copy of something. **replicate** *(v).*

Some words that begin with a "r" sound are spelled "wr."

reply replies replying replied *(v)* to give an answer or a response. **reply** *(n).*

report reporting reported
1 *(v)* to give a written or spoken account of things that have happened. **report** *(n).*
2 *(v)* If you **report** someone, you make an official complaint about them.
3 *(v)* to appear for duty. *Please report for work on Monday morning.*

report card *(n)* a listing of a student's grades that is compiled and sent home several times a year.

reporter *(n)*
someone who reports the news for radio, television, or a newspaper.

represent representing represented
1 *(v)* to act on behalf of someone else.
2 *(v)* to stand for something. *On a map, water is usually represented by the color blue.* **representation** *(n).*

representative *(n)* someone who is sent on behalf of someone else. *A sales representative.*

repress
represses repressing repressed
1 *(v)* If you **repress** an emotion, such as anger, you keep it under control and do not show it. **repressed** *(adj).*
2 *(v)* to keep people under very strict control. *The cruel Emperor repressed his people.* **repression** *(n),* **repressed** *(adj).*

reprieve *(rih-preeve)* reprieving reprieved *(v)* to postpone or cancel a punishment, especially a death sentence. **reprieve** *(n).*

reprimand reprimanding reprimanded *(v)* to tell someone off formally. **reprimand** *(n).*

reprisal *(n)* an act of revenge.

reproach reproaches reproaching reproached *(v)* to blame someone or to show that you disapprove of them. *Annie reproached me for forgetting her birthday.* **reproach** *(n).*

reproduce
reproducing reproduced
1 *(v)* to make a copy of something. **reproduction** *(n).*
2 *(v)* When animals **reproduce**, they breed and produce babies. **reproduction** *(n).*

reptile *(n)* a cold-blooded animal with a scaly skin that lays eggs. Lizards, crocodiles, snakes, turtles, and tortoises are all reptiles. *The picture shows a range of reptiles from around the world.* **reptilian** *(adj).*

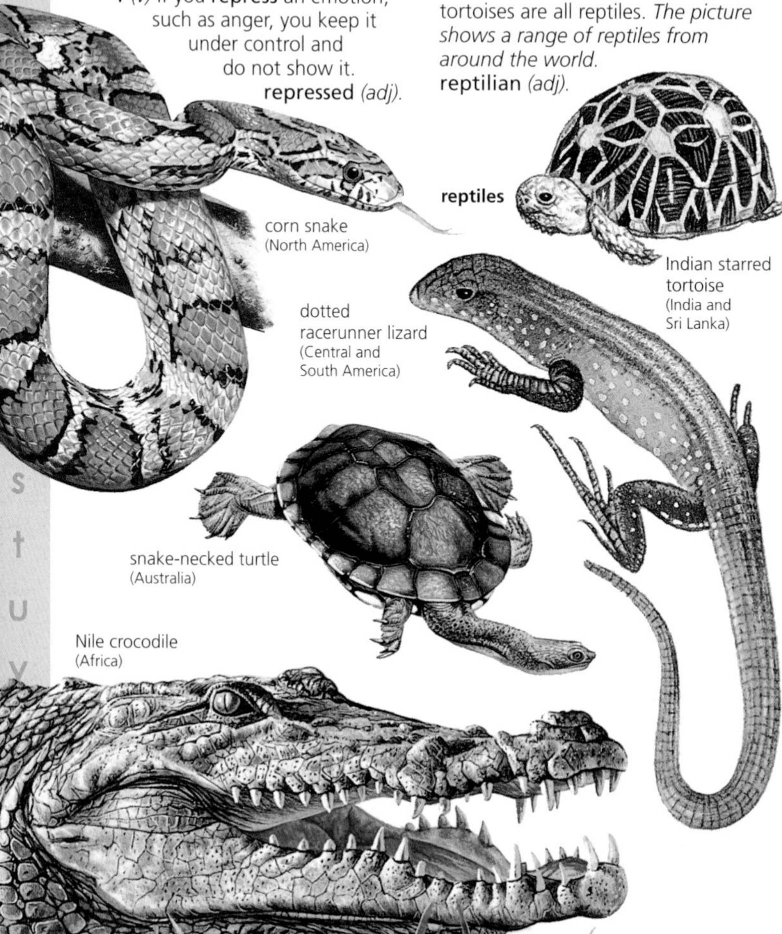

republic *(n)* a country or state that elects its government and does not have a king or queen. *The leader of a republic is the president. France is a republic.*

republican
1 *(adj)* having to do with a republic or in favor of a republic.
2 **Republican Party** *(n)* the name of one of the two main political parties in the United States.

repugnant *(adj)* very unpleasant and disgusting. *Melissa found the job of cleaning out the pigpens totally repugnant.* **repugnance** *(n).*

repulse repulsing repulsed
1 *(v)* to drive or to force back. *The crew repulsed the alien's attack.*
2 *(v)* to reject something. *Ben repulsed my offer of help.*

repulsive *(adj)*
very ugly or disgusting. *A repulsive monster.* **repulsively** *(adv).*

reputable *(adj)*
reliable and trustworthy. *It's wise to buy electrical equipment from a reputable dealer.* **reputably** *(adv).*

reputation *(n)*
the opinion that other people have of you. *Abe has a reputation for hard work.*

repute *(n)* fame.

reputed *(adj)* supposed to be or thought to be. *Dominic is reputed to be very good at chess.* **reputedly** *(adv).*

request requesting requested
1 *(v)* to ask for something politely. *Visitors are requested not to take photographs.*
2 *(n)* something that you ask for. *That's a very strange request!*

requiem *(rek-wee-em)*
1 *(n)* a church service where prayers are said for someone who has died.
2 *(n)* a piece of music composed in memory of a dead person, often a musical setting of the requiem service.

require requiring required
1 *(v)* to need something. *Do you require anything to eat?*
2 *(v)* If someone **requires** you to do something, you must do it.

requirement *(n)*
something that you need to do or have. *The ability to swim 100 yards is a requirement of this sailing course.*

reread rereading reread *(v)*
to read something again. *Kerry reread the train schedule anxiously.*

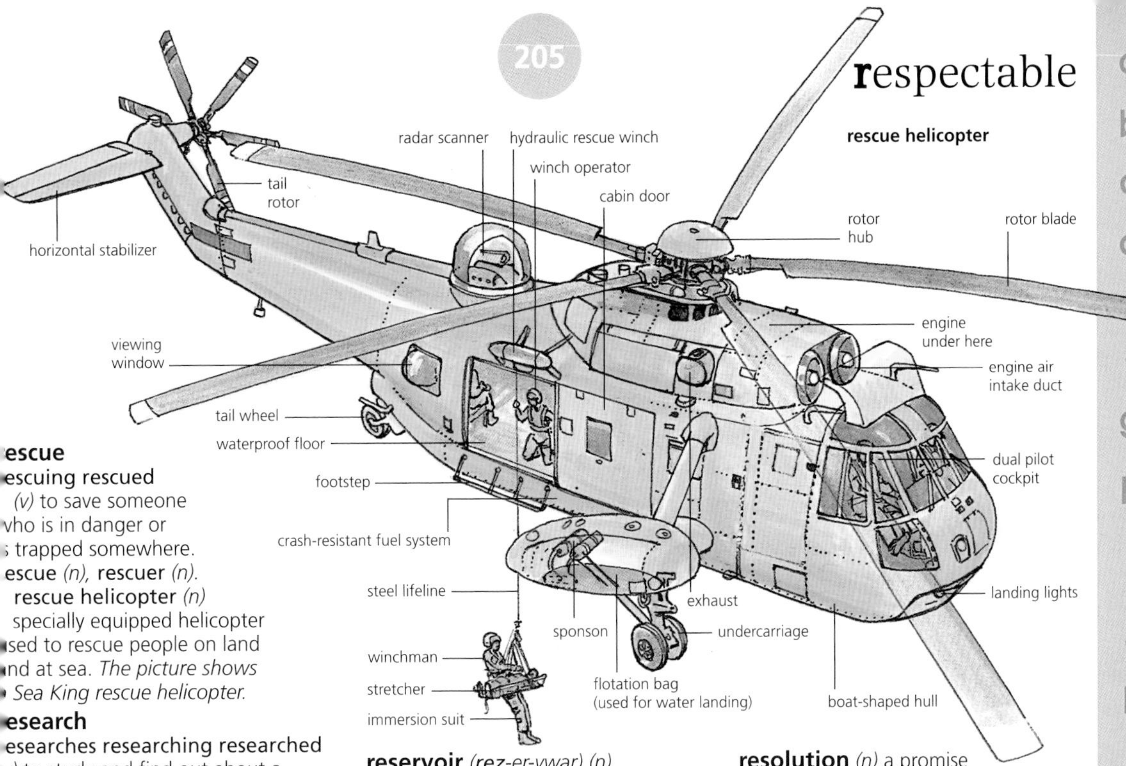

escue
escuing rescued
(v) to save someone vho is in danger or ; trapped somewhere. **escue** *(n)*, **rescuer** *(n)*.
rescue helicopter *(n)* specially equipped helicopter sed to rescue people on land nd at sea. *The picture shows Sea King rescue helicopter.*

esearch
esearches researching researched
v) to study and find out about a ubject, usually by reading about it, or y doing experiments. **research** *(n)*.

esemble
esembling resembled *(v)*
o be or look like somebody or omething. *Lucy resembles her unt Matilda.* **resemblance** *(n)*.

esent **resenting resented** *(v)*
o feel hurt or angry about something hat has been done or said to you. *resent being treated like an idiot.* **esentment** *(n)*, **resentful** *(adj)*.

eservation
(n) an area of land set side for native people. *Native American reservation.*
(n) a booking. *Do you have reservation for this flight?*
(plural n) If you have **reservations** bout something, you feel doubtful nd unsure about it.

eserve **reserving reserved**
(v) to arrange for something o be kept for you. *Harvey eserved a seat on the train.*
2 *(n)* an extra member of a team vho plays if one of the team is njured or cannot play.
3 *(n)* a protected place where nimals can live and breed safely.

eserved
(adj) If a seat, table, or oom is **reserved**, it is kept or someone to use later.
(adj) Someone who is **reserved** ehaves in a quiet, shy way and loes not show their feelings much.

reservoir *(rez-er-vwar) (n)*
a natural or artificial lake used for storing a large amount of water.

residence *(n)*
the place where someone lives. *Where do you reside?*

resident *(n)* someone who lives in a particular place. *The village residents.* **residential** *(adj)*.

residue
1 *(n)* remains or leftovers. **residual** *(adj)*.
2 *(n)* a substance that is left after combustion or evaporation.

resign *(rez-ine)*
resigning resigned
1 *(v)* to give up a job. **resignation** *(rez-ig-**nay**-shun) (n)*.
2 *(v)* If you **resign yourself** to something, you accept it without complaining or worrying about it. *I've resigned myself to losing.* **resignation** *(n)*, **resigned** *(adj)*.

resist **resisting resisted**
1 *(v)* to refuse to accept something. *Jessie resisted all offers of help.*
2 *(v)* to fight back. *The citizens resisted the advancing army.*
3 *(v)* to stop yourself doing something that you would like to do. *I resisted the temptation to tickle Theo's feet.*

resistance
1 *(n)* fighting back. *Resistance is useless. We must surrender!*
2 *(n)* the ability of a substance or an electrical circuit to oppose an electrical current passing through it. Resistance is measured in ohms.

resolution *(n)* a promise to yourself that you will try hard to do something. *New Year's resolutions.*

resolve **resolving resolved**
1 *(v)* to decide that you will try hard to do something. *Shane resolved to find a part-time job.* **resolve** *(n)*.
2 *(v)* to deal with a problem or difficulty successfully. *We need to resolve this misunderstanding quickly.*

resort **resorting resorted**
1 *(n)* a place where people go on vacation. *A ski resort.*
2 *(v)* If you **resort to** something, you turn to it because you do not have any other choices.
3 If you do something **as a last resort**, you do it because everything else has failed to work.

resource *(n)* something valuable or useful to a place or person. *Oil is one of the Earth's most valuable resources.* **resourceful** *(adj)*.

respect **respecting respected**
1 *(v)* to admire and have a high opinion of someone.
2 *(n)* a feeling of admiration or consideration for someone that makes you take them seriously.
3 *(n)* a detail or particular part of something. *I liked Guy's plan in many respects.*

respectable
1 *(adj)* If someone is **respectable**, they behave in a decent way that does not offend anyone. **respectably** *(adv)*.
2 *(adj)* reasonably good. *Brody got a respectable score.*

Some words that begin with a "r" sound are spelled "wr."

respiration *(n)* breathing or the process of taking in oxygen and sending out carbon dioxide. *The diagram shows the main organs used in respiration. Air is drawn into the lungs and travels to the alveoli where oxygen from the air passes into the blood. Carbon dioxide from the blood passes into the alveoli and is breathed out.*

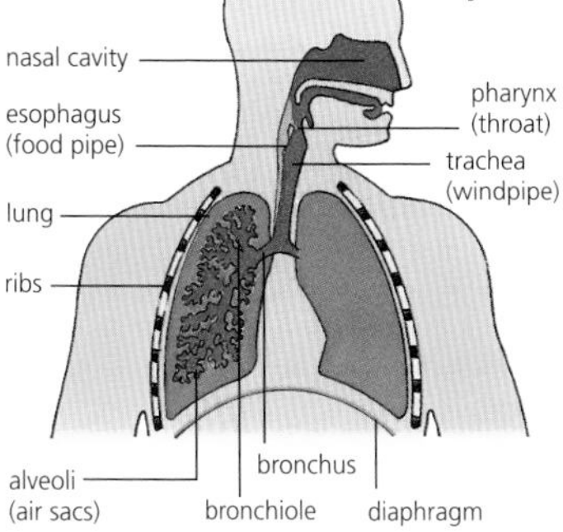

human respiration system

nasal cavity
esophagus (food pipe)
lung
ribs
alveoli (air sacs)
bronchiole
bronchus
diaphragm
pharynx (throat)
trachea (windpipe)

respond responding responded
1 *(v)* to reply. **response** *(n).*
2 *(v)* to react to something. *Rosie did not respond to her brother's taunts.*

responsibility responsibilities
1 *(n)* a duty. *It's my responsibility to provide coffee.*
2 If you **take responsibility** for something bad that has happened, you agree that you are to blame for it.

responsible
1 *(adj)* If someone is **responsible** for something, they have to do it and it is their fault if it goes wrong.
2 *(adj)* If a person is **responsible**, they are sensible and can be trusted. **responsibly** *(adv).*

rest resting rested
1 *(v)* to relax or to sleep. **rest** *(n).*
2 *(n)* the others or the remaining part of something. *I came first and beat all the rest.*
3 *(v)* to lean on something. *Rest your rackets against the wall.*
4 *(v)* to stop and stay in one place. *The spotlight rested on his face.*
5 *(n)* a period of silence in a piece of music. See **notation**.

restaurant *(n)*
a place where people pay to eat meals.

restless *(adj)* If someone is **restless**, they find it hard to keep still or to concentrate on anything. **restlessness** *(n),* **restlessly** *(adv).*

restore restoring restored
1 *(v)* to repair something that has been damaged.
2 *(v)* to give or bring something back. *The teacher soon restored order.*

restrain restraining restrained *(v)*
to prevent someone from doing something. *We managed to restrain Harry from eating another ice cream.* **restraint** *(n).*

restrained *(adj)*
If someone is **restrained**, they are very quiet and controlled.

restrict restricting restricted *(v)*
to keep something within limits. *Please restrict yourselves to one cookie each.* **restriction** *(n),* **restricted** *(adj).*

rest room *(n)* a bathroom, especially in a public building.

result resulting resulted
1 *(n)* something that happens because of something else. *The result of our efforts was a delicious meal.*
2 *(v)* If one thing **results in** something else, it causes it.
3 *(n)* a final score or mark. *Test results.*

resume resuming resumed *(v)*
to start doing something again after a break. *We will resume our discussion after lunch.*

résumé *(re-zuh-may) (n)*
a brief list of all the education, jobs and awards a person has had.

Resurrection *(n)*
In the Christian religion, the **Resurrection** is Christ's coming back to life three days after his death.

resuscitate *(re-suss-it-ate)* resuscitating resuscitated *(v)*
to make someone conscious again after they have stopped breathing. **resuscitation** *(n).*

retail retailing retailed
1 *(v)* to sell goods to the public.
2 The **retail price** of goods is the price at which they are sold in the stores.

retailer *(n)* someone who sells goods to the public. *An online retailer.*

retain retaining retained *(v)*
to keep something. **retention** *(n).*

retainer *(n)* a removable metal and plastic device designed to hold a person's teeth in a certain position.

retaliate retaliating retaliated *(v)*
to do something unpleasant to someone because they have done something unpleasant to you. **retaliation** *(n),* **retaliatory** *(adj).*

retard retarding retarded *(v)*
to slow down. *The children's poor diet retarded their growth.* **retarded** *(adj).*

retch retches retching retched *(v)*
When you **retch**, you feel your throat and stomach move as if you are going to vomit. **retch** *(n).*

reticent *(ret-i-sent) (adj)*
If someone is **reticent**, they are unwilling to tell people what they know or feel. **reticence** *(n).*

retire retiring retired
1 *(v)* to give up work, usually because of your age. **retirement** *(n),* **retired** *(adj).*
2 *(v)* to leave a sports competition, usually because of injury.
3 *(v)* to go to a quieter place. *The jury has retired to consider its verdict.*
4 *(v) (old-fashioned)* to go to bed.

retort retorting retorted
1 *(v)* to answer someone quickly and sharply. **retort** *(n).*
2 *(n)* a glass container with a round body and a long neck used in a laboratory.

retrace retracing retraced *(v)*
to go back over something. *I retraced my steps to see if I had missed the turn.*

retreat retreating retreated
1 *(v)* to move back or withdraw from a difficult situation. **retreat** *(n).*
2 *(n)* a quiet place where you can go to think or be alone.

retrieve retrieving retrieved *(v)*
to get or bring something back. *Fran retrieved her umbrella from the lost property office.* **retrieval** *(n).*

return returning returned
1 *(v)* to go back. *It's time to return home.* **return** *(n).*
2 *(v)* to give or send something back. *Please return my book.* **return** *(n).*
3 *(n)* money made as a profit. *The returns from the book fair were excellent.*
4 **in return** (n) in exchange for something, or as a payment for something.
5 **return ticket** *(n)*
a ticket that allows you to travel to a place and back again.

reunion *(n)* a meeting between people who have not seen each other for a long time.

reusable *(adj)* If something is **reusable**, it can be used again rather than being thrown away.

rev revving revved
1 *(v) (informal)* to make an engine run quickly and noisily.
2 **revs** *(plural n) (informal)* the speed at which an engine turns. Revs is short for revolutions per minute.

reveal revealing revealed *(v)*
to allow something to be seen or known. *Carmen would not reveal the whereabouts of her secret hiding place.* **revealing** *(adj).*

Some words that begin with a "r" sound are spelled "wr."

evel reveling reveled *(v)*
you **revel in** something,
ɔu enjoy it very much.

evelation *(n)* a very surprising ıct that is made known to people.

evenge *(n)*
:tion that you take to pay someone ack for harm that they have done) you or to your friends.

evenue
(n) the money that a ɔvernment makes from taxes.
(n) the money that is ıade from investments.

everberate reverberating everberated *(v)* to echo loudly and peatedly. *Jo's screams reverberated ound the cave.* **reverberation** *(n)*.

everence *(n)*
eat respect and admiration. everent *(adj)*, **reverently** *(adv)*.

everse reversing reversed
(n) the opposite. *You may think this fun, but in fact it's quite the reverse.*
(v) to turn something around inside out. *You can reverse is jacket.* **reversible** *(adj)*.
(v) to move a vehicle backwards. *everse the car into the parking space.*
(v) to cancel something. *The verdict as reversed by the court.* **reversal** *(adj)*.

evert reverting reverted *(v)* to go ıck to the way things were. *Despite ɛr resolutions, Gina soon reverted her old habits.* **reversion** *(n)*.

view reviewing reviewed
(n) a piece of writing that gives opinion about a new book, play, ɔvie, etc. **reviewer** *(n)*, **review** *(v)*.
(v) to study something carefully see whether changes are ɛcessary. *We will review the udget each year.* **review** *(n)*.
(v) to look at your school work ıd try to learn it before an exam.

vise revising revised *(v)*
change and correct something, r example to bring it up to te. *The new city guide has been oroughly revised.* **revision** *(n)*.

vive reviving revived
(v) to bring someone back consciousness after they ve been unconscious.
(v) to bring something back :o use. *We've revived a play ɔm the 1980s.* **revival** *(n)*.
(v) to refresh or strengthen. *e hot drinks revived us.*

volt revolting revolted
(v) to fight against authority. **volt** *(n)*.
(v) If something **revolts** you, u find it horrible and disgusting.

revolting *(adj)*
disgusting. *A revolting smell.*

revolution
1 *(n)* a violent uprising by the people of a country, intended to change its political system. **revolutionary** *(n)*, **revolutionary** *(adj)*.
2 *(n)* a very large important change. **revolutionary** *(adj)*.
3 *(n)* one complete turn of a wheel.

revolutionize
revolutionizing revolutionized *(v)* to change something totally. *The introduction of the printing press revolutionized communication.*

revolve revolving revolved
1 *(v)* to turn around in a circle.
2 *(v)* If something **revolves around** a person or thing, that person or thing is the most important part of it. *Hester's life revolves around television.*

revolver *(n)*
a small handgun that can fire several shots before it needs to be reloaded.

reward *(n)* something that you receive as a gift for doing something good or useful. **reward** *(v)*.

rewarding *(adj)* If something is **rewarding**, it gives you pleasure and satisfaction. *A rewarding job.*

rheumatism *(room-uh-tizm) (n)*
a condition that causes the joints and muscles to become stiff and painful. **rheumatic** *(room-**at**-ik) (adj)*.

rhinoceros rhinoceroses *or* **rhinoceros** *(n)* a large heavy mammal that comes from Africa and Asia and has one or two large horns on its nose. *The picture shows a rhinoceros with a cattle egret and two oxpeckers on its back.*

rhinoceros

rhizome *(rye-zome) (n)*
the thick stem of some plants that grows just under the ground and from which roots and leaves grow.

rhombus *(rom-buss)* **rhombuses** *or* **rhombi** *(n)* a shape that has four straight sides of equal length but usually does not have right angles. *See* **shape**.

rhubarb *(roo-barb) (n)*
a plant with long red or green stems that can be cooked and eaten.

rhyme *(rime)* rhyming rhymed
1 *(v)* If words **rhyme**, they end with the same sound. *"Seat" rhymes with "beat" and "feet."* **rhyme** *(n)*.
2 *(n)* a short poem.

rhythm *(**rith**-um) (n)*
a regular beat in music, poetry, or dance. **rhythmic** *(adj)*, **rhythmical** *(adj)*, **rhythmically** *(adv)*.

rib
1 *(n)* one of the curved bones that protect your lungs. *See* **skeleton**.
2 *(n)* the main vein of a leaf. *See* **leaf**.

ribbon *(n)* a long, thin piece of material used for tying up hair, or for decorating a gift, for example.

rice *(n)* a kind of tall grass that is grown in flooded fields, the seeds of which can be cooked and eaten. *See* **paddy**.

rich riches; richer richest
1 *(adj)* Someone who is **rich** has a lot of money and possessions.
2 *(adj)* If something is **rich in** a particular thing, it contains a lot of it. *Milk is rich in calcium.* **richly** *(adv)*.
3 *(adj)* Food that is **rich** contains a lot of fat or sugar and makes you feel full very quickly.
4 **riches** *(plural n)* great wealth.

rickety *(adj)* old, weak, and likely to break. *A rickety chair.*

ricochet *(**rick**-uh-shay)*
ricocheting ricocheted *(v)*
If a stone or bullet **ricochets**, it hits a wall or other hard surface and flies off in a different direction.

rid ridding rid
1 *(v)* to remove something that is unwanted. *I must rid myself of this ridiculous costume.*
2 *(v)* If you **get rid of** something, you throw it away.

riddle *(n)* a question that seems to make no sense but which has a clever answer.

ride riding rode ridden
1 *(v)* to sit on a horse, bicycle, or motorcycle and travel along on it. **rider** *(n)*.
2 *(n)* a journey on a horse, bicycle, or motorcycle, or in a car or other vehicle.

ridge
1 *(n)* a narrow, raised piece of land.
2 *(n)* a narrow, raised strip on something. **ridged** *(adj)*.

ridicule ridiculing ridiculed *(v)*
to make fun of someone or something. **ridicule** *(n)*.

ridiculous *(adj)* extremely silly or foolish. **ridiculously** *(adv)*.

rifle *(n)* a long-barreled gun that you hold against your shoulder as you fire it.

rig rigging rigged
1 *(n)* a large structure on land or in the sea, used to drill for oil or gas under the ground. *See* **oil rig**.
2 *(v)* to control something dishonestly. *Natalie rigged the competition so that she came first.*
3 *(v)* to equip a ship with masts, ropes, etc.
4 *(n)* a carriage led by a horse or horses for carrying people or goods.
5 *(v)* If you **rig up** something, you make it quickly from whatever you can find. *We rigged up a tent from broom handles and sheets.*

rigging *(n)* the ropes on a boat or ship that support and control the sails.

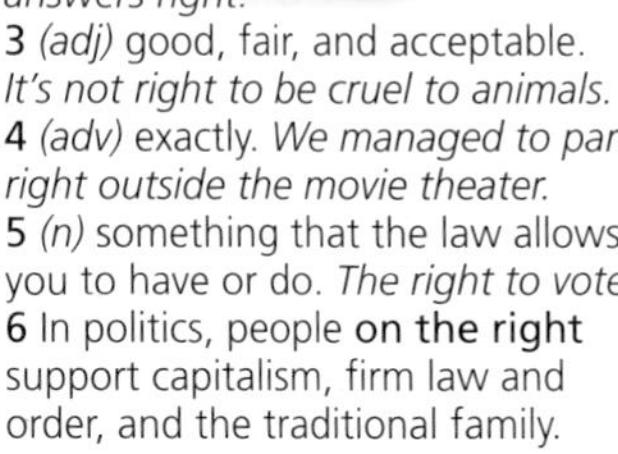

right
1 *(adj)* This page faces the **right** side of the book. **right** *(n)*, **right** *(adv)*.
2 *(adj)* correct. *I got the answers right.*
3 *(adj)* good, fair, and acceptable. *It's not right to be cruel to animals.*
4 *(adv)* exactly. *We managed to park right outside the movie theater.*
5 *(n)* something that the law allows you to have or do. *The right to vote.*
6 In politics, people **on the right** support capitalism, firm law and order, and the traditional family.

right angle *(n)* an angle of 90°, like one of the angles of a square.

righteous
1 *(adj)* Someone who is **righteous** does not do anything that is bad or against the law. **righteousness** *(n)*.
2 *(adj)* with good reason. *When I saw the mess in my room, I was filled with righteous indignation.*

right-handed *(adj)* If you are **right-handed**, you use your right hand to write. **right-hander** *(n)*.

right triangle *(n)* a triangle that includes one right angle.

rigid *(rij-id)*
1 *(adj)* stiff and difficult to bend. **rigidity** *(n)*, **rigidly** *(adv)*.
2 *(adj)* very strict and difficult to change. *A rigid rule.* **rigidly** *(adv)*.

rim *(n)* the outside or top edge of something. *The jug has a blue rim.*

rind *(n)* the outer layer on cheese, and some fruits. *Lemon rind.*

ring ringing rang rung
1 *(n)* a circle. *The mushrooms grew in a ring around the tree.* **ring** *(v)*.
2 *(n)* a thin band worn on your finger as a piece of jewelry.
3 *(v)* When a bell **rings**, it makes a musical sound.
4 *(v)* to call someone on the phone.
5 *(n)* the area in which a boxing or wrestling match takes place.

ringleader *(n)* the leader of a group of people who commit crimes or do things that are wrong.

ringlet *(n)* a long, tight curl of hair.

rink *(n)* an indoor area with a specially prepared surface that is used for ice-skating or roller-skating, or hockey.

rinse rinsing rinsed
1 *(v)* to wash something in clean water without using any soap. **rinse** *(n)*.
2 *(v)* to wash lightly.
3 *(n)* a special liquid that you can put on your hair to color it slightly.

riot rioting rioted *(v)*
If people **riot**, they behave in a noisy, violent, and usually uncontrollable way. **riot** *(n)*, **riotous** *(adj)*.

rip ripping ripped
1 *(v)* to tear something. **rip** *(n)*.
2 **rip off** *(v) (slang)* If someone **rips you off**, they sell you a faulty product or charge you an unfair amount of money for something. **rip-off** *(n)*.

ripe riper ripest *(adj)* ready to be harvested, picked, or eaten. *Ripe fruit.* **ripeness** *(n)*, **ripen** *(v)*.

ripple
1 *(n)* a very small wave on the surface of a lake, pond, etc. **ripple** *(v)*.
2 *(n)* a small wave of sound. *A ripple of laughter.*

rise rising rose risen
1 *(v)* to go or move upward. *The balloon rose slowly into the air.*
2 *(v)* to stand up.
3 *(v)* to increase. *A rise in prices.* **rise** *(n)*.
4 *(n)* the process by which a person, country, etc. becomes more powerful. *The rise of the British Empire.*

risk risking risked *(v)*
to do something that might cause something unpleasant to happen. *Joel risked his life to rescue the kitten.* **risk** *(n)*, **risky** *(adj)*.

ritual
1 *(n)* a set of actions that are always performed in the same way as part of a religious ceremony or social custom. **ritual** *(adj)*, **ritually** *(adv)*.
2 *(n)* a set of actions that you repeat often. *Eating a good breakfast is part of my morning ritual.*

rival rivaling rivaled
1 *(n)* someone whom you are competing against. **rivalry** *(n)*, **rival** *(adj)*.
2 *(v)* to be as good as something or someone else. *No team can rival us at hockey.*

river *(n)*
a large stream of fresh water that flows into a lake or sea. *The picture shows how a river develops and changes as it flows from its source to its mouth.*

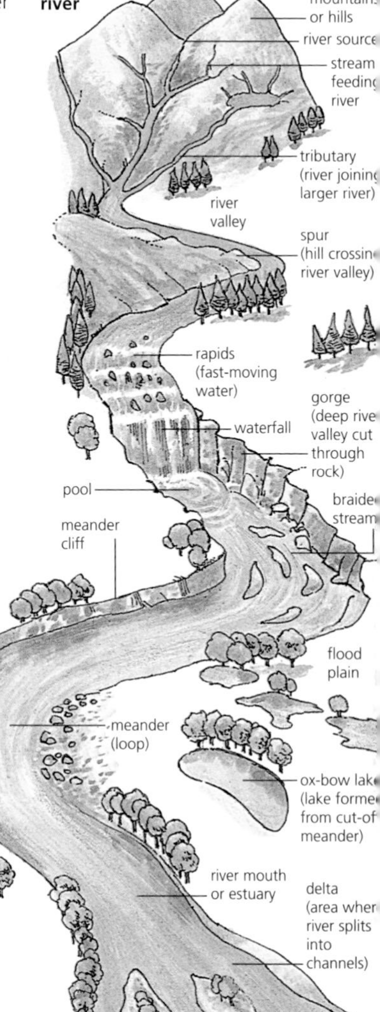

Some words that begin with a "r" sound are spelled "wr."

ivet riveting riveted
1 *(n)* a strong metal bolt that is used to fasten pieces of metal together. **rivet** *(v)*.
2 *(v)* If you are **riveted** by something, you find it so interesting that you cannot stop watching it or listening to it. **riveting** *(adj)*.

road *(n)* a wide path with a smooth surface on which vehicles travel.

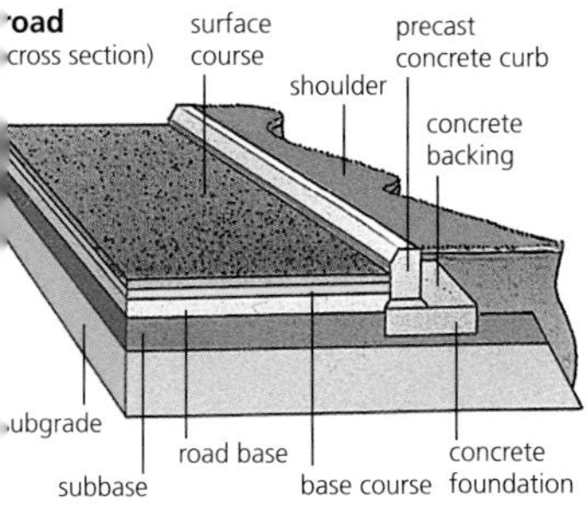

roadside *(n)* the area beside the road. **roadside** *(adj)*.

roadworthy *(adj)* A car that is **roadworthy** is in good enough condition to be driven on the roads. **roadworthiness** *(n)*.

roam roaming roamed *(v)* to wander around without any particular purpose. *I roamed the streets until dark.* **roam** *(n)*.

roar roaring roared *(v)* to make a loud, deep noise. *The lion roared. The crowd roared.* **roar** *(n)*.

roaring *(adj)* If you do a **roaring** trade, you sell a lot of things.

roast roasting roasted
1 *(v)* to cook meat or vegetables in a hot oven. **roast** *(adj)*.
2 *(n)* a piece of meat that has been cooked in a hot oven.
3 *(v)* to be very hot. *We were roasted by the sun.* **roasting** *(adj)*.

rob robbing robbed *(v)* to steal something from someone. **robber** *(n)*.

robbery robberies *(n)* the crime of stealing money or goods.

robe *(n)* a piece of clothing resembling a long, loose coat.

robin *(n)* a bird with a red breast. *The American robin is much larger than the European robin.*

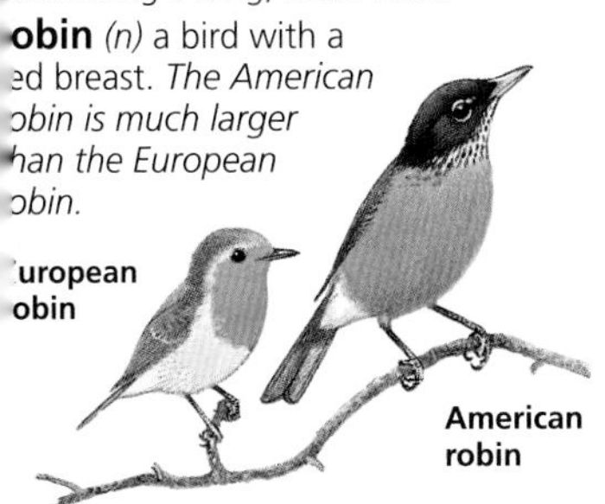

robot *(n)* a machine that is programmed to do jobs that are usually performed by a person. **robotic** *(adj)*.

robotic arm *(n)* an electronically controlled mechanical arm that can use tools and work like a human arm. *The arrows on this picture of a robotic arm show the six directions in which it can move. Also see* **underwater**.

robotics *(singular n)* the science and study of making and using robots.

robust *(adj)* strong. *A robust child. A robust cheese.* **robustly** *(adv)*.

rock rocking rocked
1 *(n)* the very hard substance of which the Earth is made.
2 *(n)* a large stone.
3 *(v)* to move gently backward and forward or from side to side.
4 *(v)* to shake or move violently. *The bomb blast rocked the building.*
5 **rock music** *(n)* music with a very strong beat and a simple tune.

rock climbing *(n)* the sport of climbing steep rock faces, usually with the help of ropes and other equipment. *The picture shows a climber with various pieces of equipment that are used in rock climbing.*

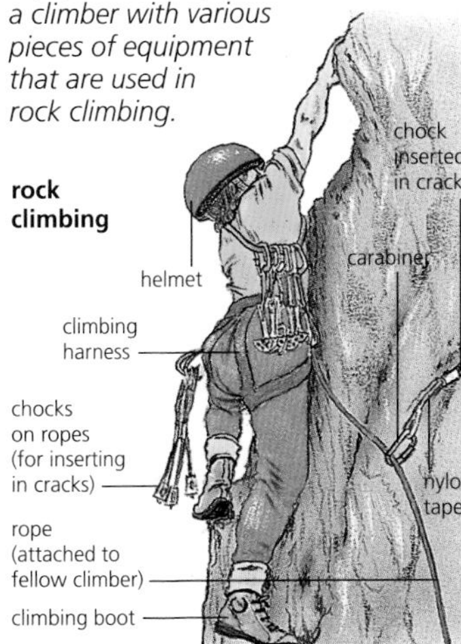

rockery rockeries *(n)* an area of a garden where small plants are grown among rocks and stones.

rocket rocketing rocketed
1 *(v)* to increase very quickly. *The price of oil has rocketed.*
2 *(n)* a firework, which shoots high into the air and then explodes.
3 *(n)* a vehicle shaped like a long tube with a pointed end, that can travel very fast through the air. Rockets are used for space travel and for carrying missiles.

rocking chair *(n)* a chair with curved runners that enable the sitter to rock back and forth.

rock 'n' roll *(n)* a kind of dance music with a strong beat and a simple tune. "Rock 'n' roll" is short for rock and roll. **rock 'n' roll** *(adj)*.

rod *(n)* a long, thin pole.

rodent *(n)* a mammal with large, sharp front teeth that it uses for gnawing things. *Rats, beavers, and squirrels are all rodents.*

rodeo *(n)* an entertainment in which cowboys show off their skills, such as riding untamed horses and catching cattle with lassos.

roe
1 *(n)* a type of small deer.
2 *(n)* a mass of eggs or sperm found inside a fish and often eaten as food.

rogue *(rohg)* *(n)* a dishonest person.

role
1 *(n)* the job or purpose of a person or thing.
2 *(n)* the part that a person acts in a play. *Julian played the role of Hamlet.*

roll rolling rolled
1 *(v)* to move along by turning over and over. *The ball rolled down the hill.*
2 *(v)* to make something into the shape of a ball or tube.
3 *(n)* something that has been made into the shape of a tube.
4 *(v)* to flatten something by pushing a rounded object over it. *Roll out the pastry.*
5 *(n)* a small round loaf of bread to be eaten by one person.
6 *(n)* a continuous, deep, vibrating sound. *A roll of thunder.*

roller
1 *(n)* an object shaped like a tube that can turn around and around and is used in machines. *An ink roller.*
2 *(n)* a small plastic tube that you wind hair around to make it curl.

Rollerblade *(n)* Trademark name for an inline skate.

roller coaster *(n)* an amusement park ride consisting of a train of cars that travels fast over a track that rises, falls, and curves.

roller-skating *(n)* the sport of moving around on shoes or boots with wheels attached to them. **roller skate** *(n)*, **roller-skate** *(v)*.

rolling pin *(n)* a smooth cylinder with handles at each end, used to roll out dough or pastry.

ROM *(n)* permanent computer memory that can be read but not changed. The initials ROM stand for read-only memory.

romance
1 *(n)* a love affair.
2 *(n)* an exciting story, usually about love.
3 *(n)* mystery and excitement. *The romance of the East.*

Roman numerals *(n)* letters used by the ancient Romans to represent figures. Roman numerals are sometimes used today, for example, on some clocks.

Roman numerals

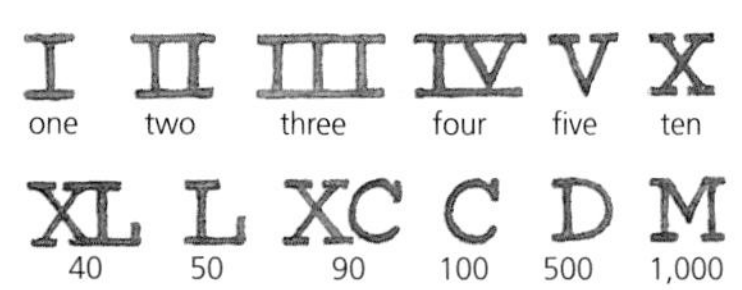

romantic
1 *(adj)* like a love story. *How romantic of Gary to send you roses!*
2 *(adj)* like a fairy tale. *A romantic castle.*

romp romping romped *(v)* to play in a noisy and energetic way. *The boys love romping in the ocean.* **romp** *(n)*.

roof
1 *(n)* the covering on the top of a building.
2 *(n)* the top part of something. *The roof of your mouth. The roof of a car.*

rook
1 *(n)* a large, black bird like a crow that lives in a big group called a rookery.
2 *(n)* a chess piece, also known as a castle, that can move in straight lines across the board but not diagonally. *See* **chess**.

rookie
1 *(n)* someone who has just joined a group and lacks experience and training, such as a new police officer.
2 *(n)* an athlete who is in his or her first season with a professional sports team.

room
1 *(n)* one of the separate parts of a house or building, with its own door and walls.
2 *(n)* enough space for something. *Is there room for us all to go in your car?*

roost roosting roosted
1 *(n)* a place where birds rest or build their nests.
2 *(v)* When birds **roost**, they settle somewhere for the night.

rooster *(n)* a fully grown male chicken.

root rooting rooted
1 *(n)* the part of a plant that grows under the ground. *Water and dissolved foods are absorbed from the soil through root hairs and travel up the roots to the plant's stem through xylem and phloem vessels.*
2 *(v)* to form roots. *I took some plant cuttings, but they didn't root.*
3 *(plural n)* Your **roots** are where your family comes from, where you grew up, and where you feel that you belong.

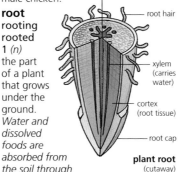

phloem (carries dissolved foods)
root hair
xylem (carries water)
cortex (root tissue)
root cap
plant root (cutaway)

rope *(n)* a strong, thick cord made from twisted fibers.

rose
1 *(n)* a garden flower that usually has a sweet smell and grows on bushes with thorns.
2 *(n)* a light-pink color. **rose** *(adj)*.

rosette *(n)* a large, round badge with ribbons attached to it, worn to show that you have won something or that you support a particular person, team, or political party.

Rosh Hashanah *(n)* the Jewish New Year.

rostrum *(n)* a raised platform for a speaker or conductor.

rosy rosier rosiest
1 *(adj)* pink. *Rosy cheeks.*
2 *(adj)* hopeful. *A rosy future.*

rot rotting rotted *(v)* When something **rots**, it becomes weak and starts to break up because it is old or damp. **rot** *(n)*.

rotary *(adj)* turning around and around, or rotating. *This lawn mower has a rotary action.*

rotate rotating rotated
1 *(v)* to turn round and round like a wheel. **rotation** *(n)*.
2 *(v)* to do things or use things in a fixed order, one after the other. **rotation** *(n)*.

rotor
1 *(n)* the part of an engine that turns or rotates.
2 *(n)* the blades of a helicopter that turn and lift the helicopter into the air. *See* **helicopter**.

rotten
1 *(adj)* Food that is **rotten** has gone bad and cannot be eaten.
2 *(adj)* If floorboards, furniture, etc. are **rotten**, they have become weak and have started to break up.
3 *(adj) (informal)* very bad or unpleasant. *A rotten trick.*

rough *(ruff)* roughing roughed; rougher roughest
1 *(adj)* A **rough** surface is not smooth but has dents or bumps in it.
2 *(adj)* Someone who is **rough** is not gentle or polite and may fight with people. **roughly** *(adv)*.
3 *(adj) (informal)* difficult and unpleasant. *Daria had a rough time in her last job.*
4 *(adj)* vague or not exact. *I've got a rough idea of where Dean lives.* **roughly** *(adv)*.
5 *(adj)* **Rough** work is work that you do as preparation for the final version.
6 *(v) (informal)* If you **rough it**, you manage without the usual comforts of home.

roughage *(ruff-ij) (n)* the fiber found in foods such as cereals and vegetables, which passes through the body but is not digested. Roughage helps you to digest food.

round rounder roundest
1 *(adj)* shaped like a circle or ball.
2 *(adj)* returning to a place. *A round-trip from New York to London.*
3 *(n)* a series of visits made by a mail carrier, doctor, etc.
4 *(n)* a set of matches or games in a competition.
5 *(n)* a simple song in which people start singing one after another, so that they are singing different parts of the song at the same time.
6 *(n)* a single shot fired from a weapon

Some words that begin with a "r" sound are spelled "wr."

7 round number *(n)* a number that ends in zero or five.
8 *(v)* If you **round a number up or down**, you increase it or decrease it to the nearest round number.
9 **round up** *(v)* to gather a group of people, animals or things. *Round up the usual suspects.*

roundabout *(adj)* indirect in travel, thought, or conversation. *Charles told me the facts in a roundabout sort of way.*

rouse rousing roused
1 *(v)* to wake someone up.
2 *(v)* to make someone feel interested or excited. **rousing** *(adj).*

route *(root or rout)*
1 *(n)* the set of roads or paths that you follow to get from one place to another.
2 *(n)* a series of places or customers visited on a regular basis by someone who delivers or sells something.

routine *(root-een)*
1 *(n)* a regular way of doing things.
2 *(adj)* Something that is **routine** is normal and not at all difficult or unusual.

row rowing rowed
1 *(rhymes with low) (n)* a line of people or things, side by side.
2 *(rhymes with low) (v)* to use oars in order to move a boat through water. **row** *(n).*
3 *(rhymes with cow) (n)* an angry argument or quarrel. **row** *(v).*
4 *(rhymes with cow) (n)* a dreadful noise.

rowdy rowdier rowdiest *(adj)* wild and noisy. *Don't play such rowdy games!* **rowdiness** *(n),* **rowdily** *(adv).*

royal *(adj)* having to do with a king or queen or a member of their family. **royalty** *(n).*

R.S.V.P. the initials of the French phrase *Répondez s'il vous plaît,* which means "please reply." R.S.V.P. is often written at the bottom of an invitation.

rub rubbing rubbed
1 *(v)* to press one thing against another and move them backward and forward. *Frank rubbed his chin thoughtfully.*
2 *(v)* to apply to a surface using pressure. *Rub some lotion onto your skin.*
3 *(v) (informal)* If you **rub it in**, you keep telling someone about their mistakes.

rubber *(n)* a substance made from the juice of a rubber tree, or produced artificially. Rubber is strong, elastic, and waterproof, and is used for making things like tires. *The picture shows liquid rubber, or latex, being collected by a method called tapping.*

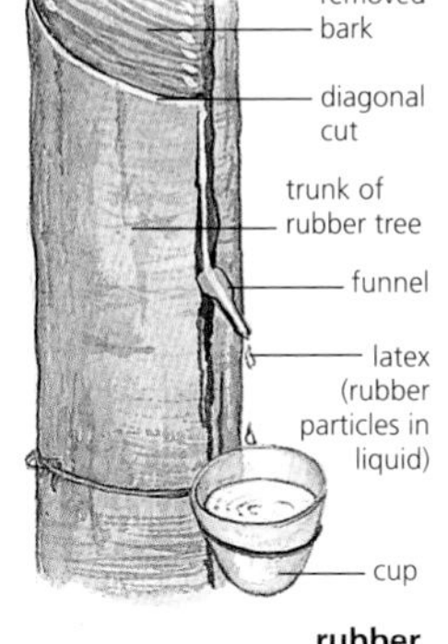

rubber tapping

rubber band *(n)* a loop of thin rubber that can be stretched and used to hold things together.

rubbish
1 *(n)* things that you throw away because they are not useful or valuable.
2 *(n)* nonsense. *Don't talk rubbish!*

rubble *(n)* broken bricks and stones. *All that was left of their house was a pile of rubble.*

ruble *(n)* the main unit of money in Russia.

ruby rubies *(n)* a dark-red precious stone.

rudder *(n)* a hinged plate attached to the back of a boat or airplane and used for steering. *See* **aircraft**, **dinghy**, **ship**.

rude ruder rudest
1 *(adj)* not polite, as in *rude behavior*. **rudeness** *(n),* **rudely** *(adv).*
2 *(adj)* crudely or roughly made.

ruffian *(n)* a violent person.

ruffle ruffling ruffled
1 *(v)* to disturb something that was smooth so that it becomes uneven or messy. *Gail ruffled Miguel's hair.*
2 *(v)* to make someone feel annoyed or worried. *Woody's questioning really ruffled me.*

rug *(n)* a thick mat made from wool or other fibers.

rugby *(n)* a game played by two teams with an oval-shaped ball that they can kick, pass, or carry while running.

rugged *(rug-id)*
1 *(adj)* wild and rocky. *Rugged countryside.*
2 *(adj)* tough and strong. *I have always admired Kirk's rugged good looks.*

ruin ruining ruined
1 *(v)* to spoil something completely. **ruin** *(n).*
2 *(n)* a building that has been destroyed or very badly damaged.
3 *(v)* to make someone lose all their money. *Jeffrey was almost ruined by the legal costs of the case.*

rule ruling ruled
1 *(n)* an official instruction that tells you what you must or must not do.
2 *(v)* to govern a country or to have power over it.
3 *(n)* the time during which a person rules a country.
4 *(v)* to make an official decision or judgment. *The judge ruled that the father should be allowed to see his children.* **ruling** *(n).*
5 If you do something **as a rule**, you usually do it.
6 **rule out** *(v)* If you **rule something out**, you decide that it is not possible.

ruler
1 *(n)* a long, flat piece of wood, plastic, or metal that you use for measuring and drawing straight lines.
2 *(n)* someone who rules a country.

rumba *(n)* a rhythmic dance originally from Cuba. **rumba** *(v).*

rumble rumbling rumbled *(v)* to make a low, rolling noise like the sound of thunder. **rumble** *(n).*

rummage *(rum-ij)* rummaging rummaged *(v)* to look for something by moving things around in an untidy or careless way. *Ned rummaged in his backpack for a candy bar.*

rumor *(n)* something that lots of people are saying although it may not be true.

rump *(n)* the back part of an animal, above its hind legs.

run running ran run
1 *(v)* to move quickly, using your legs. **run** *(n).*
2 *(v)* to take someone somewhere in a car. *Shall I run you home?*
3 *(v)* to function or to work. *Most trucks run on diesel.*
4 *(v)* to be in charge of something. *Olivia runs a small business.*
5 *(n)* a small enclosure for animals. *A chicken run.*
6 *(v)* If you **run away**, you escape from a place or leave it secretly.
7 *(v)* If you have **run out** of something, you have used it all and have none left.
8 If someone is **run over**, they are hit by a car or other vehicle.

runaway
1 *(n)* a child who has run away from home.
2 *(adj)* out of control. *A runaway train.*
3 *(adj)* very easy. *A runaway victory.*

rundown *(adj)* old, tired, or weak.

rung *(n)* one of the horizontal bars on a ladder.

runner
1 *(n)* someone who runs in a race.
2 *(n)* a rod or bar on which something slides.

runner-up runners-up *(n)* the person or team that comes in second in a race or competition.

runny runnier runniest
1 *(adj)* If something is **runny**, it flows or moves like a liquid. *Runny paint.*
2 *(adj)* If you have a **runny** nose, mucus is dripping from it.

runway *(n)* a strip of land that aircraft use for taking off and landing.

rural *(adj)* having to do with the countryside or farming.

rush rushes rushing rushed
1 *(v)* to go somewhere quickly, or to do something quickly. *Eddie rushed to the store before it closed.* **rush** *(n).*
2 **rushes** *(plural n)* tall plants with rounded stems that grow in damp places.

rust rusting rusted
1 *(n)* the red-brown substance that can form on iron and steel when they get wet. **rusty** *(adj).*
2 *(v)* to become covered with rust. *The door hinges have rusted.*

rustle rustling rustled
1 *(v)* When leaves, papers, etc. **rustle**, they make a soft, crackling sound as they move together gently.
2 *(v)* to steal horses or cattle. **rustler** *(n),* **rustling** *(n).*

rut
1 *(n)* a deep narrow track made in the ground by wheels.
2 *(n)* If someone is **in a rut**, they do the same sort of thing all the time.

ruthless *(adj)* Someone who is **ruthless** is cruel and has no pity. **ruthlessness** *(n),* **ruthlessly** *(adv).*

rye
1 *(n)* a cereal grown in cold countries and used to make flour.
2 *(n)* a dark brown bread made from rye flour.

Ss

Sabbath *(n)* the weekly day of rest in some religions. The Jewish Sabbath is Saturday, while the Christian Sabbath is Sunday.

saber *(say-bur)*
1 *(n)* a heavy sword with a curved blade.
2 **saber-toothed tiger** *(n)* an extinct big cat with very long saber-shaped fangs.

sabotage *(sab-uh-tahj) (n)* deliberate damage intended to cause difficulties for an enemy, employer, etc. **saboteur** *(n),* **sabotage** *(v).*

saber-toothed tiger

sack sacking sacked
1 *(n)* a large bag made from strong material, used for carrying coal, potatoes, flour, etc.
2 *(v)* If an employer **sacks** someone, the employer tells them that they no longer have a job and must leave. **sack** *(n).*

sacred *(say-krid) (adj)* holy or connected with religion.

sacrifice sacrificing sacrificed
1 *(n)* the killing of an animal or person as an offering to a god. **sacrifice** *(v),* **sacrificial** *(adj).*
2 *(v)* to give up something important or enjoyable for a good reason. *Mabel sacrificed her career for her children.* **sacrifice** *(n).*

sacrilege *(sak-ril-ij) (n)* disrespect for something holy or very important. **sacrilegious** *(adj).*

sad sadder saddest
1 *(adj)* unhappy. **sadness** *(n),* **sadden** *(v),* **sadly** *(adv).*
2 *(adj)* Something that is **sad** makes you feel unhappy. *Sad news.*

saddle saddling saddled
1 *(n)* a leather seat on the back of a horse on which a rider sits. *See* **tack**.
2 *(n)* a seat for a bicycle. *See* **bicycle.**
3 *(v)* If someone **saddles** you with an unpleasant job or responsibility, they leave you to deal with it.

safe safer safest
1 *(adj)* If something is **safe**, it is not in danger of being harmed or stolen. **safety** *(n),* **safely** *(adv).*
2 *(adj)* not dangerous, or not risky. *Is this ladder safe?*
3 *(n)* a strong box in which you can lock away money or valuables.

safeguard safeguarding safeguarded
1 *(v)* to protect something.
2 *(n)* a law or regulation that is meant to protect something.

safety belt *(n)* a belt you wear across your chest in a car or plane to make you safer.

sag sagging sagged *(v)* to hang down or sink down.

sage
1 *(n)* a herb, the leaves of which are often used in cooking. *See* **herb**.
2 *(adj)* wise. *A sage remark.*
3 *(n) (old-fashioned)* a wise person.

sail sailing sailed
1 *(n)* a large sheet of strong cloth, such as canvas, that makes a boat or ship move when it catches the wind. *The picture below shows the main parts of the sails on a sailing dinghy. Also see* **ship**.
2 *(v)* to travel in a boat or ship. **sailing** *(n).*
3 *(v)* When a boat or ship **sails**, it starts out on a voyage.
4 *(n)* an arm of a windmill. *See* **windmill**.

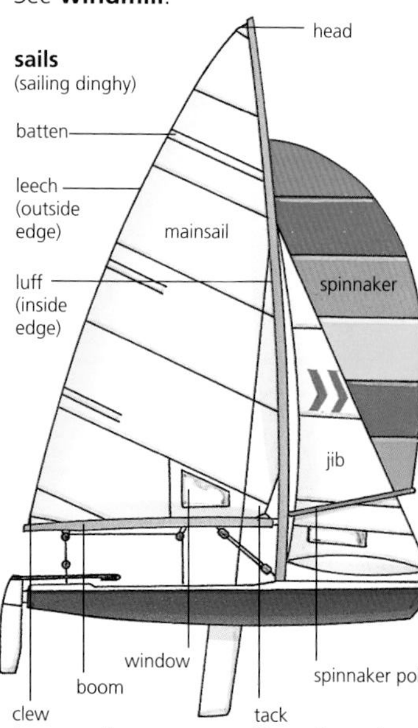

sails (sailing dinghy)

ailboard *(n)* a flat board with mast and sail fixed to it, used or windsurfing. *See* **windsurfing**.

ailor *(n)* someone who works on a ship as a member of the crew.

aint
(n) a man or woman honored by the Christian Church, because of their very holy fe. The short orm of Saint is St. *he picture shows painting of aint Peter from 13th-century nanuscript.*
(n) a very good and kind person. **aintly** *(adj).*

Saint Peter

ake *(n)* If you do something or someone else's **sake**, you do it to help or please them.

alad
(n) a mixture of raw vegetables.
(n) a mixture of cold foods. *Rice salad. Fruit salad.*

alamander
(n) an amphibian, similar o a newt, which lives on and but breeds in water.
(n) In some myths nd legends, **salamander** s a newt-like reature that ves in fire.

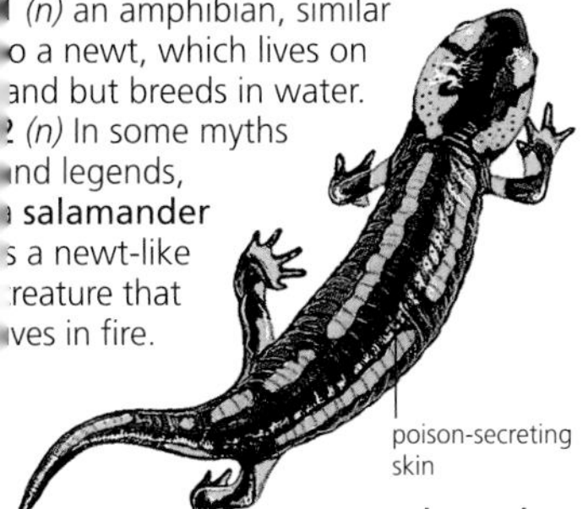

salamander

alary salaries *(n)* the money omeone is paid for their work.

ale
(n) a time when goods are sold t cheaper than usual prices.
(n) the act of selling something. *How's the sale of your house going?*
for sale *(adj)* available for people to buy.
on sale *(adj)* available in the stores.

aliva *(n)* the liquid in your mouth hat keeps it moist and helps you o swallow and begin to digest food.

almon salmon *(n)* a large fish vith a silvery skin and pink flesh. *almon can leap up to nine eet to jump a waterfall.*

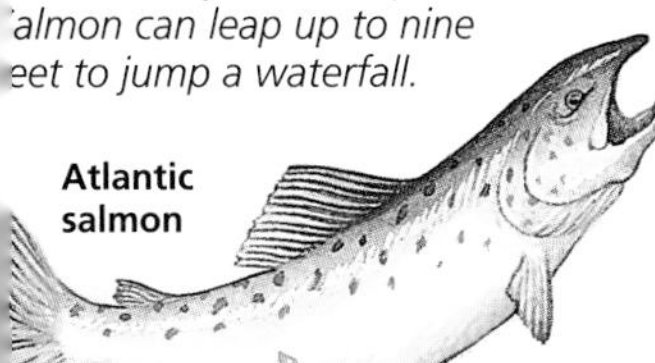
Atlantic salmon

salt
1 *(n)* a common white substance, found in sea water and under the ground and used for adding flavor to food. **salty** *(adj).*
2 *(n)* a chemical compound formed from an acid and a metal.
3 If you take something with **a grain of salt**, you do not believe that it is absolutely true.

salute saluting saluted
1 *(v)* When soldiers **salute**, they raise their hand to their forehead as a sign of respect. **salute** *(n).*
2 *(v)* to praise or honor someone for something that they have done. *The school saluted Jill for her bravery.*

salvage salvaging salvaged *(v)* to rescue something from a shipwreck, fire, etc.

salvation *(n)* the state of being saved from evil, harm, or destruction.

salve *(n)* an ointment or cream that relieves pain and helps heal wounds, burns, or sores.

same *(adj)* exactly alike or not different.

sample sampling sampled
1 *(n)* a small amount of something that shows what the whole of it is like. *The doctor took a blood sample.*
2 *(v)* to try a small amount of something to see if you like it. *Jerry sampled the cheese before buying it.*

samurai *(sam-er-eye)* **samurai** *(n)* a Japanese warrior. *This samurai is defending himself from attack with his naginata, a long rod with a curved blade at the end.*

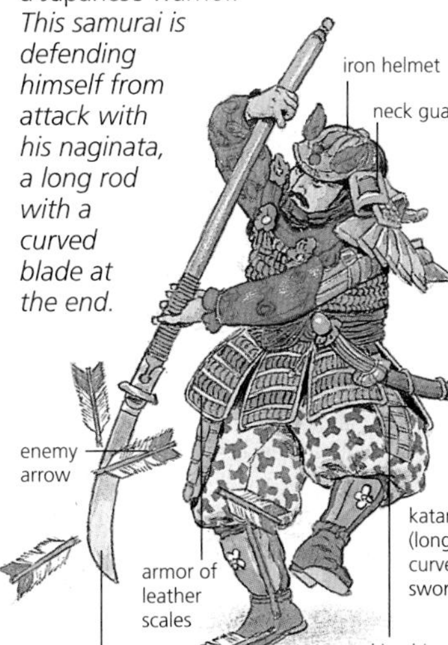

samurai warrior

sanction sanctioning sanctioned
1 *(v)* to allow something or to give approval to something.
2 sanctions *(plural n)* punishment for breaking the law or for unacceptable behavior. *One country sometimes applies sanctions against another country by refusing to trade with them.*

sanctuary sanctuaries
1 *(n)* a holy place.
2 *(n)* a place where someone who is being hunted can be safe.
3 *(n)* a place where birds or animals are protected.

sand sanding sanded
1 *(n)* the tiny grains of rock that make up beaches and deserts. **sandy** *(adj).*
2 *(v)* to smooth or polish a surface with sandpaper or a sanding machine.

sandal *(n)* a light open shoe with straps that go over your foot.

sandbag *(n)* a sack filled with sand, used as protection against flood water, bullets, or explosions.

sandpaper *(n)* paper with grains of sand stuck to it that you rub over surfaces to make them smooth.

sandwich sandwiches *(n)* pieces of bread around a filling of cheese, meat, or some other food.

sane saner sanest
1 *(adj)* Someone who is **sane** has a healthy mind. **sanity** *(n),* **sanely** *(adv).*
2 *(adj)* sensible or not at all crazy. *We can rely on Janet to make a sane decision.* **sanity** *(n),* **sanely** *(adv).*

sanitary *(adj)* clean and free from germs.

sanitation *(n)* a system for protecting people from dirt and disease, for example by a clean water supply and sewage disposal.

sap sapping sapped
1 *(n)* the liquid in the stems of plants.
2 *(v)* to weaken something gradually. *Hunger had sapped Ali's strength.*

sapling *(n)* a young tree.

sapphire *(saf-fire) (n)* a bright-blue precious stone.

sarcastic *(adj)* If you are **sarcastic**, you say the opposite of what you really mean as a way of criticizing or mocking someone. **sarcasm** *(n),* **sarcastically** *(adv).*

sardine *(n)* a small sea fish, often sold in cans as food.

sari *(sah-ree) (n)* a long piece of light material worn draped around the body. Saris are worn mainly by Indian women and girls. *The picture shows an Indian woman wearing a sari.*

sarong *(sa-rong) (n)* a piece of cloth wrapped around the body like a skirt or dress, originally worn by Malaysian men and women.

sash sashes
1 *(n)* a strip of material worn around the waist or diagonally across the chest.
2 **sash window** *(n)* a window with two frames that can slide up or down.

satchel *(n)* a bag often carried over the shoulder or on the back.

satellite
1 *(n)* a machine that is sent into orbit around the Earth. *The picture shows the main parts of a communications satellite that receives and sends television and telephone signals.*
2 *(n)* a moon or other natural object that moves in orbit around a planet. *See* **Moon**.

satellite dish satellite dishes *(n)* a dish-shaped receiver for signals sent by satellite. Satellite dishes are often attached to outside walls.

satellite television *(n)* television programs that are transmitted by satellite and received by a satellite dish.

satire *(n)* a type of clever, mocking humor that points out the faults in certain people or ideas. **satirical** *(adj)*.

satisfaction *(n)* a feeling of contentment, because you have done something that you wanted to do or have done something well.

satisfactory *(adj)* good enough. **satisfactorily** *(adv)*.

satisfy satisfies satisfying satisfied
1 *(v)* to please someone by doing enough or giving them enough. *The pizzas soon satisfied the hungry children.* **satisfied** *(adj)*.
2 *(v)* to convince someone that something is true. *John's alibi satisfied the police.*

saturate saturating saturated
1 *(v)* to make something very wet. **saturated** *(adj)*.
2 *(v)* to fill something so full that there is no room for anything else. **saturation** *(n)*, **saturated** *(adj)*.

sauce *(n)* a thick liquid served with food.

saucepan *(n)* a metal cooking pot with a handle and, sometimes, a lid.

saucer *(n)* a small curved plate that is placed under a cup.

sauna *(saw-nuh) (n)* a room filled with steam where people sit and sweat a lot.

sausage *(n)* chopped and seasoned meat in a thin case shaped like a tube.

savage savaging savaged
1 *(adj)* wild and vicious. *A savage dog.* **savagery** *(n)*, **savagely** *(adv)*.
2 *(v)* to attack a person or an animal by biting or scratching them.
3 *(n)* an uncivilized person.

save saving saved
1 *(v)* to rescue someone or something from danger.
2 *(v)* If something **saves** time, space, energy, etc., it does not waste it.
3 *(v)* to keep money to use in the future rather than spending it now.
4 *(v)* to stop a ball or puck from scoring. **save** *(n)*.

savings *(plural n)* money that you have saved.

savory *(adj)* Food that is **savory** has a salty or spicy flavor, not a sweet one.

saw sawing sawed sawn
1 *(n)* a tool with a toothed blade used for cutting wood.
2 *(v)* to cut something with a saw.

sawdust *(n)* the powder that you get when you saw wood.

saxophone *(n)* a musical instrument made of brass, often played in jazz and dance bands. **saxophonist** *(n)*.

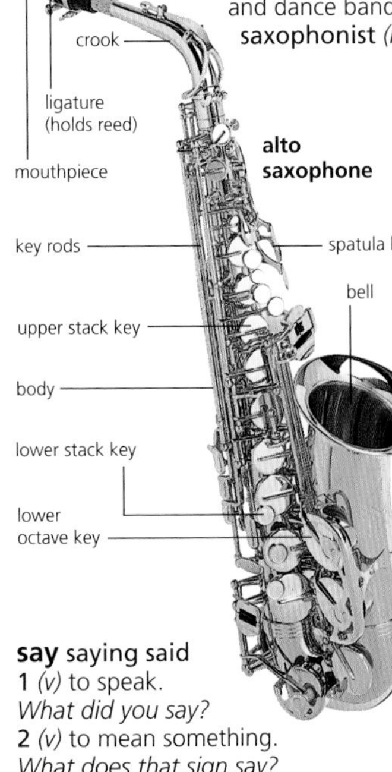

say saying said
1 *(v)* to speak. *What did you say?*
2 *(v)* to mean something. *What does that sign say?*
3 If you **have a say** in something, you are one of the people involved in deciding it.

saying *(n)* a well-known phrase that gives advice.

scab *(n)* the hard covering that forms over a wound when it is healing.

scaffolding *(n)* the structure of metal poles and wooden planks that workers stand on when they are working on a building.

scald scalding scalded *(v)* to burn yourself with very hot liquid. scald *(n)*, scalding *(adj)*.

scale scaling scaled
1 *(n)* one of the small, hard pieces of skin that cover the body of a fish, snake, or other reptile. scaly *(adj)*.
2 *(n)* a series of numbers, units, etc. that are used to measure something. *The Richter scale measures the energy released during an earthquake.*
3 *(n)* a series of musical notes going up or down in order.
4 *(n)* the relationship between the measurements on a map or model and the actual measurements.
5 scales *(plural n)* an instrument used for weighing things.
6 *(v)* to climb up something. *Joel scaled the mountain.*

scallop *(n)* a shellfish with two hinged shells or valves. Scallops move around by opening and closing their valves rapidly.

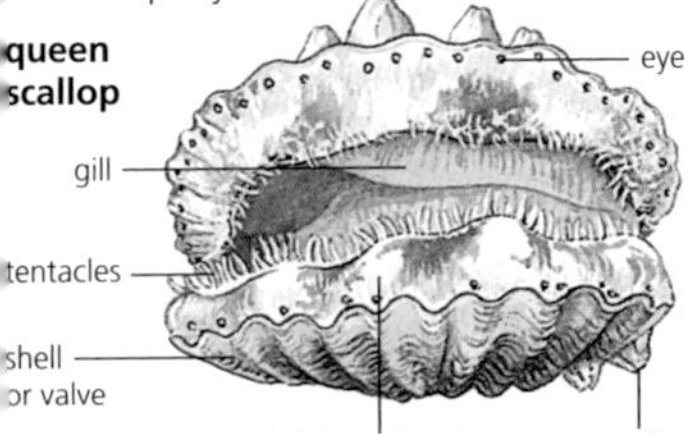

scalp *(n)* the skin on the top of your head. See **brain**.

scalpel *(n)* a small, sharp knife used by surgeons.

scamper scampering scampered *(v)* to run with short, quick steps.

scan scanning scanned
1 *(v)* to look through a piece of writing to search for something. *Max scanned the email.*
2 *(v)* to look carefully along something. *We scanned the horizon for ships.*
3 *(v)* When a machine **scans** something, it copies pictures or text from paper onto a computer.

scandal
1 *(n)* gossip about someone's dishonest or immoral behavior.
2 *(n)* something that you think is disgraceful. scandalous *(adj)*.

scanner
1 *(n)* a machine used by medical staff to view inside a patient's body. scan *(n)*, scan *(v)*.
2 *(n)* a machine used to copy pictures or text from paper into a computer. scan *(n)*, scan *(v)*.

scant *(adj)* not enough or not big enough. *There were scant supplies.*

scanty scantier scantiest *(adj)* not enough or not big enough.

scapegoat *(n)* someone who is made to take all the blame for something.

scar *(n)* a mark left on your skin by an old cut or wound. scar *(v)*.

scarce *(adj)* Something that is **scarce** is hard to find because there is so little of it. *Freshwater is scarce on the island.* scarcity *(n)*.

scarcely *(adv)* hardly. *I've scarcely seen Suzie today.*

scare scaring scared *(v)* to frighten a person or an animal. scare *(n)*, scared *(adj)*, scary *(adj)*.

scarecrow *(n)* a model of a person, put in a field to frighten birds away from crops.

scarf scarfs *or* scarves *(n)* a strip of material worn around your neck or head.

scarlet *(n)* a bright red color. scarlet *(adj)*.

scatter scattering scattered
1 *(v)* to throw things over a wide area. *We scattered the seeds over the earth.*
2 *(v)* to run off in different directions.

scatterbrained *(adj)* If you are **scatterbrained**, you are always forgetting things.

scavenge scavenging scavenged *(v)* to search among garbage for food or something useful. scavenger *(n)*.

scene *(seen)*
1 *(n)* a view or a picture. *Duane paints country scenes.*
2 *(n)* a part of a play or movie where the events all happen in the same place. *My favorite part was the scene with the car chase.*
3 *(n)* the place where something happens. *The ambulance rushed to the scene of the accident.*
4 *(n) (informal)* an area of interest or activity. *Terry is very interested in the jazz scene.*
5 If you **make a scene**, you get very angry with someone in public.

scenery *(seen-er-ee)* sceneries
1 *(n)* the natural countryside of an area, such as trees, hills, and lakes.
2 *(n)* the painted boards and curtains that are used on stage as the background to a play, opera, or ballet.

scenic *(seen-ik) (adj)* A **scenic** place has beautiful surrounding countryside.

scent *(sent)* scenting scented
1 *(n)* a pleasant smell. *The scent of roses.* scented *(adj)*.
2 *(n)* a liquid that you can put on your skin to make you smell pleasant.
3 *(n)* an animal's smell.
4 *(v)* If you **scent** danger or victory, you start to feel that it will happen.

schedule *(sked-djool)* scheduling scheduled
1 *(n)* a plan, program, or timetable. *We must stick to the schedule.*
2 *(v)* If you **schedule** an event, you plan it for a particular time. *We've scheduled a road trip in June.*

scheme *(skeem)* scheming schemed
1 *(n)* a plan or an arrangement.
2 *(v)* to plan or plot something, especially something secret or dishonest. schemer *(n)*, scheming *(adj)*.

scholar *(skol-er)*
1 *(n)* a student who has won a scholarship.
2 *(n)* a very clever and educated person.

scholarship *(n)* a prize that pays for you to go to a school or college.

school
1 *(n)* a place where people go to be taught.
2 *(n)* a group of fish or other sea creatures. *A school of porpoises.*

science *(n)* the study of nature and the physical world by testing, experimenting, and measuring. Biology, physics, and chemistry are all types of science. scientist *(n)*, scientific *(adj)*, scientifically *(adv)*.

science fiction *(n)* stories about life in the future or life on other planets.

scissors *(plural n)* a sharp tool with two blades used for cutting paper, fabric, etc.

scoff scoffing scoffed *(v)* to be scornful and mocking about someone or something. *Nat scoffed at the idea of ballet lessons.*

scold scolding scolded *(v)* to tell someone in an angry way that he or she has done something wrong. *Melanie's mother scolded her for staying out after her curfew.*

scoop scooping scooped
1 *(v)* to lift or pick up something. *Jason scooped up a handful of snow.*
2 *(n)* a serving utensil used to pick things up. *An ice-cream scoop.*
3 *(n)* a story in a newspaper that other papers do not have.

scooter
1 *(n)* a vehicle with two wheels, a flat board, and a handlebar. The rider stands on the board with one foot while pushing on the ground with the other.
2 *(n)* a small motorcycle.

scope *(n)* the range of opportunity that something gives. *There is plenty of scope for improving this garden.*

scorch
scorches scorching scorched
1 *(v)* to burn slightly. **scorch** *(n).*
2 *(v)* to dry something up. *The blazing sun scorched the earth.*
3 *(adj)* If the weather is **scorching**, it is extremely hot.

score scoring scored
1 *(v)* to get a goal or win a point in a game.
2 *(n)* the number of points or goals that each team wins in a game.
3 *(n)* a written piece of music.
4 *(v)* to cut a line or lines in a surface.
5 *(n)* twenty. *Seth lived for four score years.*
6 **scores** *(plural n)* a large number. *I've received scores of letters.*

scorn *(n)* a strong feeling of contempt and superiority. *Gwen poured scorn on my idea of becoming a doctor.* **scornful** *(adj).*

scorpion *(n)* a creature with eight legs and a venomous stinger in its tail.

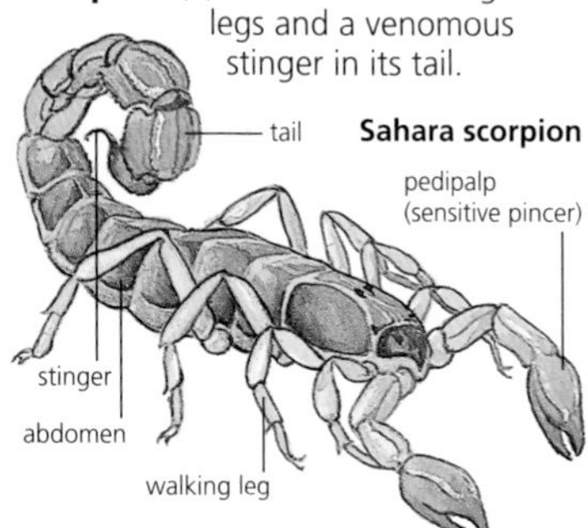

Sahara scorpion

scoundrel *(n)* someone who cheats and lies.

scour scouring scoured
1 *(v)* to clean something by rubbing it hard. **scourer** *(n).*
2 *(v)* to search an area thoroughly. *Police scoured the building for clues.*

scourge *(skurj) (n)* a cause of great harm and suffering.

scout scouting scouted
1 *(n)* a soldier sent ahead of the main army to find the enemy.
2 *(v)* to look for something. *We scouted around for firewood.*
3 *(n)* a member of a scouting organization.

scowl scowling scowled *(v)* to make an angry face. **scowl** *(n).*

scrabble scrabbling scrabbled *(v)* to dig or scratch with your hands or feet, usually to find something.

scraggy scraggier scraggiest *(adj)* skinny and lean. **scragginess** *(n).*

scramble scrambling scrambled
1 *(v)* to climb over rocks or hills.
2 *(v)* to rush or struggle to get somewhere. **scramble** *(n).*
3 *(v)* to mix up sounds or words.
4 **scrambled egg** *(n)* a mixture of eggs and milk, cooked in a pan.

scrap scrapping scrapped
1 *(n)* a small piece of paper, food, etc.
2 *(n)* metal from old cars or machines.
3 *(v)* to get rid of something. *We had to scrap our plans due to the weather.*
4 *(v) (informal)* to fight or to quarrel. **scrap** *(n).*

scrapbook *(n)* a book in which you stick pictures, cuttings, etc.

scrape scraping scraped
1 *(v)* to clean, peel, or scratch something with a sharp object. **scraper** *(n).*
2 *(n) (informal)* an awkward situation. *Miranda's always getting into scrapes.*
3 *(v)* If you **scrape through** an examination, you only just pass it.

scratch
scratches scratching scratched
1 *(v)* to make a mark or a cut. **scratch** *(n).*
2 *(v)* to rub a part of you that itches. **scratch** *(n),* **scratchy** *(adj).*
3 If you do something **from scratch**, you start from the beginning.
4 *(informal)* If something is **not up to scratch**, it is not good enough.

scrawl scrawling scrawled *(v)* to write in a quick careless way. *Mike scrawled his name.* **scrawl** *(n).*

scream screaming screamed
1 *(v)* to cry out loudly or to shriek. **scream** *(n).*
2 *(n) (informal)* a very funny thing or person. *Zak's such a scream!*

screech screeches screeching screeched *(v)* to make a high, unpleasant sound. *The car screeched to a halt.* **screech** *(n).*

screen screening screened
1 *(n)* a wall or a barrier. **screen** *(v).*
2 *(n)* the front of a television set or computer monitor, or the white surface on which movies are shown.
3 *(v)* to show on a screen. *The movie will be screened tonight.*
4 *(v)* to test someone to see if they have a disease. **screening** *(n).*

screw screwing screwed
1 *(n)* a metal fastener resembling a nail, with a groove or cross in its head and a spiral thread.
2 *(v)* to fasten something with screws.
3 *(v)* to twist into an unnatural position. *The boy screwed up his face.*
4 *(v) (informal)* If you **screw up**, you make a bad mistake.

screwdriver *(n)* a tool with a tip that fits into the head of a screw to turn it. *See* **tool**.

scribble scribbling scribbled
1 *(v)* to write carelessly or quickly. *Joy scribbled the answer.* **scribble** *(n).*
2 *(v)* to make meaningless marks with a pencil, pen, or crayon. **scribble** *(n).*

scribe *(n)* A **scribe** was someone who copied books by hand, before printing was invented. *This picture shows a statue of an ancient Egyptian scribe.*

Egyptian scribe

script
1 *(n)* an alphabet.
2 *(n)* the written text of a play, a movie, or a television or radio show.
3 *(n)* a series of instructions for a computer program.

scripture *(n)* religious writing, especially the Bible.

scroll

scroll scrolling scrolled
1 *(n)* a rolled-up piece of paper or parchment with writing on it.
2 *(v)* to move the text on a screen up and down so that you can see more of it.

scrounge
scrounging scrounged *(v)* *(informal)* to get things free from people by asking for them. *Can I scrounge a sandwich from you?*

scrub scrubbing scrubbed
1 *(v)* to clean something by rubbing it hard with a brush.
2 *(n)* low bushes or short trees that cover a piece of ground.

scruffy scruffier scruffiest *(adj)* shabby and untidy. **scruffily** *(adv).*

scruples *(plural n)* strong feelings about what is right or wrong that keep you from doing something wrong.

scrupulous *(scroo-pyoo-luss) (adj)* careful and exact. *Tanya is scrupulous about money.* **scrupulously** *(adv).*

scrutinize scrutinizing scrutinized *(v)* to examine something closely. **scrutiny** *(n).*

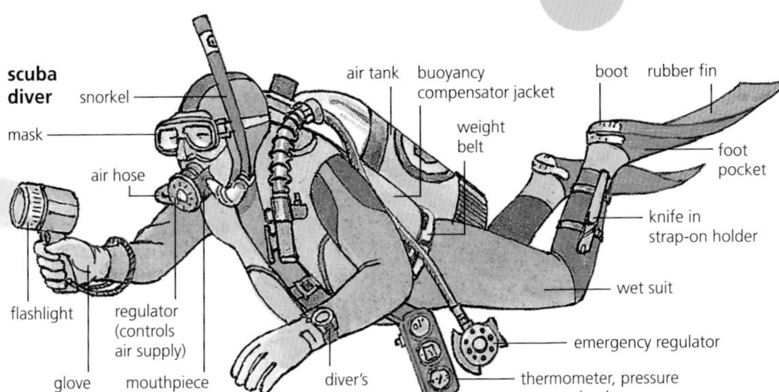

scuba diving *(n)* underwater swimming with an air tank on your back that is connected to your mouth by a hose. **scuba diver** *(n).*

scuffle *(n)* a small fight. **scuffle** *(v).*

scull sculling sculled
1 *(v)* to row a boat using oars on both sides of the boat.
2 *(n)* a small, light boat that is propelled by oars, also called sculls.

sculpture
1 *(n)* something carved or shaped out of stone, wood, metal, etc. *This sculpture by Henry Moore is called "Recumbent Figure."*
2 *(n)* the art or work of making sculpture. **sculptor** *(n),* **sculpt** *(v).*

sculpture

scum *(n)* a layer of dirty froth on top of a liquid.

scurry scurries scurrying scurried *(v)* to hurry, or to run with short quick steps.

scuttle scuttling scuttled
1 *(v)* to dash.
2 *(n)* a coal bucket.
3 *(v)* to make a hole in a ship so that it sinks.

scuzzy scuzzier scuzziest *(adj)* disgusting or dirty.

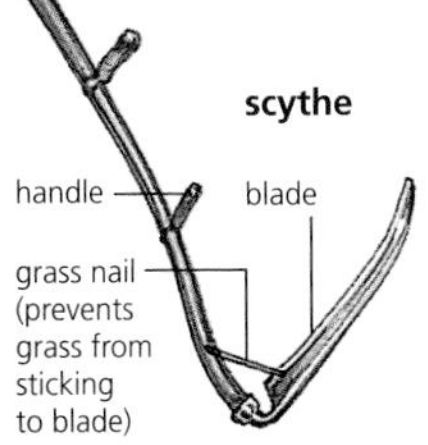

scythe *(sythe) (n)* a tool with a large, curved blade, used for cutting grass or crops. **scythe** *(v).*

sea *(n)* a large area of salt water.

seafarer *(n)* a sailor or someone who travels by sea. **seafaring** *(adj).*

seafood *(n)* fish or shellfish that are eaten as food.

seagull *(n)* a large gray or white bird that is commonly seen near the sea.

sea horse

sea horse *(n)* a fish with a head shaped like a horse's head, and a long curling tail.

seal sealing sealed
1 *(n)* a sea mammal with small flippers that breeds on land. *See* **polar**.
2 *(v)* to close something. **seal** *(n).*
3 *(n)* a stamp, pressed into wax, used to make a document official or to close up a letter or an envelope.

sea level *(n)* the average level of the surface of the sea, which is used to measure land heights. *This mountain is 2,000 feet above sea level.*

sea lion *(n)* a sea-mammal similar to a seal with sticking-out ears and large flippers.

sea lion

flipper

seam
1 *(n)* a line of sewing that joins two pieces of material.
2 *(n)* a band of a different kind of rock between layers of other rock. *A coal seam.*

seaplane *(n)* an aircraft that can take off and land on water.

search searches searching searched *(v)* to explore or examine something closely. **search** *(n).*

search engine *(n)* a computer program on the internet that finds items containing or showing particular words that you type in.

searching *(adj)* deep and thorough. *Searching questions.*

searchlight *(n)* a large, powerful light that can be turned in a particular direction.

search warrant *(n)* an order from a court that allows the police to go into a building to look for things or people.

seashell *(n)* the shell of a sea creature, such as a mussel or cockle.

seashore *(n)* the sandy or rocky land next to the sea.

seasick *(adj)* If you are **seasick**, you feel ill because of the rolling movement of a boat or ship.

season seasoning seasoned
1 *(n)* a time of the year. The four seasons are spring, summer, fall, and winter. **seasonal** *(adj).*
2 *(v)* to add flavor to food with salt, spices, etc.
3 If a food is **in season**, it is fresh and easily available.

seasoning *(n)* herbs and spices that are added to food to give it more flavor.

seat seating seated
1 *(n)* a place where you can sit.
2 *(v)* to sit. *Jack seated himself on the arm of the sofa.*
3 *(v)* to have room for people to sit down. *This table seats six.*

seat belt *(n)* a belt that you wear across your lap and chest in a car or plane to make you safer. *See* **car**.

seaweed *(n)* a type of algae that grows in the sea. *The picture shows examples of brown, green, and red seaweed growing underwater.*

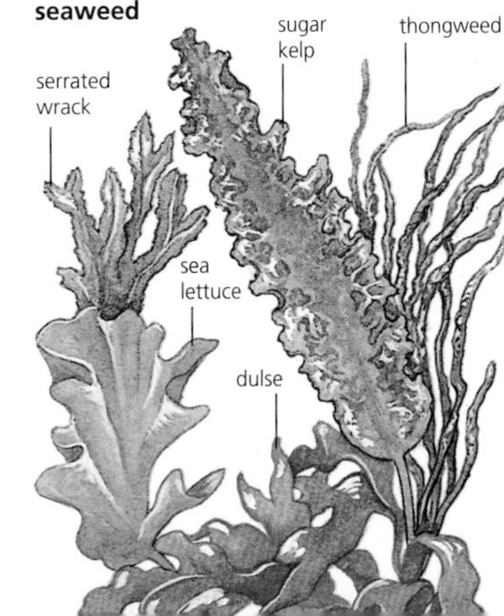

secede *(si-seed) (v)*
to formally withdraw from a group. secession *(n).*

secluded *(adj)*
quiet and private. *The farm is in a secluded valley.* **seclusion** *(n).*

second seconding seconded
1 *(adj)* next or after the first. **second** *(adv),* **secondly** *(adv).*
2 *(v)* If you **second** a proposal at a meeting, you support it. **seconder** *(n).*
3 *(n)* a sixtieth of a minute.

secondary
1 *(adj)* having to do with the second stage of something. *Secondary education.*
2 *(adj)* less important. *A secondary problem.* **secondarily** *(adv).*

secondhand *(adj)*
If something is **secondhand**, it has belonged to another person first.

second-rate *(adj)* not very good.

secret
1 *(n)* a mystery or something that only a few people know.
2 *(adj)* not known by many people. **secrecy** *(n),* **secretly** *(adv).*
3 **in secret** *(adv)* privately.

secret agent *(n)* a spy or someone who obtains secret information.

secretary secretaries
1 *(n)* someone whose job is to prepare letters, make appointments, keep records, and do other office work for an employer. **secretarial** *(adj).*
2 *(n)* a government minister or representative. *The Secretary of State.*

secrete secreting secreted
1 *(v)* to produce a liquid. *Some snakes secrete venom.* **secretion** *(n).*
2 *(v)* to hide. *The spy secreted the message in the heel of his shoe.*

section
1 *(n)* a part or division of something. *The tail section of an airplane.*
2 *(n)* a drawing or plan that shows a slice through an object.

sector
1 *(n)* a part of a circle made by drawing two straight lines from the center to different places on the circumference. *See* **circle**.
2 *(n)* a part of a business or an area of trade. *The marketing sector.*

secure securing secured
1 *(adj)* If you feel **secure**, you feel safe and sure of yourself. **security** *(n).*
2 *(adj)* safe, firmly closed, or well-protected. **security** *(n),* **securely** *(adv).*
3 *(v)* If you **secure** something, you make it safe, especially by closing it tightly.

sedan *(n)* a covered car for four or more people.

sedate sedating sedated
1 *(adj)* calm and unhurried. **sedately** *(adv).*
2 *(v)* to make someone calm or sleepy, especially by giving them medicine. **sedation** *(n).*

sedative *(n)*
a drug that makes you quiet and calm.

sediment
1 *(n)* solid pieces that settle at the bottom of a liquid.
2 **Sedimentary rock** is formed by layers of material in the ground being pressed together. **sedimentation** *(n).*

seduce seducing seduced *(v)*
If you **seduce** someone, you tempt or persuade them to do something. **seduction** *(n),* **seductive** *(adj),* **seductively** *(adv).*

see seeing saw seen
1 *(v)* to use your eyes to look at or to notice something or someone.
2 *(v)* to understand or to recognize. *I see what you mean.*
3 *(v)* to visit or spend time with someone.
4 If you **see about** something, you deal with it or think it over.
5 *(v)* If you **see through** someone or something, you are not deceived or tricked by them.

seed *(n)* a small, hard object that grows into a plant. *See* **germinate**.

seedling *(n)* a young plant that has been grown from a seed.

seek seeking sought *(v)* to look for something or search for something.

seem seeming seemed *(v)*
to appear to be or to give the impression of being. *They seem to be happy.*

seep seeping seeped *(v)* to flow or trickle slowly. *Some water has seeped through the ceiling.* **seepage** *(n).*

seethe seething seethed
1 *(v)* If a liquid **seethes**, it bubbles or boils.
2 *(v)* to be very angry or excited. **seething** *(adj).*

see-through *(adj)* able to be seen through, or transparent.

segment
1 *(n)* a piece of something. *Lucy divided the orange into segments.*
2 *(n)* a part of a circle made by drawing a straight line across it.

segregate segregating segregated *(v)* to keep groups of people apart from each other. **segregation** *(n),* **segregated** *(adj).*

seize *(seez)* seizing seized
1 *(v)* to take something quickly or by force. *Molly seized a rolling pin.*
2 *(v)* If a machine **seizes up**, it jams or stops working.

seizure *(see-zher) (n)*
A **seizure** is a sudden attack of illness.

seldom *(adv)* rarely. *We seldom see our neighbors.*

select selecting selected
1 *(v)* to pick or choose. **selector** *(n).*
2 *(adj)* carefully chosen and exclusive. *Hugh has a house in the select part of town.*

selective *(adj)* If you are **selective**, you choose carefully.

self selves *(n)*
your individual nature or personality.

self-centered *(adj)*
thinking only about yourself.

self-confident *(adj)*
If you are**self-confident**, you know that you are all right, and that you can do things well. **self-confidence** *(n),* **self-confidently** *(adv).*

self-conscious *(adj)*
If you are **self-conscious**, you think that people are looking at you, and you worry about what they are thinking. **self-consciously** *(adv).*

self-control *(n)*
control of yourself and your feelings. **self-controlled** *(adj).*

self-defense *(n)*
the act of protecting yourself against an attacker.

self-employed *(adj)*
If you are **self-employed**, you work for yourself, not an employer.

self-explanatory *(adj)*
If something is **self-explanatory**, it does not need any further explanation. *These instructions are self-explanatory.*

selfish *(adj)* Someone who is **selfish** puts their own feelings and needs first. **selfishness** *(n),* **selfishly** *(adv).*

self-respect *(n)*
reasonable pride in yourself and your abilities. **self-respecting** *(adj).*

self-rising flour *(n)*
flour containing baking powder, which makes cakes or bread rise.

self-service *(adj)*
If a store or gas station is **self-service**, you help yourself to what you want, and then pay for it at the checkout.

self-sufficient *(adj)*
If a family or community is **self-sufficient**, they grow or make everything that they need themselves. **self-sufficiency** *(n).*

sell selling sold
1 *(v)* to give something in exchange for money. **seller** *(n)*.
2 *(v)* to make someone believe or want something. *Sasha tried to sell us on the idea of a Caribbean vacation.*
3 *(v)* to offer for sale. *This store sells sports equipment.*
4 *(v)* If a person **sells out**, it means they abandon their principles for money or fame. **sellout** *(n)*.

sellout *(n)* If a show is a **sellout**, all the tickets have been sold.

semaphore *(n)* a way of sending a message by signaling with your arms or with flags. *The picture shows the message SOS in semaphore.*

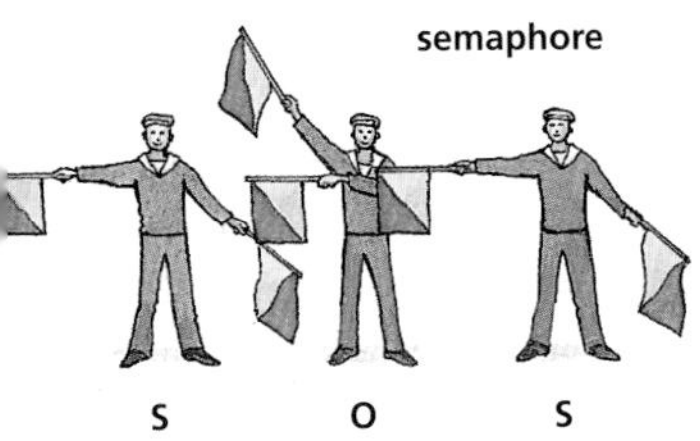

semester *(n)* one half of a school year.

semicircle *(n)* half a circle. **semicircular** *(adj)*.

semicolon *(n)* the punctuation mark (;) used to separate parts of a sentence.

semifinal *(n)* a match to decide who will play in the final. **semifinalist** *(n)*.

semitone *(n)* the smallest possible space, or interval, between two musical notes.

senate *(sen-it) (n)* a governing group or council. *The American Senate.* **senator** *(sen-uh-ter) (n)*.

send sending sent
1 *(v)* to make someone or something go somewhere. *Send Tammy to the store for a paper.* **sender** *(n)*.
2 *(v)* If you **send for** something or someone, you make them come to you. *Let's send for some take-out.*

send off sending off sent off
1 *(v)* to make a player leave the sports field as a punishment.
2 *(v)* to write to ask for something. *We sent off for the free offer.*

send-off *(n)* If you are given a **send-off**, people gather to wish you well for a journey, new job, etc.

senile *(adj)* weak in mind and body because of old age. **senility** *(n)*.

senior
1 *(adj)* Someone who is **senior** to you is older or more important than you are. **seniority** *(n)*.
2 *(n)* a student in the fourth year of high school or college. **senior** *(adj)*.
3 *(n)* When a father and son have identical names, **Senior** or **Sr.** is placed after the surname to indicate the father. *James Smith, Sr.*

senior citizen *(n)* an old person, especially a person who has retired.

sensation
1 *(n)* a feeling. *Amelia was so cold, she had no sensation in her toes.*
2 *(n)* something that causes a lot of excitement and interest. **sensational** *(adj)*, **sensationally** *(adv)*.

sense sensing sensed
1 *(n)* good judgement or understanding. *Kirk has no sense.*
2 *(n)* the ability to feel or be aware of something. *A sense of direction.*
3 *(n)* Your five **senses** are sight, hearing, touch, taste, and smell.
4 *(n)* meaning. *I can't make sense of this story.*
5 *(v)* to feel or be aware of something. *I sensed that Gary was angry.*

senseless
1 *(adj)* pointless or without meaning. *What a senseless attack on an old man!* **senselessly** *(adv)*.
2 *(adj)* unconscious.

sensible *(adj)* If you are **sensible**, you think carefully and do not do stupid or dangerous things. **sensibly** *(adv)*.

sensitive
1 *(adj)* easily offended or easily hurt. **sensitivity** *(n)*, **sensitively** *(adv)*.
2 *(adj)* aware of other people's feelings. **sensitivity** *(n)*, **sensitively** *(adv)*.
3 *(adj)* able to react to the slightest change. *Sensitive measuring equipment.* **sensitivity** *(n)*, **sensitively** *(adv)*.

sensor *(n)* an instrument that can detect changes in heat, sound, etc.

sentence
1 *(n)* a group of words that make sense. A sentence starts with a capital letter and ends with a period.
2 *(n)* a punishment given to a criminal in court. *A short prison sentence.* **sentence** *(v)*.

sentimental *(adj)* having to do with emotion, romance, or feelings. *This ring has sentimental value: it belonged to my mother.* **sentimentally** *(adv)*.

sentry sentries *(n)* a person, often a soldier, who stands guard.

separate separating separated
1 *(sep-er-ate) (v)* to part or divide something or some people. **separation** *(n)*.
2 *(sep-er-rut) (adj)* different, individual, or not together. *The three children have separate bedrooms.* **separately** *(adv)*.
3 *(sep-er-ate) (v)* If a husband and wife **separate**, they stop living together. **separation** *(n)*.
4 **separates** *(sep-er-ruts) (plural n)* clothes, such as a skirt and blouse, that you can wear together or on their own.

septic *(adj)* infected with bacteria. *Maria's cut finger went septic.*

septic tank *(n)* a tank where sewage is treated outside homes not connected to the sewage system.

sequel *(see-kwell) (n)* a second book or movie that continues the story from the first.

sequence *(see-kwence) (n)* a series of things that follow in order. *My life is a sequence of disasters.*

serene *(adj)* calm and peaceful. **serenity** *(n)*, **serenely** *(adv)*.

serf *(n)* a farm worker in medieval times who belonged to the lord of the manor. **serfdom** *(n)*. *See* **feudalism**.

sergeant *(sar-jent) (n)* an officer in the armed forces or police force.

serial
1 *(n)* a story that is told in several parts. *A television serial.* **serialization** *(n)*, **serialize** *(v)*.
2 *(adj)* Something that is **serial** happens in a row or in order.
3 *(n)* A **serial number** is a number that identifies a machine or other product.

series series
1 *(n)* a group of related things, that follow in order. *A series of lessons.*
2 *(n)* a number of television or radio programs that are linked in some way. *A detective series.*
3 Electrical parts that are connected **in series** allow electricity to pass through them one after the other.

serious
1 *(adj)* solemn and thoughtful. **seriousness** *(n)*, **seriously** *(adv)*.
2 *(adj)* sincere or not joking. *Are you serious about leaving school?* **seriousness** *(n)*, **seriously** *(adv)*.
3 *(adj)* very bad or worrying. *A serious illness.* **seriousness** *(n)*, **seriously** *(adv)*.
4 *(adj)* important. *Stop kidding around, this match is serious!* **seriousness** *(n)*, **seriously** *(adv)*.

a b c d e f g h i j k l m n o p q r s t u v w x y z

sermon *(n)* a religious talk given during a church service.

serpent *(n) (poetic)* a snake. Serpents often represent evil in pictures and stories. *This Aztec pendant is made in the shape of a two-headed serpent.*

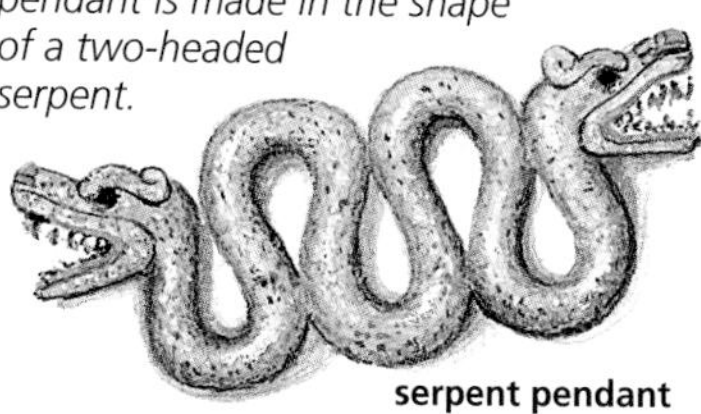

serpent pendant

serrated *(adj)* A **serrated** knife has teeth like a saw.

servant *(n)* someone who works in someone else's house, doing housework, cooking, etc.

serve serving served
1 *(v)* to work for someone.
2 *(v)* to give someone food or help them in a store.
3 *(v)* to begin play in games such as tennis, by hitting the ball. **serve** *(n).*

server *(n)* a computer that provides a service for other computers in a network. The server may run the network or provide a link to a printer or some other piece of equipment.

service
1 *(n)* The **service** in a store, café, etc. is the way that you are looked after.
2 *(n)* a business or organization that provides you with something. *The police service.*
3 *(n)* a religious ceremony or meeting.
4 *(n)* a check on a car or machine to make sure that it is working properly. **service** *(v).*
5 **services** *(plural n)* work that helps others. *He needs the services of a nurse.*
6 *(n)* a complete set of matched dishes. *A dinner service.*

session
1 *(n)* a period of time used for an activity. *A training session.*
2 *(n)* a formal meeting. *A court session.*

set setting set
1 *(n)* a group of things that go together. *A chess set.*
2 *(n)* the scenery for a play or movie.
3 *(adj)* ready. *Are we all set to go to the movie?*
4 *(adj)* fixed. *We eat at set times.*
5 *(v)* to put, fix, or arrange. *Set the alarm for 6 a.m. Set the table.*
6 *(v)* If a liquid **sets**, it becomes solid.
7 *(v)* When the Sun **sets**, it goes below the horizon.

setback *(n)* something that delays you or stops you from making progress.

settee *(n)* a small sofa.

settle settling settled
1 *(v)* to decide or agree on something. *We settled the argument by tossing a coin.*
2 *(v)* to make yourself comfortable. *Phillip settled down with a good book.*
3 *(v)* to go and live somewhere. **settler** *(n).*
4 *(v)* to sink. *The sidewalk has settled and cracked.*
5 *(v)* If you **settle in**, you get used to your new house, school, etc.
6 *(v)* If you **settle up**, you pay a bill or an account.

setup *(n)* the way that something is organized or arranged.

sever severing severed
1 *(v)* to cut off or apart. *A severed limb.*
2 *(v)* to end or break off. *The two countries have severed all ties.*

several *(adj)* a small number of people, things, etc. *We have several umbrellas at home.* **several** *(pronoun).*

severe severer severest *(adj)* strict, harsh, or demanding. *Steve's dad is very severe with him.* **severity** *(n),* **severely** *(adv).*

sew *(so)* sewing sewed sewn *(v)* to stitch using a needle and thread. **sewing** *(n).*

sewage *(n)* liquid and solid waste that is carried away in sewers and drains.

sewer *(n)* an underground pipe that carries away liquid and solid waste.

sewing machine *(n)* a machine for sewing very fast, worked by hand, foot, or electric motor.

sex sexes *(n)* A person's **sex** is their identity as male or female. *The symbols below are often used to denote the male and female sexes.*

sexist *(adj)* Someone who is **sexist** discriminates against members of one or the other sex. *It is sexist to assume that girls can't play football.* **sexism** *(n),* **sexist** *(n).*

male

female

shabby shabbier shabbiest
1 *(adj)* worn, neglected, or in need of repair. *Shabby clothes.* **shabbiness** *(n),* **shabbily** *(adv).*
2 *(adj)* unfair or mean. *That was a shabby trick.* **shabbily** *(adv).*

shack *(n)* a small roughly built hut or house.

shackles *(plural n)* a pair of linked metal rings put around the wrists or ankles of a prisoner.

shade shading shaded
1 *(v)* to shelter something from the light. *A large hat shaded her face.* **shade** *(n).*
2 *(n)* an area that is sheltered from the light. *Come and sit in the shade.* **shady** *(adj).*
3 *(n)* a level of color or meaning. *A lighter shade of blue. This poem has several shades of meaning.*
4 *(v)* to make part of a drawing darker than the rest. **shading** *(n).*
5 **shades** *(plural n) (informal)* sunglasses.

shadow shadowing shadowed
1 *(n)* a dark shape made by something blocking out light. **shadowy** *(adj).*
2 *(v)* to follow someone closely and watch them carefully, and usually secretly. *We shadowed the thieves all the way back to their den.*

shaft
1 *(n)* the long, narrow bar of a spear, arrow, or paddle. See **kayak**.
2 *(n)* a rotating bar that transmits power to wheels or a propeller.
3 *(n)* a thin beam of light.
4 *(n)* a hole in the ground through which you enter a mine.
5 *(n)* the central stem of a feather. See **feather**.

shaggy shaggier shaggiest *(adj)* **Shaggy** hair or fur is long, rough, and uncombed.

shake shaking shook shaken
1 *(v)* to tremble or to quiver.
2 *(v)* to take hold of something and move it quickly up and down. *Shake the bottle before opening.*

Shakespearean *or* **Shakespearian**
1 *(adj)* having to do with the works of playwright William Shakespeare.
2 *(adj)* written in the style of William Shakespeare.

shaky shakier shakiest
1 *(adj)* unsteady and wobbly. *The calf stood up on shaky legs.*
2 *(adj)* not very good or not very strong. *Tim's spelling is rather shaky.*

shale *(n)* a kind of rock often formed from clay and mud that breaks easily and sometimes contains fossils.

shallow shallower shallowest *(adj)* not deep. *Shallow water.*

sham *(n)* something that is not what it seems to be. **sham** *(adj).*

shaman *(n)* a priest or doctor, often in connection with a tribal culture.

shambles *(singular n)* If something is a **shambles**, it is very badly organized and chaotic. *The game turned into a shambles after the crowd invaded the field.* **shambolic** *(adj)*

shame
1 *(n)* a feeling of guilt and sadness about something that you have done.
2 *(n)* a pity, or a sad thing to have happened. *It's a shame that Alexandra can't come tonight.*

shameless *(adj)* having or showing no sense of shame for your behavior.

shampoo *(n)* a soapy liquid used for washing hair, carpets, etc. **shampoo** *(v)*.

shamrock *(n)* a small green plant, the leaves of which are divided into three parts. The shamrock is the national emblem of Ireland.

shanty shanties
1 *(n)* a roughly built hut or cabin, usually made of wood.
2 *(n)* a song with a strong rhythm that was sung by sailors as they worked.

shantytown *(n)* an area of very poor temporary housing.

shape shaping shaped
1 *(n)* the form or outline of something. *The picture shows a range of flat and solid shapes.*
2 *(v)* to mold something into a shape.
3 **shape up** *(v) (informal)* to develop. *The new team is shaping up well.*

share sharing shared
1 *(v)* to divide what you have between two or more people.
2 *(n)* the portion of something that you receive.

shares *(plural n)* the equal portions into which the overall value of a business is divided. People can pay money for shares in many companies, receiving in return regular, smaller amounts of money, based on how profitable the company is.

shark
1 *(n)* a large and often fierce sea fish with very sharp teeth.
2 *(n)* someone who cheats people.

tiger shark

sharp sharper sharpest
1 *(adj)* A **sharp** edge is fine or pointed and is likely to prick or cut.
2 *(adj)* quick-witted or smart.
3 *(adj)* sudden and dramatic. *A sharp turn in the road.*
4 *(adj)* slightly sour. *Lemon juice tastes sharp.*
5 *(adj)* clearly defined and in focus. *A sharp picture.*
6 *(adv)* exactly. *Be here at three o'clock sharp.*
7 *(adj)* In music, a **sharp** note is higher in pitch than the usual note. *C sharp is a semitone higher than C.*
8 *(adj)* tense and abrupt. **sharply** *(adv)*.

flat shapes

circle

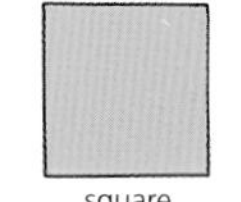
square

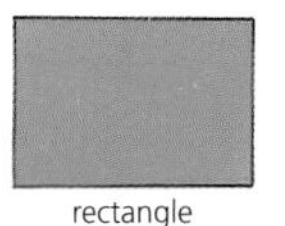
rectangle

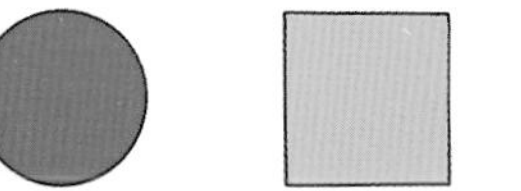
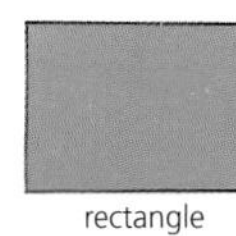

equilateral triangle / isosceles triangle / right triangle

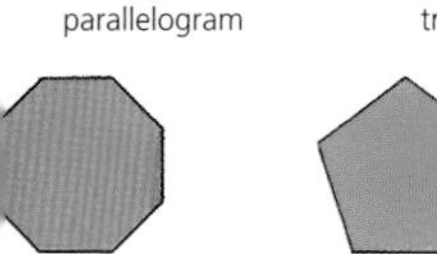
parallelogram

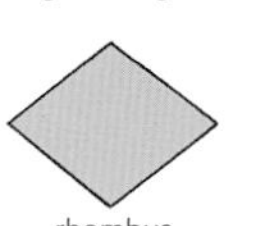
trapezoid

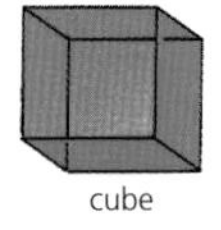
rhombus

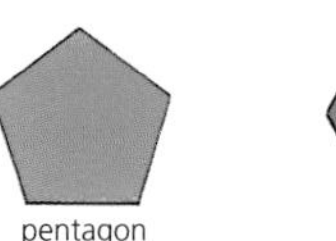
octagon

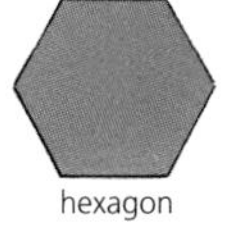
pentagon

hexagon

solid shapes

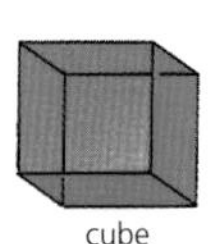
cube

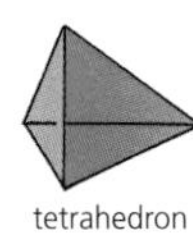
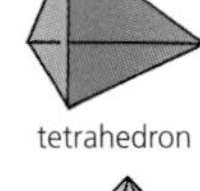
tetrahedron

pyramid

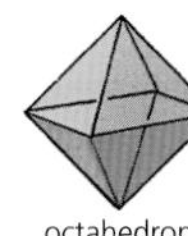
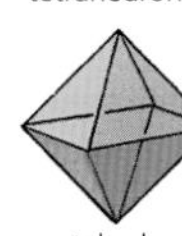
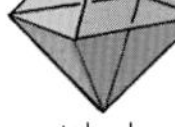
octahedron

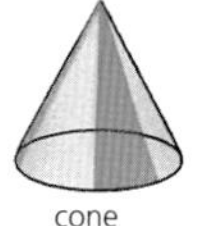
cone

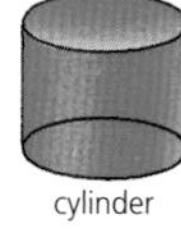
cylinder

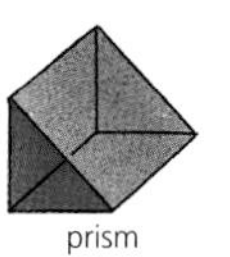
prism

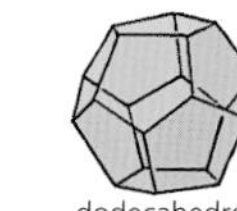
dodecahedron

shatter shattering shattered
1 *(v)* to break into tiny pieces.
2 *(v)* to destroy completely or ruin. **shattered** *(adj)*, **shattering** *(adj)*.

shave shaving shaved *(v)*
1 *(v)* to remove hair with a razor.
2 *(v)* to cut off or slice in thin layers.
3 *(n)* If you have a **close shave**, you only just manage to escape from something.

shawl *(n)* a piece of soft material, sometimes wrapped around a baby or worn by women over their shoulders.

sheaf sheaves *(n)* a bundle. *A sheaf of corn. A sheaf of papers.*

shear shearing sheared shorn
1 *(v)* to cut the fleece off a sheep. *The picture shows a farmer shearing a sheep with electric clippers.*
2 **shears** *(plural n)* a large cutting tool with two blades, used for cutting hedges, trimming grass, etc.

sheepshearing

sheath *(n)* a holder for a knife or dagger. *See* **dagger**.

shed shedding shed
1 *(n)* a small hut used for storing things.
2 *(v)* to let something fall or drop off. *Some reptiles shed their skin.*

sheen *(n)* a shine on a surface.

sheep sheep *(n)* a farm animal kept for its wool and meat.

sheepdog *(n)* a working farm dog that guards and rounds up sheep.

sheepish *(adj)* If someone looks **sheepish**, they look embarrassed or ashamed, often because they have done something foolish. **sheepishly** *(adv)*.

sheer sheerer sheerest
1 *(adj)* extremely steep. *There was a sheer drop down to the sea.*
2 *(adj)* total and complete. *Our vacation was sheer bliss.*
3 *(adj)* extremely thin and transparent. *Sheer stockings.*

sheet
1 *(n)* a large, thin, rectangular piece of cloth used to cover a bed.
2 *(n)* a thin flat piece of paper, glass, metal, etc.

sheik *or* **sheikh** *(sheek or shake) (n)* the head of an Arab tribe, village, or family.

shelf shelves *(n)* a horizontal board on a wall or in a closet, used for storing things.

shell
1 *(n)* a protective outer case. Nuts, tortoises, shellfish, and eggs all have shells.
2 *(n)* a type of bomb that is fired from a gun.

seashells

shellfish shellfish *(n)* a sea creature with a shell, such as a crab, lobster, or mussel. Many shellfish are edible.

shelter *(n)* a place where you can keep dry in wet weather or stay safe. *We took shelter under the tree.*

shelve shelving shelved
1 *(v)* to put something off for a while.
2 *(v)* to put something on a shelf or on shelves.

shepherd *(n)* someone whose job is to look after sheep.

sheriff *(n)* the chief person in charge of enforcing the law.

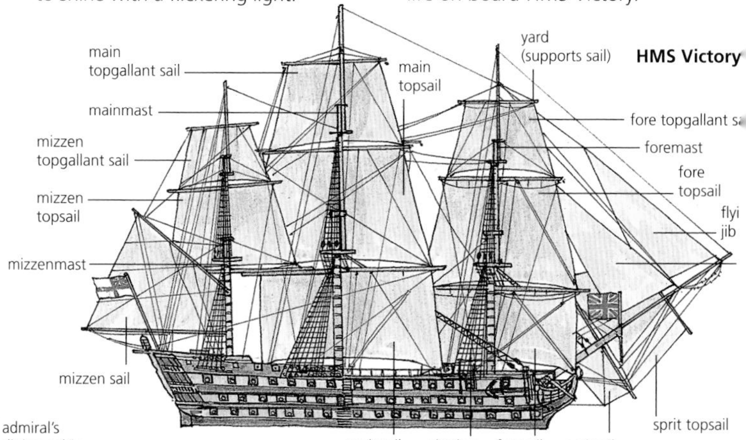

shield shielding shielded
1 *(n)* a piece of armor, carried to protect your body from attack. *Soldiers used to carry shields in battle.*
2 *(n)* a protective barrier. *A heat shield.*
3 *(v)* to protect someone or something. *Henry shielded me from the bullies. The umbrella shielded us from the sun.*

shift shifting shifted
1 *(v)* to move something heavy.
2 *(n)* a set period of several hours' continuous work. *A night shift.*

shimmer shimmering shimmered *(v)* to shine with a flickering light.

shin *(n)* the front part of your leg between your knee and ankle.

shine shining shone
1 *(v)* to give off a bright light.
2 *(v)* If someone **shines** at something, they are very good at it.

Shinto *(n)* a Japanese religion that involves the worship of ancestors and the spirits of nature.

ship *(n)* a large boat used for sea travel. *The two pictures below show* HMS Victory, *the ship on which Admiral Nelson was killed in 1805, during the battle of Trafalgar. The cutaway view shows a reconstruction of life on board* HMS Victory.

HMS Victory

main topgallant sail
main topsail
yard (supports sail)
mainmast
fore topgallant sa
foremast
mizzen topgallant sail
fore topsail
mizzen topsail
flyi jib
mizzenmast
mizzen sail
mainsail
rigging
foresail
spritsail
sprit topsail

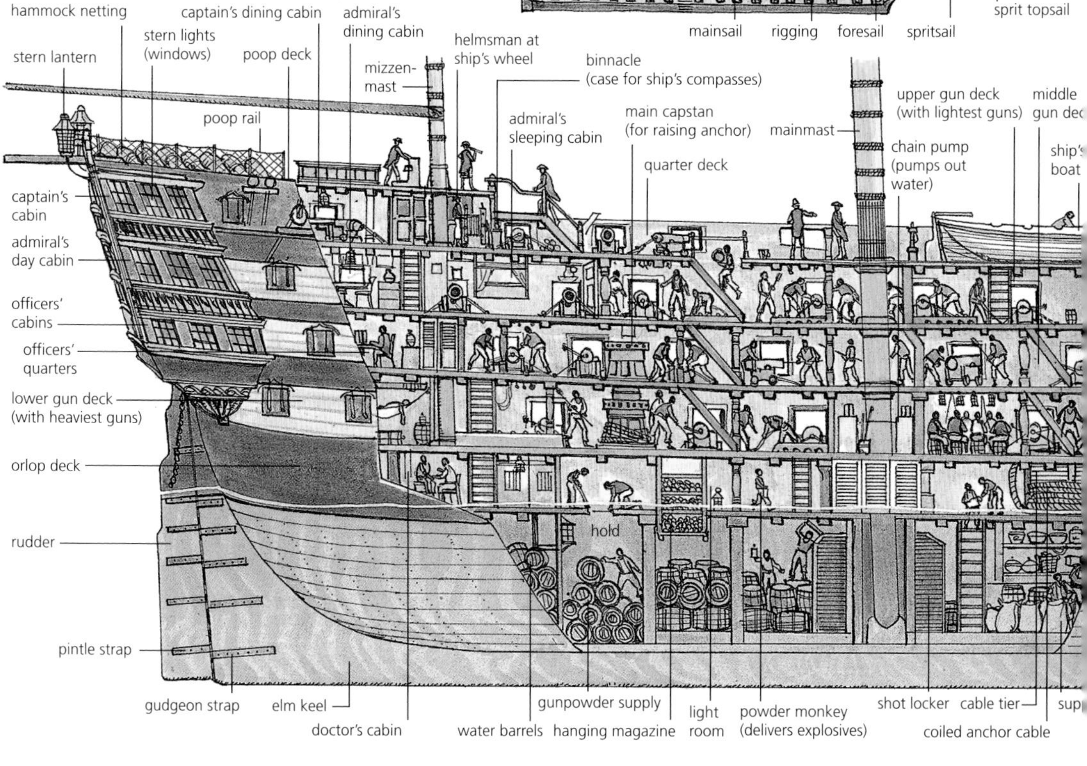

hammock netting
captain's dining cabin
admiral's dining cabin
stern lantern
stern lights (windows)
poop deck
helmsman at ship's wheel
mizzen-mast
binnacle (case for ship's compasses)
poop rail
admiral's sleeping cabin
main capstan (for raising anchor)
mainmast
upper gun deck (with lightest guns)
middle gun dec
quarter deck
chain pump (pumps out water)
ship's boat
captain's cabin
admiral's day cabin
officers' cabins
officers' quarters
lower gun deck (with heaviest guns)
orlop deck
hold
rudder
pintle strap
gudgeon strap
elm keel
doctor's cabin
water barrels
gunpowder supply
hanging magazine
light room
powder monkey (delivers explosives)
shot locker
cable tier
coiled anchor cable
sup

shipshape *(adj)*
clean, tidy, and in good order.

shipwreck
1 *(n)* the wrecking or destruction of a ship.
2 *(n)* the remains of a wrecked ship.

shipyard *(n)* a place where ships are built or repaired.

shirk shirking shirked *(v)*
to avoid doing much work. **shirker** *(n)*.

shirt *(n)* a piece of clothing that you wear on the top half of your body. Shirts usually have a collar, sleeves, and buttons down the front.

shish kabob *(n)*
small pieces of meat on a skewer.

shiver shivering shivered *(v)*
to shake with cold or fear.
shiver *(n)*, **shivering** *(adj)*.

shoal *(n)* a stretch of shallow water.

shock shocking shocked
1 *(n)* a sudden, violent fright.
2 *(v)* to give someone a fright.
3 *(v)* to horrify and disgust someone. *The news of the freeway crash shocked us all.* **shocking** *(adj)*.
4 *(n)* the violent effect of an electric current passing through someone's body.
5 *(n)* a thick, untidy mass. *Daniel has a shock of golden curls.*

shoddy shoddier shoddiest *(adj)*
carelessly produced and of poor quality. **shoddiness** *(n)*.

shoe *(n)* an outer covering for the foot, often made of leather.

shoehorn *(n)* a narrow piece of plastic or metal that you use to help your heel slip easily into a shoe.

shoelace *(n)*
a cord or lace used for fastening shoes.

shoot shooting shot
1 *(v)* to fire a gun. **shot** *(n)*.
2 *(v)* to make a movie or video.
3 *(v)* to move very fast.
4 *(n)* a young plant that has just appeared above the surface, or a new part of a plant that is just beginning to grow. *See* **germinate**, **plant**.

shooting star *(n)* a meteorite, or piece of rock from space, which burns up as it enters the Earth's atmosphere.

shop
1 *(n)* a place where goods are displayed and sold.
2 *(v)* to go to the stores to buy goods. **shopper** *(n)*, **shopping** *(n)*.

shopkeeper *(n)*
someone who runs a small shop or store.

shoplifter *(n)* someone who steals goods from a store. **shoplifting** *(n)*.

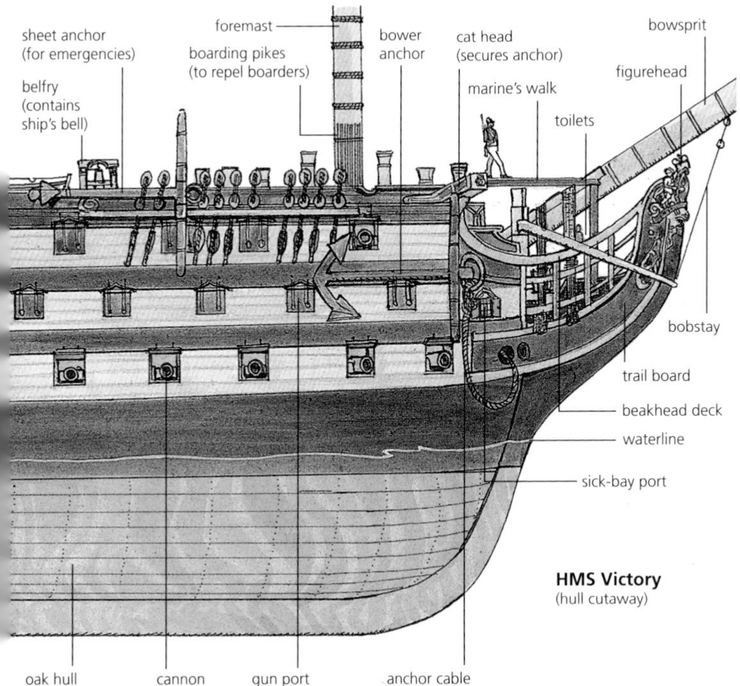

HMS Victory
(hull cutaway)

shopworn *(adj)*
Goods that are **shopworn** are dirty or slightly damaged because they have been on display in a store.

shore *(n)* the edge of the land where it meets a sea, river, or lake.

short shorter shortest
1 *(adj)* less than the average length, distance, time, etc. *A short book.* **shortness** *(n)*, **short** *(adv)*.
2 If you are **short of** something, you have less of it than you need. *Barry is very short of money at the moment.*
3 *(n)* a **short circuit.**

shortage *(n)* When there is a **shortage** of something, there is not enough of it. *A food shortage.*

shortbread *(n)*
a rich cookie made with shortening.

shortcoming *(n)*
a failing or a weak point in someone or something. *One of Marvin's shortcomings is that he is always late.*

shortening *(n)* butter, lard, or other fat used in baking.

shorthand *(n)* a system of writing symbols instead of words, used for very quick note-taking.

shorthanded *(adj)*
If you are **shorthanded**, you do not have enough people to do a job.

shortly *(adv)* soon or presently. *The train will be arriving shortly.*

short-range *(adj)* small in time or distance. *A short-range shot.*

shortsighted
1 *(adj)* If you are **shortsighted**, you cannot see things clearly when they are far away. **shortsightedness** *(n)*.
2 *(adj)* not aware of future consequences. *A shortsighted decision.* **shortsightedness** *(n)*.

short-tempered *(adj)* Someone who is **short-tempered** becomes angry very quickly and easily.

shot
1 *(n)* the firing of a gun.
2 *(n)* a photograph.
3 *(n)* a heavy metal ball thrown in an athletic event.
4 *(n)* *(informal)* an injection.
5 *(n)* *(informal)* an attempt. *Fiona had a shot at beating the record.*
6 *(n)* a person who shoots. *Mary is a good shot.*

shotgun *(n)*
a gun with a long barrel that fires cartridges full of tiny pellets.

shot put *(n)* an athletic event in which you throw a heavy metal ball as far as possible. **shot-putter** *(n)*.

shoulder *(n)* the part of your body between your neck and your arm.

shout shouting shouted *(v)* to call out loudly. **shout** *(n)*.

shove *(shuv)* shoving shoved *(v)* to push roughly. **shove** *(n)*.

shovel shoveling shoveled
1 *(n)* a spade with a flattened scoop.
2 *(v)* to move things with a shovel or spade. *Maggie shoveled the snow off the path.*

show showing showed shown
1 *(v)* to let something be seen. *Show me the picture!*
2 *(v)* to explain or to demonstrate. *Show me how to do it!*
3 *(v)* to guide or lead someone. *Let me show you to your seat.*
4 *(v)* to be visible. *That stain won't show.*
5 *(n)* a public performance or an exhibition. *An art show.*

show business *(n)* the world of theater, movies, television, and other entertainments.

shower showering showered
1 *(n)* a brief rain. **showery** *(adj)*.
2 *(n)* a piece of equipment that produces a fine spray of water for washing your body.
3 *(v)* to wash yourself under a shower.
4 *(v)* to fall in large numbers. *Leaves showered from the tree.*
5 *(v)* to give someone a lot of things. *Rosie showered me with presents.*
6 *(n)* a party to celebrate a change in someone's life, and to give them gifts. *A baby shower.*

show-off *(n)* someone who behaves in a boastful way to impress people. **show off** *(v)*.

showroom *(n)* a large room used to display goods that are for sale. *A car showroom.*

shrapnel *(n)* small pieces of metal scattered by an exploding shell or bomb.

shred *(n)* a long, thin strip of cloth or paper that has been torn off something. **shred** *(v)*.

shredder *(n)* a machine for cutting used documents into tiny pieces so that no one can read them.

shrew *(n)* a small, insect-eating mammal with a long nose and small eyes. *The picture shows a white-toothed shrew with her young.*

shrew with young

shrewd shrewder shrewdest *(adj)* clever, experienced, and cunning in dealing with practical situations. **shrewdly** *(adv)*.

shriek shrieking shrieked *(v)* to cry out or scream in a shrill, piercing way. **shriek** *(n)*.

shrill shriller shrillest *(adj)* harsh, high-pitched, and piercing. *The shrill blast of a whistle.*

shrimp *(n)* a small shellfish you can cook and eat.

shrine *(n)* a holy place that often contains sacred relics.

shrink shrinking shrank shrunk
1 *(v)* If something **shrinks**, it becomes smaller, often after being wet. *My shirt has shrunk in the wash.*
2 *(v)* to move away because you are frightened. *The children shrank closer to the wall as the creature approached them.*

shrivel shriveling shriveled *(v)* If something **shrivels**, it becomes smaller, often after drying in heat. **shriveled** *(adj)*.

shrub *(n)* a small plant or bush with woody stems.

shrubbery shrubberies *(n)* an area where shrubs are planted.

shrug shrugging shrugged *(v)* to raise your shoulders to show doubt or lack of interest. **shrug** *(n)*.

shudder shuddering shuddered *(v)* to shake violently from cold or fear.

shuffle shuffling shuffled
1 *(v)* to walk slowly, hardly raising your feet from the floor.
2 *(v)* to mix together playing cards, papers, etc.

shun shunning shunned *(v)* to avoid someone or something. *Mo shunned any contact with the outside world.*

shunt shunting shunted *(v)* to move things from one place to another.

shut shutting shut
1 *(v)* to block an opening or close something with a door, lid, cover, etc. *Shut the door behind you, please.* **shut** *(adj)*.
2 **shut down** *(v)* to stop or to close down. *The local factory has shut down.*
3 **shut up** *(informal) (v)* to keep quiet.

shutter
1 *(n)* a cover that protects the outside of a window and keeps out the light.
2 *(n)* the part of a camera that opens to let in light.

shuttle
1 *(n)* the part of a loom that carries threads from side to side.
2 *(n)* a bus or other form of transportation that travels frequently between two places. **shuttle** *(v)*.

shy shier shiest; shying shied
1 *(adj)* If someone is **shy**, they are timid and do not enjoy meeting new people. **shyness** *(n)*.
2 *(adj)* lacking or short. *Joe is ten dollars shy of the amount he needs to buy the video game.*
3 *(v)* If a horse **shies**, it moves backward or sideways suddenly, because it is frightened.

sibling *(n)* a brother or a sister.

sick sicker sickest
1 *(adj)* unwell or suffering from a disease. **sickness** *(n)*.
2 If you are **sick**, you vomit.
3 *(adj) (informal)* If you are **sick of** something, you have had too much of it. *I'm sick of your crazy ideas.*

sicken sickening sickened *(v)* If something **sickens** you, it makes you feel shocked and disgusted. **sickening** *(adj)*.

sickly sicklier sickliest *(adj)* weak and often ill.

side siding sided
1 *(n)* a surface of a shape or an object.
2 *(n)* an outer part of something that is not the front or the back. **side** *(adj)*.
3 *(n)* a team. *Please play on our side.*
4 *(v)* If you **side** with someone, you support them in an argument.

sideboard *(n)* a piece of furniture with a large, flat surface and drawers or cabinets below. Sideboards are usually found in dining rooms.

sideburns *(plural n)* the hair that grows down the sides of a man's face.

side effect *(n)* an effect of taking a medicine aside from the intended effect.

sideshow *(n)* a small entertainment at a fair.

sidetrack sidetracking sidetracked *(v)* to distract someone from what they are doing or saying.

sidewalk *(n)* a raised path beside a street.

sideways *(adv)* moving toward the side. **sideways** *(adj)*.

siding *(n)* a section of railroad track used for storing or shunting cars.

Some words that begin with a "si" sound are spelled "ci," "cy," or "psy."

siege *(seej) (n)* the military action of surrounding a place, such as a castle or city, and waiting for its defenders to surrender.

sierra *(n)* a chain of hills or mountains with sharp, jagged peaks.

siesta *(see-**est**-a) (n)* an afternoon rest, taken in hot countries.

sieve *(siv) (n)* a container with a lot of very small holes in it, used for separating large from small pieces or liquids from solids.

sift sifting sifted
1 *(v)* to put substances through a sieve to get rid of lumps.
2 *(v)* to examine something carefully. *Police sifted through the evidence for clues.*

sigh *(rhymes with lie)* sighing sighed *(v)* to breathe out deeply, often to express sadness or relief. sigh *(n).*

sight
1 *(n)* the ability to see. *Nancy lost her sight in an accident.*
2 *(n)* a view or a scene. *The New York skyline is a marvelous sight.*

sightseer *(n)* someone who travels to see interesting places for pleasure. sightseeing *(n).*

sign signing signed
1 *(n)* a symbol that stands for something. *A dollar sign. A minus sign.*
2 *(n)* a public notice giving information. *A road sign.*
3 *(v)* to write your name in your own way.
4 **sign language** *(n)* a way of communicating by using hands, not speech, used especially by deaf people. sign *(v).*

signal
1 *(n)* a form of communication that does not use speech. *A traffic signal.* signal *(v).*
2 *(n)* Television and radio **signals** are pictures and sounds sent through the air by electrical pulses.

William Shakespeare

Shakespeare's signature

signature *(n)* the individual way that you write your name.

significant *(adj)* important or meaning a great deal. significance *(n),* significantly *(adv).*

signpost *(n)* a roadside sign giving directions.

Sikh *(seek) (n)* a member of an Indian religious sect that believes in a single god. Sikhism *(n).*

silage *(n)* cut grass or hay that is stored in a large sealed container, called a silo, and used as animal feed.

silent *(adj)* absolutely quiet. silence *(n),* silently *(adv).*

silhouette *(sil-oh-**ett**) (n)* a dark outline seen against a light background.

silicon *(n)* a very common chemical element used to make microchips, transistors, etc.

silicone *(n)* a man-made material used to make rubber, grease and oil.

silk *(n)* a soft smooth fabric made from fibers produced by silkworms. silky *(adj).*

silkworm *(n)* a caterpillar that spins a cocoon of silk threads and then turns into a moth.

life cycle of a silkworm

1 silkworm hatches

2 silkworm feeds and grows

3 silkworm spins silk cocoon

4 silkworm moth emerges from cocoon

silly sillier silliest *(adj)* foolish or not sensible. silliness *(n).*

silo
1 *(n)* a tower or pit for storing grain, grass for silage, etc.
2 *(n)* an underground shelter for a guided missile.

silt *(singular n)* the fine particles that are carried by running water and that settle on riverbeds.

silver
1 *(n)* a shiny, gray, precious metal used in jewelry and coins.
2 *(n)* coins made from silver or silver-colored metal.
3 *(n)* the color of silver. silver *(adj),* silvery *(adj).*

silverware *(n)* knives, forks and spoons.

similar *(adj)* alike or of the same type. similarity *(n),* similarly *(adv).*

simile *(**sim**-ill-ee) (n)* a way of describing something by comparing it with something else, for example, "Her eyes are like stars."

simmer simmering simmered
1 *(v)* to boil very gently.
2 **simmer down** *(v) (informal)* to calm down.

simple simpler simplest
1 *(adj)* easy or not hard to understand or do. simplicity *(n),* simply *(adv).*
2 *(adj)* plain and not fussy. *A simple meal.* simplicity *(n),* simply *(adv).*

simplify simplifies simplifying simplified *(v)* to make something easier or less complicated. simplification *(n).*

simply
1 *(adv)* in a simple way.
2 *(adv)* absolutely. *Simply marvelous.*

simulator *(n)* a machine that allows you to experience what it is like to fly a plane, drive a speedboat, etc. by using computer technology, video footage and mechanical movement.

simultaneous *(adj)* happening at the same time. simultaneously *(adv).*

sin *(n)* bad behavior that goes against moral and religious laws. sinful *(adj),* sinfully *(adv).*

since
1 *(conj)* from the time that. *I've lived here since I was three.*
2 *(conj)* as or because. *Since you've been so helpful, we'll give you a treat.*

sincere *(sin-**seer**)* sincerer sincerest *(adj)* If you are **sincere**, you are honest and truthful in what you say and do. sincerity *(n),* sincerely *(adv).*

sinew *(**sin**-yoo) (n)* a tough fiber that connects a muscle to a bone.

sing singing sang sung *(v)* to make a musical noise with your voice. singer *(n).*

singe singeing singed *(v)* to scorch or burn something at the tip or the surface.

single
1 *(adj)* individual or only one.
2 *(adj)* unmarried.
3 *(n)* a hit in baseball that allows the runner to get to first base.
4 *(n)* a music recording featuring one main song.

single out *(v)* to select.

single-minded *(adj)* If you are **single-minded**, you concentrate on achieving one objective.

singular *(adj)* having to do with one thing or one person.

sinister *(adj)* If something is **sinister**, it seems evil and threatening.

Some words that begin with a "si" sound are spelled "sci," "ci," "sy," or "cy."

sink sinking sank sunk
1 *(n)* a basin with faucets and a drain, used for washing.
2 *(v)* to go down slowly. *The ship sank. Sophie sank to her knees.*
3 *(v)* to make a ship sink. **sinking** *(n).*

sinus *(sy-nuss)* **sinuses** *(n)* one of the hollow spaces in your skull at the top of your nose. *See* **brain**.

sip sipping sipped *(v)* to drink slowly in small amounts. **sip** *(n).*

siphon *(sy-fun) (n)* a tube through which liquid is drained upward and then down to a lower level. **siphon** *(v).*

sir
1 *(n)* a formal name for a man, used in speaking and writing. *Can I help you, sir? Dear Sir.*
2 *(n)* the title given to a knight. *Sir Lancelot.*

sister *(n)* a girl or woman who has the same parents as you. **sisterly** *(adj).*

sit sitting sat
1 *(v)* to rest on your buttocks.
2 *(v)* to pose. *Jane sat for a photograph.*

site *(n)* the place where something is or happens. *The site of the battle.*

sitting room *(n)* a room in which people can sit and relax.

situation
1 *(n)* the circumstances that exist at a particular time. *The flood has produced a desperate situation.*
2 *(n)* the position of something. *The house is in a pleasant situation overlooking the sea.*

size *(n)* the measurement of how large or small something is.

sizable *or* **sizeable** *(adj)* quite big.

sizzle sizzling sizzled *(v)* to make a hissing noise, like bacon frying.

skate skating skated
1 *(n)* a boot with a blade on the bottom, used for moving across ice.
2 *(v)* to move smoothly across ice, wearing skates.

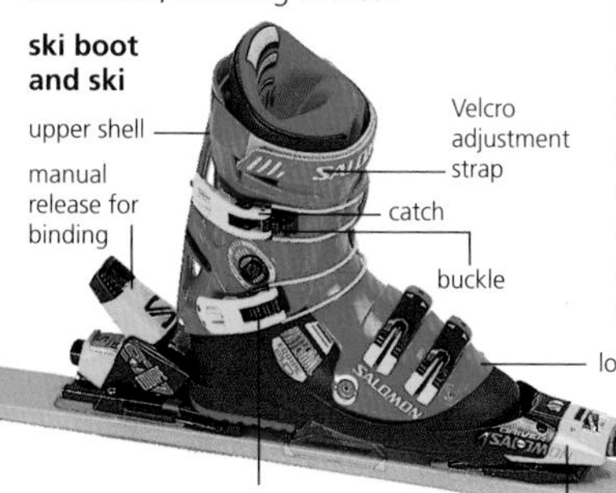

skateboard *(n)* a small board with wheels that you stand on and ride.

skeleton *(n)* the framework of bones in a body.

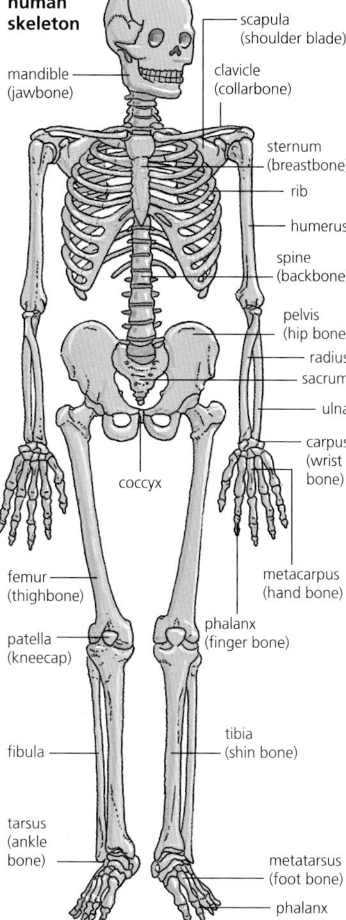

skeptical *(adj)* doubtful about whether something is true. **skeptic** *(n)*, **skepticism** *(n)*, **skeptically** *(adv).*

sketch sketches
1 *(n)* a quick, rough drawing of something. **sketch** *(v).*
2 *(n)* a short, often funny, acting piece.

skewer *(n)* a long pin for holding meat or vegetables while they cook.

ski *(n)* one of a pair of long, narrow runners that you fasten to boots, and use for traveling over snow. **ski** *(v)*, **skiing** *(n).*

skid skidding skidded
1 *(v)* to slide on a slippery surface.
2 *(n)* a runner on the bottom of a helicopter. *See* **helicopter**.

skill *(n)* an ability to do something well. **skillful** *(adj)*, **skilled** *(adj).*

skim skimming skimmed
1 *(v)* to take something off the top of a liquid. **skimmed** *(adj).*
2 *(v)* to glide across a surface.

skin
1 *(n)* the outer covering of tissue on the bodies of humans and animals.
2 *(n)* the outer layer of a fruit or vegetable. *A banana skin.*

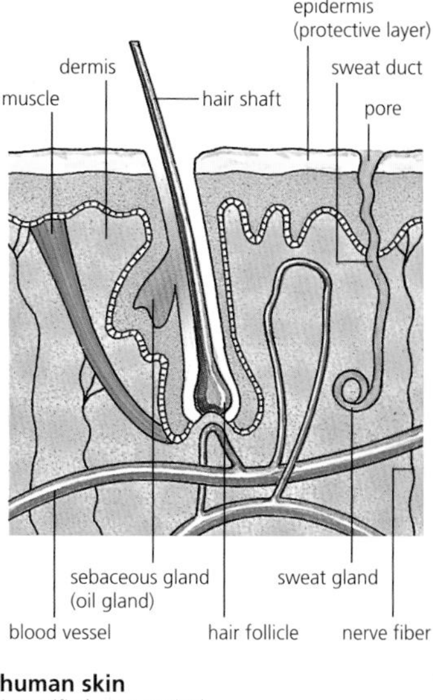

human skin
(magnified cross section)

skinny skinnier skinniest *(adj)* very thin.

skip skipping skipped
1 *(v)* to jump over a turning rope.
2 *(v)* to move along in a bouncy way, hopping on each foot in turn.
3 *(v) (informal)* to leave something out deliberately. *I skipped the gory scenes in my book.*

skirt *(n)* a piece of clothing worn by women and girls that hangs from the waist.

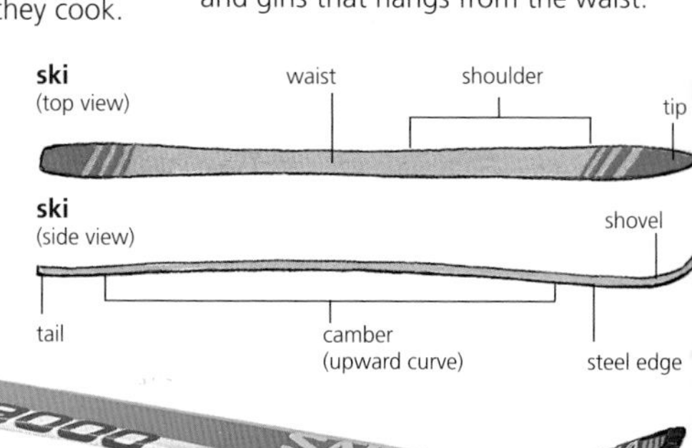

Some words that begin with a "si" sound are spelled "ci," "cy," "sy," or "sci."

skull *(n)* the bony framework of your head. *See* **skeleton**.

skunk *(n)* a black and white mammal with a bushy tail. Skunks give off a foul smell when they are threatened.

skunk

sky skies *(n)* the upper atmosphere as seen from the Earth.

skydiving *(n)* parachute jumping that involves stunts or formation work. *This picture of skydiving shows a formation called a star.* **skydiver** *(n)*, **skydive** *(v)*.

skydiving

skylight *(n)* a window in a roof.

skyscraper *(n)* a very tall building with many stories.

slab *(n)* a large flat block of stone, wood, or other heavy material.

slack slacker slackest
1 *(adj)* loose or not tight. **slacken** *(v)*.
2 *(adj)* not busy. *In a recession, trade is slack for many stores.*
3 *(adj)* If you are **slack** in your work, you do not try very hard at it.

slalom *(slah-lum) (n)* an event in which competitors ski downhill, between poles.

slalom skier

slam slamming slammed *(v)* to close something heavily and loudly. *Jessica slammed the book shut.*

slander *(n)* an untrue, spoken statement that damages someone's name or reputation. **slander** *(v)*.

slang *(n)* words and expressions used by particular groups of people, but not in formal speech or writing.

slant slanting slanted
1 *(v)* to slope or to be at an angle. *My handwriting slants to the right.*
2 *(n)* a point of view. *These new facts give a very different slant to the story.*

slap slapping slapped *(v)* to hit someone or something with the palm of your hand. **slap** *(n)*.

slapdash *(adj)* **Slapdash** work is done carelessly and hurriedly.

slapstick *(n)* rough and noisy comedy, often performed by clowns.

slash slashes slashing slashed
1 *(v)* to make a sharp, sweeping cut in something with a knife or blade.
2 *(v)* to reduce something dramatically. *The store has slashed all its prices.*

slate
1 *(n)* a blue-gray rock that can be split into thin pieces and is often used for roofing.
2 *(n)* a roofing or flooring tile made from slate.

slaughter *(slaw-ter)* slaughtering slaughtered
1 *(v)* to kill animals for their meat.
2 *(n)* the brutal killing of large numbers of people. **slaughter** *(v)*.

slave slaving slaved
1 *(n)* someone who is forced to work for someone else without being paid. **slavery** *(n)*.
2 *(v)* to work very hard. *I've slaved all day over my homework.*

slay slaying slayed *or* slew slain *(v)* *(poetic)* to kill someone in a violent way. *The knight slew the dragon.*

sled *(n)* a vehicle with wooden or metal runners, used for traveling over snow and ice.

sledgehammer *(n)* a heavy hammer.

sleek sleeker sleekest *(adj)* smooth and shiny.

sleep sleeping slept *(v)* to rest in an unconscious state. **sleep** *(n)*.

sleeping bag *(n)* a padded bag in which you sleep, especially when you are camping.

sleeping car *(n)* a railroad car fitted with beds or compartments for people to sleep in.

sleepwalker *(n)* someone who walks in their sleep. **sleepwalk** *(v)*.

sleepy sleepier sleepiest *(adj)* tired or drowsy. **sleepiness** *(n)*.

sleet *(n)* partly melted falling snow or partly frozen rain.

sleeve *(n)* the part of a garment that covers your arm.

sleigh *(slay) (n)* a sled, usually pulled by horses or other animals. *The picture shows a reindeer pulling a sleigh in Lapland.*

sleigh

slender slenderer slenderest
1 *(adj)* slim or thin.
2 *(adj)* small and inadequate in amount. *A slender income.*

slice *(n)* a thin piece or wedge of food cut from a larger piece. **slice** *(v)*.

slick slicker slickest
1 *(adj)* very fast, efficient, and professional. *A slick performance.*
2 *(n)* a pool of oil covering an area of water or road.

slide sliding slid
1 *(v)* to move smoothly over a surface. *Amy is sliding down the banister.*
2 *(n)* a smooth surface for sliding along, especially in a playground.
3 *(n)* a small piece of glass on which you place a specimen to view it under a microscope. *See* **microscope**.

slight slightest *(adj)* small or not very important. *A slight delay.* **slightly** *(adv)*.

slim slimmer slimmest
1 *(adj)* very thin or narrow. **slim** *(v)*.
2 *(adj)* very small. *A slim chance.*

slime *(n)* a slippery substance, such as produced by a slug. **slimy** *(adj)*.

sling slinging slung
1 *(n)* a piece of cloth used to support an injured arm.
2 *(v)* *(informal)* to throw something in a rough way. *Sling your bag on the top bunk.*

slip slipping slipped
1 *(v)* to lose your balance on a slippery surface.
2 *(v)* to move quickly and easily. *Georgia slipped away silently.*
3 *(n)* a small mistake.
4 *(n)* a light garment worn under a skirt or dress.

slipper *(n)* a soft, light shoe that you wear indoors.

slippery *(adj)* smooth, oily, or wet, and very hard to grip.

slipshod *(adj)* careless and untidy.

slit slitting slit *(v)* to make a long, narrow cut in something. **slit** *(n).*

slither slithering slithered *(v)* to slip and slide along like a snake.

sliver *(n)* a very thin piece or slice of something.

slog slogging slogged
1 *(v)* to work hard. **slog** *(n).*
2 *(n)* a long, hard walk. **slog** *(v).*
3 *(v)* to hit a ball hard.

slogan *(n)* an easily-remembered word or phrase used in advertising.

sloop *(n)* a sailboat with a single mast, and sails that are set from front to back.

slop slopping slopped *(v)* to splash or spill liquid.

slope sloping sloped *(v)* to be at an angle. *The wall slopes to the left.* **slope** *(n).*

sloppy sloppier sloppiest
1 *(adj)* wet or slushy. **sloppiness** *(n).*
2 *(adj) (informal)* careless and untidy. *Sloppy work.* **sloppiness** *(n),* **sloppily** *(adv).*
3 *(adj) (informal)* very sentimental.

slot *(n)* a small, narrow space or groove in which something is fitted.

sloth *(rhymes with cloth)*
1 *(n)* a very slow-moving South American mammal with a shaggy coat.
2 *(n)* laziness. **slothful** *(adj).*

slouch slouches slouching slouched
1 *(v)* to sit, stand, or walk in a lazy way, with your shoulders and head drooping.
2 *(n) (slang)* a slow and lazy person. *Dan's no slouch at football.*

slovenly *(adj)* careless, untidy, and dirty. **slovenliness** *(n).*

slow slower slowest
1 *(adj)* not fast. **slowness** *(n),* **slowly** *(adv).*
2 *(adj)* behind the right time. *My watch is five minutes slow.*

sludge *(n)* soft, thick mud.

slug
1 *(n)* a soft, slimy creature that is similar to a snail, but has no shell. *A slug moves in a series of waves in which it lifts part of its sole and then puts it down further forward. The sole is covered with mucus for protection and to help it cling to surfaces.*
2 *(n)* a bullet.

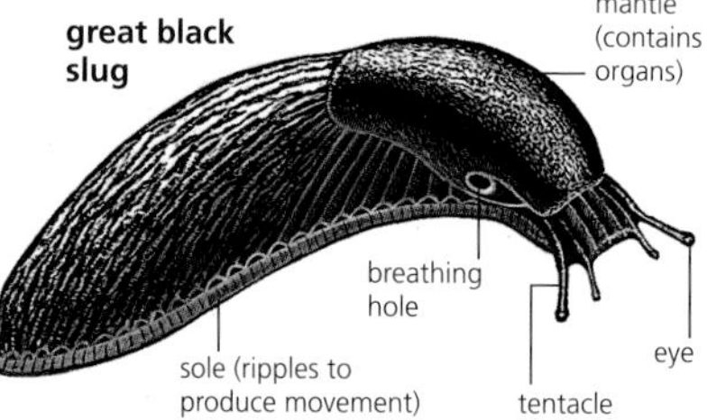

sluggish *(adj)* slow-moving and lacking in energy. **sluggishness** *(n).*

slum *(n)* an overcrowded, poor, and neglected area of housing in a town or city.

slump slumping slumped
1 *(v)* to fall in a heavy or uncontrolled way. *Maurice slumped to the ground.*
2 *(n)* a time of decline in industry and trade, when demand for products is greatly reduced.

slur slurring slurred
1 *(v)* to pronounce words unclearly by running sounds into one another.
2 *(n)* If something is a **slur** on your character, it is insulting or damaging.

slush *(singular n)* snow that has partly melted. **slushy** *(adj).*

sly slier sliest *(adj)* crafty, cunning, and secretive. **slyly** *(adv).*

smack smacking smacked *(v)* to hit someone with the palm of your hand as a punishment. **smack** *(n).*

small smaller smallest
1 *(adj)* little or tiny.
2 **small talk** conversation about unimportant things.

smart smarting smarted; smarter smartest
1 *(adj)* clever or quick-thinking. **smartness** *(n).*
2 *(v)* to sting, or to hurt.
3 *(adj)* well-dressed, tidy, and clean. **smartness** *(n),* **smartly** *(adv).*

smash smashes smashing smashed
1 *(v)* to break something into a lot of pieces by hitting or dropping it.
2 *(n)* a tennis stroke in which you hit the ball downward very hard.

smear smearing smeared
1 *(v)* to rub something sticky or greasy over a surface. **smear** *(n).*
2 *(v)* to try to damage someone's reputation by telling untrue stories about them.

smell smelling smelled
1 *(v)* to sense through your nose. *I can smell dinner cooking.*
2 *(n)* an odor, or a scent.
3 *(v)* to give off a smell, especially an unpleasant one. *Your socks smell!*
4 *(n)* the ability to notice smells. *Dogs have an excellent sense of smell.*

smelt smelting smelted
1 *(v)* to heat rock containing metal so that the metal melts and can be removed.
2 *(n)* a silver-colored fish that lives in cold ocean waters, and swims up rivers to lay eggs.

smile smiling smiled *(v)* When you **smile**, your mouth widens and turns up at the corners to show that you are happy or amused. **smile** *(n).*

smirk smirking smirked *(v)* to smile in an unpleasant way. **smirk** *(n).*

smog *(n)* a mixture of fog and smoke that sometimes hangs in the air over cities and industrial areas.

smoke smoking smoked
1 *(n)* the mixture of gas and tiny particles that is given off when something burns. **smoky** *(adj).*
2 *(v)* to give off smoke. *The bonfire was still smoking.*
3 *(v)* to hold a cigarette or cigar in your mouth and breathe in its smoke. **smoker** *(n),* **smoking** *(n).*
4 *(v)* to treat food by hanging it in smoke. **smoked** *(adj).*

smolder smoldering smoldered *(v)* If something **smolders** it burns slowly, with no flames.

smooth smoothing smoothed; smoother smoothest
1 *(adj)* A **smooth** surface is even and flat, not rough or bumpy. *A smooth road.* **smoothness** *(n),* **smooth** *(v).*
2 *(adj)* happening easily, with no problems or difficulties. **smoothness** *(n),* **smoothly** *(adv).*
3 *(v)* to make things more even and flat. *Amy smoothed down her hair.*
4 *(adj)* Someone who is **smooth** seems too pleasant and confident.

smother *(smuh-ther)*
smothering smothered
1 *(v)* to cover someone's nose and mouth so that they cannot breathe.
2 *(v)* to cover something completely.
3 *(v)* to protect someone too closely.

SMS message *(n)* a message that you type into your cell phone and send to another person who reads it on the screen of their cell phone. SMS stands for Short Messaging Service. Often called a text message.

smudge smudging smudged *(v)* to make a messy mark by rubbing ink, paint, etc. **smudge** *(n).*

smug smugger smuggest *(adj)* If you are **smug**, you are too pleased with yourself. **smugness** *(n),* **smugly** *(adv).*

smuggle smuggling smuggled
1 *(v)* to take goods into a country illegally. **smuggler** *(n).*
2 *(v)* to take something into or out of a place secretly.

snack *(n)* a small, light meal.

snag *(n)* a small problem or difficulty.

snail *(n)* a small creature with no legs, a soft, slimy body and a shell on its back.

garden snail

snake *(n)* a long, thin reptile that has no legs and slithers along the ground. Some snakes have venomous bites. *The diagram shows the internal organs of a snake. Also see* **adder**, **venom**.

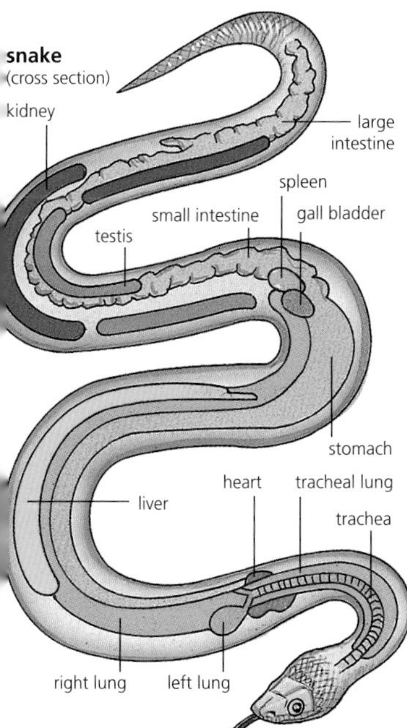

snap snapping snapped
1 *(v)* to break with a sudden, loud, cracking sound. *The twigs snapped beneath our feet.* **snap** *(n).*
2 *(v)* to try to bite someone. *The dog snapped at me.*
3 *(v)* to speak sharply and angrily to someone. **snappy** *(adj).*
4 *(n) (informal)* a photograph.
5 *(v)* in football, to pick the ball up off the ground and pass it to another player.
6 *(n)* **cold snap** a brief period of cold weather.
7 A **snap decision** is a decision that is made very quickly.

snapshot *(n)* a photograph taken with a simple camera.

snare snaring snared
1 *(n)* a trap for birds or animals.
2 *(v)* to catch a bird or an animal in a snare.
3 **snare drum** *(n)* a small drum, with strings or wires stretched across its base, that produces a rattling sound when hit. *See* **drum**.

snarl snarling snarled
1 *(v)* If an animal **snarls**, it shows its teeth and makes a growling sound.
2 *(v)* to say something angrily.

snatch
snatches snatching snatched
1 *(v)* to take or grab something roughly.
2 *(n)* a small part. *I overheard snatches of their conversation.*

sneak sneaking sneaked
1 *(v)* to move quietly and secretly. *Melissa sneaked up on me from behind.* **sneaky** *(adj),* **sneakily** *(adv).*
2 *(v)* to bring someone or something in where it's not supposed to be. *Emily sneaked the cat into her bedroom when her mom wasn't looking.*
3 *(v)* done secretly. *A sneak attack.*
4 *(n)* someone who is tricky and dishonest.

sneakers *(n)* soft, casual shoes with rubber soles.

sneer sneering sneered *(v)* to smile in an unpleasant, mocking way. **sneer** *(n).*

sneeze sneezing sneezed *(v)* to push out air through your nose and mouth suddenly, often because you have a cold. **sneeze** *(n).*

snicker snickering snickered *(v)* to laugh quietly or secretly.

sniff sniffing sniffed
1 *(v)* to breathe in strongly and often noisily through your nose. **sniff** *(n).*
2 *(v)* to smell something. **sniff** *(n).*

sniffle
sniffling sniffled *(v) (informal)* to breathe noisily through your nose, usually because you have a cold.

snip snipping snipped *(v)* to cut something using small, quick scissor cuts. **snip** *(n).*

snipe
1 *(v)* to shoot at a person or people from a hidden place.
2 *(n)* a wading bird with a long slender bill.

sniper *(n)* someone who shoots at people while staying hidden. **snipe** *(v).*

snivel
sniveling sniveled *(v)* to cry or complain in a noisy, whining way.

snob
1 *(n)* someone who looks down on people who are not rich and powerful. **snobbery** *(n).*
2 *(n)* a person who thinks that he or she is better or superior to others.

snoop
snooping snooped
1 *(v) (informal)* to look around somewhere secretly. **snooper** *(n).*
2 *(n)* a nosy person who pries into other people's business.

snooze
snoozing snoozed *(v) (informal)* to sleep lightly for a short time, usually during the day. **snooze** *(n).*

snore snoring snored *(v)* to breathe noisily through your mouth while you are asleep. **snore** *(n).*

snorkel and mask

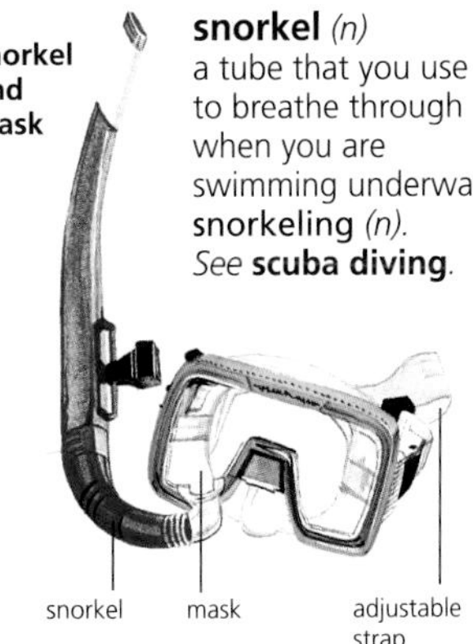

snorkel *(n)* a tube that you use to breathe through when you are swimming underwater. **snorkeling** *(n).* *See* **scuba diving**.

snort
snorting snorted *(v)* to breathe out air noisily through your nose. *Janice was laughing so hard she suddenly snorted like a pig.* **snort** *(n).*

snout *(n)*
the nose and mouth of a pig or similar animal.

snow
snowing snowed
1 *(n)* light flakes of ice that fall from the sky when it is very cold.
2 *(v)* When it **snows**, snow falls from the sky.
snowy *(adj)*.

snowball
snowballing snowballed
1 *(n)* snow pressed into a ball.
2 *(v)* If something **snowballs**, it grows rapidly. *Once we started inviting friends, the party snowballed.*

snowplow
snowplowing snowplowed
1 *(n)* a vehicle used to push snow off a road or railroad line.
2 *(v)* When you **snowplow** in skiing, you go down the slope slowly with the tips of your skis pointing inward and the ends pointing out.

snub snubbing snubbed
1 *(v)* to behave in a rude, unfriendly way toward someone. **snub** *(n)*.
2 **snub nose** a small, turned-up nose.

snuffle snuffling snuffled *(v)*
to breathe noisily and with difficulty.

snug snugger snuggest *(adj)*
warm, cozy, and comfortable. *The cottage was warm and snug.* **snugly** *(adv)*.

snuggle snuggling snuggled *(v)*
to sit or lie close to someone or something, so that you are warm and comfortable.

soak soaking soaked
1 *(v)* to put something in water and leave it there.
2 *(v)* When something **soaks up** liquid, it absorbs it or takes it in.

soaking *(adj)* very wet.

soap *(n)*
a substance that you rub onto your skin when you wash yourself. **soapy** *(adj)*.

soap opera *(n)*
a television series about the everyday lives of a group of people.

soar soaring soared
1 *(v)* to fly very high in the air.
2 *(v)* to rise or increase very quickly. *Inflation has soared to ten percent.*

sob sobbing sobbed *(v)*
to breathe in short bursts because you are crying. **sob** *(n)*.

sober soberer soberest
1 *(adj)* careful and serious. *A sober warning.* **soberly** *(adv)*.
2 *(v)* to make someone more serious.
3 *(adj)* **Sober** colors are dark and dull.

sob story sob stories *(n)*
a sad tale about yourself, intended to make people feel sorry for you.

soccer *(n)* a game played by two teams of eleven players who try to score goals by kicking a ball into a net at each end of a field. *The picture shows half a soccer field with a team in 4-4-2 formation.*

soccer field and players

sociable *(adj)* Someone who is **sociable** enjoys talking to people and spending time with them. **sociability** *(n)*, **sociably** *(adv)*.

social
1 *(adj)* having to do with the way that people live together. *This town has many social problems.* **socially** *(adv)*.
2 *(adj)* having to do with activities that you take part in with other people in your spare time. *Joss has an exciting social life.* **social** *(n)*, **socially** *(adv)*.
3 *(adj)* **Social** animals or insects live in groups rather than on their own.

social network *(n)*
a group of friends and acquaintances that you maintain online or through your phone. **social networking** *(v)*.

Social Security *(n)*
a U.S. government program that pays money to people who are elderly, retired, or disabled.

social services *(plural n)*
services provided by the government for people who have problems with health, childcare, housing, etc.

society societies
1 *(n)* all of the people who live in the same country or area and share the same laws and customs.
2 *(n)* an organization for people who share the same interests. *Polly is a member of the local music society.*

sociology *(n)*
the study of the ways in which people live together in different societies. **sociologist** *(n)*, **sociological** *(adj)*.

sock socking socked
1 *(n)* a piece of clothing that you wear on your foot.
2 *(v) (slang)* to hit someone very hard.

socket
1 *(n)* a hole or set of holes into which an electrical plug or bulb fits.
2 *(n)* a bone with a hole into which another bone fits. *See* **joint**.

soda
1 *(n)* a soft drink made with soda water.
2 *(n)* a drink made with soda water, flavoring and ice cream.
3 *(n)* baking soda.

soda water *(n)* water mixed with carbon dioxide gas to produce bubbles.

sodden *(adj)* extremely wet. *Patti fell in a pond and her clothes are sodden.*

sodium *(n)* a chemical found in salt.

sodium bicarbonate *(n)*
a chemical substance used to help cakes rise. Also called baking soda.

sofa *(n)*
a long soft seat with arms and a back and room for two or more people.

soft softer softest
1 *(adj)* Something that is **soft** is not stiff or hard and is easily pressed or bent into a different shape. *A soft cushion.* **softness** *(n),* **soften** *(v).*
2 *(adj)* smooth and gentle to touch. *Babies have very soft skin.*
3 *(adj)* pleasantly quiet and gentle. *Soft music.* **softly** *(adv).*
4 *(adj)* not strict or tough enough. *My Dad's so soft, he'll let me do anything.*
5 **soft drink** *(n)* a cold drink.

softball *(n)* a type of baseball played with a large ball.

softhearted *(adj)* If someone is **softhearted**, they are very kind, sympathetic, and generous to others.

software *(n)* a general name for computer programs.

soggy soggier soggiest *(adj)* very wet and heavy.

soil soiling soiled
1 *(n)* ground or earth in which plants grow.
2 *(v)* If you **soil** something, you make it dirty or stained.

solar *(adj)* having to do with the Sun. *A solar eclipse.*

solar energy *(n)* energy from the Sun that can be used for heating, lighting, etc. *Solar panels, like the one shown below, are fixed to roofs and use solar energy to produce hot water.*

solar panel (cutaway)

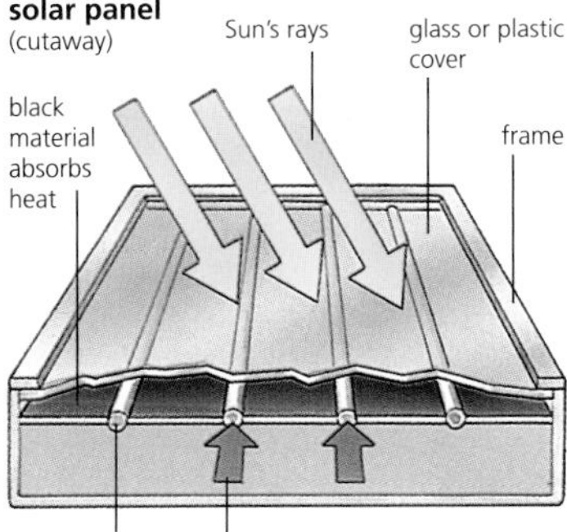

solar system *(n)* the Sun and the planets that move around it. In our solar system there are eight planets, many moons, and also asteroids and comets, all of which move around the Sun. *See* **planet**.

solder soldering soldered *(v)* to join pieces of metal together by putting a small amount of hot, liquid metal between them, which hardens as it cools.

soldier soldiering soldiered
1 *(n)* someone who is in the army. **soldierly** *(adj).*
2 *(v)* If you **soldier on**, you keep doing something difficult.

soldiers

Roman legionnaire | 11th-century European knight | 15th-century European knight | 17th-century British cavalryman | 18th-century Prussian musketeer | 19th-century U.S. private

sole
1 *(n)* the underneath part of the foot.
2 *(n)* the underneath part of a shoe, boot or sock.
3 *(n)* a kind of flat sea fish.
4 *(adj)* only. *I was the sole survivor.* **solely** *(adv).*

solemn *(adj)* very serious. *Mike had a solemn look on his face.* **solemnity** *(n),* **solemnly** *(adv).*

solid
1 *(adj)* hard and firm. *The water had frozen solid.* **solidity** *(n).*
2 *(adj)* not hollow. *A solid chocolate egg.*
3 *(adj)* not mixed with anything else. *It was made of solid gold.*
4 *(adj)* dependable. *Solid citizens.*
5 *(n)* a three-dimensional geometric figure.

solidarity *(n)* agreement between a group of people that they will work or fight together to achieve something.

solidify solidifies solidifying solidified *(v)* to become hard and firm.

solidly
1 *(adv)* firmly and strongly. *This house is very solidly built.*
2 *(adv)* without interruption. *Alma worked solidly for two hours.*

solitary
1 *(adj)* If someone is **solitary**, they spend a lot of time alone.
2 *(adj)* single. *There was not one solitary person on the beach.*
3 **solitary confinement** *(n)* a punishment in which a prisoner is put in a cell alone and is not allowed to see or talk to anyone.

solo *(n)* a piece of music played or sung by one person. **solo** *(adj),* **soloist** *(n).*

soluble *(adj)* A substance that is **soluble** can be dissolved in liquid.

solution
1 *(n)* the answer to a problem.
2 *(n)* a liquid that has something dissolved in it.

solve solving solved *(v)* to find the answer to a problem.

solvent *(n)* a liquid that makes other substances dissolve.

somber *(som-bur) (adj)* dark and gloomy. *Carl is in a somber mood.*

some
1 *(adj)* a number of things or an amount of something. *There were some children in the park. Would you like some cake?*
2 *(pronoun)* a certain number of people or things. *Some of us are going abroad.*

somebody *(pronoun)* someone.

someday *(adv)* at some future time.

somehow *(adv)* in some way. *Somehow, the rabbit managed to wiggle free.*

someone *(pronoun)* a person. *Someone has taken my pen!*

somersault *(n)* When you do a **somersault**, you tuck your head into your chest and roll over forwards on the ground or in the air. **somersault** *(v).*

something *(pronoun)* a thing. *There's something moving in the bushes.*

sometime *(adv)* at some time in the past or the future. *I'll do my homework sometime tomorrow.*

sometimes *(adv)* at some times but not at others. *Gertie sometimes has a nap in the afternoon.*

somewhere *(adv)* to or in some place. *My aunt lives somewhere in Ohio. Let's go somewhere else.*

son *(n)*
Someone's **son** is their male child.

sonar *(n)* a piece of equipment that is used on ships to calculate how deep the water is or where underwater objects are. It works by sending sound waves through the water and listening for when they bounce back off something. Sonar stands for *SOund Navigation And Ranging*.

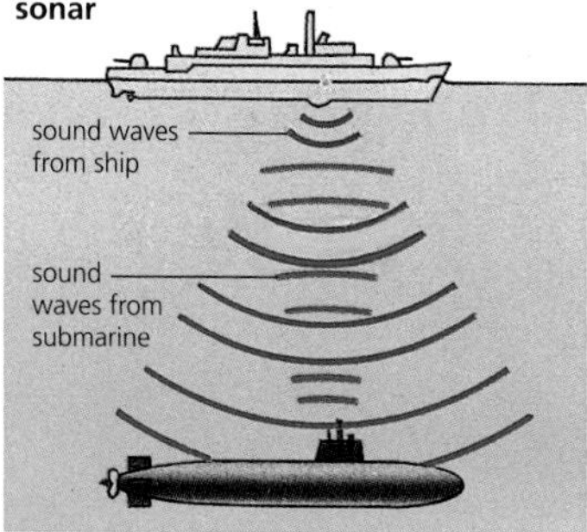

sonata *(n)* a piece of music for one or two instruments.

song
1 *(n)* a piece of music with words for singing.
2 *(n)* the musical sounds made by a bird.

sonic
1 *(adj)* to do with sound waves.
2 **sonic boom** *(n)* the loud noise produced by a vehicle when it breaks through the sound barrier and travels faster than the speed of sound. *This picture shows the shape of a sonic boom created by an airplane.*

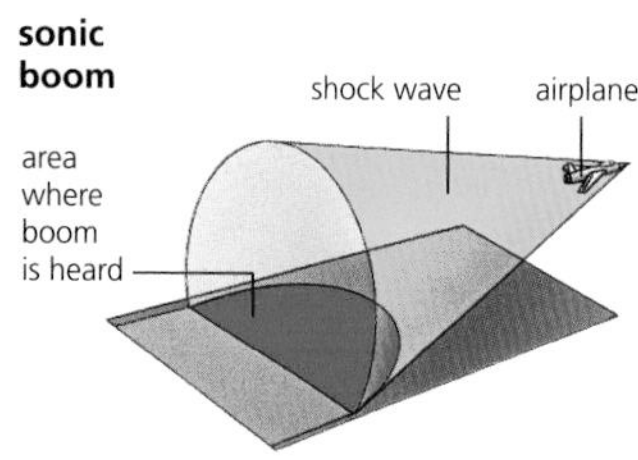

sonnet *(n)* a poem with 14 lines and a fixed pattern of rhymes.

soon sooner soonest
1 *(adv)* in a short time. *I'll visit you soon.*
2 If you would **sooner** do something, you would prefer to do that thing.

soot *(n)*
black powder that is produced when something is burned, and that often collects in chimneys. **sooty** *(adj).*

soothe soothing soothed
1 *(v)* to make someone less angry or upset. *Frankie tried to soothe the screaming baby.* **soothing** *(adj).*
2 *(v)* to make something less painful. *This cream should soothe your rash.* **soothing** *(adj).*

sophisticated *(sof-iss-tik-ate-id)*
1 *(adj)* People who are **sophisticated** have a lot of knowledge and experience of social life, fashion, and culture. **sophistication** *(n).*
2 *(adj)* A **sophisticated** machine is cleverly designed and able to do difficult or complicated things. **sophistication** *(n).*

sophomore *(n)*
a student in their second year at either high school or college.

sopping *(adj)* extremely wet.

soprano
1 *(n)* a high singing voice. **soprano** *(adj).*
2 *(n)* a woman or young boy with a soprano voice.

sordid
1 *(adj)* dishonest and shameful.
2 *(adj)* dirty and messy. *A sordid room.*

sore sorer sorest
1 *(adj)* painful. **soreness** *(n).*
2 *(n)* an area of infected and painful skin on your body. *A cold sore.*

sorrow *(n)* great sadness. **sorrowful** *(adj),* **sorrowfully** *(adv).*

sorry sorrier sorriest
1 *(interject)* a word that you say when you feel unhappy or upset because you have done something wrong or because someone is suffering. **sorry** *(adj).*
2 *(adj)* If you feel **sorry** for someone, you have sympathy and compassion for them.
3 If someone or something is **in a sorry state**, they are in a bad condition.

sort sorting sorted
1 *(n)* a type or a kind. *What sort of dog is that?*
2 *(v)* to arrange things into groups.

SOS *(n)* a signal sent out by a ship or plane that is in need of urgent help. The initials SOS stand for Save Our Souls. *See* **semaphore**.

soul
1 *(n)* your spirit, which many people believe lives on after you have died.
2 *(n)* a person. *Don't tell another soul.*
3 *(adj)* having to do with African-American culture. *Soul food.*

sound sounding sounded
1 *(n)* something that you hear.
2 *(v)* If a horn or bell **sounds**, it makes a noise.
3 *(v)* to give an impression. *Your vacation sounds wonderful.*
4 *(adj)* reliable, practical, or strong. *A sound idea.* **soundly** *(adv).*

sound barrier *(n)*
When a vehicle goes through the **sound barrier**, it meets a sudden increase in the force of the air against it because it has passed the speed of sound. *See* **sonic boom**.

sound effects *(plural n)*
noises that accompany a play or movie to make it more realistic.

soundproof *(adj)* A **soundproof** room does not let any sound in or out of it. **soundproof** *(v).*

soundtrack *(n)*
the recorded sound for a movie.

soup *(n)* a liquid food made with vegetables, meat or fish.

sour
1 *(adj)* Something that is **sour** has a bitter taste. **sourness** *(n).*
2 *(adj)* bad-tempered. *Lorenzo has a very sour expression.* **sourness** *(n),* **sourly** *(adv).*

source
1 *(n)* the place, person, or thing from which something comes. *We must find the source of the problem.*
2 *(n)* the place where a stream or river starts.
3 *(n)* someone or something that provides information.

south
1 *(n)* one of the four main points of the compass, the direction to your left when you face the setting Sun, in the northern hemisphere. **south** *(adj),* **southern** *(adj),* **south** *(adv).*
2 *(adj)* A **south** wind blows from the south. **southerly** *(adj).*
3 **South Pole** *(n)* the most southerly part of the Earth, located at the bottom tip of the Earth's axis. *See* **polar**.

souvenir *(soo-ven-ear) (n)*
an object that you keep to remind you of a place, event, etc.

sovereign *(sov-rin) (n)*
a king or queen.

sow sowing sowed sown *or* sowed
1 *(rhymes with go) (v)* to put seeds into the ground so that they will grow.
2 *(rhymes with how) (n)* a female pig.

soybean *(n)* a kind of bean that can be cooked and eaten or made into milk, oil, or flour.

soy sauce *(n)* a dark liquid that is made from fermented soybeans. It's used as a sauce to flavor foods.

space
1 *(n)* an empty or available area. *We'll need a lot of space for dancing.*
2 *(n)* the universe beyond the Earth's atmosphere.
3 *(n)* a period of time. *Everyone arrived within a space of five minutes.*
4 *(v)* to leave an empty area between things. *Space the stitches evenly as you sew.*

spacecraft *(n)*
a vehicle that travels in space.

space shuttle *(n)*
a spacecraft designed to carry passengers and spacecraft into space and back to Earth.

space station *(n)* a spacecraft large enough to house crew for long periods of time. Space stations are placed in orbit and are used for making scientific observations and as launching sites for other spacecraft.

spacesuit *(n)* the protective clothing that an astronaut wears in space. *See* **astronaut**.

spacious *(adj)*
very large. *A spacious kitchen.*

spade
1 *(n)* a tool with a flat blade and a long handle, used for digging.
2 **spades** *(plural n)* one of the four suits in a pack of cards, with a black symbol like a heart with a stalk.

spaghetti *(n)*
long, thin strings of pasta. *See* **pasta**.

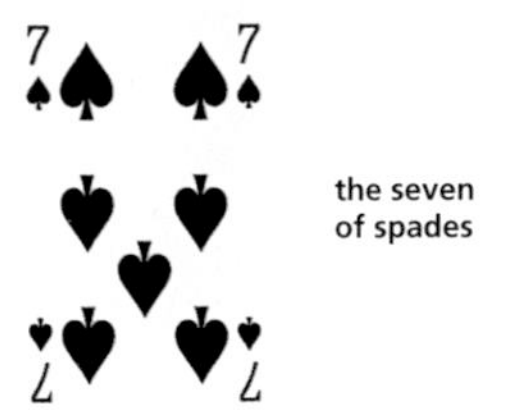

the seven of spades

spam *(n)* messages or advertisements sent by e-mail to people who have not asked for them.

span
1 *(n)* Your **span** is the distance between your little finger and thumb when your hand is outstretched.
2 *(n)* The **span** of something is its length from one end to the other. *This bridge has a span of over a mile.* **span** *(v)*.
3 *(n)* a length of time. **span** *(v)*.

spank spanking spanked *(v)*
to smack someone as a punishment.

spar
1 *(n)* a strong pole.
2 *(v)* a boxing practice or exhibition.

spare sparing spared
1 *(adj)* free for extra use. *Spare time. A spare tire.*
2 *(v)* to make something available. *Can you spare me a few minutes?*
3 *(v)* to let someone live instead of killing them. *Thankfully, the hostages were spared.*

spark sparking sparked
1 *(n)* a red-hot speck caused by fire, electricity, or friction. **spark** *(v)*.
2 **spark off** *(v)* to make something happen. *The concert sparked off my interest in music.*

spark plug

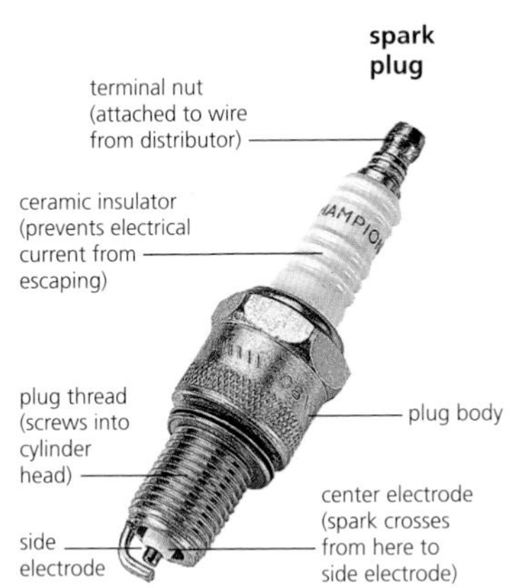

sparkle sparkling sparkled *(v)*
to shine with a lot of flashing points of light. **sparkle** *(n)*.

spark plug *(n)* one of the parts of a gasoline engine that supplies an electrical spark to ignite the gas and air mixture in a cylinder. Spark plugs are screwed into the cylinders and connected to the distributor, which supplies the current to create the spark. *Also see* **engine**.

sparrow *(n)* a small, brown bird.

sparse *(adj)* thinly spread or scattered. *Sparse vegetation.*

spasm *(n)* a short, sudden attack of pain or emotion. *A spasm of laughter.*

spatula
1 *(n)* a kitchen utensil with a broad, flat blade, used for lifting and stirring food.
2 *(n)* an instrument with a flat blade, used by doctors and scientists. *See* **apparatus**.

spawn *(n)* the eggs produced by fish and amphibians. *See* **frog**.

speak speaking spoke spoken *(v)*
to talk or to say words.

speaker
1 *(n)* someone who gives a speech in public.
2 *(n)* a piece of equipment that turns electrical signals into sound, usually attached to a stereo system. Speaker is short for loudspeaker. *The diagram shows a cutaway view of a speaker.*

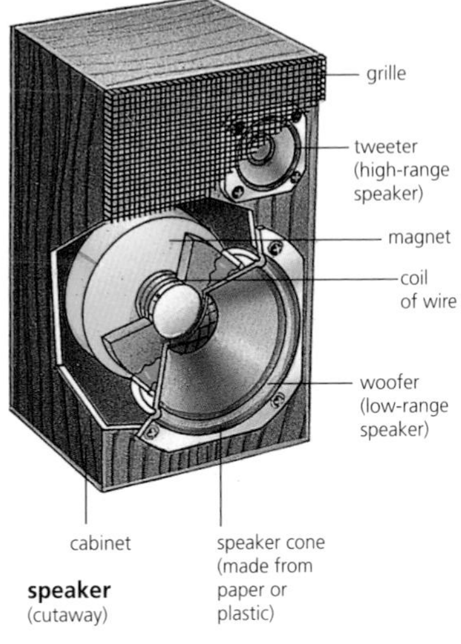

speaker (cutaway)

spear *(n)*
a long, pointed weapon that used to be thrown in battle.

Spartan warrior

This picture shows a warrior from ancient Sparta wielding a spear.

special
1 *(adj)* extraordinary and important. *A special day.* **specially** *(adv)*.
2 *(adj)* particular. *You need a special badge to get into the exhibition.*

specialist *(n)* an expert at one particular job. **specialism** *(n)*.

specialize
specializing specialized *(v)*
to concentrate on one thing that you are good at or interested in. *Alice specializes in medieval art.*

specialty specialties *(n)* the thing that you are particularly good at. *Simon's specialty is cooking.*

species *(spee-sheez)* **species** *(n)* one of the groups into which animals and plants are divided, according to their characteristics. *The domestic dog is a species of mammal.*

specific *(adj)* particular, definite, or individually named. *Hilda insists on a specific type of tea.* **specifically** *(adv).*

specification *(n)* detailed information and instructions about something that is to be built or made.

specify specifies specifying specified *(v)* to mention something in an exact way. *Please specify which course you would like to attend.*

specimen *(n)* a sample or an example. *Please supply a specimen of your signature.* **specimen** *(adj).*

speck *(n)* a minute piece of something, like dust or dirt.

speckled *(adj)* covered with small, irregular marks. *A speckled egg.*

spectacle *(n)* a remarkable and dramatic sight. *The fireworks were quite a spectacle.*

spectacular
1 *(adj)* remarkable and dramatic to look at. *A spectacular waterfall.*
2 *(n)* a show that contains dramatic effects and acts.

spectator *(n)* someone who watches an event. **spectate** *(v).*

specter *(spek-tur)* *(n)* a ghost. **spectral** *(adj).*

spectrum spectra
1 *(n)* a wide range of things or ideas.
2 *(n)* the range of colors that is revealed when light shines through a prism or through drops of water. When white light travels through a prism it is bent or refracted. Since each of the colors in light travels at a slightly different speed, they each bend at a different angle and spread out in a spectrum.

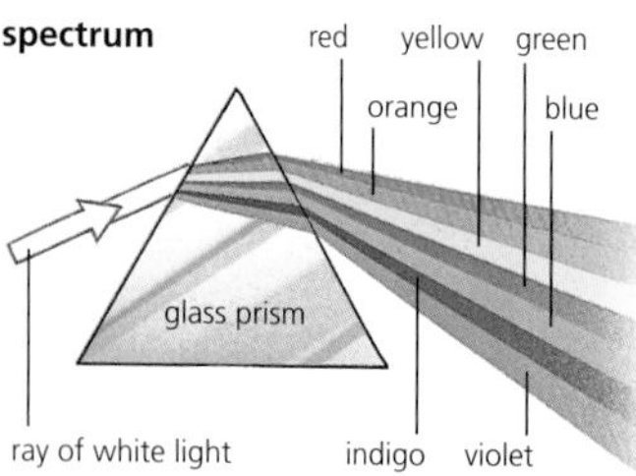

speculate speculating speculated
1 *(v)* to wonder or guess about something when you do not know all the facts. **speculation** *(n).*
2 *(v)* to buy shares on the stock market or to put money into other projects that carry some risk. **speculation** *(n).*

speech speeches
1 *(n)* the ability to speak.
2 *(n)* a talk given to a group of people.

speechless *(adj)* unable to speak. *Dad was speechless with rage.*

speed
speeding sped *or* speeded
1 *(n)* the rate at which something moves.
2 *(v)* to travel very fast or to travel faster than is allowed.
3 *(n)* quickness of movement.

speedometer *(n)* an instrument in a vehicle that shows you how fast you are traveling.

spell spelling spelled
1 *(v)* to write or say the letters of a word in their correct order.
2 *(n)* a period of time, usually a short one. *A spell of silence.*
3 *(n)* words that are supposed to have magical powers.

spelunking
If you **go spelunking**, you explore caves (caving, *U.K.*) **spelunker** *(n).*

spend spending spent
1 *(v)* to use money to buy things.
2 *(v)* If you **spend** time or energy, you use it.

sphere *(sfear)* *(n)* a shape like a ball or globe. **spherical** *(sfeer-ik-al)* *(adj).*

sphinx

sphinx *(sfinks)* **sphinxes** *(n)* a mythical monster with a woman's head and a lion's body. *The picture above shows the statue of the sphinx at Giza, in Egypt.*

spice *(n)* a substance with a distinctive smell or taste, used to flavor foods. *The picture shows a range of spices.*

spider *(n)* an insect-like eight-legged creature that weaves a web to trap insects for food. *This picture shows a selection of spiders from around the world.*

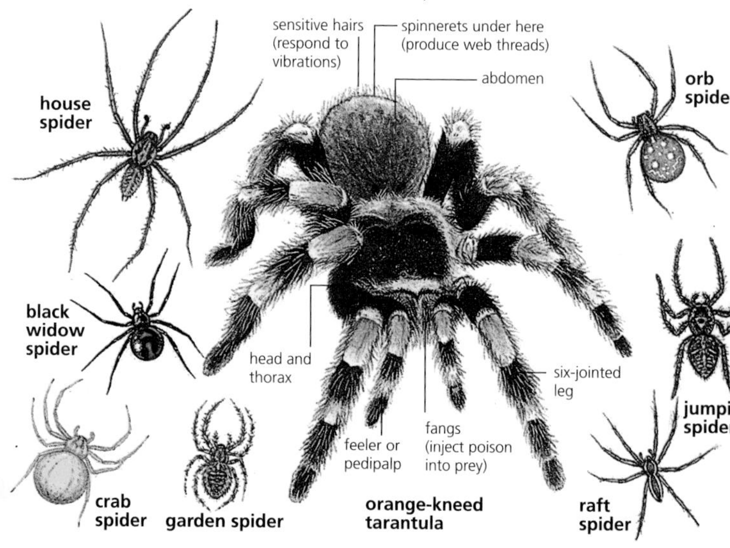

spike *(n)* a sharp point. spiky *(adj).*

spill spilling spilled *(v)* If you **spill** something, you let the contents of a container fall out accidentally.

spin spinning spun
1 *(v)* to turn around fast on the spot.
2 *(v)* to create a thread by twisting fine fibers together. *The picture shows a spinning jenny, a machine invented in the 18th century, which could spin up to eight threads at once.*

spinning jenny

spinach *(n)*
a dark-green leafy vegetable. *See* **vegetable**.

spindly spindlier spindliest *(adj)*
long, thin, and rather weak.

spine
1 *(n)* the backbone.
spinal *(adj). See* **skeleton**.
2 *(n)* part of a book's cover that joins the front and the back. *See* **book**.

spinster *(n)*
a woman who has never been married.

spiral *(adj)*
A **spiral** pattern winds around in circles like a spring.
The chambers inside a nautilus shell are arranged in a spiral pattern.
spiral *(n)*, **spiral** *(v).*

nautilus shell
(cutaway)

spire *(n)*
the pointed cone on top of some church towers. *See* **cathedral**.

spirit
1 *(n)* the part of a person that is not physical and is expressed in their deepest thoughts and feelings.
2 *(n)* enthusiasm and determination in a person or group of people. *We shared a spirit of hope.* **spirited** *(adj).*
3 *(n)* a ghost or a being with no physical form.
4 **spirit away** *(v)* to carry off quickly and mysteriously.
5 **spirit level** *(n)* an instrument used for checking whether a surface is level. *See* **woodwork**.

spiritual
1 *(adj)* having to do with beliefs, thoughts, and feelings and not physical things. **spiritually** *(adv).*
2 *(n)* a folk song, often religious, originated by African-Americans.
3 *(adj)* to do with religion.

spit spitting spat *or* spit
1 *(v)* to force saliva out of your mouth.
2 *(n)* saliva.
3 *(n)* a long, thin metal rod which is pushed through meat to hold and turn it while it is being cooked over a fire.

spite
1 *(n)* deliberate nastiness.
spiteful *(adj),* spitefully *(adv).*
2 **in spite of** without taking notice of.

splash
splashes splashing splashed *(v)*
to scatter liquid. **splash** *(n).*

splendid *(adj)* impressive, excellent, or very good. **splendidly** *(adv).*

splint *(n)* a piece of wood, plastic, or metal used to support a broken or damaged limb.

splinter *(n)*
a thin, sharp piece of wood, glass, metal, etc. **splinter** *(v).*

split splitting split
1 *(v)* to break something into separate pieces.
2 *(n)* a crack.
3 *(v)* If a couple **splits up**, they stop going out together or living together.

spoil spoiling spoiled *or* spoilt
1 *(v)* to ruin or wreck something.
2 *(adj)* If children are **spoiled**, their parents have allowed them to have their own way too often.

sponge
1 *(n)* a sea animal with a rubbery absorbent skeleton. The skeletons of sponges can be used for washing.
2 *(n)* soft man-made material, filled with holes, used for washing and cleaning. **sponge** *(v),* **spongy** *(adj).*
3 *(n)* a light cake.

sponsor sponsoring sponsored
1 *(v)* to give money to people who are doing something worthwhile, often for charity. **sponsorship** *(n).*
2 *(n)* an organisation that gives money to a sports team or TV show in return for advertising.

spontaneous *(adj)*
without previous thought or planning.
spontaneity *(n),* **spontaneously** *(adv).*

spool *(n)* a reel on which film, tape, thread, etc. is wound. *See* **angling**.

spoon *(n)* a utensil used for eating, stirring, and measuring.

spoor *(n)*
the trail left behind by an animal.

moss spore cases

spore *(n)*
a cell produced by non-flowering plants such as fungi, mosses, and ferns, which develops into a new plant. *The picture shows some moss spore cases. When the cases open, the spores are spread by the wind.*
Also see **fern**.

sports *(n)*
a general name for games involving physical activity. Sports can be played professionally or for pleasure.

spot spotting spotted
1 *(n)* a small mark that is usually round. **spotted** *(adj).*
2 *(n)* a sore, red place on the skin.
3 *(n)* a place or a location. *This looks like a good spot for a picnic.*
4 *(v)* to notice something.
Angelina has spotted a friend.

spotless *(adj)*
absolutely clean. **spotlessly** *(adv).*

spotlight *(n)*
a powerful light used to light up a small area.

spouse *(n)*
a husband or a wife.

spout spouting spouted
1 *(n)* a tube through which liquid is poured, for example the spout of a kettle.
2 *(v) (informal)* to talk about something in a boring, pompous way.

sprain spraining sprained *(v)*
to injure a joint by twisting it.
Liza sprained her ankle when she fell.

sprawl sprawling sprawled
1 *(v)* to sit or lie with your arms and legs spread out carelessly.
2 *(v)* to spread out in all directions.
The city sprawled for miles.

spray spraying sprayed *(v)*
to scatter liquid in very fine drops. **spray** *(n).*

spread spreading spread
1 *(v)* to unfold or to stretch out.
Hilary spread out the map on the table. Joel spread his arms wide.
2 *(v)* to cover a surface with something. *We spread the bread with peanut butter.* **spread** *(n).*
3 *(v)* to scatter or to make known.
Spread the news.

sprightly sprightlier sprightliest *(adj)*
lively and energetic.

spring springing sprang sprung
1 *(n)* the season between winter and summer, when it becomes warmer and leaves grow on the trees.
2 *(v)* to jump suddenly. *The lion sprang at the antelope.*
3 *(n)* a coil of metal that moves back to its original position after being compressed or pushed down.
4 *(n)* a place where water rises up from underground and becomes a stream.

springboard *(n)*
a flexible board that people jump on in order to increase their height or force in diving or gymnastics. *The picture shows a diver using a springboard.*

springboard jump

spring-cleaning *(n)*
thorough cleaning of a place, usually done once a year.

sprinkle sprinkling sprinkled *(v)*
to scatter liquid or powder in small amounts. *Sprinkle the top of the dish with grated cheese.*

sprint sprinting sprinted
1 *(v)* to run fast. *Gerry sprinted to the stores.*
2 *(n)* a very fast race run over a short distance.
sprinter *(n)*, **sprint** *(adj)*.

sprint start

sprocket *(n)*
a wheel with a toothed edge, usually driven by a chain. *See* **bicycle**.

sprout sprouting sprouted
1 *(v)* When a plant **sprouts**, it starts to grow and produce shoots or buds.
2 **sprouts** *(plural n)* shoots of various plants, often eaten raw. *Bean sprouts.*

spur spurring spurred
1 *(n)* a spike or spiked wheel on the heel of a rider's boot, used to make a horse go more quickly.
2 **spur on** *(v)* If something **spurs you on**, it encourages or motivates you.

spurt spurting spurted
1 *(v)* When liquid **spurts**, it flows or gushes suddenly. **spurt** *(n)*.
2 *(n)* a sudden burst of energy, growth, or speed.

spy spies spying spied
1 *(v)* to watch something closely from a hidden place.
2 *(n)* someone who secretly collects information about an enemy. **spy** *(v)*.

squabble *(n)* a childish argument or quarrel. **squabble** *(v)*.

squad *(n)* a small group of people involved in the same activity, such as soldiers or football players.

squalid *(adj)* dirty and unpleasant.

squander
squandering squandered *(v)*
to spend money wastefully.

square squaring squared
1 *(n)* a shape with four equal sides and four right angles. *See* **shape**.
2 *(v)* to multiply a number by itself. *4 squared equals 16.*
3 **square root** *(n)*
the number that, when multiplied by itself, gives a particular number. *5 is the square root of 25.*

squash
squashes squashing squashed
1 *(v)* to crush or flatten something.
2 *(n)* a racket game played by two people who hit a small rubber ball against the walls of an enclosed court.
3 *(n)* a fleshy fruit that grows on a vine in many shapes, sizes and colors. *See* **vegetable**.

squash court

side wall line
front boundary line
service line
tin
back boundary line
half-court line
short line
service box

squat squatting squatted
1 *(v)* to crouch with your knees bent.
2 *(v)* to live, without permission, in a place that does not belong to you. **squat** *(n)*, **squatter** *(n)*.
3 *(adj)* short and broad.

squawk squawking squawked *(v)*
to make a loud, harsh cry like the noise of a parrot. **squawk** *(n)*.

squeak squeaking squeaked *(v)*
to make a short, high-pitched sound like the noise of a mouse. **squeak** *(n)*.

squeal squealing squealed *(v)*
to make a shrill, high-pitched sound, usually because you are frightened or in pain. **squeal** *(n)*.

squeamish *(adj)* easily sickened or shocked. **squeamishly** *(adv)*.

squeeze squeezing squeezed
1 *(v)* to press something firmly together from opposite sides. **squeeze** *(n)*.
2 *(v)* to force something into or through a space. *We squeezed into the bus.* **squeeze** *(n)*.

squid *(n)*
a sea creature with a long, soft body and ten tentacles. *Squids swim by squirting water out of their bodies with great force.*

squid

squint
squinting squinted
1 *(v)* If you **squint** at something, you nearly close your eyes to see it more clearly.
2 *(n)* Someone who has a **squint** has eyes that look in different directions from one another.

squire *(n)*
In medieval times, a **squire** was a young nobleman who accompanied and helped a knight.

squirm squirming squirmed
1 *(v)* to wiggle around uncomfortably. *Stop squirming!*
2 *(v)* to feel uncomfortable because you are embarrassed or ashamed. *Alex squirmed in his new suit.*

squirrel *(n)* a tree-climbing rodent with a bushy tail. *The gray squirrel shown here is found in Europe and North America.*

gray squirrel

squirt squirting squirted *(v)* to send out a stream of liquid. *Misha turned on the hose and squirted her brothers.* **squirt** *(n).*

squishy squishier squishiest *(adj)* *(informal)* soft and soggy.

St. *see* **saint**.

stab stabbing stabbed
1 *(v)* to wound someone by piercing their skin with a knife or other sharp instrument. **stab** *(n).*
2 *(informal)* If you **make a stab** at something, you try to do it.

stable
1 *(n)* a building or a part of a building where a horse is kept.
2 *(adj)* firm and steady. *Before you climb the ladder, check that it is stable.* **stability** *(n),* **stabilize** *(v).*
3 *(adj)* safe and secure. *The children had a stable upbringing.* **stability** *(n).*

staccato *(sta-**kah**-toh) (adv)* When you play notes **staccato**, you make them short and separate.

stack stacking stacked *(v)* to pile things up, one on top of another. **stack** *(n).*

stadium stadiums *or* stadia *(n)* a large building, often open air, in which sports events and concerts are held.

staff
1 *(plural n)* the people who work in an organization. *The office staff.*
2 *(n) (old-fashioned)* a thick wooden stick.

stag *(n)* an adult male deer. *The picture shows a stag roaring. Stags roar to one another in the mating season when they compete for females.*

red deer stag

stage staging staged
1 *(n)* a period of development. *Our plans are still at an early stage.*
2 *(n)* a level of progress. *You have done so well that you can move to the next stage.*
3 *(n)* an area where plays and concerts are performed.
4 *(v)* to organize a public performance or event. *Our school is staging a play.*
5 If you **go on the stage**, you become an actor.

stagecoach stagecoaches *(n)* a horse-drawn vehicle used in the past to carry passengers and mail for long distances. Stagecoaches traveled in stages and were supplied with fresh horses at each stage.

stagecoach

stage-manage
stage-managing stage-managed *(v)* to organize a play, concert, or other event. **stage manager** *(n).*

stagestruck *(adj)* Someone who is **stagestruck** thinks that the theater is very glamorous and wants to become an actor.

stagger staggering staggered
1 *(v)* to walk or stand unsteadily.
2 *(adj)* If you are **staggered** by something, you are astonished.
3 *(v)* When you **stagger** events, you time them so that they do not happen at the same time. *The guards staggered their breaks.*

staggering *(adj)* amazing or astonishing. *Julio bought the house for a staggering amount of money.*

stagnant *(adj)* **Stagnant** water cannot flow and is dirty and smelly.

stagnate stagnating stagnated
1 *(v)* When water **stagnates**, it changes color, and becomes stale and often smelly.
2 *(v)* If a situation or person **stagnates**, they remain the same for a long time. **stagnation** *(n).*

staid *(adj)* If someone is **staid**, they are not lively and do not like change.

stain staining stained
1 *(n)* a mark on something that is hard to remove.
2 *(v)* to make a mark that is hard to remove from something. *The paint stained my coat.*
3 *(n)* coloring used on wood.

stained glass *(n)* colored pieces of glass held together by lead strips. Stained glass is often used in church windows. *The picture shows a stained glass window from Chartres Cathedral in France.*

stainless steel *(n)* a type of steel that does not rust or tarnish.

stairway *(n)* steps that allow you to walk from one level of a building to another.

stake staking staked
1 *(n)* a thick, pointed post that can be driven into the ground.
2 *(v)* to bet. *Jim staked his money on the race.*
3 *(n)* If you have a **stake** in something, you are involved in it or you have put money into it.
4 If something is **at stake**, it is at risk.

stained glass

stalactite *(n)* a thin piece of rock, shaped like an icicle, that hangs from the roof of a cave. Stalactites are made from calcium minerals, dissolved in dripping water, that have slowly solidified. *The picture below shows stalactites in a cave.*

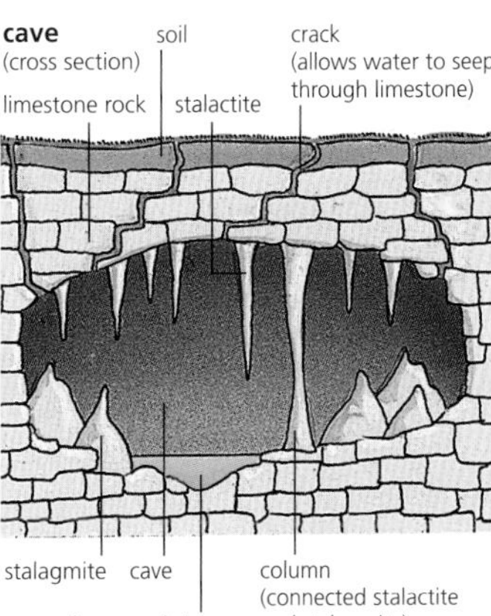

stalagmite *(n)* a piece of rock that sticks up from the floor of a cave. Stalagmites are made from calcium minerals, dissolved in dripping water, which have slowly solidified. *The picture above shows stalagmites in a cave.*

stale staler stalest *(adj)* no longer fresh. *Stale bread.*

stalemate *(n)* a situation in an argument or game of chess in which neither side can win.

stalk *(stawk)* **stalking stalked**
1 *(n)* the long, main part of a plant from which the leaves, flowers, and fruit grow.
2 *(n)* a thin branch that holds a leaf, flower, or fruit.
3 *(v)* to hunt, track or follow someone or something in a quiet, secretive way. *The leopard stalked its prey.* **stalker** *(n).*

stall stalling stalled
1 *(v)* When a car **stalls**, its engine stops suddenly.
2 *(n)* a table or booth from which things are sold in a market or rummage sale.
3 *(n)* a section in a stable or barn where one animal is kept.
4 *(v)* to delay doing something until later.

stallion *(n)* a male horse.

stamina *(n)* the energy to keep doing something for a long while. *You need stamina for long-distance running.*

stammer
stammering stammered *(v)* If you **stammer** when you speak, you repeat the first sound of a word before you manage to say the whole word. **stammer** *(n).*

stamp
stamping stamped
1 *(n)* a small piece of paper that you stick on a letter or package to show that you have paid for it to be sent. **stamp** *(v).*
2 *(n)* an object used to print a mark on paper. You press the stamp first onto an ink pad and then onto paper. **stamp** *(v).*
3 *(v)* to bang your foot down.

penny black, Britain, 1840

Japan, 1956

stamps

U.S.A., 1969

U.S.S.R., 1959

Australia, 1994

stampede stampeding stampeded *(v)* When people or animals **stampede**, they suddenly rush somewhere wildly. **stampede** *(n).*

stand standing stood
1 *(v)* to be on your feet with your body upright.
2 *(v)* to put something somewhere. *Stand the vase on the table.*
3 *(v)* to continue unchanged. *My offer still stands.*
4 *(n)* an object on which you put things.
5 *(n)* a covered area within a stadium.
6 *(n)* a small, outdoor store. *A hot dog stand.*
7 **stand for** *(v)* to represent. *U.S. stands for United States.*
8 *(v)* If you **cannot stand** something, you hate it or are unable to bear it.
9 *(v)* If you **stand by** someone, you support them when they are in trouble.
10 *(v)* If something **stands out**, it can be seen or noticed easily.

standard
1 *(adj)* usual or average.
2 *(n)* a rule or model for judging or measuring how good something is. *Standards of math seem to be falling.*
3 *(n)* a flag or banner used by an organization, such as the army.

standby
1 *(n)* something or someone that is ready to be used if needed.
2 *(n)* If a computer is **on standby-mode**, it means it has power running through it and can be activated quickly.

stand-in *(n)* someone who takes the place of another person when that person cannot be there. **stand in** *(v).*

standstill *(n)* If something is **at a standstill**, it has stopped completely.

stanza *(n)* one of the groups of lines into which a poem is divided. Another name for stanza is verse.

staple
1 *(n)* a small piece of wire, which is punched through sheets of paper to hold them together. **staple** *(v).*
2 *(adj)* A **staple** food is the main food eaten as part of a person's diet.

star starring starred
1 *(n)* a ball of burning gases in space, seen from the Earth as a tiny point of light in the sky at night. **starry** *(adj).*
2 *(n)* a shape with several points, usually five or six.
3 *(n)* a well-known actor or entertainer in a movie, television show, or play.
4 *(v)* to take the main part in a movie, television show or play.

starboard *(n)* the right side of a ship or aircraft. **starboard** *(adj).*

starch starches
1 *(n)* a substance found in such foods as potatoes, bread, and rice. Starch is very filling and gives you energy.
2 *(n)* a substance used for making cloth stiff. **starch** *(v).*

stare staring stared *(v)* to look at someone or something for a long time without moving your eyes. **stare** *(n).*

starfish starfish *(n)* a star-shaped sea animal with five or more arms.

branch of intestine
flexible outer wall
anus
branch of water canal with tube feet attached
central water canal
stomach
arm with spines and pincers to attack enemies
tube foot

starfish (cutaway)

stark starker starkest
1 *(adj)* bare and plain. *A stark landscape. The stark truth.*
2 *(adj)* complete or total. *Stark poverty.*

start starting started
1 *(v)* to begin to act, move, happen, etc. or to make something begin to act, move, happen, etc.
2 *(n)* the beginning of something.
3 *(v)* to jump in surprise.
4 *(n)* an advantage at the beginning of a race. *You can have a 20-yard start.*

startle startling startled *(v)* to surprise someone and make them jump. **startled** *(adj),* **startling** *(adj).*

starve starving starved *(v)* to suffer or die from hunger. **starvation** *(n).*

starving
1 *(adj)* suffering or dying from hunger.
2 *(adj) (informal)* very hungry.

state stating stated
1 *(v)* to say something clearly. *Please state your name.*
2 *(n)* the government of a country. *Affairs of state.*
3 *(n)* an area within a country that makes its own laws. *The State of Texas.*
4 *(n)* the way that something is or the condition that something or someone is in. *Your room is in a terrible state. Betty is in a state of confusion.*
5 *(informal)* If someone is **in a state**, they are upset.
6 **state-of-the-art** *(adj)* very advanced and up to date. *A state-of-the-art computer.*

tatement
(n) something
hat is said formally.
(n) a list of all
he amounts paid
nto and out of
bank account.

stay staying stayed
1 *(v)* to remain where you are.
2 *(v)* to spend time somewhere. *We didn't stay long at the party.*
3 *(n)* a period of time spent somewhere as a visitor. *Have you had an enjoyable stay?*

steam locomotive *(n)* an engine powered by steam and used for pulling trains. *The steam produced by this steam locomotive forces the pistons to move. The pistons drive the connecting rods and crank rods, which are connected to the driving wheels.*

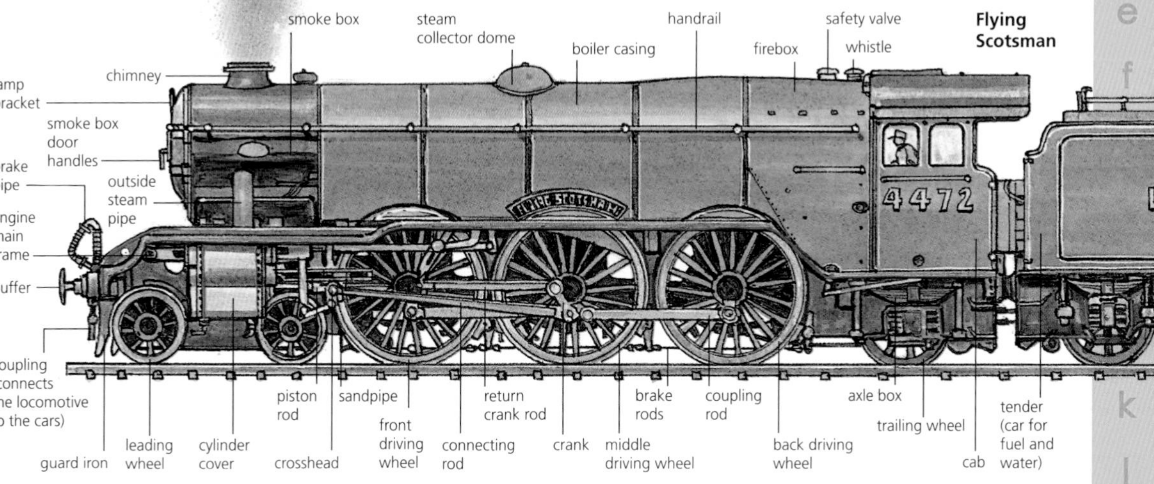

tatic
(adj) not moving or not changing.
static situation.
(n) electricity that is produced
y friction. Static is short for
tatic electricity.
(n) the crackling noises that
ou hear when static electricity
the air causes interference
a radio or television signal.

tation
(n) a place where trains
r buses stop. *A bus station.*
(n) a building used as the base
r a police force, ambulance
ervice, or fire department.
(n) a radio or television channel.

tationary *(adj)*
t rest or not moving.

tationery *(n)* writing materials,
uch as paper, envelopes, and pens.

tatistic *(n)*
fact or a piece of information,
xpressed as a number or percentage.
atistical *(adj)*, **statistically** *(adv)*.

tatue *(n)* a model of a person or
nimal made from metal, stone, etc.

tatus statuses *(n)*
person's rank or position in society.

tatute *(n)* a rule or a law.

tave staving staved *or* stove
(n) the set of five lines on which
usic is written. *See* **notation**.
stave off *(v)*
you **stave something off**,
u manage to keep it away.

steady steadies steadying steadied; steadier steadiest
1 *(adj)* continuous and not changing much. *Steady progress.* **steadily** *(adv)*.
2 *(adj)* not moving around or not shaking. *A steady hand.*
3 *(v)* to stop something from moving around or shaking.
4 *(adj)* sensible and dependable.

steak *(n)* a thick slice of meat or fish.

steal stealing stole stolen
1 *(v)* to take and keep something that does not belong to you.
2 **steal away** *(v)* to leave quietly.

stealthy *(rhymes with wealthy)* **stealthier stealthiest** *(adj)* secret and quiet. *We crept away with stealthy steps.* **stealth** *(n)*, **stealthily** *(adv)*.

steam steaming steamed
1 *(n)* the vapor formed when water boils.
2 *(v)* When glass **steams up**, it gets covered with condensation.
3 *(informal)* If you **let off** or **blow off steam**, you release your stored-up energy or feelings.
4 *(informal)* If you **run out of steam**, you have no more energy left.

steam engine *(n)*
an engine powered by steam. Coal or wood burned in a boiler produces hot air that travels in pipes through a water tank. As the water in the tank boils, it creates steam. Steam is forced into cylinders where it pushes pistons to operate machinery. *See* **steam locomotive**.

steamroller *(n)* a steam-driven vehicle used to flatten road surfaces.

steel
1 *(n)* a hard strong metal made mainly from iron.
2 **steel band** *(n)* a group that plays music on drums called steel pans made from oil barrels. *See* **instrument**.

steep
steeping steeped; steeper steepest
1 *(adj)* sharply sloping up or down. *A steep hill.* **steeply** *(adv)*.
2 *(adj)* sharp or rapid. *A steep drop in student numbers.*
3 *(v)* to soak something in a liquid.
4 If something is **steeped** in something, it is full of it.

steeplechase *(n)*
a long race over obstacles such as fences, water jumps, ditches, etc.

steer steering steered
1 *(v)* to make a vehicle go in a particular direction.
2 *(n)* a young bull.

steering wheel *(n)* the wheel in a vehicle used to control its direction.

stem stemming stemmed
1 *(n)* the long, main part of a plant from which the leaves, flowers, and fruit grow. *See* **plant**.
2 *(v)* If something **stems from** a place or thing, it comes from it. *The quarrel stemmed from a misunderstanding.*
3 *(v)* to stop something from flowing or spreading. *The rescue team tried to stem the flow of oil from the tanker.*

stench stenches *(n)*
a strong, unpleasant smell.

stencil *(n)* a piece of card, plastic, or metal with a design cut out of it, which can be painted over to transfer the design onto a surface. **stencil** *(v)*.

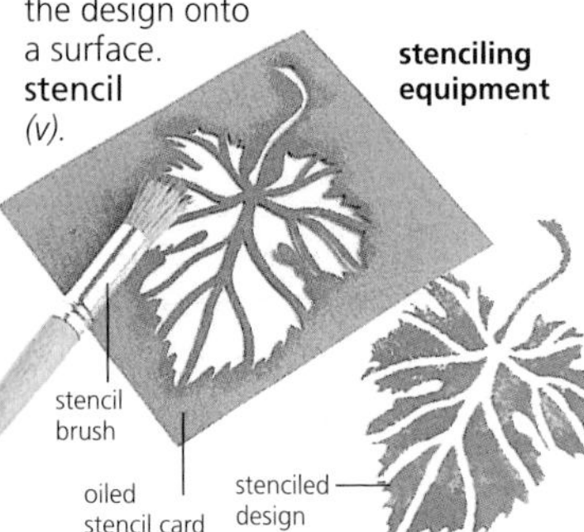

stenciling equipment

step stepping stepped
1 *(v)* to move your foot forward and put it down. **step** *(n)*.
2 *(n)* the sound of someone walking. *Can you hear steps behind you?*
3 *(n)* one of the flat surfaces on a staircase. *The first step.*
4 *(n)* one of the things that you need to do to make or achieve something. *This recipe is in six steps.*
5 *(informal)* If someone says that you should **watch your step**, they are telling you to be careful.

stepfamily stepfamilies *(n)*
the family of your stepfather or stepmother.

stepfather *(n)*
the man who is married to your mother but is not your father.

stepmother *(n)*
the woman who is married to your father but is not your mother.

stereo
1 *(n)* sound that comes from two different directions at the same time. Stereo is short for stereophonic.
2 *(n)* a CD player or radio with stereo speakers.

stereotype *(n)* a simplified idea of a person or thing. *We've created a teenage stereotype for this advertising campaign.* **stereotypical** *(adj)*.

sterile
1 *(adj)* free from germs.
2 *(adj)* unable to have babies.

sterilize sterilizing sterilized *(v)*
to clean something so thoroughly that you make it free from germs. **sterilization** *(n)*.

sterling *(n)*
the currency of the U.K.

stern sterner sternest
1 *(adj)* serious and severe. *Paula gave me a stern look.*
2 *(n)* the back end of a ship.

steroid *(n)*
a chemical substance used as a drug to treat various illnesses and conditions.

stethoscope *(n)*
a Y-shaped tube connected to two earpieces, used by a doctor to listen to a patient's heart or lungs.

ear piece
ear tube
non-chill rim
Y-joint
stainless steel chest piece
flexible tubing
stethoscope

stew
1 *(n)* meat and vegetables, cooked slowly in liquid. **stew** *(v)*.
2 If you are **in a stew** about something, you are upset and worried about it. **stew** *(v)*.

steward
1 *(n)* a man who looks after passengers on a ship or airplane.
2 *(n)* someone who helps to direct people at a large public event, such as a race or concert.

stewardess stewardesses *(n)*
a woman who looks after passengers on a ship or airplane.

stick sticking stuck
1 *(n)* a long, thin piece of wood.
2 *(n)* a long, thin piece of something. *A stick of gum.*
3 *(v)* to glue or fasten one thing to another. **sticky** *(adj)*.
4 *(v)* to push something with a point into something else. *Wanda stuck a pin into her pincushion.*
5 *(v)* If something **sticks**, it becomes fixed in a particular position. *This door keeps sticking.*
6 *(v)* If someone **sticks to** an idea, friend, etc. they support them and do not give them up.
7 *(v) (informal)* If you **stick up for** someone, you support them.

sticker *(n)* a sticky paper or plastic badge that you can attach to things.

stick insect *(n)* an insect with a long body that looks like a twig.

stiff stiffer stiffest
1 *(adj)* difficult to bend or turn. **stiffen** *(v)*, **stiffly** *(adv)*.
2 *(adj)* If you feel **stiff**, your muscles hurt because you have overworked them.
3 *(adj)* difficult or severe. *Stiff competition.*
4 *(adj)* formal and distant.

stifle stifling stifled
1 *(v)* If you **stifle** a cough, sneeze, or yawn, you close your mouth to prevent it from being noticed.
2 *(n)* a knee joint in some animals. *See* **dog**.

stigma
1 *(n)* a mark of shame or embarrassment.
2 *(n)* the part of a flower that receives the pollen when the flower is pollinated. *See* **flower**.

still stiller stillest
1 *(adj)* not moving. *Stand still!*
2 *(adj)* quiet or silent. *A still night.*
3 *(adv)* even now. *Are you still here?*
4 *(adv)* however.
5 *(adj)* yet or even. *It grew still hotter.*

stimulate stimulating stimulated
1 *(v)* If someone or something **stimulates** you, they fill you with exciting new ideas. **stimulating** *(adj)*.
2 *(v)* to encourage something to grow or develop.

sting stinging stung
1 *(v)* to wound with a sharp point.
2 *(v)* to hurt with a sharp or throbbing pain. *My eyes are stinging.*

stinger *(n)*
the sharp part of an insect, animal, or plant that can pierce your skin and leave some venom in it. *See* **scorpion**.

stingray *(n)* a flat-bodied fish that has large, wing-like fins and a long tail with venomous spines.

stingray

stingy *(stin-jee)* stingier stingiest *(adj)* very cheap. **stingily** *(adv)*.

stink stinking stank stunk
1 *(v)* to have an unpleasant smell. **stink** *(n)*.
2 *(v) (slang)* to be very bad. *Robyn's plan stinks!*

stir stirring stirred
1 *(v)* to mix a liquid by moving a spoon or stick around and around in it.
2 *(v)* to move slightly.
3 If you **cause a stir**, you make people excited about something.

stitch stitches stitching stitched
1 *(v)* to make loops of thread or wool in sewing or knitting. **stitch** *(n)*. *See* **embroidery**.

? *(v)* to close up a wound
ɔy sewing. **stitch** *(n)*.
3 *(n)* a sudden, sharp pain in
your side, caused by exercise.
4 *(informal)* If you are **in stitches**,
you cannot stop laughing.

stock stocking stocked
1 *(v)* If a store **stocks** a product, it
keeps a supply of the product to sell.
2 *(n)* all the products that a factory,
warehouse, or store has to sell.
3 *(n)* a liquid used in cooking, made
from the juices of meat or vegetables.
4 *(v)* If you **stock up** on something,
you buy a large supply of it.

stockade
1 *(n)* a fence or enclosure made
of posts set in the ground
to protect against attacks.
2 *(n)* a jail for people in the military.

stockbroker *(n)* someone whose
job is buying and selling stocks and
shares in companies for other people.

stock car *(n)* a car driven in rough
races in which the cars crash into
one another on purpose.

stocking *(n)* a close-fitting garment
that covers your leg and foot.

stocks
1 *(plural n)* a heavy wooden frame
with holes in it, used in the past
to hold criminals by their legs.
The picture below shows
some medieval stocks.
2 *(plural n)* If you have **stocks**
in a company, you have invested
money in it and receive regular small
amounts in return, based on how
profitable the company is.

stocks

stocky stockier stockiest *(adj)*
A **stocky** person is short, broad,
and strong. **stockily** *(adv)*.

stodgy stodgier stodgiest *(adj)*
Stodgy food is very heavy and filling.

stoke stoking stoked *(v)* to put
more fuel on a fire to keep it burning.

stomach
1 *(n)* the part of the body where food
is digested. *See* **digestion**, **organ**.
2 *(n)* the front part of your
body, just below your waist.

stone stoning stoned
1 *(n)* a small piece of rock, usually
found on the ground. **stony** *(adj)*.
2 *(n)* a hard material used for
building, making sculptures, etc.
3 *(n)* a valuable jewel or
gem. Emeralds and rubies
are precious stones.
4 *(v)* to hit with stone.

Stone Age *(n)* a very early period
in human history, when people used
stone to make tools and weapons.

stone circle *(n)* a circle of large
tall stones put up in prehistoric times.
The picture shows the remains of
Stonehenge, a prehistoric stone
circle in Wiltshire, England.

Stonehenge

stool *(n)*
a small seat with no back.

stoop stooping stooped
1 *(v)* to bend down low.
2 *(v)* to walk, sit, stand, etc.
with your head and shoulders
bent forward. **stoop** *(n)*.

stop stopping stopped
1 *(v)* When something **stops**, it
comes to an end. *The music stopped.*
2 *(v)* If you **stop** something, you put
an end to it or do not do it anymore.
3 *(v)* to be no longer moving or
working. *My watch has stopped.*
4 *(n)* one of the places on
a route where a bus or train
picks up passengers.
5 *(v)* If you **stop** or **stop up**
a hole, you fill it or plug it.

stopper *(n)*
a piece of cork or plastic that
fits into the top of a test tube,
jar, or bottle to close it.

stopwatch *(n)*
a watch that you can start and stop
at any time, used for timing races.

storage *(n)*
If you put something **in storage**, you
put it in a place where it can be kept
until it is needed. **storage** *(adj)*.

store storing stored
1 *(n)* a place where things are sold.
A grocery store. A toy store.
2 *(n)* a place where things are kept.
3 *(v)* to put things away
until they are needed.
4 *(v)* to keep information
on a computer, by saving
it as a computer file.

stork *(n)* a large bird with
long thin legs and a long bill.

storm storming stormed
1 *(n)* a period of bad weather
with strong wind and rain, and
sometimes thunder and lightning.
stormy *(adj)*.
2 *(n)* a show of strong and angry
feelings. *A storm of protest.*
stormy *(adj)*.
3 *(v)* to attack a place suddenly.
The army stormed the castle.
4 *(v)* If you **storm out**, you
rush out of a place angrily.

story stories
1 *(n)* a spoken or written account
of someone's life or adventures.
2 *(n)* a tale made up by an author.
3 *(n)* a lie. *Are you telling stories?*
4 *(n)* one layer or floor of a building.

stout stouter stoutest
1 *(adj)* quite fat.
2 *(adj)* strong and thick. *Stout boots.*

stove *(n)* a piece of equipment used
for cooking or for heating a room.

stowaway *(n)* someone who hides
in an airplane, ship, or other vehicle
because they want to escape
secretly or cannot afford a ticket.

straggle straggling straggled *(v)*
to follow slowly behind a group
of people. **straggler** *(n)*.

straight straighter straightest
1 *(adj)* not bent or not curved.
2 *(adj)* level or neat.
Put your hat straight. **straighten** *(v)*.
3 *(adj)* honest or correct.
A straight answer.
4 *(adv)* immediately.
Gus arrived straight after me.

straightaway *(adv)* at once.

straightforward
1 *(adj)* simple and uncomplicated.
The operation was straightforward.
2 *(adj)* honest or to the point.
John gave a straightforward answer.

strain straining strained
1 *(n)* stress or tension. **strained** *(adj)*.
2 *(v)* If you **strain** a muscle in your
body, you damage it by pulling
it or overusing it. **strain** *(n)*.
3 *(v)* If you **strain** to do something,
you try very hard to do it.
4 *(v)* If you **strain** a mixture, you
pour it through a sieve or colander
to separate the solids from the liquid.
strainer *(n)*, **strained** *(adj)*.

strait
1 *(n)* a narrow strip of water between two seas or two countries. *The picture shows the Strait of Gibraltar between Spain and Morocco.*
2 If you are in **dire straits**, you are in trouble.

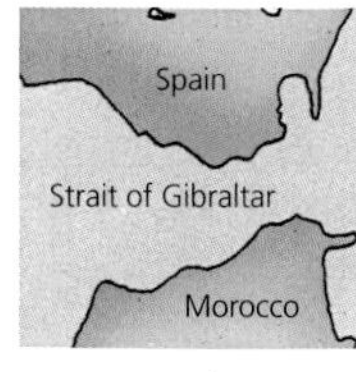

strait

strand
1 *(n)* one of the threads or wires that are twisted together to form a rope.
2 *(n)* a single length of hair, yarn, etc.

stranded
1 *(adj)* washed up on a shore. *A stranded whale.*
2 *(adj)* If you are **stranded** somewhere, you are stuck there and cannot get away.

strange stranger strangest *(adj)* odd, unusual, or unfamiliar. **strangeness** *(n)*, **strangely** *(adv)*.

stranger
1 *(n)* someone you do not know.
2 *(n)* someone in a place where they have not been before. *I am a stranger in this city.*

strangle strangling strangled *(v)* to kill someone by squeezing their throat so that they cannot breathe. **strangler** *(n)*, **strangulation** *(n)*.

strap strapping strapped
1 *(n)* a strip of leather or material used to fasten things together.
2 *(v)* to fasten things or hold things in place with straps.

strategy strategies *(n)* a clever plan for winning or achieving something. **strategic** *(adj)*, **strategically** *(adv)*.

straw
1 *(n)* dried stalks of barley, wheat, etc.
2 *(n)* a thin hollow tube through which you can drink.

strawberry strawberries *(n)* a soft red fruit. *See* **fruit**.

stray straying strayed
1 *(v)* to wander away or to get lost. **stray** *(adj)*.
2 *(n)* a lost cat or dog.

streak streaking streaked
1 *(n)* a stripe of color. **streaky** *(adj)*.
2 *(v)* to move very fast. *The sprinter streaked past us.*

stream streaming streamed
1 *(n)* a small river.
2 *(n)* a long line of moving people, cars, etc.
3 *(v)* to move or flow fast.

streamer *(n)* a long thin strip of colored paper used as a decoration.

streamlined *(adj)* If a car, plane, or other vehicle is **streamlined**, it is designed so that it can cut through air or water very quickly and easily. *See* **aerodynamic**.

street
1 *(n)* a road with houses or other buildings along it.
2 *(n)* everyone who lives and works on a street. *The whole street is having a party.*

streetwise *(adj)* If you are **streetwise**, you know how to survive in towns or cities without getting into trouble.

strength
1 *(n)* If you have **strength**, you are physically strong. **strengthen** *(v)*.
2 *(n)* Someone's **strengths** are their good points, or the things that they can do well.

strenuous *(stren-yoo-uss) (adj)* Something that is **strenuous** needs a lot of energy or effort. **strenuously** *(adv)*.

stress stresses stressing stressed
1 *(n)* worry, strain, or pressure. **stressful** *(adj)*.
2 *(adj)* If you are **stressed**, you feel anxious and under pressure.
3 *(v)* If you **stress** something, you show that it is important. **stress** *(n)*.

stretch
stretches stretching stretched
1 *(v)* to make something bigger, longer, or greater.
2 *(v)* to reach out with your arms. **stretch** *(n)*.
3 *(v)* to extend or to spread out. *The path stretches for miles.*
4 *(n)* a period of time, especially time spent in a prison.
5 **stretch out** *(v)* to lie full length.

stretcher *(n)* a narrow bed stretched between two poles, and used for carrying an injured or sick person.

strict stricter strictest
1 *(adj)* If someone is **strict**, they make you obey the rules and behave properly. **strictness** *(n)*, **strictly** *(adv)*.
2 *(adj)* complete or total. *This trick needs strict concentration.* **strictly** *(adv)*.

stride striding strode stridden *(v)* to walk with long steps. **stride** *(n)*.

strife *(n)* trouble or arguing.

strike striking struck
1 *(v)* to hit or attack someone or something. **strike** *(n)*.
2 *(v)* When a clock **strikes**, it chimes to show the time.
3 *(v)* to make an impression on someone. *Simon struck me as silly.*
4 *(v)* If you **strike** a match, you light it
5 *(v)* When people **strike**, they refuse to work because of an argument or disagreement with their employer. **strike** *(n)*.
6 *(n)* In baseball, a **strike** is a pitch that is swung at and missed.

striking *(adj)* unusual or noticeable in some way. **strikingly** *(adv)*.

string stringing strung
1 *(n)* a thin cord or rope.
2 *(n)* a thin wire on a musical instrument such as a guitar. **string** *(v)*.
3 *(n)* a number of things of a similar kind all in a row. *A string of beads. A string of thefts.*
4 **string out** *(v)* If you **string something out**, you stretch or lengthen something. *We strung out the game until bedtime.*

strings *(plural n)* the section of an orchestra that is made up of stringed instruments, such as violins and cellos. *The picture shows the main parts of a violin, and other instruments in the string section of an orchestra.*

strip stripping stripped
1 *(v)* to take something off. *Jo stripped the wallpaper off the wall.*
2 *(v)* to undress.
3 *(n)* a narrow piece of paper, material, etc.

stripe *(n)* a band of color. **striped** *(adj)*, **striped** *(adj)*.

strive striving strove striven *(v)* to make a great effort to do something. *Strive to do your best.*

strobe *(n)* a light that keeps flashing on and off very quickly.

stroke stroking stroked
1 *(n)* a hit. *A backhand stroke. A stroke of lightning.*
2 *(v)* to pass your hand gently over something. *You may stroke the kitten.* **stroke** *(n)*.
3 *(n)* When someone has a **stroke**, a part of their brain is damaged, which sometimes causes part of their body to be paralyzed.
4 *(n)* a line drawn by a pen or brush.
5 *(n)* a method of moving in swimming or rowing.
6 *(n)* an unexpected action that has a powerful effect. *A stroke of luck.*

stroll *(n)* a short relaxed walk. **stroll** *(v)*.

stroller *(n)* a small collapsible chair on wheels for a baby or child to sit in and be pushed around.

strong stronger strongest
1 *(adj)* powerful or having great force. *A strong wind.* **strongly** *(adv)*.
2 *(adj)* hard to break. *A strong shelf.* **strongly** *(adv)*.
3 *(adj)* full of taste, spices, etc. *A strong smell.* **strongly** *(adv)*.

stronghold *(n)* a fortress or a place that is well defended.

structure
1 *(n)* the organization of something or the way that it is made up. **structure** *(v)*, **structural** *(adj)*.
2 *(n)* a building or something that has been put together. **structural** *(adj)*.

struggle struggling struggled
1 *(v)* If you **struggle** with someone, you fight or wrestle with them. **struggle** *(n)*.
2 *(v)* If you **struggle** with something, you find it difficult to do. **struggle** *(n)*.

strum strumming strummed *(v)* to play a guitar, banjo, etc. by brushing the tips of your fingers over the strings.

strut strutting strutted
1 *(v)* to walk proudly and stiffly with your chest pushed out.
2 *(n)* a wooden or metal supporting bar. *See* **acoustic guitar**, **hydrofoil**.

stub stubbing stubbed
1 *(n)* a short end of something, such as a pencil or ticket. **stubby** *(adj)*.
2 *(v)* to hurt your toe by banging it against something.

stubble
1 *(n)* short spiky pieces of barley, wheat, etc. left in a field after harvesting. **stubbly** *(adj)*.
2 *(n)* the short hair that grows on a man's face if he does not shave. **stubbly** *(adj)*.

stubborn *(adj)* obstinate, or determined not to give way. **stubbornness** *(n)*, **stubbornly** *(adv)*.

stuck-up *(adj) (informal)* conceited and snobbish.

student *(n)* someone who is studying, especially in a college or university.

studio
1 *(n)* a room in which an artist or a photographer works.
2 *(n)* a place where movies, CDs, etc. are filmed or recorded.
3 *(n)* a place that transmits radio or television programs.
4 *(n)* a one-room apartment.

studious *(stew-dee-us) (adj)* If you are **studious**, you like to study and work carefully. **studiousness** *(n)*, **studiously** *(adv)*.

study studies studying studied
1 *(n)* an office or room where someone works.
2 *(v)* to spend time learning a subject or skill. **study** *(n)*.
3 *(v)* to examine something carefully. *Amanda studied the baseball scores.*

stuff stuffing stuffed
1 *(n)* a substance or a material.
2 *(v)* to fill something tightly.
3 *(v)* to put something into something else. *Don't forget to stuff the turkey.*
4 *(n)* personal belongings. *I put my stuff in the drawers.*
5 *(adj)* If you feel **stuffed**, you have eaten too much. *I felt stuffed after the Thanksgiving dinner.*
6 If you are **stuffed up**, you have a cold and cannot breathe through your nose.

stuffing *(n)* a filling, especially a mixture of chopped food that you cook inside a chicken, pepper, etc.

stuffy stuffier stuffiest
1 *(adj)* A **stuffy** room has stale air in it. **stuffiness** *(n)*.
2 *(adj)* A **stuffy** person is prim and easily shocked. **stuffily** *(adv)*.

stumble stumbling stumbled
1 *(v)* to trip up or to walk in an unsteady way.
2 *(v)* to make mistakes when you are talking or reading aloud.

stump
1 *(n)* the part that is left when a tree is cut down.
2 *(n)* a short broken-off piece of something, such as a pencil stub.

stumpy stumpier stumpiest *(adj)* short and thick. *A stumpy tail.*

stun stunning stunned *(v)* If you are **stunned**, you are shocked, dazed, or knocked out.

stunning
1 *(adj)* beautiful or amazing. **stunningly** *(adv)*.
2 *(adj)* hard enough to knock you out. *A stunning blow.*

stunt stunting stunted
1 *(n)* a dangerous trick or act.
2 *(v)* to stop the proper growth of something. **stunted** *(adj)*.
3 **publicity stunt** *(n)* a trick to get public attention for a company, organization, event, etc.
4 *(n)* A **stunt man** or **stunt woman** takes the place of an actor to perform the dangerous actions in a movie.

stupendous *(adj)* very good or very big. **stupendously** *(adv)*.

stupid stupider stupidest *(adj)* silly or unintelligent. **stupidity** *(n)*, **stupidly** *(adv)*.

sturdy sturdier sturdiest *(adj)* strong and firm. *A sturdy tree.*

stutter stuttering stuttered *(v)* If you **stutter** when you speak, you sometimes repeat one sound of a word before you manage to say the whole word. **stutter** *(n)*.

sty sties
1 *(n)* a pen in which pigs live.
2 *(n)* a painful red swelling on the eyelid.

style styling styled
1 *(n)* a way of doing something, such as writing, dressing, building, etc.
2 *(n)* If you do something with **style**, you do it fashionably or elegantly. **stylish** *(adj)*, **stylishly** *(adv)*.
3 *(v)* to arrange or design something. *The model's hair was styled by Philippe of Paris.* **style** *(n)*.
4 *(n)* the part of a flower that extends from the ovary and supports the stigma. *See* **flower**.

subconscious *(n)* part of your mind that influences you without your being aware of it. **subconsciously** *(adv)*.

subcontinent *(n)* a large area of land that is smaller than a continent. *The Indian subcontinent.*

subdivide
subdividing subdivided *(v)* to divide something into smaller, even parts. *I cut the apple in half, then subdivided each half into quarters.* **subdivision** *(n).*

subdued
1 *(adj)* unusually quiet and restrained.
2 *(adj)* not bright. *Subdued lighting.*

subject **subjecting subjected**
1 *(sub-jekt) (n)* the topic of a book, article, conversation, etc.
2 *(sub-jekt) (n)* an area of study, such as geography or mathematics.
3 *(sub-jekt) (n)* A **subject** of a king or queen is someone who lives in their country.
4 *(sub-jekt)* If you are **subject to** something, you are likely to be affected by it. *Laura is subject to terrible colds.*
5 *(sub-**jekt**) (v)* If you **subject** someone to something, you force them to suffer it. *Our neighbors subjected us to loud music all night.*

subjective *(adj)* having to do with opinions rather than actual facts. *Donna's essay on animal rights was purely subjective.* **subjectively** *(adv).*

submarine *(n)* a ship that can travel under the water for long periods.

submerge
submerging submerged *(v)* to put something underwater.

submit **submitting submitted**
1 *(v)* to hand in or put something forward. *Can I submit a proposal to the committee?* **submission** *(n).*
2 *(v)* to agree to obey something. *Reluctantly, I submitted to their decision.* **submission** *(n).*

subordinate
1 *(adj)* less important.
2 *(n)* someone who is low in rank and can be told what to do.

subscribe **subscribing subscribed**
1 *(v)* to pay money regularly for a newspaper, magazine, cable television channel, etc. **subscriber** *(n),* **subscription** *(n).*
2 *(v)* to give money to a charity or an appeal.

subsequent *(adj)* coming after or following. *Felix lost the first match, but played better in subsequent ones.* **subsequently** *(adv).*

subside **subsiding subsided**
1 *(v)* If the ground **subsides**, it caves in or sinks down. **subsidence** *(n).*
2 *(v)* to become less. *Gradually, the noise subsided.*

subsidiary *(adj)* minor or less important. *A subsidiary role.*

subsidy **subsidies** *(n)*
money that a government or organization contributes to make goods cheaper. **subsidize** *(v).*

substance
1 *(n)* a material. Objects, powders, and liquids are all substances.
2 *(n)* the important part of something. *The substance of an argument.*

substantial *(adj)* solid, large, or important. **substantially** *(adv).*

substitute *(n)* something or someone used instead of another, such as a teammate who plays when another player is injured. **substitution** *(n),* **substitute** *(v).*

subtitle
1 *(n)* the second, less important title of a book, movie, etc.
2 **subtitles** *(plural n)* the translated words that appear on the screen when a foreign movie is shown.

subtle *(sut-ul)* **subtler subtlest**
1 *(adj)* delicate, or not easy to notice. *A subtle flavor.* **subtly** *(adv).*
2 *(adj)* using clever or disguised methods. *A subtle plan.* **subtlety** *(n),* **subtly** *(adv).*

subtract
subtracting subtracted *(v)* to take one number away from another. *If you subtract four from six, you are left with two.* **subtraction** *(n).*

suburb *(n)* an area of housing at the edge of a large town or city. **suburbia** *(n),* **suburban** *(adj).*

subway *(n)* an underground system of electric trains.

succeed *(suk-**seed**)*
succeeding succeeded
1 *(v)* to manage to do something. *Brendan succeeded in fixing the car.*
2 *(v)* to take over from someone in an important position. *Travis succeeded his father as company director.*
3 *(v)* to do well or to get what you want. **success** *(n),* **successful** *(adj).*

succulent *(suk-yu-lent) (adj)* juicy. *A succulent peach.* **succulence** *(n).*

suck **sucking sucked**
1 *(v)* to draw something into your mouth using your tongue and lips. *George still sucks his thumb.* **suck** *(n).*
2 *(v)* to pull strongly. *The vacuum cleaner sucked up my hairpin.*

suction *(n)* the creation of a vacuum, so that air or liquid is sucked in, or so that two surfaces stick together.

sudden *(adj)* quick or unexpected. **suddenness** *(n),* **suddenly** *(adv).*

sue **suing sued** *(v)*
If you **sue** someone, you take them to court to make them pay for the harm that they have done to you.

suede *(swayd) (n)* soft leather with a smooth, velvet-like surface.

suffer **suffering suffered**
1 *(v)* to experience something bad, such as unhappiness or pain. **sufferer** *(n),* **suffering** *(n).*
2 *(v)* If you **suffer** from an illness, you get it often or have it for a long time. *Jacob suffers from hay fever.*

sufficient *(suf-**ish**-unt) (adj)*
If something is **sufficient**, it is enough or adequate. *We left sufficient food for the cats while we were away.* **sufficiently** *(adv).*

suffix **suffixes** *(n)* a group of letters added at the end of a word to create a new but related word. For example, "ness," "ly," and "ful" are all suffixes. *The suffix "ness" is used in "sadness," "happiness" and "sickness."*

suffocate **suffocating suffocated**
1 *(v)* If someone **suffocates**, they die because they cannot breathe. **suffocation** *(n).*
2 *(v)* to stop someone from breathing, so that they die.

sugar
1 *(n)* a sweet substance that comes from plants and is used in foods and drinks. **sugary** *(adj).*
2 **sugar beet** *(n)* a root vegetable from which sugar is produced.
3 **sugar cane** *(n)* a tall, tropical plant that has sugar in its stems.

sugar beet

suggest
suggesting suggested *(v)* to put something forward as an idea or a possibility. *I suggested going to China for our next vacation.* **suggestion** *(n).*

suicide *(soo-iss-ide) (n)* If someone commits **suicide**, they kill themselves. **suicidal** *(adj),* **suicidally** *(adv).*

suit **suiting suited**
1 *(n)* a set of elegant, matching clothes, usually a man's jacket and pants.
2 *(n)* one of the four types of playing card in a pack of cards. The four suits are clubs, diamonds, hearts, and spades.
3 *(v)* to be acceptable and convenient. *Does Wednesday suit you?*

4 *(v)* If a hairstyle or an outfit **suits** you, it makes you look good.

suitable *(adj)*
If something is **suitable**, it is right for a particular purpose. **suitability** *(n)*, **suitably** *(adv)*.

suitcase *(n)* a container used for carrying clothes when you travel.

suite *(sweet)*
1 *(n)* a set of matching furniture.
2 *(n)* a set of rooms in a hotel.

sulfur *(sul-fer)*
1 *(n)* a yellow chemical element used in gunpowder and matches. *See* **mineral**.
2 **sulfur dioxide** *(n)* a poisonous gas found in some industrial waste, which causes air pollution.

sulk sulking sulked *(v)*
If you **sulk**, you are angry and silent. **sulk** *(n)*, **sulky** *(adj)*.

sullen *(adj)* gloomy, silent, and bad-tempered. **sullenly** *(adv)*.

sultan *(n)* an emperor or ruler of a Muslim country.

sultana
1 *(n)* a small, brown, dried fruit made from grapes.
2 *(n)* the wife or daughter of a sultan.

sultry sultrier sultriest
1 *(adj)* If the weather is **sultry**, it is hot and humid. **sultriness** *(n)*.
2 *(adj)* If a person is **sultry**, they are passionate. **sultriness** *(n)*.

sum summing summed
1 *(n)* an amount of money.
2 *(n)* an arithmetic problem.
3 *(v)* If you **sum up**, you go through the main points of what has been said to reach a conclusion.
4 **sum total** *(n)* the whole or the final amount. *What is the sum total of your savings?*

summary summaries *(n)*
a short statement of the main points of something that has been said or written. **summarize** *(v)*.

summer *(n)* the season between spring and fall, when the weather is warmest. **summery** *(adj)*.

summit
1 *(n)* the top of a mountain.
2 *(n)* a meeting of leaders from different countries.

summon summoning summoned
1 *(v)* to call or request someone to come. *Summon the next witness.*
2 *(v)* If you **summon up** courage, you make a great effort to be brave.

summons summonses *(n)* an order to appear in court. **summons** *(v)*.

sun sunning sunned
1 **the Sun** *(n)* the star that the Earth moves around, and that gives us light and warmth. *See* **planet**.
2 *(n)* light and warmth from the Sun. *Don't stay too long in the sun.*
3 *(v)* If you **sun** yourself, you sit or lie in the sunlight.

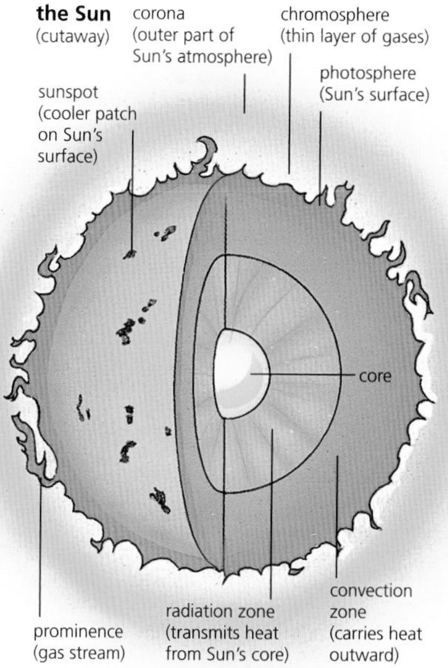

the Sun (cutaway)
corona (outer part of Sun's atmosphere)
chromosphere (thin layer of gases)
photosphere (Sun's surface)
sunspot (cooler patch on Sun's surface)
core
prominence (gas stream)
radiation zone (transmits heat from Sun's core)
convection zone (carries heat outward)

sunbathe sunbathing sunbathed *(v)* to sit or lie in sunlight to make your body suntanned.

sunburn *(n)* sore red skin caused by staying in sunlight too long. **sunburned** *(adj)*.

sundial *(n)*
an instrument that shows the time by using the Sun's light. A pointer casts a shadow that moves around a flat, marked dial.

sundial

sunglasses *(plural n)*
dark glasses that protect your eyes from sunlight.

sunrise *(n)*
the time in the morning when the Sun appears above the horizon.

sunset *(n)*
the time in the evening when the Sun sinks below the horizon.

sunshine *(n)* the light from the Sun.

sunstroke *(n)* an illness, caused by staying in hot sunlight for too long.

suntan *(n)* If you have a **suntan**, your skin is darker than usual because you have been in sunlight. **suntanned** *(adj)*.

super *(adj)* very good.

superb *(adj)* excellent or magnificent. **superbly** *(adv)*.

superficial *(soo-per-fish-ul)*
1 *(adj)* on the surface. *A superficial cut.* **superficially** *(adv)*.
2 *(adj)* not deep or not thorough. *My interest in music is only superficial.* **superficially** *(adv)*.

superfluous *(soo-per-floo-uss) (adj)* more than is needed or wanted. *A superfluous remark.*

superhero *(n)* a fictional character with superhuman powers, such as the ability to fly.

superintendent
1 *(n)* someone in charge of something. *An apartment superintendent.*
2 *(n)* a senior police officer.

superior
1 *(adj)* better. *Daisy thinks that butter is superior to margarine.*
2 *(n)* someone who is in a more important position than you.
3 *(adj)* If someone acts in a **superior** way, they behave as if they are better than other people. **superiority** *(n)*.

superlative *(soo-per-la-tiv)*
1 *(adj)* **Superlative** adjectives and adverbs are used to describe the greatest or highest degree of things or actions. *"Biggest" is the superlative of "big," and "most quickly" is the superlative of "quickly."* **superlative** *(n)*.
2 *(adj)* very good. **superlatively** *(adv)*.

supermarket *(n)* a large store that sells food and other household items.

supernatural *(adj)* If something is **supernatural**, it involves things that natural laws cannot explain, such as ghosts. **supernaturally** *(adv)*.

supersonic *(adj)* faster than the speed of sound.

Concorde

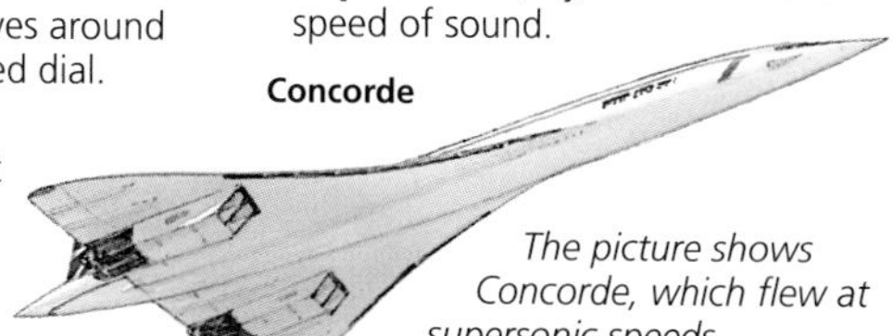

The picture shows Concorde, which flew at supersonic speeds.

superstitious *(adj)*
People who are **superstitious** are afraid that something bad will happen if they do not follow certain rules. **superstition** *(n)*.

superstore *(n)* a very large store.

supervise supervising supervised *(v)* to watch over and be in charge of someone while they do something. **supervision** *(n)*, **supervisor** *(n)*.

supper *(n)* an evening meal.

supple supple**r** supple**st** *(adj)* If you are **supple**, you can move or bend your body easily. **suppleness** *(n).*

supplement supplementing supplemented *(n)* an additional item. *A food supplement or dietary supplement. This newspaper has a color supplement.* **supplement** *(v),* **supplementary** *(adj).*

supplies *(plural n)* food and equipment taken on an expedition.

supply supplies supplying supplied *(v)* to provide someone with what they want or need. **supply** *(n),* **supplier** *(n).*

support supporting supported
1 *(v)* to hold something up to keep it from falling. **support** *(n).*
2 *(v)* to help and encourage someone. **support** *(n),* **supportive** *(adj).*
3 *(v)* to believe in someone or something. *Sally supports the Chicago Bears.* **support** *(n),* **supporter** *(n).*

suppose supposing supposed *(v)* to think that something is true or to expect something. *I suppose you're right. I suppose that Justin will be late.*

suppress suppresses suppressing suppressed
1 *(v)* to stop something from happening. *The dictator suppressed the revolution.* **suppression** *(n).*
2 *(v)* to hide or control something. *Carly tried to suppress her giggles.*

supreme *(adj)* the greatest, best, or most powerful. **supremacy** *(n),* **supremely** *(adv).*

sure surer surest *(adj)* certain and definite. *Are you sure that he's here?* **surely** *(adv).*

surf surfing surfed
1 *(n)* the spray produced by waves as they break on the shore.
2 *(v)* to ride on breaking waves using a surfboard. **surfer** *(n),* **surfing** *(n).*
3 *(v)* to move from one website to another on the internet. **surfing** *(n).*

surfing

surface surfacing surfaced
1 *(n)* the outer face or top of something.
2 *(v)* to come to the surface or to appear. *The submarine surfaced after it had been hit. The lost coins finally surfaced.*

surfboard *(n)* a narrow board that surfers stand on to ride breaking waves. *See* **surf**.

surge surging surged *(v)* to rush forward or upward. *The crowd surged forward as the gate was opened.* **surge** *(n).*

surgeon *(sur-jun) (n)* a doctor who performs operations.

surgery *(ser-jer-ee) (n)* medical treatment that involves cutting the patient open and repairing, removing, or replacing body parts. **surgical** *(adj).*

surly surlier surliest *(adj)* If someone is **surly**, they are bad-tempered and unfriendly. *Mandy is a sweet girl, but I find her brother a little surly.*

surname *(n)* a person's last name or family name.

surpass surpasses surpassing surpassed *(v)* to do better than you have done before. *Today, Patrick surpassed his previous record.*

surplus *(adj)* spare or more than what is needed. *The thrift store is asking for any surplus clothes.*

surprise surprising surprised *(v)* to do or say something unexpected. *Alvin's outburst surprised us all.* **surprise** *(n),* **surprising** *(adj).*

surrender surrendering surrendered *(v)* to give up or to admit that you are beaten in a fight or battle. **surrender** *(n).*

surround surrounding surrounded *(v)* to be on every side of something. *Robin Hood and his men surrounded Nottingham Castle.*

surroundings *(plural n)* the things around something or someone. *People work better in cheerful surroundings.*

survey surveying surveyed
1 *(ser-vay) (n)* a report on what people think about something. *We are producing a survey of reactions to the new mall.*
2 *(ser-**vay**) (v)* to look at the whole of a scene or situation. *Mom surveyed the mess with horror.*
3 *(ser-**vay**) (v)* to measure an area to make a map or plan. **survey** *(ser-vay) (n),* **surveyor** *(n).*

survive surviving survived *(v)* to stay alive, especially after some dangerous event. *Only a handful of passengers survived the plane crash.* **survival** *(n),* **survivor** *(n).*

sushi

sushi *(soo-shee) (n)* a Japanese food made from vinegared rice mixed with other ingredients, such as raw fish or vegetables. *The picture shows sushi packed in bamboo leaves.*

suspect suspecting suspected
1 *(suss-**pekt**) (v)* to think someone should not be trusted. **suspicion** *(n).*
2 *(suss-**pekt**) (v)* to think that something is wrong with a situation. *The doctor suspected something more serious than the flu.* **suspicion** *(n),* **suspect** *(**suss**-pekt) (adj).*
3 *(**suss**-pekt) (n)* someone thought to be responsible for a crime.

suspend suspending suspended
1 *(v)* to hang something downward. *Phoebe suspended a banner from her bedroom window.*
2 *(v)* to stop something for a short time. *Work was suspended for the holidays.*
3 *(v)* to punish someone by keeping them from taking part in an activity for a short while. *Sophie was suspended from school for a week.* **suspension** *(n).*

suspenders *(plural n)* a pair of elastic straps worn over the shoulders and attached to pants or a skirt to hold the garment up.

suspense *(n)* an anxious and uncertain feeling caused by having to wait to see what will happen.

suspicious
1 *(adj)* If you feel **suspicious**, you think that something is wrong, but have no firm proof. **suspicion** *(n).*
2 *(adj)* If something is or looks **suspicious**, it makes people think that something is wrong.

sustain sustaining sustained
1 *(v)* to keep something going. *Curtis sustained a conversation with his cat for over ten minutes.*
2 *(v)* If something **sustains** you, it gives you energy. *The hot soup sustained the hikers for hours.*
3 *(v)* to suffer something. *Sebastian sustained serious injuries.*

swagger swaggering swaggered *(v)* to walk or act in a conceited way.

swallow swallowing swallowed
1 *(v)* to make food or drink pass down your throat.
2 *(n)* a migrating bird with long wings and a forked tail.

barn swallow

swamp *(n)* an area of wet, marshy ground

swan *(n)* a large water bird with webbed feet and a long neck. *The picture shows a female swan with her young.*

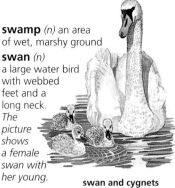

swan and cygnets

swap swapping swapped *(v)* to exchange one thing for another. **swap** *(n).*

swarm swarming swarmed
1 *(v)* When bees or other insects **swarm**, they fly together in a thick mass. **swarm** *(n).*
2 *(adj)* If a place is **swarming** with people, it is very crowded.

swarthy swarthier swarthiest *(adj)* A **swarthy** person has dark skin.

swastika *(n)* an ancient symbol consisting of a cross with the arms bent at right angles. It was adopted as the emblem of the Nazi party during Hitler's rule in Germany.

swat swatting swatted *(v)* to kill a fly or other insect with a quick blow.

sway swaying swayed
1 *(v)* to move or swing from side to side. *Swaying branches.*
2 *(v)* to move or influence the way someone thinks.

swear swearing swore sworn
1 *(v)* to use rude words.
2 *(v)* to make a formal, solemn promise. *I swear to tell the truth.*

sweat sweating sweated *(v)* When you **sweat**, you let out moisture through the pores in your skin because you are hot or anxious. **sweat** *(n).*

sweater *(n)* a knitted piece of clothing that you wear on the top half of your body.

sweatshirt *(n)* a collarless, casual top with long sleeves.

sweep sweeping swept
1 *(v)* to clean up somewhere, using a broom.
2 *(v)* to move rapidly and forcefully. *The duchess swept into the room.*
3 *(v)* to move or pass over an area quickly and steadily.

sweeping *(adj)* Something that is **sweeping** affects many things or people. *Sweeping changes in the firm have resulted in many job losses.*

sweet sweeter sweetest
1 *(adj)* Food that is **sweet** has a sugary flavor, not a savory one.
2 *(adj)* pleasant or cute. **sweetly** *(adv).*

sweet potato *(n)* the thick, sweet, orange root of a plant that's eaten as a vegetable.

swell swelling swelled swollen
1 *(v)* to grow larger or fatter. *Jake's knee swelled where he had bumped it.* **swollen** *(adj).*
2 *(adj) (slang)* wonderful.

sweltering *(adj)* When the weather is **sweltering**, it is very hot indeed. **swelter** *(v).*

swerve swerving swerved *(v)* to change direction quickly, usually to avoid something. *Rick swerved away from the ducklings just in time.*

swift swifter swiftest
1 *(adj)* fast or rapid. **swiftness** *(n),* **swiftly** *(adv).*
2 *(n)* a migrating bird with long narrow wings, similar to a swallow. *See* **bird**.

swig swigging swigged *(v)* *(informal)* to drink in large gulps, usually from a bottle, etc.

swim swimming swam swum *(v)* to propel yourself through water using your arms and legs. **swimmer** *(n).*

swimsuit *(n)* a costume worn by a woman or girl when she goes swimming.

swindle swindling swindled *(v)* to cheat someone out of something, especially money. **swindle** *(n),* **swindler** *(n).*

swine swine
1 *(n)* a pig or a hog.
2 *(n)* a very unpleasant person.

swing swinging swung
1 *(v)* to move from side to side.
2 *(n)* a piece of play equipment that you sit on and move backward and forward.
3 *(n)* the amount by which votes move from one party to another. *There was a swing of 20 percent against the government.*

swipe swiping swiped
1 *(v) (informal)* to hit something or somebody hard. **swipe** *(n).*
2 *(v) (slang)* to steal something. *Max swiped my chocolate!*

swirl swirling swirled *(v)* to move in circles. *The water swirled around the drain.*

switch switches switching switched
1 *(v)* to exchange one thing for another. *Can I switch my potato chips for your chocolate bar?*
2 *(v)* to change from one thing to another. *Miles switched courses.*
3 **switch on** *(v)* to turn on a piece of electrical equipment. *Switch the lights on, please.* **switch** *(n).*

switchboard *(n)* a control center for a telephone system for connecting calls.

swivel swiveling swiveled *(v)* to turn or rotate on the spot.

swollen *(swoh-len) (adj)* enlarged or increased. *Jane's bank balance had swollen.*

swoop swooping swooped *(v)* When a bird **swoops**, it pounces on another creature by flying downward suddenly.

sword *(sord) (n)* a weapon with a handle and a long sharp blade. Swords were used in the past for man-to-man fighting and are still used in some ceremonies such as coronations. *The picture shows one type of sword used by Vikings in the 10th century.*

Viking sword

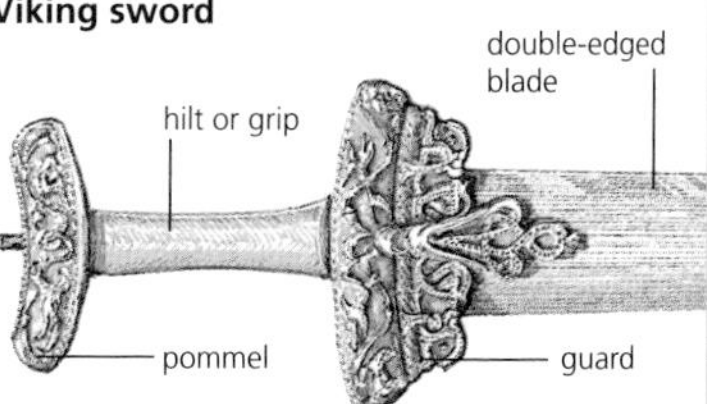

sycamore *(n)* a tree with smooth brown bark that peels off in layers.

syllable *(n)* one of the sounds in a word. *The word "America" has four syllables: A-me-ri-ca.*

syllabus syllabuses *or* syllabi *(n)* a program of work that must be covered for a particular course of study.

symbol *(n)* a design or object that represents something else. *A dove is a symbol of peace.* **symbolic** *(adj),* **symbolically** *(adv).*

symbolize *(v)* to stand for or represent something else.

symmetrical *(adj)* One half of a **symmetrical** shape exactly mirrors the other. **symmetry** *(n),* **symmetrically** *(adv).*

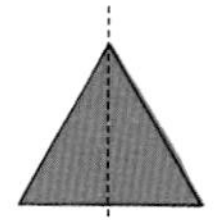

symmetrical shapes

sympathy sympathies
1 *(n)* the understanding and sharing of other people's troubles. *After her accident, Polly's friends gave her a lot of sympathy.* **sympathize** *(v),* **sympathetic** *(adj),* **sympathetically** *(adv).*
2 If you are **in sympathy** with someone's aims or actions, you agree with them and support them.

symphony symphonies *(n)* a long piece of music for an orchestra, usually in four parts, called movements. **symphonic** *(adj).*

symptom *(n)* something that shows that you have an illness. *A rash is one of the symptoms of measles.*

synagogue *(sin-a-gog) (n)* a building used by Jews for worship.

synchronize *(sin-kron-ize)* **synchronizing synchronized** *(v)* to make things happen at exactly the same time. *Let's synchronize our watches before we arrange a meeting time.* **synchronization** *(n).*

syncopate syncopating syncopated *(v)* to stress beats in a piece of music that are not normally stressed. **syncopation** *(n).*

synonym *(sin-uh-nim) (n)* a word that means the same, or nearly the same, as another word. *Rapid is a synonym of quick.*

synopsis synopses *(n)* a brief summary of a longer piece of writing.

syntax *(n)* the rules of grammar that govern the way that words are put together to make phrases and sentences.

synthesizer *(n)* an electronic keyboard instrument that can make a variety of sounds, and can imitate other musical instruments.

synthetic *(adj)* Something that is **synthetic** is manufactured or artificial. **synthetically** *(adv).*

syringe *(n)* a tube with a plunger and a hollow needle, used for giving injections and taking blood samples.

syrup *(n)* a sweet, sticky, substance made from sugar. *Maple syrup.* **syrupy** *(adj).*

system
1 *(n)* a group of things that exist or work together in an organized way. *The Solar System. A heating system.*
2 *(n)* a way of organizing or arranging things. *The education system.* **systematic** *(adj),* **systematically** *(adv).*

Tt

tab
1 *(n)* a small piece of paper, metal, etc. that you can hold or pull. *Most drink cans have ring tabs.*
2 *(informal)* If you **keep tabs on** someone, you watch them closely to see what they are doing.
3 *(informal)* If you **pick up the tab**, you pay the check in a restaurant.

tabby tabbies
1 *(n)* a cat with a gray or yellow-brown striped coat.
2 *(n)* any domestic cat, especially a female. *See* **cat**.

tabernacle *(tab-er-nak-ul)*
1 *(n)* a building used for worship.
2 *(n)* a container or shrine for holy objects.

table
1 *(n)* a piece of furniture with a flat top resting on legs.
2 *(n)* a chart showing figures or information.

tablecloth *(n)* a piece of material used to protect or decorate a table.

table manners *(plural n)* the way you behave when you are eating.

tablespoon *(n)* a large spoon that you use as a measure in cooking or to serve food. **tablespoonful** *(n).*

tablet
1 *(n)* a small solid piece of medicine that you swallow.
2 *(n)* a portable computer that you operate by touching the screen.
3 *(n)* a piece of stone with writing carved on it.

table tennis *(n)* a game for two or four players, who hit a small light ball over a low net on a table, using round paddles.

tabloid *(n)* a newspaper printed on small pages, with large headlines and a lot of pictures. **tabloid** *(adj).*

taboo *(adj)* If a subject is **taboo**, you may upset or offend people if you talk about it. *Death is a taboo subject in some societies.* **taboo** *(n).*

tabular *(adj)* set out in the form of a table or chart. **tabulate** *(v).*

tacit *(tass-it) (adj)* If something is **tacit**, it is understood or agreed without being stated. *My parents have given their tacit agreement to my staying up late.* **tacitly** *(adv).*

taciturn *(adj)* If someone is **taciturn**, they are shy and do not talk much.

tack tacking tacked
1 *(n)* a small, sharp nail.
2 *(v)* to attach or fix something using tacks. *We tacked a picture to the wall.*
3 *(v)* If you **tack** material, you sew it loosely before doing it neatly. **tack** *(n).*
4 *(v)* to sail in a zigzag course against the wind. **tack** *(n).*
5 *(n)* equipment that you need to ride a horse, such as a saddle and bridle. *The picture shows the main parts of a bridle and saddle. The horse on the right wears western-style tack.*

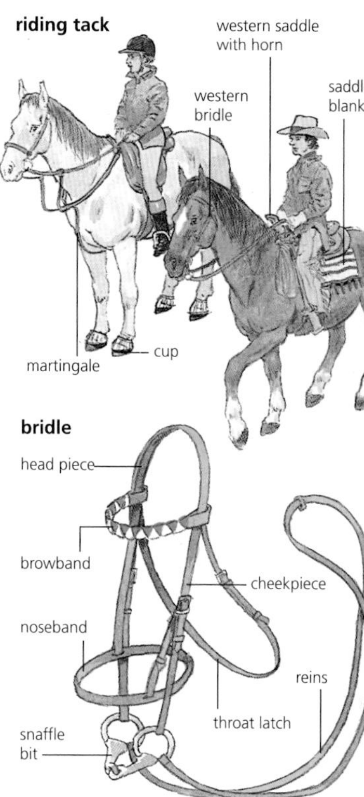

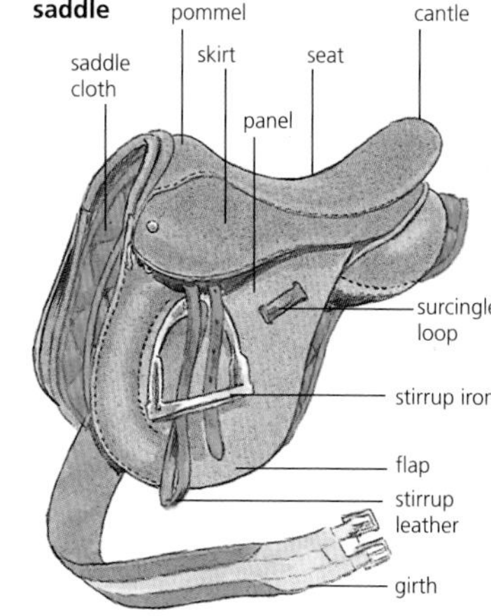

tackle tackling tackled
1 *(v)* If you **tackle** someone in a ball game, you try to get the ball away from them. **tackle** *(n)*.
2 *(v)* to deal with a problem or difficulty. *We must tackle the litter problem.*
3 *(n)* the equipment that you need to do something. *Fishing tackle.*

tact *(n)* If you handle a person or situation with **tact**, you are sensitive and do not upset anyone. **tactful** *(adj)*, **tactfully** *(adv)*.

tactics *(plural n)* plans or methods to win a game or battle. **tactical** *(adj)*, **tactically** *(adv)*.

tag tagging tagged
1 *(n)* a label. *A price tag.*
2 *(n)* a children's chasing game.
3 *(v)* If you **tag along** with someone, you go with them. *Henry wasn't part of the gang; he just tagged along.*

tail tailing tailed
1 *(n)* the long part at the end of an animal's body.
2 *(n)* something that is like a tail. *We joined the tail of the procession.*
3 *(v) (informal)* If you **tail** someone, you follow them closely. **tail** *(n)*.
4 *(v)* If something **tails off**, it gets less or weakens. *Misha's enthusiasm for the project has started to tail off.*

tailor tailoring tailored
1 *(n)* someone who makes or alters clothes, especially men's suits.
2 *(v)* to design or alter something so that it suits someone perfectly. *The computer company will tailor the system to suit our needs.*

take taking took taken
1 *(v)* to move or carry something. *Take your plate into the kitchen.*
2 *(v)* to get, seize, or capture something. *Ken's taken my pen!*
3 *(v)* to accept something. *Do you take credit cards?*
4 *(v)* to use something. *Does your camera take batteries?*
5 *(v)* If you **take after** someone in your family, you look like them or have the same characteristics as them.
6 **take in** *(v) (informal)* If somebody **takes you in**, you believe the lies that they tell you.

takeoff *(n)* the beginning of a flight, when the aircraft leaves the ground. **take off** *(v)*.

takeout
1 *(n)* a restaurant selling meals that you take and eat somewhere else.
2 *(n)* food you buy from a takeout restaurant.

takeover *(n)* If there is a **takeover** of a company, another company buys enough shares in it to control the company. **take over** *(v)*.

takings *(plural n)* money received from customers in a store, café, etc.

talcum powder *(n)* a fine, white powder that you can use to dry your body or to make it smell nice.

tale
1 *(n)* a story.
2 *(n)* a lie or a complaint about someone. *Don't tell tales!*

talent *(n)* an ability or a skill. **talented** *(adj)*.

talk talking talked
1 *(v)* to speak.
2 *(n)* a conversation.
3 *(n)* a speech or a lecture.

talkative *(adj)* If you are **talkative**, you talk a lot.

tall taller tallest
1 *(adj)* higher than usual. *A tall tree. A tall woman.*
2 *(adj)* having a certain height. *He was six feet tall.*
3 *(adj)* hard to believe. *A tall story.*

tally tallies tallying tallied
1 *(n)* a count or a record. *Keep a tally of what I owe you.*
2 *(v)* to add up or match. *These figures don't quite tally.*

Talmud *(n)* the collection of Jewish civil and religious laws.

talon *(n)* a sharp claw.

tambourine *(n)* a small, round musical instrument that is similar to a drum. It has jingling metal discs around its rim and you play it by shaking or hitting it with your hand. *See* **percussion**.

tame tamer tamest
1 *(adj)* A **tame** animal is not wild and can live with people. **tame** *(v)*.
2 *(adj)* not very exciting. **tamely** *(adv)*.

tamper tampering tampered *(v)* to interfere with something so that it becomes damaged or broken.

tan tanning tanned
1 *(n)* a light yellow-brown color.
2 *(n)* If you have a **tan**, your skin has become darker because you have been out in the sun a lot. **tan** *(v)*.
3 *(v)* Animal skin is **tanned** to make it into leather. **tanner** *(n)*, **tannery** *(n)*.

tandem bicycle *(n)* a bicycle for two people.

tandoori *(n)* an Indian method of cooking meat, bread, etc. by baking it in a clay oven.

tangent
1 *(n)* a straight line that touches the edge of a curve in one place. *See* **circle**.
2 If you **go off on a tangent**, you start talking about something different from the main discussion.

tangerine *(n)* a small sweet orange that you can peel easily.

tangle tangling tangled *(v)* to make things twisted and mixed-up. **tangle** *(n)*.

tank
1 *(n)* a large container for liquid or gas. *See* **aquarium**.
2 *(n)* an armored vehicle used by soldiers. *See* **armored vehicle**.

tanker *(n)* a ship or truck that carries gas or liquid. *The picture below shows an oil tanker.*

oil tanker

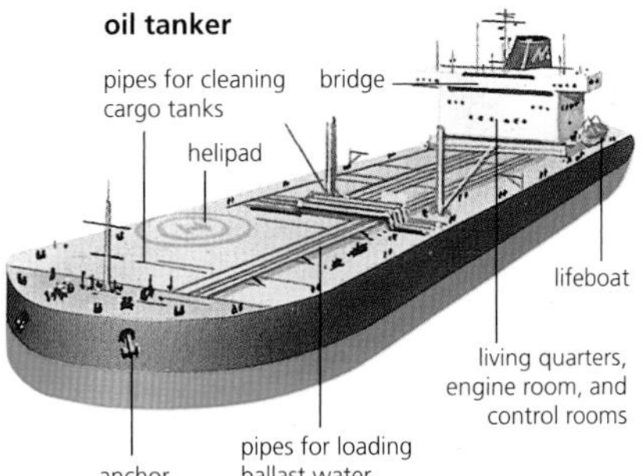

tantrum *(n)* a fit of temper.

tap tapping tapped
1 *(n)* a piece of equipment used to control the flow of a liquid; a faucet.
2 *(v)* to hit or knock something gently. **tap** *(n)*.
3 *(v)* to listen to a telephone conversation using a secret device. **tap** *(n)*.
4 *(v)* to make a hole to draw off liquid. *See* **rubber**.
5 **tap dancing** *(n)* dancing with shoes that have metal plates on their soles, which make a clicking noise. **tap dancer** *(n)*, **tap-dance** *(v)*.

tape taping taped
1 *(n)* a thin strip of material, paper, plastic, etc. *Adhesive tape.*
2 *(v)* to record sound or pictures on audio or video tape.
3 *(n)* a long piece of magnetic ribbon used for recording sound or pictures, usually contained in a plastic case or cassette.
4 *(v)* to fasten together, wrap, or bind with tape.

tape measure *(n)* a long, thin strip of material or steel marked in inches or centimeters so that you can measure things with it.

taper tapering tapered
1 *(v)* to become narrower at one end.
2 **taper off** *(v)* to become gradually smaller.
3 *(n)* a wooden strip or thin candle used for carrying a flame. *We lit the candles with a taper.*

tape recorder *(n)* an electrical machine that you use to play or record music or sound. **tape-record** *(v)*.

tapestry tapestries *(n)* a heavy piece of cloth with pictures or patterns woven into it. *The picture shows a tapestry being sewn.*

tapestry

single canvas (made from hemp or linen thread)
tapestry wool
tapestry needle with rounded head

tar *(n)* a thick, black, sticky substance used for making roads. Tar is made from coal or wood.

tarantula *(n)* a large, hairy, venomous spider. *See* **spider**.

target targeting targeted
1 *(n)* something that you aim at or attack. **target** *(v)*.
2 *(n)* a round object marked with circles, at which an archer aims his arrows.
3 *(v)* If you **target** something, you concentrate on it. *The publicity campaign is targeting a very young audience.*

tariff
1 *(n)* a tax on imports and exports.
2 *(n)* a list of prices in a hotel or restaurant.

tarmac *(n)* a mixture of tar and small stones that is used on road surfaces. *Tarmac is short for Tarmacadam.* **tarmac** *(v)*.

tarnish tarnishes tarnishing tarnished *(v)* If something **tarnishes**, it becomes duller or less bright.

tarpaulin *(n)* a heavy waterproof sheet.

tart tarter tartest
1 *(n)* an open fruit pie or pastry. *An apple tart.*
2 *(adj)* If food is **tart**, it tastes sour or sharp. **tartness** *(n)*.
3 *(adj)* A **tart** reply is unkind or sarcastic. **tartly** *(adv)*.

tartan *(n)* woolen cloth patterned with squares of different colors. Tartan is used especially for Scottish kilts.

task *(n)* a job or a duty.

task force *(n)* a team, especially of soldiers, formed to deal with a problem.

tassel *(n)* a bunch of threads tied at one end, used as a decoration on clothing, furniture, etc. **tasseled** *(adj)*.

taste tasting tasted
1 *(n)* Your sense of **taste** tells you what food you are eating.
2 *(n)* The **taste** of a food is whether it is sweet, sour, bitter, salty, etc. **taste** *(v)*, **tasty** *(adj)*.
3 *(n)* If you have good **taste**, you make good choices of furnishings, clothes, etc. **tasteful** *(adj)*.
4 *(v)* to try a bit of food or drink to see if you like it. **taste** *(n)*.

tattered *(adj)* old and torn, or scruffy. *Tattered jeans.*

tattoo *(n)* a picture or words that have been permanently printed on somebody's skin, using ink and needles. **tattooist** *(n)*, **tattoo** *(v)*.

taunt taunting taunted *(v)* to try to make someone angry or upset by teasing them. **taunt** *(n)*.

taut *(adj)* stretched tight. *A taut rope.*

tavern *(n)* an inn.

tawny *(n)* a light sandy-brown color. **tawny** *(adj)*.

tax taxes *(n)* money that has to be paid to the government for public services. **taxation** *(n)*, **tax** *(v)*.

taxi taxiing taxied
1 *(n)* a car with a driver whom you pay to take you where you want to go.
2 *(v)* When planes **taxi**, they move along the ground.

taxing *(adj)* If something is **taxing**, it is demanding and puts a strain on you.

tea
1 *(n)* a drink made from the leaves of a tea plant. *The picture below shows tea leaves being picked on a hillside plantation in southern India.*
2 *(n)* an afternoon gathering in which small snacks and tea are served.

tea-picking

teach teaches teaching taught *(v)* to give a lesson or show someone how to do something. *Joel taught me how to swim.* **teacher** *(n)*.

teakettle *(n)* a kettle with a handle and a spout. It is used for boiling water.

teal
1 *(n)* any of several small ducks with short necks. Teal live in rivers and marshes.
2 *(adj)* a dark color between green and blue.

team teaming teamed
1 *(n)* a group of people who work together or play a sport together. *A hockey team.* **teamwork** *(n)*.
2 *(n)* two or more horses or oxen that are harnessed together to do work.
3 *(v)* If two people **team up**, they join together to do something.

teammate *(n)* a fellow member of a team.

tear tearing tore torn
1 *(rhymes with dear) (n)* a drop of liquid that comes from your eye. **tearful** *(adj)*.
2 *(rhymes with dare) (n)* a rip in a piece of paper or material.
3 *(rhymes with dare) (v)* to pull one part of something away from the rest. *Ben has torn his jeans.*
4 *(rhymes with dare) (v)* to move very fast. *Louise tore down the street.*

tease teasing teased *(v)* to mock someone by saying unkind things to them; to kid.

teaspoon *(n)* a small spoon that you use for stirring drinks or as a measure in cooking. **teaspoonful** *(n)*.

technical
1 *(adj)* having to do with science, machines, industry, etc. **technically** *(adv)*.
2 *(adj)* using words that only experts understand. *Once we started to talk about computers, the conversation became very technical.*

technician *(n)* someone who looks after scientific equipment or does practical laboratory work.

technique *(tek-neek) (n)* a skillful way of doing something.

techno *(tek-no) (n) (slang)* electronic dance music, often based around repeated rhythms.

technology technologies *(n)* the use of science to do practical things. **technological** *(adj)*.

eddy bear
ı) a stuffed
oy bear
nade from
oft furry
naterial.
*'he teddy
ear shown
ere was made
ı the Steiff
actory in Germany.*

teddy bear

.edious *(tee-dee-us) (adj)*
ɔng and boring. **tediously** *(adv)*.

eeming *(adj)* If a place is **teeming**,
t is full of people or animals.

:eenager *(n)* a person who is
etween the ages of 13 and 19.
:**eenage** *or* **teenaged** *(adj)*.

:eens *(plural n)*
he years between 13 and
19. *Tanya is in her teens.*

:eepee *see* **tepee**.

tee shirt *see* **T-shirt**.

:eeth *(plural n)* the white,
ɔone-like structures in your
nouth that you use for biting
and chewing food. *The diagram
shows a lower set of adult teeth.*

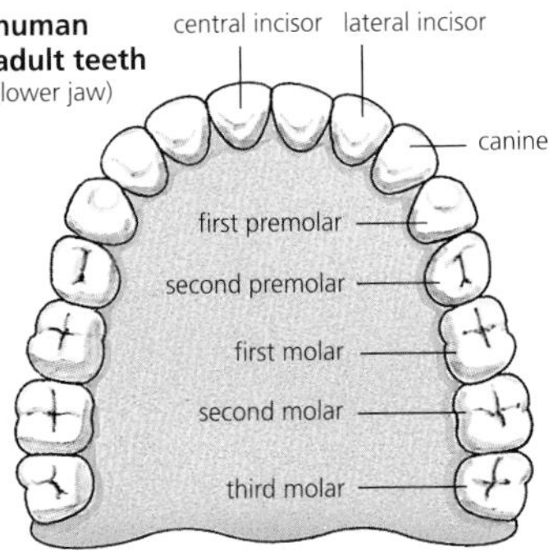

numan adult teeth (lower jaw)

teethe teething teethed *(v)*
If a baby is **teething**, new teeth are
coming through his or her gums.

teetotal *(adj)* If a person is
teetotal, they never drink
alcohol. **teetotaler** *(n)*.

telecast *(n)* a program
broadcast by television.

telecommunication
1 *(n)* the science that deals with the
sending of messages by telephone,
satellite, radio, etc. Also known
as **telecommunications**.
2 *(n)* any message sent this way.
See **satellite**.

telegram *(n)* a written message that
is sent by radio or electrical signals.
Telegrams were used to give urgent
news or send congratulations.

telegraph *(n)*
a way of sending messages
using radio or electrical
signals. **telegraph** *(v)*.

telemarketing *(n)*
the selling of goods and
services by telephone.

telemetry *(n)* the use
of radio waves to transmit
and record information
from a measuring instrument.

telepathy *(tel-ep-uh-thee) (n)*
If you use **telepathy**, you
send your thoughts to
someone else without
speaking, writing, or
making signs. **telepathic**
(tell-uh-path-ik) (adj).

telephone *(n)* a machine
that uses electrical wires
or radio waves to enable you
to speak to someone far away.
*The image on the right shows
a selection of early telephones.
The mechanism inside each version
is the same: the sound of a voice
makes the mouthpiece vibrate,
sending a signal along a wire.
The earpiece matches the vibrations,
reproducing the sound.* **telephone** *(v)*.

telephoto lens *(n)*
a camera lens that makes things that
are far away look closer and larger.

telescope *(n)* a tube-shaped
instrument, which makes things
that are far away look closer and
larger. Telescopes are used especially
for looking at stars. *The picture
shows a refracting telescope, and
describes how light travels through it.*
telescopic *(adj)*.

A 'candlestick' design from 1905.
earpiece
mouthpiece
An early experimental telephone made by Bell in 1875.
number dial
A plastic 'phone from the 1930s.

early telephones

television
1 *(n)* a piece of equipment
with a screen, which receives
and shows moving pictures
with sound.
2 *(n)* the sending of sounds and
moving pictures along radio waves
to be picked up by a television.

tell telling told
1 *(v)* to speak to someone.
2 *(v)* to show something.
The red light tells you to stop.
3 *(v)* to recognize or be
certain. *It was difficult to
tell who it was in the dark.*
4 **tell off** *(v)*
If you **tell someone off**,
you scold them because they
have done something wrong.

temper *(n)*
an angry or impatient mood.

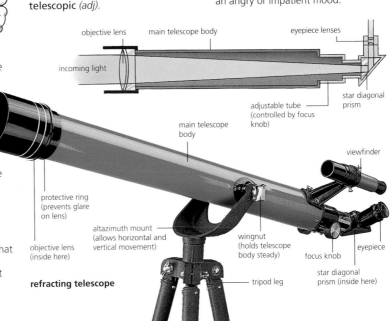

objective lens
main telescope body
eyepiece lenses
incoming light
adjustable tube (controlled by focus knob)
star diagonal prism
main telescope body
viewfinder
protective ring (prevents glare on lens)
altazimuth mount (allows horizontal and vertical movement)
wingnut (holds telescope body steady)
objective lens (inside here)
focus knob
eyepiece
star diagonal prism (inside here)
tripod leg

refracting telescope

temperament *(n)* your nature or your personality. *Laura has a very calm temperament.*

temperamental
1 *(adj)* excited, unpredictable, or moody. *A temperamental artist.*
2 *(adj)* caused by your temperament. **temperamentally** *(adv).*

temperate *(adj)* If an area has a **temperate** climate, it has neither very high nor very low temperatures.

temperature
1 *(n)* a measure of how cold or hot something is.
2 *(n)* If you have a **temperature**, your body is hotter than normal because you are ill.

tempest *(n)* a violent storm.

template *(n)* a shape or pattern that you draw or cut around to make the same shape in paper, metal, material, etc. *See* **geometry**.

temple *(n)* a building used for worship. *This reconstruction of the Parthenon, a temple dedicated to the Goddess Athene, shows how it would have looked in the 5th century B.C.*

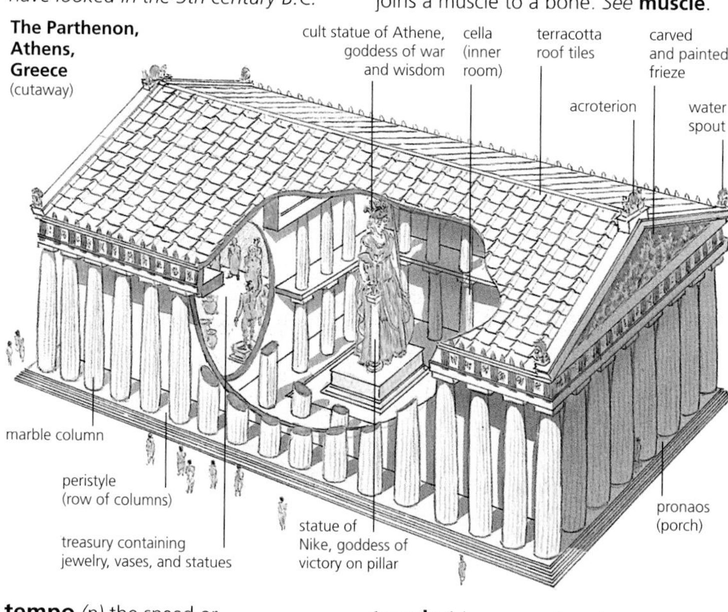

tempo *(n)* the speed or timing of a piece of music.

temporary *(adj)* If something is **temporary**, it lasts for only a short time. **temporarily** *(adv).*

tempt tempting tempted
1 *(v)* If you **tempt** someone, you make them want something by telling them how good it is. **tempting** *(adj).*
2 *(v)* If you are **tempted**, you are attracted to doing something wrong.

temptation
1 *(n)* the act of being tempted. *Try to resist temptation.*
2 *(n)* something that you want to have or do, although you know it is wrong. *That cake is such a temptation!*

tenant *(n)* someone who rents a room, house, office, etc.

tend tending tended
1 *(v)* If something **tends** to happen, it often or usually happens.
2 *(v)* If you **tend** to a person, animal, or plant, you take care of it.

tendency tendencies *(n)* If you have a **tendency** to do something, you often or usually do it.

tender
1 *(adj)* sore or sensitive. *Sal's bruises were still tender.* **tenderness** *(n).*
2 *(adj)* soft. *A tender steak.* **tenderness** *(n).*
3 *(adj)* gentle and kind. *A tender kiss.* **tenderness** *(n),* **tenderly** *(adv).*

tendon *(n)* a strong, thick cord that joins a muscle to a bone. *See* **muscle**.

tennis *(n)* a game played on a court by two or four players who use rackets to hit a ball over a net.

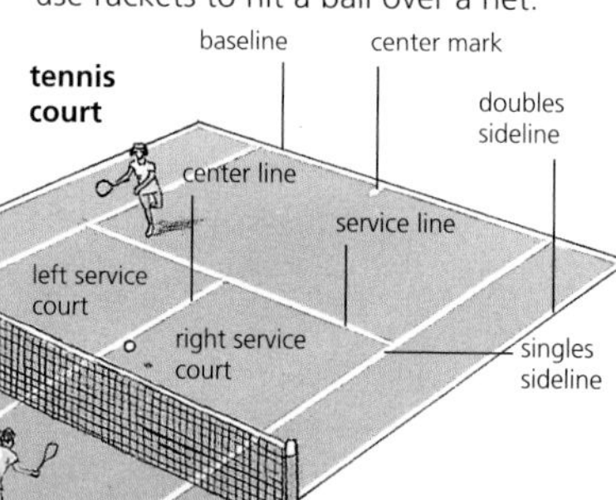

tenor
1 *(n)* a male singing voice that is quite high. **tenor** *(adj).*
2 *(n)* a singer with a tenor voice.

tense tenser tensest
1 *(adj)* If you are **tense**, you are nervous or worried. *Miriam is always tense before an exam.* **tenseness** *(n),* **tensely** *(adv).*
2 *(adj)* stretched tight and stiff. *Your muscles will be tense if you don't warm up before a game.* **tenseness** *(n),* **tense** *(v).*
3 *(n)* a form of a verb that shows whether an action happened in the past, is happening in the present, or will happen in the future. "I was," "I am," and "I will be" are examples of past, present, and future tenses of the verb *to be*.

tension
1 *(n)* the tightness or stiffness of a rope, wire, etc. *After you've put up your tent, you need to test the tension of all the guy ropes.*
2 *(n)* a feeling of worry, nervousness, or suspense. *Tension mounted as the boxers entered the ring.*
3 *(n)* If there is **tension** between two people, there is difficulty or strain in their relationship.

tent *(n)* a shelter made of polyester or canvas, supported by poles and ropes.

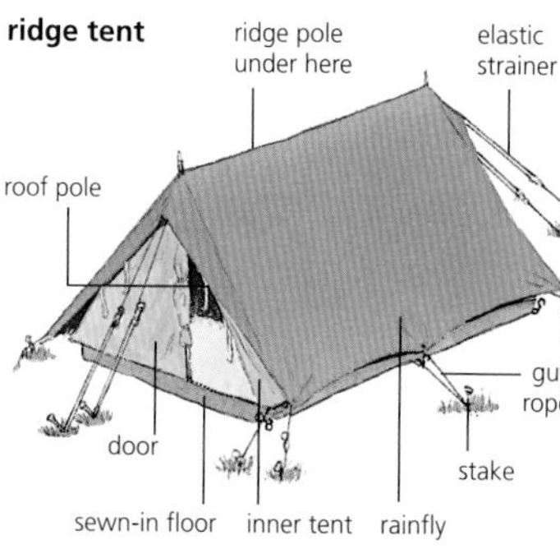

tentacle *(n)* one of the long, flexible limbs of some animals such as octopuses and squids. Tentacles are used for moving and feeling. *See* **jellyfish**, **octopus**, **slug**, **squid**.

tentative *(adj)* hesitant or unsure. *Joe made a tentative attempt to join in the game.* **tentatively** *(adv).*

tenterhooks If you are **on tenterhooks**, you are in suspense, waiting for something to happen.

tenuous *(ten-yoo-uss) (adj)* not very important or not very significant. **tenuously** *(adv).*

opening for smoke to escape

tepee

avois (for arrying oods)

stitched and painted buffalo hide

epee *or* **teepee** *(n)* round tent made rom animal skins r canvas, used by lorth American lains Indians.

epid *(adj)* slightly warm.

erm
(n) a part of the school ear. **termly** *(adv).*
(n) a length of time. *The job is or a limited term of eight months.*
(n) a word. *Musical terms.*
terms *(plural n)* ne conditions of an agreement.

erminal
(n) a building where passengers rrive and leave. *An airport terminal.*
(n) a computer keyboard nd screen linked to a network.
(adj) If someone has a **terminal** lness, they cannot be cured and vill die from it. **terminally** *(adv).*

erminate terminating **erminated** *(v)* to stop or to end. *'he train terminates here.*

ermite *(n)* an ant-like insect that lestroys wood. Termites live together n colonies inside large mounds hat they build hemselves. *'he picture hows a nound nade by ligerian ermites.*

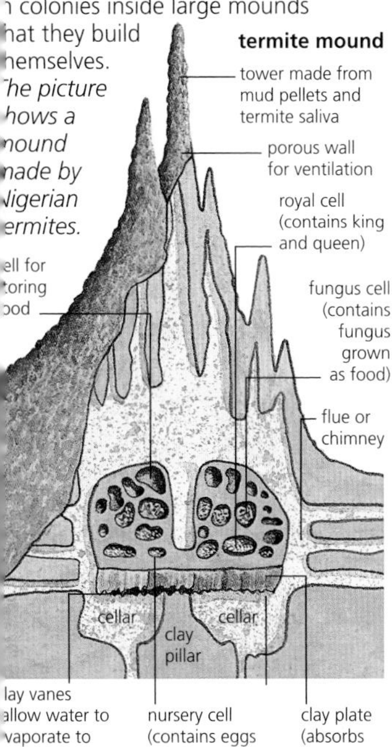

terrace *(n)*
1 a paved, open area next to a house, café, etc. where you can sit.
2 a balcony of an apartment building.
3 a raised flat platform of land with sloping sides.

terracotta *(n)* a type of clay used for ornaments, pots, or roofs.

terrain *(n)* ground or land.

terrestrial *(adj)* having to do with the Earth or living on the Earth.

terrible *(adj)* very bad, shocking, or awful. *Donna has a terrible singing voice.* **terribly** *(adv).*

terrific
1 *(adj)* very good or wonderful. *We had a terrific time at the bowling alley last night.*
2 *(adj)* great. *Rod set off at terrific speed.* **terrifically** *(adv).*

terrify terrifies terrifying terrified *(v)* to frighten someone very much. *Ruth was terrified when she saw the size of the spider.* **terrifying** *(adj),* **terrifyingly** *(adv).*

terrine
1 *(n)* a kind of cooking pot.
2 *(n)* a kind of food, similar to pâté, usually prepared in a terrine.

territory territories *(n)* an area of land, especially land that belongs to someone. **territorial** *(adj).*

terror
1 *(n)* great fear. *His eyes were filled with terror.*
2 *(n)* a person or thing that causes immense terror or fear.

terrorist *(n)* someone who uses violence for example, bombing or hijacking, for political reasons. **terrorism** *(n).*

terrorize terrorizing terrorized *(v)* to frighten someone very much. *Wild dogs have been terrorizing the town for weeks now.*

terse terser tersest *(n)* brief and abrupt. *When I asked Aunt Agatha her age, she gave a very terse reply.*

tertiary *(adj)* third in order.

tessellate tessellating tessellated *(v)* When shapes **tessellate**, they fit together exactly, without leaving gaps. *The picture shows how hexagons tessellate.* **tessellated** *(adj).*

tessellating shapes

test testing tested
1 *(n)* a set of questions or actions that check your knowledge or skill. **test** *(v).*
2 *(n)* a medical examination or check-up. *A blood test.* **test** *(v).*
3 *(v)* to try something out. *Esther tested the new recipe before her dinner party.* **test** *(n).*

testify testifies testifying testified *(v)* to state the truth, or to give evidence in a court of law.

testimony testimonies *(n)* a statement given by a witness who is under oath, in a court of law.

test pilot *(n)* a pilot who flies new airplanes to test them.

test tube
1 *(n)* a small thin glass tube used in a science laboratory. *See* **apparatus**.
2 **test-tube baby** *(n)* a baby that develops from an egg that has been fertilized outside the mother's body but which then grows normally inside her womb.

tetanus *(n)* a serious disease caused by bacteria getting into a cut or wound. Tetanus makes your muscles, and especially your jaw, become stiff.

tether tethering tethered
1 *(v)* to tie up an animal so that it cannot move far. **tether** *(n).*
2 If you are **at the end of your tether**, you have run out of patience.

text
1 *(n)* the main section of writing in a book, rather than the pictures or index.
2 *(n)* a text message.

textbook *(n)* a book used at school or college as part of a course.

text message *(n)* a message that you type into your cell phone and send to another person who reads it on the screen of their cell phone.

textile *(n)* a fabric or cloth.

texture *(n)* the feel of something, such as its roughness or smoothness.

thank thanking thanked
1 *(v)* to tell someone that you are grateful for what they have done. *Donald thanked the stranger for stopping to see if he was all right.*
2 **thanks** *(plural n)* spoken or written words showing that you are grateful.

thankful *(adj)* glad or grateful. *Helena was thankful for a decent meal.* **thankfully** *(adv).*

thatch thatches *(n)* straw or reeds used for making roofs. *The picture shows some features of a roof made of thatch.* **thatch** *(v)*, **thatched** *(adj)*.

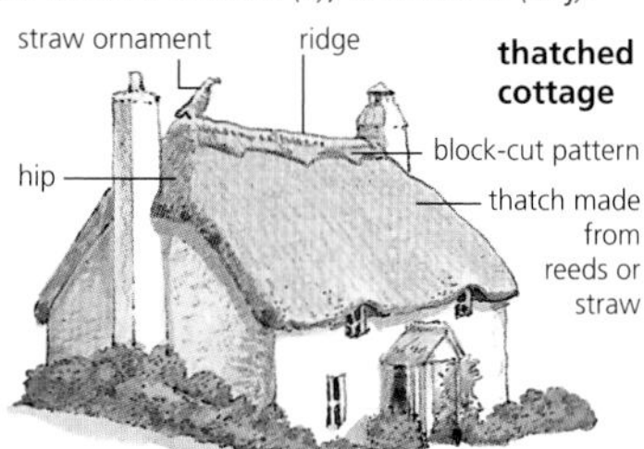

thaw thawing thawed
1 *(v)* to become soft or liquid after being frozen. *Leave the turkey to thaw overnight.*
2 *(n)* a time when snow and ice melt because the weather has become warmer.

theater
1 *(n)* a place where you go to watch plays, shows, etc.
2 *(n)* a part of a hospital where surgeons operate.

theatrical
1 *(adj)* having to do with the theater. *Theatrical costumes.*
2 *(adj)* If something is **theatrical**, it is intended to create a dramatic effect.

theft *(n)* the crime of stealing. *Kit is being punished for theft.*

their *(pronoun)* belonging to them. *Have the girls brought their books?* **theirs** *(pronoun)*.

them *(pronoun)* the things, people, etc. just mentioned. *Sam and Alex will be here soon, so look out for them.*

theme *(theem)*
1 *(n)* the subject of a speech, book, movie, etc.
2 *(n)* a melody or a tune.
3 **theme park** *(n)* a park with rides and attractions based on a subject, such as the Wild West.

themselves *(pronoun)* them and no one else. *The children dressed themselves.*

then
1 *(adv)* at that time. *I didn't know Pandora then.*
2 *(adv)* after that. *Eat first, then talk.*
3 *(adv)* as a result. *If you stay up late, then you'll be tired tomorrow.*

theology theologies *(n)* the study of religion and religious beliefs. **theological** *(adj)*.

theorem *(n)* a statement, especially in math, that can be proved to be true.

theory *(rhymes with weary)* theories
1 *(n)* an idea that is intended to explain something.
2 *(n)* the rules and principles of a subject, rather than its practice. **theoretical** *(adj)*.
3 If something should happen **in theory**, you expect it to happen, but it may not. **theoretically** *(adv)*.

therapy therapies *(n)* a treatment for an illness, injury or disability, for example psychotherapy and speech therapy. **therapist** *(n)*.

there
1 *(adv)* to, in, or at that place. *Let's not go there again!*
2 *(pronoun)* The word **there** is often used as a subject in sentences. *There is a man outside.*

therefore *(adv)* as a result. *Stanley is sick; therefore Joe must take his place.*

therm *(n)* a unit for measuring heat, especially heat from burning gas.

thermal
1 *(adj)* having to do with heat or holding in heat. *Thermal underwear.*
2 *(n)* a rising current of warm air.

thermometer *(n)* an instrument used to measure temperature. *The picture shows an old-style liquid thermometer, which was used to measure body temperature. The bulb was usually placed under the tongue, and as the liquid heated up it expanded and rose up the capillary tube.*

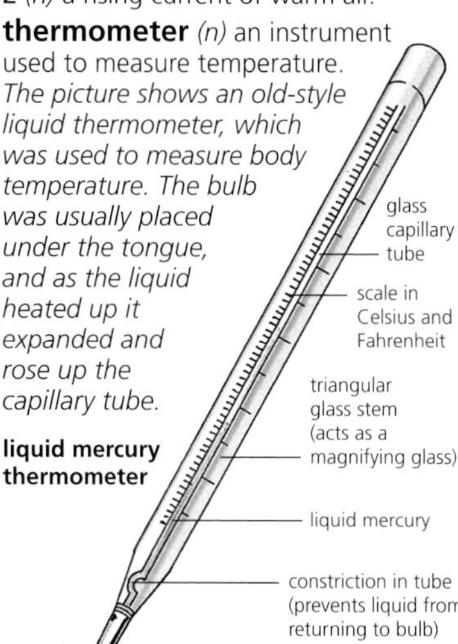

liquid mercury thermometer

thermostat *(n)* a device connected to a radiator, iron, etc., that controls the temperature. *See* **refrigerator**.

thesaurus *(thi-sar-rus)* thesauruses *or* thesauri *(n)* a book containing lists of words with similar or related meanings.

these *(plural pronoun)* the things here, or the things being talked about. *Let's move these boxes.* **these** *(adj)*.

thesis theses *(n)* an idea to be debated or proved.

they
1 *(pronoun)* the people, animals, or things being talked about.
2 *(pronoun)* people in general. *They say that it will snow.*

thick thicker thickest *(adj)* wide, fat, or dense. *Thick walls. Thick soup.* **thickness** *(n)*, **thicken** *(v)*, **thickly** *(adv)*.

thicket *(n)* a thick growth of plants, bushes, or small trees.

thief thieves *(n)* someone who steal things. **thieve** *(v)*, **thieving** *(adj)*.

thigh *(n)* Your **thigh** is the top part of your leg between your knee and your hip.

thin thinner thinnest *(adj)* not fat, not thick, or not dense. *A thin cat. A thin sauce.* **thinness** *(n)*, **thin** *(v)*, **thinly** *(adv)*.

thing
1 *(n)* an object, idea, or event.
2 **things** *(plural n)* belongings. *Don't leave your things here.*
3 **things** *(plural n)* the general state of affairs. *How are things with you?*

think thinking thought
1 *(v)* to use your mind. *Try to think of the answer.* **thinker** *(n*
2 *(v)* to have an idea or opinion. *Sophie thinks boys are silly.*

third
1 *(n)* one of three equal parts.
2 *(adj)* If you come **third** in a race, you finish behind two other people. **thirdly** *(adv)*.

thirst
1 *(n)* a need for liquid. **thirst** *(v)*.
2 *(n)* a longing for something. *Jesse has a great thirst for adventure.* **thirst** *(v)*.

thirsty thirstier thirstiest *(adj)* If you are **thirsty**, you need or want to drink something. **thirstily** *(adv)*.

this *(pronoun)* the thing here or the thing being talked about. **this** *(adj)*.

thistle *(n)* a wild plant with prickly leaves and purple, white, blue, or yellow flowers.

spear thistle

thorax thoraxes
1 *(n)* the part of your body between your neck and your stomach.
2 *(n)* the part of an insect's body between its head and its abdomen. *See* **beetle**.

thorn *(n)* a sharp point on the stem of a plant, such as a rose.

thorny thornier thorniest
1 *(adj)* covered with thorns.
2 *(adj)* difficult. *A thorny problem.*

thorough *(adj)* If you are **thorough**, you do a job carefully and completely. **thoroughness** *(n)*, **thoroughly** *(adv)*.

thoroughfare *(n)* a main road.

those *(plural pronoun)* the people or things there. *The purple boots are all right, but I prefer those in the window.* **those** *(adj)*.

though
1 *(conj)* even if or despite the fact that. *I'm still hungry, though I've just had breakfast.*
2 *(adv)* nevertheless. *He's very friendly; I don't like him, though.*

thought
1 *(n)* the act or process of thinking.
2 *(n)* an idea or opinion.
3 If you are **deep in thought**, you are thinking hard about something.

thoughtful
1 *(adj)* serious or involving a lot of thought. *A thoughtful essay.*
2 *(adj)* A **thoughtful** person considers other people's feelings and needs. **thoughtfully** *(adv)*.

thoughtless *(adj)*
A **thoughtless** person does not consider other people's feelings and needs. **thoughtlessly** *(adv)*.

thrash
thrashes thrashing thrashed
1 *(v)* to beat with a stick or a whip.
2 *(v)* to beat someone thoroughly in a game. *Gemma always thrashes me at tennis.* **thrashing** *(n)*.
3 *(v)* If you **thrash out** an idea or a problem, you talk about it until something is decided.

thread threading threaded
1 *(n)* a strand of cotton, silk, etc. used for sewing.
2 *(v)* to pass a thread through something, such as the eye of a needle or a set of beads.
3 *(n)* the raised, spiral ridge around a screw.

threadbare *(adj)* If your clothes are **threadbare**, they are old and worn out.

threaten
threatening threatened
(v) If someone or something **threatens** you, it frightens you or puts you in danger.

three-dimensional *or* **3-D**
(adj) solid or not flat.
Cubes and spheres are three-dimensional shapes.

thresh threshes threshing threshed *(v)* to separate the grain of a crop, such as wheat, from the chaff and straw. *The picture shows 19th-century farmers threshing by beating the corn with flails. Nowadays, most farmers use combine harvesters to thresh their crops.*
Also see **harvest**.

threshold
1 *(n)* the base of a doorway.
2 *(n)* the beginning of something. *We are on the threshold of a great adventure!*

thrifty thriftier thriftiest *(adj)*
Someone who is **thrifty** does not waste money, food, supplies, etc. **thrift** *(n)*.

thrill *(n)* a feeling of excitement and pleasure. **thrill** *(v)*, **thrilling** *(adj)*.

thriller *(n)* an exciting story about mystery, danger, or crime.

thrive thriving thrived *(v)*
to do well and flourish. *Yasmin is thriving at her new school.* **thriving** *(adj)*.

throat
1 *(n)* the front of your neck.
2 *(n)* the passage that runs from your mouth into your stomach or lungs.

throb throbbing throbbed *(v)*
to beat in a regular way. *The drumbeat throbbed in my ears.* **throb** *(n)*.

throne
1 *(n)* an elaborate chair for a king or queen. *This picture from the Bayeux Tapestry shows Harold Godwinson seated on his throne, as King of England.*
2 If someone **comes to the throne**, they become king or queen.

throne

throng *(n)* a large crowd of people. **throng** *(v)*.

throttle throttling throttled
1 *(v)* If you **throttle** someone, you squeeze their throat so that they cannot breathe.
2 *(n)* a valve in a vehicle's engine that opens to let fuel, or fuel and air, flow into it.

through
1 *(prep)* from one end or side to the other. *Lily squeezed through the crowd.* **through** *(adv)*.
2 *(prep)* by way of, or because of. *Elsa got the job through a friend.*
3 *(adv)* completely. *Johnny was wet through.* **through** *(adj)*.

throughout *(prep)*
all the way through. *Chickenpox spread throughout the school.* **throughout** *(adv)*.

throw throwing threw thrown
1 *(v)* to make something move, especially through the air. *Dean threw the ball.* **throw** *(n)*.
2 *(v) (informal)* If something **throws** you, it confuses you.
3 **throw away** *(v)*
to get rid of something.
4 **throw up** *(v) (informal)* to vomit.

thrush thrushes *(n)*
a garden bird with a brown back and a spotted breast.

thrust thrusting thrust
1 *(v)* to push something suddenly and hard. **thrust** *(n)*.
2 *(n)* The **thrust** of an argument is its main point.

thud *(n)*
a noise like the sound of a heavy object falling on the ground. **thud** *(v)*.

thug *(n)* a violent person.

thumb thumbing thumbed
1 *(n)* the short, thick digit that you have on each hand.
2 *(v)* to turn over the pages of a book.
3 *(informal)* If someone is **all thumbs**, they are very clumsy.

thumbtack *(n)*
a small pin with a flat round head used for fastening paper on bulletin boards, walls, etc.

thump thumping thumped
1 *(v)* to hit someone or something with your fist. **thump** *(n)*.
2 *(n)* a dull sound. *The paper landed on the mat with a thump.* **thump** *(v)*.

thunder thundering thundered
1 *(n)* the loud, rumbling sound that you hear during a storm.
2 *(v)* to make a loud noise like thunder. *The trucks thundered past.*

thwart thwarting thwarted *(v)*
If you **thwart** someone's plans, you prevent them from happening.

tiara *(n)*
a piece of jewelry like a small crown.

tick ticking ticked
1 *(n)* a small creature similar to a spider that lives on the skin of some animals and feeds on blood. Some ticks carry diseases and can pass them on to humans.
2 *(n)* the sound that a clock or watch makes. **tick** *(v)*.
3 **tick off** *(v) (informal)* If you **tick someone off**, you make them angry.

ticket *(n)* a printed piece of paper or card that proves that you have paid to do something. *A train ticket.*

tickle tickling tickled *(v)*
to keep touching or poking someone gently, often causing them to laugh or feel irritated. **ticklish** *(adj)*.

tiddledywinks or **tiddlywinks** *(plural n)* a game in which each player tries to flick plastic counters into a cup.

tide *(n)* the constant change in sea level caused by the pull of the Sun and the Moon. **tidal** *(adj)*.

tidings *(plural n)*
news or information.

tidy tidier tidiest *(adj)* neat or in proper order. **tidiness** *(n)*, **tidy** *(v)*.

tie ties tying tied
1 *(v)* to join two pieces of string, cord, etc. together with a knot.
2 *(n)* a long piece of fabric that is worn knotted around the collar of a shirt; a necktie.
3 *(n)* a situation in which two people finish even in a competition. *There was a tie for second place.* **tie** *(v)*.

tiebreaker *(n)*
a special game or question played or asked to decide the result of a match or competition when the players have won the same number of points.

tier *(teer) (n)* one of several levels placed one above the other, for example a row of seats in a theater or a layer of a wedding cake. **tiered** *(adj)*.

tiger *(n)* a large striped wild cat found in Asia.

tiger and cubs

tight tighter tightest
1 *(adj)* fitting closely or fastened closely. *Tight jeans.* **tighten** *(v)*, **tightly** *(adv)*.
2 *(adj)* fully stretched. **tighten** *(v)*.
3 *(adj)* difficult to deal with or get out of. *You have put me in a tight spot.*

tightrope *(n)* a stretched high wire on which circus performers balance.

tights *(plural n)*
a close-fitting garment that covers your hips, legs, and feet.

tile *(n)* a small, flat piece of baked clay, cork, slate, etc., often used for covering floors, roofs, or walls. *The picture shows a baked clay, or ceramic, tile.* **tile** *(v)*.

Dutch ceramic tile

till tilling tilled
1 *(n)* a drawer or box in a store used to hold money, and often part of a cash register.
2 *(v)* to plow the soil ready for planting crops.

tilt tilting tilted *(v)*
to lean to one side. **tilt** *(n)*.

timber *(n)* cut wood used for furniture making, building, etc.

time timing timed
1 *(n)* the passing of seconds, minutes, hours, days, etc.
2 *(n)* a particular moment shown on a clock or watch. *What is the time now?*
3 *(n)* a particular period. *A time of great happiness.*
4 *(v)* to measure how long something takes. *I'll time you while you run.*
5 *(v)* to choose the moment for something. *Harry timed his entrance perfectly.*

timetable *(n)*
a chart of the times when travel departures, events, lessons, etc. are planned to happen; a schedule. **timetable** *(v)*.

timid *(adj)* shy and easily frightened. **timidly** *(adv)*.

tin *(n)* a soft, silvery metal used to make alloys and food cans.

tinge *(tinj)*
1 *(n)* a very small amount of added color. *White with a tinge of pink.*
2 *(n)* a slight feeling. *Ira's smile had a tinge of sadness to it.*

tingle tingling tingled *(v)*
to feel a stinging, pricking, or tickling sensation. **tingle** *(n)*.

tinker tinkering tinkered *(v)*
to work at or fiddle with something, with the objective of repairing it or improving it.

tint *(n)* a small amount of added color. **tint** *(v)*, **tinted** *(adj)*.

tiny tinier tiniest *(adj)*
very small or minute.

tip tipping tipped
1 *(v)* to make something lean or fall over.
2 *(v)* to lean or to fall over.
3 *(n)* the thin end of something. *The tip of a pool cue.*
4 *(n)* a useful hint.
5 *(n)* a sum of money given, in addition to the bill, to a waitress, taxi driver, etc. as thanks for their services.
6 *(v)* to raise or touch your hat as a greeting to someone.

tiptoe tiptoeing tiptoed *(v)*
to walk quietly, without putting your heels down.

tire tiring tired
1 *(n)* a circle of rubber around the rim of a wheel.
2 *(v)* to become bored. *I soon tired of Terry's chatter.*
3 *(v)* to make someone tired or to become tired and weak. **tiring** *(adj)*, **tiredness** *(n)*, **tired** *(adj)*.

tiresome *(adj)* boring, irritating, or annoying. **tiresomely** *(adv)*.

tissue *(tish-yoo)*
1 *(n)* soft thin paper used for wiping, wrapping, etc.
2 *(n)* a mass of cells that form the flesh and muscle of a living creature. *Muscle tissue.*

title
1 *(n)* the name of a book, movie, etc.
2 *(n)* the very first part of a person's name, for example, Ms., Mrs., Mr.
3 *(n)* a special name showing a high position in society, for example, Sir, Dame, Lord, Lady. **titled** *(adj)*.
4 *(n)* a championship.

midwife toad

toad *(n)* an amphibian similar to a frog, but with a rougher skin, that lives mainly on land. *The male midwife toad carries strands of eggs wrapped around its back legs for several weeks before depositing them in a pond to hatch.*

toadstool *(n)* a usually poisonous fungus with a rounded top on a stalk.

toast toasting toasted
1 *(n)* bread browned by heat. **toast** *(v)*.
2 *(v)* to drink in honor of someone. *Let's toast the bride and bridegroom.* **toast** *(n)*.

Some words that begin with a "ti" sound are spelled "ty."

oboggan
obogganing tobogganed
(n) a long flat sled.
(v) to travel by toboggan,
specially downhill.

oday
(n) on this day. *I'm going out today.*
(n) nowadays, or at the present
me. *Today, most adults in the*
estern world can read and write.

toga

toddler *(n)* a young child who has just learned to walk.

toe *(n)* one of the five digits at the end of your foot.

toffee *(n)*
a hard, chewy candy made from boiled sugar and butter.

toga *(n)* a piece of clothing worn by ancient Romans. It was wrapped around the body and over the left shoulder.

ogether *(adv)* with another person
thing. *The boys arrived together.*

oil toiling toiled *(v)* to work very
ard and continuously. **toil** *(n)*.

oilet
(n) a large bowl with flushing water,
sed for disposing of urine and feces.
(n) a room containing
toilet; a bathroom.

oken
(n) a small, physical object used to
epresent something larger or to show
omeone's feelings. *Rod gave Sue*
ring as a token of his love.
(n) a piece of stamped metal
hat can be used in place of money.

olerate tolerating tolerated *(v)*
you **tolerate** something, you put
p with it or endure it. *It is difficult to*
olerate rude people. **tolerant** *(adj)*.

oll tolling tolled
(v) to ring a bell, usually
a slow, solemn way.
(n) a charge for using
private road or bridge.
If something **takes its toll**, it
esults in serious damage or suffering.
ears of hard labor have taken their
oll on Jed's health.

omahawk *(n)*
war ax used by North American
ndians. *This*
ecorated
omahawk
vas used by the
hawnee people.

tomahawk

tomato tomatoes *(n)* a sweet red fruit often eaten in salads.

tomb *(n)* a grave, usually for an important person. *The picture shows the tomb of Robert Curthose, Duke of Normandy.*

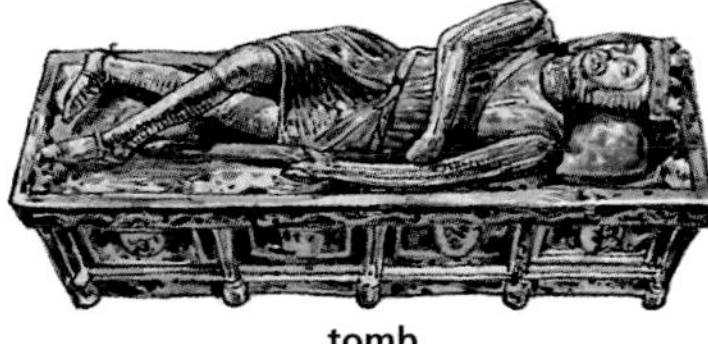
tomb

tomboy *(n)*
a girl who enjoys activities usually associated with boys, such as climbing trees or playing baseball.

tombstone *(n)*
a carved block of stone that marks the place where someone is buried.

tonic
1 *(n)* something that makes you feel stronger or refreshed. *Our vacation was a real tonic.*
2 *(n)* a slightly bitter-tasting mineral water.

tonight *(n)*
this evening or night.

tonsillitis *(n)* a disease that makes your tonsils infected and painful.

tonsils *(plural n)*
two flaps of soft tissue in your throat at the back of your mouth.

too
1 *(adv)* as well or in addition. *Is Janey coming too?*
2 *(adv)* very, extremely, or more than enough. *The heavy metal band was too noisy for Grandma.*

tool *(n)* a piece of equipment that you use to do a particular job.

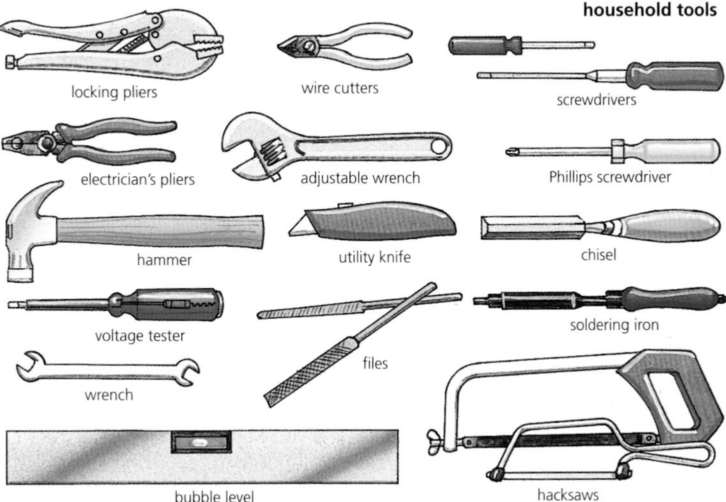

household tools

tomorrow *(n)* the day after today.

tone
1 *(n)* the way that something sounds.
2 *(n)* the general atmosphere of a place or situation. *The tone of our conversation was cheerful.*
3 *(n)* In music, a **tone** is an interval between two notes that is equal to two semitones.
4 *(n)* a shade of a color. *A pink tone.*

tongs *(plural n)*
a tool with two connected arms, used for picking up things.

tongue *(tung)*
1 *(n)* a flap of muscle in your mouth, used for tasting, eating, and talking.
2 *(n)* a language. *Native tongue.*

tongue twister *(n)* a sentence or verse that is very hard to say fast, for example, "Red leather, yellow leather."

tooth teeth
1 *(n)* one of the white, bonelike structures in your mouth, used for biting and chewing food. *Also see* **teeth**.
2 *(n)* one of a row of sticking out parts on a saw, comb, cogwheel, etc. *See* **gear**.

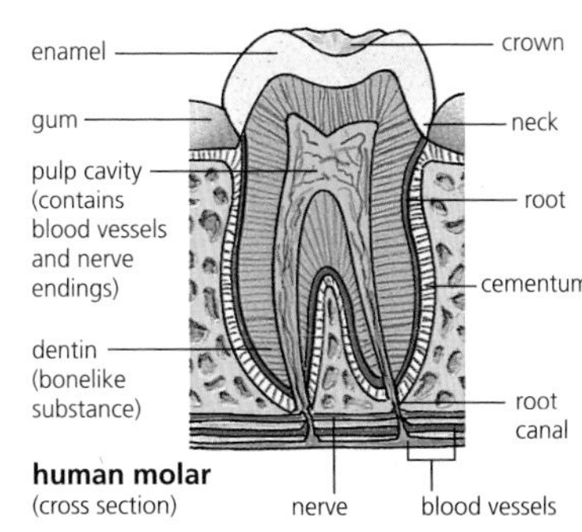

human molar
(cross section)

top topping topped
1 *(n)* the highest point of something.
2 *(adj)* very good or best. *A top singer.*
3 *(n)* a covering or a lid. *A bottle top.*
4 *(n)* a piece of clothing for the upper part of your body.
5 *(v)* to be the best or to lead. *Fred topped the class in spelling.*

top-heavy *(adj)*
If something is **top-heavy**, it is heavier toward the top, and therefore likely to fall over.

topic *(n)* the subject of a discussion, study, lesson, speech etc.

topical *(adj)* relevant now or in the news at present.

topple toppling toppled *(v)*
to fall over, usually from a height.

Torah *(n)* the sacred scroll in a Jewish synagogue on which is written, in Hebrew, the books of Genesis, Exodus, Leviticus, Numbers, and Deuteronomy.

torch torches *(n)* a piece of wood dipped in wax or fat used to provide light for buildings in medieval times.

toreador *(tor-ee-a-dor) (n)*
a bullfighter mounted on a horse.

torment tormenting tormented
1 *(tor-**ment**) (v)* to upset or annoy someone deliberately.
2 *(**tor**-ment) (n)* great pain.

tornado tornados *or* tornadoes *(n)*
a windstorm that swirls in a circle.

torpedo torpedoes *(n)*
an underwater missile that explodes when it hits something.

torrent *(n)* a large mass of flowing or falling water. **torrential** *(adj)*.

torso *(n)* the part of your body between your neck and your waist.

tortilla *(n)*
a round flat bread made from corn or wheat meal. Tortillas are often served with a topping or a filling.

tortoise *(n)*
a slow-moving reptile with a shell and thick, scaly skin. *The giant tortoise in the picture is allowing finches to crawl over its body in search of parasites.*

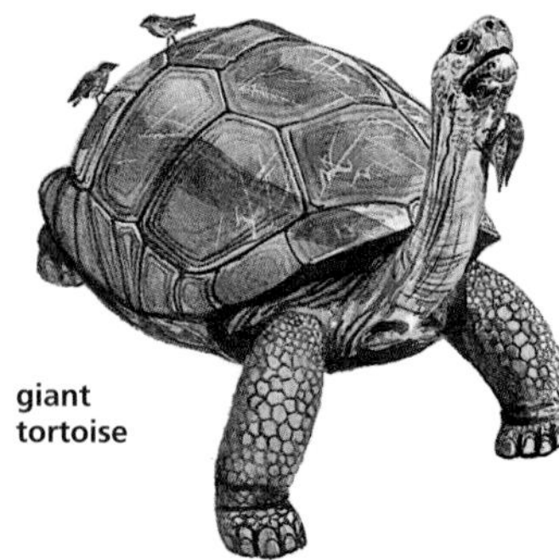
giant tortoise

torture
torturing tortured *(v)*
to cause someone extreme pain. **torture** *(n)*.

toss
tosses tossing tossed
1 *(v)* to throw something around or upward.
2 *(v)* to throw something away casually.

total
1 *(n)* the result of an addition or multiplication calculation. *Add these figures and give me the total.* **total** *(v)*.
2 *(adj)* complete and utter. *The party was a total surprise.*
totally *(adv)*.

totem pole *(n)* a carved pole that acts as a sacred emblem for a tribe or family of North American Indians. *The painted totem pole shown here is in Stanley Park, Vancouver, Canada.*

totem pole

totter
tottering tottered *(v)*
to sway and stagger.

toucan *(too-kan) (n)*
a brightly colored tropical bird that has a huge beak.

toucan

touch touches touching touched
1 *(v)* to make contact with something using your hands or other areas of your body.
2 *(v)* to make gentle contact with another object. *The ship touched the quay as it docked.*
3 Your **sense of touch** is your ability to feel things with your fingers or with other parts of your body.
4 If you **keep in touch** with someone, you contact them regularly by telephone, email, etc.

touchdown
1 *(n)* in football, a play in which the ball is carried over the opponent's goal line, scoring six points.
2 *(n)* the moment when an aircraft or a spacecraft lands.

touching *(adj)*
Something that is **touching** appeals to your emotions. **touchingly** *(adv)*.

touchy touchier touchiest *(adj)*
irritable and easily annoyed. **touchiness** *(n)*.

tough *(tuff)* tougher toughest
1 *(adj)* strong and difficult to damage, either physically or mentally. *Tough boots. A tough personality.*
2 *(adj)* difficult. *A tough decision.*

toupee *(too-**pay**) (n)*
a piece of false hair, usually used to disguise a man's baldness.

tour
1 *(n)* a journey around a set route, often for sightseeing. **tour** *(v)*.
2 When a band or team go **on tour**, they go to different places to play.

tourist *(n)* someone who travels and visits places for pleasure. **tourism** *(n)*.

tournament
1 *(n)* a competition for players of sports, chess, cards, etc. *A tennis tournament.*
2 *(n)* In the Middle Ages, **tournaments** were events where knights jousted against each other. *See* **joust**.

tourniquet *(turn-uh-kit) (n)*
a very tight bandage or band put around a wounded limb to stop the flow of blood.

tow towing towed *(v)*
to pull something behind you, usually with a rope, chain, etc. **tow** *(n)*.

toward *or* **towards** *(prep)*
in the direction of. *Oscar marched toward the door.*

towel *(n)* a thick, soft, absorbent cloth for drying yourself.

tower
towering towered
1 *(n)* a tall structure that is thin in relation to its height. *The picture shows the Leaning Tower of Pisa in Italy.*
2 *(v)* to be very tall and dominant. *The skyscraper towered over the houses.*

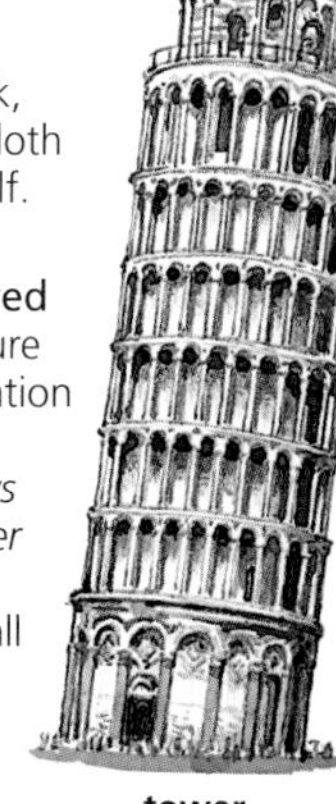
tower

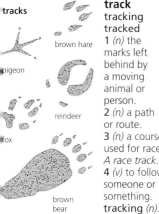

town *(n)*
a place with houses, stores, offices, schools, etc. where many people live.

towpath *(n)*
a path beside a canal or river.

toxic *(adj)* poisonous. **toxin** *(n)*.

toy toying toyed
1 *(n)* an object that children play with.
2 *(v)* If you **toy with** something, you play with it in a halfhearted, unenthusiastic way.

trace tracing traced
1 *(v)* to find out where something or someone is.
2 *(v)* to draw over the outline of a shape. **tracing** *(n)*.
3 *(n)* a visible sign that something has happened or that someone has been somewhere. *Traces of blood.*

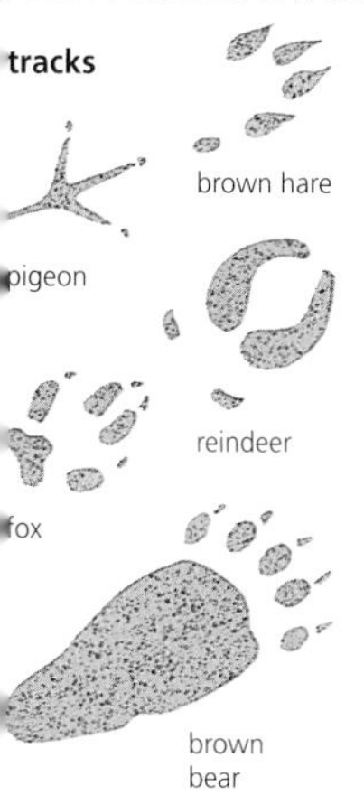

track tracking tracked
1 *(n)* the marks left behind by a moving animal or person.
2 *(n)* a path or route.
3 *(n)* a course used for races. *A race track.*
4 *(v)* to follow someone or something. **tracking** *(n)*.

track and field *(n)*
competitive athletic sports that involve running, jumping, or throwing. *The picture shows the standard layout of a stadium used for track and field.* **track-and-field** *(adj)*.

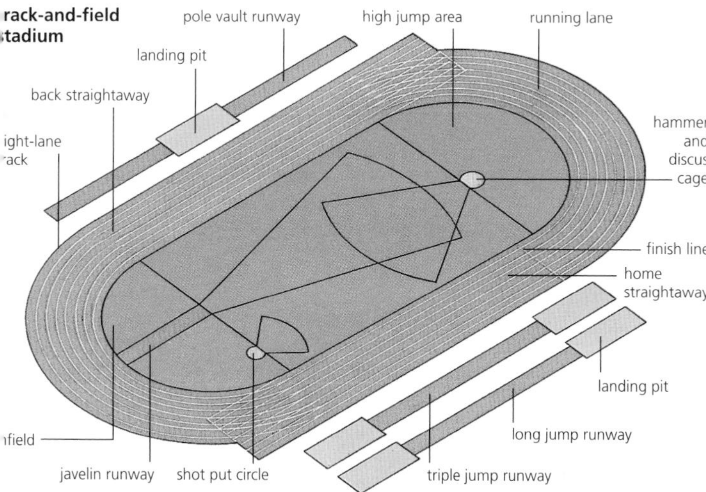

traction *(n)* the friction or gripping power that stops something from slipping on a surface as it moves.

tractor
1 *(n)* a powerful vehicle used on farms. Tractors are often used to pull farm machinery or heavy loads. *Also see* **farm**.
2 *(n)* a truck that has a cab and no body, used for pulling a trailer.

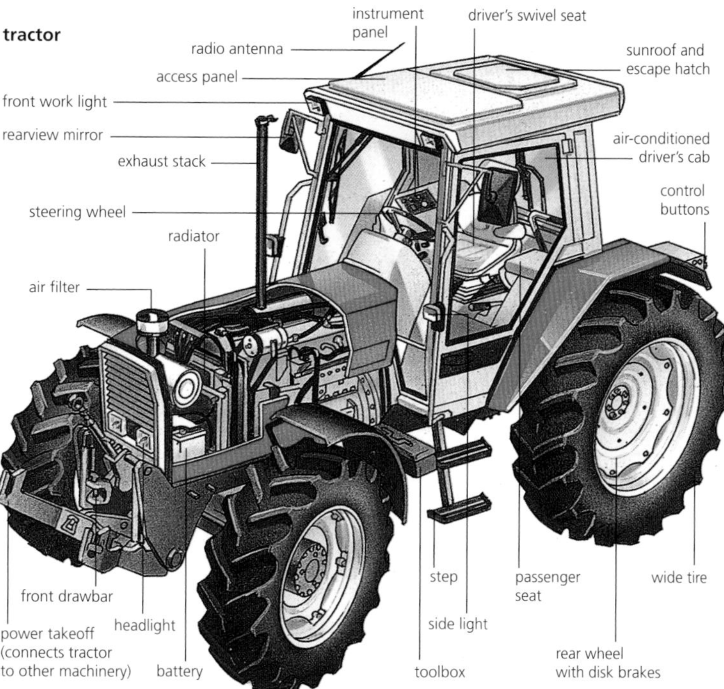

trade trading traded
1 *(n)* the business of buying and selling things; commerce. **trader** *(n)*, **trade** *(v)*.
2 *(n)* a particular job or craft, especially one that requires working with the hands or with a machine. *Bob is a decorator by trade.*
3 *(v)* to exchange one thing for another. *We've started a club to trade computer games.*

trademark *(n)* a name, sign, or design that shows that a product is made by a particular company.

tradition *(n)* a custom that has been passed down from generation to generation. **traditional** *(adj)*.

traffic trafficking trafficked
1 *(n)* moving vehicles. *Heavy traffic.*
2 *(v)* to buy and sell goods illegally. **trafficking** *(n)*.

traffic jam *(n)* a line of vehicles that can hardly move because there are so many cars on the road.

traffic lights *(plural n)* a set of lights that controls traffic on roads.

tragedy tragedies
1 *(n)* a serious play with a sad ending.
2 *(n)* a very sad event.

tragic *(adj)* having to do with, or in the style of, a tragedy.

trail trailing trailed
1 *(n)* a track or path for people to follow.
2 *(v)* to follow someone or something to check up on them or catch them.
3 *(v)* to follow slowly behind others.

a b c d e f g h i j k l m n o p q r s t u v w x y z

trailer
1 *(n)* a vehicle that is towed by a car or truck and used to carry things.
2 *(n)* a mobile home.
3 *(n)* a short piece of film used to advertise a movie or program to be shown in the future.

train **training** **trained**
1 *(n)* a string of railroad cars pulled by an engine. *The train shown below is a French TGV Atlantic, which is powered by electricity from overhead wires.*
2 *(v)* to learn how to do something, such as a job. **training** *(n).*
3 *(v)* to teach a person or animal how to do something.
4 *(v)* to practice and prepare for a sports event. **training** *(n).*
5 *(n)* the long piece of fabric that trails behind a bride's dress.

trampoline *(n)* a piece of thick, stretchy fabric attached to a frame by elastic rope or springs. Trampolines are used for jumping, either for sport or for pleasure. **trampolining** *(n).*

trance *(n)*
If you are **in a trance**, you are conscious but not really aware of what is happening around you.

tranquil *(tran-kwil) (adj)*
calm and peaceful. **tranquility** *(n).*

transaction *(n)*
a business deal. **transact** *(v).*

transatlantic
1 *(adj)* crossing the Atlantic Ocean. *A transatlantic telephone call.*
2 *(adj)* on or from the other side of the Atlantic. *A transatlantic fashion.*

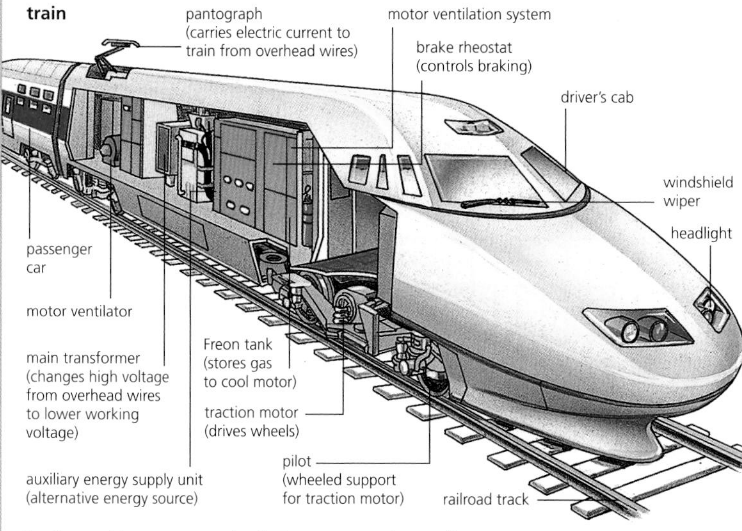

trainer *(n)* someone who helps a person or an animal become good enough to compete in a sport or competition.

traitor *(n)*
someone who betrays their country or friends by working for an enemy.

tram *(n)* a large vehicle that carries passengers. Trams run on rails laid in roads and are usually powered by electricity from overhead wires.

tramp **tramping** **tramped**
1 *(v)* to go for a long walk. *We tramped over the hills.* **tramp** *(n).*
2 *(v)* to walk or tread with heavy steps. **tramp** *(n).*
3 *(n)* someone who does not have a permanent home.

trample **trampling** **trampled** *(v)*
to damage something by walking all over it.

transfer
transferring **transferred**
1 *(trans-**fur**) (v)* to move a person or thing from one place to another. *I transferred the ball to my right hand.* **transfer** *(**trans**-fur) (n).*
2 *(**trans**-fur) (n)* a printed ticket that permits you to change from one vehicle or route to another without paying more money.

transform **transforming** **transformed** *(v)* to make a great change in something. *Meeting Alphonso has transformed my life.* **transformation** *(n).*

transformer *(n)*
a piece of equipment that changes the voltage of an electric current.

transfusion *(n)* the injection of blood from another person into the body of someone who is injured or ill.

transient *(adj)* lasting for a short time only. **transience** *(n).*

transistor *(n)*
a small electrical component that controls the flow of a current.

transit
1 *(n)* a public transportation system.
2 *(n)* If goods are **in transit**, they are being moved from one place to another.

transition *(n)* a change from one situation to another.

transitive *(adj)* A **transitive** verb usually needs a direct object to make sense. *The verbs "to hit," "to pull," and "to cut" are all transitive.*

translate
translating **translated** *(v)* to put something into another language. **translation** *(n),* **translator** *(n).*

translucent *(adj)*
A **translucent** substance is not clear, like glass, but nevertheless will let light through. *Frosted glass is translucent.* **translucency** *(n).*

transmit **transmitting** **transmitted**
1 *(v)* to send something from one place or person to another. **transmission** *(n).*
2 *(v)* to send out radio or television signals. *The program will be transmitted next Friday.* **transmission** *(n),* **transmitter** *(n).*

transparency *(n)*
operating in a way that makes it easy for others to see and understand what is being done, especially in business, finance and government.

transparent
1 *(adj)* A **transparent** substance is clear, like glass, and lets light through.
2 *(adj)* obvious or clear. *The woman was a transparent liar.* **transparency** *(n).*

transpiration *(n)* the process by which plants lose moisture into the atmosphere. **transpire** *(v).*

transplant
transplanting **transplanted**
1 *(trans-**plant**) (v)* to remove something, such as a plant, and put it somewhere else.
2 *(**trans**-plant) (n)* a surgical operation in which a diseased organ, such as a kidney, is replaced by a healthy one.

transport **transporting** **transported** *(trans-**port**)* *(v)* to move people and goods from one place to another.

transportation *(n)*
all types of vehicles that carry people or goods.

trap trapping trapped *(v)*
to capture a person or an animal by using some sort of trick or bait. **trap** *(n)*.

trap door *(n)*
a horizontal door in a floor or ceiling.

trapeze *(trap-**eez**) (n)*
a bar hanging from two ropes, used by circus performers and gymnasts.

trapezoid *(n)*
a four-sided shape with one pair of opposite parallel sides. *See* **shape**.

trash *(singular n)* things that you have thrown away because they are not useful or valuable.

traumatic *(adj)* If something is **traumatic**, it is shocking and very upsetting. **trauma** *(n)*.

travel traveling traveled *(v)*
to go from one place to another. **travel** *(n)*.

travel agent *(n)*
a person or company that organizes travel and vacations for its customers. **travel agency** *(n)*.

traveler *(n)*
someone who is traveling or who travels regularly.

trawler *(n)*
a fishing boat that drags a large bag-shaped net through the water. **trawl** *(v)*.

tray *(n)* a flat board used for carrying food and drinks.

treacherous *(**tretch**-er-uss) (adj)*
dangerous or not to be trusted. *A treacherous path.* **treacherously** *(adv)*.

tread
treading trod trodden
1 *(v)* to put your foot down on the ground. *I have trodden in some mud.*
2 *(n)* the ridges on a tire or on the sole of a shoe that help to prevent slipping.

treason *(n)* the crime of betraying your country, for example by spying for another country.

treasure treasuring treasured
1 *(n)* very precious and valuable objects, such as gold and jewels.
2 *(v)* to love and value very highly something that you have or own. *I treasure my independence.* **treasure** *(n)*, **treasured** *(adj)*.

treasurer *(n)*
the person who looks after the money for an organization, club, etc.

treasury treasuries
1 *(n)* a place where treasure is stored. *See* **temple**.
2 *(n)* the funds of an organization, government, etc.

treat treating treated
1 *(v)* to deal with people or things in a certain way. *In China, old people are treated with great respect.* **treatment** *(n)*.
2 *(v)* Doctors **treat** people to try to cure them of illness. **treatment** *(n)*.
3 *(v)* to process something in order to change it in some way. *Sewage is treated with chemicals to make it harmless.* **treatment** *(n)*.
4 *(v)* to give someone a special gift or take someone somewhere special. *Uncle Jerry treated us to a movie.* **treat** *(n)*.

treaty treaties *(n)*
a formal agreement between two or more countries.

treble
1 *(adj)* three times as big, or three times as many.
2 *(n)* a boy's singing voice that is very high. **treble** *(adj)*.
3 *(v)* to increase to three times the original amount. *His income trebled over the course of two years.*

tree treeing treed
1 *(n)* a large woody plant with a trunk, roots, branches, and leaves. *See* **trunk**.
2 *(v)* to chase up a tree. *The dog treed a cat.*

trek trekking trekked *(v)*
to walk a long way, often in difficult conditions. **trek** *(n)*.

trellis trellises *(n)* a crisscross framework of thin strips of wood, used to support growing plants.

tremble trembling trembled *(v)*
to shake, especially from fear or excitement.

tremendous
1 *(adj)* huge or enormous. *A tremendous explosion.* **tremendously** *(adv)*.
2 *(adj)* very good or excellent. *We had a tremendous time surfing.* **tremendously** *(adv)*.

tremor *(n)* a shaking movement. *Earth tremors are very common in the earthquake belt.*

trench trenches *(n)* a long thin channel dug in the ground.

trend
1 *(n)* the general direction in which things are changing. *Recently, there has been a trend toward smaller families.*
2 *(n)* the latest fashion. *The trend this season is for shorter skirts.* **trendy** *(adj)*.

trespass
trespasses trespassing trespassed
1 *(v)* to enter someone's private property without permission. **trespasser** *(n)*.
2 *(n) (old-fashioned)* a sin.

tress tresses *(n)* a lock of long hair.

trial
1 *(n)* a test. *A trial of strength.*
2 *(n)* the examination of someone who appears in court accused of a criminal offense.

triangle
1 *(n)* a three-sided shape. **triangular** *(adj)*. *See* **shape**.
2 *(n)* a triangular percussion instrument. You play the triangle by striking it with a metal rod. *See* **percussion**.

tribe *(n)* a group of people who share the same ancestors, customs, and laws. **tribal** *(n)*.

tribunal *(n)* a law court.

tributary tributaries *(n)*
a stream or river that flows into a larger stream or river. *See* **river**.

tribute *(n)*
If you **pay tribute to** someone or something, you praise them.

trick tricking tricked
1 *(v)* If you **trick** someone, you make them believe something that is not true. *Kevin tricked me into believing that he was related to the Kennedys.* **trick** *(n)*.
2 *(n)* a clever and entertaining act. *A magic trick.*

trickle trickling trickled *(v)*
to flow very slowly in small quantities. *Water trickled constantly from the faucet.* **trickle** *(n)*.

tricky trickier trickiest *(adj)*
difficult or awkward. *A tricky situation.*

tricycle *(n)* a three-wheeled vehicle, usually powered by pedals.

trifle
1 *(n)* something that is not very important. **trifling** *(adj)*.
2 *(n)* a small amount; a bit.

trigger triggering triggered
1 *(n)* the lever on a gun that you pull to fire it.
2 *(v)* to cause something to happen, as a reaction. *The man's arrest triggered riots in the streets.*

trim trimming trimmed;
trimmer trimmest
1 *(v)* to cut small pieces off something to improve its shape. *Now that winter is over, we need to trim the hedges.* **trim** *(n)*.
2 *(adj)* slim and shapely.

trimming
1 *(n)* something used as a decoration.
2 **trimmings** *(plural n)* the things that go with something. *Roast turkey and all the trimmings.*

trio
1 *(n)* a group of three things or people.
2 *(n)* a piece of music that is played or sung by three people.

trip tripping tripped
1 *(v)* to stumble or to fall over.
2 *(n)* a journey, or a visit. *A trip to the zoo.* **tripper** *(n)*.

triple
tripling tripled
1 *(v)* to make something three times as big or three times as many. **triple** *(adj)*.
2 *(adj)* made up of three parts. *The triple jump involves a hop, a step, and a jump.*

triplet *(n)* one of three children born to the same mother at almost the same time.

tripod *(n)* a three-legged stand used to support a camera or other piece of equipment. *See* **apparatus**.

trireme *(try-reem) (n)* an ancient Greek warship propelled by oars.

triumph *(n)* a victory or a great achievement. **triumph** *(v)*, **triumphant** *(adj)*.

trivial *(adj)* If something is **trivial**, it is not very important. *Don't bother me with such trivial questions.* **trivia** *(plural n)*, **trivialize** *(v)*.

trolley *(n)* an electric streetcar that runs on tracks and gets its power from an overhead wire.

troop trooping trooped
1 *(n)* an organized group of soldiers, scouts, etc.
2 *(v)* to move in a group. *Sam and his friends trooped back to the house.*

trophy *(troh-fee)* **trophies** *(n)* a prize or award, such as a cup or plaque.

tropical *(adj)* having to do with, or living in, the hot, rainy area of the tropics.

tropical fish tropical fish *(n)* fish that originally come from the tropics. Tropical fish are often kept as pets in aquariums.

tropics *(plural n)* the extremely hot area of the Earth near the equator.

tropical fish
freshwater
saltwater

spotted grouper
French angelfish
long-nosed filefish
common clownfish
yellow long-nose butterflyfish
swordtail
Siamese fighting fish
neon tetra
multi-spotted catfish

trot trotting trotted *(v)* When a horse **trots**, it moves briskly at a pace between a walk and a canter. **trot** *(n)*.

trouble troubling troubled
1 *(n)* a difficult or dangerous situation. **troublesome** *(adj)*.
2 *(v)* to disturb or worry someone. *The letter troubled Millie.*
3 *(n)* a cause of difficulty, worry, or annoyance. *The trouble with James is that he is too serious.*
4 If you **take the trouble** to do something, you make an effort to do it.
5 *(v)* to ask someone for help or to make an extra effort.

trough *(troff) (n)* a long, narrow container from which animals can drink or feed.

trout trout *(n)* an edible freshwater fish.

trowel
1 *(n)* a tool with a small, curved blade used for planting and other light garden work.
2 *(n)* a tool with a flat, diamond-shaped blade used for laying cement, filling holes in plaster, etc.

truant *(n)* a student who stays away from school without permission. **truancy** *(n)*.

truce *(n)* a temporary agreement to stop fighting.

truck *(n)* a large motor vehicle used for carrying goods by road. *The picture shows a semitrailer, which is made up of a cab and a trailer, linked by a flexible joint.*

semitrailer truck

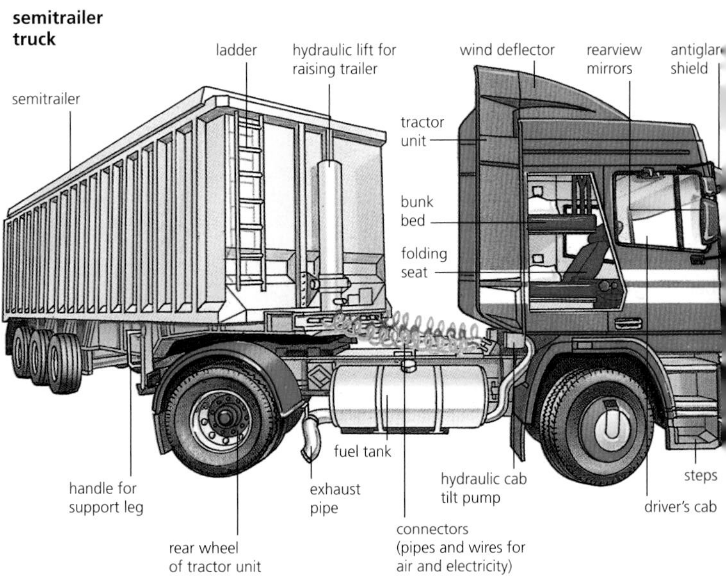

trudge trudging trudged *(v)*
to walk slowly and heavily.
We trudged through the mud.

true truer truest
1 *(adj)* accurate or correct. **truly** *(adv).*
2 *(adj)* loyal or faithful.
He was a true friend.
3 *(adj)* real or genuine.
Sarah felt she had found true love.

trumpet
1 *(n)* a brass wind instrument that makes a loud, blaring sound. *See* **brass, orchestra**.
2 *(n)* a loud blaring sound, such as the noise an elephant makes.

trunk
1 *(n)* the main stem of a tree. Tree trunks contain xylem and phloem vessels that transport fluids up and down the tree.
In the section of a tree trunk below, you can see the rings of xylem, or sapwood, that are created each year.
2 *(n)* a large case or box used for storage or for carrying clothes on a long journey.
3 *(n)* the upper part of your body, not including your head and arms.
4 *(n)* the long nose of an elephant.

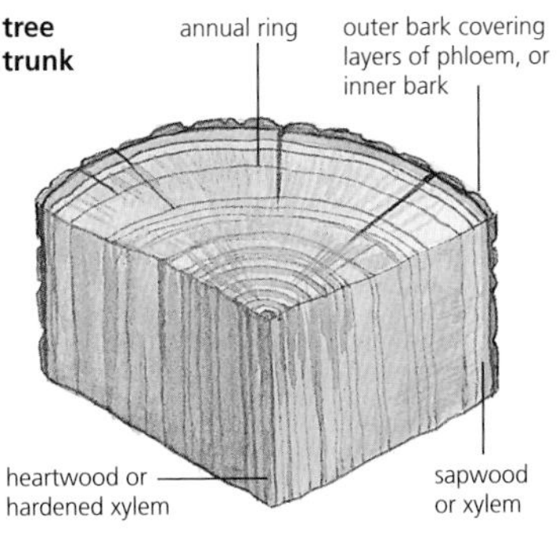

5 *(n)* the place, usually at the back of a car, where luggage can be carried.
6 **trunks** *(plural n)*
close-fitting shorts worn by men or boys for swimming.

trust trusting trusted *(v)*
If you **trust** someone, you believe that they are honest and reliable. **trust** *(n).*

trustworthy *(adj)*
honest, reliable, and able to be trusted. **trustworthiness** *(n).*

truth *(n)* the real facts.
truthful *(adj),* **truthfully** *(adv).*

try tries trying tried
1 *(v)* to attempt to do something or to do the best you can. **try** *(n).*
2 *(v)* to examine someone accused of a criminal offense in a court of law.

trying *(adj)* If a person is **trying**, they make you feel annoyed and impatient.

tryout *(n)*
a test or trial to see if a person is qualified to do something, such as perform in a play or play on a team.

tsar *see* **czar**.

T-shirt, t-shirt *or* **tee shirt** *(n)*
a light cotton top, usually with short sleeves and a round neck.

tsunami *(n)* a very large, destructive wave caused by an underwater volcano or earthquake.

tub
1 *(n)* a plastic container used for storing foods. *A tub of ice cream.*
2 *(n)* a large wide container used for bathing in or for washing clothes.

tuba *(n)* a large brass wind instrument. *See* **brass, orchestra.**

tube *(n)* a long hollow cylinder.
The poster came rolled in a tube.

tubular *(adj)* shaped like a tube.

tuck tucking tucked
1 *(v)* to fold or push something into a restricted space.
Tuck the sheets in well.
2 *(n)* a small fold sewn in material.

tuft *(n)* an upright bunch of hair, grass, feathers, etc. **tufted** *(adj).*

tug tugging tugged
1 *(v)* to pull hard. **tug** *(n).*
2 **tug** *or* **tugboat** *(n)* a small powerful boat that tows large ships.
3 **tug-of-war** *(n)*
a contest between two teams, each at one end of a rope, who try to pull each other over a center line.

tuition *(too-ish-un) (n)*
the money a student has to pay to attend school, a private high school or university.

tulip *(n)* a plant with a tall stem and a colorful flower shaped like a cup.

tumble tumbling tumbled
1 *(v)* to fall, often with a rolling motion.
2 *(v)* to do somersaults, handsprings, and other athletic feats.
3 **tumble dryer** *(n)*
a machine that dries clothes by tossing them around in hot air.

tumbler *(n)*
a tall glass with straight sides.

tummy tummies *(n) (informal)*
your stomach.

tumor *(n)* a swelling or lump caused by the abnormal growth of a mass of new cells.

tumult *(n)* loud noise and confusion.
There was a tumult when the fire bell rang. **tumultuous** *(adj).*

tuna tuna *or* tunas *(n)*
a large edible sea fish.

tundra *(n)* the cold areas of northern Europe and Asia where there are no trees and the soil under the surface is permanently frozen.

tune tuning tuned
1 *(n)* a series of musical notes, arranged in a pattern. **tuneful** *(adj).*
2 *(v)* to adjust a radio, the pitch of a musical instrument, etc.
3 **in tune** producing the right notes.
Can you sing in tune?

tunic *(n)* a loose sleeveless garment.

tuning fork *(n)*
a piece of metal with two prongs, used for tuning musical instruments.

tunnel *(n)* an underground passage.
The picture below shows cutaway sections of the Channel Tunnel, that runs under the seabed between England and France. **tunnel** *(v).*

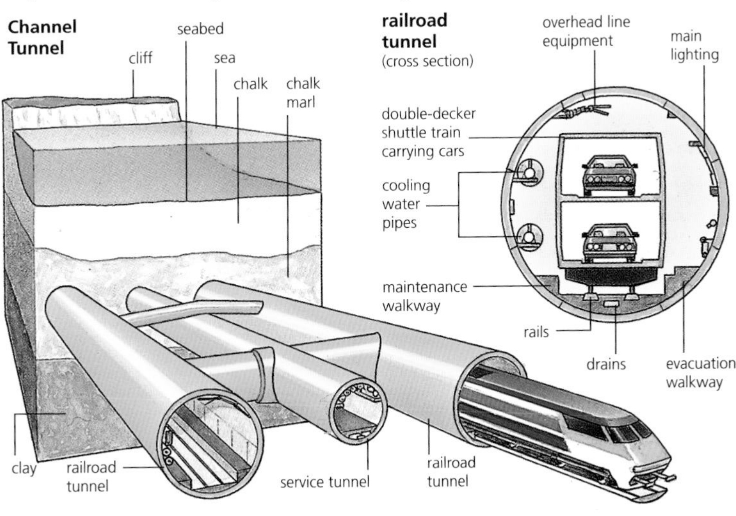

turban *(n)* a headdress made from a long cloth wound around the head. Some Muslims, Hindus, and Sikhs wear turbans.

turbine *(n)* an engine driven by water, steam, or gas that passes through the blades of a wheel and makes it revolve. *See* **jet engine**.

turbo *(adj)* A **turbo** or **turbocharged** engine has high-pressure air forced into its cylinders by a turbine to produce extra power.

turbofan *(n)* a type of aircraft engine in which a large fan, driven by a turbine, pushes air into the hot exhaust at the rear of the engine, giving extra power. *See* **jet engine**.

turbulent *(adj)* wild, confused, or unpredictable. *Turbulent waters.*

turf *(n)* the surface layer of grass and earth on a lawn or athletics field.

turkey
1 *(n)* a large flightless bird, usually reared for its meat. *The picture shows a North American wild turkey.*
2 *(n) (slang)* a hopeless or useless person or thing.

wild turkey

turmoil *(n)* violent confusion. *The class was in turmoil.*

turn turning turned
1 *(v)* to change direction. *Turn left at the junction.* **turn** *(n)*.
2 *(v)* to spin or to revolve. *Turn the wheel.*
3 *(v)* to change appearance or state. *The liquid turns into a vapor when heated.*
4 *(v)* to move a switch, faucet, etc. to control the supply of something. *Turn down the volume.*
5 *(n)* If it is your **turn** to do something, it is your chance or duty to do it.
6 *(n)* A **good turn** is a helpful action.
7 **turn down** *(v)* If you **turn something down**, you refuse it.
8 *(v)* If someone **turns up**, they appear.
9 **turn on** *(v) (slang)* If something **turns you on**, it makes you enthusiastic and excited. **turn-on** *(n)*.

turnip *(n)*
a round white root vegetable.

turnstile *(n)*
a revolving gate that turns in only one direction, and controls admission to a stadium, theme park, etc.

turntable *(n)*
a circular, revolving surface. Turntables of different sizes can be used for playing records or turning engines.

turpentine *(n)*
a mixture of tree resin and oil, used in paint and medicines.

turquoise *(tur-kwoyz)*
1 *(n)* a blue-green semiprecious stone. *See* **mineral**.
2 *(n)* a blue-green color.
turquoise *(adj)*.

turtle *(n)*
a water reptile with flippers and a large shell. *The shell of the mata mata turtle looks like a dead leaf.*

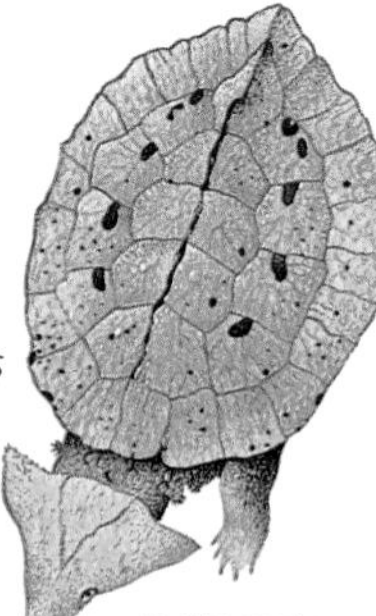
mata mata turtle

tusk *(n)*
one of the pair of long, curved, pointed teeth of an elephant, walrus, etc.

tussle tussling tussled *(v)* to fight or wrestle vigorously. **tussle** *(n)*.

tutor *(n)* a teacher, usually one who teaches people individually or in small groups. **tutorial** *(n)*.

tutu *(n)* a short ballet skirt made of several stiff layers of net.

tuxedo *(n)* a man's dinner jacket with silk lapels, worn with a bow tie for formal occasions. Tuxedo is often shortened to tux.

TV *(n) short for* **television**.

tweezers *(plural n)* small pincers used for pulling out hairs or for picking up very small objects.

twice *(adv)* two times.

twig *(n)*
a small, thin branch.

twilight *(n)*
the time of day when the Sun has just set and it is beginning to get dark.

twin
1 *(n)* one of two children born to the same mother at almost the same time.
2 *(n)* one of a matching pair.

twine
1 *(n)* a very strong string made of two or more strands twisted together.
2 *(v)* to wind or grow in a coil.

twinge *(twinj) (n)*
a sudden pain or unpleasant feeling. *A twinge of regret.*

twinkle twinkling twinkled *(v)* to shine and sparkle. *The stars twinkle in the sky.* **twinkle** *(n)*.

twirl twirling twirled *(v)* to turn or spin around and around. **twirl** *(n)*.

twist twisting twisted
1 *(v)* to turn or to bend. *Andrew twisted the top off the jar.*
2 *(v)* to wind two strands of something together.

twitch
twitches twitching twitched *(v)* to make small, jerky movements. **twitch** *(n)*, **twitchy** *(adj)*.

type typing typed
1 *(n)* a kind or a sort. *What type of car do you have?*
2 *(v)* to write something using a keyboard.
3 *(n)* printed letters and numbers. *This picture shows two kinds of type. Serif has a small line, or serif, at the end of each letter's main strokes. Sans serif has no serifs.*

typewriter *(n)*
a machine that people used to use to print letters and numbers by pressing its keys with their fingers.

typhoid *(ty-foyd) (n)*
a serious infectious disease that causes fever, diarrhea, and sometimes death. It is caused by germs in food or water.

typhoon *(ty-foon) (n)*
a violent tropical storm.

typical
1 *(adj)* Something that is **typical** has the usual features that you associate with that kind of thing. *A typical English village.*
typically *(adv)*.
2 *(adj)* If someone does something that is **typical**, they behave in their usual way. *It's typical of Toby to forget my birthday!* **typically** *(adv)*.

tyrannosaur *(n)*
a huge dinosaur that walked upright on two legs and fed on meat.

tyrant *(n)* someone who rules other people in a cruel and unkind way. **tyranny** *(n)*, **tyrannical** *(adj)*.

U u

udder *(n)* the bag-like part of a cow, sheep, etc. that hangs down near its back legs and produces milk.

UFO *(n)* a strange object seen flying in the sky, which is believed by some people to be a spaceship from another planet. UFO is short for Unidentified Flying Object.

ugly **uglier ugliest**
1 *(adj)* If something or someone is **ugly**, they are unattractive and unpleasant to look at.
2 *(adj)* dangerous and violent. *There were ugly scenes as police and demonstrators clashed.*

ulcer *(ul-ser) (n)*
a sore area, either on your skin or inside your mouth or stomach.

ultimate
1 *(adj)* last or final. **ultimately** *(adv).*
2 *(adj)* original or basic. *The Sun is the ultimate source of almost all our energy.* **ultimately** *(adv).*
3 *(n)* the greatest, or the best. *This car is the ultimate in luxury.*

ultimatum *(n)* a final warning.

ultrasound *(n)* sound that is of too high a frequency for the human ear to hear it. **Ultrasound waves** are used in medical scans.

ultraviolet light *(n)*
light that cannot be seen by the human eye, which is given off by the Sun and causes your skin to tan.

umbilical cord *(n)*
the tube that connects an unborn baby to its mother's body and through which it gets oxygen and food. *See* **pregnant**.

umbrella *(n)*
a frame with a circular cloth stretched over it that you hold over your head to protect you from the rain.

umpire *(n)* someone who makes sure that a baseball or tennis match is played according to the rules.

unable *(adj)* If you are **unable** to do something, you cannot do it.

unacceptable *(adj)* If something is **unacceptable**, it is not good enough to be allowed or accepted.

unaccustomed *(adj)*
If you are **unaccustomed** to something, you are not used to it.

unadulterated *(adj)*
If a substance is **unadulterated**, it has not had anything extra added to it.

unaided *(adj)*
If you do something **unaided**, you do it on your own without any help.

unanimous *(yoo-nan-im-uss) (adj)* agreed on by everyone. *A unanimous decision.* **unanimously** *(adv).*

unapproachable *(adj)* Someone who is **unapproachable** is not friendly, or is not easy to get to know.

unarmed *(adj)*
Someone who is **unarmed** is not carrying any weapons.

unauthorized *(adj)*
If something is **unauthorized**, it is done without official permission.

unavoidable *(adj)* If something is **unavoidable**, it is impossible to prevent. **unavoidably** *(adv).*

unaware *(adj)* If you are **unaware** of something, you do not know that it exists or is happening.

unbalanced
1 *(adj)* Something that is **unbalanced** cannot balance and falls over.
2 *(adj)* Someone who is **unbalanced** has mental health problems.
3 *(adj)* A piece of writing or a speech that is **unbalanced** puts forward only one side of an argument.

unbearable *(adj)* If something is **unbearable**, it is so bad or unpleasant that you cannot stand it.

unbelievable *(adj)* If something is **unbelievable**, it is so strange, surprising, or wonderful that you find it hard to accept that it is true.

unbending *(adj)* If someone is **unbending**, they are very firm and will not change their mind.

unburden
unburdening unburdened *(v)*
If you **unburden yourself**, you get rid of a load or a worry. *Jim unburdened himself by confessing.*

uncanny *(adj)*
very strange and difficult to explain or understand. **uncannily** *(adv).*

uncertain *(adj)* If you are **uncertain** about something, you are not sure about it. **uncertainty** *(n).*

uncivilized
1 *(adj)* not yet civilized or educated. *An uncivilized country.*
2 *(adj)* **Uncivilized** behavior is rude and rough.

uncle *(n)*
the brother of your father or mother, or the husband of your aunt.

uncomfortable
1 *(adj)* If you are **uncomfortable**, you do not feel relaxed in your body or your mind. **uncomfortably** *(adv).*
2 *(adj)* Something that is **uncomfortable** makes you feel uneasy or unhappy. *An uncomfortable situation.*

uncomplimentary *(adj)*
If someone says **uncomplimentary** things about you, they are insulting or rude.

uncompromising *(adj)*
If you are **uncompromising**, you refuse to change your mind. **uncompromisingly** *(adv).*

unconditional *(adj)*
not depending on anything else. *Maxine has an unconditional college place.* **unconditionally** *(adv).*

unconfirmed *(adj)* not yet known to be true. *Unconfirmed rumors.*

unconscious
1 *(adj)* not awake or unable to see, hear, think, etc., because you have fainted or been knocked out.
2 *(adj)* unaware of something. *George was unconscious of the fact that the bus was leaving.*

uncontrollable *(adj)*
Something that is **uncontrollable** cannot be stopped or controlled. **uncontrollably** *(adv).*

uncooperative *(adj)*
If you are **uncooperative**, you refuse to help people or do things for them.

uncouth *(adj)* rough and rude.

uncover **uncovering uncovered**
1 *(v)* to take a cover off something.
2 *(v)* to reveal something. *The police investigation uncovered a major fraud.*

undaunted *(adj)*
If you are **undaunted**, you are not put off by dangers or difficulties.

undecided *(adj)*
If you are **undecided** about something, you have not made up your mind about it.

undeniable *(adj)*
Something that is **undeniable** is certainly true. **undeniably** *(adv).*

under
1 *(prep)* below or beneath something. *The key is under the doormat.*
2 *(prep)* less than a number or amount. *Children under 12 will not be admitted.*
3 *(prep)* If you have people **under** you, you give them orders.

underarm *(adv)*
throwing with your arm swinging under your shoulder. **underarm** *(adj).*

undercarriage *(n)* the part of an aircraft, including the wheels, which supports it when it is on the ground. Also called landing gear.

underclothes *(plural n)* clothes that you wear under your other clothes. *The picture shows European underclothes from four centuries.*

underdog *(n)* a person or team that is expected to be the loser in a situation or competition.

underestimate underestimating underestimated
1 *(v)* to think that something is not as good or as great as it really is. *Freddie feels that his mother underestimates his talents.*
2 *(v)* to make a guess that is too low. *Calvin underestimated the amount of food we would need.*

underfoot *(adv)* under your feet or on the ground. *It's slippery underfoot.*

undergo undergoes undergoing underwent undergone *(v)* to experience or suffer something. *Dan underwent a serious operation.*

underground
1 *(adj)* below the ground. *An underground stream.* **underground** *(adv).*
2 *(adj)* secret and often illegal. *An underground organization.*

undergrowth *(n)* bushes and plants that grow in a thick mass under trees, usually in the woods or forest.

underline underlining underlined
1 *(v)* to draw a line under a word or sentence.
2 *(v)* to stress how important something is.

undermine undermining undermined *(v)* to weaken something gradually.

underneath *(prep)* under or below something. **underneath** *(adj).*

undernourished *(adj)* Someone who is **undernourished** is weak and unhealthy through lack of food.

underpants *(plural n)* clothes worn by men or boys as underwear.

underpass underpasses *(n)* a road or path that passes underneath another road.

underprivileged *(adj)* Someone who is **underprivileged** is poor and does not have the opportunities that most people have.

understand understanding understood
1 *(v)* to know what something means or how something works. *Luke understands engines.*
2 *(v)* to know what someone is like or why they behave in the way that they do. *I can understand why you're so happy.* **understanding** *(adj).*
3 *(v)* to believe that something is true. *I understand that Drew's family is moving to Melbourne.*

understandable
1 *(adj)* easy to grasp or understand.
2 *(adj)* easy to sympathize with. *It's understandable that Justin's upset.* **understandably** *(adv).*

undertake undertaking undertook undertaken *(v)* If you **undertake** something, you agree to do a particular job. **undertaking** *(n).*

undertaker *(n)* someone whose job is to arrange funerals and prepare dead bodies to be buried or cremated.

underwater *(adj)* living or happening under the surface of water. *The picture shows a submersible and a remote-operated vehicle, which are both used for underwater exploration.* **underwater** *(adv).*

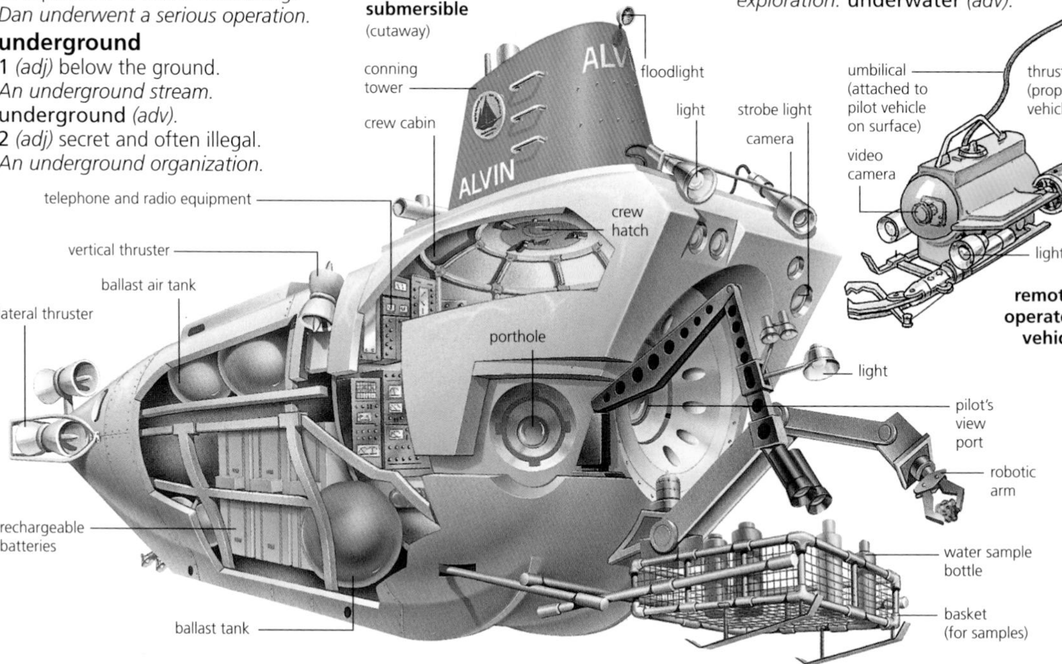

underwear *(singular n)* clothes that you wear next to your skin, under your other clothes. *See* **underclothes**.

underworld
1 *(n)* the secret world of criminals.
2 *(n)* In legends, **the Underworld** is the place under the ground where the spirits of dead people live.

undesirable *(adj)* unpleasant.

undeveloped
1 *(adj)* An **undeveloped** country is poor and does not have many modern industries.
2 *(adj)* **Undeveloped** land does not have buildings on it.

undo
undoes undoing undid undone
1 *(v)* to untie or unfasten something.
2 *(v)* to remove or destroy the effects of something.

undress undresses undressing undressed *(v)* to take off your clothes.

unearth unearthing unearthed
1 *(v)* to dig something up. *John unearthed an old arrowhead in his yard.*
2 *(v)* to find something after searching for it. *At last, I unearthed my pen.*

uneasy *(adj)* If you feel **uneasy** about something, you feel slightly worried or unhappy about it. **uneasiness** *(n)*, **uneasily** *(adv)*.

unemployed *(adj)* Someone who is **unemployed** does not have a paid job. **unemployment** *(n)*.

unequal *(adj)* not the same as something else in size, value, or amount. **unequally** *(adv)*.

uneven
1 *(adj)* not flat or not smooth.
2 *(adj)* not regular or not consistent. *An uneven essay.* **unevenly** *(adj)*.

uneventful *(adj)* not interesting or not exciting.

unexpected *(adj)* Something that is **unexpected** is surprising because you did not think it would happen. **unexpectedly** *(adv)*.

unfair unfairest *(adj)* not reasonable or not right. **unfairly** *(adv)*.

unfaithful *(adj)* not loyal or not trustworthy. *The unfaithful employee sold confidential information to a newspaper.* **unfaithfully** *(adv)*.

unfamiliar
1 *(adj)* not well known or not easily recognized. *The room was full of unfamiliar people.*
2 *(adj)* If you are **unfamiliar with** something, you do not know it well.

unfit
1 *(adj)* not healthy or not strong.
2 *(adj)* not suitable or not good enough. *The king was unfit to rule.*

unfold unfolding unfolded
1 *(v)* to open something that was folded. *I unfolded the letter.*
2 *(v)* When a story or plan **unfolds**, more of it becomes known.

unforgettable *(adj)* so good, bad, etc. that you will never forget it.

unforgivable *(adj)* If someone does something **unforgivable**, they do something so bad that you cannot forgive them. **unforgivably** *(adv)*.

unfortunate
1 *(adj)* unlucky. *An unfortunate accident.* **unfortunately** *(adv)*.
2 *(adj)* If you say that something was **unfortunate**, you mean that you wish it had never happened.

unfriendly
unfriendlier unfriendliest *(adj)* unkind, or unhelpful. **unfriendliness** *(n)*.

ungrateful *(adj)* If you are **ungrateful** for something, you are not thankful for it and do not appreciate it. **ungratefully** *(adv)*.

unhappy unhappier unhappiest *(adj)* miserable or upset. **unhappiness** *(n)*, **unhappily** *(adv)*.

unhealthy
unhealthier unhealthiest
1 *(adj)* unfit or not well.
2 *(adj)* Something that is **unhealthy** makes you unfit. *An unhealthy diet.*

unhygienic *(adj)* unclean and not free from germs.

unicorn *(n)* an imaginary animal resembling a horse with one straight horn growing from its forehead. *This unicorn comes from a series of tapestries called "The Lady and the Unicorn," made in about 1500.*

unicorn

unicycle *(n)* a vehicle with only one wheel, usually powered by pedals.

unidentified *(adj)* If something is **unidentified**, no one knows what it is. **unidentifiable** *(adj)*.

uniform
1 *(n)* a special set of clothes worn by all the members of a particular group or organization. **uniformed** *(adj)*.
2 *(adj)* Things that are **uniform** are all the same and not different or changing in any way. *The houses were all of uniform height.* **uniformity** *(n)*, **uniformly** *(adv)*.

unify unifies unifying unified *(v)* to bring together different people or groups to form a larger group. **unification** *(n)*.

unimportant *(adj)* Something that is **unimportant** will not have a great effect and does not need to be taken seriously.

uninhabited *(adj)* If a place is **uninhabited**, no one lives there.

unintelligible *(adj)* If something is **unintelligible**, it cannot be understood. **unintelligibly** *(adv)*.

unintentional *(adj)* Something that is **unintentional** is done by accident, not deliberately. **unintentionally** *(adv)*.

uninterested *(adj)* If you are **uninterested** in something, you do not want to know about it.

union
1 *(n)* an organized group of workers set up to help improve work conditions and pay.
2 *(n)* the joining together of two or more things or people.

unique *(yoo-neek) (adj)* If something is **unique**, it is the only one of its kind. **uniquely** *(adv)*.

unisex *(adj)* able to be used by both men and women. *Unisex clothing.*

unison *(n)* If people say or do something **in unison**, they say or do it together.

unit
1 *(n)* a single, complete thing.
2 *(n)* a group of people who work together to do a job. *An army unit.*
3 *(n)* a piece of furniture that fits together with others of the same type. *Kitchen units.*
4 *(n)* an amount used as a standard of measurement. *An ounce is a unit of weight.*

unite uniting united *(v)* If people **unite**, they join together or work together to achieve something. **unity** *(n)*.

universal
1 *(adj)* Something that is **universal** applies to everyone or everything. *This movie has universal appeal.* **universally** *(adv)*.
2 **universal indicator** *(n)* a solution or a piece of paper that turns a different color to show how acidic or alkaline a substance or solution is.

universe *(n)*
everything in space, including the Earth, Sun, Moon, and stars.

university universities *(n)*
a place where people can study for degrees or do research.

unjust *(adj)*
not fair or not right. **unjustly** *(adv).*

unkempt *(adj)* untidy and neglected.

unkind unkinder unkindest *(adj)*
unfriendly, unhelpful, and not generous. **unkindly** *(adv).*

unknown *(adj)* unfamiliar or not known about. *An unknown planet.*

unless *(conj)* except or if not. *I can't come unless someone gives me a lift.*

unlike *(prep)*
If one thing is **unlike** another, the two things are very different.

unlikely unlikelier unlikeliest *(adj)*
not probable.

unlimited *(adj)*
If there is an **unlimited** amount of something, you can have or use as much of it as you want.

unload unloading unloaded *(v)*
to remove things from a container or vehicle.

unlock unlocking unlocked *(v)*
to unfasten something with a key.

unlucky unluckier unluckiest
1 *(adj)* Someone who is **unlucky** is unfortunate and bad things seem to happen to them.
2 *(adj)* Something that is **unlucky** happens by chance and is unfortunate. **unluckily** *(adv).*
3 *(adj)* An **unlucky** number, date, etc. is one that you think will bring you bad luck.

unmistakable *(adj)* If someone or something is **unmistakable**, they are very individual and cannot be confused with someone or something else. **unmistakably** *(adv).*

unnatural
1 *(adj)* unusual or not normal. *An unnatural sound.* **unnaturally** *(adv).*
2 *(adj)* false or not sincere. *Stan sounded nervous and unnatural.* **unnaturally** *(adv).*

unnecessary *(adj)* If something is **unnecessary**, you do not need to do it or have it. **unnecessarily** *(adv).*

unobserved *(adj)*
unseen or unnoticed.

unofficial
1 *(adj)* not approved by someone in authority. *An unofficial report.*
2 *(adj)* informal. *An unofficial visit.*

unpack unpacking unpacked *(v)*
to take objects out of a box, case, etc.

unpleasant *(adj)* horrible or not likable. **unpleasantly** *(adv).*

unplug
unplugging unplugged *(v)* to remove a plug from an electric socket.

unpopular *(adj)*
not liked or enjoyed by many people.

unpredictable *(adj)* If something or someone is **unpredictable**, you do not know what they will do or say next. **unpredictably** *(adv).*

unprepared *(adj)*
not ready for something.

unprovoked *(adj)* If an action is **unprovoked**, no one has done anything to cause it or encourage it.

unravel unraveling unraveled
1 *(v)* to unwind a tangled mass of string, yarn, etc.
2 *(v)* to search for and discover the truth about a complex situation. *The detectives unraveled the mystery.*

unreasonable *(adj)* not fair. *The movie star's demands were totally unreasonable.* **unreasonably** *(adv).*

unrecognizable *(adj)* If someone or something is **unrecognizable**, they have totally changed so that you do not immediately know who or what they are.

unreliable *(adj)* Something or someone who is **unreliable** cannot be depended on or trusted.

unrest *(n)* disturbance and trouble.

unrestricted *(adj)* without rules or restrictions. *This ticket gives you unrestricted use of the pool.*

unripe *(adj)* not yet ready to be harvested, picked, or eaten.

unrivaled *(adj)*
better than anything else.

unroll unrolling unrolled *(v)*
to open out something that is rolled up. *We unrolled our sleeping bags.*

unruly unrulier unruliest *(adj)*
badly behaved and disobedient.

unscathed *(adj)*
not hurt. *The driver survived the crash unscathed.*

unscrupulous *(adj)*
Unscrupulous people have few principles and are not concerned about whether their actions are right or wrong. **unscrupulously** *(adv).*

unseen *(adj)*
hidden or not able to be seen.

unsettle unsettling unsettled *(v)*
to disturb someone or to make someone feel uneasy.

unsightly *(adj)*
ugly and unpleasant to look at.

unskilled *(adj)* An **unskilled** worker has no particular skill or training.

unstable
1 *(adj)* not firm or not steady.
2 *(adj)* An **unstable** person has rapid changes of mood and behavior.

unsteady *(adj)*
shaky or wobbly. **unsteadily** *(adv).*

unstuck *(adj)*
If something has come **unstuck**, it is not glued together any more.

unsuccessful *(adj)*
If you are **unsuccessful**, you do not do well or do not get what you want. **unsuccessfully** *(adv).*

unsuitable *(adj)*
not right for a particular purpose. *Richard was wearing unsuitable clothes for the expedition.* **unsuitability** *(n),* **unsuitably** *(adv).*

unsure *(adj)*
not certain or not definite. *Katie is unsure about the future.*

unthinkable *(adj)* If something is **unthinkable**, it is out of the question and cannot be considered.

untidy untidier untidiest *(adj)*
not neat. **untidiness** *(n),* **untidily** *(adv).*

untie untying untied *(v)*
to undo knots or bows.

until *(conj)* up to the time that. *You can stay until tomorrow.*

unto *(prep) (old-fashioned)* to.

untold
1 *(adj)* too great to be counted or worked out. *Untold damage.*
2 *(adj)* not told or not revealed. *The true story remains untold.*

untouched
1 *(adj)* not handled by anyone.
2 *(adj)* left alone or ignored. *The thieves took the money but left the jewelry untouched.*

untrue *(adj)* false or incorrect.

unused *(adj)*
An **unused** item has never been used.

unusual *(adj)* strange, abnormal, or odd. **unusually** *(adv).*

unwaged *(adj)* without a paid job.

unwanted *(adj)*
If something is **unwanted**, you do not need or want it.

unwelcome *(adj)* If someone or something is **unwelcome**, they are not gladly received or accepted.

unwell *(adj)* sick or poorly.

unwieldy *(adj)* difficult to hold or hard to manage. *An unwieldy package.*

unwilling *(adj)*
reluctant or not keen to do something. **unwillingly** *(adv).*

unwind unwinding unwound
1 *(v)* to undo something that has been wound up. *Tina unwound the hose.*
2 *(v)* to relax and become less worried or tense. *Ann plays sports to unwind.*

unworthy *(adj)*
not deserving or below standard. *The wooden crate made an unworthy seat for the President.*

unwrap unwrapping unwrapped
(v) to take the packaging or outer layer off something.

up *(prep)* from a lower to a higher place. **upward** *(adj),* **up** *(adv).*

upbeat *(adj) (informal)*
optimistic and cheerful.

upbringing *(n)* the way that a child is raised or brought up.

update updating updated
1 *(v)* to give someone the latest information. *Please update us on your plans.* **update** *(n).*
2 *(v)* to change something to include the latest style or information. *We are updating our catalog.*

upgrade upgrading upgraded
1 *(v)* to improve something. *Jamal upgraded his computer by adding extra memory.*
2 *(v)* to promote someone to a better or more important job.

upheaval *(n)* a big change or disturbance. *Moving was a great upheaval for us all.*

uphill *(adj)* sloping upward.

upholstery *(n)* the stuffing, covering, etc., that is put in or on furniture.

upkeep *(n)* the work or cost of looking after something or someone.

upon *(prep)* on.

upper *(adj)* higher in position or rank. *An upper window. An upper house of a legislature.*

uppercase *(adj)*
Uppercase letters are capital letters.

upright
1 *(adj)* standing up or standing straight. **upright** *(adv).*
2 *(adj)* honest and fair. *An upright citizen.*
3 *(n)* a vertical post.

uprising *(n)*
a rebellion or a revolt.

uproar *(n)* shouting, noise, and confusion. *The lesson ended in uproar.* **uproarious** *(adj).*

uproot uprooting uprooted
1 *(v)* to take a plant out of the earth.
2 *(v)* to move someone from where they are settled in their home or work.

upset upsetting upset
1 *(v)* to make someone unhappy or distressed. **upset** *(adj).*
2 *(v)* to overturn something. *Sara upset the milk.*
3 *(v)* to make someone feel sick. *Oysters always upset my stomach.*

upside down
1 *(adj)* the wrong way up.
2 *(adv)* in a confused or untidy condition. *The thieves turned the place upside down.*

upstairs *(adv)*
to or on a higher floor.

uptight *(adj) (informal)*
tense, nervous, or anxious.

up-to-date *(adj)*
If something is **up-to-date,** it contains the most recent information or is in the latest style.

urban *(adj)* to do with or living in towns or cities. *Urban wildlife.*

Urdu *(n)* a language spoken in Pakistan and India.

urge urging urged
1 *(v)* to encourage or persuade someone strongly. *Dad urged me to try harder.*
2 *(n)* a strong wish or need to do something. *Todd felt a sudden urge to throw something.*

urgent *(adj)*
If something is **urgent**, it needs very quick or immediate action. **urgency** *(n),* **urgently** *(adv).*

urinate *(yoor-in-ate)*
urinating urinated *(v)* to pass urine from your body. **urination** *(n).*

urine *(yoor-in) (n)*
the liquid waste that people and animals pass out of their bodies.

URL (n) the series of letters (and sometimes numbers) that you type into your computer to enable a browser to find a particular website or page. URL stands for Uniform Resource Locator. Another name for URL is web address.

urn

urn
1 *(n)* a vase used as an ornament or as a container for the ashes of a dead person. *The picture shows an urn made in ancient Greece.*
2 *(n)* a large insulated container, used for serving tea or coffee and for keeping them hot.

usage
1 *(n)* the way that something is used or treated. *Careless usage.*
2 *(n)* the way that a language is spoken and written. *English usage.*

use using used
1 *(yooz) (v)* to do a job with something. *I used a pocketknife to cut through the wrapping.*
2 *(yooce) (n)* the action of using something. *I'm sure I can find a use for your gift. Put away the tools after use.*
3 *(yooz) (v)* If you **use** someone, you take advantage of them in order to get something that you want.
4 **use up** *(yooz) (v)* If you **use something up**, you finish it.

used
1 *(yoozed) (adj)* already made use of. *A used car.*
2 *(yoost)* If you are **used to** something, you know it well.
3 *(yoost)* If you **used to do** something, you did it in the past.

useful *(yooce-ful) (adj)*
Something that is **useful** is helpful and can be used a lot. **usefulness** *(n).*

useless *(yooce-less)*
1 *(adj)* Something that is **useless** cannot be used or is not helpful.
2 *(adj) (informal)* not very good. *I'm useless at French.*

user-friendly *(adj)* If something is **user-friendly**, it is easy to use.

usher *(n)* someone who shows people to their seats in a court, at a wedding, etc. **usher** *(v).*

usual *(adj)*
normal or regular. **usually** *(adv).*

utensil *(n)* a tool or container, often one used in the kitchen.

utmost *(n)* the most, or the greatest possible. *The government said they would do their utmost to help the refugees.* **utmost** *(adj).*

utter uttering uttered
1 *(v)* to speak or to make some sort of sound from your mouth. *Anna uttered a low moan.* **utterance** *(n).*
2 *(adj)* complete, total, or absolute. *The play was an utter disaster.* **utterly** *(adv).*

U-turn
1 *(n)* a U-shaped turn made by a vehicle, to change its direction.
2 *(n)* a complete reversal of policy or attitude. *A government U-turn.*

vacant
1 *(adj)* empty or not occupied. *A vacant house.*
2 *(adj)* available. *This job is vacant.* **vacancy** *(n).*
3 *(adj)* If someone looks **vacant**, they have a blank expression on their face.

vacate vacating vacated *(v)* to leave or to make somewhere empty. *Hotel guests should vacate their rooms by 10 a.m.*

vacation *(n)* time away from school or work, especially a trip away from home.

vaccinate vaccinating vaccinated *(v)* to protect someone against a disease, usually by giving them an injection. **vaccination** *(n).*

vaccine *(vak-seen) (n)* a substance injected or given by mouth to protect someone from disease.

vacuum *(vak-yoom) (n)* a sealed space from which all air or gas has been emptied.

vacuum cleaner *(n)* a machine that sucks up dirt from carpets, furniture, etc.

vague *(vayg)* vaguer vaguest *(adj)* not clear or not definite. *I have only vague memories of Miranda.*

vain vainer vainest
1 *(adj)* If you are **vain**, you are too proud of yourself, especially of the way that you look.
2 *(adj)* unsuccessful or futile. *Bill made a vain attempt to stop the bus.*

valentine
1 *(n)* a gift or greeting card that you send to a friend, relative or loved one on Valentine's Day.
2 *(n)* a sweetheart or loved one chosen on Valentine's Day.

Valentine's Day *(n)* February 14, a day dedicated to St. Valentine, a Christian martyr of the third century A.D. It is celebrated by sending valentines.

valiant *(adj)* brave or courageous. **valiantly** *(adv).*

valid
1 *(adj)* sensible and acceptable. *You can leave early only if you have a valid reason.* **validity** *(n).*
2 *(adj)* acceptable, or legal. *To travel on the train, you need a valid ticket.*

valley *(n)* an area of low ground between two hills, usually containing a river.

valor *(n)* bravery or courage.

valuable
1 *(adj)* Something that is **valuable** is worth a lot of money, or is very important in some other way. *Valuable jewels. Valuable information.*
2 **valuables** *(plural n)* possessions that are worth a lot of money. *My father keeps his valuables in a safe.*

value valuing valued
1 *(n)* what something is worth. *What is the value of this watch?*
2 *(v)* to think that something is important. *I value Posy's friendship greatly.*
3 *(v)* to assess how much something is worth. *The auctioneer valued the paintings before the sale.*
4 *(plural n)* People's **values** are their beliefs and ideas about what is most important in life.

valve *(n)* a type of faucet that controls the flow of fluid, air, etc. *See* **engine**, **heart**.

vamoose *(v)* to leave quickly.

van *(n)* a closed vehicle for carrying goods. *A delivery van.*

vandal *(n)* someone who needlessly damages or destroys other people's property. **vandalism** *(n),* **vandalize** *(v).*

vane
1 *(n)* A **weathervane** is a pointer that swings around to show the direction of the wind.
2 *(n)* the flat part of a bird's feather. *See* **feather**.

vanilla *(n)* the pod or bean of a tropical orchid. It is used for flavoring ice cream, cakes, candies, cookies, and other foods

vanilla

vanish vanishes vanishing vanished *(v)* to disappear suddenly.

vanity *(n)* a feeling of extreme pride and conceit.

vapor *(n)* a gas, usually one that has been changed from a liquid or solid. *Water vapor is visible as clouds, mist, or steam.*

variable
1 *(adj)* likely to change. *Variable weather.* **variability** *(n).*
2 *(n)* In math, a **variable** is a value, given to a symbol, such as x or y, that may change.

variation *(n)* a change in something.

variety varieties
1 *(n)* a selection of different things.
2 *(n)* a different type of the same thing. *A new variety of rose.*

various
1 *(adj)* several. *I have various hobbies.*
2 *(adj)* different. *The cakes were many and various.*

varnish varnishes *(n)* a clear coating that you paint on wood to protect it and give it a shiny finish. **varnish** *(v).*

vary varies varying varied
1 *(v)* to change or be different. *Mimi's handwriting varies depending on her mood.*
2 *(v)* If you **vary** something, you make changes to it.

vase *(n)* an ornamental container, often used for flowers. *The picture shows an Art Deco style enameled vase, made in the 1930s.*

vase

vast vaster vastest *(adj)* huge in area or extent. *The vast Sahara Desert. Polly has a vast fund of jokes.* **vastness** *(n),* **vastly** *(adv).*

vat *(n)* a large tank or container used for storing liquids.

vault vaulting vaulted
1 *(v)* to leap over something, using your hands or other support. **vault** *(n).*
2 *(n)* an underground burial chamber.
3 *(n)* a room for keeping money and other valuables safe. *A bank vault.*

VDU *(n)* the screen of a computer and the keyboard connected to it. The initials VDU stand for Visual Display Unit.

veal *(n)* the meat from a calf.

veer veering veered *(v)* to change direction. *The wind veered from east to northeast.*

vegan *(vee-gan) (n)* someone who does not use or eat any animal products. **veganism** *(n),* **vegan** *(adj).*

vegetable *(n)* a plant grown to be used as food. Vegetables are usually eaten with savory foods. *The picture shows a variety of different vegetables.*

2 *(n)* the soft skin on the growing antler of deer, elk, etc. *See* **antler**.

vendetta *(n)* a long-running feud between two families, gangs, etc.

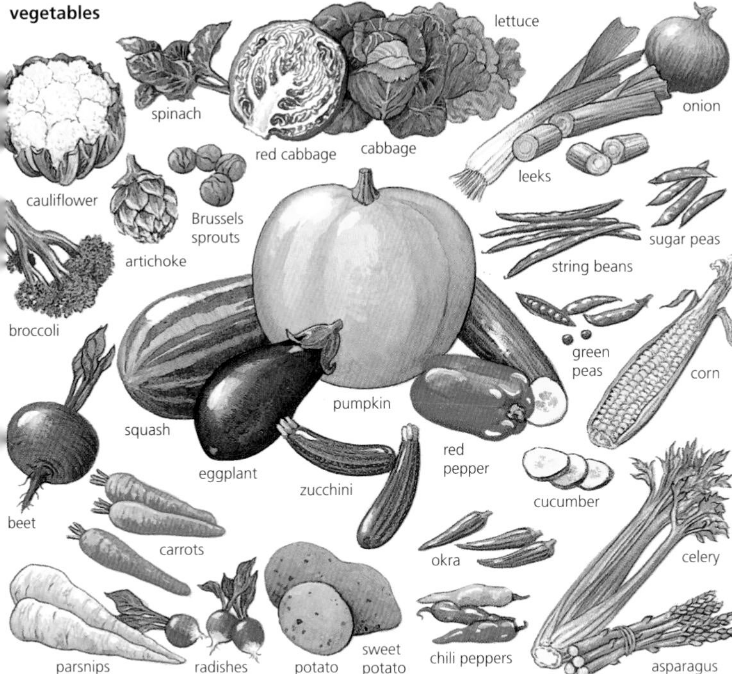

vegetarian *(n)* someone who does not eat meat or fish. **vegetarianism** *(n)*, **vegetarian** *(adj)*.

vegetation *(n)* plant life of all types.

vehement *(vee-hem-ent) (adj)* If you are **vehement** about something, you express your feelings about it very strongly. **vehemence** *(n)*, **vehemently** *(adv)*.

vehicle *(vee-hik-ul) (n)* something in which people or goods are carried from one place to another. Vehicles can range in size and power from a sled to an express train.

veil *(vale) (n)* a fine piece of material worn by women to hide their faces.

vein *(vane) (n)* one of the tubes through which blood is carried back to the heart from other parts of the body. *See* **circulation**.

vellum
1 *(n)* fine parchment made from the skin of a calf, lamb, etc.
2 *(n)* very high-quality writing paper.

velocity *(vel-oss-it-ee)* **velocities** *(n)* speed. *The velocity of the rocket is 3,000 mph at top speed.*

velvet
1 *(n)* a soft thick fabric made from cotton or silk. **velvety** *(adj)*.

vending machine *(n)* a coin-operated machine from which you can buy food, drinks, or other products.

venetian blind *(n)* an indoor blind made from thin strips that can be raised or tilted to alter the amount of light coming in.

vengeance *(n)* action that you take to pay someone back for harm that they have done to you or to your friends or family.

venom *(n)* poison produced by some snakes and spiders and injected through their fangs into their victims' bodies. *This diagram of a snake's jaws shows where its venom is stored.*

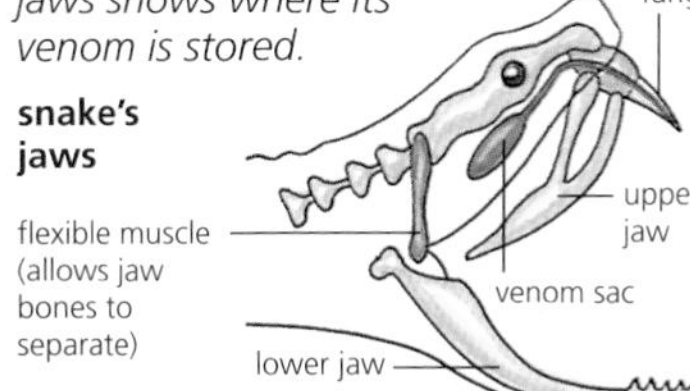

vent venting vented
1 *(n)* an opening through which waste can escape.
2 *(n)* the shaft of a volcano through which smoke and lava escape. *See* **volcano**.
3 *(v)* If you **vent** your feelings, you show them in an obvious way.

ventilate ventilating ventilated *(v)* to let fresh air into a place and to send stale air out. **ventilation** *(n)*.

ventriloquism *(n)* the art of speaking without moving your lips so that your words seem to come from somewhere else, for example, from a dummy's mouth. **ventriloquist** *(n)*.

venture venturing ventured
1 *(v)* to put yourself at risk by doing something daring or dangerous. *The explorers ventured bravely into the dense jungle.*
2 *(n)* a project that is rather risky.

venue *(ven-yoo) (n)* a place where an event is held.

veranda *or* **verandah** *(n)* a raised platform around the outside of a house, often with a roof.

verb *(n)* a word that describes what someone or something does, thinks, or feels. "Sing," "have," and "come" are all verbs. *See page 3.*

verbal
1 *(adj)* having to do with words. *A verbal-reasoning test.*
2 *(adj)* spoken. *Verbal abuse.*
3 *(adj)* having to do with verbs.

verdict
1 *(n)* the decision of a judge or jury as to whether someone is guilty or not guilty.
2 *(n)* a decision or an opinion. *What's your verdict on my chicken casserole?*

verge verging verged
1 *(n)* land at the side of a road, often with grass on it.
2 If you are **on the verge** of doing something, you will do it soon. *Harry is on the verge of leaving.*
3 *(v)* to be very near to something. *Pearl's behavior was verging on madness.*

verify verifies verifying verified *(v)* to confirm or to back up something. *Roberta verified that what the witness said was true.* **verification** *(n)*, **verifiable** *(adj)*.

versatile *(adj)* talented or useful in many ways. *A versatile entertainer. A versatile tool.* **versatility** *(n)*.

verse
1 *(n)* one part of a poem or song, made up of several lines.
2 *(n)* a general name for poetry.

version
1 *(n)* one way of expressing something. *Holly gave her version of the events.*
2 *(n)* a revised form or model of a book, car, piece of software, etc.

versus *(prep)* against. *Today's match is U.S. versus Canada.*

vertebra vertebrae *(n)* one of the bones that make up your spine.

vertebrate *(n)* a creature with a backbone. *Humans, elephants, and snakes are all vertebrates.* **vertebrate** *(adj).*

vertex vertexes *or* vertices
1 *(n)* the highest point of something.
2 *(n)* the point where two lines meet to form an angle.

vertical *(adj)* upright and perpendicular to the ground. *A vertical post.* **vertically** *(adv).*

very
1 *(adv)* to a great extent, much, or most. *I am very pleased to see you.*
2 *(adj)* exact. *You're the very person I wanted to see.*

vessel
1 *(n)* a general name for a ship.
2 *(n)* a container for liquids.

vest *(n)* a sleeveless piece of clothing, often worn over a shirt or blouse.

vestige *(vest-ij) (n)* a trace of something. *There's a vestige of truth in what Bill says.*

vet vetting vetted
1 *(n) (informal)* a veterinarian.
2 *(n) (informal)* a veteran. *A Vietnam vet.*

veteran
1 *(n)* someone with a lot of experience in something.
2 *(n)* a soldier who has returned from war.

veterinarian *(n)* someone who is trained to treat sick animals.

veterinary *(adj)* having to do with the treatment of animals.

veto *(vee-toe)* vetoes vetoing vetoed *(v)* If someone **vetoes** something, they use their power to put a stop to a plan. **veto** *(n).*

vex vexes vexing vexed *(v)* to annoy or irritate someone. **vexation** *(n),* **vexatious** *(adj).*

VHF *(n)* the waveband most commonly used for high-frequency reception of local radio and TV signals. The initials VHF stand for Very High Frequency.

via *(prep)* by way of. *This train goes to Los Angeles via Denver.*

viable *(adj)* workable or capable of succeeding. *A viable plan.* **viability** *(n).*

viaduct *(n)* a large bridge that carries a railroad track, pipeline, or road across a valley.

vibrant *(adj)* bright or lively. *Vibrant colors.* **vibrancy** *(n),* **vibrantly** *(adv).*

vibrate vibrating vibrated *(v)* to shake rapidly. **vibration** *(n).*

vice *(n)* immoral or criminal behavior.

vice-captain *(n)* a deputy who helps the captain and takes over duties when the captain is unable to act.

vice president *(n)* a deputy who helps the president and takes over duties when the president is unable to act.

vice versa *(adv)* a Latin phrase meaning "the other way around." *You help me and vice versa.*

vicinity *(vis-in-it-ee)* **vicinities** *(n)* the area near a particular place. *After the robbery, the police sealed off all the roads in the vicinity.*

vicious *(adj)* bad-tempered, aggressive, and violent. **viciousness** *(n),* **viciously** *(adv).*

victim *(n)* someone who suffers or is killed because of something or someone else. *There were many victims of the plane crash.*

victimize victimizing victimized *(v)* to pick someone out for unfair treatment. **victimization** *(n).*

victor *(n)* the winner in a battle or contest.

victory victories *(n)* a win in a battle or contest. **victorious** *(adj),* **victoriously** *(adv).*

video videoing videoed
1 *(v)* to record sound and pictures. **video** *(adj).*
2 *(n)* a recording of sound and pictures.

videotape *(n)* magnetic tape used in the past to store recordings of sound and pictures.

vie vying vied *(v)* If you **vie with** someone, you compete with them. *The brothers vied for attention.*

view viewing viewed
1 *(n)* what you can see from a certain place. *The view from my window.*
2 *(v)* to look at something to see if you want to buy it. *May we view the house next weekend?* **viewing** *(n).*
3 *(n)* what you think about something.
4 *(n)* the range or field of vision. *The ship has disappeared from view.*

vigilant *(adj)* watchful and alert. **vigilance** *(n),* **vigilantly** *(adv).*

vigorous *(adj)* energetic, lively, or forceful. *Vigorous exercise.* **vigor** *(n),* **vigorously** *(adv).*

Viking *(n)* one of the Scandinavian peoples who invaded England and parts of northern Europe between the 8th and 11th centuries. *See* **longship**.

vile viler vilest *(adj)* horrible and disgusting. **vileness** *(n).*

villa
1 *(n)* In ancient Roman times, a **villa** was a country house, usually built around a courtyard and including farm buildings.
2 *(n)* a large luxurious house, especially one in the country.

village *(n)* a small group of houses and other buildings that make up a community. **villager** *(n).*

villain *(vill-un) (n)* a wicked person, often an evil character in a story, movie, or play. **villainous** *(adj).*

vindictive *(adj)* Someone who is **vindictive** is unforgiving and wants revenge. **vindictiveness** *(n),* **vindictively** *(adv).*

vine *(n)* a climbing plant on which grapes and some other fruits grow.

vinegar *(n)* a sour-tasting liquid made from fermented wine, cider, etc. and used to flavor food.

vineyard *(vin-yard) (n)* an area of farmland where grapes are grown.

vintage *(vin-tij)*
1 *(adj)* very good or the best of its kind. *Maxine gave a vintage performance.*
2 *(adj)* having to do with the past. *Vintage clothing.*

violate violating violated
1 *(v)* to break a promise, a rule, or a law. **violation** *(n).*
2 *(v)* to treat a person or place with no respect. **violation** *(n).*

violence *(n)* the use of physical force to hurt or kill. **violent** *(adj),* **violently** *(adv).*

violet *(n)*
a blue-purple color. **violet** *(adj).*

violin *(n)*
a musical instrument with four strings, played with a bow. *See* **strings**.

VIP *(n)*
a famous or important person. The initials VIP stand for Very Important Person.

viper *(n)*
a type of venomous snake, sometimes called an adder. *See* **adder**.

virgin *(adj)* untouched or in its natural state. *Virgin snow.*

virile *(adj)* Someone who is **virile** has qualities that are supposed to be typical of men. **virility** *(n).*

virtually *(adv)*
nearly or almost. *We have virtually finished.* **virtual** *(adj).*

virtual reality *(n)* an environment created by a computer that seems real to the person who experiences it.

virtue *(n)*
a good quality. *Patience is a virtue.* **virtuous** *(adj),* **virtuously** *(adv).*

virtuoso *(n)*
a highly skilled performer, especially a musician.

virulent
1 *(adj)* If a disease is **virulent**, it is very severe or harmful. **virulence** *(n),* **virulently** *(adv).*
2 *(adj)* **Virulent** criticism is very severe or bitter. **virulence** *(n),* **virulently** *(adv).*

virus viruses
1 *(n)* an organism that multiplies in body cells, often causing disease.
2 *(n)* the disease caused by a virus.
3 *(n)* hidden instructions within a computer program, designed to damage data or destroy a computer system.

visa *(vee-zuh) (n)*
a document giving permission for someone to enter a foreign country.

vise *(n)* a tool that holds an object between two jaws so that you can work on it.

visible *(adj)*
Something that is **visible** is able to be seen. *The island was visible on the horizon.* **visibility** *(n),* **visibly** *(adv).*

vision
1 *(n)* sight.
2 *(n)* something that you see in a dream or trance, which is often strange or beautiful.
3 *(n)* the ability to think ahead.

visit visiting visited *(v)*
to go to see people or places. **visit** *(n),* **visitor** *(n).*

visual
1 *(adj)* having to do with seeing. *A visual guide.* **visually** *(adv).*
2 *(n)* an image or a picture.

visualize visualizing visualized *(v)*
to picture something or to see something in your mind. *I can visualize myself winning the race.* **visualization** *(n).*

vital *(adj)* essential or absolutely necessary. **vitally** *(adv).*

vitality *(n)* energy and liveliness. *Puppies are usually full of vitality.*

vitamin *(n)*
one of the substances in food that is necessary for good health.

vivacious *(adj)* A **vivacious** person has a lively personality. **vivacity** *(n),* **vivaciously** *(adv).*

vivid *(adj)* very bright, clear, or realistic. *A vivid dream.* **vividness** *(n),* **vividly** *(adv).*

vivisection *(n)*
the use of live animals for scientific and medical research.

vocabulary vocabularies *(n)*
the range of words that a person uses and understands. *Carolina has a very large vocabulary.*

vocal
1 *(adj)* having to do with the voice.
2 *(adj)* If someone is **vocal** they are outspoken and often express their opinions. **vocally** *(adv).*
3 *(plural n)* In music, the **vocals** are the parts that are sung.

vocalist *(n)*
a singer.

vocation
1 *(n)* a strong feeling that you want to do a particular job.
2 *(n)* a job or profession, especially one that needs special training. **vocational** *(adj).*

vociferous
*(vo-**sif**-er-us) (adj)*
If someone is **vociferous**, they are noisy and talkative and insist on being heard. **vociferously** *(adv).*

vogue *(vohg) (n)*
If something is **in vogue**, it is the current fashion.

voice voicing voiced
1 *(n)* the power to speak and sing. *Lois has lost her voice.*
2 *(n)* the sound produced when you speak or sing. *Minnie has a high voice.*
3 *(v)* When you **voice** an opinion, you express it. **voice** *(n).*

void
1 *(n)* an empty space. *The spaceship careered into the void.*
2 *(adj)* If a result is declared **void**, it does not count any more.

volatile
1 *(adj)* A **volatile** chemical evaporates very easily or is unstable in some other way. **volatility** *(n).*
2 *(adj)* Someone who is **volatile** has rapid mood changes.

volcano volcanoes *(n)*
a mountain with vents through which molten lava, ash, cinders, and gas erupt, sometimes violently. Volcanoes occur along the boundaries of the Earth's plates, where molten rock is forced upward from magma reservoirs. Some volcanoes are extinct, others are dormant, and a few are active. **volcanic** *(adj).*
This picture shows a cutaway view of an erupting volcano.

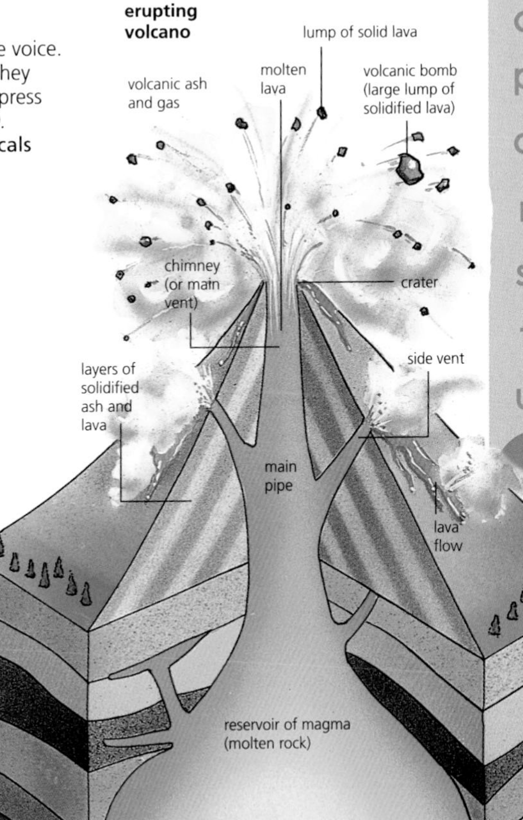

volley *(n)*
a shot in games, such as tennis and soccer, where the ball is hit or kicked before it can bounce.

volleyball *(n)*
a six-a-side game in which teams use their hands to hit a large ball over the net and try to make it hit the ground on their opponents' side.

volt *(n)* a unit of electrical force. Volts are used to measure voltage.

voltage *(n)* the force of an electrical supply, expressed in volts. *12 volts is the voltage of most car batteries.*

volume
1 *(n)* the amount of space taken up by a three-dimensional shape, such as a box or room. To figure out the volume of an object, you multiply its length by its width by its breadth.
2 *(n)* the degree of sound produced by a radio, a pop group, etc.
3 *(n)* a large book, often one of a series of titles.
This encyclopedia has 12 volumes.

voluntary
1 *(adj)* willing and unforced.
A voluntary decision.
2 **voluntary work** *(n)* unpaid work, usually done to help others.

volunteer
volunteering volunteered *(v)*
to offer to do a job. **volunteer** *(n).*

vomit vomiting vomited *(v)*
When you **vomit**, you bring up food from your stomach through your mouth. **vomit** *(n).*

vote voting voted *(v)*
to make a choice in an election or other poll. **vote** *(n).*

vow vowing vowed *(v)* to make a serious and important promise.

vowel *(n)* one of the letters a, e, i, o, and u. Y is also a vowel in words such as gymnastics, but a consonant in words such as yo-yo.

voyage *(n)*
a sea journey. **voyager** *(n).*

vulgar *(adj)*
rude or coarse. **vulgarity** *(n).*

vulnerable *(adj)*
If someone or something is **vulnerable**, they are in a weak position and likely to be hurt or damaged in some way.
vulnerability *(n),* **vulnerably** *(adv).*

vulture
1 *(n)* a large bird of prey with a bald head and dark feathers.
2 *(n) (informal)*
a greedy or mean person who takes advantage of other people.

Ww

wad *(wod) (n)* a thick pad or a bundle. *A wad of cash.*

waddle waddling waddled *(v)*
to walk awkwardly, swaying from side to side. *The geese waddled into the farmyard.*

wade wading waded *(v)*
to walk through water.

wader
1 *(n)* a wading bird.
2 *(n)* a thigh-high waterproof boot, used for fishing in deep water.

wafer *(n)*
a thin, light, crispy type of cracker.

waffle waffling waffled
1 *(n)* a type of square pancake, sometimes eaten with syrup.
2 *(v) (informal)*
to speak in a long-winded, rambling way. **waffle** *(n).*

wag wagging wagged *(v)*
to move something from side to side. *Fido wagged his tail.*

wage waging waged
1 **wage** *or* **wages** *(n)* the money someone is paid for their work.
2 *(v)* If you **wage** a war or a campaign, you start it and carry on with it.

wagon
1 *(n)* a horse-drawn cart.
2 *(n)* a cart with four wheels that children play with, or ride in.

wail wailing wailed *(v)*
to let out a long cry of sadness or distress. **wail** *(n).*

waist *(n)* the middle part of your body, between your hips and your ribs, where your body narrows.

wait waiting waited
1 *(v)* to pause, or to stop doing something for a period of time.
2 *(v)* If you **wait on** someone, you serve them food and drink in a restaurant.

waiter *(n)*
a man who serves people with food and drink in a restaurant.

waiting room
(n) a room where people sit and wait for something, such as a train or an appointment.

walruses

waitress waitresses *(n)*
a woman who serves people with food and drink in a restaurant.

wake waking woke woken
1 *(v)* to become fully conscious after being asleep.
Dora always wakes at dawn.
2 *(v)* to rouse someone from their sleep. *My dog woke me up.*
3 *(n)* the trail left by a moving boat.
4 *(n)* a watch kept over the body of a dead person before a funeral.

walk walking walked
1 *(v)* to move along on your feet.
walker *(n).*
2 *(n)* a journey on foot.
3 *(v) (informal)*
If you **walk all over** somebody, you take advantage of them.

walking stick *(n)* a stick held by someone to help them to walk.

walkway *(n)*
a path or passage for walking.

wall *(n)*
a solid structure that separates two areas or supports a roof.

wallaby wallabies *(n)*
a plant-eating animal similar to a kangaroo.

red-necked wallaby

wallet *(n)* a pouch for holding money, usually made of leather.

wallop walloping walloped *(v)*
(informal) to hit someone very hard, usually as a punishment. **wallop** *(n).*

wallow wallowing wallowed
1 *(v)* to roll around in mud or water.
2 *(v)* If you **wallow in** something, you enjoy it greatly.

wallpaper *(n)* patterned or colored paper that is stuck in strips to a wall to decorate a room.

walrus walruses *(n)* a large sea animal from the Arctic with long tusks and flippers.

waltz waltzes *(n)*
a ballroom dance with a regular 1-2-3 beat.
waltz *(v).*

wand *(rhymes with pond) (n)*
a thin stick that is supposed to have magical powers.

Some words that begin with a "w" sound are spelled "wh."

wander wandering wandered
1 *(v)* to walk around without going in any particular direction. **wander** *(n)*.
2 *(v)* to move around.
Don't let your eyes wander.

wane waning waned
1 *(v)* to get smaller or less.
As the job progressed, Jasmine's enthusiasm waned.
2 *(v)* When the Moon **wanes**, it appears to get smaller. *See* **Moon**.

wangle wangling wangled *(v)*
(informal) to gain something by crafty or dishonest methods.
I wangled a front row seat.

want wanting wanted
1 *(v)* to feel that you would like something.
I want a chocolate bar. **want** *(n)*.
2 *(v)* to need something.
What Gerry wants is a good meal. **want** *(n)*.

war
1 *(n)* fighting between opposing forces.
2 *(n)* a struggle against something.
A war against hunger.

ward warding warded
1 *(n)* a large room in a hospital where patients are looked after.
2 *(n)* a young person who is under the care of a guardian.
3 **ward off** *(v)* to prevent something from attacking or hurting you.
I'm trying to ward off a cold.

warden *(n)*
someone in charge of a prison.

wardrobe
1 *(n)* a tall closet used for storing clothes. Also called an armoire.
2 *(n)* a collection of clothes or theatrical costumes.

warehouse *(n)* a large building used for storing goods.

warfare *(n)* a general term for the fighting of wars. *Jungle warfare.*

warlike *(adj)* hostile, aggressive, or likely to start a war.

warm warming warmed;
warmer warmest
1 *(adj)* fairly hot.
warmth *(n)*.
2 *(v)* to increase the temperature of something.
3 *(adj)* very friendly.
We were given a warm welcome.
warmth *(n)*, **warmly** *(adv)*.
4 *(v)* If you **warm up** before playing a sport, you exercise gently to prepare yourself for it. **warm-up** *(n)*.
5 *(v)* When an engine **warms up**, it starts to run smoothly.

warm-blooded *(adj)*
Warm-blooded animals have a body temperature that remains approximately the same, whatever their surroundings.

warn warning warned *(v)*
If you **warn** someone, you tell them about a danger or a bad thing that might happen. **warning** *(n)*.

warp warping warped *(v)*
If an object **warps**, it gets twisted or bent by heat or dampness.

warrant *(n)* an official piece of paper that gives permission for something. *A search warrant.*

warren *(n)* a group of underground tunnels where rabbits live.

warrior *(n)* a soldier or someone who fights. *See* **samurai**.

warship *(n)* a ship with guns on it, used in war. *See* **ship**.

wart *(rhymes with port) (n)*
a small hard lump on your skin. **warty** *(adj)*.

wary warier wariest *(adj)*
cautious and careful. *Dustin is always very wary of dogs.*
wariness *(n)*, **warily** *(adv)*.

wash
washes washing washed
1 *(v)* to clean something with water, soap, etc. **wash** *(n)*.
2 *(n)* the trail of disturbed water behind a moving boat.
3 *(v)* If the sea **washes up** something, it leaves it on the shore.

washable *(adj)*
If a material is **washable**, you can wash it without damaging it.

washer *(n)* a plastic or metal ring that fits under a bolt or nut to give a tighter fit or to prevent a leak.

washing machine *(n)*
a machine that washes clothes.

wasp *(n)*
a flying insect that has black and yellow stripes and can sting.
See **insect**, **nest**.

wastage *(n)* loss. *You'll need three meters of fabric, allowing for wastage.*

waste wasting wasted
1 *(v)* If you **waste** something, you use it wrongly or throw it away when you do not need to.
Don't waste your time. **waste** *(n)*.
2 *(n)* trash or something left over and not needed.
Chemical waste. **waste** *(adj)*.
3 *(v)* If someone **wastes away**, they get thinner and weaker because of illness or starvation.

wasteful *(adj)* If you are **wasteful**, you use things up needlessly and do not think about saving them.
wastefulness *(n)*, **wastefully** *(adv)*.

wasteland *(n)*
land that is not used for anything.

watch
watches watching watched
1 *(n)* a small clock, usually worn on your wrist.
2 *(v)* to look at something.
Alma was watching the news on the television.
3 *(v)* to notice or to be careful about something. *Watch what you're doing with those scissors!*
4 *(v)* to keep guard over. *Will you watch my purse while I go to the rest room?*

water watering watered
1 *(n)* a colorless liquid that you can drink.
2 *(v)* to pour water on something.
Can you water the plants?
3 *(v)* If your mouth **waters**, you see or smell food and feel hungry.
4 *(v)* If your eyes **water**, tears come from them.
5 **water down** *(v)* If you **water something down**, you make it weaker, usually by adding water.

watercolors *(plural n)*
paints that are mixed with water, not oil. *See* **artist**.

water cycle *(n)*
the constant movement of the Earth's water. Plants transpire, and water from rivers and oceans evaporates, making water vapor. This vapor rises, forms clouds and then falls as rain, hail, or snow. Some water enters plants and soil and the rest runs off into rivers and oceans.

water cycle

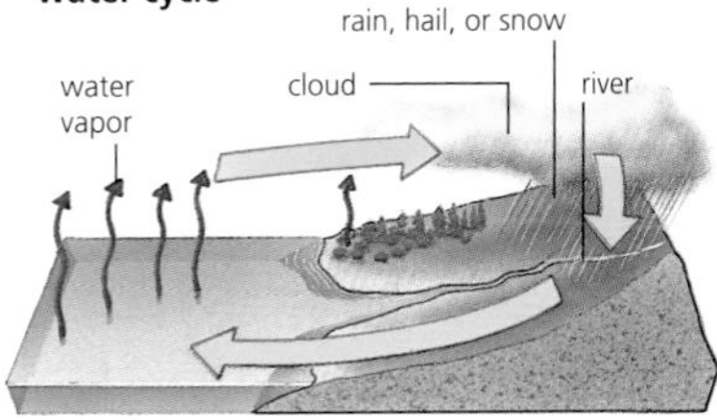

waterfall *(n)* water from a stream or river that falls down over rocks.

watering can *(n)* a metal or plastic container with a handle and a long spout, used for watering plants.

waterlogged *(adj)* If something is **waterlogged**, it is completely flooded or filled with water.
A waterlogged baseball outfield.

Some words that begin with a "w" sound are spelled "wh."

water main *(n)* a large supply pipe that carries water under the ground.

watermark *(n)* a mark in paper that you can see when you hold it up to the light.

waterproof *(adj)* If something is **waterproof**, it keeps water out.

water-ski **water-skiing water-skied** *(v)* to travel on skis over water, towed by a boat. **water-skier** *(n)*, **water-skiing** *(n)*.

watertight *(adj)* If something is **watertight**, it is completely sealed so that water cannot enter.

water vapor *(n)* the gas produced when water evaporates.

watt *(n)* a unit of electrical power. **wattage** *(n)*.

wave waving waved
1 *(v)* to move your hand, for example when you are saying hello or good-bye to someone. **wave** *(n)*.
2 *(v)* to move something from side to side in the air. *The fairy godmother waved her magic wand.* **wave** *(n)*.
3 *(n)* a moving ridge on the surface of water, especially the ocean.
4 *(n)* a curl in your hair. **wavy** *(adj)*.
5 *(n)* a vibration of energy that travels through air or water, for example, sound waves or radio waves.

wavelength
1 *(n)* the distance between one wave of light, sound, etc. and another.
2 *(n)* the size of wavelength that a radio station uses to transmit its programs.
3 *(informal)* If you are **on the same wavelength** as someone, you think in the same way as they do.

waver wavering wavered *(v)* to be uncertain or unsteady. *Nadia never wavered in her determination to win.*

wax waxes waxing waxed
1 *(n)* a substance made from fats or oils and used to make crayons, polish, and candles. **waxy** *(adj)*.
2 *(v)* to put wax polish on something, such as a car.
3 *(v)* When the Moon **waxes**, it appears to get larger. *See* **Moon**.

way
1 *(n)* a direction. *Which way is north?*
2 *(n)* a road or route. *Do you know the way home?*
3 *(n)* a method or style of doing something. *Is this the right way to spell your name?*
4 **ways** *(plural n)* habits or customs.

weak weaker weakest
1 *(adj)* not powerful or not having much force. **weakness** *(n)*, **weaken** *(v)*, **weakly** *(adv)*.
2 *(adj)* easy to break.
3 *(adj)* lacking flavor. *Weak tea.*
4 Your **weak points** are the things that you are not very good at.

weakling *(n)* a weak person or animal.

wealthy wealthier wealthiest *(adj)* Someone who is **wealthy** has a lot of money or property. **wealth** *(n)*.

wean weaning weaned
1 *(v)* When you **wean** babies, you start giving them food instead of just milk.
2 *(v)* If you **wean someone off** something, you help them to give it up gradually.

weapon *(n)* something that can be used for fighting, such as a sword or a gun. **weaponry** *(n)*.

wear *(wair)* wearing wore worn
1 *(v)* to be dressed in something or to have something attached to you. *Rosie wore a red brooch.* **wearer** *(n)*.
2 *(n)* clothes. *Boys' wear.*
3 *(n)* the gradual damage done to something by constant use. *My coat is showing signs of wear.*
4 **wear out** *(v)* If an activity **wears you out**, it makes you very tired.
5 *(v)* If you **wear out** your clothes, you make them ragged and useless.
6 **wear away** *(v)* to destroy something slowly, bit by bit.
7 **wear off** *(v)* to become less. *The effects of the painkiller have worn off.*

weary *(wihr-ee)* wearier weariest *(adj)* very tired or exhausted. **weariness** *(n)*, **wearily** *(adv)*.

weather weathering weathered
1 *(n)* the state of the atmosphere, for example how hot or cold it is and whether it is raining, snowing, etc.
2 *(v)* If wood or stone **weathers**, it changes after being outside for a long time.
3 *(v)* If you **weather** a storm or a crisis, you get through it.

weather-beaten *(adj)* Something that is **weather-beaten** is damaged or worn by the weather.

weather forecast *(n)* a prediction about the weather for the next few days.

weave weaving wove *or* weaved woven *or* weaved
1 *(v)* to make cloth, baskets, etc. by passing threads, canes or strips over and under each other. **weaver** *(n)*.
2 *(v)* to move from side to side to get through something. *Dan wove his way through the crowd.*

web
1 **the web** *(n)* a collection of linked pages stored on computers all over the world, that people can look at by using the internet. The web is short for the World Wide Web.
2 *(n)* a very fine net of sticky threads made by a spider to catch flies and other insects.
3 **webcam** *(n)* a camera that records video footage directly onto a website.
4 **web page** *(n)* a computer document on the web.
5 **website** *(n)* a collection of linked web pages, set up by an individual or organization.

webbed *(adj)* Animals with **webbed** feet have skin connecting their toes, which helps them to swim.

wedding *(n)* a marriage ceremony.

wedge
1 *(n)* a piece of food, wood, etc. that is thin at one end and thick at the other. *A wedge of cheese.*
2 *(v)* If you **wedge** something, you fix it tightly, or force it into a space. *Wedge open the door.*

wee *(adj)* very small, or tiny.

weed weeding weeded
1 *(n)* a wild plant, growing in a garden or a field.
2 *(v)* If you **weed** your garden, you pull the weeds out.

week *(n)* a period of seven days, usually from Sunday to Saturday. **weekly** *(adj)*.

weekday *(n)* one of the five days of the week, from Monday to Friday.

weekend *(n)* Saturday and Sunday.

weep weeping wept *(v)* to cry because you feel very sad or very emotional. **weepy** *(adj)*.

weigh weighing weighed
1 *(v)* to measure how heavy or light someone or something is, on scales or on a weighing machine.
2 *(v)* If you **weigh up** an idea or a situation, you think about it carefully.
3 *(adj)* If you are **weighed down**, you have too much to carry.

weight
1 *(n)* Someone or something's **weight** is how heavy they are.
2 *(n)* a heavy object. *This backpack is a weight!*
3 *(n)* a heavy object that people lift as an exercise to make their muscles stronger.

Some words that begin with a "w" sound are spelled "wh."

weightlifting *(n)*
a sport in which people lift weights to get stronger. **weightlifter** *(n)*.

weir *(rhymes with fear) (n)*
a wall built across a river to control the flow of water.

weird *(adj)* strange, or mysterious. **weirdness** *(n)*, **weirdly** *(adv)*.

welcome welcoming welcomed
1 *(v)* If you **welcome** someone, you greet them in a friendly way. **welcome** *(n)*, **welcoming** *(adj)*, **welcome** *(interject)*.
2 *(adj)* If something is **welcome**, you like it or are glad to have it. **welcome** *(v)*.

weld welding welded *(v)*
to join two pieces of metal by heating them and then fixing them together. **welder** *(n)*.

welfare *(n)* Someone's **welfare** is their state of health, happiness, and comfort. *Animal welfare.*

welfare state *(n)* a system in which the government uses money from taxes to pay for education, healthcare, and social services.

well
1 *(adv)* If you do something **well**, you do it successfully.
2 *(adv)* thoroughly. *Wash your hands well.*
3 *(adj)* healthy. *You're looking well.*
4 *(n)* a hole from which you can draw water or oil from under the ground.
5 *(interject)* You say **well** at the start of a sentence to show surprise or doubt. *Well, look who's here!*

wellbeing *(n)* health and happiness.

well-known *(adj)*
known by many people. *A well-known fact.*

well-off *(adj)* If someone is **well-off**, they are wealthy or rich.

west
1 *(n)* one of the four main points of the compass; the direction in which the sun sets. **west** *(adj)*, **west** *(adv)*.
2 *(adv, adj* or *n)* A **west wind** blows from the west. **westerly** *(adj* or *n)*.

western
1 *(adj)* having to do with the west of a country or the west of the world. *Western Australia. Western civilization.*
2 *(n)* a cowboy movie, set in the western part of the United States.

wet wetting wet *or* wetted; wetter wettest
1 *(adj)* covered with, or full of liquid.
2 *(v)* to make something wet. *Wet the cloth before you wipe those shelves.*

wetland *(n)* marshy land.

whack
1 *(n)* a hard, sharp hit. **whack** *(v)*.
2 *(n)* an attempt. *I'll take a whack at this math problem.*

whale *(n)* a large sea mammal, shaped like a fish. Whales take air into their lungs, but live in water.

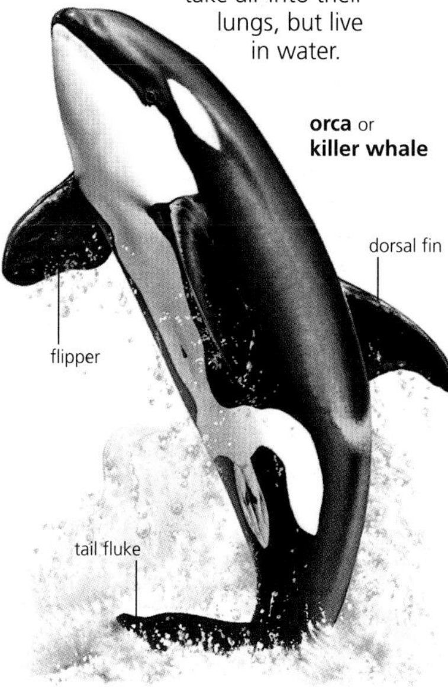

whaler
1 *(n)* someone who hunts whales for their meat and oil. **whaling** *(n)*.
2 *(n)* a boat used to catch whales.

wharf *(worf)* **wharfs** *or* **wharves** *(n)*
a place where boats and ships can be loaded or unloaded.

what
1 *(adj)* The word **what** is used in questions to discover more about something. *What music do you like?*
2 *(pronoun)* the thing or things that. *I heard what you said.*
3 *(adj)* The word **what** is used to emphasize how great, small, strange, etc., something or someone is. *What a surprise! What an idiot!*

whatever
1 *(pronoun)* anything that. *Wear whatever you like.*
2 *(pronoun)* what. *Whatever have you done that for?*

wheat *(n)*
a cereal plant whose grain is used for making flour. *See* **grain**.

wheel wheeling wheeled
1 *(n)* a circular object that turns on an axle, used to work machinery or move a vehicle.
2 *(v)* to push something on wheels. *Wheel your bicycle up the hill.*

wheelbarrow *(n)*
a small cart with one wheel at the front, often used to carry things around in yards or gardens.

wheelchair *(n)*
a chair on wheels for people who are ill, injured, or disabled.

wheelie *(n) (informal)*
If you do a **wheelie** on a bicycle or motorcycle, you ride with the front wheel off the ground.

wheeze wheezing wheezed *(v)*
to breathe with difficulty, making a whistling noise in your chest. **wheeziness** *(n)*, **wheezy** *(adj)*.

when
1 *(conj)* at the time that. *I told Jake the news when I saw him.*
2 *(adv)* The word **when** is used to ask about the time that something happened. *When was Warhol born?*

whenever *(conj)* at any time. *We'll eat whenever you're hungry.*

where
1 *(conj)* at the place that. *I visited the house where my friend lives.*
2 *(adv)* The word **where** is used to ask about the place or position of something. *Where is Emma?*

whereabouts
1 *(adv)* roughly where. *Whereabouts in Maine did you stay?*
2 *(n)* the place where someone or something is. *I'm afraid we don't know Billy's whereabouts.*

whereas *(conj)* but. *My parents eat meat, whereas I am a vegetarian.*

wherever *(conj)*
to any place. *We'll go wherever you suggest.* **wherever** *(adv)*.

whether *(conj)* if. *I wonder whether it will rain.*

whey *(n)*
When you separate milk to make cheese, the watery part is **whey**.

which
1 *(adj)* The word **which** is used to ask about a choice of things. *Which dress shall I wear?*
2 *(pronoun)* what one or ones. *Which is yours?*

whichever *(pronoun)*
any or no matter which. *You can have whichever you want.*

whiff *(n)* a smell in the air.

while
1 *(n)* a period of time. *It was a long while before I ate noodles again.*
2 **while** *(conj)* during the time that. *Can you feed my dog while I'm away?*
3 *(conj)* in contrast to. *Hannah likes skating while I prefer swimming.*

whim *(n)* a sudden idea or wish, which is often rather silly.

whimper
whimpering whimpered *(v)* to make weak, crying noises. whimper *(n)*.

whine whining whined
1 *(v)* to make a long, drawn-out sound that is sad or unpleasant.
2 *(v)* to complain or moan about something in an irritating way.

whinny *(n)*
a horse's low, gentle neigh.

whip whipping whipped
1 *(n)* a long piece of leather used for hitting people or animals. whip *(v)*.
2 *(v)* to move something suddenly. *Cal whipped the present behind his back.*
3 *(v)* to beat cream, eggs, etc. into a foam.
4 *(v)* to defeat badly. *Our team whipped the Giants last week.*

whirl whirling whirled
1 *(v)* If something **whirls**, it moves around quickly. *Leaves were whirling across the playground.*
2 *(n)* a fast or confused movement. *A whirl of activity.*
3 *(informal)* If you **give something a whirl**, you try it out.

whirlwind
1 *(n)* a wind like a cyclone, which moves in a tall column and goes around and around very fast.
2 *(adj)* very quick or sudden. *A whirlwind tour of the city.*

whisk whisking whisked
1 *(n)* a metal tool that you use for beating eggs or cream. whisk *(v)*.
2 *(v)* to move something quickly or suddenly. *Our plates were whisked away before we finished eating.*

whisker *(n)* one of the long, stiff hairs near the mouth of some animals.

whisper
whispering whispered *(v)* to talk very quietly or to make a soft sound. whisper *(n)*.

whistle
whistling whistled
1 *(n)* an instrument that makes a high loud sound when you blow it.
2 *(v)* to blow air through your lips to make a sound or a tune. whistle *(n)*.
3 *(v)* to move very fast with a whistling sound. *The train whistled past.*

white whiter whitest
1 *(n)* the color of snow. white *(adj)*.
2 *(adj)* **White** people have naturally light skin, or are descended from people with light skin.
3 *(n)* The **white** of an egg is the part around the yolk. *See* **egg**.

whitewash
1 *(n)* a mixture of lime, chalk and water used for painting things white. whitewash *(v)*.
2 *(v)* to cover up someone's mistakes or wrongdoings.

whiz *or* **whizz**
whizzes whizzing whizzed
1 *(v)* to move very fast, often with a buzzing sound.
2 *(n) (slang)* someone who is very good at something. *A math whiz.*

who *(hoo)*
1 *(pronoun)* The word **who** is used to ask questions about people. *Who is that man?*
2 *(pronoun)* The word **who** is used to show which person you are talking about, or to give more information about someone. *The man who lives next door.*

whoever *(hoo-**ev**-er)*
1 *(pronoun)* anyone at all or no matter who. *Whoever made this mess will have to clean it up.*
2 *(pronoun)* who. *Whoever could that be at the door?*

whole *(hole)*
1 *(adj)* the total amount of something. *I've eaten a whole loaf of bread.*
2 *(adj)* complete or not broken.
3 *(n)* the entire thing or all the parts of something. *Two halves make a whole.*

whole food *(**hole** food) (n)* food that has been processed as little as possible, such as brown rice.

wholesale *(**hole**-sayl) (adv)* When store owners buy things **wholesale**, they buy them cheaply in large quantities, to sell them in their stores. wholesaler *(n)*.

wholesome *(**hole**-sum)*
1 *(adj)* healthy or good for you. *A wholesome diet.*
2 *(adj)* suggesting good health, or good or moral behaviour.

whole wheat *(**hole** weet) (adj)* Whole wheat flour has all the grain left in it.

wholly *(**hoe**-lee) (adv)* completely.

whooping cough *(**hoo**-ping koff) (n)* an infectious disease that makes children cough violently and breathe in a noisy way.

whose *(hooz)*
1 *(pronoun)* The word **whose** is used to ask to whom something belongs. *Whose skateboard is this?*
2 *(pronoun)* The word **whose** is used to indicate the person or thing about which you are talking. *That's the girl whose party I've been invited to.*

why *(adv)* The word **why** is used to ask about the reason for something. *Why did you leave?* why *(conj)*.

wick *(n)* the twisted cord running through a candle, which you light.

wicked
1 *(adj)* very bad, cruel, or evil. wickedness *(n)*, wickedly *(adv)*.
2 *(adj) (slang)* very good.

wide wider widest
1 *(adj)* from one side to the other, or from edge to edge. *This room is fourteen feet wide.*
2 *(adj)* large from side to side. widen *(v)*.
3 *(adj)* covering a large number of things. *We stock a wide range of magazines.* widely *(adv)*.

widespread *(adj)* happening in many places or among many people. *There is widespread concern about climate change.*

widow *(n)* a woman whose husband has died and who has not married again. widowed *(adj)*.

widower *(n)* a man whose wife has died and who has not married again. widowed *(adj)*.

width *(n)* the distance from one side of something to the other. *What is the width of this carpet?*

wife *(n)*
the female partner in a marriage.

wig *(n)* a covering of artificial or real hair made to fit someone's head.

wiggle wiggling wiggled *(v)* to make small movements from side to side or up and down. wiggly *(adj)*.

wild wilder wildest
1 *(adj)* natural and not tamed by humans. *Wild animals.* wildness *(n)*.
2 *(adj)* uncontrolled, often in an angry or crazy way. *Mom went wild when she saw the mess.* wildly *(adv)*.
3 *(adj)* crazy, fantastic, or reckless. *He had a wild plan to walk from Argentina to New York.*

wilderness wildernesses *(n)* an area of wild, uninhabited land, such as a desert.

wildlife *(n)* wild animals and plants.

will
1 *(n)* written instructions stating what should happen to someone's property and money when they die.
2 *(n)* Your **will** is your determination to do something. *Eleanor has an amazing will to succeed.*

willful
1 *(adj)* deliberate. willfully *(adj)*.
2 *(adj)* Someone who is **willful** is determined to have their own way. willfulness *(n)*.

willing *(adj)* People who are **willing** are eager and pleased to offer their help. **willingness** *(n),* **willingly** *(adv).*

willow *(n)* a tree with thin narrow leaves and branches, often near water.

wilt wilting wilted
1 *(v)* If a plant **wilts**, it begins to droop.
2 *(v)* If a person **wilts**, they become tired through lack of energy or food.

wimp *(n) (informal)* a feeble or cowardly person. **wimpy** *(adj).*

win winning won
1 *(v)* to come first in a contest. **win** *(n),* **winner** *(n).*
2 *(v)* to gain or deserve something. *Julius won his brother's respect.*

wince wincing winced *(v)* to twitch or flinch because you are in pain, embarrassed, or disgusted. **wince** *(n).*

winch winches *(n)* a cable wound around a rotating drum, which you use for pulling or hoisting things. **winch** *(v).* *See* **portcullis**, **rescue**.

wind winding wound
1 *(rhymes with pinned) (n)* moving air. **windy** *(adj).*
2 *(rhymes with kind) (v)* to wrap something around something else. *Verity wound her scarf several times around her neck.*
3 *(rhymes with kind) (v)* to twist and turn. *The road winds up the mountain.*
4 *(rhymes with kind) (v)* to turn the key of a clock.
5 **wind up** *(rhymes with kind) (v) (slang)* If you **wind something up**, you finish it.

winded *(adj)* If you are **winded**, you are out of breath because of exercise or a sudden hit in the stomach.

windfall
1 *(n)* a fruit that has been blown off a tree.
2 *(n)* a sudden piece of good fortune, usually an unexpected gain of money.

wind instrument *(n)* an instrument played by blowing, for example, the trombone, harmonica, and clarinet. *See* **brass**, **harmonica**, **woodwind**.

windmill *(n)* a machine for grinding grain to make flour, worked by the wind turning a set of sails. *The picture above shows a 19th-century windmill. Its sails turn the wallower, which is connected by a series of shafts and cogwheels to the greater spur wheel, which turns the millstones to grind grain into flour.*

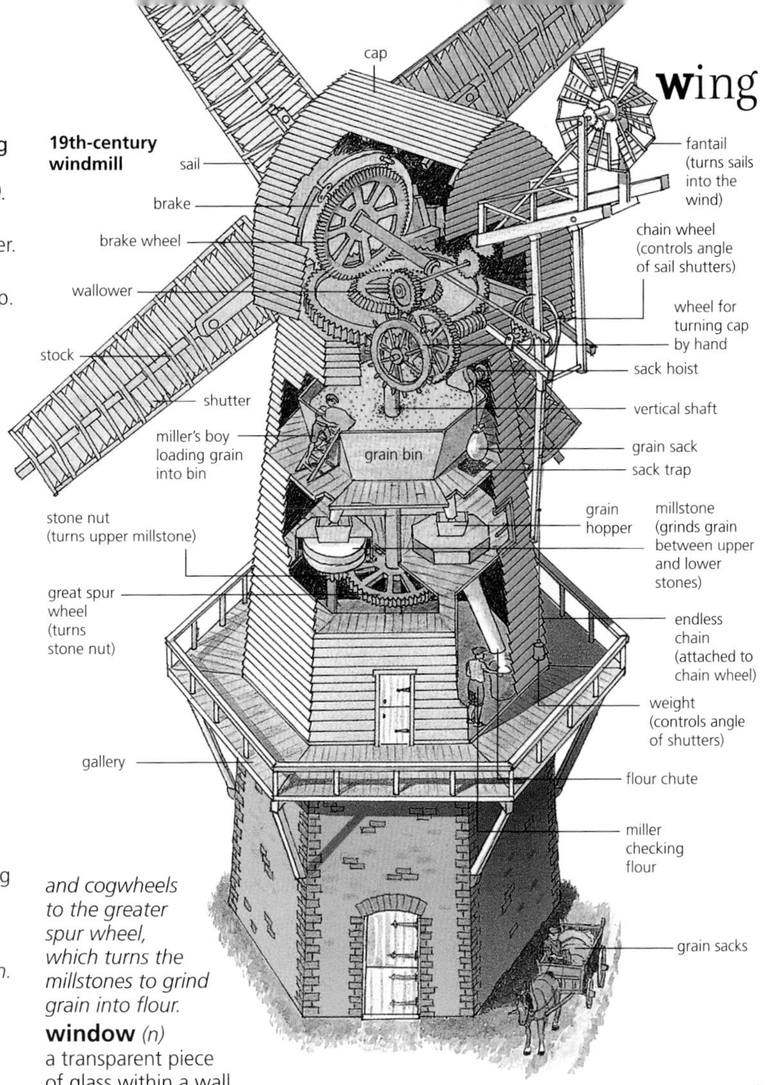

19th-century windmill

window *(n)* a transparent piece of glass within a wall.

window-shopping *(n)* If you go **window-shopping**, you look in store windows but do not buy anything.

windpipe *(n)* the tube that links the lungs with the nose and mouth. *See* **respiration**.

windsurfing *(n)* the sport of sailing by standing on a board with a flexible mast and a sail, and holding onto a curved boom. *This picture of windsurfing at sea shows a windsurfer riding a wave called a rollercoaster.* **windsurfer** *(n).*

windswept *(adj)* exposed and blown by the wind.

wind turbine *(n)* a machine, with blades shaped like propellers, that uses energy from the wind to make electricity.

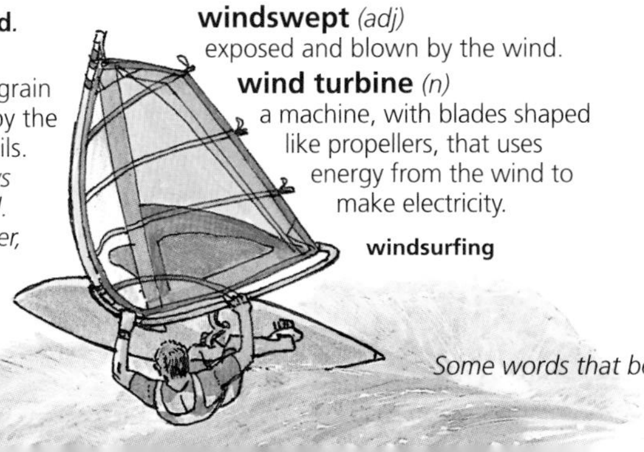

windsurfing

Wind turbines are often erected in groups called wind parks or wind farms.

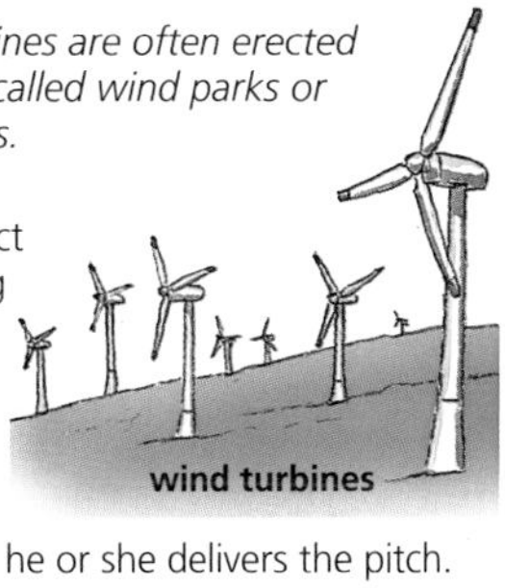

wind turbines

windup
1 *(n)* the act of bringing to an end.
2 *(n)* the pose struck by a pitcher, just before he or she delivers the pitch.

wing
1 *(n)* one of the feather-covered limbs of a bird, which the bird flaps to fly. *See* **bird**.
2 *(n)* a movable part of an insect or a bat that allows it to fly.
3 *(n)* an outer part or extension of something. *Hospital wing.*
4 *(n)* a wing-like structure on an aircraft that makes it able to fly.
5 **wings** *(plural n)* the sides of a theater stage, which cannot be seen by the audience.

Some words that begin with a "w" sound are spelled "wh."

wingspan *(n)*
the distance between the outer tips of the wings of a bird or an aircraft.

wink winking winked *(v)*
to close one eye briefly as a signal or a friendly gesture.

winner
1 *(n)* a person, a team, an animal, or thing that wins a contest.
2 *(n) (informal)* an excellent idea or plan that seems likely to succeed.

winter *(n)*
the season between fall and spring, when the weather is coldest. wintry *(adj).*

wipe wiping wiped
1 *(v)* to clear or clean a surface with your hand or a cloth, using a sweeping motion.
2 *(v)* to rub something to clean it. *Wipe the dishes. Wipe your feet.*
3 wipe out *(v)*
to destroy something totally. *The earthquake wiped out the village.*

wire wiring wired
1 *(n)* a long, thin, flexible piece of metal. Wire can be used to pull or support things or to conduct an electrical current.
2 *(v)* to connect electrical wires to equipment. *Marco wired up the new stove.*

wiry wirier wiriest
1 *(adj)* tough and stiff. *Wiry hair.*
2 *(adj)* A **wiry** person is thin but tough.

wisdom *(n)* knowledge, experience, and understanding.

wise wiser wisest *(adj)*
Wise people know what is right to say and do in different situations. wisely *(adv).*

wish wishes wishing wished
1 *(v)* to think or say that you would like something. wish *(n).*
2 *(v)* to hope for something for someone else. *I wish you a very happy New Year!*

wisp *(n)*
a small and delicate piece of something. *A wisp of hair. A wisp of smoke.* wispy *(adj).*

wit
1 *(n)* the ability to say clever and funny things.
2 *(n)* someone who can say clever and funny things.
3 *(n)* the ability to think quickly and clearly. *Donny had the wit to find an escape route.*

with *(prep)* attached to or accompanying. *Chicken with fried noodles.*

withdraw withdrawing withdrew withdrawn
1 *(v)* to remove or to take away something. *Sadie withdrew the cash from her bank. Alex withdrew his support for the project.* withdrawal *(n).*
2 *(v)* to drop out or to go away. *Lee had to withdraw from the team because of injury.*

withdrawn *(adj)* A **withdrawn** person is very shy and quiet.

wither withering withered
1 *(v)* When something **withers**, it shrivels up because it has lost moisture.
2 *(adj)* A **withering** look or remark is a very scornful one.

withhold withholding withheld *(v)*
to keep something back or to refuse to give something. *My parents withheld their permission for a party.*

within
1 *(prep)* inside. *Within the cave was a dragon.* within *(adv).*
2 *(prep)* not beyond the limits of. *I want you back here within ten minutes!*

without *(prep)* If you are **without** something, you do not have it.

withstand withstanding withstood *(v)* to bear or to stand something. *The sea wall withstood the pounding of the waves.*

witness witnesses *(n)* someone who sees something happen and who may be called to give evidence in court. witness *(v).*

witty wittier wittiest *(adj)*
A **witty** person says or writes humorous things. wittily *(adv).*

wobble wobbling wobbled *(v)*
to move from side to side in an unsteady manner. *The cups wobbled on the tray.* wobbly *(adj).*

Asiatic wolf

woe *(n)* (old-fashioned) great sadness or grief. woeful *(adj),* woefully *(adv).*

wolf wolves *(n)*
a wild mammal that looks like a large dog and hunts in a pack.

woman *(n)*
an adult female human being. womanhood *(n),* womanly *(adj).*

wombat

womb *(woom) (n)*
the part of a woman in which a baby develops before it is born. *See* **pregnant**.

wombat *(n)*
a short-legged marsupial that looks like a small bear. The female carries her young in a pouch.

wonder
wondering wondered
1 *(v)* to think about something in a casual or curious way. *I wonder whether it is time for dinner.*
2 *(v)* to be amazed at something. *We wondered at Linda's ability to talk for hours.*
3 *(n)* someone or something that is amazing or impressive.

wonderful
1 *(adj)* amazing, splendid, or magnificent. *The Himalayan mountains were a wonderful sight.*
2 *(adj)* extremely pleasant. *It was wonderful to see Hugh again.* wonderfully *(adv).*

wood *(n)* the substance that forms the trunk and branches of a tree. wooden *(adj).*

woods *(n)* an area of trees that is smaller than a forest. wooded *(adj).*

woodland *(n)*
land covered mainly by trees.

great spotted woodpecker

woodpecker *(n)*
a bird that can drill through bark and wood with its bill. Most woodpeckers live in forests.

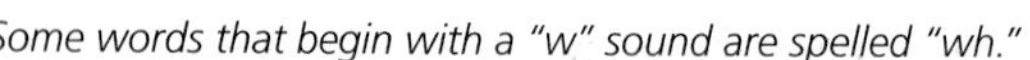
Some words that begin with a "w" sound are spelled "wh."

oboe
flute
piccolo
bassoon
English horn
clarinet
barrel
ligature
mouthpiece containing reed
upper joint
key
ring key
lower joint
bell

woodwind *(n)*
The **woodwind** section of an orchestra is made up of instruments that you blow into and that were originally made of wood. *The illustration above shows a clarinet, with its main parts labeled, and five other instruments from the woodwind section of an orchestra.*

woodwork
1 *(n)* things made out of wood. *An exhibition of woodwork.*
2 *(n)* the craft of making things from wood. *The picture shows a range of tools used for woodwork.* **woodworking** *(adj).*

wool *(n)*
the hair of a sheep, spun into a thread for knitting, weaving, etc. **woolen** *(adj).*

word
1 *(n)* a group of spoken sounds or written letters that has a meaning.
2 *(n)* an order.
Jump when I give the word!
3 *(n)* news or a message.
Is there any word from the Alamo?
4 If you **give your word**, you promise something.

word processing *(n)*
the use of a computer and software to type and print documents. Words are viewed onscreen and can easily be changed, copied, and stored. **word processor** *(n).*

work working worked
1 *(v)* to study, or to do a job. **work** *(n).*
2 *(v)* to function properly.
Does your computer work?
3 *(n)* a piece of music, painting, sculpture, etc. *A work of art.*
4 *(n)* a task. *We finished work on the house yesterday.*
5 *(v)* When you **work out** in a gym, you do physical exercise. **workout** *(n).*

workable *(adj)* If a plan is **workable**, it can be carried out.

worker *(n)* someone who is employed to do a job.

workman workmen *(n)*
a man who does manual work.

workshop
1 *(n)* a room, shed, or other building where things are made or repaired.
2 *(n)* a group of people who meet to discuss, learn about, or practice a particular skill. *A writer's workshop.*

world
1 *(n)* the planet Earth.
2 *(n)* an area of activity.
The world of sports.

worldly worldlier worldliest
1 *(adj)* concerned with the world of money and material things, rather than with spiritual or religious matters. **worldliness** *(n).*
2 *(adj)* used to the way that people behave.

worldwide *(adj)* to do with, or reaching most parts of the world.

World Wide Web *(n)*
a collection of linked pages stored on computers all over the world, which people can look at by using the internet.

worm *(n)*
a small creature that lives in the soil. Worms have long, thin, soft bodies and no backbones.

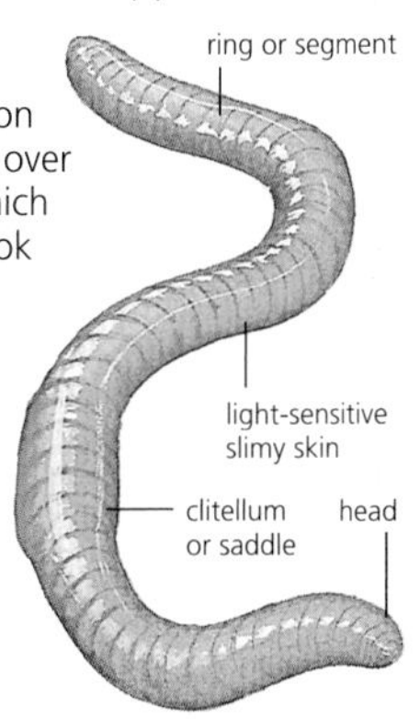

earthworm

Some words that begin with a "w" sound are spelled "wh."

worn *(adj)* Something that is **worn** is old and less useful because it has been used a lot. *Worn tires can be dangerous.*

worry worries worrying worried
1 *(v)* to be anxious or uneasy about something. **worrier** *(n)*, **worrying** *(adj)*, **worryingly** *(adv)*.
2 *(n)* something that makes you anxious. *Dustin is a worry to his mom.*

worse *(adj)* less good. *Your handwriting is worse than mine.*

worship worshiping worshiped
1 *(v)* to express your love and devotion to God or a god. **worship** *(n)*.
2 *(n)* a church service.
3 *(v)* If you **worship** someone, you think that they are wonderful.

worst *(adj)* worse than anything else. *Carl's self-portrait is the worst I've ever seen.*

worth
1 *(adj)* having a certain value. *This painting is worth a fortune.* **worth** *(n)*.
2 *(adj)* deserving or good enough for. *It's worth going to the sale for the bargains.*

worthless *(adj)* If something is **worthless**, it has no value or is useless. **worthlessness** *(n)*.

worthwhile *(adj)* useful and valuable. *Learning French is a worthwhile activity.*

worthy worthier worthiest *(adj)* deserving. *I'm happy to give money to a worthy cause.*

wound *(n)* an injury in which the skin is cut, usually caused by an accident, violence, etc. **wound** *(v)*.

wraith *(rayth) (n)* a ghost or ghostlike figure.

wrangle wrangling wrangled *(v)* to argue or debate in a noisy or angry way. **wrangle** *(n)*.

wrap wrapping wrapped *(v)* to cover something in paper, material, etc. to protect it.

wrapper *(n)* the protective material in which something is wrapped. *A candy wrapper.*

wrath *(rath) (n)* anger.

wreak *(reek)* wreaking wreaked *(v)* to cause or to inflict. *The bull wreaked havoc in the china shop.*

wreath *(reeth)*
1 *(n)* a circle of flowers or leaves worn on the head. *A laurel wreath.*
2 *(n)* an arrangement of flowers, leaves, etc. in memory of the dead.

wreck wrecking wrecked
1 *(v)* to destroy or ruin something completely.
2 *(n)* something that has been ruined, for example, a ship.

wreckage *(n)* the broken remains at the site of a crash or explosion.

wrench
wrenches wrenching wrenched
1 *(v)* to pull something suddenly and forcefully. *I wrenched open the door.*
2 *(n)* an adjustable tool for gripping and pulling nuts, bolts, etc. *See* **tool**.

wrestle wrestling wrestled
1 *(v)* to fight by gripping an opponent and trying to throw them to the floor.
2 *(v)* If you **wrestle** with a problem, you try to solve it by thinking very hard.

wrestling *(n)* a sport in which you fight according to rules. *The picture shows the ancient Japanese sport of Sumo wrestling.* **wrestler** *(n)*.

Sumo wrestling

wretch wretches
1 *(n)* a miserable and unfortunate person. **wretched** *(adj)*.
2 *(n)* a mean and unpleasant person.

wriggle wriggling wriggled *(v)* to twist and turn.

wring wringing wrung *(v)* to squeeze the moisture from wet material by twisting it with both hands.

wrinkle *(n)* a crease or line in someone's skin or in material.

wrist *(n)* the joint that connects your hand and your arm.

write writing wrote written
1 *(v)* to put down letters, words, or numbers on paper or another surface, using a pen, pencil, etc.
2 *(v)* to compose poetry, prose, music, etc. **writer** *(n)*.
3 *(v)* If someone **writes off** a car in a crash, it is a total wreck and cannot be repaired. **write-off** *(n)*.

writhe writhing writhed *(v)* to twist about. *Sammy writhed in agony.*

writing
1 *(n)* anything that has been written. *Who did this writing on the wall?*
2 *(n)* literature, stories, poems, etc.

wrong
1 *(adj)* incorrect or not right. *Wrong answers.* **wrongly** *(adv)*.
2 *(adj)* bad and sinful. *It is wrong to steal.* **wrong** *(n)*, **wrongful** *(adj)*.

WWW *(n)*
WWW is short for World Wide Web.

Xmas *see* **Christmas**.

X-ray
1 *(n)* a beam of energy that can pass through some solids. **X-ray** *(adj)*.
2 *(n)* a photograph of the inside of a person's body, taken using X-rays. *The picture shows an X-ray of a hand.* **X-ray** *(v)*.

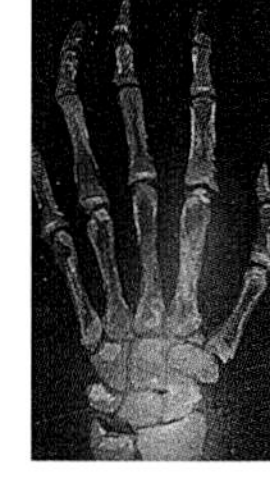

X-ray

xylophone *(zy-luh-fone) (n)* a musical instrument with wooden bars of different sizes, which are struck to give different notes.

yacht *(rhymes with dot)*
1 *(n)* a large sailboat, used for pleasure or for racing. **yachting** *(n)*.
2 *(n)* a large, luxury motor cruiser.

yaks

yak *(n)* a long-haired ox from Tibet and central Asia.

yank yanking yanked *(v)* to pull something sharply and strongly. **yank** *(n)*.

yap yapping yapped *(v)* to bark repeatedly, with short, high-pitched sounds.

yard
1 *(n)* an enclosed area with a hard surface, usually next to a building.
2 *(n)* a unit of measurement. *See* page 284.
3 *(n)* an area of grass surrounding or next to a house.

yardstick *(n)* a standard used to judge things or people. *I judge comedians by the yardstick of whether they make me laugh.*

yarn
1 *(n)* a very long strand of wool or cotton, used for sewing, knitting, etc.
2 *(informal)* If someone **spins a yarn**, they tell a long and exaggerated story.

yashmak *(n)*
a veil worn by some Muslim women to cover all of their face except for their eyes.

yawn yawning yawned
1 *(v)* to open your mouth wide and breathe in, often because you are tired or bored. **yawn** *(n)*.
2 *(v)* to make a wide opening or gap. *A huge gulf yawned between the two rocks.*

year *(n)*
a period of 365 days, or 366 days in a leap year, which is the time that it takes the Earth to circle the Sun once.

yearn *(rhymes with burn)* yearning yearned *(v)* to wish or long for something very strongly. **yearning** *(n)*.

yeast *(n)*
a yellow fungus used to make bread.

yell yelling yelled *(v)*
to shout or scream very loudly. **yell** *(n)*.

yellow *(n)* the color of lemons or butter. **yellow** *(adj)*.

yelp yelping yelped *(v)* When a dog **yelps**, it makes a sharp, high-pitched cry, showing that it is in pain. **yelp** *(n)*.

yen
1 *(n)* the main unit of money in Japan.
2 *(n) (informal)* If you have a **yen** for something, you want it very much.

yes *(interject)*
a word used to show agreement.

yesterday *(n)*
the day before today.

yet
1 *(adv)* so far. *I haven't received an answer yet.*
2 *(adv)* up to now. *You're not allowed out yet.*
3 *(adv)* still or even. *There were yet more surprises in store.*
4 *(conj)* but. *Celia passed all her exams yet couldn't find a job.*

yield yielding yielded
1 *(v)* to produce something. *The field yielded 90 tons of potatoes.* **yield** *(n)*.
2 *(v)* to surrender. *Yield, Sir Jasper!*

yodel yodeling yodeled *(v)*
to sing in a voice that changes rapidly between high and low sounds. Yodeling is popular in Switzerland. **yodeler** *(n)*.

yoga *(n)* a system of exercises and meditation that helps people to become mentally relaxed and physically fit. Yoga came originally from Hindu teachings.

yogurt *(n)*
a slightly sour-tasting food prepared from milk curdled by bacteria.

yoke *(n)* a wooden frame attached to the necks of oxen to link them together for plowing. *See* **plow**.

yolk *(rhymes with poke) (n)*
the yellow part of an egg. If the egg is fertilized, the protein and fat from the yolk nourish the developing embryo. *See* **egg**.

Yom Kippur *(n)*
the most important Jewish holy day of the year, when Jews fast all day.

yonder *(adj) (old-fashioned)*
over there. **yonder** *(adv)*.

you
1 *(pronoun)* the person or people to whom someone is talking.
2 *(pronoun)* anyone or people in general. *You never know.*

young younger youngest
1 *(adj)* Someone who is **young** has lived for a short time.
2 *(adj)* Something that is **young** has existed for a short time. *A young country.*
3 *(plural n)* the offspring of an animal.

youngster *(n)* a young person.

your *(pronoun)* belonging to you.

yours *(pronoun)* the one or ones belonging or having to do with you. *Is this pen yours?*

yourself yourselves *(pronoun)*
you and nobody else. *Help yourself to some food.*

youth
1 *(n)* the time of life when a person is young.
2 *(n)* a young person, usually aged between 13 and 18.
3 *(plural n)* young people in general. *Today's youth face many challenges.*
4 **youth hostel** a place where people can stay very cheaply while on vacation. Youth hostels are usually used by young people.

yo-yo *(n)* a toy consisting of a string wound around a flat reel. You loop the string over your finger and flick the reel up and down on the string.

Yuletide *(n) (old-fashioned)*
the Christmas season.

Zz

zany zanier zaniest *(adj)* humorous in an unusual, crazy way. **zanily** *(adv)*.

zap zapping zapped *(v) (slang)*
to kill someone, usually in a game.

zeal *(zeel) (n)* enthusiasm and eagerness. **zealous** *(zel-uss) (adj)*.

zebra *(n)* an African wild animal, similar to a horse, with black and white stripes on its body.

zebras

zenith *(zee-nith) (n)*
the highest point of a structure, or the peak of a mountain.

zero *(n)* nothing, naught, or nil.

zest
1 *(n)* enthusiasm and liveliness.
2 *(n)* the outer skin of a citrus fruit.

zigzag *(n)* a line with sharp, diagonal turns. **zigzag** *(v)*.

zinc *(n)* a blue-white metal that is used in some alloys and for coating metals so that they will not rust.

zip zipping zipped
1 *(v)* to fasten clothes with a zipper.
2 *(v)* to move fast.

zip code *(n)*
the set of numbers and letters at the end of an address, used to help sort letters, packages, etc., more quickly.

zipper *(n)*
a fastener for fabrics. A zipper consists of two strips of metal or plastic teeth that link when pulled together.

zit *(n)* a spot or pimple on the skin.

zodiac *(n)* a circular, imaginary belt in the sky that includes the path of the Sun, the Moon, and the planets. The zodiac is divided into twelve equal parts whose names are the names of constellations. The names, or signs of the zodiac are used in astrology.

zombie *(n) (informal)*
someone who seems lifeless or dull.

zone *(n)* an area that is separate from other areas and used for a special purpose. *A conservation zone.*

zoo *(n)* a place where animals are kept for people to see or study them.

zoology *(n)*
the study of animals.
zoologist *(n)*, **zoological** *(adj)*.

zoom zooming zoomed *(v)*
to move very fast. *Ann zoomed off on her bike.*

zucchini *(n)*
a long, fleshy vegetable similar to a small squash. *See* **vegetable**.

COUNTRIES AND NATIONALITIES

If a nationality is not given with the country, you refer to people from that country as a citizen of .....

Afghanistan - *Afghan*
Albania - *Albanian*
Algeria - *Algerian*
Andorra - *Andorran*
Angola - *Angolan*
Antigua and Barbuda
Argentina - *Argentine*
Armenia - *Armenian*
Australia - *Australian*
Austria - *Austrian*
Azerbaijan - *Azerbaijani*
Bahamas - *Bahamian*
Bahrain - *Bahraini*
Bangladesh - *Bangladeshi*
Barbados - *Barbadian*
Belarus - *Belarussian*
Belgium - *Belgian*
Belize - *Belizean*
Benin - *Beninese*
Bhutan - *Bhutanese*
Bolivia - *Bolivian*
Bosnia-Herzegovina
Botswana - *Batswana/Motswana*
Brazil - *Brazilian*
Brunei
Bulgaria - *Bulgarian*
Burkina Faso - *Burkinian*
Burma - *Burmese*
Burundi
Cambodia - *Cambodian*
Cameroon - *Cameroonian*
Canada - *Canadian*
Cape Verde - *Cape Verdean*
Central African Republic
Chad - *Chadian*
Chile - *Chilean*
China - *Chinese*
China (Taiwan) - *Nationalist Chinese*
Colombia - *Colombian*
Comoros - *Comoran*
Congo - *Congolese*
Congo (Democratic Republic)
Costa Rica - *Costa Rican*
Croatia - *Croat*
Cuba - *Cuban*
Cyprus - *Cypriot*
Czech Republic - *Czech*
Denmark - *Dane*
Djibouti - *Djiboutian*
Dominica - *Dominican*
Dominican Republic
East Timor
Ecuador - *Ecuadorian*
Egypt - *Egyptian*
El Salvador - *Salvadorean*
Equatorial Guinea - *Equatorial Guinean*
Eritrea - *Eritrean*
Estonia - *Estonian*
Ethiopia - *Ethiopian*
Fiji
Finland - *Finn*
France - *Frenchman, Frenchwoman*
Gabon - *Gabonese*
Gambia, The - *Gambian*
Georgia - *Georgian*
Germany - *German*
Ghana - *Ghanaian*
Greece - *Greek*
Grenada - *Grenadian*
Guatemala - *Guatemalan*
Guinea - *Guinean*
Guinea-Bissau
Guyana - *Guyanese*
Haiti - *Haitian*
Honduras - *Honduran*
Hungary - *Hungarian*
Iceland - *Icelander*
India - *Indian*
Indonesia - *Indonesian*
Iran - *Iranian*
Iraq - *Iraqi*
Ireland, Republic of
Israel - *Israeli*
Italy - *Italian*
Ivory Coast
Jamaica - *Jamaican*
Japan - *Japanese*
Jordan - *Jordanian*
Kazakhstan - *Kazakh*
Kenya - *Kenyan*
Kiribati
Korea, North - *North Korean*
Korea, South - *South Korean*
Kosovo - *Kosovan*
Kuwait - *Kuwaiti*
Kyrgyzstan - *Kyrgyz*
Laos - *Laotian*
Latvia - *Latvian*
Lebanon - *Lebanese*
Lesotho
Liberia - *Liberian*
Libya - *Libyan*
Liechtenstein
Lithuania - *Lithuanian*
Luxembourg - *Luxembourger*
Macedonia - *Macedonian*
Madagascar - *Malagsy*
Malawi - *Malawian*
Malaysia
Maldives - *Maldivian*
Mali - *Malian*
Malta - *Maltese*
Marshall Islands - *Marshall Islander*
Mauritania - *Mauritanian*
Mauritius - *Mauritian*
Mexico - *Mexican*
Micronesia - *Micronesian*
Moldova - *Moldovan*
Monaco - *Monegasque*
Mongolia - *Mongolian*
Montenegro
Morocco - *Moroccan*
Mozambique - *Mozambican*
Namibia - *Namibian*
Nauru - *Nauruan*
Nepal - *Nepalese*
Netherlands - *Dutchman, Dutchwoman*
New Zealand - *New Zealander*
Nicaragua - *Nicaraguan*
Niger
Nigeria - *Nigerian*
Norway - *Norwegian*
Oman - *Omani*
Pakistan - *Pakistani*
Palau - *Palauan*
Palestine - *Palestinian*
Panama - *Panamanian*
Papua New Guinea - *Papua New Guinean*
Paraguay - *Paraguayan*
Peru - *Peruvian*
Philippines, The - *Filipino, Filipina*
Poland - *Pole*
Portugal - *Portuguese*
Qatar - *Qatari*
Romania - *Romanian*
Russia - *Russian*
Rwanda
St. Kitts and Nevis
St. Lucia - *St Lucian*
St. Vincent and the Grenadines
Samoa - *Samoan*
San Marino
São Tomé and Príncipe
Saudi Arabia - *Saudi Arabian*
Senegal - *Senegalese*
Serbia - *Serbian*
Seychelles
Sierra Leone - *Sierra Leonean*
Singapore - *Singaporean*
Slovakia - *Slovak*
Slovenia - *Slovene*
Solomon Islands - *Solomon Islander*
Somalia - *Somali*
South Africa - *South African*
South Sudan, Republic of
Spain - *Spaniard*
Sri Lanka
Sudan - *Sudanese*
Suriname - *Surinamer*
Swaziland - *Swazi*
Sweden - *Swede*
Switzerland -*Swiss*
Syria - *Syrian*
Tajikistan - *Tajik*
Tanzania - *Tanzanian*
Thailand - *Thai*
Togo - *Togolese*
Tonga -*Tongan*
Trinidad and Tobago
Tunisia - *Tunisian*
Turkey - *Turk*
Turkmenistan - *Turkmen*
Tuvalu - *Tuvaluan*
Uganda - *Ugandan*
Ukraine - *Ukrainian*
United Arab Emirates
United Kingdom
United States - *American*
Uruguay - *Uruguayan*
Uzbekistan - *Uzbek*
Vanuatu
Vatican City
Venezuela - *Venezuelan*
Vietnam - *Vietnamese*
Yemen - *Yemeni*
Zambia - *Zambian*
Zimbabwe - *Zimbabwean*

MONTHS OF THE YEAR

January	July
February	August
March	September
April	October
May	November
June	December

MEASUREMENTS

Length

US Customary
1 inch (in)
1 foot (ft) = 12in
1 yard (yd) = 3ft
1 mile = 1,760yd

METRIC
1 millimeter (mm)
1 centimeter (cm) = 10mm
1 meter (m) = 100cm
1 kilometer (km) = 1,000m

Volume

US Customary
1 fluid ounce (fl oz)
1 pint (pt) = 16fl oz
1 quart = 2pt
1 gallon (gal) = 8pt

METRIC
1 milliliter (ml)
1 centiliter (cl) = 10ml
1 liter (l) = 100cl
1 kiloliter (kl) = 1,000l

Weight

US Customary
1 ounce (oz)
1 pound (lb) = 16oz
1 hundredweight (cwt) = 100lbs
1 ton = 20cwt

METRIC
1 milligram (mg)
1 gram (g) = 1,000mg
1 kilogram (kg) = 1,000g
1 tonne (t) = 1,000kg

Area

US Customary
1 square inch (in^2)
1 square foot (ft^2) = $144in^2$
1 square yard (yd^2) = $9ft^2$
1 acre = $4,840yd^2$
1 square mile = 640 acres

METRIC
1 square cm (cm^2)
1 square m (m^2) = $10,000cm^2$
1 hectare = $10,000m^2$
1 square kilometer (km^2) = 100 hectares

NUMBERS

1 - one	**16** - sixteen
2 - two	**17** - seventeen
3 - three	**18** - eighteen
4 - four	**19** - nineteen
5 - five	**20** - twenty
6 - six	**21** - twenty-one
7 - seven	**30** - thirty
8 - eight	**40** - forty
9 - nine	**50** - fifty
10 - ten	**60** - sixty
11 - eleven	**70** - seventy
12 - twelve	**80** - eighty
13 - thirteen	**90** - ninety
14 - fourteen	**100** - hundred
15 - fifteen	**1000** - thousand

INDEX OF PICTURE LABELS

Some words that do no have their own entry appear as labels to the illustrations in this dictionary. You can use this index to find those words.

N

O

P

Q

R

S

Internet links

There are lots of great websites on the internet to help with English writing, grammar, spelling and punctuation. At the Usborne Quicklinks Website, you can search online dictionaries, use handy thesauruses and find help with homework. There are also test-yourself quizzes, word searches, puzzles and games to build skills and understanding. To visit the recommended websites for this book, go to the Usborne Quicklinks Website at **www.usborne.com/quicklinks** and type the keyword "**dictionary**".

When using the internet, please follow the internet safety guidelines shown on the Usborne Quicklinks Website. The recommended websites in Usborne Quicklinks are regularly reviewed and updated, but Usborne Publishing Ltd. is not responsible and does not accept liability for the content or availability of any website other than its own. We recommend that children are supervised while using the internet.

ADDITIONAL EDITORIAL WORK: Rachel Firth, Alex Frith, Hannah Wood and Rachel Wardley
ADDITIONAL DESIGN WORK: Sue Grobecker and Stephanie Jones
COVER DESIGN: Michael Hill **PHOTOGRAPHY**: Mark Mason Studio
US PROOFREADERS: WordSharp.net
EDITORIAL DIRECTOR: Felicity Brooks
ADVISORS: Colin Hope, Susan Hitch, George Phillipson, Richard Hatton, John Rostron, Margaret Rostron, Anne Rooney, Bill Chambers, Anne Millard, Michael Reiss

THE PUBLISHERS ARE GRATEFUL TO THE FOLLOWING: Benetton Formula Ltd. (196); Boss Trucks Ltd. (102); Corporation of Trinity House (144); Douglas MacKenzie, Visitor Services Manager, HMS Victory, Portsmouth (222-223); Flight International (14-15); Ford Motor Company Ltd. (46);Massey Ferguson (259); Minolta Cameras (179); Mitsui Machinery Sales (UK) Ltd. (158); New Holland Ford Sales Promotion & Product Support Department (117); Renault UK Ltd. (192); Rolls Royce plc (135); Shell UK Exploration and Production (167); Stephen Bateman (164); Thames Barrier Visitor's Centre (28); Vickers PLC, Defence Systems (21); Yamaha-Kemble Music (UK) Ltd. (200). The picture on page 203 is based on the drawing "Study for the Head of Leda" by Leonardo da Vinci, The Royal Collection, Windsor.

First published in 2014 by Usborne Publishing Ltd, 83-85 Saffron Hill, London EC1N 8RT, England. **www.usborne.com**